300.184
B58c

120479

DATE DUE			
Sept 25 '72			

CAUSAL MODELS IN THE SOCIAL SCIENCES

CAUSAL MODELS IN THE SOCIAL SCIENCES

edited by H. M. BLALOCK, JR.

University of Washington

ALDINE PUBLISHING COMPANY/ *New York*

ABOUT THE EDITOR

H. M. Blalock, Jr. is Professor, Department of Sociology,
the University of Washington, Seattle. He was educated at
Dartmouth College, Brown University, and the University of
North Carolina, where he received his Ph.D. He previously
taught at the University of North Carolina, Yale University
and the University of Michigan. Professor Blalock has
written or edited seven books, including *Measurement in the
Social Sciences: Theories and Strategies* (Aldine 1974) and
has contributed numerous articles to academic and professional
journals. He is a former Chairman of the Methodology Section
of the American Sociological Association, and has served on a
number of other professional councils and as associate editor
of several journals. He was recipient of the 1973 ASA Samuel
Stouffer Prize.

First published 1971
Aldine Publishing Company
200 Saw Mill River Road
Hawthorne, New York 10532

Library of Congress Catalog Card Number 70-133304
ISBN 202-30076-5, cloth; 202-30228-5, paper
Printed in the United States of America

Sixth printing, 1981

To Paul F. Lazarsfeld

Preface

There is a growing literature on causal models and structural systems of equations that crosscuts a number of different fields. However, much of this material is widely scattered throughout the journal literature and varies considerably in terms of both level of difficulty and substantive application. It therefore seemed wise to attempt to capture the essential flavor of the main developments of this methodological approach through an edited volume that may be used to supplement textual materials of a more integrated nature.

The most systematic discussions of this general approach have appeared in the econometrics literature, where several general texts are available. Many of these discussions are too technical for most sociologists, political scientists, and others who lack strong backgrounds in mathematics, however. In editing this volume I have attempted to integrate a few of the less technical papers written by econometricians such as Koopmans, Wold, Strotz, and Fisher with discussions of causal approaches in the biological sciences and with relatively more exploratory treatments by sociologists and other social scientists.

It is assumed that the reader has some rudimentary familiarity with the subject, as can be obtained by reading nontechnical discussions such as contained in my *Causal Inferences in Nonexperimental Research* (Chapel Hill: University of North Carolina Press, 1964). Those readers who wish to study the subject seriously should learn the basic elements of matrix algebra and then take up treatments of simultaneous-equation approaches in textbooks on econometrics. Many of the papers in this volume can be understood by those who have been exposed to simple least-squares procedures but who lack training in mathematical statistics. However, there can be no getting around the fact that many of the most important methodological problems we face in the social sciences involve highly technical issues. One of my major purposes in editing this volume is to convince the reader that there *are* ways of handling the kinds of complexities that have been loosely discussed in the verbal literature, but that we cannot expect to obtain definitive answers without first mastering at least some of this rapidly accumulating technical literature.

This book is dedicated to Paul F. Lazarsfeld, whose pioneering work in methodology has sensitized numerous generations of sociologists and political scientists to the basic problems and issues pertaining to the interrelationship between theory and research. It is hoped that the present volume will constitute an additional contribution in this same tradition.

Contents

PART I

Simple Recursive Models

This first part focuses on the kinds of relatively simple causal models that have served for many years as first approximations for political scientists and sociologists. These models all involve one-way causation and can be handled by what are referred to as recursive systems of equations. Such models provide a heuristic device for broadening the scope of simple regression approaches that commonly focus on a single dependent variable and a set of "predictors." In fact, they justify the procedure of treating each such equation as separate from the rest so that its coefficients can be estimated by ordinary least squares. As we shall see in Part III, there are numerous instances where more complex kinds of estimating procedures must be used and indeed many situations where there will be too many unknowns in the system to permit any estimation at all. These latter kinds of complications do not arise in the case of one-way causation, provided we are willing to make certain kinds of simplifying assumptions about the omitted variables.

Sociologists and political scientists, in particular, are well aware of the hiatus or gap between our verbal theories, on the one hand, and our research techniques, on the other. The causal modeling approach offers a systematic way out of this impasse, although at the same time it makes one well aware of the limitations of the inference procedures involved. In effect, it provides a set of rules for making causal inferences on the basis of empirical interrelationships. These rules alone can never provide infallible guides nor can they assure one that any particular causal explanation is correct. But they can give us a systematic way of building block upon block, so that our theories can become cumulative and so that alternative explanations that are not consistent with the data can be rejected.

The notion of recursive equations is fundamental to both this section and the discussions of path analysis contained in Part II. The basic idea is that variables can be hierarchically arranged in terms of their causal priorities

1

in such a way that it becomes possible to neglect variables that are clearly dependent on a given subset of variables. Suppose we are considering four variables X_1, X_2, X_3, and X_4. If we are willing to assume that X_4 does not affect X_1, X_2, and X_3, then regardless of the influence that any of these latter variables may have on X_4, we are justified in ignoring X_4 when considering the interrelationships among these first three variables. Similarly, if we assume that X_3 does not influence X_1 and X_2, we are justified in ignoring X_3 in studying their interrelationship. In fact, if we were to introduce X_3 into their relationship, say by relating X_2 and X_1 controlling for X_3, we might be badly misled. Finally, if we are willing to assume that X_2 cannot affect X_1, then we may write the following set of equations:

$$X_1 = e_1$$
$$X_2 = b_{21}X_1 + e_2$$
$$X_3 = b_{31}X_1 + b_{32}X_2 + e_3$$
and $$X_4 = b_{41}X_1 + b_{42}X_2 + b_{43}X_3 + e_4$$

where the e_i are disturbance terms representing the effects of all omitted variables. Obviously this basic idea can be extended to any number of variables as long as we are willing to assume such a causal ordering.

Much of the literature on causal models and simultaneous equations consists of elaborations on this basic kind of model. As we shall see in Part III, the simple recursive model can be replaced by one in which there are sets or blocks of variables that are recursively related but where one can allow for reciprocal causation within blocks. In these more complex models, however, there may be too many unknowns in the system, in which case we refer to the system as being underidentified. Furthermore, as soon as we allow for reciprocal causation we are forced to think more carefully about our assumptions concerning the disturbance terms e_i. In order to justify the use of ordinary least squares, we commonly assume that these disturbances are uncorrelated with the *independent* variables in each equation as well as with each other. It can be shown that in the case of the more general nonrecursive system this kind of assumption breaks down, and we must therefore find alternatives to ordinary least-squares estimating procedures.

A whole host of problems revolves around the very simple assumptions about these error terms commonly made in connection with recursive systems, and these involve the very core issues of causal inferences. We ordinarily conceive of these disturbances as having been brought about by variables that have been omitted from the theoretical system. In the case of recursive systems, the use of ordinary least squares therefore requires the assumption that the aggregate effect of omitted variables that affect the dependent variable in any given equation must be such that the error term is uncorrelated with each of the independent variables. For example, in the case of the equation for X_4 we assume that omitted variables that affect X_4 are uncorrelated in the aggregate with X_1, X_2, and X_3. This is a somewhat weaker form of the assumption that "other things" are equal, in that we do not need to assume that all relevant variables are literally constant. They are merely assumed not to disturb the basic relationships within the system.

In the first selection of Part I, Simon shows how this assumption about the disturbance terms is utilized to provide the rationale behind our more intuitive ideas about spurious correlations. He notes that whenever one is not satisfied by this particular simplifying assumption, he must expand the theoretical system to include those variables thought to be violating the assumption about the disturbance terms. My own paper on four-variable models extends the Simon approach by showing its implications for the use of control variables.

The recursive models appropriate to one-way causation, as well as the more general models discussed in Part III, assume perfect measurement in all variables that appear as "independent" variables somewhere in the causal system. Obviously, this assumption is unrealistic in the case of all research, but it is especially so in the case of the social sciences. Nevertheless, it is useful to ignore problems of measurement error when studying other kinds of complications in the models. Approaches to the study of measurement errors and their implications will be considered in Parts IV and V. There are other kinds of elaborations, however, that cannot be extensively discussed in this single volume. These include nonlinear or nonadditive models, the handling of correlated disturbance terms that are especially likely in the case of time-series and ecological data, and the use of truly dynamic formulations that explicitly involve the time dimension. The reader who wishes to pursue these additional topics will find extensive bibliographies suggested in many of the papers in this volume.

Among the most difficult tasks confronting social scientists are those of making the appropriate translations of methodological problems across substantive areas and of seeing the connections between technical discussions of methodology and the theoretical issues posed in the individual social sciences. In order to facilitate this translation process I have included in each section one or two substantive papers. Some readers may prefer to read these illustrations of applications before turning to the more abstract methodological materials. In Part I, the paper by Goldberg applies the causal model approach to the testing of alternative theories to data involving voting behavior.

The final paper in Part I, by Costner and Leik, relates the causal modeling approach to so-called "axiomatic theories" that are found in the social science literature. Costner and Leik confine themselves to very simple causal chains of the form X causes Y which, in turn, causes Z. They point to the fact that verbal propositions of the form "the greater the X, the greater the Y" are often ambiguous with respect to whether or not causal asymmetry is implied. The general implication is that verbal theories can be translated into causal models involving mathematical equations only if the direction of causality is specified. As we shall see in Part III, this does not restrict us to simple one-way causation, since if a theorist clearly indicates that X is to be taken as both a cause and an effect of Y, we may translate this into mathematical terms by writing two separate equations, one for X and the other for Y. But in doing so we destroy the simplicity that is made possible in the case of recursive systems.

Chapter 1

SPURIOUS CORRELATION:
A CAUSAL INTERPRETATION

HERBERT A. SIMON*
Carnegie Institute of Technology

Even in the first course in statistics, the slogan "Correlation is no proof of causation!" is imprinted firmly in the mind of the aspiring statistician or social scientist. It is possible that he leaves the course (and many subsequent courses) with no very clear ideas as to what *is* proved by correlation, but he never ceases to be on guard against "spurious" correlation, that master of imposture who is always representing himself as "true" correlation.

The very distinction between "true" and "spurious" correlation appears to imply that while correlation in general may be no proof of causation, "true" correlation does constitute such proof. If this is what is intended by the adjective "true," are there any operational means for distinguishing between true correlations, which do imply causation, and spurious correlations, which do not?

A generation or more ago, the concept of spurious correlation was examined by a number of statisticians, and in particular by G. U. Yule [8]. More recently important contributions to our understanding of the phenomenon have been made by Hans Zeisel [9] and by Patricia L. Kendall and Paul F. Lazarsfeld [1]. Essentially, all these treatments deal with the three variable case—the clarification of the relation between two variables by the introduction of a third. Generalizations to *n* variables are indicated but not examined in detail.

Reprinted by permission of the author and publisher from the *Journal of the American Statistical Association*, 1954, Vol. 49, pp. 467–479.

* I am indebted to Richard M. Cyert, Paul F. Lazarsfeld, Roy Radner, and T. C. Koopmans for valuable comments on earlier drafts of this paper.

Meanwhile, the main stream of statistical research has been diverted into somewhat different (but closely related) directions by Frisch's work on confluence analysis and the subsequent exploration of the "identification problem" and of "structural relations" at the hands of Haavelmo, Hurwicz, Koopmans, Marschak, and many others.[1] This work has been carried on at a level of great generality. It has now reached a point where it can be used to illuminate the concept of spurious correlation in the three-variable case. The bridge from the identification problem to the problem of spurious correlation is built by constructing a precise and operationally meaningful definition of causality—or, more specifically, of causal ordering among variables in a model.[2]

1. Statement of the problem

How do we ordinarily make causal inferences from data on correlations? We begin with a set of observations of a pair of variables, x and y. We compute the coefficient of correlation, r_{xy}, between the variables and whenever this coefficient is significantly different from zero we wish to know what we can conclude as to the causal relation between the two variables. If we are suspicious that the observed correlation may derive from "spurious" causes, we introduce a third variable, z, that, we conjecture, may account for this observed correlation. We next compute the partial correlation, $r_{xy.z}$, between x and y with z "held constant," and compare this with the zero order correlation, r_{xy}. If $r_{xy.z}$ is close to zero, while r_{xy} is not, we conclude that either: (a) z is an intervening variable—the causal effect of x on y (or vice versa) operates through z; or (b) the correlation between x and y results from the joint causal effect of z on both those variables, and hence this correlation is spurious. It will be noted that in case (a) we do not know whether the causal arrow should run from x to y or from y to x (via z in both cases); and in any event the correlations do not tell us whether we have case (a) or case (b).

The problem may be clarified by a pair of specific examples adapted from Zeisel.[3]

1. See Koopmans [2] for a survey and references to the literature.
2. Simon [6] and [7]. See also Orcutt [4] and [5]. I should like, without elaborating it here, to insert the *caveat* that the concept of causal ordering employed in this paper does not in any way solve the "problem of Hume" nor contradict his assertion that all we can ever observe are covariations. If we employ an ontological definition of cause—one based on the notion of the "necessary" connecton of events—then correlation cannot, of course, prove causation. But neither can anything else prove causation, and hence we can have no basis for distinguishing "true" from "spurious" correlation. If we wish to retain the latter distinction (and working scientists have not shown that they are able to get along without it), and if at the same time we wish to remain empiricists, then the term "cause" must be defined in a way that does not entail objectionable ontological consequences. That is the course we shall pursue here.
3. Zeisel [9], pp. 192–195. Reference to the original source will show that in this and the following example we have changed the variables from attributes to continuous variables for purposes of exposition.

I. The data consist of measurements of three variables in a number of groups of people: x is the percentage of members of the group that is married, y is the average number of pounds of candy consumed per month per member, z is the average age of members of the group. A high (negative) correlation, r_{xy}, was observed between marital status and amount of candy consumed. But there was also a high (negative) correlation, r_{yz}, between candy consumption and age; and a high (positive) correlation, r_{xz}, between marital status and age. However, when age was held constant, the correlation $r_{xy.z}$, between marital status and candy consumption was nearly zero. By our previous analysis, either age is an intervening variable between marital status and candy consumption; or the correlation between marital status and candy consumption is spurious, being a joint effect caused by the variation in age. "Common sense"—the nature of which we will want to examine below in detail—tells us that the latter explanation is the correct one.

II. The data consist again of measurements of three variables in a number of groups of people: x is the percentage of female employees who are married, y is the average number of absences per week per employee, z is the average number of hours of housework performed per week per employee.[4] A high (positive) correlation, r_{xy}, was observed between marriage and absenteeism. However, when the amount of housework, z, was held constant, the correlation $r_{xy.z}$ was virtually zero. In this case, by applying again some common sense notions about the direction of causation, we reach the conclusion that z is an intervening variable between x and y: that is, that marriage results in a higher average amount of housework performed, and this, in turn, in more absenteeism.

Now what is bothersome about these two examples is that the same statistical evidence, so far as the coefficients of correlation are concerned, has been used to reach entirely different conclusions in the two cases. In the first case we concluded that the correlation between x and y was spurious; in the second case that there was a true causal relationship, mediated by the intervening variable z. Clearly, it was not the statistical evidence, but the "common sense" assumptions added afterwards, that permitted us to draw these distinct conclusions.

2. Causal relations

In investigating spurious correlation we are interested in learning whether the relation between two variables persists or disappears when we introduce a third variable. Throughout this paper (as in all ordinary correlation analyses) we will assume that the relations in question are linear, and without loss

---

4. Zeisel [9], pp. 191–192.

of generality, that the variables are measured from their respective means.

Now suppose we have a system of three variables whose behavior is determined by some set of linear mechanisms. In general we will need three mechanisms, each represented by an equation—three equations to determine the three variables. One such set of mechanisms would be that in which each of the variables *directly influenced* the other two. That is, in one equation x would appear as the dependent variable, y and z as independent variables; in the second equation y would appear as the dependent variable, x and z as the independent variables; in the third equation, z as dependent variable, x and y as independent variables.[5]

The equations would look like this:

$$\text{(2.1)} \qquad x + a_{12}y + a_{13}z = u_1,$$
$$\text{(I)} \qquad \text{(2.2)} \qquad a_{21}x + y + a_{23}z = u_2,$$
$$\text{(2.3)} \qquad a_{31}x + a_{32}y + z = u_3,$$

where the u's are "error" terms that measure the net effects of all other variables (those not introduced explicitly) upon the system. We refer to $A = \|a_{ij}\|$ as the *coefficient matrix* of the system.

Next, let us suppose that not all the variables directly influence all the others—that some independent variables are absent from some of the equations. This is equivalent to saying that some of the elements of the coefficient matrix are zero. By way of specific example, let us assume that $a_{31} = a_{32} = a_{21} = 0$. Then the equation system (I) reduces to:

$$\text{(2.4)} \qquad x + a_{12}y + a_{13}z = u_1,$$
$$\text{(II)} \qquad \text{(2.5)} \qquad y + a_{23}z = u_2,$$
$$\text{(2.6)} \qquad z = u_3.$$

By examining the equations (II), we see that a change in u_3 will change the value of z directly, and the values of x and y indirectly; a change in u_2 will change y directly and x indirectly, but will leave z unchanged; a change in u_1 will change only x. Then we may say that y *is causally dependent on* z in (II), and that x is causally dependent on y and z.

If x and y were correlated, we would say that the correlation was genuine in the case of the system (II), for $a_{12} \neq 0$. Suppose, instead, that the system were (III):

$$\text{(2.7)} \qquad x + a_{13}z = u_1,$$
$$\text{(III)} \qquad \text{(2.8)} \qquad y + a_{23}z = u_2,$$
$$\text{(2.9)} \qquad z = u_3.$$

In this case we would regard the correlation between x and y as spurious,

5. The question of how we distinguish between "dependent" and "independent" variables is discussed in Simon (7), and will receive further attention in this paper.

because it is due solely to the influence of z on the variables x and y. Systems (II) and (III) are, of course, not the only possible cases, and we shall need to consider others later.

3. *The* a priori *assumptions*

We shall show that the decision that a partial correlation is or is not spurious (does not or does indicate a causal ordering) can in general only be reached if *a priori* assumptions are made that certain *other* causal relations do *not* hold among the variables. This is the meaning of the "common sense" assumptions mentioned earlier. Let us make this more precise.

Apart from any statistical evidence, we are prepared to assert in the first example of Section 1 that the age of a person does *not* depend upon either his candy consumption or his marital status. Hence z cannot be causally dependent upon either x or y. This is a genuine empirical assumption, since the variable "chronological age" really stands, in these equations, as a surrogate for physiological and sociological age. Nevertheless, it is an assumption that we are quite prepared to make on evidence apart from the statistics presented. Similarly, in the second example of Section 1, we are prepared to assert (on grounds of other empirical knowledge) that marital status is not causally dependent upon either amount of housework or absenteeism.[6]

The need for such *a priori* assumption follows from considerations of elementary algebra. We have seen that whether a correlation is genuine or spurious depends on which of the coefficients, a_{ij}, of A are zero, and which are non-zero. But these coefficients are not observable nor are the "error" terms, u_1, u_2 and u_3. What we observe is a sample of values of x, y, and z.

Hence, from the standpoint of the problem of statistical estimation, we must regard the $3n$ sample values of x, y, and z as numbers given by observation, and the $3n$ error terms, u_i, together with the six coefficients, a_{ij}, as variables to be estimated. But then we have $(3n + 6)$ variables ($3n$ u's and six a's) and only $3n$ equations (three for each sample point). Speaking roughly in "equation-counting" terms, we need six more equations, and we depend on the *a priori* assumptions to provide these additional relations.

The *a priori* assumptions we commonly employ are of two kinds:

(1) *A priori* assumptions that certain variables are not directly dependent on certain others. Sometimes such assumptions come from knowledge of the time sequence of events. That is, we make the general assumption about the world that if y precedes x in time, then $a_{21} = 0$—x does not directly influence y.

---

6. Since these are empirical assumptions it is conceivable that they are wrong, and indeed, we can imagine mechanisms that would reverse the causal ordering in the second example. What is argued here is that these assumptions, right or wrong, are implicit in the determination of whether the correlation is true or spurious.

(2) *A priori* assumptions that the errors are uncorrelated—i.e., that "all other" variables influencing x are uncorrelated with "all other" variables influencing y, and so on. Writing $E(u_i u_j)$ for the expected value of $u_i u_j$, this gives us the three additional equations:

$$E(u_1 u_2) = 0; \qquad E(u_1 u_3) = 0; \qquad E(u_2 u_3) = 0.$$

Again it must be emphasized that these assumptions are "a priori" only in the sense that they are not derived from the statistical data from which the correlations among x, y, and z are computed. The assumptions are clearly empirical.

As a matter of fact, it is precisely because we are unwilling to make the analogous empirical assumptions in the two-variable case (the correlation between x and y alone) that the problem of spurious correlation arises at all. For consider the two-variable system:

$$
\begin{array}{lll}
 & (3.1) & x + b_{12} y = v_1 \\
(\text{IV}) & & \\
 & (3.2) & y = v_2
\end{array}
$$

We suppose that y precedes x in time, so that we are willing to set $b_{21} = 0$ by an assumption of type (1). Then, if we make the type (2) assumption that $E(v_1 v_2) = 0$, we can immediately obtain a unique estimate of b_{12}. For multiplying the two equations, and taking expected values, we get:

$$(3.3) \qquad E(xy) + b_{12} E(y^2) = E(v_1 v_2) = 0.$$

Whence

$$(3.4) \qquad b_{12} = -\frac{E(xy)}{E(y^2)} = -\frac{\sigma_y}{\sigma_x} r_{xy}.$$

It follows immediately that (sampling questions aside) b_{12} will be zero or non-zero as r_{12} is zero or non-zero *Hence correlation is proof of causation in the two-variable case if we are willing to make the assumptions of time precedence and non-correlation of the error terms.*

If we suspect the correlation to be spurious, we look for a common component, z, of v_1 and v_2 which might account for their correlation:

$$(3.5a) \qquad v_1 \equiv u_1 - a_{13} z,$$

$$(3.5b) \qquad v_2 \equiv u_2 - a_{23} z.$$

Substitution of these relations in (IV) brings us back immediately to systems like (II). This substitution replaces the unobservable v's by unobservable u's. Hence, we are not relieved of the necessity of postulating independence of the errors. We are more willing to make these assumptions in the three-variable case because we have explicitly removed from the error term the component z which we suspect is the source, if any, of the correlation of the v's.

Stated otherwise, introduction of the third variable, z, to test the genuineness or spuriousness of the correlation between x and y, is a method for determining whether in fact the v's of the original two-variable system were uncorrelated. But the test can be carried out only on the assumption that the unobservable error terms of the three variable system are uncorrelated. If we suspect this to be false, we must further enlarge the system by introduction of a fourth variable, and so on, until we obtain a system we are willing to regard as "complete" in this sense.

Summarizing our analysis we conclude that:

(1) Our task is to determine which of the six off-diagonal matrix coefficients in a system like (I) are zero.

(2) But we are confronted with a system containing a total of nine variables (six coefficients and three unobservable errors), and only three equations.

(3) Hence we must obtain six more relations by making certain *a priori* assumptions.

(a) Three of these relations may be obtained, from considerations of time precedence of variables or analogous evidence, in the form of direct assumptions that three of the a_{ij} are zero.

(b) Three more relations may be obtained by assuming the errors to be uncorrelated.

4. Spurious correlation

Before proceeding with the algebra, it may be helpful to look a little more closely at the matrix of coefficients in systems like (I), (II), and (III), disregarding the numerical values of the coefficients, but considering only whether they are non-vanishing (X), or vanishing (0). An example of such a matrix would be

$$\left\| \begin{array}{ccc} X & 0 & 0 \\ X & X & X \\ 0 & 0 & X \end{array} \right\|$$

In this case x and z both influence y, but not each other, and y influences neither x nor z. Moreover, a change in u_2—u_1 and u_3 being constant—will change y, but not x or z; a change in u_1 will change x and y, but not z; a change in u_3 will change z and y, but not x. Hence the causal ordering may be depicted thus:

In this case the correlation between x and y is "true," and not spurious.

Since there are six off-diagonal elements in the matrix, there are $2^6 = 64$ possible configurations of X's and 0's. The *a priori* assumptions (1), however, require 0's in three specified cells, and hence for each such set of assumptions there are only $2^3 = 8$ possible distinct configurations. If (to make a definite assumption) x does not depend on y, then there are three possible orderings of the variables $(z, x, y; x, z, y; x, y, z)$, and consequently $3.8 = 24$ possible configurations, but these 24 configurations are not all distinct. For example, the one depicted above is consistent with either the ordering (z, x, y) or the ordering (x, z, y).

Still assuming that x does not depend on y, we will be interested, in particular, in the following configurations:

$$
\left\| \begin{matrix} X & 0 & 0 \\ X & X & X \\ 0 & 0 & X \end{matrix} \right\|
\qquad
\left\| \begin{matrix} X & 0 & X \\ X & X & 0 \\ 0 & 0 & X \end{matrix} \right\|
\qquad
\left\| \begin{matrix} X & 0 & 0 \\ X & X & 0 \\ X & 0 & X \end{matrix} \right\|
$$
$$
(\alpha) \qquad\qquad\qquad (\beta) \qquad\qquad\qquad (\gamma)
$$

$$
\left\| \begin{matrix} X & 0 & X \\ 0 & X & X \\ 0 & 0 & X \end{matrix} \right\|
\qquad
\left\| \begin{matrix} X & 0 & 0 \\ 0 & X & X \\ X & 0 & X \end{matrix} \right\|
$$
$$
(\delta) \qquad\qquad\qquad (\epsilon)
$$

In Case α, either x may precede z, or z, x. In Cases β and δ, z precedes x; in Cases γ and ϵ, x precedes z. The causal orderings that may be inferred are:

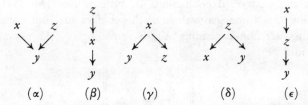

$$
(\alpha) \qquad (\beta) \qquad (\gamma) \qquad (\delta) \qquad (\epsilon)
$$

The two cases we were confronted with in our earlier examples of Section 1 were δ and ϵ, respectively. Hence, δ is the case of spurious correlation due to z; ϵ the case of true correlation with z as an intervening variable.

We come now to the question of which of the matrices that are consistent with the assumed time precedence is the correct one. Suppose, for definiteness, that z precedes x, and x precedes y. Then $a_{12} = a_{31} = a_{32} = 0$; and the system (I) reduces to:

$$(4.1) \qquad\qquad x \quad + a_{13}z = u_1,$$

$$(4.2) \qquad\qquad a_{21}'x + y + a_{23}z = u_2,$$

$$(4.3) \qquad\qquad z = u_3.$$

Next, we assume the errors to be uncorrelated:

(4.4) $$E(u_1u_2) = E(u_1u_3) = E(u_2u_3) = 0.$$

Multiplying equations $(4.1) - (4.3)$ by pairs, and taking expected values we get:

(4.5) $\quad a_{21}E(x^2) + E(xy) + a_{23}E(xz) + a_{13}[a_{21}E(xz) + E(yz) + a_{23}E(z^2)]$
$$= E(u_1u_2) = 0,$$

(4.6) $$E(xz) + a_{13}E(z^2) = E(u_1u_3) = 0,$$

(4.7) $$a_{21}E(xz) + E(yz) + a_{23}E(z^2) = E(u_2u_3) = 0.$$

Because of (4.7), the terms in the bracket of (4.5) vanish, giving:

(4.8) $$a_{21}E(x^2) + E(xy) + a_{23}E(xz) \equiv 0.$$

Solving for $E(xz)$, $E(yz)$ and $E(xy)$ we find:

(4.9) $$E(xz) = -a_{13}E(z^2),$$

(4.10) $$E(yz) = (a_{13}a_{21} - a_{23})E(z^2),$$

(4.11) $$E(xy) = a_{13}a_{23}E(z^2) - a_{21}E(x^2).$$

Case α: Now in the matrix of case α above, we have $a_{13} = 0$. Hence:

(4.12a) $\quad E(xz) = 0;$ (4.12b) $E(yz) = -a_{23}E(z^2),$

(4.12c) $\quad E(xy) = -a_{21}E(x^2).$

Case β: In this case, $a_{23} = 0$, hence,

(4.13a) $\quad E(xz) = -a_{13}E(z^2);$ (4.13b) $E(yz) = a_{13}a_{21}E(z^2);$

(4.13c) $\quad E(xy) = -a_{21}E(x^2);$

from which it also follows that:

(4.14) $$E(xy) = E(x^2)\frac{E(yz)}{E(xz)}.$$

Case δ: In this case, $a_{21} = 0$. Hence,

(4.15a) $\quad E(xz) = -a_{13}E(z^2);$ (4.15b) $E(yz) = -a_{23}E(z^2);$

(4.15c) $\quad E(xy) = a_{13}a_{23}E(z^2);$

and we deduce also that:

(4.16) $$E(xy) = \frac{E(xz)E(yz)}{E(z^2)}.$$

We have now proved that $a_{13} = 0$ implies (4.12a); that $a_{23} = 0$ implies (4.14); and that $a_{21} = 0$ implies (4.16). We shall show that the converse also holds.

To prove that (4.12a) implies $a_{13}=0$ we need only set the left-hand side of (4.9) equal to zero.

To prove that (4.14) implies that $a_{23}=0$ we substitute in (4.14) the values of the cross-products from (4.9)–(4.11). After some simplification, we obtain:

$$(4.17) \qquad a_{23}[E(x^2) - a_{13}{}^2 E(z^2)] = 0.$$

Now since, from (4.1)

$$(4.18) \qquad E(x^2) - E(u_1{}^2) + 2a_{13}E(zu_1) = a_{13}{}^2 E(z^2),$$

and since, by multiplying (4.3) by u_1, we can show that $E(zu_1)=0$, the second factor of (4.17) can vanish only in case $E(u_1{}^2)=0$. Excluding this degenerate case, we conclude that $a_{23}=0$.

To prove that (4.16) implies that $a_{21}=0$, we proceed in a similar manner, obtaining:

$$(4.19) \qquad a_{21}[E(x^2) - a_{13}{}^2 E(z^2)] = 0,$$

from which we can conclude that $a_{21}=0$.

We can summarize the results as follows:

1) If $E(xz)=0$, $E(yz)\neq0$, $E(xy)\neq0$, we have Case α

2) If none of the cross-products is zero, and

$$E(xy) = E(x^2)\frac{E(yz)}{E(xz)},$$

we have Case β.

3) If none of the cross-products is zero, and

$$E(xy) = \frac{E(xz)E(yz)}{E(z^2)},$$

we have Case δ.

We can combine these conditions to find the conditions that two or more of the coefficients a_{13}, a_{23}, a_{21} vanish:

4) If $a_{13}=a_{23}=0$, we find that:

$$E(xz)=0, \ E(yz)=0. \text{ Call this Case } (\alpha\beta).$$

5) If $a_{13}=a_{21}=0$, we find that:

$$E(xz)=0, \ E(xy)=0. \text{ Call this Case } (\alpha\delta).$$

6) If $a_{23}=a_{21}=0$, we find that:

$$E(yz)=0, \ E(xy)=0. \text{ Call this Case } (\beta\delta).$$

7) If $a_{13}=a_{23}=a_{21}=0$, then

$$E(xz)=E(yz)=E(xy)=0. \text{ Call this Case } (\alpha\beta\delta).$$

8) If none of the conditions (1)–(7) are satisfied, then all three co-efficients a_{13}, a_{23}, a_{21} are non-zero. Thus, by observing which of the conditions

(1) through (8) are satisfied by the expected values of the cross products, we can determine what the causal ordering is of the variables.[7]

We can see also, from this analysis, why the vanishing of the partial correlation of x and y is evidence for the spuriousness of the zero-order correlation between x and y. For the numerator of the partial correlation coefficient $r_{xy.z}$, we have:

$$(4.20) \qquad \mathcal{N}(r_{xy.z}) = \frac{E(xy)}{\sqrt{E(x^2)E(y^2)}} - \frac{E(xz)E(yz)}{E(z^2)\sqrt{E(x^2)E(y^2)}}.$$

We see that the condition for Case δ is precisely that $r_{xy.z}$ vanish while none of the coefficients, r_{xy}, r_{xz}, r_{yz} vanish. From this we conclude that the first illustrative example of Section 1 falls in Case δ, as previously asserted. A similar analysis shows that the second illustrative example of Section 1 falls in Case ϵ.

In summary, our procedure for interpreting, by introduction of an additional variable z, the correlation between x and y consists in making the six *a priori* assumptions described earlier; estimating the expected values, $E(xy)$, $E(xz)$, and $E(yz)$; and determining from their values which of the eight enumerated cases holds. Each case corresponds to a specified arrangement of zero and non-zero elements in the coefficient matrix and hence to a definite causal ordering of the variables.

5. *The case of experimentation*

In sections (3)–(4) we have treated u_1, u_2 and u_3 as random variables. The causal ordering among x, y, and z can also be determined without *a priori* assumptions in the case where u_1, u_2, and u_3 are controlled by an experimenter. For simplicity of illustration we assume there is time precedence among the variables. Then the matrix is triangular, so that $a_{ij} \neq 0$ implies $a_{ji} = 0$; and $a_{ij} \neq 0$, $a_{jk} \neq 0$ implies $a_{ki} = 0$.

Under the given assumptions at least three of the off-diagonal a's in (I) must vanish, and the equations and variables can be reordered so that all the non-vanishing coefficients lie on or below the diagonal. If (with this ordering) u_2 or u_3 are varied, at least the variable determined by the first equation will remain constant (since it depends only on u_1). Similarly, if u_3 is varied, the variables determined by the first and second equations will remain constant.

In this way we discover which variables are determined by which equations. Further, if varying u_i causes a particular variable other than the ith to change in value, this variable must be causally dependent on the ith.

---

7. Of course, the expected values are not, strictly speaking, observables except in a probability sense. However, we do not wish to go into sampling questions here, and simply assume that we have good estimates of the expected values.

Suppose, for example, that variation in u_1 brings about a change in x and y, variation in u_2 a change in y, and variation in u_3 a change in x, y, and z. Then we know that y is causally dependent upon x and z, and x upon z. But this is precisely the Case β treated previously under the assumption that the u's were stochastic variables.

6. Conclusion

In this paper I have tried to clarify the logical processes and assumptions that are involved in the usual procedures for testing whether a correlation between two variables is true or spurious. These procedures begin by imbedding the relation between the two variables in a larger three-variable system that is assumed to be self-contained, except for stochastic disturbances or parameters controlled by an experimenter.

Since the coefficients in the three-variable system will not in general be identifiable, and since the determination of the causal ordering implies identifiability, the test for spuriousness of the correlation requires additional assumptions to be made. These assumptions are usually of two kinds. The first, ordinarily made explicit, are assumptions that certain variables do *not* have a causal influence on certain others. These assumptions reduce the number of degrees of freedom of the system of coefficients by implying that three specified coefficients are zero.

The second type of assumption, more often implicit than explicit, is that the random disturbances associated with the three-variable system are uncorrelated. This assumption gives us a sufficient number of additional restrictions to secure the identifiability of the remaining coefficients, and hence to determine the causal ordering of the variables.

References

[1] KENDALL, PATRICIA L., and LAZARSFELD, PAUL F., "Problems of Survey Analysis," in Merton and Lazarsfeld (eds.), *Continuities in Social Research*, The Free Press, 1950, 133–196.

[2] KOOPMANS, TJALLING C., "Identification Problems in Economic Model Construction," *Econometrica* 17: 125–144 (April 1949), reprinted as Chapter II in *Studies in Econometric Methods*, Cowles Commission Monograph 14.

[3] ———, "When Is an Equation System Complete for Statistical Purposes?" Chapter 17 in *Statistical Inference in Dynamic Economic Models*, Cowles Commission Monograph 10.

[4] ORCUTT, GUY H., "Toward Partial Redirection of Econometrics," *The Review of Economics and Statistics*, 34 (1952), 195–213.

[5] ———, "Actions, Consequences, and Causal Relations," *The Review of Economics and Statistics*, 34 (1952), 305–314.

[6] SIMON, HERBERT A., "On the Definition of the Causal Relation," *The Journal of Philosophy*, 49 (1952), 517–528.

[7] ———, "Causal Ordering and Identifiability." Chapter III in *Studies in Econometric Methods*, Cowles Commission Monograph 14.

[8] YULE, G. UDNY, *An Introduction to the Theory of Statistics*, Charles Griffin and Co., 10th ed., 1932, Chapters 4, 12. (Equivalent chapters will be found in all subsequent editions of Yule and Yule and Kendall, through the 14th.)

[9] ZEISEL, HANS, *Say It With Figures*, New York, Harper and Brothers, 1947.

Chapter 2

FOUR-VARIABLE CAUSAL MODELS
AND PARTIAL CORRELATIONS

H. M. BLALOCK, JR.
University of Washington

In several recent papers the writer has discussed the use of Simon's method for making causal inferences from correlational data.[1] Simon's method yields results which are consistent with those obtained through partial correlations, but it also forces one to make explicit assumptions about both outside disturbing influences and the nature of the various causal links among an entire set of variables. It thereby serves to keep our attention focused on the complete network of causal relationships rather than on a single dependent variable.

But Simon's method can also be used to provide a rationale for predicting what should happen to empirical intercorrelations under various control situations. Our major purpose in systematically treating the four-variable case is to gain certain insights into what happens to a zero-order correlation when controls are introduced for variables which are causally related to the original variables in different ways. A secondary purpose of the paper is to provide a set of prediction equations for four-variable causal models for the

Reprinted by permission of the publisher from the *American Journal of Sociology*, Vol. 68, pp. 182–194. Copyright 1962, The University of Chicago Press.

1. See H. M. Blalock, "Correlation and Causality: The Multivariate Case," *Social Forces*, XXXIX (March, 1961), 246–251; "Evaluating the Relative Importance of Variables," *American Sociological Review*, XXVI (December, 1961), 866–874; and "Spuriousness versus Intervening Variables: The Problem of Temporal Sequences," *Social Forces*, Vol. XL (May, 1962). Discussions of the general method and the rationale for expressing causal relations in terms of simultaneous equations can be found in H. A. Simon, *Models of Man* (New York: John Wiley & Sons, 1957), pp. 37–49; and "Causal Ordering and Identifiability," in W. C. Hood and T. C. Koopmans (eds.), *Studies in Econometric Method* (New York: John Wiley & Sons, 1953), pp. 49–74.

convenience of the non-mathematically inclined social scientist, who may not wish to carry out the computations required by Simon's method.

Why focus on the four-variable case to study what happens in the controlling process? Since even the five-variable case will involve over a thousand distinct models, a systematic treatment of most of these possibilities would be out of the question. Why not merely make an exhaustive study of the three-variable case? First, the three-variable case has been more or less systematically treated in the literature, and there is no need to repeat these discussions.[2] But second, the three-variable case is too simple for our purposes. For example, we may wish to consider models in which a relationship between two variables could be partly spurious but also partly indirect through an intervening variable. Although in the present paper we cannot discuss the important problem of *when* and *why* we control in such instances, we can at least deal with the question of *what* will happen if controls are made.[3]

Rationale and limitations of the method

We cannot attempt a formal definition of causality without becoming involved with issues which are outside our present focus. Metaphysically, it is difficult to think without the aid of notions such as causes or forces. According to Bunge, the essential idea behind causal thinking is that of some agent *producing* some change of state in a system.[4] It is not necessary that there be a definite temporal sequence or even a constant conjunction of events, though we do require that an effect can never precede its cause in time.[5] Simon argues that the really essential aspect of a causal relationship is that it is asymmetrical in nature and not that it always involves temporal sequences.[6] In view of the difficulties in actually demonstrating causal relationships empirically, Simon prefers to confine the notions of cause and effect to *models* of the real world which consist of only a finite number of explicitly defined variables.[7] We shall follow Simon in this respect.

We begin by postulating a causal model involving a given number of

2. See esp. Simon, *Models of Man;* S. Nowak, "Some Problems of Causal Interpretation of Statistical Relationships," *Philosophy of Science*, XXVII (January, 1960), 23–38; and H. Hyman, *Survey Design and Analysis* (Glencoe, Ill.: Free Press, 1955), pp. 275–329.

3. Here we shall deal only with the sort of control situation in which one is interested in seeing whether or not a relationship between two variables disappears in controlling for antecedent or intervening variables. In such instances, we may suspect that there is no direct link between the two variables being related and that the relationship is either spurious or can be interpreted through an intervening variable.

4. M. Bunge, "Causality, Chance, and Law," *American Scientist*, XLIX (December, 1961,) 432–448.

5. *Ibid.*, p. 438.

6. Simon, "Causal Ordering and Identifiability," *op. cit.*, p. 51.

7. *Ibid.*

variables X_i. We make certain simplifying assumptions about how these variables are interrelated and about the behavior of variables which have not been included in the causal network. In particular, we shall assume additive and linear models, as is commonly done in regression analyses. It should be specifically noted that the presence of non-linear relationships may invalidate our conclusions. We also make the explicit assumption that variables which have been left out of the causal model create "error" terms which are essentially random. Whatever factors produce variations in one of the X_i should be uncorrelated with factors which give rise to disturbances in any of the remaining X's.

In non-experimental situations, such as cross-sectional studies, this particular kind of assumption may not be as plausible as in the case of experimental designs in which randomization has been possible. Our only alternative in such non-experimental studies is to bring as many outside disturbing influences as possible into the causal picture as explicit variables. This will ordinarily necessitate the use of a larger number of variables, and more complex causal models, than would be required to handle experimental data. And, unfortunately, the more variables we use, the simpler our assumptions usually have to be about *how* these variables are interrelated. The reader is therefore cautioned concerning the possibility of reaching erroneous conclusions with the method when one or more of these assumptions are violated.

Having committed ourselves on a particular set of variables, we can then define a causal relationship in terms of manipulations that might be carried out in an ideal experiment. We shall say that X is a direct cause of Y (written $X \rightarrow Y$) if and only if we can produce a change in the mean value of Y by changing X, holding constant *all* other variables which have been explicitly introduced into the system and which are not causally dependent upon Y. Since there is a finite number of such variables, and since they have been explicitly defined, there is no problem of determining whether or not one has controlled for all "relevant" variables.

The causal notion is confined to this particular model, as is the directness of the causal relationship. The introduction of a single additional variable might therefore change a causal relationship from direct to indirect, or even to a non-causal one. By an indirect causal relationship we mean one in which a change in X produces a change in certain other variables, which in turn affect Y. More precisely, we can say that X is an indirect cause of Y, within a particular causal model, if and only if it is possible to find certain variables $U, V, \ldots W$, explicitly included in the system, which are such that $X \rightarrow U \rightarrow V \rightarrow \ldots \rightarrow W \rightarrow Y$.

We now write a set of equations, which must hold simultaneously, and which express the various causal relationships mathematically. In a one-way linear causal system these will be of the form

$$X_1 = e_1$$
$$X_2 = b_{21}X_1 + e_2$$
$$X_3 = b_{31.2}X_1 + b_{32.1}X_2 + e_3$$
$$X_4 = b_{41.23}X_1 + b_{42.13}X_2 + b_{43.12}X_3 + e_4.$$

These particular equations indicate that X_1 depends causally only on outside variables, the effects of which are represented by e_1. But X_2 depends on X_1 as well as outside factors, X_3 depends upon both X_1 and X_2, and finally X_4 depends upon all of the remaining X's. Such a system is referred to as "recursive," as contrasted with a possible set of equations in which there may be reciprocal causation in which X_1 depends upon X_2 and vice versa.[8] Recursive equations have the property that the various b's can all be estimated without bias by means of simple least-squares methods.[9]

A particular recursive set of equations involves the *assumption* that a given causal arrangement is appropriate. If some of the b's can be assumed to be equal to zero, certain restrictions will be imposed on the data if the equations are to be mutually consistent. For each of the b's set equal to zero we impose the condition that the comparable partial correlation should also be zero, thus obtaining a prediction which can actually be tested from the data. But setting one of the b's equal to zero is equivalent to our postulating that there is no *direct* causal link between the two variables concerned. Thus, if we set $b_{31.2} = 0$, we are saying that there is no direct causal link between X_1 and X_3 and that a partial correlation between X_1 and X_3 (in this case $r_{13.2}$) should vanish. Similarly, if $b_{42.13} = 0$, this means that we are assuming that X_2 is no longer a direct cause of X_4 and therefore $r_{24.13}$ should be zero. But X_2 may of course be an indirect cause of X_4 through X_3.

Before considering four-variable causal models, one further caution should be introduced. There will always be a number of alternative models which will give the same predictions (e.g., the same vanishing partials) as any particular model under study. We can only proceed by *eliminating* inadequate models which give incorrect predictions, since it will ordinarily be impossible to rule out all the logical alternatives on the basis of the data at hand. In this sense, one can never "establish" any given causal model.

Specific four-variable models

Let us designate the four variables as X_1, X_2, X_3, and X_4. Since, for any given set of data, the variables can always be labeled arbitrarily, we shall

---

8. See H. Wold and L. Juréen, *Demand Analysis* (New York: John Wiley & Sons, 1953), p. 50. As Wold and Juréen point out, recursive systems can also be used to handle instances of reciprocal causation, provided that "feedback" is not more or less instantaneous. By lagging certain variables and collecting data at several points in time, we may take a given variable as independent at time t-1 and also as dependent at time t.

9. *Ibid.*, p. 51.

suppose that X_4 cannot be a cause of the other three variables, that X_3 cannot cause either X_1 or X_2, and that X_2 cannot cause X_1. In effect, then, we are ruling out two-way causation, and we are supposing that, unless the appropriate arrows have been omitted, we are moving in the direction $X_1 \rightarrow X_2 \rightarrow X_3 \rightarrow X_4$ rather than the other way around.

With four variables there will be six pairs of relationships. Since any given arrow may be either present or absent, there will be 2^6, or 64, possible causal situations. Certain of these models can be eliminated as either trivial or uninteresting, however. If all six arrows are present, Simon's method cannot be used. Cases involving no arrows or one arrow are completely trivial. In instances where there are only two arrows, these arrows will either by-pass one variable completely, in which case we are dealing with only three variables, or they will connect two completely unrelated pairs of variables. Therefore we need be concerned only with situations in which there are three, four, or five arrows.

The various possible causal models involving three, four, and five arrows are given in Chart 1. Before discussing some of these cases individually, we should first clarify the notation and organization used. The six possible models involving five arrows have been presented at the top of the chart. These models have been labeled in terms of the particular arrow omitted from the diagram. In model A the arrow between X_1 and X_2 has been left out; in B the arrow between X_1 and X_3 is missing; and, finally, in F we are dealing with the situation in which there is no direct link between X_3 and X_4.

Single numerical subscripts have been used to denote subtypes for the four-arrow cases. For example, in model A_1 not only is there no link between X_1 and X_2 (as is true for all A's), but there is also no arrow between X_1 and X_3. similarly, in A_2 there are no arrows between X_1 and X_2 and also between X_2 and X_3. In A_3 there is no arrow between X_1 and X_4, and so on. Notice that when we come to the B series in four arrows, there is no B_1 because of the fact that if we use the same subscripts as in the A series, a subscript of 1 would indicate no link between X_1 and X_3, and this is already covered by B. But we have used the symbol B_2 for the B model involving no link between X_2 and X_3. When we come to the C series, there will be no need for either C_1 or C_2, since both of these cases have been handled previously. Finally, there will be only one four-arrow case in the E series (i.e., E_5) and none in the F series. There are $6 \times 5/2$, or 15, four-arrow cases in all.

Double numerical subscripts have been used in the three-arrow cases in analogous fashion. For example, the symbol A_{12} is associated with the three-arrow model which represents a combination of A_1 and A_2, with arrows missing between X_1 and X_2, X_1 and X_3, and X_2 and X_3. Likewise, B_{23} is a composite of B_2 and B_3, with no arrows between X_1 and X_3, X_2 and X_3, and X_1 and X_4. Once the reader has become familiar with this particular notational scheme, it should be relatively easy to pass back and forth from one model to another whenever comparisons are to be made.

Notice that we have one prediction equation for each five-arrow model, two equations for each four-arrow model, and three for every model involving only three arrows. This is in line with the fact that Simon's method yields a prediction equation for each pair of variables which have *not* been connected by an arrow. Each prediction equation involves the disappearance of some partial or zero-order correlation between a pair of unconnected variables. For example, if X_2 and X_4 have not been linked with an arrow, then either r_{24} or one of the partials, with X_1 and X_3 as controls, will vanish. Conceivably, all correlations between X_2 and X_4 (zero, first, and second order) may be zero. But they may not, and our problem becomes that of determining exactly which ones will vanish under a particular set of causal conditions.

As we shall see in the four-variable case, and as appears to be true more generally, certain higher-order partials can always be expected to disappear. These vanishing partials involve controls for *all* variables which are either antecedent to, or intervening between, the particular variables being related, but they do *not* involve controls for variables taken to be dependent upon *both* of these variables. Thus if there were no arrow between X_1 and X_3 the value of $r_{13.2}$ should be approximately zero, but if we were to control for X_4 we would not expect the partial to disappear. Conceivably, however, the *total* association between X_1 and X_3 might be zero. In relating X_3 and X_4, supposing no direct link between these variables, the value of $r_{34.12}$ should be approximately zero. But we do not, as yet, know whether or not $r_{34.1}$, $r_{34.2}$, or r_{34} should also vanish.

THE A SERIES

In all of the *A*-series models there is no direct link between X_1 and X_2, the two variables which are taken as causally prior to the remaining variables X_3 and X_4. This will mean that under these models the *total* association between X_1 and X_2 should be approximately zero, subject to the possibility of sampling error. Suppose we were to control for one or both of the two variables which are taken to be dependent upon X_1 and X_2. It can be seen that the resulting partials will *not* be equal to zero, except in those situations in which certain other arrows linking the first two variables with X_3 and X_4 have also been erased. An examination of the formula for a first-order partial will clarify the point:

$$r_{12.3} = \frac{r_{12} - r_{13}r_{23}}{\sqrt{1 - r_{13}{}^2}\sqrt{1 - r_{23}{}^2}}.$$

Since the denominator on the right cannot be greater than unity, it is clear that the partial will vanish only when the numerator is zero. Simon's

Chart 2.1. *Prediction equations for four-variable causal models.*

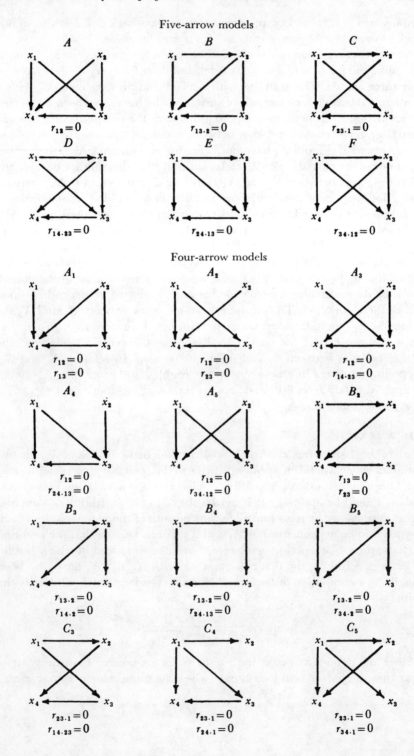

Five-arrow models

A

$r_{12} = 0$

B

$r_{13 \cdot 2} = 0$

C

$r_{23 \cdot 1} = 0$

D

$r_{14 \cdot 23} = 0$

E

$r_{24 \cdot 13} = 0$

F

$r_{34 \cdot 12} = 0$

Four-arrow models

A_1

$r_{12} = 0$
$r_{13} = 0$

A_2

$r_{12} = 0$
$r_{23} = 0$

A_3

$r_{12} = 0$
$r_{14 \cdot 23} = 0$

A_4

$r_{12} = 0$
$r_{24 \cdot 13} = 0$

A_5

$r_{12} = 0$
$r_{34 \cdot 12} = 0$

B_2

$r_{13} = 0$
$r_{23} = 0$

B_3

$r_{13 \cdot 2} = 0$
$r_{14 \cdot 2} = 0$

B_4

$r_{13 \cdot 2} = 0$
$r_{24 \cdot 13} = 0$

B_5

$r_{13 \cdot 2} = 0$
$r_{34 \cdot 2} = 0$

C_3

$r_{23 \cdot 1} = 0$
$r_{14 \cdot 23} = 0$

C_4

$r_{23 \cdot 1} = 0$
$r_{24 \cdot 1} = 0$

C_5

$r_{23 \cdot 1} = 0$
$r_{34 \cdot 1} = 0$

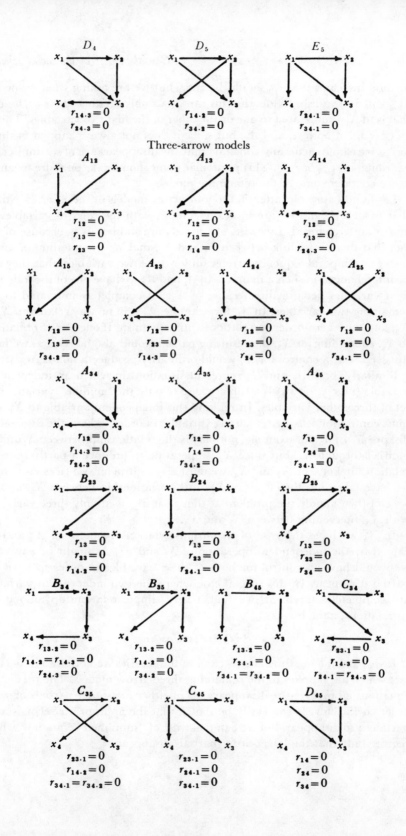

Three-arrow models

method indicates that r_{12} should be zero, but we are asking whether or not $r_{12.3}$ will also vanish. Evidently, this can occur only if either r_{13} or r_{23} is zero, that is, if X_3 is unrelated to one or the other of the first two variables. This in fact occurs in both A_1 and A_2, but since it does not always happen in the A series, we cannot generally conclude that the disappearance of r_{12} implies the vanishing of $r_{12.3}$ or $r_{12.4}$. This particular point should take on more meaning as we consider some of the remaining models.

Let us now turn our attention to four-arrow models in the A series. Notice that models A_1 and A_2 are basically similar, with the roles of variables X_1 and X_2 interchanged. Likewise, A_3 and A_4 are similar. It is because of the fact that there is no link between X_1 and X_2, making the question of asymmetry or temporal sequences irrelevant for these two variables, that they can be interchanged in such a manner. In A_1 and A_2 we have one of the independent variables being a direct cause of X_4 but completely unrelated to the remaining two variables. In A_1, for example, X_1 is in no way related to X_2 or X_3, and these zero-order correlations with X_1 vanish. If one were to relate X_1 to X_2, controlling for X_3, the resulting partial would also be zero, as we have just seen. But a control for X_4 would ordinarily produce a non-zero partial.

Similarly, both A_3 and A_4 represent situations in which an independent variable (i.e., X_1 or X_2) is a direct cause of only the "middle" variable in a set of three other variables. In relating this independent variable to X_4, one must control for *both* the remaining variables in order to have the association disappear. In A_3, for example, not only is the relationship between X_1 and X_4 indirect through X_3, but since X_2 is operating to produce a partly spurious relationship between X_3 and X_4, we must also control for X_2. In essence, once we have taken out the effects of X_2 on the relationship between X_3 and X_4, we can then handle the problem as though it involved only three variables, with X_3 intervening between X_1 and X_4.

In A_5 we have the case of a spurious relationship between X_3 and X_4 caused by the independent operation of X_1 and X_2. As might be expected, we would have to control for both of these variables in order to have the partial disappear. In this special case where the two independent variables are completely unrelated, we find a very simple relationship among the correlations, namely,

$$r_{34} = r_{13}r_{14} + r_{23}r_{24}.$$

If we examine the three-arrow cases in the A series we notice an important fact which also applies to the remaining three-arrow models. The prediction equations all involve the disappearance of either first-order partials or zero-order coefficients. It can easily be shown that the appropriate second-order partials also disappear, but we can make use of "simplified" equations which require only that the lower-order partials disappear.

We can see numerically why this will occur. If we compare, for example, A_{14} with the four-arrow model A_4, we note that for the latter model we have $r_{24.13} = 0$, whereas we need only control for X_3 in A_{14} in order to have the relationship between X_2 and X_4 disappear, This is true because in A_{14} we also have $r_{13} = 0$ (see A_1). With both r_{12} and r_{13} being zero, we then know that $r_{12.3}$ must be zero as well. But

$$r_{24.31} = \frac{r_{24.3} - r_{12.3} r_{14.3}}{\sqrt{1 - r_{12.3}^2} \sqrt{1 - r_{14.3}^2}}.$$

Since from A_4 we know that $r_{24.31}$ is zero, and since $r_{12.3} = 0$, we must also have $r_{24.3} = 0$. Thus the combined facts that the second-order partial is zero and $r_{12} = r_{13} = 0$ imply that the first-order partial (with X_3 as control) will likewise be zero.

Notice what has happened when A_1 and A_4 have been combined into A_{14}. We have dropped the diagonal arrows and have reduced the situation to one in which there is a single independent variable X_1 operating on only one variable (in this case X_4) of a set of variables (X_2, X_3, and X_4) which are interrelated by only two arrows. When we now obtain the prediction equation linking X_2 and X_4, we find that we can actually ignore the effects of the first variable and still have the partial reduced to zero.

Similarly, in A_{15} we can ignore X_1 and still have $r_{34.2}$ vanish. Since X_2 affects only X_4 in A_{23}, we likewise obtain the result that $r_{14.3} = 0$. In A_{35} we see that X_1 affects only X_3, and therefore $r_{34.2}$ vanishes as well as $r_{34.12}$. These facts can easily be verified by an examination of the appropriate formulas.

The particular phenomenon we are noting did not arise in the four-arrow models because of the fact that if only a single arrow connected any one variable to the others, there must have been *three* additional arrows linking the triad of remaining variables, making it impossible for Simon's method to yield a prediction equation among these latter variables. After we have examined the B series, we shall be in a position to make a more general assertion about this sort of situation found in the three-arrow models.

Several of the three-arrow situations are worthy of comment. Notice that in both A_{13} and A_{24} (as well as B_{25} and D_{45}) we have trivial cases in which one variable has been completely cut out and where we are essentially dealing with only three variables. In each of these instances the prediction equations involve vanishing zero-order correlations with the isolated variable. But there are no predictions for the remaining three variables. Model A_{12} is another simple case in which we have three unrelated variables operating on a single dependent variable. In A_{34} we have two independent variables causing X_3, which in turn causes X_4. In relating either of these former variables to X_4, we may merely control for X_3 in order to have the partial vanish. It will not be necessary to control for the remaining independent variable.

THE B SERIES

In the B series we have no direct link between X_1 and X_3, though we are now assuming that X_1 is a cause of X_2. A control for the intervening variable X_2 gives a zero partial between X_1 and X_3, but since X_4 is assumed not to cause either X_1 or X_3, directly or indirectly, an additional control for X_4 ordinarily produces a non-vanishing partial.

We see that B_2 involves basically the same type of situation as A_1 and A_2, with a variable causing X_4 completely independently of the other two variables. We again find that two total correlations (in this case, r_{13} and r_{23}) should disappear. Both $r_{13.2}$ and $r_{23.1}$ will also be zero because of the fact that X_3 is unrelated to *both* X_1 and X_2.

The situations represented in B_3 and B_5, as well as certain of the models appearing in later series, pose a more difficult problem. In B_3 the prediction equation tells us that it should be unnecessary to control for X_3 in order for the partial between X_1 and X_4 to vanish. Similarly in B_5 the partial between X_3 and X_4 (controlling for X_2) is zero even without a control for X_1. An examination of the formula for $r_{14.23}$ shows us that for B_3 the pair of prediction equations $r_{13.2}=0$ and $r_{14.2}=0$ automatically implies that $r_{14.23}$ must also be zero since

$$r_{14.23} = \frac{r_{14.2} - r_{13.2}r_{34.2}}{\sqrt{1-r_{13.2}{}^2}\sqrt{1-r_{34.2}{}^2}}.$$

Likewise in B_5 we can show that the equations $r_{13.2}=0$ and $r_{34.2}=0$ give us the result that $r_{34.21}$ is also zero. Notice that in both B_3 and B_5 we have two prediction equations involving first-order partials using the *same control variable* (in each case, X_2). We shall find this again happening in certain other models (i.e., C_4, C_5, D_4, D_5, and E_5).

In B_3 we see that the link between X_2 and X_4 is both direct and indirect through X_3. The numerical value of r_{24} will reflect the influence of X_3 as well as the direct effect of X_2. It will therefore be unnecessary to control for X_3 in relating X_1 and X_4. Similarly, in B_5 the relationship between X_2 and X_4 is both direct and partly spurious, and the numerical value of r_{24} will reflect this fact. We thus need only control for X_2 in order to reduce the partial between X_3 and X_4 to zero.

There is an apparent similarity between both B_3 and B_5 and two of the models in the A series, namely, A_3 and A_4. In the latter two models we have an independent variable connected to a triad of variables by an arrow to the middle variable of the triad. In relating this independent variable to X_4, the dependent variable of the triad, we found it necessary to control for *both* remaining variables in order for the partial to vanish. One might raise the question as to why it was necessary in A_3, for example, to control for X_2 as well as X_3, since the numerical value of r_{34} reflects the fact that the relationship between X_3 and X_4 is partly spurious. The essential difference between these two A models and B_3 and B_5, as well as certain other models in later series, seems to be that in both A_3 and A_4 we have two variables operating completely independently of each other on the remaining variables. Even though the diagrams may look similar to some of those for models in other series, the algebra shows that when one of these independent variables is related to the dependent variable, the effects of the other cannot be ignored if we expect the partial to vanish.

The remaining four-arrow case in the B series can be handled briefly. In B_4 the relationship between X_2 and X_4 is partly spurious and partly indirect through X_3. Controls for both X_1 and X_3 will therefore be necessary in order to reduce the relationship between X_2 and X_4 to zero. We have, here, an instance where the two control variables operate in different ways, a fact which can easily be overlooked if one does not develop the habit of drawing causal diagrams before attempting to interpret his findings.

Turning finally to the three-arrow models in the B series, we note only one new type of result. In both B_{34} and B_{45} we see instances in which *either* one of two first-order partials will disappear. In B_{34} we have a simple causal chain in which X_1 causes X_2, X_2 causes X_3, and X_3 causes X_4. When we come to the correlation between X_1 and X_4 we obtain the very simple result that

$$r_{14} = r_{12} r_{23} r_{34} .$$

A control for either X_2 or X_3, the two variables which are intermediate in the chain, will produce a zero partial between X_1 and X_4.

In B_{45} we do not have a causal chain, but it again turns out that we can control for either of the two "middle" variables and still produce a zero partial between X_3 and X_4.[10] In this particular model we also get the simple result that

$$r_{34} = r_{14} r_{12} r_{23} .$$

In the case of the three-arrow models in the A series we noted that none of the prediction equations involved second-order partials. We saw that, in instances where there was an independent variable affecting only one of the three remaining variables, the effects of this independent variable could be ignored and still have the appropriate partials reduced to zero. But actually in the A series the single independent variable always operated on a dependent or intervening variable in the triad of remaining variables. In B_{34} and

10. By "middle variables" we do not necessarily mean X_2 and X_3, but whatever variables are connected to two of the remaining variables. By "end variables" we shall mean the two variables, in a simple sequence, which are connected directly to only one other variable. The type of results found in models B_{34} and B_{45}, as well as C_{34} and C_{35}, seem to hold in the general case. For example, in the k variable causal chain, a control for any of the middle variables will produce a zero partial.

B_{35}, however, we have instances in which X_1 affects only X_2, the variable which would be taken as *independent* in the triad (X_2, X_3, X_4). Nevertheless, we still find it unnecessary to control for X_1 in order for the appropriate partials to disappear.

We thus seem to have a general rule that *whenever a given variable affects directly only one of the remaining variables, its effects on the partials for the latter variables can safely be ignored.* It appears as though this general rule will also hold for more than four variables, though to the writer's knowledge this has not been proven mathematically.

THE REMAINING SERIES

We can discuss the C, D, E, and F series much more briefly since there are no basically new problems posed by these models. In the C series there is no direct link between X_2 and X_3, these variables being spuriously related through X_1. The value of $r_{23.1}$ should be zero, although if we were to control for the dependent variable X_4 the value of $r_{23.14}$ would ordinarily not be zero.

In C_3 we have the case in which X_1 and X_4 are related indirectly by means of two intervening variables, themselves not directly related, both of which must be controlled if the partial between X_1 and X_4 is to vanish. Models C_4 and C_5 are basically the same, with the roles of X_2 and X_3 being interchanged. In each case, X_1 causes both X_2 and X_3. But in C_4 there is no link between X_2 and X_4, whereas in C_5 there is no arrow from X_3 to X_4. Examining the relationship between X_4 and whichever of these variables is *not* linked to it with an arrow, we find that when we control for X_1 the partial disappears. No control for the remaining variable is needed.

Models C_{34} and C_{35} have prediction equations which are similar to those of B_{34} and B_{45}. When relating the two "end variables" we can obtain a zero partial by controlling for either of the variables falling intermediate in the sequence. Model C_{45} represents the special case where X_2 X_3 and X_4 are all spuriously related through X_1, so that a control for this latter variable produces vanishing partials among the former variables.

In the D series, X_1 and X_4 are only indirectly related through the intervening variables X_2 and X_3. In D_4 there is no need to control for X_2 in relating X_1 and X_4 since the indirect effects of X_1 on X_3 through X_2 will be taken into consideration in the value of r_{13}. Likewise, in this same model, we do not need to control for X_1 in order for the partial between X_2 and X_4 to disappear. Essentially the same kinds of control situations occur in D_5. No special comments are necessary concerning D_{45}, which represents the trivial case in which X_4 is completely unrelated to any of the remaining variables.

Model E is the situation in which the relationship between X_2 and X_4 is partly spurious and partly indirect but with the added complication that X_1 also directly affects X_3. In F the relationship between X_3 and X_4 is spurious owing to the effects of the two related variables X_1 and X_2. In E_5 we find another example of a situation in which it becomes unnecessary to control for more than one variable in order to have a partial disappear.

Extensions to more than four variables

Considering the present stage in the development of sociological theory, as well as the fact that a number of variables in any particular study will usually be only weakly related to most of the remainder, it will probably seldom be necessary to make use of models involving more than five or six variables. By using an alternative computing routine, which will be described elsewhere, it should not be too difficult to work out the prediction equations for any particular five-variable model, although even the six-variable case begins to involve rather tedious computations.

Certain relatively simple procedures can be suggested, however, for situations in which the investigator wishes to test the adequacy of any particular causal model but is not interested in determining exactly which of the lower-order partials will disappear. First, one can often eliminate certain variables, either because of their low correlations with other variables or because they appear in positions analogous, say, to that of X_3 in model B_3 or of X_1 in model B_5. Second, one may then single out the first four of the remaining variables, leaving out of the picture those variables which stand in dependent relationships to these four variables. The prediction equations among these four variables can then be found from Chart 2.1. Here, we are making use of the fact that prediction equations never involve controls for variables which are dependent, directly or indirectly, upon *both* variables being interrelated.

Finally, it can be shown for the general case, assuming one-way causation, that we may reintroduce the remaining variables, writing a prediction equation for each arrow which has been omitted when these remaining variables are related to each other and to the four variables taken as causally prior. Each of these latter prediction equations will involve the disappearance of the highest-order partials, using controls for *all* variables except those taken to be causally dependent upon the two variables being related. In any particular case, certain lower-order partials may also vanish, but it may not be feasible to carry out the algebra to determine exactly which of these partials can be expected to do so under the assumed model.

Concluding remarks

We have seen that Simon's method for making causal inferences from correlational data can be used to provide a systematic basis for predicting what should happen when we control under a given causal model. The four-variable situation has been taken up in detail, and certain suggestions have been made for handling larger numbers of variables. In discussing the various specific four-variable models, we have attempted to make sense intuitively out of the prediction equations derived by Simon's method. It is possible that many, if not all, of these equations might have been developed by using "common sense." The value of Simon's method, however, is in providing a rationale for whatever intuitive ideas we may have and in giving us a check whenever common sense might lead us astray.

Strictly speaking, Simon's method provides us with such a rationale only when we have made use of interval scales and linear models. Since a dichotomy can be considered a special case of an interval scale, the rationale would also seem appropriate for attribute data, though results with such data should be interpreted cautiously in view of possible peculiarities produced by extreme marginals or the use of arbitrary cut-points.[11] At present, there seems to be no comparable rationale for making causal inferences from rank-order correlations, but even in the absence of such a rationale, one might still wish to make causal inferences on the basis of a measure such as Kendall's tau. Provided he considered the study exploratory and provided he interpreted the results with extreme caution, he might thereby gain valuable theoretical insights that otherwise would have been lost.

The problems of evaluating sampling error and developing a satisfactory set of criteria for deciding on the adequacy of the goodness of fit of a particular model to a given set of data are too complex to be discussed in the present paper. Provided one is willing to assume multivariate normality, he might make a series of significance tests for the disappearance of the various partials. However, it should be noted that (1) the researcher may often be on the wrong end of the test, actually wishing to accept the null hypothesis that a particular model is correct; and (2) the results of a significance test are dependent not only upon the degree to which a particular partial departs from zero, but upon the size of the sample as well.

Finally, it must be recalled that, since a number of different causal models all yield the same set of prediction equations, the mere fact that we cannot reject a particular model does not mean that we have established its validity.[12] We can, however, determine which models successfully resist elimination.

11. For excellent discussions of causality in terms of attribute data, see Nowak, *op. cit.*, and R. G. Francis, *The Rhetoric of Science* (Minneapolis: University of Minnesota Press, 1961), chap. iii. It should be noted, however, that if the concept of causality is defined or conceived in terms of attributes (e.g., in terms of necessary and/or sufficient conditions for the presence of an attribute), one runs into difficulties in conceptualizing causal relationships among continuous variates.

12. Chart 2.1 has been set up in such a manner that it appears as though all causal models yield different predictions. But it must be remembered that the variables could have been reordered and that the particular variable labeled X_1 might have been taken as X_3 instead.

Chapter 3

DISCERNING A CAUSAL PATTERN AMONG DATA ON VOTING BEHAVIOR

ARTHUR S. GOLDBERG*
University of Rochester

1. Causal explanations: Simon's model

The present analysis is devoted to making an empirically based choice among alternate causal explanations. This entails making causal inferences from statistical correlations. While this might, at one time, have constituted a heresy, I believe that the procedure to be followed here will soon be a part of statistical orthodoxy.[1]

This is not the place for an extended philosophical discussion of the problem of causality. Yet I would like to make my position on the problem as clear as concise presentation will permit. My basic sympathies are with that school which argues that scientifically relevant causal explanation inheres only in our theories, i.e., that the explained event takes the shape which it does because our postulates and logic preclude any other shape on

Reprinted by permission of the author and publisher from the *American Political Science Review*, Vol. 60, pp. 913–922. Copyright 1966, The American Political Science Association.

* While I have incurred a great many intellectual debts in the conduct of this inquiry, I am most particularly indebted to Hayward R. Alker, Jr., at Yale University, for so generously making available to me his understanding of causal inference strategies. I also wish to thank the University of Rochester for the research fellowship which enabled me to devote the summer of 1964 to the study of causality and causal inference techniques. Of course, neither mentor nor patron is responsible for such errors as may have been perpetrated herein. For these I alone am culpable.

1. Cf. Warren E. Miller and Donald E. Stokes, "Constituency Influence in Congress," *American Political Science Review* (March, 1963), 45–56; Donald C. Pelz and Frank M. Andrews, "Causal Priorities in Panel Study Data," *American Sociological Review*, 24 (December, 1964), 836–847; Hayward R. Alker, Jr., *Mathematics and Politics* (New York: The Macmillan Company, 1965), chap. VI.

pain of being themselves incorrect.[2] However, the development of such theory, containing such postulates, is usually the product of an inspired insight on the part of one thoroughly immersed in the manifestations of the empirical phenomenon under consideration. The production and verification of such insight in a systematic and reproducible way is the goal of inductive research. Where controlled experimentation is possible, Mill's canons may apply. Where such experiments are either impossible or impracticable, statistical inference becomes necessary. It is in this situation that the present approach, based upon a model developed by Herbert Simon and others, seems justified.[3]

Simon's model is designed to capture the asymmetry in our notions of causality. When one speaks of A as a cause of B, one usually has in mind a unidirectional forcing, and not merely a covariation, or phased covariation. Thus, if one speaks of rains as a cause of floods, one expects that a variation in rainfall will be accompanied by a variation in flooding, *but* one does *not* expect that variations in flooding deriving from other causes, e.g., faulty dam construction, will be accompanied by variations in rainfall. Again, it should be noted that the concept of alternate causes is alien to deductive theory, which seeks to postulate the most inclusive principles. However, inductive inference is concerned with perceiving an ever-increasing proportion of the total set of alternate causes in order to facilitate formulation of a principle of commonality.

Simon suggests that a patterned causal ordering can and should be described as a recursive set of simultaneous equations dealing sequentially with each of the variables in the causal ordering and describing each in terms of the regression of its causal antecedents upon it. Thus if one had four variables, $x_1 \ldots x_4$, in which x_1 was considered causally independent of all of the rest, and x_4 was considered causally dependent upon all of the rest, and in which x_2 and x_3 were causally intervening, this could be described as follows:[4]

$$x_1 = e_1$$
$$x_2 = b_{21}x_1 + e_2$$
$$x_3 = b_{31.2}x_1 + b_{32.1}x_2 + e_3$$
$$x_4 = b_{41.23}x_1 + b_{42.13}x_2 + b_{43.12}x_3 + e_4$$

2. Cf. Robert Brown, *Explanation in Social Science* (Chicago: Aldine Publishing Company, 1963), chap. XI. See also Norwood Russell Hanson, *Patterns of Discovery* (Cambridge: Cambridge University Press, 1958, chap. III; and William H. Riker, "Causes of Events," *Journal of Philosophy*, 55 (1958), 281–291.

3. See Herbert A. Simon, *Models of Man* (New York: John Wiley & Sons Inc., 1957), chaps. I–III; and Hubert M. Blalock, Jr., *Causal Inferences in Nonexperimental Research* (Chapel Hill: The University of North Carolina Press, 1964), chaps. I–III. These authors, in turn, have drawn heavily upon the work of econometricians. Among basic sources are, for example, Ragnar Frisch, *Statistical Confluence Analysis by Means of Complete Regression Systems* (Oslo: Universitets Økonomiske Institutt, 1934) and T. C. Koopmans (ed.), *Statistical Inference in Dynamic Economic Models* (New York: John Wiley and Sons, 1950).

4. Simon, *op. cit.*, chap. I.

The non-zero regression coefficients describe the impact of each of the causal antecedents upon a given variable; the pattern of impacts is inferable from the zero regression coefficients, and asymmetry is accomplished in that manipulation of the value of a given variable leaves unaltered the relationships among its causal antecedents, and can affect only causally subsequent variables.[5]

Since it is the case that causal impacts should appear as non-zero value regression coefficients, causal models in which any of the variables contribute directly to less than the full set of subsequent variables have implied zero value regression coefficients. Hubert Blalock points out that such regression coefficients imply zero value correlation coefficients. It thus becomes possible with the aid of partial correlation coefficients to make an empirically based decision among alternate causal models purporting to describe the causal relationships within the same set of variables. This is the technique which will be used in the present analysis.

It should be noted that there are several assumptions being made which bear substantially upon the logic of the analysis. These are: that the effects on the dependent variable of variables excluded from the model are not related to effects produced by any of the independent variables in the model; that all variables which have a substantial impact on the dependent variable and are correlated with independent variables in the model are also included in the model (i.e., the error terms are uncorrelated); that the phenomena to be explained entail no reciprocal causation.[6]

It should also be noted that there is a serious controversy among econometricians with regard to the uncorrelated error term assumption.[7] Although I do not wish to indulge in an extended discussion of the subject, it is perhaps only fair that I make my own position explicit. In general, I believe that this assumption is almost always invalid, and that science proceeds not only in spite of this invalidity, but to a large extent through efforts to cope with it. When the limit of a theory is encountered, in the form of the occurrence of a theoretically precluded phenomenon, the search is begun for some component of the error term which is correlated in the relevant sense, and in conjunction with its discovery, the substance of the theory is revised. This is but one form of the retroductive process.[8]

2. Causal relations among six variables

The present analysis is concerned with making inferences about the pattern of causal relationships among six variables: father's sociological characteristics

5. Blalock, *op. cit.*, pp. 52–60.
6. See *ibid.*, pp. 46–54.
7. See, for example, Fritz C. Holte, *Economic Shock-Models* (Oslo: Norwegian Universities Press, 1962), pp. 14–17.
8. See Hanson, *op. cit.*, chap. IV.

(FSC); father's party identification (FPI); respondent's sociological characteristics (RSC); respondent's party identification (RPI); respondent's partisan attitudes (RPA); and respondent's vote for President in 1956 (RV). The assumed causal ordering is the sequence in which the variables are listed above, except when otherwise noted. In each case to be examined, the model will be presented schematically, and the variables will be numbered in accordance with their assumed causal sequence.

Variables were selected for inclusion in the analysis on the bases of their repeated occurrence in the voting literature and their availability in a reliable body of data.[9] The sociological characteristics of the respondent's father and the father's party identification were taken as indicators of the context in which the respondent underwent his early political socialization. The literature is replete with the importance of this early socialization for political behavior in general and for voting behavior in particular.[10] The respondent's sociological characteristics were taken as an indicator of the constraints placed upon him by his current social environs. This variable represents the approach taken by Berelson *et al.* in *Voting*, and thus the general sociological explanation of voting behavior.[11] The respondent's party identification was included because of its well established and substantial correlation with direction of vote in a number of major studies.[12] Finally, the respondent's partisan attitudes were included as an indicator of his perceptions of the political arena, on the basis of the argument made in *The American Voter*, and because of the high correlation of these attitudes with voting behavior in that study.[13]

9. The body of data used consisted of that generated in the 1956 election study (#417) by the Survey Research Center at The University of Michigan, and made available to me through the Inter-University Consortium for Political Research. The exact operationalization of the variables is described in the Technical Note at the end of the article. The number of respondents in the present analysis is 645 out of the 1762 provided in the SRC survey. The 645 are those who had full information on the full set of variables. There is thus a slight overrepresentation of Republicans and upper SES respondents. This bias is slight and there appears to be no other systematic bias in the sub-sample. For more detailed discussion, see Arthur S. Goldberg, *The Intergenerational Transmission of Party Identification* (unpublished doctoral dissertation, Yale University, 1966), Appendix B.

10. Surveys of the literature on this point are available in Herbert H. Hyman, *Political Socialization* (Glencoe, Illinois: The Free Press. 1959); and Robert E. Lane and David O. Sears, *Public Opinion* (Englewood Cliffs: Prentice-Hall, Inc., 1964).

11. See, for example, Bernard R. Berelson, Paul F. Lazarsfeld, and William N. McPhee, *Voting* (Chicago: The University of Chicago Press, 1954), chaps. IV–VII. See also Seymour Martin Lipset, *Political Man* (Garden City, New York: Doubleday & Company, Inc., 1960), Part II.

12. See, for example, Angus Campbell, Gerald Gurin, and Warren E. Miller, *The Voter Decides*, (Evanston, Illinois: Row, Peterson and Company, 1954), chap. VII. See also Angus Campbell, Philip E. Converse, Warren E. Miller, and Donald E. Stokes, *The American Voter* (New York: John Wiley & Sons, Inc., 1960), chap. VI.

13. *The American Voter*, chap. IV. See also Donald E. Stokes, Angus Campbell, and Warren E. Miller, "Components of Electoral Decision," this REVIEW, 52 (June, 1958), 367–387.

Model I. Attitude as final mediator.

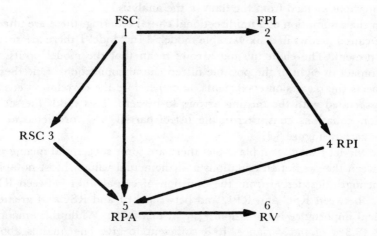

Prediction equations | Actual values

$r_{41 \cdot 23} = 0$ 0.017
$r_{61 \cdot 2345} = 0$ −0.019
$r_{32 \cdot 1} = 0$ 0.101
$r_{52 \cdot 134} = 0$ 0.032
$r_{62 \cdot 1345} = 0$ 0.053
$r_{43 \cdot 12} = 0$ 0.130
$r_{63 \cdot 1245} = 0$ −0.022
$r_{64 \cdot 1235} = 0$ 0.365

Figure 3.1.

3. Model I

As a point of departure, let us consider one version of an attitude-field theory model, that presented in *The American Voter*.[14] The authors have told us very little about what to expect in such a model, except that in pure Gestalt theory, the attitude field is the final mediator of all causes of the behavior in question. Based upon this requirement, let us consider one plausible model. In this model the attitude field is taken to be the result of two causal streams, one consisting in the sociological conditioning of childhood and adult life,[15] and the other consisting in affective conditioning to the party label.[16] This model is presented in Figure 3.1. Let us call this Model I, Attitude as Final Mediator. Figure 3.1 contains a schematic of the model, the theoretical

14. Cf. *The American Voter*, pp. 24–37.
15. Cf. Berelson, Lazarsfeld, and McPhee, *loc. cit.*
16. Cf. Lane and Sears, *op. cit.*, pp. 18–19.

prediction equations implied by the model, and the empirical values which those equations yielded from the data in the analysis.[17]

Given the assumption of a unidirectional causal ordering, there are fifteen possible causal arrows in a six variable model.[18] In Model I there are seven arrows present. The eight missing arrows mean that the model posits no causal impact in eight of the possible fifteen causal connections. One therefore expects the regression coefficients, and therefore the correlation coefficients associated with the missing arrows to be zero. This yields the set of prediction equations consisting in the list of partial "*r*'s" predicted to be equal to zero in Figure 3.1.

While Model I may seem plausible, there are some substantial incongruities between the prediction equations and the actual values. Most notably, these incongruities derive from the omission of causal links between RPI and RV, between RSC and RPI, and between FPI and RSC. Of greatest theoretical importance is the size of $r_{64.1235}$, i.e., 0.365. While this amounts to only 13.3% of the variance, it is sufficient to give one qualms about regarding attitudes, as operationalized by *The American Voter*, as the final mediator. Clearly party identification has an impact not caught in the screen which those researchers drew across their funnel of causality.[19] The need for a link between RSC and RPI, based upon the actual value of $r_{43.12}$ being equal to 0.130 instead of zero, reflects the idea that adult sociological characteristics play a role in party identification. The fact that this role accounts for a miniscule proportion of the variance (1.7%) suggests that the adult sociological environs are supportive of earlier learned behavior, rather than the primary source of this behavior. The need for a link between FPI and RSC is suggested by the value of $r_{32.1} = 0.101$. The size of this value suggests that the link is quite weak, and a more parsimonious model might well do without it. A possible explanation may be in upwardly aspirational parents

17. Although the aid of a computer was enlisted for the statistical computations in the present article, the lower order partials could be calculated with a slide rule or desk calculator. The appropriate formulae are available in Hubert M. Blalock, *Social Statistics* (New York: McGraw-Hill Book Company, Inc. 1960), pp. 333–336. For those who wish to check the computation of some of the lower order partials, the matrix of simple correlations is provided below:

	FSC	FPI	RSC	RPI	RPA	RV
FSC	1.000					
FPI	0.454	1.000				
RSC	0.808	0.420	1.000			
RPI	0.400	0.603	0.411	1.000		
RPA	0.318	0.453	0.289	0.710	1.000	
RV	0.282	0.466	0.271	0.722	0.742	1.000

18. Assuming that reciprocal causation is not involved, there are always $n!/2(n-2)!$ possible arrows among n variables.

19. *The American Voter*, p. 35. The relative size of this impact is a function of factors which will be dealt with later in the present analysis. See pp. 42–44, below.

Model II. Party identification as final mediator.

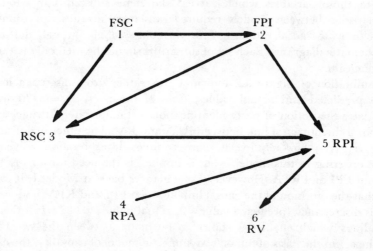

Prediction Equations	Actual Values
$r_{41 \cdot 23} = 0$	-0.017
$r_{51 \cdot 234} = 0$	0.037
$r_{61 \cdot 2345} = 0$	-0.019
$r_{42 \cdot 13} = 0$	0.357
$r_{62 \cdot 1345} = 0$	0.053
$r_{43 \cdot 12} = 0$	0.031
$r_{63 \cdot 1245} = 0$	-0.022
$r_{64 \cdot 1235} = 0$	0.470

Figure 3.2.

adopting a party identification normally associated with higher status groups and transmitting their status aspirations to their offspring with sufficient impact to have them realized to some extent. This is, to be sure, a most tentative explanation, but then this particular linkage is also rather tentative.

4. *Model II*

On the basis of the experience provided by Model I, a second model is proposed. In Model II party identification is taken as the final arbiter. Three arrows have been dropped: those linking FSC and RPA, RSC and RPA, and RPA and RV. The first two were dropped in a search for parsimony, and the third was dropped to implement the central idea of this particular model. Finally the lessons of Model I have been incorporated in Model II presented in Figure 2. Note that in Model II the time sequence between RPI and RPA is the reverse of what it was in Model I. Thus the subscripts do not necessarily refer to those variables which carried the same subscripts in Model I. Comparisons between models require translation of subscript numbers, which indicate causal ordering, into variable symbols through the use of the schematic diagrams. Each set of subscripts should be used only within its own diagram.

Examination of Figure 3.2 indicates two rather gross discrepancies between predicted and actual values. One of these, $r_{64.1235} = 0.470$ simply invalidates the notion of party identification as final arbiter. It suggests the need for a direct causal link between RPA and RV. The other major discrepancy, $r_{42.13} = 0.357$ requires a more complex interpretation. Given the causal ordering in this model, what is implied is the need for a causal link between FPI and RPA. However, if one glances back at Model I, it can be seen that the omission of the causal link between FPI and RPA produced no serious discrepancy (predicted value $= 0$, actual value $= 0.032$). It is this pair of findings which enables a choice to be made between the two causal orderings. On the basis of Simon's asymmetric model of causality, the causal link between two variables may be affected by all of the variables antecedent to the dependent variable, but *cannot* be affected by any of the variables subsequent to the dependent variable.[20] Thus, in Model I the antecedents to RPA are FSC, FPI, RSC, and RPI. In describing the impact of FPI upon RPA, it was therefore necessary to control for FSC, RSC, and RPI. However, in Model II, RPA is assumed to be antecedent to RPI. Therefore, in describing the impact of FPI upon RPA in this model, one is prohibited from including RPI as a control. Clearly, the omission of the control yields a poor fit with the data and suggests that to the extent that unidirectionality is assumed and parsimony desired, the RPI ought to be regarded as prior to RPA. Support is thus lent to the positions of Lane and Sears, Greenstein, and others who have urged the importance of the early socialization of political symbols.[21]

5. Model III

Reverting, then, to the causal ordering in Model I, and incorporating the lessons taught by Models I and II, a third model is proposed, that of dual mediation. The schematic, prediction equations, and findings are presented in Figure 3.3. Here, in Model III, one has a model which fits the data relatively well. Its distinctive features are: it hypothesizes *both* party identification and partisan attitudes as direct causes of vote direction; it assigns a

20. Blalock, *Causal Inference* . . ., p. 59.
21. Lane and Sears, *loc. cit.* Fred I. Greenstein, "The Benevolent Leader: Children's Images of Political Authority," *American Political Science Review*, 54 (1960), 934–943.

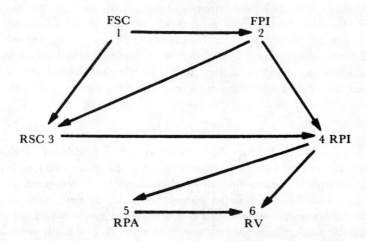

Model III. Dual mediation.

Prediction Equations | Actual Values
$r_{41 \cdot 23} = 0$	-0.017
$r_{51 \cdot 234} = 0$	0.083
$r_{61 \cdot 2345} = 0$	-0.019
$r_{52 \cdot 134} = 0$	0.032
$r_{62 \cdot 1345} = 0$	0.053
$r_{53 \cdot 124} = 0$	-0.073
$r_{63 \cdot 1245} = 0$	-0.022

Figure 3.3.

pivotal position to party identification in denying that any of the antecedents to party identification have a direct bearing on partisan attitudes or vote direction; within the framework of the model, no causes are hypothesized for partisan attitudes other than party identification. The last point, of course, suggests that the framework of the model is too restricted, since party identification in its total impact accounts for only about 50% of the variance in partisan attitudes ($r = .710$, see n. 17, above). This point will be elaborated upon. However, before launching into a serious critique of Model III, one ought to consider that while the model fits the data rather well, it is not a perfect fit. Since it is possible to make perfectly valid direct inferences from correlation coefficients to regression coefficients only where the former are actually zero, and since the inferences here have been based upon correlation coefficients slightly different from zero, a further analytic step seems warranted, i.e., calculation of standardized regression coefficients (beta weights). Based upon the causal ordering of Model III, such coefficients were generated for all of the linkages possible within that ordering. In general, the inferences made from the correlation coefficients are supported. That is, the implied zero impacts prove to be very small and statistically insignificant at the .05 level.[22] However, there is one exception: the FSC to RPA linkage, while relatively small, proved to be significant at the .05 level. Thus there is occasioned the revision presented in Model IV, in Figure 3.4. Within the assumptions made with regard to unidirectional causality and causal ordering, this is the model which best fits the data, and which requires critical assessment.

6. Model IV

From the viewpoint of theory, Model IV has both desirable and undesirable features. Let us first look at the happier side of this situation. Certainly the model achieves a certain amount of parsimony. Of fifteen possible causal arrows, six have been eliminated and of the remaining nine, two are clearly of secondary importance, leaving a dominant seven-arrow model. Moreover, the model is theoretically informative, both in terms of what it omits and in terms of its dominant patterns. The omission of direct causal links between sociological characteristics, both childhood (FSC) and adult (RSC), and voting behavior, as well as the omission of such a link between childhood sociological characteristics and adult party identification certainly justify the qualms of the authors of *The American Voter* about the sociological explanations of voting behavior.[23] However, it can also be seen, in this empirically supported model, that sociological characteristics do have a substantial *indirect* impact on voting behavior, exerted primarily through party identification. The mediating role of party identification as described in Model IV suggests that father's sociological characteristics, father's party identification, and respondent's sociological characteristics have almost no impact upon voting behavior save as they act through respondent's party identification. Therefore one expects $r_{65 \cdot 4} = r_{65 \cdot 1234}$. The actual values are: $r_{65 \cdot 4} = 0.472$, $r_{65 \cdot 1234} = 0.470$.

The fact that party identification rather than partisan attitudes proves to be the pivotal encapsulator of political socialization, substantiates the

---

22. The decision to accept or reject linkages on the basis of significance tests poses some problems. The significance test is designed to deal with the type I error (rejection of the null hypothesis when it is true). That is to say, it provides a statement of the probability that a strength of association as great as that found in the sample could have been drawn from a population in which there was in fact no relationship between the variables in question. However, in deciding to omit a link, one is concerned with the risk of a type II error (acceptance of the null hypothesis when it is false). The information desired in this case is the probability that a strength of association as weak as that in the sample could have been drawn from a population in which there was a stronger association. Unless one has an *a priori* expectation of the strength of association in the population, it is not possible to calculate this probability.

23. *The American Voter*, pp. 32–37.

Model IV. Dual mediation, revised.

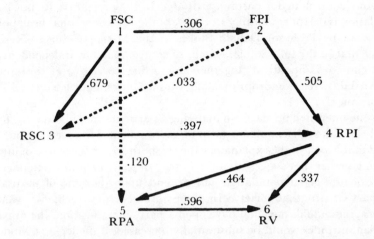

Key: The beta weights of the implied linkages appear either immediately above or immediately to the right of their representational arrows. The beta weights of the linkages represented by solid arrows prove significant at the .001 level. Those represented by broken arrows prove significant at the .05 level but not at the .01 level. None of the possible linkages which have been omitted have beta weights which are significant even at the .05 level.

Figure 3.4.

position that such socialization entails an affective relationship to symbols rather than a conscious evaluative relating of political means to ends. This position is given still further support by the absence of a direct link between childhood sociological characteristics and adult party identification; there is a relationship, but it is dependent upon mediation by paternal party identification. However, this is not to say that there is no rational calculus involved in voting. The fact that partisan attitudes have a substantial impact beyond that of party identification, suggests that such a calculus is operative, but operative against a set of predispositions dominated by party identification.[24] Thus, the model suggested by this study comports well with the data of other studies and imposes a certain order upon their findings.

Yet certain caveats are in order. One should bear in mind that the present study has dealt, to this point, only with respondents who claimed a Republican or a Democratic party identification for themselves. Those who were classified as Independents or as apolitical have been excluded. This has an

24. Cf. Berelson, Lazarsfeld, and McPhee, *op. cit.*, pp. 227–233. See also *The American Voter*, pp. 128–131; and Lane and Sears, *op. cit.* pp. 81–82.

important bearing upon the partial correlation between party identification and vote, controlling for partisan attitudes. In the present study, this partial correlation is 0.415, amounting to 17.2% of the variance. It has been pointed out to me by Professor Donald Stokes of the Michigan Survey Research Center that in the full sample, which, of course, includes Independents and those classed as apolitical (together amounting to 12.6% of the sample), this partial correlation drops to 0.238, thus accounting for less than 5.7% of the variance.

To one interested primarily in mapping a particular population, the figures based upon the full sample ought to be more salient. However, for one interested in the logic of the explanatory theory, both sets of figures are of interest. Taken together they suggest that the impact of party identification on voting behavior in a given population will depend upon the ratio of partisans to non-partisans in that society. In those instances in which, for whatever reasons, individuals have not developed a party identification, the impact of partisan attitudes would be substantially increased, if the logic of Model IV is correct. As the proportion of such instances in a population increased, the net impact of party identification on vote would be expected to diminish.[25] Essentially this is the obverse of the argument made in *The American Voter* about the efficacy of partisan attitudes as a guide to voting behavior.[26]

At this point attention is directed to certain unsatisfactory features of the model itself. While it leaves room for a rational calculus prior to the voting act, it does not permit party identification to benefit from this calculus. This prohibition derives from the requirements of the mathematical model of causality used in the analysis. A major requirement of that model, it will be recalled, was unidirectionality. Yet this is a limitation which, in the long run, must be circumvented, if theory is to be relevant to events. As this model stands, party identification is nearly immutable. There is very little if any variation over time in its antecedents, nor is there any provision for what V. O. Key calls a critical election.[27] This derives from two factors. First the model does not permit partisan attitudes to have an impact upon party identification. Second, the model does not include among its components the political events in the environment in which it is assumed to operate. The failure of partisan attitudes to feed back upon party identification would mean that even if the correlation between partisan attitudes and party identification were substantially reduced, voting behavior would be influenced, but party identification would be unaffected. Clearly the model needs

25. Note that this "net impact" refers to a population parameter, or statistic thereof, rather than to the impact of party identification on the vote of any single individual in the population. While the latter would doubtless be of interest, it would be extremely difficult to come by in non-experimental data.

26. See *The American Voter*, pp. 139–142.

27. V. O. Key, Jr., "A Theory of Critical Elections," *Journal of Politics*, 18 (1955), 3–18.

revision on this point. Moreover, unless one includes an additional variable there is no source within the model for variation of partisan attitudes. Thus, the model is itself a partial description of the impact of the past upon the present, but its connection with the future rests almost entirely in the error factors of the recursive equations which define the model—a situation both undesirable and unnecessary.

Let us first consider amending the model to permit partisan attitudes to have an impact upon party identification. This could be done within a recursive set of equations by "lagging" some of the variables, as Blalock suggests.[28] This entails treating a single variable through time as a set of discrete variables, and treating two interacting variables as two sets of discrete variables. Thus in the time interval $t_o \ldots t_n$, an interaction between X and Y could be schematized as follows: $Y_{t_o} \rightarrow Y_{t_1} \rightarrow Y_{t_2} \rightarrow Y_{t_3} \rightarrow X_{t_4} \ldots$. This technique, of course, requires data through time, and will not be utilized with the data of the present study, but is presented for future research purposes.

Introjection of political events into the model presents rather more difficult problems. All of the variables in the model are, in some sense, attributes or activities of the actors. Political events, on the other hand, are external to the actors and cannot be brought into the model directly. They can however, be brought in through his perceptions. Now to some extent these perceptions are measured in partisan attitudes. These attitudes are, however, assessed only immediately prior to the election itself. What would have to be done in a more dynamic and adaptive model would be to sample perceptions of political events as they arise in the political arena, probing in each case for evaluation of the party's handling of the event. The adequacy of the series of events selected would depend upon the astuteness of the analyst and could be tested by the amount of variance in partisan attitudes immediately prior to the election which is accounted for by the attitudes on the full set of events. Moreover, selected probing techniques, such as factor analysis, could be applied to draw inferences about the factors underlying shifts in partisanship over time.

A model incorporating these modifications is presented in Figure 3.5 below. The model exploits the mediating roles of partisan attitudes and party identification in order to avoid reincorporation of political socialization characteristics over time. This is not to say that these are not operative. On the contrary, they form the background, encapsulated largely in party identification, against which partisan attitudes are formed and operate. The model represents a continual reality-testing and adjustment process. To the extent that party identification exceeds the impact of partisan attitudes, little learning is taking place. To the extent that partisan attitudes exceed and have the same directional impact as party identification, reinforcement

28. Blalock, *Causal Inferences . . .*, pp. 53–57.

Model V. A proposed dynamic.

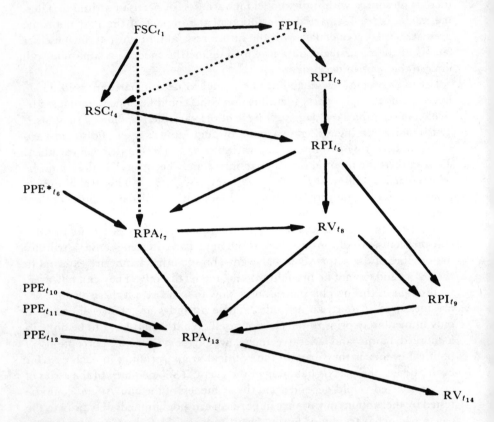

* PPE = perception of political events.

Figure 3.5.

is taking place. Finally, to the extent partisan attitudes operate in a direction opposite to party identification, that identification is being eroded. There are several other points in the proposed model that bear discussion, e.g., the requirement that partisan attitudes operate on party identification through vote (or vote intention). However, this and other excluded arrows had best wait upon the systematic analysis of data in future studies.

7. *Conclusion*

In concluding the present analysis, it is important to bear in mind that we are as yet very far from concluding the inquiry into causality in voting behavior. First, it should be noted that the full set of independent variables accounts for only 50% of the variance in voting. This suggests, of course, that one or more important variables have been excluded from the model. In itself, this is only an indication of the need for a broader searching effort. However, there is a distinct possibility that the omitted variable(s) may be correlated with both the dependent variable and one or more of the independent variables in the present model. In such a case the regression coefficients in the model might be substantially affected, even to the extent of reducing to zero some of the now non-zero coefficients, and of reasserting causal linkages estimated as zero in the present model.[29] The present model is thus tentative, an initial approximation to be continually retested not only with the same variables in different populations at different times, but against the impact of the inclusion of new variables.

Technical note

The variables were operationalized from the source decks of the 1956 election study (Project 417) of the Survey Research Center at the University of Michigan in the following manner:

1. Father's Sociological Characteristics (FSC)

This variable consists in an index generated by running five sociological characteristics of the father against the father's party identification in order to generate an expected value of his being Republican. This value constituted the index. The variables utilized, their sources, and their categorizations are presented below:

Variable (Source Deck: Column)	Categories	(Rows)
Religion (5:27)	Protestant	(1)
	Catholic	(2)
	Jewish	(3)
Class (8:11)	Working	(1, 2, 3)
	Middle	(4, 5, 6)
Size of community (6:34)	Farm	(1)
	Town	(2, 3, 4, 5, 6, 8)
	Metropolis	(7, 9)
Region (6:31–32)	South	
	(1 in col. 31, 4 or 5 in col. 32)	
	Non-South	(all others)
Race (6:10)	White	(1)
	Negro	(2)

29. *Ibid.*, pp. 46–47. See also Herman Wold and Lars Juréen, *Demand Analysis* (New York: John Wiley & Sons, 1953), pp. 37–38, and Fritz C. Holte, *loc. cit.* 1

2. Father's Party Identification (FPI)

This was established on the basis of data gathered in a later wave with the same panel, i.e., the 1958 election study, project 431. Within that study, the information was taken from Deck CO4: column 23, and the only categories used were Democrat (Row 1) and Republican (Row 2).

3. Respondent's Sociological Characteristics (RSC)

The procedure here was the same as that entailed in building the index of father's sociological characteristics, except that the variables used in the regression were characteristics of the respondent rather than of the father.

Variable (Source Deck: Column)	Categories	(Rows)
Religion (5:27)	Protestant	(1)
	Catholic	(2)
	Jewish	(3)
Class (8:10)	Working	(1, 2, 3)
	Middle	(4, 5, 6)
Size of community (1:17)	Farm	(6, -, &)
	Town	(3, 4, 5, 8, 9, 0)
	Metropolis	(1, 2, 7)
Region (1:15)	South	(8, 9, 0)
	Non-South	(1-7)
Race (6:10)	White	(1)
	Negro	(2)

4. Respondent's Party Identification (RPI)

This information was taken from Deck 4, column 9. It was dichotomized as follows: Democrat (rows 1-3), Republican (rows 5-7).

5. Respondent's Partisan Attitudes (RPA)

This variable was received directly from the Survey Research Center at the University of Michigan as an index, drawn from their analysis deck number 86, columns 3-9, and based upon their regression of six dimensions of partisan attitudes against reported vote in 1956.

6. Respondent's Vote

Deck 7: Column 26,   Democrat (row 1),   Republican (row 2).

Chapter 4

DEDUCTIONS FROM "AXIOMATIC THEORY"

HERBERT L. COSTNER
ROBERT K. LEIK*
University of Washington

The term "axiomatic theory" has, among sociologists, become associated with the name of Hans Zetterberg and with the form of the propositions Zetterberg utilized in his seminal essay, "On Axiomatic Theories in Sociology."[1] Axiomatic theories, generally speaking, are not restricted to propositions of any given form; the term applies to a set of propositions "summarizing our knowledge in a given field and for finding further knowledge deductively."[2] Zetterberg's guidelines, however, apparently have a special appeal for sociologists, presumably because the propositions are simple statements of relationship and because the mode of deduction can be summarized in a simple rule of signs. Several axiomatic theories with propositions and deductions in this form or very similar form now appear in the sociological literature.[3]

Reprinted by permission of the authors and publisher from the *American Sociological Review*, Vol. 29, pp. 819–835. Copyright 1964, The American Sociological Association.

* The authors wish to thank J. David Martin for writing the computer program for the data shown in Figures 3 through 8.

1. Hans L. Zetterberg, "On Axiomatic Theories in Sociology," in Zetterberg, *On Theory and Verification in Sociology*, Stockholm: Almquist and Wiksell, 1954. See also Zetterberg, *On Theory and Verification in Sociology* (*A Much Revised Edition*), Totowa, N. J.: The Bedminster Press, 1963.

2. Oskar Morgenstern, "Limits to the Uses of Mathematics in Economics," in James C. Charlesworth (ed.), *Mathematics and the Social Sciences*, The American Academy of Political and Social Science, 1963.

3. See William R. Catton, Jr., "The Functions and Dysfunctions of Ethnocentrism: A Theory," *Social Problems*, 8 (Winter, 1961), pp. 201–211; Jack P. Gibbs and Walter T. Martin, "Urbanization, Technology, and the Division of Labor: International Patterns," *American Sociological Review*, 27 (October, 1962), pp. 667–677; Leroy C. Gould and Clarence Schrag, "Theory Construction and Prediction in Juvenile Delinquency," *Proceedings of the Social Statistics Section of the American Statistical Association*, 1962, pp. 68–73; Kent P. Schwirian and John W. Prehn, "An Axiomatic Theory of Urbanization," *American Sociological Review*, 27 (December, 1962), pp. 812–825.

Commenting on one of these theories, O. D. Duncan flatly asserted that "the reasoning is not valid."[4] In their plaintive reply to Duncan's criticisms, Schwirian and Prehn defended their reasoning by suggesting that they had originally assumed "very high" associations in their postulates[5]—an assumption not previously made explicit in their own or other published statements of axiomatic theories. Unfortunately, Schwirian and Prehn are forced to admit that "the empirical observations conflicted with [this] assumption,"[6] thus making the assumption and the reasoning invalid. They complain, however, that Duncan imposes a severe restriction on the theorist:

> Duncan is stating that, before one attempts to derive any basic hypotheses, one ought first to observe the size of the relationships between the variables to be treated. This is possible when the basic hypotheses derive from other empirical knowledge about the subject matter. It cannot be done however, when one's basic hypotheses derive primarily from a conceptual process.[7]

The future of axiomatic theory would be bleak indeed if it were true that one must observe the size of the relationships—and obtain very high relationships—before making any valid deductions. The point to be elaborated in this paper is that although deductions from such simple statements of relationship as are found in current axiomatic theories are not valid, sociologists may find postulates of a somewhat different form useful in constructing deductive theories with perfectly valid deductions.

Zetterberg's propositional form and mode of deduction are illustrated by the following:

> The greater the A, the greater the B (postulate).
> The greater the B, the greater the C (postulate).

From these, Zetterberg derives a third:

> The greater the A, the greater the C (deduction).

These propositions are statements of relationship between two variables. Zetterberg does not explicitly state a rule for deduction, suggesting instead that "derivation rules implied in ordinary language" will be sufficient.[8] His rule for deduction, however, may be summarized by the statement: *The*

4. Otis Dudley Duncan, "Axioms or Correlations?" *American Sociological Review*, 28 (June, 1963), p. 452.

5. John W. Prehn and Kent P. Schwirian, "Reply to Duncan," *American Sociological Review*, 28 (June, 1963), pp. 452–453.

6. *Ibid.*

7. *Ibid.*

8. Zetterberg, 1954 edition, p. 17. In the 1963 edition, Zetterberg again refers to "the deduction rules of ordinary language" (p. 75).

sign of the deduced relationship is the algebraic product of the signs of the postulated relationships. Hereafter we shall refer to this deductive rule simply as the "sign rule." It is the rule followed by all of the axiomatic theories cited in this paper, and it is the rule that Duncan asserts to be invalid.

A proposition of the form, "The greater the A, the greater (or less) the B," presumes that both A and B are at least ordinal variables and implies a positive (or negative) relation between them as measured by some measure of association such as gamma or r.[9] We shall first consider the case where all relationships in a system of three propositions are measured by r and then proceed to consider the case where relationships are measured by gamma for a 2×2 table only.

Relationships measured by r[10]

If r_{AB} and r_{BC} (the postulates) are positive, the degree and sign of r_{AC} (the "deduced" relationship) cannot be expressed as a function of r_{AB} and r_{BC} alone. The correlation between A and C may, however, be expressed as a function of r_{AB}, r_{BC} and $r_{AC \cdot B}$, where the partial, $r_{AC \cdot B}$, represents the relationship between A and C controlling for B, i.e., the correlation between the errors of estimate in the regression of A on B and the errors of estimate in the regression of C on B. Except in the trivial case where r_{AB} or r_{BC} is exactly $+1$ or -1 (in which case the partial is indeterminate), this partial may range from -1 to $+1$, independently of r_{AB} and r_{BC}.[11]

9. In the 1963 edition of *On Theory and Verification in Sociology*, Zetterberg delineates several "varieties of linkage between determinants and results" (pp. 14–17). He does not make perfectly clear the relevance of these distinctions to deductive reasoning from relational postulates. He states, "So long as all propositions used in our theorizing are of the same type, there are few dangers involved. However, when they are of different varieties, pitfalls appear; and one must proceed with caution." In his re-statement of what had been the core illustration in the 1954 edition, Zetterberg states that the "linkage between determinant and result in these propositions is stochastic and reversible" (p. 74). Since these linkages are not identified as deterministic, we therefore assume that a proposition of the form "The greater the A, the greater the B," may appropriately be equated with a proposition of the form, "A positive relationship exists between A and B as measured by r or gamma."

This equation may not, however, do justice to Zetterberg's intent. In the 1963 edition, Zetterberg indicates that it is appropriate to speak of determinants and results only when "we know or assume the direction in which the variates influence each other" (p. 12). Hence, although Zetterberg does not emphasize the point in the 1963 edition and does not even mention it in the 1954 edition, he apparently intended his propositions to assert a cause and effect relation between variables and not simply a correlation.

10. Although the reasoning utilized in this section can be applied to systems of more than three variables, we consider here the case of three variables only, deferring for future exploration the case of more complex systems.

11. The mathematical proof for this statement consists of showing that for any valu r_{AB} and r_{BC} greater than -1 and less than $+1$, and for any value of $r_{AC \cdot B}$ between -1 $+1$, there exists an r_{AC} between -1 and $+1$ that satisfies Equation (1) on p. 52.

By simple algebraic manipulation of the familiar computing formula for a first order partial

$$r_{AC \cdot B} = \frac{r_{AC} - r_{AB} \, r_{BC}}{\sqrt{1 - r^2_{AB}} \, \sqrt{1 - r^2_{BC}}}, \tag{1}$$

we may express r_{AC} as a function of r_{AB}, r_{BC} and $r_{AC \cdot B}$ (ignoring sampling and measurement errors) as follows:

$$r_{AC} = r_{AB} \, r_{BC} + r_{AC \cdot B} \, \sqrt{1 - r^2_{AB}} \, \sqrt{1 - r^2_{BC}}. \tag{2}$$

When the partial assumes its maximum value of $+1$, we have the maximum r_{AC} possible for given values of r_{AB} and r_{BC}, or

$$r_{AC_{max}} = r_{AB} \, r_{BC} + \sqrt{1 - r^2_{AB}} \, \sqrt{1 - r^2_{BC}}. \tag{3}$$

And when the partial assumes its minimum value of -1, we have the minimum r_{AC} possible for given values of r_{AB} and r_{BC}, or

$$r_{AC_{min}} = r_{AB} \, r_{BC} - \sqrt{1 - r^2_{AB}} \, \sqrt{1 - r^2_{BC}}. \tag{4}$$

For two postulates of like sign, the sign rule specifies a positive deduced relationship. Hence, if the sign rule is to be valid, the minimum possible r_{AC} must be greater than zero. By setting $r_{AC_{min}}$ at zero, squaring the equation and solving for r_{BC}, we may therefore find, for a given value of r_{AB}, the value of r_{BC} that must be exceeded if the sign rule is to yield a valid deduction Thus, for a given r_{AB}, the minimum r_{BC} for which the sign rule (when applied to postulates of like sign) is valid is given by

$$r_{BC_{min}} = \sqrt{1 - r^2_{AB}}. \tag{5}$$

Similarly, for two postulates of unlike sign, the sign rule specifies a negative deduced relationship. Hence, if the rule is to be valid, the maximum possible r_{AC} must be less than zero. By setting the maximum at zero, we again obtain (5). In general, without making further assumptions, the sign rule yields valid deductions if and only if

$$r^2_{AB} + r^2_{BC} > 1.^{12} \tag{6}$$

Consider the magnitude of r's that must be assumed in the postulates if the sign rule is to yield valid deductions with no additional assumptions. The shaded area of Figure 4.1 shows the combinations of postulated r's for which the deduction by the sign rule is valid. In other words, for combinations of

12. This condition, which was basic to Duncan's critique of Schwirian and Prehn, is implied by G. Udny Yule and M. G. Kendall, *An Introduction to the Theory of Statistics*, New York: Hafner, 1950, pp. 301–302. It is the same condition which many years ago was shown to imply a common factor underlying the observed correlations. See J. Ridley Thompson, "Boundary Conditions for Correlation Coefficients Between Three and Four Variables," *The British Journal of Psychology*, 19 (July, 1928) pp. 77–94, and "The Limits of Correlation Between Three Variables," *The British Journal of Psychology*, 19 (January, 1929), pp. 240–252.

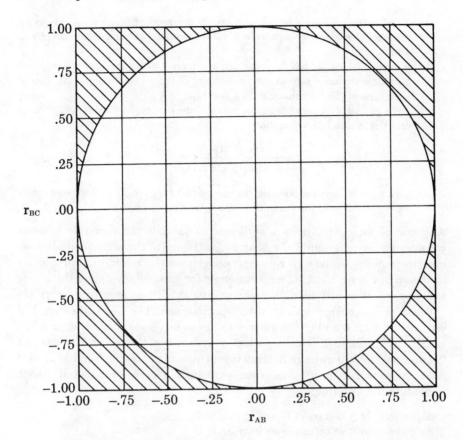

If no assumptions are made about the AB and BC relationships, such as asym-. metric causality, then the point (r_{AB}, r_{BC}) must fall in the shaded area in order for the sign rule to hold.

Figure 4.1. Requirements for the sign rule when relations are measured by r.

r_{AB} and r_{BC} represented in the shaded area of Figure 4.1 and falling in the positive quadrants (upper right and lower left), r_{AC} cannot fall below zero even if the partial, $r_{AC \cdot B}$, takes its minimum value of -1. And for combinations of r_{AB} and r_{BC} represented in the shaded area and falling in the negative quadrants (upper left and lower right) r_{AC} cannot fall above zero even if the partial takes its maximum value of $+1$. Evidently, high relationships must be assumed if the sign rule is to be valid without further assumptions.

Are there, however, alternative assumptions that render the sign rule valid without requiring such high degrees of relationship? Referring to (2) above, it is evident that

(a) if the partial, $r_{AC \cdot B}$, is zero, r_{AC} is simply the product (r_{AB}) (r_{BC}). Hence, if the partial is zero, the sign rule is valid regardless of the magnitude of r_{AB} and r_{BC};

(b) if the partial, $r_{AC \cdot B}$, has the same sign as the product (r_{AB}) (r_{BC}), then r_{AC} will also have the same sign as the product (r_{AB}) (r_{BC}) and the sign rule is valid regardless of the magnitude of r_{AB} and r_{BC};

(c) if the partial, $r_{AC \cdot B}$, has a sign opposite to the sign of the product (r_{AB}) (r_{BC}) and less in absolute value than

$$\frac{(r_{AB})\ (r_{BC})}{\sqrt{1 - r^2_{AB}}\ \sqrt{1 - r^2_{BC}}},$$

then r_{AC} will have the same sign as the product (r_{AB}) (r_{BC}), and the sign rule is valid regardless of the magnitude of r_{AB} and r_{BC}.

Any one of these conditions is sufficient to validate the sign rule without considering the magnitude of r_{AB} and r_{BC}. If none of the above conditions is met, the validity of the sign rule rests entirely on the assumption of high r's as shown in Figure 4.1. Is there a rationale for making any one of the above assumptions, thereby making the sign rule valid without requiring high r's?

Condition (a) above, requiring a zero partial, would be met if the errors of estimate of A on B and of C on B are random (i.e., uncorrelated) errors. We usually interpret such a zero partial as indicating that A and C are not "connected" except through B. Drawing on the work of Simon[13] and Blalock[14] we may state two propositions implying such a zero partial and hence validating the sign rule:

An increase in A will result in an increase in B;
An increase in B will result in an increase in C.

We have modified Zetterberg's form of proposition, intending thereby to indicate quite explicitly that these statements postulate not simply covariation between two variables, but an asymmetric causal relationship. Zetterberg's introduction of the language of "determinants and results," in his 1963 edition of *On Theory and Verification in Sociology*, may imply a "causal" relationship even though the propositions themselves remain in covariation form, i.e., "The greater the A, the greater the B." The axiomatic theories that

13. Herbert A. Simon, "Spurious Correlation: A Causal Interpretation," *Journal of the American Statistical Association*, 49 (September, 1954), pp. 467–479. (This article is reproduced in Simon's *Models of Man*, New York: Wiley, 1957, pp. 37–49.)

14. Hubert M. Blalock, "Correlational Analysis and Causal Inferences," *American Anthropologist*, 62 (August, 1960), pp. 624–631; "Correlation and Causality: The Multivariate Case," *Social Forces*, 39 (March, 1961), pp. 246–251; "Evaluating the Relative Importance of Variables," *American Sociological Review*, 26 (December, 1961), pp. 866–874; "Four-Variable Causal Models and Partial Correlation," *American Journal of Sociology*, 68 (September, 1962), pp. 182–194.

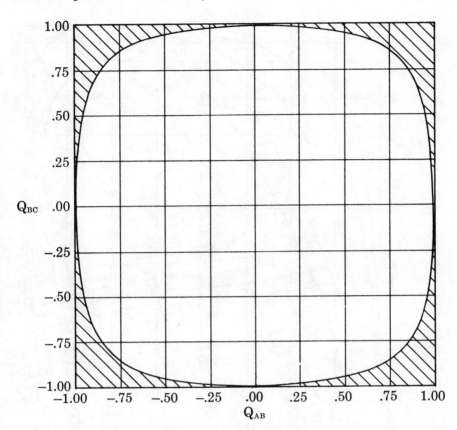

If no assumptions are made about the AB and BC relationships, then the point (Q_{AB}, Q_{BC}) must fall in the shaded area in order for the sign rule to hold.

Figure 4.2. Requirements for the sign rule when relations are measured by Q.

have come to our attention do not stress the "causal" nature of their propositions, although in their discussions, such terms as "consequences of", "give rise to," "makes for," etc., indicate that "causal" propositions are intended. The causal assumption is crucial in the present discussion because only with that assumption can the nature of the partial be derived, and only if the nature of the partial is known can the sign rule be definitely judged valid.

The "asymmetric" assumption is equally crucial, and for the same reason. Zetterberg distinguishes, in the 1963 edition, between "linkages" that are "reversible" and those that are "irreversible," a distinction apparently parallel to "symmetric" and "asymmetric" in the language of Simon and Blalock. But this distinction plays no explicit part in Zetterberg's deductions,

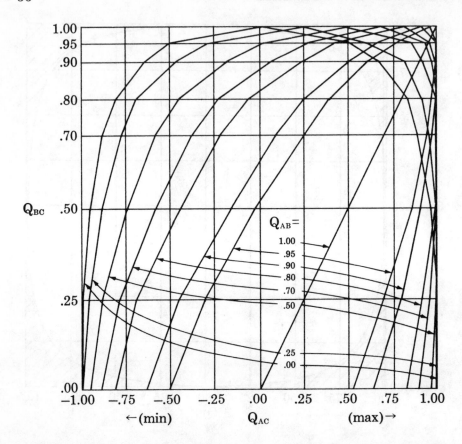

To use Figure 4.3, locate the curve representing a given value of Q_{AB}. This curve intersects the horizontal line representing the value of Q_{BC} at Q_{AC}(max) on the right side and Q_{AC}(min) on the left side. If either Q_{AB} or Q_{BC} is negative and the other positive, then Q_{AC}(max) $= -Q_{AC}$(min) as shown in the figure, and Q_{AC}(min) $= -Q_{AC}$ as shown.

Figure 4.3. Limits on the range of Q_{AC} for given values of Q_{AB} and Q_{BC}. All marginal distributions are .50—.50.

and he makes deductions where postulates are explicitly identified as symmetrical. Some of the axiomatic theories in the literature have also been accompanied by discussion that indicates recognition of a distinction between symmetrical and asymmetrical propositions, while others have not, and some of the theories that recognize the distinction continue, like Zetterberg, to make deductions from propositions assumed to be symmetrical. Nothing in our present discussion can be construed as validating the sign rule for symmetric propositions.

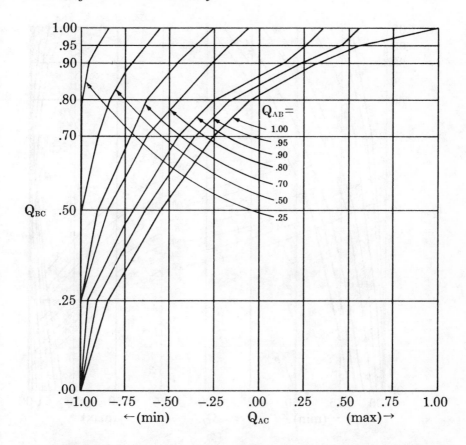

To use Figure 4.4, locate the curve representing a given value of Q_{AB}. This curve intersects the horizontal line representing the value of Q_{BC} at $Q_{AC}(\min)$. All $Q_{AC}(\max)$ equal 1.00. If either Q_{AB} or Q_{BC} is negative and the other positive, then $Q_{AC}(\max) = -Q_{AC}(\min)$ as shown in the figure, and $Q_{AC}(\min) = 1.00$.

Figure 4.4. Limits on the range of Q_{AC} for given values of Q_{AB} and Q_{BC}. Marginal distributions of A and B are .50—.50, and marginal distribution of C is .75—.25.

An asymmetric causal relationship is a relationship that would be verified by an experiment in which the first-named variable is manipulated while controlling for or randomizing all other variables, whereas the relationship would not be verified by an experiment in which the second-named variable is manipulated while controlling for or randomizing all other variables. In making a proposition of this form we do not, however, necessarily assume that such an experiment has been carried out. Propositions of this form may have the status of assumptions rather than findings; if those assumptions allow deductions about matters of fact, those deductions, when tested, provide

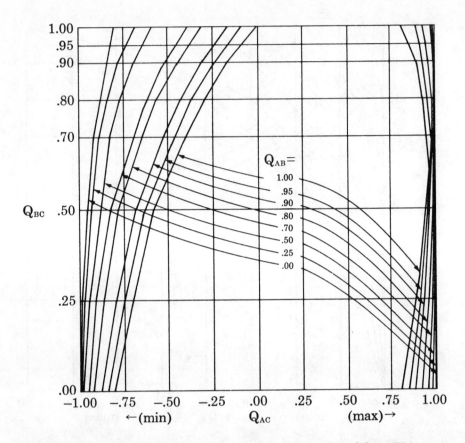

To use Figure 4.5, locate the curve representing a given value of Q_{AB}. This curve intersects the horizontal line representing the value of Q_{BC} at Q_{AC}(max) on the right side and Q_{AC}(min) on the left side. If either Q_{AB} or Q_{BC} is negative and the other positive, then Q_{AC}(max) $= -Q_{AC}$(min) as shown in the figure, and Q_{AC}(min) $= -Q_{AC}$(max) as shown.

Figure 4.5. Limits on the range of Q_{AC} for given values of Q_{AB} and Q_{BC}. Marginal distribution of A is .75—.25, and marginal distributions of B and C are .50—.50.

an indirect test of the assumptions that may supplant or supplement direct tests in the familiar manner of scientific theories generally. The "asymmetric causal" propositions stated above may be more formally stated in a form adapted from Simon[15] as follows:

$$(A - \overline{A}) = e_1$$
$$(B - \overline{B}) = b_{21}(A - \overline{A}) + e_2$$
$$(C - \overline{C}) = b_{32}(B - \overline{B}) + e_3.$$

15. Simon, *op. cit.*, p. 470.

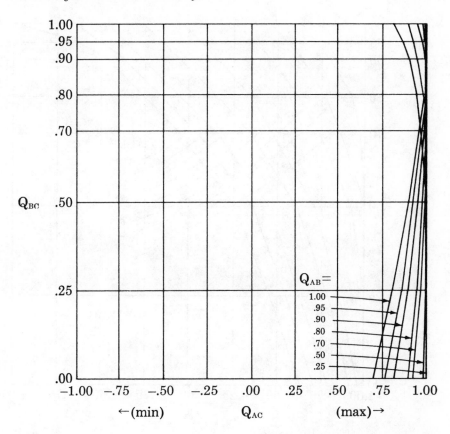

To use Figure 4.6, locate the curve representing a given value of Q_{AB}. This curve intersects the horizontal line representing the value of Q_{BC} at Q_{AC} (max) on the right side. All Q_{AC}(min) equal -1.00. If either Q_{AI} or Q_{BC} is negative and the other positive, then Q_{AC}(max) $= 1.00$, and Q_{AC}(min) $= -Q_{AC}$(max) as shown in the figure.

Figure 4.6. Limits on the range of Q_{AC} for given values of Q_{AB} and Q_{BC}. Marginal distributions of A and C are .75—.25, and marginal distribution of B is .50—.50.

In other words, A "is causally dependent on"[16] neither B nor C but on other variables not explicit in this three-variable system; hence A is expressed as a function of an "error term" only. On the other hand, B is causally dependent on A, but not C, and on its own error term. Finally, C is causally dependent on B and its own error term. Simon has shown that, with the assumption of uncorrelated error terms, this set of equations implies that the partial, $r_{AC \cdot B}$, is zero. Since the sign rule is valid if the partial is zero and since the

16. *Ibid.*

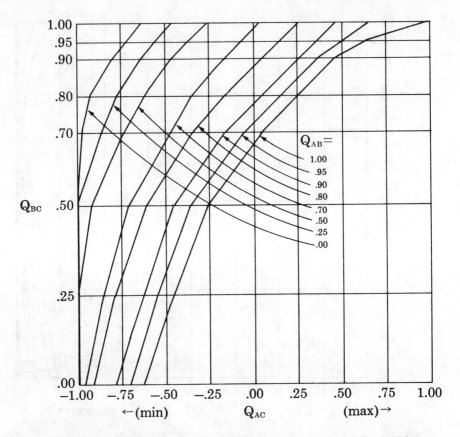

To use Figure 4.7, locate the curve representing a given value of Q_{AB}. This curve intersects the horizontal line representing the value of Q_{BC} at $Q_{AC}(\text{min})$. All $Q_{AC}(\text{max})$ equal 1.00. If either Q_{AB} or Q_{BC} is negative and the other positive, then $Q_{AC}(\text{max}) = -Q_{AC}(\text{min})$ as shown in the figure, and $Q_{AC}(\text{min}) = -1.00$.

Figure 4.7. Limits on the range of Q_{AC} for given values of Q_{AB} and Q_{BC}. Marginal distributions of A and B are .75—.25, and marginal distribution of C is .50—.50.

conditions outlined above imply a zero partial, we may conclude that the conditions are sufficient for the validity of the sign rule. Hence the appropriate conclusion is:

An increase in A will result in an increase in C.

In general, then, we may outline one set of sufficient conditions for the validity of the sign rule as follows: If

 i. postulates are stated in asymmetric causal form;
 ii. the common variable in the two postulates is prior to one but not to both of the other two variables; and

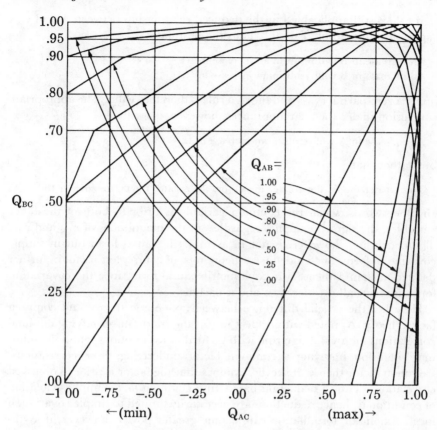

To use Figure 4.8, locate the curve representing a given value of Q_{AB}. This curve intersects the horizontal line representing the value of Q_{BC} at Q_{AC} (max) on the right side and Q_{AC}(min) on the left side. If either Q_{AB} or Q_{BC} is negative and the other positive, then Q_{AC}(max) = $-Q_{AC}$(min) as shown in the figure, and Q_{AC}(min) = $-Q_{AC}$(max) as shown.

Figure 4.8. Limits on the range of Q_{AC} for given values of Q_{AB} and Q_{BC}. All marginal distributions are .75—.25.

iii. a "closed system" is assumed, i.e., it is assumed that there is no connection between the variables in the postulates except those connections stated or implied in the postulates (otherwise, the assumption of uncorrelated error terms would be unwarranted and the propositions would not imply a zero partial),

then the sign rule is valid, regardless of the magnitude of r_{AB} and r_{BC}.

When the common variable in two "asymmetric causal" postulates is prior to both of the other two variables (i.e., condition ii above is not met), the sign rule is still applicable but the deduced relationship between A and C is "spurious" instead of "causal." Thus the postulates,

An increase in B will result in an increase in A;
An increase in B will result in an increase in C,

imply a zero partial $r_{AC \cdot B}$ and the sign rule is therefore valid. The appropriate conclusion under these circumstances, however, is *not* that

An increase in A will result in an increase in C,

but rather that

The greater the A, the greater the C (or, the greater the C, the greater the A).

In other words, when the common variable is prior to both of the other variables, the sign rule applies regardless of the magnitudes of r_{AB} and r_{BC}. The conclusion, however, is not in asymmetric causal form but in simple covariation form. Such a deduced theorem is, of course, less useful in further deduction than a theorem in asymmetric causal form since the covariation form does not allow inferences about partials.

Here lies the crucial difference between axiomatic theory and common factor theory. As noted with respect to (6), the condition specifying minimal correlations for a valid sign rule with no further assumptions is also the minimal condition implying a common factor underlying those correlations. Common factor theory, however, assumes that the factor is prior to observed correlations. Thus a deduction based on a common factor implies violation of condition ii; hence deductions are necessarily limited to simple covariation form. Axiomatic formulation can assume greater power, however, if asymmetric causality under condition ii can be assumed, allowing directional deductions that permit chained inferences.

It should also be evident that when the postulates are in asymmetric causal form and the common variable in the two postulates is prior to *neither* of the other two variables, no conclusion about the partial (controlling for the common variable) can be drawn. Hence no theorem could be deduced by the sign rule unless conditions other than condition (a) validate the rule.

Condition (*b*), requiring a partial of the same sign as the product $(r_{AB})(r_{BC})$, renders a deduction by the sign rule valid but of limited utility. If, for example one states as postulates,

The greater the A, the greater the B,
The greater the B, the greater the C,

and assumes further that condition (b) is met, i.e., that partialling out B, the relation between A and C remains positive, it is evident from (2) that r_{AC} must be positive.

This assumption states, in effect, that if the already known relation between two variables, with all others controlled, has the same sign as that implied by the deduction through an intermediate third variable, then the sign of the relation between the two will remain unchanged when the third is not controlled. In other words, if an increase in A leads to an increase in C (implying a zero partial), and if B is positively related to both A and C, then the relation between A and C must remain positive even when B is allowed to operate. This type of deduction may be useful in determining whether or not a given variable must be controlled when experimentally manipulating a system. It is difficult to see much utility for such deductions, however, when developing axiomatic theories.

Condition (*c*), requiring a partial opposite in sign to the sign of the product (r_{AB}) (r_{BC}) but less in absolute value than

$$\frac{(r_{AB}) \ (r_{BC})}{\sqrt{1-r^2_{AB}} \ \sqrt{1-r^2_{BC}}},$$

is an exceedingly demanding condition to assume. It requires that the partial not exceed, in absolute value, an amount that would ordinarily not be specifiable from the statement of the postulates alone. We are unable to specify any additional assumptions, with or without evident intuitive meaning, which would imply that condition (c) had been met.

We may, however, consider briefly the meaning of a partial, of whatever magnitude, opposite in sign to the sign of the product (r_{AB}) (r_{BC}). Referring back to (2), it is evident that the partial $r_{AC.B}$ must be opposite in sign to the sign of the product (r_{AB}) (r_{BC}) if the sign rule is ever to be *invalid*, regardless of the magnitudes of r_{AB} and r_{BC}. It is, therefore, appropriate to ask whether partials opposite in sign to the product (r_{AB}) (r_{BC}) are in any way "unreasonable" or "freak" occurrences. It can be shown mathematically that such partials are not impossible (see footnote 11). But if such partials, while mathematically possible, occur only under very unusual circumstances, the potential invalidity of the sign rule would, perhaps, be a small concern in the methodology of theory construction. For postulates in simple covariation form, however, a partial of a given sign is neither more nor less reasonable than a partial of opposite sign. For example, in the two postulates,

The greater the A, the greater the B;
The greater the B, the greater the C,

the positive relation between A and B may be "spurious" (in Simon's sense), i.e., both may be causally dependent on a fourth variable, D. Similarly, the positive relation between B and C may be "spurious" through some variable, E. If either or both is spurious, no "direct connection" between A and C is implied by the postulates, and the negative partial $r_{AC.B}$ is neither more nor less reasonable than a positive partial. Under these circumstances, the sign and magnitude of the partial would depend on other "connections" between A and C not specified in the postulates.

Thus, although a partial opposite in sign to the sign of the product (r_{AB}) (r_{BC}) is neither impossible nor "unreasonable," the unknown value in condition (c) still makes it a "demanding" condition. The assumption that the partial is less in absolute value than some describable, but ordinarily unknown, quantity appears to be an assumption for which no rationale is available.

We have considered above the magnitude of the postulated r's that must be assumed if the sign rule is to yield valid conclusions, without further assumptions. The magnitudes required are high and exceed those usually found. Of the three conditions we have outlined, each of which would render the sign rule valid regardless of the magnitude of the postulated r's, one, (c), has no rationale. Another, (b), is such that its utility is limited in building axiomatic theories. The third condition, (a), is subject to neither of these handicaps. On the contrary, we have shown that by making assumptions identical to those made by Simon in his development of asymmetric causal models, condition (a) is implied and the sign rule for deductions is therefore valid, regardless of the magnitude of the postulated r's.

We therefore conclude that to make valid deductions from postulated relations between variables through the application of the sign rule, it is sufficient to

   i. state postulates in asymmetric causal form;

  ii. make deductions only from postulates in which the common variable is prior to one or both of the other two variables included in two postulates; and

 iii. assume a "closed system," i.e., there is no "connection" (causal or "spurious") between the variables in the postulates except those stated or implied in the postulates.

These requirements are, of course, more stringent than those explicitly suggested by Zetterberg or applied by others who have published axiomatic theories in which the sign rule provides the mode of deduction. These requirements, furthermore, specify "causal" propositions as the postulational form for axiomatic theories, and some may consider "causal" propositions inappropriate when the data are correlational. These requirements, however, allow not only the *valid* deduction of theorems but also the deduction of *more* propositions, i.e., for each pair of postulates an additional proposition may be deduced, thereby permitting a more complete empirical test of the postulates than would one deduction alone. For example, assuming a "closed system" in Simon's sense, the postulates,

An increase in A will result in an increase in B;
An increase in B will result in an increase in C,

not only imply

An increase in A will result in an increase in C.

but also imply

$r_{AC.B} = 0$.

Postulates of this form in sociology must ordinarily have the status of assumptions, not findings,[17] and if empirical data are incompatible with *either* of the above deductions from the postulates, then either the postulates or the assumption of a "closed system" must be modified. On the other hand, if empirical data are incompatible with neither of the above deductions, a "stronger" theory has met the test of data without rejection than would have been the case if postulates and deductions were in simple covariation form. Careful reading of axiomatic theories in the literature suggests that "causal" propositions are being discussed, although the formal statements make no causal claims. The result of failing to recognize explicitly the causal nature of the postulates is not simply that the deductions are invalid, as Duncan has charged, but that the use of partials in the empirical test of the theory is not recognized.

Relationships measured by gamma: the 2 × 2 case

Throughout the discussion above, we have assumed that product moment correlation, r, provides an appropriate measure for the relationships postulated and deduced; in other words we have implicitly assumed interval measures and linear relationships. But interval measures may not be obtainable for data of theoretical interest, and the assumption of linear relationships may not be theoretically or empirically appropriate. An ordinal measure of association, gamma, makes neither of these assumptions.[18] An older measure, Yule's Q, is a special case of gamma for the 2 × 2 table. We consider here only the case of the 2 × 2 table and explore the applicability of the reasoning in the above section to this case.

Evidently, the 2 × 2 cross-classification table is one way of representing the familiar relationships treated in the logic of classes, i.e., necessary, sufficient, and necessary-and-sufficient. But when represented in a 2 × 2 table, these

17. Failure to recognize the fact that the "asymmetric" coefficients in Simon's model have the status of assumptions, to be accepted or rejected on the basis of an empirical outcome (i.e., the nature of the partial correlation), appears to underlie Polk's charge that asymmetric coefficients are "logically inconsistent and empirically impossible as long as symmetrical measures of correlation are assumed." See Kenneth Polk, "A Note on Asymmetric Causal Models," *American Sociological Review*, 27 (August, 1962), p. 540.

18. Leo A. Goodman and William H. Kruskal, "Measures of Association for Cross Classifications," *Journal of the American Statistical Association*, 49 (December, 1954), pp. 732–764.

traditional logical relationships imply at least one zero cell, i.e., a "perfect" relationship when measured by gamma for the 2×2 table. Here we do not question the venerable and highly respectable logic of classes, but rather the appropriateness of assuming the "perfect" relationships that make such logic applicable. We are inclined to agree with Zetterberg that "deterministic [i.e., "perfect"] relations seem very rare in sociology."[19] Our interest, then, focuses on less than "perfect" relationships.

An equation "decomposing" a relationship into its "partial" and "marginal" components has become familiar to sociologists through the work of Lazarsfeld.[20] Lazarsfeld's equation is an adaptation of the following equation from Yule and Kendall:[21]

$$\delta_{AC} = \delta_{AC \cdot B1} + \delta_{AC \cdot B2} + \frac{n}{(C_1)\,(C_2)}\,(\delta_{AC})\,(\delta_{BC}) \qquad (7)$$

where δ_{AC} is the discrepancy between the observed frequency in a given cell of the AC table and the expected frequency for that cell under the hypothesis of statistical independence. In other words, the "original" relation between A and C may be "decomposed" into the "partials" (i.e., the relation between A and C when B is at level 1 and the relation between A and C when B is at level 2) and the "marginal" relationships, AC and BC. Equation (7) bears an obvious similarity to (2), which expresses r_{AC} as a function of the partial, $r_{AC \cdot B}$, and the "marginals," r_{AB} and r_{BC}. But whereas (2) was utilized to obtain combinations of r_{AB} and r_{BC} for which the sign rule must be valid, (7) is not convenient for finding analogous combinations of gammas for which the sign rule must be valid, since the gammas are a function not only of the deltas of (7) but also of marginal frequencies not represented there. The similarity of the two equations, however, suggests a high degree of similarity between systems of relationships measured by r and systems of relationships measured by Q (gamma) in 2×2 tables.

A more convenient, if less elegant, procedure for finding combinations of Q values for which the sign rule must be valid, for given marginal frequencies,[22] yields the information represented in Figure 4.2. Given 50-50 marginals for all three variables, Figure 4.2 is analogous to Figure 4.1 for r: for all combinations of Q in the shaded area of Figure 4.2, the sign rule is valid. For combinations of Q not in the shaded area, the deduced relationship does not necessarily have the sign implied by the sign rule unless further

19. Zetterberg, *op. cit.* (1954 edition), p. 15.
20. See, for example, Paul F. Lazarsfeld, "Interpretation of Statistical Relations as a Research Operation," in Lazarsfeld and Morris Rosenberg (eds.), *The Language of Social Research*, Glencoe, Ill.: The Free Press, 1955.
21. Yule and Kendall, *op. cit.*, p. 36.
22. In this procedure, computations are made directly with cell frequencies. Let cells be

assumptions are made. It is clear that for 2×2 tables in which relationships are measured by Q, like systems of relationships measured by r, very high relationships must be assumed if the sign rule is to yield valid conclusions without further assumptions.

Skewed marginals do not remove the necessity for assuming high independent Q's, but the necessary magnitude of independent Q's differs from the positive to the negative quadrants. This lack of symmetry varies as the degree of skew in the marginals varies. Figures 4.3 through 4.8 present the limits of

---

lettered a, b, c and d in the usual manner, with subscripts attached to these letters to designate the various cell entries as follows:

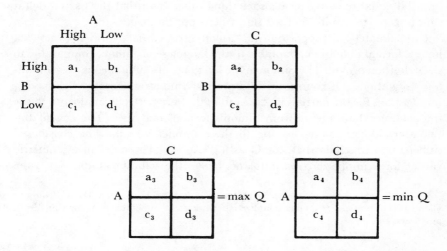

Consider the maximum possible Q (i.e., maximum possible product ad, or $a_3 d_3$). The cases that are high on both A and B are represented by a_1. The cases that are high on both C and B are represented by a_2. Some of the a_1 cases high on both A and B may also be high on C, but no more than a_2 of them can possibly be. Alternately, some of the a_2 cases high on both C and B may also be high on A, but no more than a_1 of them can possibly be. Hence, the number of high B cases that are high on both A and C cannot be greater than the lesser of the two quantities, a_1 and a_2. Similarly, the number of low B cases that are high on both A and C cannot be greater than the lesser of the two quantities c_1 and c_2. Hence

$$a_3 = [\min (a_1, a_2)] + [\min (c_1, c_2)].$$

Now consider the minimum possible Q, (i.e., minimum possible product ad, or $a_4 d_4$). The cases that are high on both A and B are represented by a_1. The high B, low C cases are represented by b_2. Some of the a_1 cases high on both A and B might be low on C, but no more than b_2 of them. Alternately, some of the b_2 cases high on B and low on C might be high on A, but no more than a_1 of them. Hence, the number of high B cases that are high on A and low on C cannot be greater than the lesser of the two values a_1 and b_2. Similarly, the number of low B cases that are high on A and low on C cannot be greater than the lesser of the two quantities c_1 and d_2. Hence

$$b_4 = [\min (a_1, b_2)] + [\min (c_1, d_2)].$$

Q_{AC} for given independent conditions. These figures show maximum and minimum Q_{AC} for all possible pairs of independent Q's with the values 1.00, .95, .90, .80, .70, .50, .25 and 0, and for all combinations of marginal distributions .75-.25 and .50-.50. It is apparent at a glance that Q_{AC} is highly variable and quite susceptible to influence from marginal distributions.

Is it also true for Q's as for r's that the statement of postulates in asymmetric causal form, plus the "closed system" assumption, is sufficient to render the sign rule valid regardless of the magnitude of the postulated Q's? Equation (7) indicates that when the "partial" deltas are both zero, or when they sum to zero, the relation between A and C is a product function of the "marginals:" hence the sign rule must be valid under these conditions. If a "partial equal to zero" means something other than that the partial deltas sum to zero, the validity of the sign rule is not implied.[23]

Unfortunately, a proposition in "asymmetric causal" form does not yet have a formal definition adaptable to the language of gamma comparable to the definition provided by Simon in the language of simultaneous "regression-like" equations. Of course, we interpret "asymmetric causality" as having implications for the partials in 2×2 tables that are perfectly analogous to the implications that emerge from Simon's formal analysis.[24] The cogent but "non-formal" reasoning leading to those implications may be considered sufficient to conclude that, for Q as for r, postulates stated in asymmetric causal form imply zero partials and hence the validity of the sign rule.

23. For example, a formula for partial Q has been suggested by James A. Davis ("Notes on Gamma: Interpretation, Computation, Partials, Multiples," unpublished manuscript, 1963), as follows:

Given	C	$\overline{C}$
B A	a	b
B $\overline{A}$	c	d
B̄ A	e	f
B̄ $\overline{A}$	g	h

$$Q_{AC \cdot B} = \frac{(ad + eh) \ - \ (bc + fg)}{(ad + eh) \ + \ (bc + fg)}$$

Although we would prefer a formal analysis that leads to these implications, we will not attempt to present one here.

Conclusions: The methodology of theory construction

The gap between the techniques relevant to "theory building" and those relevant to "empirical research" appears to be narrowing; statistical techniques developed in the service of data analysis are not irrelevant to the construction of theory and the valid deduction of theorems therefrom. We have shown that although the sign rule applied to pairs of postulates in simple correlational form does not yield logically valid theorems, the sign rule applied to pairs of postulates in "asymmetric causal" form does lead to logically valid theorems. The formal argument underlying this conclusion, drawing heavily on the work of Simon, ignores measurement and sampling errors and is restricted to systems of relationships measurable by r. However, a "non-formal" but nonetheless cogent argument, drawing heavily on the work of Lazarsfeld, Kendall and Hyman, suggests the extension of this same reasoning to systems of relationships measurable by gamma in 2×2 tables. We have not explored the more general case of gamma in $r \times c$ tables.

Examination of the Davis partial shows, however, that $Q_{AC \cdot B} = 0$ is *not* a sufficient condition to validate the sign rule. Consider the following frequencies:

		C	C̄
B	A	18	18
	Ā	9	0
B̄	A	27	18
	Ā	9	12

For this illustration, $Q_{AB} = .30$, $Q_{BC} = .11$, $Q_{AC \cdot B}$ (Davis) $= 0$, yet, $Q_{AC} = -.09$. Although the Davis partial is zero, the two partial deltas do not sum to zero, and the difference between them is greater in absolute value than, and opposite in sign to, the product function of the marginals constituting the third term on the right in (7). Hence, the sign rule does not apply.

24. See Lazarsfeld, *op. cit.*; Patricia Kendall and Paul F. Lazarsfeld, "Problems of Survey Analysis," in R. K. Merton and P. F. Lazarsfeld (eds.), *Continuities in Social Research*, Glencoe, Ill.: The Free Press, 1950, pp. 133–196; and Herbert Hyman, *Survey Design and Analysis*, Glencoe, Ill.: The Free Press, 1955, chaps. 6 and 7.

Many other issues in the methodology of theory construction may well be clarified if they are examined with regard to implied mathematical and statistical relationships. For example, how can "conditional" or "contingent"[25] causal connections best be worked into postulational theories? Such relationships represent a special type of interaction; and the reasoning employed in analysis of covariance, with its explicit recognition of the possibility of interaction, may be useful in developing a postulational form and rules of deduction for contingent propositions. Similarly, how are "cumulative" or "interdependent" relations to be represented in axiomatic (or other formal) theories so that their implications may be deduced in detail for comparison with relevant data? This type of relation is described by Zetterberg as one in which "a small increment in one variable results in a small increment in a second variable; then, the increment in the second variable makes possible a further increment in the first variable which in turn affects the second one, and so this process goes on until no more increments are possible."[26] For its substantive rather than its methodological interest precisely this type of process is described by Cohen as a process of "mutual conversion" in subcultural differentiation.[27] The substantive relevance of such a process is also indicated in Kirkpatrick's description of "cumulative-circular-social-interaction."[28] Perhaps the statistical techniques developed by economists for treating interdependent systems of variables in time sequence[29] will be helpful in representing such a process in postulational form and in drawing testable implications from such postulates.

Examples may be found of mathematical as well as statistical formulations providing deductions about the type of process just indicated. Simon's simultaneous differential equations representing Homans' postulates on activity, interaction and sentiment indicate one approach.[30] Economic input-output models, which are readily adapted to such problems as interdependent status systems,[31] constitute another.

25. The circumstance "if X, then Y, but only if Z" is described by Zetterberg as a "contingent" relation. Zetterberg, *op. cit.* (1963 edition), p. 16. Hyman suggests a similar relation in his discussion of the type of "elaboration" he calls "specification." Hyman, *op. cit.*, pp. 283 ff.

26. Zetterberg, *op. cit.* (1963 edition), p. 17.

27. Albert K. Cohen, *Delinquent Boys*, Glencoe, Ill.: The Free Press, 1955, pp. 59 ff.

28. Clifford Kirkpatrick, *The Family as Process and Institution*, New York: Ronald Press, 1955, pp. 198–446 *passim*.

29. See, for example, Herman Wold, "Causal Inference from Observational Data," *Journal of the Royal Statistical Society Series A*, 119 (Part I, 1956), pp. 28–60, and Herman Wold and L. Jureen, *Demand Analysis*, New York: Wiley, 1953.

30. Herbert A. Simon, "A Formal Theory of Interaction in Social Groups," *American Sociological Review*, 17 (April, 1952), pp. 202–211. (This article is reproduced in Simon's *Models of Man, op. cit.*, pp. 99–114.)

31. See, for example, Charles H. Hubbell, "An Input-Output Approach to Clique Identification," paper read at the American Sociological Association meeting, Los Angeles, August, 1963.

The foregoing examples suggest a problem we have not addressed. Much of the popularity of Zetterberg's initial work on axiomatic theory was undoubtedly a consequence of its relative simplicity, particularly its non-mathematical character. To many theoretically inclined sociologists, mathematical and statistical reasoning appears cumbersome, overly restrictive, or simply obscure. Is it necessary to conclude from our discussion that only mathematically or statistically trained persons will be able to construct valid axiomatic theories? We think not.

Mathematical and statistical reasoning can, however, clarify the logical guidelines for theory construction. Once necessary assumptions for given types of deductions have been established, the theoretician need only decide whether he is willing to make the requisite assumptions or to forego the particular deductions. This, of course, is what has been done all along, with somewhat less certainty as to the rules of the game.

PART II

Path Analysis

Part II is concerned with an approach to causal model building that has taken on the name of "path analysis" following the terminology of Sewall Wright who introduced the procedure into the biometric literature fully fifty years ago. Since there are many misunderstandings concerning the similarities and differences between path analysis, the approach suggested by Simon, and the simultaneous-equation methods developed within the econometric tradition, certain introductory comments would seem necessary. The fact that these approaches have retained some of the distinctive features introduced by their originators should not blind one to their basic similarities. In sociology, in particular, something of a false dichotomy seems to have developed between "path analysis" and what has been termed the "Simon-Blalock" approach, and there has been additional confusion as a result of Boudon's introduction of the term "dependence analysis" as a synonym for path analysis.[1]

The reader will notice that all of the models discussed in the present section are recursive in nature, and that they involve basically the same assumptions as those utilized in Part I. But whereas in Part I the major focus was on *testing* alternative models in order to select those most compatible with the data, the focus in Part II is primarily on *estimating* the numerical values of the coefficients once one has already settled on the appropriate model. Contrary to the impressions that have been left by some authors, this is *not* a basic distinction between "path analysis" and the "Simon-Blalock" approach. For it is a simple matter to estimate the regression coefficients in each equation of a recursive model. As I argue in the paper on closed populations, one's focus should be on the magnitudes of these regression coefficients, rather than on partial correlation coefficients. Of course, in the testing phase of the model-building enterprise one is often interested in predictions

1. Raymond Boudon, "A Method of Linear Causal Analysis: Dependence Analysis," *American Sociological Review*, 30 (June 1965), pp. 365–374.

that some of the regression coefficients or structural parameters are zero, and these tests can therefore be translated into predictions that certain partial correlations will be zero.

The papers by Turner and Stevens and by Sewall Wright should help to clarify one of the basic issues that has tended to confuse many sociologists and political scientists. Turner and Stevens utilize path-analytic terminology and diagrams, but they tend to prefer the kinds of unstandardized regression coefficients that appear in the econometric literature and that are explicit in the recursive model. Wright's paper points out that path coefficients, which are standardized measures, have certain advantages over the unstandardized coefficients, which Wright has termed "path regression coefficients." Thus one of the issues that divides those who utilize "path analysis" from those who have followed Simon or who have been trained in the econometric tradition is that of whether standardized coefficients are preferable to unstandardized ones. Duncan's discussion of sociological applications of path analysis utilizes the standardized measures, whereas in my paper on causal inferences and closed populations I attempt to argue in favor of the unstandardized measures. Thus the differences between perspectives partly involve the question of the *kinds* of measures to utilize, but the models and assumptions involved are fundamentally the same.

There is also another difference that may be important in terms of the psychological process of theory building. The path-analytic perspective involves more explicit attention to the "error" or "residual" components of the equation. These terms are conceptualized as though they were due to a distinct though unmeasured variable, thus making each variable completely determined by the remaining "variables" in the system. The resulting algebraic manipulations and formulas therefore appear different from those utilized by Simon and in connection with ordinary least-squares procedures, but it can be shown that the two systems are mathematically equivalent, provided one begins with the same models and assumptions.

This difference in the way equations are written down, as well as the path-tracing algorithms that have been developed out of the path-analytic tradition, offers the social scientist a dual approach that may afford more insights than could be attained through the use of either approach alone. In particular, the use of curved double-headed arrows to represent unexplained correlations among exogenous variables is a practical heuristic device for adding reality to a causal system. Path analysis can be effectively applied to models containing unmeasured variables, as Sewall Wright has noted. Thus, although the two approaches are formally equivalent, there are many instances in which it is useful to retain the distinction. It is hoped that this point will be clarified in Part IV where we turn our attention to multiple indicators and various kinds of measurement errors.

Chapter 5

THE REGRESSION ANALYSIS
OF CAUSAL PATHS

Malcolm E. Turner
Charles D. Stevens*
Emory University

1. Introduction

The purpose of this presentation is to acquaint biologists and biometricians with an important tool, path analysis. This tool can be of help in dealing with complex causal networks. These often, though not always, prove amenable to common regression technics. Path analysis, originated by Sewall Wright [1918], is a convenient approach to regression problems involving two or more regression equations. For those unskilled in statistics, path analysis provides one method of depicting regression problems by simple diagram. The path diagram, commonly representing the flow of cause and effect, often permits one to write estimators of parameters immediately upon inspection. Path analysis thus facilitates the process of abstraction for both mathematician and biologist. The analytic process is here explained, two computational algorithms (rules-of-thumb) are given, and an example involving feedback is detailed. Inclusion of feedback, and thus homeostasis, is an important feature of his presentation.

Since Wright's early work [1918, 1921, 1924, 1934, and others] the treatment of multiple equations has been extensively developed in econometrics (see especially Hood and Koopmans, [1953]) but generally without use of the standardized regression coefficients used by Wright or of the path diagrams

Reprinted by permission of the authors and editor from *Biometrics*, 1959, Vol. 15, pp. 236–258.
* Given before the Cincinnati Chapter of the American Statistical Association, Winter 1956.

and algorithms which characterize Wright's technic. Wright himself [1921] used unstandardized coefficients and the term *path regression*, but in general [1954] has favored the standardized form. Tukey [1954] in a critical review pointed out advantages in working with unstandardized regression coefficients. Recently Kempthorne [1957] emphasized the use of explicitly stated equations instead of reliance upon algorithms. The explicit statement of equations will be favored here, but with the use of algorithms for manipulating these equations in simple cases.

For the best exposition of Wright's views, his 1934 and 1954 papers are to be consulted. Li [1956] gave an expository review of Wright's work especially as it concerns population genetics.

Those without mathematical inclination may wish to omit Section 2 which follows. It deals with some of the assumptions underlying the analytic technic.

2. The Structure of a System

Consider first a situation where $p + q$ quantities $\eta_1, \eta_2, \ldots, \eta_p$ and $\xi_a, \xi_b, \ldots, \xi_q$ are thought of as measurable, and where p causal relations determine the η's, absolutely and uniquely by the ξ's. Let the equations which express these causal interrelations be

$$\eta_1 = F_1(\xi_a, \xi_b, \ldots, \xi_q; \alpha_{11}, \alpha_{12}, \ldots, \alpha_{1k})$$
$$\eta_2 = F_2(\xi_a, \xi_b, \ldots, \xi_q; \alpha_{21}, \alpha_{22}, \ldots, \alpha_{2k}) \qquad (1)$$
$$\ldots \qquad \qquad \ldots$$
$$\eta_p = F_p(\xi_a, \xi_b, \ldots, \xi_q; \alpha_{p1}, \alpha_{p2}, \ldots, \alpha_{pk}).$$

These equations will be referred to as the *structural equations*. Each variable η is assumed to be absolutely and uniquely determined (or "caused") by the set of ξ-variables. The parameters, denoted by α, may be thought of as physical, chemical, biological, or psychological constants. The algebraic forms of the equations will be determined by the physical, chemical, biological or psychological theory, respectively, or in the absence of adequate theory simple empirical approximations, such as polynomials, may be employed.

In the above we have dealt solely with variables not subject to random disturbances. Now we introduce the random element. Random variation enters into the ξ's as *measurement error* but may enter as *response error* as well as measurement error in the η's. By response error is meant such things as, e.g., genetic and physiological variation. The random variation may affect the measured quantities in an additive, multiplicative, exponential, or other fashion; however, we will consider only additive errors. Often, errors can be made additive by suitable transformation but this may result in a less convenient algebraic form. Suppose now that the quantities which can be measured are not the η's and ξ's, but rather y's and x's which satisfy the *error equations*:

$$y_1 = \eta_1 + \epsilon_1 \qquad x_a = \xi_a + \delta_a$$
$$y_2 = \eta_2 + \epsilon_2 \qquad x_b = \xi_b + \delta_b \qquad (2)$$
$$\cdots \qquad\qquad \cdots$$
$$y_p = \eta_p + \epsilon_p \qquad x_q = \xi_q + \delta_q$$

where the ϵ's and δ's are distributed independently of the η's and ξ's. Note that the y's and x's are unbiased estimates of the η's and ξ's as a consequence of equations (2) if in addition the errors are all assumed to have means of zero. Also note that, while the ξ's and η's are not correlated with errors, each observable quantity $(x$ or $y)$ is correlated with its own error.

By solving the structural equations (1) and the error equations (2) simultaneously to eliminate the η and ξ variables we obtain the model equations:

$$y_1 = f_1(x_a - \delta_a, x_b - \delta_b, \ldots, x_q - \delta_q, \alpha_{11}, \alpha_{12}, \ldots, \alpha_{1k}) + \epsilon_1$$
$$y_2 = f_2(x_a - \delta_a, x_b - \delta_b, \ldots, x_q - \delta_q, \alpha_{21}, \alpha_{22}, \ldots, \alpha_{2k}) + \epsilon_2 \qquad (3)$$
$$\cdots \qquad\qquad \cdots$$
$$y_p = f_p(x_a - \delta_a, x_b - \delta_b, \ldots, x_q - \delta_q, \alpha_{p1}, \alpha_{p2}, \ldots, \alpha_{pk}) + \epsilon_p.$$

The statistical problem now is to estimate the α-parameters and if possible to place confidence limits about the estimated parameters. The statistical procedures to be employed depend upon what assumptions can be made about the distributions of the errors, the nature of their interrelations, and the kinds of functions.

It is fortunate that in biological applications we may often neglect the errors in x because the *response error*, which is contained in y but not in x, is usually of much larger magnitude than the *measurement error*. When this is the case, such neglect introduces very little bias into the estimates of the parameters. In linear systems there is a special situation of interest. Berkson [1950] pointed out that when the x variables are *controlled*, that is, when the x's correspond to the values intended but not to the values actually obtained, neglecting the x error produces no bias in the estimates. This is a consequence of absence of correlation between intended values and errors of preparation. In the succeeding sections of this paper we will neglect the error in x entirely, justifying our action on the basis of one or the other of the above arguments. In making applications of the procedures to be shown, one must be careful to ascertain if this action is valid. In some cases the analyst will not be primarily concerned with estimating the constants in the structural equations but instead will wish to predict y's for given observed x's. In these cases the "best" predictor is obtained by ignoring the error in x.

In addition to assuming that the errors in x are negligible, we will also assume that the errors in y are independently and normally distributed with a mean of zero, and that the errors are uncorrelated from one y to another and are uncorrelated with the x's. Finally, in the major portion of this paper we will assume that all relations are linear in functions of the x's but not necessarily in the α's. When these assumptions are met, it is often possible to obtain rather simple estimators in quite complex causal networks. If the assumption of negligible error in x breaks down we are in trouble unless information concerning ratios of the variances of the y-errors to the variances of the x-errors is known. See Deming [1943] for general methods of handling such situations. Non-linear structural relations can be treated by iterative procedures and a few remarks will be made later on about such applications. Again see Deming. It may not always be realistic to assume non-correlation between the errors in different y-variates. When this is the case estimation procedures will not always be affected, but due to limitation of space only the simpler situations of non-correlation between errors in y, of structural equations linear in functions of x's, and of negligible errors in x will be considered in any detail. The fact that the x's may be functions of other x's, as in the examples of Tukey [1954], sections 11 and 20, or as polynomial expressions or as various transforms of original variables, makes linear methods available to a wide variety of initially non-linear situations. Note that no assumptions whatever are made about the distributions of the ξ's and η's. It is partly due to this fact that we regard this problem as one of regression, not one of correlation. As a special case either the ξ's or η's may be *randomly distributed* in some particular fashion. More commonly, the values of the ξ's to be studied are *chosen* by the experimenter. In either case, the fact of how the ξ's and η's were selected is irrelevant to the present analysis.

3. Path regression formulation

We will suppose, as in the previous section, that we have a closed causal system consisting of q primary factors or causes (ξ's) and p resultant effects (η's). These $p + q$ variables may then be considered to be associated one with another by a network of causal pathways. It is convenient to diagram this network by the device due to Wright of representing causal pathways by single-headed arrows connecting cause (tail) to corresponding effect (head). Because among any three variables of which at least one is a ξ there are six conceivable diagrams, among four variables sixty-five diagrams, and among five variables several hundred diagrams, the selection of the most meaningful and promising diagram will be based upon the judgment of the investigator.

As an example, consider a system in which two primary causes jointly determine an effect which, in turn, determines a still different effect. The path diagram for this system is:

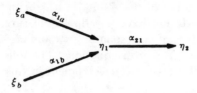

The primary factors (ξ's) are indexed by letters of the alphabet and the resultant effects (η's) by arabic numerals, in this paper.

The character of the primary factors as "causes" or "non-response variables" is represented by the restriction that *an arrow can never point toward a ξ*. There are no other restrictions whatever on the positioning of the arrows. In fact two arrows pointing in opposite directions between the same two variables is even permissible and may be given an interpretation, so long as one of the variables is not a ξ. In causal regression systems the arrows of the path diagram indicate passage of time; in other regression systems, such as calibration diagrams and prediction equations, the arrows do not necessarily represent passage of time. There is an equivalence between the methodologies appropriate to these two types of problems. The method of presentation in this article is especially suited to causal systems.

The path diagram may be interpreted in terms of the structural equations. *The variable at the head of one or more arrows is interpreted as being a function of just those variables at the tails of these same arrows*. It is quite possible for these functions to have any form whatever; however, the numerical estimation of parameters in the structural equations is usually difficult in any but the linear case. As mentioned before, the discussion in this paper for the most part will be limited to the case of linear causal relations.

Assuming linearity then, we can upon inspection write down the structural equations which are implied by any path diagram. For the previous example we have:

$$\eta_1 = \alpha_1 + \alpha_{1a}\xi_a + \alpha_{1b}\xi_b$$
$$\eta_2 = \alpha_2 + \alpha_{21}\eta_1$$

(4)

where the α's containing a double subscript are referred to as *path coefficients*[1]

---

1. Wright [1921] termed these "path regression" coefficients to distinguish the coefficients of the type discussed here from the standardized coefficients of Wright. We will use the simpler term where the distinction is not needed.

and have been inserted in the diagram. Note that the first subscript denotes the variable at the head of the arrow and the second denotes the variable at the tail. The single subscripted α's are the intercepts where the subscript corresponds to that of the left member of the equation. There are always precisely p structural equations, one equation for each effect.

As in Section 2 we think of the ξ's and η's as being "true" variables of which, in general, we do not have any direct measurement. Generally we will have obtained values of corresponding y's and x's which are related to the true variables by a set of error equations. The following conditions are assumed to hold for all subsequent development in this paper:

(1) $x_j = \xi_j$ for all j (errors in x are negligible).

(2) $y_i = \eta_i + \epsilon_i$ for all i (errors in y are additive).

Now, by combining condition (2), that is, the error equations, with the structural equations we obtain the regression equations described in the preceding section. For the previous example we obtain by direct substitution

$$
\begin{aligned}
y_1 &= \alpha_1 + \alpha_{1a}x_a + \alpha_{1b}x_b + \epsilon_1 \\
y_2 &= \alpha_2 + \alpha_{21}(y_1 - \epsilon_1) + \epsilon_2
\end{aligned}
\tag{5}
$$

as our model equations.

4. Assumptions and principles underlying estimation

In addition to assumptions (1) and (2) of the previous section, we assume:

(3) ϵ_i are normally distributed with mean zero and variance σ_i^2 for all i.

(4) ϵ_i are uncorrelated one with another for fixed i and from variable to variable.

(5) ϵ_i are uncorrelated with x_j for all i and j.

These differ slightly from the conditions assumed by Tukey [1954].

It is possible to elect any one of several estimation principles in order to obtain estimators for the path coefficients and intercepts. We prefer to use those estimators which maximize the likelihood both because of their desirable asymptotic properties and because the estimators are invariant under transformation. In an important subset of path schemata the model equations can be reparameterized such that the scheme can be separated into distinct regression equations—no two of which contain the same parameters or error terms. When these regression equations are linear, and because of assumptions (1) to (5), the Gauss-Markov theorem applies and we have the result that the maximum likelihood estimators are equivalent to least squares estimators (see Kempthorne [1952] or Rao [1952]). In fact these estimators are also equivalent to the "moment" estimators found in some older books on numerical methods. In other cases, where the Gauss-Markov theorem does not apply, discussion will revolve about the maximum likelihood estimators.

5. Estimation in some simple cases

Any causal network without closed loops or cycles can be thought of as made up of three simple kinds of relations. These are:

(1) Simple regression (ordinary multiple regression).
(2) Simultaneous regression.
(3) Chain regression.

Once the estimation problem has been discussed for these three types, the general scheme for treating cycle-free networks of any desired complexity is easily found. Networks which contain causal cycles, i.e., systems with feedback or homeostasis, require more careful consideration.

Simple regression is ordinary straight-line or multiple linear regression. For example, consider the path diagram

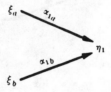

The structural equation is:

$$\eta_1 = \alpha_1 + \alpha_{1a}\xi_a + \alpha_{1b}\xi_b \tag{6}$$

and the model equation is by substitution from the error equation

$$y_1 = \alpha_1 + \alpha_{1a}x_a + \alpha_{1b}x_b + \epsilon_1. \tag{7}$$

This is, of course, the multiple linear regression model with two independent variables and the path coefficients are identical with the ordinary partial regression coefficients. In symbols

$$\alpha_{1a} = \beta_{1a.b}$$
$$\alpha_{1b} = \beta_{1b.a}$$

where $\beta_{1a.b}$ is the partial regression coefficient of y_1 on x_a holding x_b constant and $\beta_{1b.a}$ is the partial regression coefficient of y_1 on x_b holding x_a constant.

Hence, if lower case Latin letters are used to represent the maximum likelihood estimates, then the desired estimates of the unknown parameters α_{1a}, α_{1b}, and α_1 are

$$a_{1a} = b_{1a.b}$$
$$a_{1b} = b_{1b.a}$$
$$a_1 = \bar{y}_1 - a_{1a}\bar{x}_a - a_{1b}\bar{x}_b.$$

The estimates $b_{1a.b}$ and $b_{1b.a}$ are obtained in the usual way and the procedure will not be duplicated here; e.g., see Snedecor [1956] or Mather [1946]. It will be seen that many of the causal networks satisfying the five conditions of Sections 3 and 4 will have solutions in terms of ordinary total and partial regression coefficients.

The case of *simultaneous regressions* is similarly straightforward. It is the case of two or more effects which are determined by the same primary factor. As an example consider the path diagram

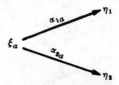

The structural equations are:

$$\eta_1 = \alpha_1 + \alpha_{1a}\xi_a$$
$$\eta_2 = \alpha_2 + \alpha_{2a}\xi_a \tag{8}$$

and the model equations are

$$y_1 = \alpha_1 + \alpha_{1a}x_a + \epsilon_1$$
$$y_2 = \alpha_2 + \alpha_{2a}x_a + \epsilon_2. \tag{9}$$

Due to the assumptions of Sections 3 and 4 the errors are independently distributed and in effect the maximum likelihood or least squares estimators can be found separately for each equation. But since each equation is just the ordinary linear model, estimators are

$$a_{1a} = b_{1a} \qquad\qquad a_{2a} = b_{2a}$$
$$a_1 = \bar{y}_1 - a_{1a}\bar{x}_a \qquad a_2 = \bar{y}_2 - a_{2a}\bar{x}_a$$

where b_{1a} is the ordinary estimated regression coefficient of y_1 on x_a and b_{2a} is the ordinary regression coefficient of y_2 on x_a.

The third basic type is less familiar. If a primary factor determines an effect and if this effect in turn determines still another effect we speak of the network as being a *chain regression*. The path diagram of the simplest example is

$$\xi_a \xrightarrow{\ \alpha_{1a}\ } \eta_1 \xrightarrow{\ \alpha_{21}\ } \eta_2$$

The structural equations are:

$$\eta_1 = \alpha_1 + \alpha_{1a}\xi_a$$
$$\eta_2 = \alpha_2 + \alpha_{21}\eta_1 \tag{10}$$

which give rise to the following model equations

$$y_1 = \alpha_1 + \alpha_{1a}x_a + \epsilon_1$$
$$y_2 = \alpha_2 + \alpha_{21}(y_1 - \epsilon_1) + \epsilon_2. \tag{11}$$

The errors ϵ_1 are common to both equations, so the parameters in the two equations cannot be separately estimated as in the previous case. However, if η_1 is eliminated from the second structural equation by substitution of the right member of the first structural equation we get a modified pair of equations which are referred to as the *reduced structural equations*. In this case we have

$$\eta_1 = \alpha_1 + \alpha_{1a}\xi_a$$
$$\eta_2 = (\alpha_2 + \alpha_1\alpha_{21}) + (\alpha_{1a}\alpha_{21})\xi_a \ . \tag{12}$$

Reduced regression equations are then found:

$$y_1 = \alpha_1 + \alpha_{1a}x_a + \epsilon_1$$
$$y_2 = (\alpha_2 + \alpha_1\alpha_{21}) + (\alpha_{1a}\alpha_{21})x_a + \epsilon_2 \ . \tag{13}$$

These are now independent and the solutions may be found in terms of the ordinary regression coefficients. The second of these is now linear in new parameters (enclosed in parentheses) and there is no common error term so that separate estimation is possible. The maximum likelihood estimators for line 1 are easily found as before to be

$$a_{1a} = b_{1a}$$
$$a_1 = \bar{y}_1 - a_{1a}\bar{x}_a$$

and since $(\alpha_{1a}\ \alpha_{21})$ is the slope of line 2 we have

$$\begin{array}{ccc} a_{1a}a_{21} = b_{2a} & & a_{21} = b_{2a}/b_{1a} \\ & \text{or} & \\ a_2 + a_1a_{21} = \bar{y}_2 - b_{2a}\bar{x}_a & & a_2 = \bar{y}_2 - a_{21}\bar{y}_1 \end{array}$$

The final estimates are maximum likelihood estimates due to the property of invariance of maximum likelihood estimators under transformation.

It can now be seen that non-cyclical combinations of the three kinds of causal networks can be treated by first eliminating all η's from the right hand members of the structural equations by substitution and then equating the resulting compound coefficients to the corresponding estimates of the appropriate ordinary and partial regression coefficients. This will give a set of simultaneous non-linear estimation equations which can sometimes be solved for the estimates of the path regression coefficients. The case of cyclical or feedback regression can be similarly handled, but consideration of this case will be delayed until after consideration of a slightly more complex example.

6. Example illustrating the process of estimation

The simplest case illustrating combination of *simple*, *simultaneous*, and *chain* regressions is diagrammed as follows:

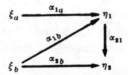

We will now obtain the estimators as functions of the ordinary partial regression coefficients. We proceed stepwise in the following manner:

(1) Write down the structural equations from the path diagram.

There are two of these since $p = 2$. We have

$$\eta_1 = \alpha_1 + \alpha_{1a}\xi_a + \alpha_{1b}\xi_b$$
$$\eta_2 = \alpha_2 + \alpha_{21}\eta_1 + \alpha_{2b}\xi_b \ . \tag{14}$$

(2) Eliminate η_1 from the right member of the second equation above by substitution of the right member of the first equation. This gives the *reduced structural equations*:

$$\eta_1 = \alpha_1 + \alpha_{1a}\xi_a + \alpha_{1b}\xi_b$$
$$\eta_2 = \alpha_2 + \alpha_1\alpha_{21} + \alpha_{21}\alpha_{1a}\xi_a + (\alpha_{2b} + \alpha_{1b}\alpha_{21})\xi_b \ . \tag{15}$$

(3) Substitute x's for ξ's and y's for η's and attach the additive errors to give the *reduced regression equations*:

$$y_1 = \alpha_1 + \alpha_{1a}x_a + \alpha_{1b}x_b + \epsilon_1$$
$$y_2 = (\alpha_2 + \alpha_1\alpha_{21}) + (\alpha_{21}\alpha_{1a})x_a + (\alpha_{2b} + \alpha_{1b}\alpha_{21})x_b + \epsilon_2 \ . \tag{16}$$

(4) The estimating equations can then be written down by inspection:

$$a_{1a} = b_{1a \cdot b} \qquad\qquad a_{21}a_{1a} = b_{2a \cdot b}$$
$$a_{1b} = b_{1b \cdot a} \qquad\qquad a_{2b} + a_{1b}a_{21} = b_{2b \cdot a}$$
$$a_1 = \bar{y}_1 - b_{1a \cdot b}\bar{x}_a - b_{1b \cdot a}\bar{x}_b \qquad a_2 + a_1 a_{21} = \bar{y}_2 - b_{2a \cdot b}\bar{x}_a - b_{2b \cdot a}\bar{x}_b .$$

These are then solved for the estimates of the intercepts and path coefficients.

7. Rules for writing down the estimators directly from the path diagram when no feedback is present

It would be convenient to be able to avoid the algebra of step (2) in the above example. This is quite simple to do if no cycles of causation or feedback exist in the system. It can be seen that, for each effect, there are exactly as many partial or simple regression coefficients available as estimators as there are primary factors which ultimately affect the particular effect. Each of these partial or simple regression coefficients may be termed *total path regressions*. Now, if a *compound path regression* is the product of the elementary path coefficients along any one path from a particular primary factor to a particular effect, then we can state:

Rule 1. A total path regression between a primary factor and an effect is the sum of the compound path regressions connecting the primary factor and the effect.

As an example of the above rule consider the problem of the previous section. Let us find the estimator associated with the partial regression coefficient of η_2 on ξ_b holding ξ_a constant $(\beta_{2b \cdot a})$. This coefficient represents the total path regression between ξ_b and η_2. This total path regression is to be set equal to the sum of the elementary paths. There are two such elementary paths between ξ_b and η_2, one direct path with coefficient α_{2b} and the other through η_1 with coefficient $\alpha_{1b}\alpha_{21}$. Hence $b_{2b \cdot a} = a_{2b} + a_{1b}a_{21}$ which is one of the four estimators based on partial regression coefficients that was obtained before.[2]

2. Note that a *total path* regression is a total derivative of an *effect* with respect to a *primary factor* and that the path coefficients are partial derivatives obtained from the functional equations. Thus in the present example

$$\frac{\partial \eta_1}{\partial \xi_a} = \alpha_{1a}, \qquad \frac{\partial \eta_1}{\partial \xi_b} = \alpha_{1b}, \qquad \frac{\partial \eta_2}{\partial \eta_1} = \alpha_{21}, \qquad \frac{\partial \eta_2}{\partial \xi_b} = \alpha_{2b}$$

and by the usual law of the total derivative

$$\beta_{1a \cdot b} = \frac{d\eta_1}{d\xi_a} = \frac{\partial \eta_1}{\partial \xi_a}\frac{d\xi_a}{d\xi_a} + \frac{\partial \eta_1}{\partial \xi_b}\frac{d\xi_b}{d\xi_a} = \alpha_{1a}$$

$$\beta_{1b \cdot a} = \frac{d\eta_1}{d\xi_b} = \frac{\partial \eta_1}{\partial \xi_a}\frac{d\xi_a}{d\xi_b} + \frac{\partial \eta_1}{\partial \xi_b}\frac{d\xi_b}{d\xi_b} = \alpha_{1b}$$

$$\beta_{2a \cdot b} = \frac{d\eta_2}{d\xi_a} = \frac{\partial \eta_2}{\partial \eta_1}\frac{d\eta_1}{d\xi_a} + \frac{\partial \eta_2}{\partial \xi_b}\frac{d\xi_b}{d\xi_a} = \alpha_{21}\alpha_{1a}$$

$$\beta_{2b \cdot a} = \frac{d\eta_2}{d\xi_b} = \frac{\partial \eta_2}{\partial \eta_1}\frac{d\eta_1}{d\xi_b} + \frac{\partial \eta_2}{\partial \xi_b}\frac{d\xi_b}{d\xi_b} = \alpha_{21}\alpha_{1b} + \alpha_{2b}.$$

We may state, similarly, a rule for writing the estimators involving the intercepts. In Rule 1 we employed the partial regression coefficients in the multiple regression equations which relate each effect η to all of its determining causes ξ. These partial regression coefficients we termed *total path regressions*. Analogously, we may speak of the *total intercepts* as being the intercepts of these same multiple regression equations. Then we have

> *Rule 2. A total intercept for a particular effect η_i is the sum of the particular intercepts α_i and the products of all intercepts of effects determining η_i by the elementary path regression connecting the determining effect and η_i.*

An example should make the application of Rule 2 clear. Again, consider the problem of Section 5. The only "effect" determining η_2 is η_1 and hence the total intercept for η_2 is to be set equal to $\alpha_2 + \alpha_1 \alpha_{21}$ where α_{21} is the elementary path regression between the determining effect η_1 and the particular effect being considered η_2. Thus we get the estimator obtained earlier

$$a_2 + a_1 a_{21} = \bar{y}_2 - b_{2b.a} \bar{x}_b - b_{2a.b} \bar{x}_a.$$

The right member of this estimator is the usual estimate of the intercept of the multiple regression equation relating η_2 to ξ_a and ξ_b.

8. Identification of parameters

In the examples of Sections 5 and 6 the parameters are said to be *just identified* because of the fact that each parameter can be uniquely expressed as a function of the simple and partial regression coefficients. For this to be so it is necessary (but not sufficient) that there be the same number of path coefficients as there are simple and partial regressions. Although many causal schemes conform to this condition the majority do not. Over-identification occurs when there are more regression coefficients than there are path coefficients, under-identification when there are fewer. We will consider briefly in the next two sections what can be done (1) if the parameters are *over-identified* and (2) if they are *under-identified*.

9. Over-identification

As an example of over-identification consider the example of Section 3. Using Rule 1 of Section 7 we get the following estimation equations for the path regressions:

$$b_{1a.b} = a_{1a} \qquad b_{2a.b} = a_{1a} a_{21}$$
$$b_{1b.a} = a_{1b} \qquad b_{2b.a} = a_{1b} a_{21} .$$

It is obvious that α_{21} can be estimated either by $b_{2a.b}/b_{1a.b}$ or by $b_{2b.a}/b_{1b.a}$.

These two estimates in general will not be the same numerically and it is apparent that any efficient estimator would have to utilize both sources of information. In cases of over-identification such as the one above, maximum likelihood estimators may be found but in general they do not have an explicit form and hence require an iterative solution. Methods utilizing only part of the available information have been developed. See Hood and Koopmans [1953]. Full information methods may present numerical difficulties but we feel that in any serious study the dictum of inductive inference that "all available information must be considered for a valid induction" should not be violated.

10. Under-identification and factor analysis

A condition considerably more serious than that of over-identification is the case of under-identified parameters. This occurs when regression information is inadequate for individual estimation of each parameter. Consider the following diagram:

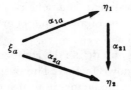

Maximum likelihood estimators are found by Rule 1 to be

$$b_{1a} = a_{1a} \qquad b_{2a} = a_{2a} + a_{1a} a_{21}.$$

This presents the impossible task of solving for three quantities knowing only two relations. For a determinate solution additional information will have to be provided. For example, if it were known that α_{1a} and α_{2a} were in some given ratio, equal, say, then a complete solution could be found. Even in the absence of such knowledge, information regarding the relative magnitudes of α_{2a} and α_{21} can be provided by supplying such restrictions as $\alpha_{2a}^2 + \alpha_{21}^2 = 1$ or $\alpha_{2a} \alpha_{21} = 1$, etc. The second of these possible restrictions assumes that the coefficients are of the same sign. The restriction $\alpha_{2a} \alpha_{21} = -1$ could be used if the signs were known to be opposite. Other restrictions will be sensible in special cases. The reader is reminded that the *character of the solution obtained will depend directly upon the character of the restrictions supplied.*

A case in point is the collection of procedures, widely used in the social sciences, known as *factor analysis*. Factor analysis may be thought of as the ultimate in under-identification, no regression information being available at all. One of the models postulated (see Lawley [1953]) is the system of linear equations corresponding to the path diagram:

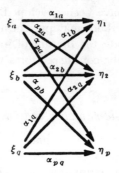

A set of observable variables whose true values are denoted by η_1, η_2, . . ., η_p are considered to be linear functions of some common factors ξ_a, ξ_b, . . ., ξ_q, where $q \leq p$. These common factors are either unknown or un-measurable. The path coefficients α_{1a}, α_{1b}, . . ., α_{pq} are referred to as *factor loadings* by the factor analysts and define the composition of each measurable variable in terms of the unknown factors. The path coefficients may just as well be thought of as defining the factors in terms of the knowables and it is in this latter sense that the factor analyst usually regards them. In any case, the problem is to estimate the path coefficients or factor loadings where no information is provided by regression. This means that pq *a priori* restrictions must be supplied. As there are infinite numbers of ways of doing this, it is not surprising that several schools of thought have arisen in regard to the matter of which restrictions to use. In general, however, methods have been advocated which maximize the contribution of a single factor and then that of a second factor, and so on until the least important factor is reached. The method of *principal components* advocated by Hotelling adds to this ordering the restrictions that the factors are orthogonal to one another (see Holzinger and Harman [1941] for a survey of models and methods of factor analysis).

The possibility should be pointed out of combining the situation of factor analysis, in which none of the ξ's is measured, with the regression situation. Thus, we envisage a model which contains some measurable factors and some non-measurable ones and either or both might be entangled in regression chains. This model is especially appropriate in biology where various kinds of collateral information are often available.

11. Feedback

A causal process often involves one or more cycles of causation. Homeostatic mechanisms provide a variety of biometric examples. Consider the diagram below:

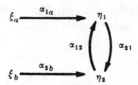

What is the meaning of this diagram? Let us suppose that the variables ξ_a, ξ_b, η_1, and η_2 have some particular value. Now suppose that ξ_a is changed by some specific amount. The effect is to change η_1 either in the same direction or in the opposite, depending upon the sign of α_{1a}. Suppose α_{1a} is positive and we increase ξ_a. Then η_1 is also increased. Since α_{21} is not zero, η_2 will also be affected. If α_{21} is positive, η_2 will also be increased. The non-nullity of α_{12} indicates that this change in η_2 will further affect η_1. In such a situation we say that there is "feed-back." If α_{12} is of the same sign as α_{21} then η_1 will increase further and this will cause a still further increase in η_2. Thus, the process continually builds up indefinitely until there is breakdown in the system. This type of system, wherein all of the processes in the loop go in the same direction, is said to possess *positive feedback*. Positive feedback is obviously unstable. On the other hand stability or equilibrium may be attained if some of the processes go in opposite directions. Then we say the system has "negative feedback." If α_{12} were negative then η_1 would decrease and perhaps the process would settle down to some stable or *equilibrium* position. Relative magnitudes as well as direction are important in producing equilibrium. In this example control is provided by ξ_b as well as ξ_a so that when both ξ_a and ξ_b are changed the flow of cause and effect cycles around the loop until equilibrium is reached, or else breakdown or oscillation occurs.

The equilibrium is said to be "stationary" if η_1 and η_2 settle down to the same final values for any particular change in ξ_a or ξ_b. The equilibrium can only be truly stationary in the degenerate case when α_{1a} and α_{2b} are zero. However, this condition is approached if the product of the path coefficients is very large in absolute magnitude. A non-stationary equilibrium is spoken of as a "moving" equilibrium.

When such a process as is diagrammed above is in equilibrium it is possible to use the methods of this paper in estimating the relevant constants. The simple rules of Section 6 require modification. However, the more general method outlined in Section 5 applies.

Wright treated the case of feedback in a manner analogous to the present treatment some years ago but did not publish this material because new algorithms would have had to be introduced. A method of handling feedback using auxiliary variables was, however, published. See Wright [1924, 1934]. The present treatment does not rely upon algorithms and hence cannot be objected to on Wright's previous grounds. The authors feel that the avoidance of the use of auxiliary variables makes logical presentation simpler. The maximum likelihood estimators are

$$a_{21} = \frac{b_{2a \cdot b}}{b_{1a \cdot b}}, \qquad a_{1a} = b_{1a \cdot b}(1 - a_{12}a_{21}), \qquad a_1 = \bar{y}_1 - b_{1a \cdot b}\bar{x}_a - b_{1b \cdot a}\bar{x}_b$$

$$a_{12} = \frac{b_{1b \cdot a}}{b_{2b \cdot a}}, \qquad a_{2b} = b_{2b \cdot a}(1 - a_{12}a_{21}), \qquad a_2 = \bar{y}_2 - b_{2a \cdot b}\bar{x}_a - b_{2b \cdot a}\bar{x}_b.$$

12. A biometrical example of feedback regression

The classical data obtained by Haldane and Priestley, from which these authors inferred a mechanism of the control of depth of breathing, affords an interesting example of feedback in a biological system. The following data for Haldane himself were given in the original memoir [1905].

Table 5.1 Haldane-Priestley data on depth of breathing

% carbon dioxide inhaled (x_a)	% carbon dioxide in the alveoli (y_1)	Depth of respiration in cubic centimeters (y_2)
.79	5.5	739
1.47	5.0	978
1.52	5.55	793.5
1.97	5.7	849
2.02	5.6	864
2.28	5.8	911
2.31	5.7	919
2.84	5.3	1154
3.07	5.5	1216
3.11	5.5	1232
3.73	5.9	1330
4.84	6.5	1662
5.14	6.2	1771
5.48	6.8	1845
6.02	6.6	2104

We suggest the following representation of the causal pathways:

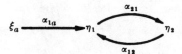

where ξ_a is the per cent carbon dioxide inhaled, η_1 is the per cent carbon dioxide in the alveoli of the lungs, and η_2 is the depth of respiration.

An advantage of path analysis is that each part of the total process is explicitly represented without regard to other parts of the process. Thus, the path coefficient in one part is invariant when other parts of the process are changed. In the present example we may ask: "What is the value of α_{1a} when α_{21} and α_{12} are both zero?" Whatever this value is, it *must* be the same for *any* values of α_{21} and α_{12}. Now, $\alpha_{21} = \alpha_{12} = 0$ is tantamount to having the lungs disconnected from the neural reflex arc. It is obvious that, if a certain time is allowed for equilibrium to be reached before observation is made, the concentration of CO_2 in the alveoli will be the same as the concentration in the inhaled air and α_{1a} must be very nearly equal to unity. From the nature of path coefficients α_{1a} must be equal to unity whatever are the true values of α_{12} and α_{21}. The structural equations are then

$$\eta_1 = \alpha_1 + \xi_a + \alpha_{12}\eta_2$$
$$\eta_2 = \alpha_2 + \alpha_{21}\eta_1 \tag{17}$$

and by substitution the reduced regression equations are

$$y_1 = (\alpha_1 + \alpha_{12}\alpha_2 + x_a)/(1 - \alpha_{12}\alpha_{21}) + \epsilon_1$$
$$y_2 = (\alpha_2 + \alpha_{21}\alpha_1 + \alpha_{21}x_a)/(1 - \alpha_{12}\alpha_{21}) + \epsilon_2. \tag{18}$$

It is seen from (17) that the response can be represented by a line which is the intersection of two planes. One of these planes is parallel to the line $\eta_1 = \alpha_{12}\eta_2$ and to the line $\eta_1 = \xi_a$; the other is parallel to the ξ_a axis and to the line $\eta_1 = (1/\alpha_{21})\eta_2$. Thus, the path coefficients may be represented as the slopes of certain projections of planes.

The degree of approach to the condition of stationary equilibrium is seen to be a function of the denominator in (18), i.e., to $1 - \alpha_{12}\alpha_{21}$. If this quantity is $\gg 1$ the equilibrium becomes nearly stationary. If the quantity is only slightly > 1 then there is poor compensation. If the quantity is < 1 then there is positive feedback and instability.

From (18) the regression coefficient for the regression of y_1 on x_a is found
to be

$$b_{1a} = \frac{S_{1a}}{S_{aa}} = \frac{9.7481}{36.0742} = 0.2702 = 1/(1 - a_{12}a_{21})$$

and for y_2 on x_a is

$$b_{2a} = \frac{S_{2a}}{S_{aa}} = \frac{9522.5}{36.0742} = 264.0 = a_{21}/(1 - a_{12}a_{21})$$

where S_{1a}, S_{2a}, and S_{aa} are the usual "corrected" sums of squares and cross-
products. Hence

$$a_{21} = \frac{b_{2a}}{b_{1a}} = 977.1$$

$$a_{12} = \frac{b_{1a} - 1}{b_{2a}} = -0.002764.$$

These estimates of the path coefficients are of opposite sign as they should be
for equilibrium or negative feedback situations. Figure 5.1 shows the estimated
line of response as the intersection of the estimated planes corresponding to
(17).

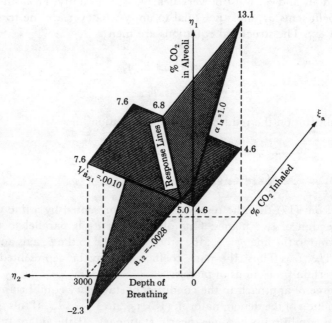

Figure 5.1. *Estimated line of response as intersection of planes fitted to data of
Haldane and Priestley.*

It is, of course, possible to test first all regression coefficients for significance before using them in estimation equations. Lack of significance of one or more regression coefficients would allow one to anticipate wide confidence limits for certain of the path coefficients. The standard test for the slope of b_{1a} yields a Student's t of 6.0 with 13 degrees of freedom. For the regression of y_a on x_a we obtain a t of 18.4 with 13 degrees of freedom. Both are, of course, highly significant and we feel justified in having estimated the path coefficients.

The results of the present analysis are consistent with the conclusion of Haldane and Priestley "that the smallest increase in the CO_2 percentage of the air breathed is accompanied by a compensatory increase in the alveolar ventilation, the latter increase being just about sufficient to keep the alveolar CO_2 percentage constant," except that a quantitative interpretation is placed upon the phrase "just about sufficient." Use might possibly be made of the estimated path coefficients in comparing individuals, in following the course of a pulmonary disease in a single individual, or in differential diagnosis of disease.

13. Confidence Limits

The problem of confidence limits for the path coefficients is not one easily resolved in general, even for the case of linear structural equations. When the path diagram is void of chain and cyclical regressions the exact confidence limits of multiple linear regression apply and the reader should refer to one of the standard sources alluded to in Section 4. In many cases, as in the example of the previous section, estimators of the path coefficients are ratios of linear functions of ordinary regression coefficients. In these cases satisfactory approximate results are easily obtained. We illustrate the technique with the example taken from Haldane and Priestley. We previously found that

Let
$$\beta_{2a} = \alpha_{21}\beta_{1a}.$$
$$T_{21} = b_{2a} - \alpha_{21}b_{1a}.$$

Then the expected value of T_{21} is zero and the estimated variance of T_{21} is given by
$$s_t^2 = s_{2a}^2 + \alpha_{21}^2 s_{1a}^2$$

where s_{2a}^2 and s_{1a}^2 are the estimated variances of b_{2a} and b_{1a}, respectively. Since the two regression coefficients are normally distributed, T_{21} is normally distributed and we may define a test criterion v by the equation
$$v^2 = \frac{T_{21}^2}{s_t^2} \frac{(b_{2a} - \alpha_{21}b_{1a})^2}{s_{2a}^2 + \alpha_{21}^2 s_{1a}^2}.$$

If we knew the value of v corresponding to a given confidence level we could invert and obtain

$$\alpha_{21} = \frac{b_{1a}b_{2a} \pm \sqrt{b_{1a}{}^2 b_{2a}{}^2 - (b_{1a}{}^2 - v^2 s_{1a}{}^2)(b_{2a}{}^2 v^2 s_{2a}{}^2)}}{b_{1a}{}^2 - v^2 s_{1a}{}^2}. \tag{19}$$

Taking the sign positive gives one limit and taking the sign negative gives the other limit, with confidence at the chosen level.

If the statistics $s_{2a}{}^2$ and $s_{1a}{}^2$ were estimates of a common variance then $s_T{}^2$ could be written $s^2(1 + \alpha_{21}{}^2)$, where s^2 is found by pooling $s_{2a}{}^2$ and $s_{1a}{}^2$, and would be distributed as χ^2 with 13 degrees of freedom. In this case v would be distributed as Student's t with 13 degrees of freedom. In the present example a common variance is not assumed and $s_T{}^2$ is a linear function of separately estimated mean squares. Satterthwaite [1946], following Fairfield Smith [1936], discusses an approximation whereby $s_T{}^2$ is taken to be distributed as χ^2 with degrees of freedom calculated by equating lower moments. If

$$s_T{}^2 = \lambda_1 s_1{}^2 + \lambda_2 s_2{}^2 + \ldots$$

then Satterthwaite proposes that $s_T{}^2$ be approximated by $\chi^2 \sigma_T{}^2$ where χ^2 has n degrees of freedom given by

$$n = \frac{(\lambda_1 s_1{}^2 + \lambda_2 s_2{}^2 + \ldots)^2}{\dfrac{(\lambda_1 s_1{}^2)^2}{n_1} + \dfrac{(\lambda_2 s_2{}^2)^2}{n_2} + \ldots};$$

$n_1 n_2, \ldots$ are the degrees of freedom available for estimating $s_1{}^2, s_2{}^2 \ldots$, respectively. In the present example $\lambda_1 = 1$ and $\lambda_2 = \alpha_{21}{}^2$, an unknown. To a first approximation we can substitute $a_{21}{}^2$ for $\alpha_{21}{}^2$. Now if $s_T{}^2$ is distributed approximately as $\chi^2 \sigma^2$, then v is distributed approximately as Student's t with n degrees of freedom. We have from the example

$$b_{1a} = 0.2702 \qquad s_{1a}{}^2 = 0.002019$$

$$b_{2a} = 264.0 \qquad s_{2a}{}^2 = 204.7$$

and n is calculated to be equal to 15.73. Interpolating in a table of Student's t distribution we find the tabular values of v for various levels of confidence given in column 2 of Table 5.2. Approximations based upon the Behrens-Fisher test and Welch's test by substituting $a_{21}{}^2$ for $\alpha_{21}{}^2$ are available in the present case since only two mean squares are involved. Values of v for these two tests are also given in Table 5.2. See Fisher and Yates [1948] and Pearson and Hartley [1954] for description of these two tests and tables of critical values. It should be mentioned in passing that these tests are not logically equivalent and test somewhat different hypotheses.

Table 5.2 Values of the test criterion v for different levels of
confidence

	For α_{21}			For α_{12}		
Level of Confidence	Smith-Satterthwaite	Welch	Behrens-Fisher	Smith-Satterthwaite	Welch	Behrens-Fisher
90%	1.75	1.75	....	1.71	1.70	....
95%	2.12	....	2.18	2.06	....	2.17
98%	2.59	2.60	....	2.48	2.47	....
99%	2.93	....	3.01	2.78	....	2.95

Taking $v = 1.8$ we get by substitution into (19) the approximate 90%
confidence limits

$$740 \leq \alpha_{21} \leq 1410$$

whereas the point estimate was 980 after rounding to two significant figures.
In order to find confidence limits for α_{12} we use

$$T_{12} = b_{1a} - \alpha_{12} b_{2a} - 1.$$

Corresponding values of v are given on the right side of Table 5.2. Taking
$v = 1.7$ at the 90% level we obtain

$$-0.0032 \leq \alpha_{12} \leq -0.0024.$$

The point estimate was previously found to be -0.0028.

14. Non-linear processes

The extension of path analysis to non-linear situations is straight-forward
although, with the exception of polynomials, simple estimators are not
available. We close this paper with an example of simple chain regression
wherein each process is exponential rather than linear. We have the diagram

$$\xi_a \xrightarrow{\gamma_{1a}} \eta_1 \xrightarrow{\gamma_{21}} \eta_2$$

The functional equations are

$$\eta_1 = \gamma_1 + \gamma_{1a} e^{\lambda_{1a} \xi_a}$$
$$\eta_2 = \gamma_2 + \gamma_{21} e^{\lambda_{21} \eta_1} \tag{20}$$

The procedure of Section 5 is applicable and the model equations are

$$y_1 = \gamma_1 + \gamma_{1a} e^{\lambda_{1a} x_a} + \epsilon_1$$
$$y_2 = \gamma_2 + \gamma_{21} \exp\{\lambda_{21}(\gamma_1 + \gamma_{1a} e^{\lambda_{1a} x_a})\} + \epsilon_2. \tag{21}$$

To estimate the unknown parameters: (1) fit the first model equation (20) by some iterative method (see Stevens [1951]); (2) replace y_1, γ_{1a} and λ_{1a} in the second of (20) by estimated values from step (1); (3) fit the second model equation by the same method as was used for the first equation.

We note that the non-linear analogues of the linear *path coefficients* are the partial derivatives

$$\eta_{1a} = \frac{\partial \eta_1}{\partial \xi_a} = \lambda_{1a}(\eta_1 - \gamma_1), \qquad \eta_{21} = \frac{\partial \eta_2}{\partial \eta_1} = \lambda_{21}(\eta_2 - \gamma_2).$$

These have been indicated in the path diagram.

Acknowledgments

The authors gratefully acknowledge the comments and suggestions (many of which have been incorporated in the final draft) generously offered by G. S. Eadie, E. K. Harris, Nathan Mantel, Horace Norton, Carl F. Schmidt, H. R. van der Vaart, E. J. Williams, and G. P. Williams.

Rather more extensive assistance was rendered by Oscar Kempthorne, Leonard J. Savage, David L. Wallace, and especially John W. Tukey.

The authors' indebtedness to Sewall Wright is manifest throughout the text. His comments on the early draft have been very useful for purposes of revision; however, complete agreement on all points has not been attained.

References

BERKSON, J. [1950]. Are there two regressions? *J. Amer. Stat. Assoc. 45*: 164.

DEMING, W. E. [1943]. *Statistical Adjustment of Data*, New York: Wiley.

FISHER, R. A., and YATES, F. [1948]. *Statistical Tables*, New York: Hafner.

HALDANE, J., and PRIESTLEY, J. [1905]. Lung ventilation. *J. Physiol. 32*: 225.

HOLZINGER, K. J., and HARMAN, H. H. [1941]. *Factor Analysis*, Chicago: University of Chicago Press.

HOOD, W. C., and KOOPMANS, T. C., editors, [1953]. *Studies in Econometric Method, Cowles Commission Monograph no. 14*, New York: Wiley.

KEMPTHORNE, O. [1952]. *The Design and Analysis of Experiments*, New York: Wiley.

[1957]. *An Introduction to Genetic Statistics*, New York: Wiley.

LAWLEY, D. N. [1953]. A modified method of estimation in factor analysis and some large sample results. *Uppsala Symposium on Psychological Factor Analysis*, Stockholm: Almquist and Wiksell.

LI, C. C. [1956]. The concept of path coefficients and its impact on population genetics. *Biometrics 12*: 190.

MATHER, K. [1946]. *Statistical Methods in Biology*, New York: Interscience Publishers.

PEARSON, E. S., and HARTLEY, H. O. [1954]. *Biometrika Tables for Statisticians*, Cambridge: Cambridge University Press.

RAO, C. R. [1952]. *Advanced Statistical Methods in Biometric Research*, New York: Wiley.

SATTERTHWAITE, F. E. [1946]. An approximate distribution of estimates of variance components. *Biometrics Bulletin 2*: 110.

SMITH, H. F. [1936]. The problem of comparing the results of two experiments with unequal errors. *J. of the Council of Scientific and Industrial Research 9*: 211.

SNEDECOR, G. W. [1956]. *Statistical Methods*, Ames: Iowa State College Press.

STEVENS, W. L. [1951]. Asymptotic regression. *Biometrics 7*: 247–267.

TUKEY, J. W. [1954]. Causation, Regression, and Path Analysis. Chapter 3, *Statistics and Mathematics in Biology*, ed. Kempthorne, Bancroft, Gowen, and Lush, Ames: The Iowa State College Press.

WRIGHT, S. [1918]. On the nature of size factors. *Genetics 3*: 367.

——— [1921]. Correlation and causation. *J. Agri. Res. 20*: 557.

——— [1924]. Corn and hog correlations. *USDA Bulletin, No. 1300*.

——— [1934]. The method of path coefficients. *Ann. Math. Stat. 5*: 161.

——— [1954]. The interpretation of multivariate systems. Chapter 2, *Statistics and Mathematics in Biology*, ed. Kempthorne, Bancroft, Gowen, and Lush, Ames: The Iowa State College Press.

Appendix on Exact Confidence Regions

by M. E. Turner

Following Anderson (1958)[3] we show how exact confidence regions can be constructed for the under- and just-identified cases of path analysis.

We are given, from experimentation, the response matrix $Y' = (y_1, y_2, \ldots, y_N)$, a set of N vector observations, y_α, drawn from the multivariate normal distribution $\mathcal{N}$ $(B\, x_\alpha, \Sigma)$. $N \geq p + q$ and the rank of $X' = (x_1, x_2, \ldots, x_N)$ is q. We take the N response vectors to be independent, although the p response variables may or may not be independent.

The maximum likelihood estimate of B, the matrix of regression coefficients in the reduced structural equations, is then given by

$$\hat{B}' = (X'X)^{-1} X'Y, \tag{22}$$

and the maximum likelihood estimate of Σ is given by

$$\hat{\Sigma} = (Y'Y - \hat{B} X'X \hat{B}')/N. \tag{23}$$

We further note that $\hat{B}' = (\hat{B}_1, \hat{B}_2, \ldots, \hat{B}_p)$ is normally distributed with mean $(B_1, B_2, \ldots, B_p)$ and covariance matrix $\{\sigma_{ij} (X'X)^{-1}\}$ where $\{\sigma_{ij}\} = \Sigma$.

Now suppose we wish to test the null hypothesis H_0: $B_1 = B_1{}^*$ where $B = (B_1, B_2)$, B_1 having q_1 columns and B_2 having $q_2 = q - q_1$ columns. The likelihood ratio test criterion is

$$\lambda = \left|\hat{\Sigma}_\Omega\right|^{N/2} / \left|\hat{\Sigma}_\omega\right|^{N/2} \tag{24}$$

where $\hat{\Sigma}_\Omega$ is found by maximizing the log-likelihood over B and Σ, and where $\hat{\Sigma}_\omega$ is found by maximizing the log-likelihood over B_2 and Σ.

3. Based on original work by M. S. Bartlett (1934) and S. S. Wilks (1934). See Anderson (1958) for citations.

It is convenient to work with $U = \lambda^{2/N}$ instead of with λ itself. We have

$$U = \frac{|N\hat{\Sigma}_\Omega|}{|N\hat{\Sigma}_\Omega + (\hat{B}_{1\Omega} - B_1^*) A_{11 \cdot 2} (\hat{B}_{1\Omega} - B_1^*)'|} \tag{25}$$

where $A_{11 \cdot 2} = A_{11} - A_{12} A_{22}^{-1} A_{21}$ and $A = X'X$. Then $a(1 - \alpha)$ confidence region in the B_1 space is given by those values of B_1^* satisfying

$$U \geq U_{p, q_1, N-q} (\alpha) \tag{26}$$

where $U_{p, q_1, N-q} (\alpha)$ is the αth critical value of $U_{p, q_1, N-q}$.

In order to construct the confidence region we need to know the distribution of U under the null hypothesis. In certain situations U may be transformed to a Snedecor's F and the standard tables employed for determining the αth critical value:

(1) If $p = 1$

$$F_{q_1, N-q} = \frac{1 - U}{U} \cdot \frac{N - q}{q_1}. \tag{27}$$

(2) If $q_1 = 1$

$$F_{p, N-p-q+1} = \frac{1 - U}{U} \cdot \frac{N - p - q + 1}{P} \tag{28}$$

(3) If $p = 2$

$$F_{2 q_1, 2(N-q-1)} = \frac{1 - \sqrt{U}}{\sqrt{U}} \cdot \frac{N - q - 1}{q_1} \tag{29}$$

(4) If $q_1 = 2$

$$F_{2 p, 2 (N-p-q+1)} = \frac{1 - \sqrt{U}}{\sqrt{U}} \cdot \frac{N - p - q + 1}{p} \tag{30}$$

In other cases we may compute the first four moments of U, form Pearson's β_1 and β_2 moment ratios and use tabulated critical values of the Pearson curves to approximately determine $U (\alpha)$. The rth moment about the origin is given by

$$\mu'_r = \prod_{i=1}^{P} \left\{ \frac{\Gamma[(n+1-i)/2+r]\Gamma[(n+q_1+1-i)/2]}{\Gamma[(n+1-i)/2]\Gamma[n+q_1+1-i)/2+r]} \right\} \tag{31}$$

where $n = N - q$.

Alternatively, we may employ an asymptotic expansion.

$$P\{-m \log U \leq z\} = P\{\chi_{pq_1}^2 \leq z\} + \frac{\gamma_2}{m_2}[P\{\chi_{pq_1}^2 + 4 \leq z\} - P\{\chi_{pq_1}^2 \leq z\}] + \ldots, \tag{32}$$

where $m = N - q_2 - (p + q_1 + 1)/2$ and $\gamma_2 = pq_1 (p^2 + {}_{q_1}^2 - 5)/48$.

Now, turning to the Haldane-Priestley example we find

$$X'X = A = \begin{pmatrix} 15 & 46.59 \\ 46.59 & 180.7827 \end{pmatrix}$$

$$X'Y = C' = \begin{pmatrix} 87.15 & 18,367.5 \\ 280.436 & 66,571.97 \end{pmatrix}$$

and
$$\hat{B}' = \begin{pmatrix} 4.970,684,844 & 404.607,607 \\ .270,223,922 & 263.970,531 \end{pmatrix}.$$

Using formula (28) with $p = 2$, $q_1 = 1$, and $N - q = 13$ we find

$$F_{2,12} (\alpha) = \frac{1-U}{U} \cdot \frac{12}{2}$$

or
$$U_{2\,1\,13} (\alpha) = \frac{6}{6 + F_{2,12} (\alpha)} = 0.607$$

if $\alpha = 0.05$.

In order to locate the boundary of the confidence region we use the equality in (26). $|N\hat{\Sigma}_{\Omega}| = 83,240.488,28$ and points lying on the confidence ellipse satisfy

$$34.155,015 \; \beta_{2a}^2 + (6,303.455 \; \beta_{1a} - 19,735.179) \; \beta_{2a} +$$
$$(3,462,389.9 \; \beta_{1a}^2 - 3,535,167.4 \; \beta_{1a} + 3,028,502.5) = 0. \qquad (33)$$

Selected values of β_{1a} are chosen and equation (33) is solved by the quadratic formula to give upper and lower confidence points for β_{2a}. Then using the identification relations from page 91, $\alpha_{21} = \beta_{2a}/\beta_{1a}$ and $\alpha_{12} = (\beta_{1a} - 1)/\beta_{2a}$ we map the calculated points (β_{1a}, β_{2a}) into points $(\alpha_{12}, \alpha_{21})$, thus defining the 95% confidence region for α_{12} and α_{21}. The results are shown in Table 5.3.

Table 5.3 Points lying on exact confidence ellipse and transformed
region for the path coefficients[1]

β_{1a}	β_{2a}		α_{21} α_{12} (from β_{2a} lower)		α_{21} α_{12} (from β_{2a} upper)	
	lower	upper				
.139,867	276	276	1973	−.00302	1973	−.00312
.140	274	278	1957	−.00314	1986	−.00309
.150	260	290	1733	−.00329	1933	−.00293
.160	253	295	1581	−.00332	1844	−.00285
.180	244	301	1356	−.00337	1672	−.00272
.200	237	304	1185	−.00338	1520	−.00262
.220	232	305	1055	−.00336	1386	−.00256
.240	228	305	950	−.00333	1271	−.00249
.260	225	305	865	−.00329	1173	−.00243
.280	223	303	796	−.00323	1082	−.00238
.300	223	300	743	−.00314	1000	−.00233
.320	223	296	697	−.00305	925	−.00230
.340	224	291	659	−.00295	856	−.00227
.360	227	284	631	−.00282	789	−.00226
.380	232	275	611	−.00267	724	−.00226
.400	248	256	620	−.00242	640	−.00234
.400,580	252	252	629	−.00238	629	−.00238

1. Haldane-Priestley data from Table 5.1, page 90.

Additional References

ANDERSON, T. W. 1958. *An Introduction to Multivariate Statistical Analysis.* New York: John Wiley.

BASMANN, R. L. 1960. An expository note on estimation of simultaneous structural equations. *Biometrics, 16*: 464–480.

CAMPBELL, E. D., TURNER, M. E., and WRIGHT, M. F. 1960. *A Handbook of Path Regression Analysis: Part I, Estimators for Simple Completely Identified Systems.* Richmond: Department of Biophysics and Biometry, Medical College of Virginia.

DEMPSTER, E. R. 1960. The question of stability with positive feedback, *Biometrics, 16*: 481–483.

TURNER, M. E., MONROE, R. J., and LUCAS, H. L. 1961. Generalized asymptotic regression and non-linear path analysis. *Biometrics, 17*: 120–143.

TURNER, M. E., and MONROE, R. J. 1963. Hypergeometric kinetics. *Biometrics, 19*: (in press).

WRIGHT, S. 1960a. Path coefficients and path regressions: alternative or complementary concepts? *Biometrics, 16*: 189–202.

———— 1960b. The treatment of reciprocal interaction with or without lag, in path analysis. *Biometrics, 16*: 423–445.

Chapter 6

PATH COEFFICIENTS AND PATH REGRESSIONS: ALTERNATIVE OR COMPLEMENTARY CONCEPTS?

SEWALL WRIGHT*

University of Wisconsin

Introduction

In a recent paper, Turner and Stevens [1959] develop a modification of the method of path coefficients (Wright [1921, 1934, 1954]). Following Tukey [1954] they advocate systematic replacement in path analysis of the dimensionless path coefficients by the corresponding concrete path regressions. The purpose of the present paper is to discuss this and other points which they raise.

(1) The authors concur with Tukey in treating the standardized and concrete forms of correlational statistics as if they were alternative conceptions between which it is necessary to make a choice. It has always seemed to me that these should be looked upon as two aspects of a single theory corresponding to different modes of interpretation which, taken together, often give a deeper understanding of a situation than either can give by itself.

(2) Even when the sole objectives of analysis are the concrete coefficients, actual path analysis takes a simpler and more homogeneous form in terms of the standardized ones. The application of the method to data usually requires algebraic manipulation of coefficients pertaining to unmeasured

Reprinted by permission of the author and editor from *Biometrics*, 1960, Vol. 16, pp. 189–202.

* Paper No. 765 from the Department of Genetics, University of Wisconsin.

variables on the same basis as measured ones. As the former can only be dealt with in standardized form, homogeneity requires that all be so dealt with in the course of the algebra. It is such a simple matter to pass from either form to the other (in the cases in which standard deviations are available to all) that the economy of effort in using the concrete coefficients as far as possible, where these are the objectives, is usually outweighed by the loss of economy in other respects.

(3) It is of first importance in path analysis to make use of all of the available data. This is not done by Turner and Stevens in most of their examples. The use of standardized coefficients leads naturally to the systematic expression of all of the available information in the form of equations to be solved simultaneously.

(4) Turner and Stevens, again following Tukey, go into the direct treatment of reciprocal interaction between variables by path analysis. This interesting topic requires more extended discussion than is appropriate here.

Review of the method of path analysis

Before taking up these points in detail, it seems necessary to review the method briefly to try to clear up certain misunderstandings.

The method is one for dealing with a system of interrelated variables. It is based on the construction of a qualitative diagram in which every included variable, measured or hypothetical, is represented (by arrows) either as *completely* determined by certain others (which may be represented as similarly determined) or as an *ultimate* factor. Each ultimate factor in the diagram must be connected (by lines with arrowheads at both ends) with each of the other ultimate factors to indicate possible correlation through still more remote unrepresented factors, except in cases in which it can safely be assumed that there is no correlation.

The necessary formal completeness of the diagram requires the introduction of a symbol for the array of unknown residual factors among those back of each variable that is not represented as one of the ultimate factors, unless it can safely be assumed that there is complete determination by the known factors. Such a residual factor can be assumed by definition to be uncorrelated with any of the other factors immediately back of the same variable, but cannot be assumed to be independent of other variables in the system without careful consideration.

It is assumed here that all relations are linear: non-linear relations may sometimes be transformed systematically throughout a diagram into linear ones. Approximate results may be obtained without transformation where deviations from linearity are small within the range of actual variation. Thus a product of uncorrelated variables XY may be treated as approximately additive $\delta(XY) = \bar{Y}\,\delta X + \bar{X}\,\delta Y$ if the coefficients of variability $\sigma_x/\bar{X}$ and $\sigma_y/\bar{Y}$ are not too large. If the latter are equal, the fraction of the variance that is excluded is less than half the squared coefficient of variability. It is also possible to deal rigorously with joint variability in restricted cases but this extension will not be dealt with here.

The validity of the system requires that variables that enter into two or more relations in the system (as a common factor of two or more, or as an intermediary in a chain) act as if point variables. If one part of a composite variable (such as a total or average) is more significant in one relation and another part in another, the treatment of the variable as if it were a unit may lead to grossly erroneous results. Fortunately, the parts of a composite variable are often known to be so strongly correlated in their values, or in their action, or both, that they may be used to obtain approximate results. It cannot be emphasized too much, however, that apart from special extensions, the strict validity of the method depends on the properties of formally complete linear systems of point variables.

The primary purpose was stated in the first general account (Wright [1921]) as follows:

"The present paper is an attempt to present a method of measuring the direct influence along each separate path in such a system and thus of finding the degree to which variation of a given effect is determined by each particular cause. The method depends on the combination of knowledge of the degrees of correlation among the variables in a system with such knowledge as may be possessed of the causal relations. In cases in which the causal relations are uncertain, the method can be used to find the logical consequences of any particular hypothesis in regard to them."

It was brought out here and later that the method

"is by no means restricted to relations that can be described as ones of cause and effect. It can be applied to purely mathematical systems of linear relations and merges into the methods of multiple regression and multivariable vectorial analysis when applied to the symmetrical systems of relations that characterize these methods" [1954].

The basic diagram in developing the theory is one in which a variable V_0 (Fig. 6.1) is represented as completely determined by a number of immediate factors $V_1, V_2, \ldots, V_m, V_u$ all of which, except the unknown residual V_u, are represented as intercorrelated. We are to consider the correlation of V_0 with any variable V_q. The latter must be represented as correlated with each of the factors of V_0 including the residual V_u if there is no reason to the contrary.

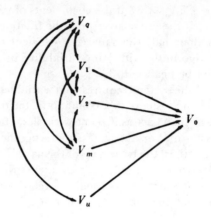

Figure 6.1.

As all relations are assumed to be linear, we have:

$$V_0 = c_0 + c_{01}V_1 + c_{02}V_2 + \ldots + c_{0m}V_m + c_{0u}V_u. \tag{1}$$

The coefficients c_{01} etc. are of the type of partial regression coefficients but are in a system that involves the residual V_u (unless there is known to be complete determination by the other immediate factors). It may involve other unmeasured hypothetical variables. The coefficients are thus ordinarily not deducible directly from the statistics in the way that is possible for a conventional partial regression coefficient such as $b_{01.23}$ where V_2 and V_3 as well as V_0 and V_1 are measured variables. They have meaning only in connection with a specified diagram. The symbol c_{01} is used to distinguish such a quantity, defined as a *path regression coefficient* (Wright [1921]), from the total regression coefficient b_{01}.

The path regression coefficient c_{01} measures the concrete contribution that V_1 is supposed to make *directly* to V_0 from the point of view represented in the diagram. If this correctly represents the causal relations, the path regression measures this contribution in an absolute sense and its value can be used in the analysis of other populations (Wright [1921, 1931]). Tukey [1954] and Turner and Stevens [1959] properly emphasize this virtue. The standardized *path coefficient* $p_{01} = c_{01}\sigma_1/\sigma_0$ obviously does not have this property, but it has other virtues including greater convenience in analysis.

Let $X_0 = (V_0 - \bar{V}_0)/\sigma_0$ etc.

Then
$$X_0 = p_{01}X_1 + p_{02}X_2 + \ldots + p_{0m}X_m + p_{0u}X_u. \tag{2}$$

In this standardized form, all correlation coefficients are reduced to product moments.

$$r_{0q} = (1/n) \sum x_0 x_q$$

$$= p_{01} r_{1q} + p_{02} r_{2q} + \ldots + p_{0m} r_{mq} + p_{0u} r_{uq} = \sum_{i=1}^{u} p_{0i} r_{iq} \tag{3}$$

If V_q is one of the immediate factors e.g. V_1, $r_{iu} = 0$,

$$r_{01} = p_{01} + p_{02} r_{12} + \ldots + p_{0m} r_{1m}. \tag{4}$$

If V_q is V_0 itself,

$$r_{00} = p_{01} r_{01} + p_{02} r_{02} + \ldots + p_{0m} r_{0m} + p_{0u}^2 = 1$$

$$r_{00} = \sum_{j=1}^{m} p_{0j} r_{0j} + p_{0u}^2 \quad \text{(where } V_j \text{ does not include } V_u\text{).} \tag{5}$$

The term $\sum p_{0j} r_{0j}$ is the squared coefficient of correlation r_{0E}^2 with the best estimate of V_0 that can be made from immediate factors other than V_u (squared coefficient of multiple correlation) and $r_{0u}^2 = p_{0u}^2 \ (= 1 - \sum p_{0j} r_{0j})$ is the squared error of estimate. Thus $r_{00} = r_{0E}^2 + r_{0u}^2$.

Returning to (3), which it may be noted does not depend on the assumption of normality of any of the variables, we note that it contains correlation coefficients which are capable of analysis by application of this formula to itself, if any of the immediate factors or V_q are represented as determined by more remote factors in a more extended diagram. The principle that is arrived at (for systems in which there are no paths that return on themselves) may be stated as follows: the correlation between any two variables in a properly constructed diagram of relations is equal to the sum of contributions pertaining to the paths by which one may trace from one to the other in the diagram without going back after going forward along an arrow and without passing through any variable twice in the same path. A coefficient pertaining to the whole path connecting two variables, and thus measuring the contribution of that path to the correlation, is known as a *compound path coefficient*. Its value is the product of the values of the coefficients pertaining to the elementary paths along its course. One, but not more than one of these, may pertain to a two-headed arrow without violating the rule against going back after going forward.

A uni-directional compound path coefficient may be indicated by listing the variables in order, from dependent to most remote independent, as subscripts. Thus in Figure 6.2, p_{013} pertains to the path $V_0 \leftarrow V_1 \leftarrow V_3$ and has the value $p_{01} p_{13}$. In a bi-directional compound path coefficient, it is convenient to list the variables in order from either end, but set off the ultimate

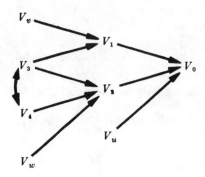

Figure 6.2.

common factor or pair of factors by parentheses. Thus $p_{01(3)2}$ in Figure 6.2 pertains to the path $V_0 \leftarrow V_1 \leftarrow V_3 \rightarrow V_2$, with value $p_{01}p_{13}p_{23}$ and $p_{01(34)2}$ pertains to the path $V_0 \leftarrow V_1 \leftarrow V_3 \leftrightarrow V_4 \rightarrow V_2$ with value $p_{01}p_{13}r_{34}p_{24}$. According to the rule above, $r_{02} = p_{02} + p_{01(3)2} + p_{01(34)2}$. In previous papers the turning point in a compound path has been indicated by a typographically somewhat awkward dot or dash over the pertinent subscript or pair of subscripts.

Concrete versus standardized coefficients

The comparison of the uses of standardized path coefficients and concrete path regressions can best be made in conjunction with a consideration of those of ordinary correlation and regression coefficients.

(1) The coefficient of correlation is a useful statistic in providing a scale from -1 through 0 to $+1$ for comparing degrees of correlation.

It is not the only statistic that can provide such a scale and these scales need not agree. There are statistics that agree at the three points referred to above without even rough agreement elsewhere (cf. r_{01}^3 with r_{01}), but, if one has become familiar with the situation implied by such values of r_{01} as .10, .50, .90 etc., the specification of the correlation coefficient conveys valuable information about the population that is under consideration. It is not a good reason to discard this coefficient because some have made the mistake of treating it as if it were an absolute property of the two variables. The term path coefficient was first used in an analysis of variability of amount of white in the spotted pattern of guinea pigs (Wright [1920]). There was a correlation of $+.211 \pm .015$ between parent and offspring and one of $+.214 \pm .018$

between litter mates in a randomly bred strain. The fact that the corresponding correlations in another population (one tracing to a single mating after seven generations of brother-sister mating) were significantly different ($+.014$ $\pm.022$ and $+.069 \pm.028$ respectively) presented in a clear way a question for analysis for which the method of path coefficients seemed well adapted, not a reason for abandoning correlation coefficients.

Path coefficients resemble correlation coefficients in describing relations on an abstract scale. A diagram of functional relations, in which it is possible to assign path coefficients to each arrow, gives at a glance the relative direct contributions of variability of the immediate causal factors to variability of the effect in each case. They differ from correlation coefficients in that they may exceed $+1$ or -1 in absolute value. Such a value shows at a glance that direct action of the factor in question is tending to bring about greater variability than is actually observed. The direct effect must be offset by opposing correlated effects of other factors. As in the case of correlation coefficients, the fact that the same type of interpretative diagram yields different path coefficients when applied to different populations is valuable for comparative purposes.

(2) The correlation coefficient seems to be the most useful parameter for supplementing the means and standard deviations of normally distributed variables in describing bivariate and multivariate distributions in mathematical form. Its value in this connection does not, however, mean that its usefulness otherwise is restricted to normally distributed variables as seems to be implied by Turner and Stevens.

The last point may be illustrated by citing one of the basic correlation arrays of population genetics, that for parent and offspring in a random breeding population, with respect to a single pair of alleles and no environmental complications.

Parent	*Offspring*			*Total*	*Grade*
	aa	*Aa*	*AA*		
AA	0	$q^2(1-q)$	q^3	q^2	$\alpha_0 + \alpha_1 + \alpha_2$
Aa	$q(1-q)^2$	$q(1-q)$	$q^2(1-q)$	$2q(1-q)$	$\alpha_0 + \alpha_1$
aa	$(1-q)^3$	$q(1-q)^2$	0	$(1-q)^2$	α_0
Total	$(1-q)^2$	$2q(1-q)$	q^2	1	

$$r_{OP} = \frac{(1-q)^2\alpha_1^2 + 2q(1-q)\alpha_1\alpha_2 + q^2\alpha_2^2}{(1-q)(2-q)\alpha_1^2 + 2q(1-q)\alpha_1\alpha_2 + q(1+q)\alpha_2^2}$$

$$= 1/2 \text{ if no dominance, } \alpha_2 = \alpha_1.$$

As each variable takes only three discrete values, as the intervals are unequal unless dominance is wholly lacking ($\alpha_2 = \alpha_1$), and as gene frequency q may take any value between 0 and 1, making extreme asymmetry possible, this distribution is very far from being bivariate normal. Obviously this ocrrelation coefficient has no application as a parameter of such a distribution. It may, however, be used rigorously in all of the other respects discussed here. It may be noted that its value may be deduced rigorously from the population array $[(1-q)a + qA]^2$, the assigned grades, and certain path coefficients that are obvious on inspection from a diagram representing the relation of parental and offspring genotypes under the Mendelian mechanism.

The correlation coefficients in a set of variables are statistical properties of the population in question that are independent of any point of view toward the relations among the variables. The dependence of calculated path coefficients on the point of view represented in a particular diagram, of course, restricts their use as parameters to this point of view.

(3) Assuming linearity, the squared correlation coefficient measures the portion of the variance of either of the two variables, that is controlled directly or indirectly, by the other, in the sense that it gives the ratio of the variance of means of one for given values of the other to the total variance of the former $[r_{12}^2 = \sigma_{1(2)}^2/\sigma_1^2]$. Correspondingly it gives the average portion of the variance of one that is lost at given values of the other $[\sigma_{1.2}^2 = \sigma_1^2(1 - r_{12}^2)]$. We are here using $\sigma_{1(2)}^2$ and $\sigma_{1.2}^2$ for the components of σ_1^2 that are dependent and independent respectively of variable V_2.

Equation (5), expressing complete determination of V_0 by its factors, can be expanded into the form

$$r_{00} = 1 = \sum_{j=1}^{m} p_{0j}^2 + 2\sum_{j,\,k=1}^{m} p_{0j}p_{0k}r_{jk} + \mathrm{p}_{0u}^2, \quad k > j. \tag{6}$$

On multiplying both sides by σ_0^2, it may be seen that the squared path coefficients measure the portions of σ_0^2 that are determined directly by the indicated factors while other terms (which may be negative) measure correlational determination.

(4) The correlation coefficient r_{01} measures the slope of the line of means of V_0 relative to V_i (or the converse) on standardized scales, and merely needs to be multiplied by the proper ratio of standard deviations to express regression in concrete terms ($b_{01} = r_{01}\sigma_0/\sigma_1$, $b_{10} = r_{01}\sigma_1/\sigma_0$).

As already noted, the abstract path coefficients have the same relation to the concrete path regressions.

(5) Another statistic of this family, the product moment,

$$M_{11}(V_1V_2) = \mathrm{cov}_{12} = (1/n)\sum_{1}^{n}(V_1 - \bar{V}_1)(V_2 - \bar{V}_2) = r_{12}\sigma_1\sigma_2$$

is useful on its own account in various ways. The product moment in a heterogeneous population may for example be analyzed into the sum of the product moment of the weighted means of the subpopulations and the average product moment within these (Wright [1917]). It was because of this additive property, analogous to that of the squared standard deviation, that Fisher later renamed this quantity the covariance in analogy with his term variance (Fisher [1918]) for the squared standard deviation.

Since the compound path coefficients analyze each correlation into additive contributions from each chain that connects the two variables, they merely need to be multiplied by the terminal standard deviations to give a similar analysis of the covariance.

(6) In certain situations (including important ones in population genetics) the correlation coefficient can be interpreted as a probability. This may be analyzable into components in terms of compound path coefficients.

(7) Finally, the formula for the correlation between linear functions is often useful and is the one that leads directly to path analysis.

If

$$
\begin{aligned}
V_S &= c_S + \sum c_{S_i} V_i, \\
\sigma_S^2 &= \sum c_{S_i}^2 \sigma_i^2 + 2 \sum c_{S_i} c_{S_j} \sigma_i \sigma_j r_{ij}, \qquad j > i \\
p_{S_i} &= c_{S_i} \sigma_i / \sigma_S, \\
r_{ST} &= \sum p_{S_i} p_{T_i} + \sum p_{S_i} p_{T_j} r_{ij}, \qquad \text{all } i \text{ and } j
\end{aligned}
\tag{7}
$$

The most extensive applications of the method have been essentially of this sort, the deduction of correlations from known functional relations in population genetics (Wright [1921, 1931, 1951]). The inverse problem, that of deducing path coefficients from known correlations and a given pattern of relations, depends on the solution of a system of simultaneous equations usually of higher degree than first and thus often requires rather tedious iteration.

We conclude that both the standardized and concrete coefficients for describing relationships between variables are useful and that the rejection of either would impoverish the theory.

The use of path coefficients in analysis

We come now to the point that even where concrete path regressions are the sole objectives, the analysis had best be carried out in terms of the standardized coefficients from which the desired concrete ones may be derived as the final step. We give below a number of simple systems. Numerical subscripts are used here for the variables that are supposed to be measured and literal ones for the hypothetical variables including the residuals necessary for completion. All of the equations that can be written from the known correlations and from cases of complete determination are expressed in terms of path coefficients and residual correlations. They can all be written from inspection by tracing connecting paths. All of them can also be written in concrete terms by use of formulae given above. This is done in some of the cases. Parentheses enclose quantities that are inseparable in analysis restricted to concrete coefficients.

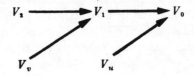

Figure 6.3.

Standardized Coefficients	Concrete Coefficients
(1) $r_{12} = p_{12}$	$b_{12} = c_{12}$
(2) $r_{01} = p_{01}$	$b_{01} = c_{01}$
(3) $r_{02} = p_{01}p_{12}$	$b_{02} = c_{01}c_{12}$
(4) $r_{00} = 1 = p_{01}^2 + p_{0u}^2$	$\sigma_0^2 = c_{01}^2\sigma_1^2 + (c_{0u}^2\sigma_u^2)$
(5) $r_{11} = 1 = p_{12}^2 + p_{1v}^2$	$\sigma_1^2 = c_{12}^2\sigma_2^2 + (c_{1v}^2\sigma_v^2)$

In this case, the first three equations are equally simple with concrete and standard coefficients and overdetermine two paths. One may (a) obtain a compromise solution as by the method of least squares or (b) may attribute any inconsistency to correlations between V_u and the variables back of V_1 (which must compensate in such a way that $r_{1u} = 0$ as required by the definition of V_u as a residual) or (c) may assume that the measurements of V_1 are in error. The hypothesis of errors in either V_0 or V_2 does not resolve any inconsistency of equations (1), (2) and (3).

The appropriate diagram and equations under (b) above are as follows:

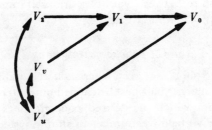

Figure 6.4.

(1) $r_{12} = p_{12}$,

(2) $r_{11} = 1 = p_{12}^2 + p_{1v}^2$,

(3) $r_{01} = p_{01}$ (since $r_{1u} = 0$),

(4) $r_{00} = 1 = p_{01}^2 + p_{0u}^2$,

(5) $r_{02} = p_{01}p_{12} + p_{0u}r_{2u}$,

(6) $r_{1u} = 0 = p_{12}r_{2u} + p_{1v}r_{uv}$.

A necessary condition for solution, that there be at least as many independent equations as paths, is met. This is not, in general, a sufficient condition since a system may be underdetermined in one part and overdetermined in another. In this case, however, the unknown path coefficients and correlations can be obtained in succession from the above equations.

The hypothesis that inconsistency of (1), (2) and (3) under Figure 6.3 is due to errors of measurement of V_1 is represented in Figure 6.5 and in the equations below.

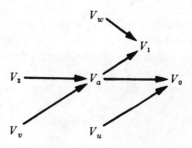

Figure 6.5.

(1) $r_{01} = p_{0a}p_{1a}$,

(2) $r_{12} = p_{1a}p_{a2}$,

(3) $r_{02} = p_{0a}p_{a2}$,

(4) $r_{00} = 1 = p_{0a}{}^2 + p_{0u}{}^2$,

(5) $r_{11} = 1 = p_{1a}{}^2 + p_{1w}{}^2$,

(6) $r_{aa} = 1 = p_{a2}{}^2 + p_{av}{}^2$.

These again are easily solved. Turner and Stevens discuss the effects of errors of measurement but not by means of path analysis, which if attempted with concrete coefficients is encumbered with symbols of variances. Thus equation (1) becomes

$$b_{01} = c_{0a}c_{1a}\sigma_a{}^2/\sigma_1{}^2 \text{ or } \text{cov}_{01} = c_{0a}c_{1a}\sigma_a{}^2.$$

There is, of course, indeterminancy if both (b) and (c) are assumed.

Encumbrance with unnecessary variances occurs wherever two variables trace to a third. The simplest case is that shown in Figure 6.6.

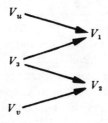

Figure 6.6.

Standardized Coefficients	Concrete Coefficients
(1) $r_{13} = p_{13}$	$b_{13} = c_{13}$
(2) $r_{23} = p_{23}$	$b_{23} = c_{23}$
(3) $r_{12} = p_{13}p_{23}$	$b_{12} = c_{13}c_{23}\sigma_3{}^2/\sigma_2{}^2$
(4) $r_{11} = 1 = p_{13}{}^2 + p_{1u}{}^2$	$\sigma_1{}^2 = c_{13}{}^2\sigma_3{}^2 + (c_{1u}{}^2\sigma_u{}^2)$
(5) $r_{22} = 1 = p_{23}{}^2 + p_{2v}{}^2$	$\sigma_2{}^2 = c_{23}{}^2\sigma_3{}^2 + (c_{2v}{}^2\sigma_v{}^2)$

There is overdetermination of two of the paths. Again a compromise solution may be obtained if there is confidence in the diagram. If not, the latter may be revised to indicate a correlation, r_{uv}, between the residuals or to indicate that there are errors of measurement in the intermediary V_3. A solution can be obtained under either of the latter two hypotheses (but not both at once).

A common situation is represented in Figure 6.7.

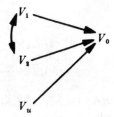

Figure 6.7.

Standardized Coefficients	Concrete Coefficients
(1) $r_{01} = p_{01} + p_{02}r_{12}$	$b_{01} = c_{01} + c_{02}b_{21}$
(2) $r_{02} = p_{01}r_{12} + p_{02}$	$b_{02} = c_{01}b_{12} + c_{02}$
(3) r_{12} given	b_{21} and b_{12} given
(4) $r_{00} = 1 = p_{01}r_{01} + p_{02}r_{02} + p_{0u}{}^2$	

The coefficients pertaining to all of the paths are readily calculated. This is a simple example of the patterns characteristic of multiple regression which are always easily solvable since only linear equations are involved. The equations (excluding 4) can be written as simply in terms of the regressions as in terms of the standardized coefficients but the former introduce an arbitrary asymmetry which is undesirable. Where only symmetrical patterns of this sort are being dealt with, the simplest procedure is, no doubt, to calculate the concrete coefficients directly from the ordinary normal equations of the method of least squares. This, however, takes us away from the sort of interpretive analysis which we are here considering, in which such symmetrical patterns are merely special cases.

Figure 6.8 is an example of another sort of symmetrical case.

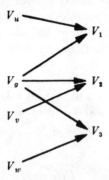

Figure 6.8.

(1) $r_{12} = p_{1g}p_{2g}$,

(2) $r_{13} = p_{1g}p_{3g}$,

(3) $r_{23} = p_{2g}p_{3g}$,

(4) $r_{11} = 1 = p_{1g}^2 + p_{1u}^2$,

(5) $r_{22} = 1 = p_{2g}^2 + p_{2v}^2$,

(6) $r_{33} = 1 = p_{3g}^2 + p_{3w}^2$.

There are six paths and six equations which permit solution for the standardized coefficients. Concrete coefficients cannot be used in this case because of ignorance of the variance of the hypothetical general factor V_g.

This is a simple example of the conventional pattern of factor analysis with one general factor as proposed by Spearman [1904]. There is over-determinancy if there are more known variables. A solution that maximizes the sum of the squared path coefficients that relate the known variables to the general factor has been given by Hotelling [1936]. Additional general factors may be postulated. The number of equations that can be written, given m known variables is $(1/2)m(m + 1)$. The number of coefficients to be determined with n common factors and m residuals is $m(n + 1)$. There may be exact determinancy, under or overdeterminancy. Hotelling has shown that with any number of known variables there is complete determinancy by the same number of factors if the sums of the squared path coefficients relating to the factors are successively maximized. Other conventions for arriving at a unique solution have been given.

The first paper on path coefficients (as square roots of coefficients of direct determination) (Wright [1918]) dealt with material of the sort to which factor analysis is applied (all possible correlations in a set of bone measurements in a rabbit population), but from a less symmetrical viewpoint. This has been developed in later papers (Wright [1932, 1954]).

Summary

The method of path coefficients and its more important pitfalls are reviewed briefly with reference to recent misunderstandings.

Reasons are discussed for looking upon standardized coefficients (correlations, path coefficients) and concrete ones (total and path regressions) as aspects of a single theory rather than as alternatives between which a choice should be made. They correspond to different modes of interpretation which taken together give a deeper understanding of a situation than either can give itself.

It is brought out that even where the sole objectives of analysis are the concrete coefficients, actual path analysis takes a simpler and more homogeneous form in terms of the standardized ones, which can easily be converted into the concrete forms as the final step.

References

FISHER, R. A. [1918]. The correlation between relatives on the supposition of Mendelian inheritance. *Trans. Roy. Soc. Edinburgh 52*, 399–433.

HOTELLING, H. [1936]. Simplified calculation of principal components. *Psychometrica 1*, 27–35.

SPEARMAN, C. [1904]. "General intelligence," objectively determined and measured. *Amer. J. Psych. 15*, 201–292.

TURNER, M. E., and STEVENS, C. D. [1959]. The regression analysis of causal paths. *Biometrics 15*, 236–258.

TUKEY, J. W. [1954]. Causation, regression and path analysis. *Statistics and Mathematics in Biology*. Edited by O. Kempthorne. T. A. Bancroft, J. W. Gowen, and J. L. Lush. Chapter 3, 35–66. Iowa State College Press, Ames, Iowa.

WRIGHT, S. [1917]. The average correlation within subgroups of a population. *J. Washington Acad. Sci. 7*, 532–535.

—— [1918]. On the nature of size factors. *Genetics 3*, 367–374.

—— [1920]. The relative importance of heredity and environment in determining the piebald pattern of guinea pigs. *Proc. Nat. Acad. Sci. 6*, 320–332.

—— [1921]. Correlation and causation *J. Agric. Research 20*, 557–585.

—— [1931a]. Evolution in Mendelian populations. *Genetics 16*, 97–159.

—— [1931b]. Statistical methods in biology. *J. Amer. Stat. Assoc. Supplement; Papers and Proceedings of the 92nd Annual Meeting 26*, 155–163.

—— [1932]. General, group and special size factors. *Genetics 17*, 603–619.

—— [1934]. The method of path coefficients. *Annals of Math. Stat. 5*, 161–215.

—— [1951]. The genetical structure of populations. *Annals of Eugenics 15*. 323–354.

—— [1954].The interpretation of multivariate systems. *Statistics and Mathematics in Biology*. Edited by O. Kempthorne. T. A. Bancroft, J. W. Gowen, and J. L. Lush. Chapter 2, p. 11–33. Iowa State College Press, Ames, Iowa.

Chapter 7

PATH ANALYSIS: SOCIOLOGICAL EXAMPLES

OTIS DUDLEY DUNCAN[1]
University of Michigan

The long-standing interest of sociologists in causal interpretation of statistical relationships has been quickened by discussions focusing on linear causal models. The basic work of bringing such models to the attention of the discipline was done by Blalock,[2] drawing upon the writings of Simon[3] and Wold[4] in particular. The rationale of this approach was strengthened when Costner and Leik[5] showed that "asymmetric causal models" of the kind proposed by Blalock afford a natural and operational explication of the notion of "axiomatic deductive theory," which had been developed primarily by sociologists working with verbal formulations. Most recently, Boudon[6] pointed out that the Simon-Blalock type of model is a "special case" or "weak form" of path analysis (or "dependence analysis," as Boudon prefers to call it). At the same

Reprinted by permission of the author and publisher from the *American Journal of Sociology*, Vol. 72, pp. 1–16. Copyright 1966, The University of Chicago Press.

1. Prepared in connection with a project on "Socioeconomic Background and Occupational Achievement," supported by contract OE-5-85-072 with the U.S. Office of Education. Useful suggestions were made by H. M. Blalock, Jr., Beverly Duncan, Robert W. Hodge, Hal H. Winsborough, and Sewall Wright, but none of them is responsible for the use made of his suggestions or for any errors in the paper.

2. Hubert M. Blalock, Jr., *Causal Inferences in Nonexperimental Research* (Chapel Hill: University of North Carolina Press, 1964).

3. Herbert A. Simon, *Models of Man* (New York: John Wiley & Sons, 1957), chap. ii.

4. Herman Wold and Lars Juréen, *Demand Analysis* (New York: John Wiley & Sons, 1953).

5. Herbert L. Costner and Robert K. Leik, "Deductions from 'Axiomatic Theory,'" *American Sociological Review*, XXIX (December, 1964), 819–835.

6. Raymond Boudon, "A Method of Linear Causal Analysis: Dependence Analysis," *American Sociological Review*, XXX (June, 1965), 365–374.

time, he noted that "convincing empirical illustrations are missing," since "moderately complicated causal structures with ·corresponding data are rather scarce in the sociological literature." This paper presents some examples (in the form of reanalyses of published work) which may be interesting, if not "convincing." It includes an exposition of some aspects of path technique, developing it in a way that may make it a little more accessible than some of the previous writings.

Path coefficients were used by the geneticist Sewall Wright as early as 1918, and the technique was expounded formally by him in a series of articles dating from the early 1920's. References to this literature, along with useful restatements and illustrations, will be found in Wright's papers of 1934, 1954, and 1960.[7] The main application of path analysis has been in population genetics, where the method has proved to be a powerful aid to "axiomatic deductions." The assumptions are those of Mendelian inheritance, combined with path schemes representing specified systems of mating. The method allows the geneticist to ascertain the "coefficient of inbreeding," a quantity on which various statistical properties of a Mendelian population depend. It also yields a theoretical calculation of the genetic correlations among relatives of stated degrees of relationship. Most of Wright's expositions of this *direct* use of path coefficients are heavily mathematical;[8] an elementary treatment is given in the text by Li.[9]

Apart from a few examples in Wright's own work, little use has been made of path coefficients in connection with the *inverse* problem of estimating the paths which may account for a set of observed correlations on the assumption of a particular formal or causal ordering of the variables involved. Of greatest substantive interest to sociologists may be an example relating to heredity and environment in the determination of intelligence.[10] Another highly suggestive study was a pioneer but neglected exercise in econometrics concerning prices and production of corn and hogs.[11] Although the subject matter is remote from sociological concerns, examples from studies in animal

7. Sewall Wright, "The Method of Path Coefficients," *Annals of Mathematical Statistics*, V (September, 1934), 161–215; "The Interpretation of Multivariate Systems," in O. Kempthorne *et al.* (eds.), *Statistics and Mathematics in Biology* (Ames: Iowa State College Press, 1954), chap. ii; "Path Coefficients and Path Regressions: Alternative or Complementary Concepts?" *Biometrics*, XVI (June, 1960), 189–202.

8. Sewall Wright, "The Genetical Structure of Populations," *Annals of Eugenics*, XV (March, 1951), 323–354.

9. C. C. Li, *Population Genetics* (Chicago: University of Chicago Press, 1955), chap. xii–xiv. See also C. C. Li, "The Concept of Path Coefficient and Its Impact on Population Genetics," *Biometrics*, XII (June, 1956), 190–210.

10. Sewall Wright, "Statistical Methods in Biology," *Journal of the American Statistical Association*, XXVI (March, 1931, suppl.), 155–163.

11. Sewall Wright, *Corn and Hog Correlations*, U.S. Department of Agriculture Bulletin 1300 (Washington: Government Printing Office, 1925); also, "The Method of Path Coefficients," pp. 192–204.

biology are instructive on methodological grounds.[12] If research workers have been slow to follow Wright's lead, the statisticians have done little better. There are only a few expositions in the statistical literature,[13] some of which raise questions to which Wright has replied.[14]

Path diagrams and the basic theorem

We are concerned with linear, additive, asymmetric relationships among a set of variables which are conceived as being measurable on an interval scale, although some of them may not actually be measured or may even be purely hypothetical—for example, the "true" variables in measurement theory or the "factors" in factor analysis. In such a system, certain of the variables are represented to be dependent on others as linear functions. The remaining variables are assumed, for the analysis at hand, to be given. They may be correlated among themselves, but the explanation of their inter-correlation is not taken as problematical. Each "dependent" variable must be regarded explicitly as *completely* determined by some combination of variables in the system. In problems where complete determination by measured variables does not hold, a residual variable uncorrelated with other determining variables must be introduced.

Although it is not intrinsic to the method, the diagrammatic representation of such a system is of great value in thinking about its properties. A word of caution is necessary, however. Causal diagrams are appearing with increasing frequency in sociological publications. Most often, these have some kind of pictorial or mnemonic function without being isomorphic with the algebraic and statistical properties of the postulated system of variables— or, indeed, without having a counterpart in any clearly specified system of variables at all. Sometimes an investigator will post values of zero order or partial correlations, association coefficients, or other indications of the "strength" of relationship on such a diagram, without following any clearly

12. Sewall Wright, "The Genetics of Vital Characters of the Guinea Pig," *Journal of Cellular and Comparative Physiology*, LVI (suppl. 1, November, 1960), 123–151; F. A. Davidson *et al.*, "Factors Influencing the Upstream Migration of the Pink Salmon (*Oncorhynchus gorbuscha*)," *Ecology*, XXIV (April, 1943), 149–68.

13. J. W. Tukey, "Causation, Regression and Path Analysis," in O. Kempthorne *et al.*, *op. cit.*, chap. iii; Oscar Kempthorne, *An Introduction to Genetic Statistics* (New York: John Wiley & Sons, 1957), chap. xiv; Malcolm E. Turner and Charles D. Stevens, "The Regression Analysis of Causal Paths," *Biometrics*, XV (June, 1959), 236–258; Eleanor D. Campbell, Malcolm E. Turner, and Mary Frances Wright, with the editorial collaboration of Charles D. Stevens, *A Handbook of Path Regression Analysis*, Part I: *Estimators for Simple Completely Identified Systems* (Preliminary Ed.; Richmond: Medical College of Virginia, Department of Biophysics and Biometry, 1960); Henri Louis Le Roy, *Statistische Methoden der Populationsgenetik* (Basel: Birkhäuser, 1960), chap. i; P. A. P. Moran, "Path Coefficients Reconsidered," *Australian Journal of Statistics*, III (November, 1961), 87–93.

14. "Paths Coefficients and Path Regressions."

defined and logically justified rules for entering such quantities into the analysis and its diagrammatic representation. In Blalock's work, by contrast, diagrams are employed in accordance with explicit rules for the representation of a system of equations. In general, however, he limits himself to the indication of the sign (positive or negative) of postulated or inferred direct relationships. In at least one instance[15] he inserts zero-order correlations into a diagram which looks very much like a causal diagram, although it is not intended to be such. This misleading practice should not be encouraged.

In path diagrams, we use one-way arrows leading from each determining variable to each variable dependent on it. Unanalyzed correlations between variables not dependent upon others in the system are shown by two-headed arrows, and the connecting line is drawn curved, rather than straight, to call attention to its distinction from the paths relating dependent to determining variables. The quantities entered on the diagram are symbolic or numerical values of *path coefficients*, or, in the case of the bidirectional correlations, the simple correlation coefficients.

Several of the properties of a path diagram are illustrated in Figure 7.1. The original data, in the form of ten zero-order correlations, are from Turner's study of determinants of aspirations.[16] The author does not provide a completely unequivocal formulation of the entire causal model shown here, but Figure 7.1 appears to correspond to the model that he quite tentatively proposes. At one point he states, "background affects ambition and ambition affects both IQ and class values; in addition . . . there is a lesser influence directly from background to class values, directly from background to IQ, and directly between IQ and class values."[17] Elsewhere, [18] he indicates that school rating operates in much the same fashion as (family) background. As for the relationship between the two, Turner notes, on the one hand, that "families may choose their place of residence," but also that "by introducing neighborhood, we may only be measuring family background more precisely."[19] Hence, it seems that there is no firm assumption about the causal ordering within this pair of variables; but since these two precede the remaining ones, it suffices to represent the link between X_1 and X_2 as merely a bidirectional correlation.

Allowing Turner to take responsibility for the causal ordering of the variables (assuming his statements are understood correctly) and deferring

15. Blalock, *op. cit.*, p. 77.
16. Ralph H. Turner, *The Social Context of Ambition* (San Francisco: Chandler Publishing Co., 1964), pp. 49 and 52, Tables 11, 17, and 20.
17. *Ibid.*, p. 107.
18. *Ibid.*, pp. 54–61.
19. *Ibid.*, p. 61.

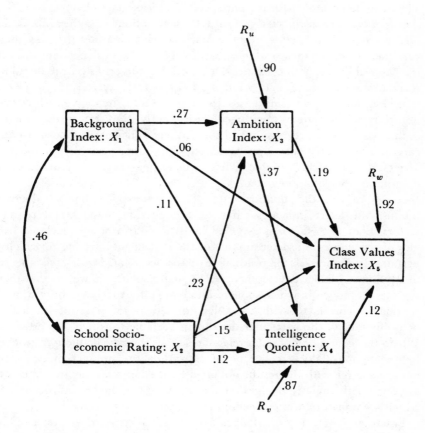

Figure 7.1. *Causal model from Turner, op. cit., with path coefficients estimated for male sample.*

the question of how the path coefficients were estimated, let us see what the system represented by Figure 7.1 is like. Each variable is taken to be in standard form; that is, if V_i is the ith variable as measured, then $X_i = (V_i - \bar{V}_i)/ \sigma_{V_i}$. The same convention holds for the residuals, R_u, R_v, and R_w, to which a literal subscript is attached to indicate that these variables are not directly measured. The system represented in Figure 7.1 can now be written:

$$X_3 = p_{32}X_2 + p_{31}X_1 + p_{3u}R_u,$$
$$X_4 = p_{43}X_3 + p_{42}X_2 + p_{41}X_1 + p_{4v}R_v, \tag{1}$$
$$X_5 = p_{54}X_4 + p_{53}X_3 + p_{52}X_2 + p_{51}X_1 + p_{5w}R_w.$$

The use of the symbol p for the path coefficient is perhaps obvious. Note that the order of the subscripts is significant, the convention being the same as that used for regression coefficients: the first subscript identifies the dependent variable, the second the variable whose direct effect on the dependent variable is measured by the path coefficient. The order of subscripts is immaterial for correlations. But note that while $r_{42} = r_{24}$ and $r_{42.123}, = r_{24.123}, p_{42} \neq p_{24}$; indeed p_{42} and p_{24} would never appear in the same system, given the restriction to recursive systems mentioned subsequently. Contrary to the practice in the case of partial regression and correlation coefficients, symbols for paths carry no secondary subscripts to identify the other variables assumed to affect the dependent variable. These will ordinarily be evident from the diagram or the equation system.

In one respect, the equation system (1) is less explicit than the diagram because the latter indicates what assumptions are made about residual factors. Each such factor is assumed by definition to be uncorrelated with any of the immediate determinants of the dependent variable to which it pertains. In Figure 7.1, the residuals are also uncorrelated with each other, as in the Simon-Blalock development.[20] We shall see later, however, that there are uses for models in which some residuals are intercorrelated, or in which a residual is correlated with variables antecedent to, but not immediate determinants of, the particular dependent variable to which it is attached. Where the assumption of uncorrelated residuals is made, deductions reached by the Simon-Blalock technique of expanding the product of two error variables agree with the results obtained by the formulas mentioned below, although path analysis involves relatively little use of the partial correlations which are a feature of their technique.

Equation system (1), as Blalock points out, is a recursive system. This discussion explicitly excludes non-recursive systems, involving instantaneous reciprocal action of variables, although Wright has indicated ways of handling them in a path framework.[21] Thus we shall not consider diagrams showing a direct or indirect feedback loop.

The principle that follows from equations in the form of (1) is that the correlation between any pair of variables can be written in terms of the paths leading from common antecedent variables. Consider

r_{35}. Since $X_3 = (V_3 - \bar{V}_3)/\sigma_3$ and $X_5 = (V_5 - \bar{V}_5)/\sigma_5$ we have $r_{35} = \Sigma(V_3 - \bar{V}_3)$ $\times (V_5 - \bar{V}_5)/N\sigma_3\sigma_5 = \Sigma X_3 X_5/N$.

We may expand this expression in either of two ways by substituting from (1)

20. Blalock, *op. cit.*, p. 64; Boudon, *op. cit.*, p. 369.
21. Sewall Wright, "The Treatment of Reciprocal Interaction, with or without Lag, in Path Analysis," *Biometrics*, XVI (September, 1960), 423–445.

the expression for X_3 or the one for X_5. It is more convenient to expand the variable which appears later in the causal sequence:

$$r_{35} = \Sigma X_3 X_5 / N$$

$$= \frac{1}{N} \Sigma X_3 (p_{54} X_4 + p_{53} X_3 + p_{52} X_2 + p_{51} X_1 + p_{5w} R_w) \qquad (2)$$

$$= p_{54} r_{34} + p_{53} + p_{52} r_{23} + p_{51} r_{13},$$

making use of the fact that $\Sigma X_3 X_3 / N = 1$ and the assumption that $r_{3w} = 0$, since X_3 is a factor of X_5. But the correlations on the right-hand side of (2) can be further analyzed by the same procedure; for example,

$$r_{34} = \frac{1}{N} \Sigma X_3 X_4 = \frac{1}{N} \Sigma X_3 (p_{43} X_3 + p_{42} X_2 + p_{41} X_1 + p_{4v} R_v) \qquad (3)$$

$$= p_{43} + p_{42} r_{23} + p_{41} r_{13},$$

and

$$r_{32} = \frac{1}{N} \Sigma X_2 X_3 = \frac{1}{N} \Sigma X_2 (p_{32} X_2 + p_{31} X_1 + p_{3u} R_u) \qquad (4)$$

$$= p_{32} + p_{31} r_{12}.$$

Note that r_{12}, assumed as a datum, cannot be further analyzed as long as we retain the particular diagram of Figure 7.1.

These manipulations illustrate the basic theorem of path analysis, which may be written in the general form:

$$r_{ij} = \sum_q p_{iq} r_{jq}, \qquad (5)$$

where i and j denote two variables in the system and the index q runs over all variables from which paths lead directly to X_i. Alternatively, we may expand (5) by successive applications of the formula itself to the r_{jq}. Thus from (2), (3), (4), and a similar expansion of r_{13}, we obtain

$$r_{53} = p_{53} + p_{51} p_{31} + p_{51} r_{12} p_{32} + p_{52} p_{32} + p_{52} r_{12} p_{31} + p_{54} p_{42} p_{32} + p_{54} p_{42} r_{12} f_{31}$$

$$+ p_{51} p_{43} + p_{54} p_{41} p_{32} r_{12} + p_{54} p_{41} p_{31}. \qquad (6)$$

Such expressions can be read directly from the diagram according to the following rule. Read *back* from variable i, *then forward* to variable j, forming the product of all paths along the traverse; then sum these products for all possible traverses. The same variable cannot be intersected more than once in a single traverse. In no case can one trace back having once started forward. The bidirectional correlation is used in tracing either forward or back, but if more than one bidirectional correlation appears in the diagram, only one can be used in a single traverse. The resulting expression, such as (6), may consist of a single direct path plus the sum of several compound paths representing all the indirect connections allowed by the diagram. The general formula (5) is likely to be the more useful in algebraic manipulation and calculation, the expansion on the pattern of (6) in appreciating the properties of the causal scheme. It is safer to depend on the algebra than on the verbal algorithm, at least until one has mastered the art of reading path diagrams.

An important special case of (5) is the formula for complete determination of X_i, obtained by setting $i = j$:

$$r_{ii} = 1 = \sum_q p_{iq} r_{iq}, \tag{7}$$

or, upon expansion,

$$r_{ii} = \sum_q p_{iq}^2 + 2\sum_{q,q'} p_{iq} r_{qq'} p_{iq'}, \tag{8}$$

where the range of q and q' $(q' > q)$ includes all variables, measured and unmeasured. A major use for (8) is the calculation of the residual path. Thus we obtain p_{3u} in the system (1) from

$$p_{3u}^2 = 1 - p_{32}^2 - p_{31}^2 - 2p_{32} r_{12} p_{31}. \tag{9}$$

The causal model shown in Figure 7.1 represents a special case of path analysis: one in which there are no unmeasured variables (other than residual factors), the residuals are uncorrelated, and each of the dependent variables is directly related to all the variables preceding it in the assumed causal sequence. In this case, path analysis amounts to a sequence of conventional regression analyses, and the basic theorem (5) becomes merely a compact statement of the normal equations of regression theory for variables in standard form. The path coefficients are then nothing other than the "beta coefficients" in a regression setup, and the usual apparatus for regression calculations may be employed.[22] Thus, the paths in Figure 7.1 are obtained from the regression of X_3 on X_2 and X_1, setting $p_{32} = \beta_{32.1}$ and $p_{31} = \beta_{31.2}$; the regression of X_4 on X_3, X_2, and X_1, setting $p_{43} = \beta_{43.12}$, $p_{42} = \beta_{42.13}$, and $p_{41} = \beta_{41.23}$; and the regression of X_5 on the other four variables, setting $p_{54} = \beta_{54.123}$, $p_{53} = \beta_{53.124}$, and so on. Following the computing routine which inverts the matrix of intercorrelations of the independent variables, one obtains automatically the standard errors of the β coefficients (or b^*-coefficients, in the notation of Walker and Lev). In the present problem, with sample size exceeding 1,000, the standard errors are small, varying between .027 and .032. All the β's are at least twice their standard errors and thus statistically significant.

22. Helen M. Walker and Joseph Lev, *Statistical Inference* (New York: Holt, Rinehart & Winston, 1953), chap. xiii.

In problems of this kind, Blalock[23] has been preoccupied with the question of whether one or more path coefficients may be deleted without loss of information. As compared with his rather tedious search procedure, the procedure followed here seems more straightforward. Had some of the β's turned out both non-significant and negligible in magnitude, one could have erased the corresponding paths from the diagram and run the regressions over, retaining only those independent variables found to be statistically and substantively significant.

As statistical techniques, therefore, neither path analysis nor the Blalock-Simon procedure adds anything to conventional regression analysis as applied recursively to generate a system of equations, rather than a single equation. As a *pattern of interpretation*, however, path analysis is invaluable in making explicit the rationale for a set of regression calculations. One may not be wholly satisfied, for example, with the theoretical assumptions underlying the causal interpretation of Turner's data provided by Figure 7.1, and perhaps Turner himself would not be prepared to defend it in detail. The point is, however, that *any* causal interpretation of these data must rest on assumptions—at a minimum, the assumption as to ordering of the variables, but also assumptions about the unmeasured variables here represented as uncorrelated residual factors.[24] The great merit of the path scheme, then, is that it makes the assumptions explicit and tends to force the discussion to be at least internally consistent, so that mutually incompatible assumptions are not introduced surreptitiously into different parts of an argument extending over scores of pages. With the causal scheme made explicit, moreover, it is in a form that enables criticism to be sharply focused and hence potentially relevant not only to the interpretation at hand but also, perchance, to the conduct of future inquiry.

Another useful contribution of path analysis, even in the conventional regression framework, is that it provides a calculus for indirect effects, when the basic equations are expanded along the lines of (6). It is evident from the regression coefficients, for example, that the direct effect of school on class values is greater than that of back-ground, but the opposite is true of the indirect effects. The pattern of indirect effects is hardly obvious without the aid of an explicit representation of the causal scheme. If one wishes a single summary measure of indirect effect, however, it is obtained as follows: indirect effect of X_2 on $X_5 = r_{52} - p_{52} = .28 - .15 = .13$; similarly, indirect effect of X_1 is $r_{51} - p_{51} = .24 - .06 = .18$. These summations of indirect effects include, in each case, the effects of one variable via its correlation with the other; hence the two are not additive. Without commenting further on the

23. *Op. cit.*, chap. iii.
24. *Ibid.*, pp. 46–47.

substantive implications of the direct and indirect effects suggested by Turner's material, it may simply be noted that the investigator will usually want to scrutinize them carefully in terms of his theory.

Decomposition of a dependent variable

Many of the variables studied in social research are (or may be regarded as) composite. Thus, population growth is the sum of natural increase and net migration; each of the latter may be further decomposed, natural increase being births minus deaths and net migration the difference between in- and out-migration. Where such a decomposition is available, it is of interest (1) to compute the relative contributions of the components to variation in the composite variable and (2) to ascertain how causes affecting the composite variable are transmitted via the respective components.

An example taken from work of Winsborough[25] illustrates the case of a variable with multiplicative components, rendered additive by taking logarithms. Studying variation in population density over the seventy-four community areas (omitting the central business district) of Chicago in 1940, Winsborough noted that density, defined as the ratio of population to area, can be written:

$$\frac{\text{Population}}{\text{Area}} = \frac{\text{Population}}{\text{Dwelling Units}} \times \frac{\text{Dwelling Units}}{\text{Structures}} \times \frac{\text{Structures}}{\text{Area}}.$$

Let $V_0 = \log$ (Population/Area), $V_1 = \log$ (Population/Dwelling Units), $V_2 = \log$ (Dwelling Units/Structures), and $V_3 = \log$ (Structures/Area); then

$$V_0 = V_1 + V_2 + V_3.$$

If each variable is expressed in standard form, we obtain,

$$\frac{V_0 - \bar{V}_0}{\sigma_0} = \frac{V_1 - \bar{V}_1}{\sigma_1} \cdot \frac{\sigma_1}{\sigma_0} + \frac{V_2 - \bar{V}_2}{\sigma_2} \cdot \frac{\sigma_2}{\sigma_0} + \frac{V_3 - \bar{V}_3}{\sigma_3} \cdot \frac{\sigma_3}{\sigma_0},$$

or

$$X_0 = p_{01} X_1 + p_{02} X_2 + p_{03} X_3,$$

where $X_0, \ldots, X_3$ are the variables in standard form and p_{01}, p_{02}, p_{03} are the path coefficients involved in the determination of X_0 by X_1, X_2, and X_3. Observe that the path coefficients can be computed in this kind of problem,

25. Hal H. Winsborough, "City Growth and City Structure," *Journal of Regional Science*, IV (Winter, 1962), 35–49.

where complete determination by measured variables holds as a consequence of definitions, without prior calculation of correlations:[26]

$$p_{01} = \sigma_1/\sigma_0 = .132 \quad \sigma_0 = .491 \quad \sigma_1 = .065$$
$$p_{02} = \sigma_2/\sigma_0 = .468 \qquad\qquad \sigma_2 = .230$$
$$p_{03} = \sigma_3/\sigma_0 = .821 \qquad\qquad \sigma_3 = .403.$$

Table 7.1 Correlation matrix for logarithms of density and its components and two independent variables: Chicago community areas, 1940

Variable	X_1	X_2	X_3	W	Z
X_0 density (log)	−.419	.636	.923	−.663	−.390
X_1 persons per dwelling unit (log)	....	−.625	−.315	.296	.099
X_2 dwelling units per structure (log) ..	....	....	.305	−.594	−.466
X_3 structures per acre (log)	....	....	....	−.517	−.226
W distance from center	....	....	....	....	.549
Z recency of growth	....	....	....	....	....

Source: Winsborough, *op. cit.*, and unpublished data kindly supplied by the author.

The intercorrelations of the components, shown in Table 7.1, are used to complete the diagram, Figure 7.2, *a*. The correlations of the dependent variable with its components may now be computed from the basic theorem, equation (5).

$$r_{01} = p_{01} + p_{02}r_{12} + p_{03}r_{13} = -.419;$$
$$r_{02} = p_{01}r_{12} + p_{02} + p_{03}r_{23} = \quad .636; \text{ and}$$
$$r_{03} = p_{01}r_{13} + p_{02}r_{23} + p_{03} = \quad .923.$$

The analysis has not only turned up a clear ordering of the three components in terms of relative importance, as given by the path coefficients, it has also shown that one of the components is actually correlated negatively with the composite variable, owing to its negative correlations with the other two components.

Winsborough considered two independent variables as factors producing variation in density: distance from the city center and recency of growth (percentage of dwelling units built in 1920 or later). The diagram can be elaborated to indicate how these factors operate via the components of log density (see Fig. 7.2, *b*).

The first step is to compute the path coefficients for the relationships of

26. Based on data kindly supplied by Winsborough.

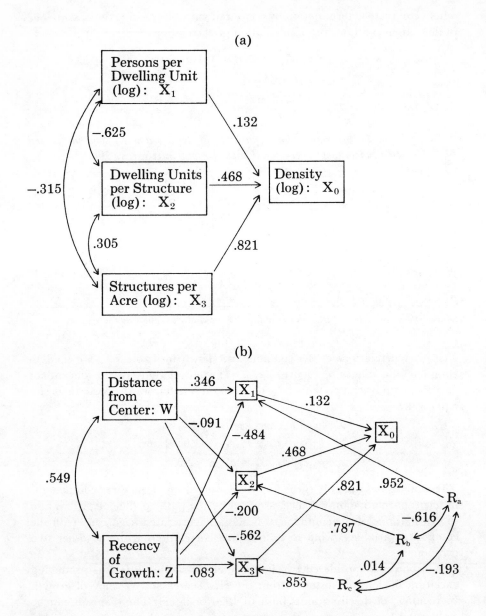

Figure 7.2. a, decomposition of log density (X_0) into components; b, effects of distance and recency of growth on log density via components. (Source: Winsborough, op. cit., and unpublished calculations kindly supplied by the author.)

each component to the two independent variables. (The requisite information is given in Table 7.1.) For example, the equations,

$$r_{1w} = p_{1w} + p_{1z}r_{zw},$$
$$r_{1z} = p_{1w}r_{zw} + p_{1z},$$

may be used to solve for p_{1z} and p_{1w}. (This is, of course, equivalent to computing the multiple regression of X_1 on W and Z, with all variables in standard form.) Substantively, it is interesting that distance, W, has somewhat larger effects on each component of density than does recency of growth, Z, while the pattern of signs of the path coefficients is different for W and Z.

The two independent variables by no means account for all the variation in any of the components, as may be seen from the size of the residuals, p_{1a}, p_{2b}, and p_{3c}, these being computed from the formula (7) for complete determination. It is possible, nevertheless, for the independent variables to account for the intercorrelations of the components and, ideally, one would like to discover independent variables which would do just that. The relevant calculations concern the correlations between residuals. These are obtained from the basic theorem, equation (5), by writing, for example,

$$r_{23} = p_{2w}r_{3w} + p_{2z}r_{3z} + p_{2b}p_{c3}r_{bc},$$

which may be solved for $r_{bc} = .014$. In this setup, the correlations between residuals are merely the conventional second-order partial correlations; thus $r_{ab} = r_{12 \cdot wz}$, $r_{ac} = r_{13 \cdot wz}$, and $r_{bc} = r_{23 \cdot wz}$. Partial correlations, which otherwise have little utility in path analysis, turn out to be appropriate when the question at issue is whether a set of independent variables "explains" the correlation between two dependent variables. In the present example, while $r_{23} = .305$, we find $r_{bc} = r_{23 \cdot wz} = .014$. Thus the correlation between the logarithms of dwelling units per structure (X_2) and structures per acre (X_3) is satisfactorily explained by the respective relationships of these two components to distance and recency of growth. The same is not true of the correlations involving persons per dwelling unit (X_1), but fortunately this is by far the least important component of density.

Although the correlations between residuals are required to complete the diagram and, in a sense, to evaluate the adequacy of the explanatory variables, they do not enter as such into the calculations bearing upon the final question: How are the effects of the independent variables transmitted to the dependent variable via its components? The most compact answer to this question is given by the equations,

$$r_{0w} = p_{01}r_{1w} + p_{02}r_{2w} + p_{03}r_{3w}$$
$$= .039 - .278 - .424 = -.663,$$

and

$$r_{0z} = p_{01}r_{1z} + p_{02}r_{2z} + p_{03}r_{3z}$$
$$= .013 - .218 - .185 = -.391.$$

Density is negatively related to both distance and recency of growth, but the effects transmitted via the first component of density are positive (albeit quite small). Distance diminishes density primarily via its intermediate effect on structures per acre (X_3), secondarily via dwelling units per structure (X_2). The comparison is reversed for recency of growth, the less important of the two factors. More detailed interpretations can be obtained, as explained earlier, by expanding the correlations r_{1W}, r_{2W}, etc., using the basic theorem (5). For further substantive interpretation, the reader is referred to the source publication, which also offers an alternative derivation of the compound paths.

The density problem may well exemplify a general strategy too seldom employed in research: breaking a complex variable down into its components before initiating a search for its causes. One egregious error must, however, be avoided: that of treating components and causes on the same footing. By this route, one can arrive at the meaningless result that net migration is a more important "cause" of population growth than is change in manufacturing output. One must take strong exception to a causal scheme constructed on the premise, "If both demographic and economic variables help explain metropolitan growth, then we may gain understanding of growth processes by lumping the two together."[27] On the contrary, "understanding" would seem to require a clear distinction between demographic *components* of growth and economic *causes* which may affect growth via one or another of its components.

A chain model

Data reported by Hodge, Siegel, and Rossi[28] seem to fit well the model of a *simple causal chain* (see Figure 7.3, *a*). These authors give correlations between the occupational prestige ratings of four studies completed at widely separated dates: Counts (1925), Smith (1940), National Opinion Research Center (1947), and NORC replication (1963). In a simple causal chain, the correlations between temporally adjacent variables are the path coefficients (this is an immediate consequence of the definition of path coefficient). Using these three correlations as reported by Hodge *et al.*, we may infer that the correlation between NORC (1963) and Smith is $(.990)$ $(.982) = .972$; between NORC (1963) and Counts is $(.990)$ $(.982)$ $(.968) = .942$; and between NORC (1947) and Counts is $(.982)$ $(.968) = .951$. The observed values of these correlations (with differences from the inferred values in parentheses) are $r_{YS} = .971$ $(-.001)$, $r_{YC} = .934$ $(-.008)$, and $r_{XC} = .955$ $(.004)$. Acceptance

27. George L. Wilber, "Growth of Metropolitan Areas in the South," *Social Forces*, XLII (May, 1964), 491.

28. Robert W. Hodge, Paul M. Siegel, and Peter H. Rossi, "Occupational Prestige in the United States, 1925–1963," *American Journal of Sociology*, LXX (November, 1964), 286–302.

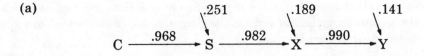

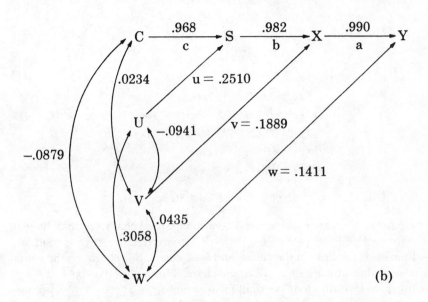

*Figure 7.3. Causal chain: a, correlations taken from Hodge et al., op. cit. (C =
Counts, 1925; S = Smith, 1940; X = NORC, 1947; Y = NORC, 1963);
b, intercorrelations of residuals implied by acceptance of chain hypothesis for
the data in a.*

of this causal chain model is consistent with the conclusion of Hodge *et al.*
that the amount of change in the relative positions of occupations in a
prestige hierarchy is a direct function of elapsed time.

Although the discrepancies between inferred and observed correlations
seem trivial, it is worth noting that acceptance of the estimates shown in
Figure 7.3, *a*, along with the assumption of a simple causal chain, requires us
to postulate a complex pattern of correlations (most of them negligible in
size) among the residuals or errors. This pattern is shown in Figure 7.3, *b*.
In obtaining this solution, we assume that each residual is uncorrelated with
the immediately preceding variable in the chain but not necessarily with
variables two or more links behind it. In the present example, then, the
crucial assumptions are that $r_{VS} = r_{WX} = 0$. We can then, using equation (5)

or the verbal algorithm, write the number of equations required to solve for the quantities to be entered on the diagram (for convenience, lower-case letters designate paths):

$$r_{YX} = a = .990,$$
$$r_{XS} = b = .982,$$
$$r_{SC} = c = .968,$$
$$r_{YY} = 1 = a^2 + w^2,$$
$$r_{XX} = 1 = b^2 + v^2,$$
$$r_{SS} = 1 = c^2 + u^2, \tag{11}$$
$$r_{XC} = .955 = bc + vr_{VC},$$
$$r_{YC} = .934 = abc + avr_{VC} + wr_{CW},$$
$$r_{YS} = .971 = ab + cwr_{CW} + uwr_{UW},$$
$$r_{VS} = 0 = ur_{UV} + cr_{CV},$$
$$r_{WX} = 0 = vr_{VW} + br_{SW}$$

(where $r_{SW} = cr_{CW} + ur_{UW}$).

In general, if we are considering a k-variable causal chain, we shall have to estimate $k-1$ residual paths, $(k-1)(k-2)/2$ correlations between residuals, $k-1$ paths for the links in the chain, and $k-2$ correlations between the initial variable and residuals 2, 3, . . ., k in the chain. This is a total of $(k^2 + 3k - 6)/2$ quantities to be estimated. We shall have at our disposal $k(k-1)/2$ equations expressing known correlations in terms of paths, $k-1$ equations of complete determination (for all variables in the chain except the initial one), and $k-2$ equations in which the correlation of a residual with the immediately preceding variable in the chain is set equal to zero. This amounts to $(k^2 + 3k - 6)/2$ equations, exactly the number required for a solution. The solution may, of course, include meaningless results (e.g., $r > 1.0$), or results that strain one's credulity. In this event, the chain hypothesis had best be abandoned or the estimated paths modified.

In the present illustration, the results are plausible enough. Both the Counts and the Smith studies differed from the two NORC studies and from each other in their techniques of rating and sampling. A further complication is that the studies used different lists of occupations, and the observed correlations are based on differing numbers of occupations. There is ample opportunity, therefore, for correlations of errors to turn up in a variety of patterns, even though the chain hypothesis may be basically sound. We should observe, too, that the residual factors here include not only extrinsic disturbances but also real though temporary fluctuations in prestige, if there be such.

What should one say, substantively, on the basis of such an analysis of the prestige ratings? Certainly, the temporal ordering of the variables is unambiguous. But whether one wants to assert that an aspect of social structure (prestige hierarchy) at one date "causes" its counterpart at a later date is perhaps questionable. The data suggest there is a high order of persistence over time, coupled with a detectable, if rather glacial, drift in the structure. The calculation of numerical values for the model hardly resolves the question of ultimate "reasons" for either the pattern of persistence or the tempo of change. These are, instead, questions raised by the model in a clear way for further discussion and, perhaps, investigation.

The synthetic cohort as a pattern of interpretation

Although, as the example from Turner indicates, it is often difficult in sociological analysis to find unequivocal bases for causal ordering, there is one happy exception to this awkward state of affairs. In the life cycles of individuals and families, certain events and decisions commonly if not universally precede others. Despite the well-known fallibility of retrospective data, the investigator is not at the mercy of respondents' recall in deciding to accept the completion of schooling as an antecedent to the pursuit of an occupational career (exceptions granted) or in assuming that marriage precedes divorce. Some observations, moreover, may be made and recorded in temporal sequence, so that the status observed at the termination of a period of observation may logically be taken to depend on the initial status (among other things). Path analysis may well prove to be most useful to sociologists studying actual historical processes from records and reports of the experience of real cohorts whose experiences are traced over time, such as a student population followed by the investigator through the first stages of postgraduation achievement.[29]

The final example, however, concerns not real cohorts but the usefulness of a hypothetical synthesis of data from several cohorts. As demographers have learned, synthetic cohort analysis incurs some specific hazards;[30] yet the technique has proved invaluable for heuristic purposes. Pending the execution of full-blown longitudinal studies on real cohorts, the synthetic cohort is, at least, a way of making explicit one's hypotheses about the sequential determination of experiences cumulating over the life cycle.[31]

In a study of the social mobility of a sample of Chicago white men with

29. For example, Bruce K. Eckland, "Academic Ability, Higher Education, and Occupational Mobility," *American Sociological Review*, XXX (October, 1965), 735–746.

30. P. K. Whelpton, "Reproduction Rates Adjusted for Age, Parity, Fecundity, and Marriage," *Journal of the American Statistical Association*, XLI (December, 1946), 501–516.

31. See, for example, A. J. Jaffe and R. O. Carleton, *Occupational Mobility in the United States: 1930–1960* (New York: King's Crown Press, 1954), p. 53 (n. 6) and Table 13.

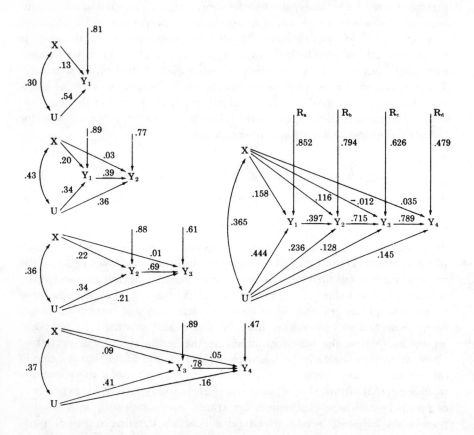

Figure 7.4. *Respondent's occupational status* (Y) *at successive ages, in relation to*
father's occupational status (X) *and respondent's educational attainment* (U).
Occupational status at age 25–34 = Y_1; *at* 35–44 = Y_2; *at* 45–54 = Y_3;
at 55–64 = Y_4. (*Source: Duncan and Hodge, op. cit., and unpublished*
calculations kindly supplied by the authors.)

nonfarm backgrounds surveyed in 1951, Duncan and Hodge[32] used data on
father's occupational status, respondent's educational attainment, and respondent's occupational status in 1940 and 1950 for four cohorts: men 25–34,
35–44, 45–54, and 55–64 years old on the survey date. Their main results,
somewhat awkwardly presented in the source publication, are compactly

32. Otis Dudley Duncan and Robert W. Hodge, "Education and Occupational Mobility,"
American Journal of Sociology, LXVIII (May, 1963), 629–644.

summarized by the first four diagrams in Figure 7.4. (The superfluous squared term in their equations has been eliminated in the present calculations. The amount of curvilinearity was found to be trivial, and curvilinear relations cannot be fitted directly into a causal chain by the procedure employed here.)

These data involve partial records of the occupational careers of the four cohorts and thus depict only segments of a continuous life history. In the original analysis, it was possible to gain some insights from the interperiod and intercohort comparisons on which that analysis was focused. Here, attention is given to a different use of the same information. Suppose we thought of the four sets of data as pertaining to a single cohort, studied at four successive points in time, at decade intervals. Then, all the data should fit into a single causal or processual sequence.

It is obvious that one cannot achieve perfect consistency on this point of view. The initial correlation, r_{UX}, varies among cohorts, for example. Moreover, age-constant intercohort comparisons of the other correlations (the Y's with X and U) suggest that some variations result from genuine differences between the conditions of 1940 and 1950. But if one is willing to suppress this information for the sake of a necessarily hypothetical synthesis, it is possible to put all the data together in a single model of occupational careers as influenced by socioeconomic origins.

The four correlations r_{UX} were averaged. The remaining correlations for adjacent cohorts were likewise averaged; for example, r_{1U} based on 1950 data for men 25–34 years old was averaged with r_{1U} based on 1940 data for men 35–44 in 1951, and so on. Only r_{4X}, r_{4U}, and the three intertemporal correlations, r_{21}, r_{32}, and r_{43}, had to be based on the experience of just one cohort. (In deriving this compromise one does, of course, lose the temporal specificity of the data by smoothing out apparently real historical fluctuations.) When the correlations had been averaged, the results shown in the "composite" model on the right of Figure 7.4 were obtained. The estimates of path coefficients here are simply the partial regression coefficients, in standard form, of Y_1 on X and U; Y_2 on Y_1, X, and U; Y_3 on Y_2, X, and U; and Y_4 on Y_3, X, and U.

The results for the synthetic cohort make explicit the following interpretations: (1) The background factors, father's education (X) and respondent's education (U), have an important direct impact during early stages of a cohort's life cycle; after age 35–44 their direct effects become small or negligible, although they exert indirect effects via preceding achieved statuses $(Y_1$ and $Y_2)$. (2) Careers tend to stabilize after age 35–44, as indicated by the sharp rise in the path coefficients representing persistence of status over a decade (compare p_{21} with p_{32} and p_{43}) and by the decreasing magnitudes of the residual paths from $R_a, \ldots, R_d$. (3) During the life cycle, many circumstances essentially independent of background factors affect occupational mobility, so that achievement in the later stages of the career becomes more and more dependent upon intervening contingencies while continuing to reflect the indirect influence of conditions determinate at the outset. Thus, for example, r_{4c}—the correlation of occupational status at age 55–64 with residual for age 45–54—may be computed as (.789) (.636) = .494, and the residual path to Y_4 itself is $P_{4d} = .479$. These are comparable in size with the correlations $r_{4X} = .301$ and $r_{4U} = .525$. The residuals are, by definition, uncorrelated with X and U and represent, therefore, the influence of factors quite unrelated to social origins and schooling. The prevailing impression that the United States enjoys a rather "loose" stratification system is thus quantified by a model such as this one. (4) While the data include observed interannual correlations of occupational statuses separated by a decade $(r_{43}, r_{32},$ and $r_{21})$, the synthetic cohort model also implies such correlations for statuses separated by two or three decades. These may be computed from the following formulas based on equation (5):

$$r_{42} = p_{4X}r_{2X} + p_{43}r_{32} + p_{4U}r_{2U},$$
$$r_{31} = p_{3X}r_{1X} + p_{32}r_{21} + p_{3U}r_{1U},$$
$$r_{41} = p_{4X}r_{1X} + p_{43}r_{31} + p_{4U}r_{1U},$$

inserting the value of r_{31} obtained from the second equation into the third. The observed and implied correlations are assembled in Table 7.2. The latter represent, in effect, hypotheses to be checked whenever data spanning twenty or thirty years of the occupational experience of a cohort become available. In the meantime, they stand as reasonable estimates, should any one have use for such estimates. If forthcoming evidence casts doubt on these estimates, the model will, of course, be called into question. It is no small virtue of a model that it is capable of being rejected on the basis of evidence.

Table 7.2. Observed and implied (*) correlations for synthetic cohort model of occupational achievement

Variable (Age and Occupational Status)	Variable		
	Y_2	Y_3	Y_4
25–34 (Y_1)	.552	.455*	.443*
35–44 (Y_2)	....	.772	.690*
45–54 (Y_3)	....	....	.866
55–64 (Y_4)	....	....	....

Source: Duncan and Hodge, *op. cit.*, and calculations from model in Figure 4.

This last example, since it rests on an explicit fiction—that of a synthetic cohort—perhaps makes clearer than previous examples the point that the role of path analysis is to *render an interpretation* and not merely to provide a format for presenting conventional calculations. In all the examples the intention has been to adhere to the purpose of path analysis as Wright formulated it:

> . . . the method of path coefficients is not intended to accomplish the impossible task of deducing causal relations from the values of the correlation coefficients.[33]
> . . . The method depends on the combination of knowledge of the degrees of correlation among the variables in a system with such knowledge as may be possessed of the causal relations. In cases in which the causal relations are uncertain, the method can be used to find the logical consequences of any particular hypothesis in regard to them.[34] . . . Path analysis is an extension of the usual verbal interpretation of statistics not of the statistics themselves. It is usually easy to give a plausible interpretation of any significant statistic taken by itself. The purpose of path analysis is to determine whether a proposed set of interpretations is consistent throughout.[35]

Neglected topics

This paper, for the lack of space and especially for lack of "convincing" examples, could not treat several potentially important applications of path analysis: (1) Models incorporating feedback were explicitly excluded. Whether our present techniques of social measurement are adequate to the development of such models is perhaps questionable. (2) The problem of two-wave, two-variable panel analysis, recently discussed by Pelz and Andrews,[36] might well be formulated in terms of path coefficients. The present writer, however, has made little progress in attempts to clarify the panel problem by means of path analysis. (3) The pressing problem of the disposition of measurement errors[37] may perhaps be advanced toward solution by explicit representation in path diagrams. The well-known "correction for attenuation," where measurement errors are assumed to be uncorrelated, is easily derived on this approach.[38] It seems possible that under very special

33. "The Method of Path Coefficients," p. 193.

34. "Correlation and Causation," *Journal of Agricultural Research*, XX (1921), 557–585 (quotation from p. 557).

35. "The Treatment of Reciprocal Interaction, with or without Lag, in Path Analysis," p. 444.

36. Donald C. Pelz and Frank M. Andrews, "Detecting Causal Priorities in Panel Study Data," *American Sociological Review*, XXIX (December, 1964), 836–854.

37. H. M. Blalock, Jr., "Some Implications of Random Measurement Error for Causal Inferences," *American Journal of Sociology*, LXXI (July, 1965), 37–47; Donald J. Bogue and Edmund M. Murphy, "The Effect of Classification Errors upon Statistical Inference: A Case Analysis with Census Data," *Demography*, I (1964), 42–55.

38. Wright, "The Method of Path Coefficients" and "Path Coefficients and Path Regressions."

conditions a solution may also be obtained on certain assumptions about correlated errors. (4) Wright has shown[39] how certain ecological models of the interaction of populations can be stated in terms of path coefficients. The inverse method of using path analysis for studies of multiple time series[40] merits consideration by sociologists. (5) Where the investigation involves unmeasured variables, path analysis may be helpful in deciding what deductions, if any, can be made from the observed data. Such unmeasured variables may, in principle, be observable; in this case, path analysis may lead to hypotheses for testing on some future occasion when measurements can be made. If the unmeasured variable is a theoretical construct, its explicit introduction into a path diagram[41] may well point up the nature of rival hypotheses. Ideally, what are sometimes called "validity coefficients" should appear explicitly in the causal model so that the latter accounts for both the "true causes" under study and the ways in which "indicator variables" are thought to represent "underlying variables." A particular case is that of factor analysis. As Wright's work demonstrates,[42] a factor analysis is prone to yield meaningless results unless its execution is controlled by explicit assumptions which reflect the theoretical structure of the problem. An indoctrination in path analysis makes one skeptical of the claim that "modern factor analysis" allows us to leave all the work to the computer.

39. "The Treatment of Reciprocal Interaction."
40. *Ibid.*
41. H. M. Blalock, Jr., "Making Causal Inferences for Unmeasured Variables from Correlations among Indicators," *American Journal of Sociology*, LXIX (July, 1963), 53–62.
42. "The Interpretation of Multivariate Systems."

Path Analysis: Sociological Examples (Addenda)[1]

1. Perhaps the most serious defect of the paper is that it glosses over the distinction between sample and population or between unobservable parameters and the coefficients computed from sample observations (which may, under certain assumptions, serve as estimates of parameters). This defect is manifest not only in the rather casual attitude taken toward the problem of statistical inference throughout the paper, but more particularly in the confused discussion of correlations involving residuals in connection with the chain model (Fig. 7.3). It should have been made clear that non-zero correlations involving residuals computed from sample data may be compatible with a model specifying zero correlations of disturbances (among themselves and with predetermined variables) in the theoretical population. Hence, the

1. Among other useful comments on the 1966 paper, I should like to acknowledge especially those of Arthur S. Goldberger.

correlations shown in Figure 7.3(b) may merely reflect sampling variation about zero parameter values. If so it is not necessary to "postulate a . . . pattern of correlations . . . among . . . the errors," but merely to acknowledge that such correlations involving residuals will inevitably appear in any sample data, even if the structural model is entirely correct as a representation of the process occurring in the population, providing that the model is over-identified, as is the simple chain model.

2. The statement on p. 130 that the solution (for correlations involving residuals) may include the result $r > 1.0$ is incorrect for the model under discussion. Implied correlations in excess of unity may, indeed, turn up in connection with other kinds of models, such as those including unmeasured variables; but this possibility is not relevant to the case at hand.

3. I now believe that the concept of "indirect effect" presented on p. 123 is not very useful and that further discussion[2] of this particular concept was ill-advised. As defined on p. 123, the indirect effect of X_j on X_i is given by $(r_{ij} - p_{ij})$. But, of course, r_{ij} includes not only the indirect effects of X_j on X_i via compound paths leading from X_j to X_i, but also the effects of common causes (if any) of X_j and X_i or the effects of variables correlated with X_j (if X_j is an exogenous variable in the system). In place of the "single summary measure of indirect effect" suggested in the paper, I would now recommend a calculation which may be illustrated with Figure 7.1. First, consider the correlation of one dependent variable with a subsequent dependent variable, e.g., r_{35}.

Correlation:	r_{35}
equals	
Direct effect:	p_{53}
plus	
Indirect effect:	$p_{54}p_{43}$
plus	
Correlation due to common or correlated causes:	$p_{52}r_{23} + p_{51}r_{13} + p_{54}(p_{42}r_{23} + p_{41}r_{13})$

This, of course, is equivalent to either of the expansions of r_{35} given by equations (2) and (6). Second. consider the correlation of an exogenous variable with a dependent variable, e.g., r_{15}.

2. Kenneth C. Land, "Principles of Path Analysis," in Edgar F. Borgatta and George W. Bohrnstedt (Eds.), *Sociological Methodology* 1969 (San Francisco: Jossey-Bass, 1969), p. 23.

Correlation: r_{15}

  equals

Direct effect: p_{51}

  plus

Indirect effect: $p_{54}\,(p_{41}+p_{43}p_{31})+p_{53}p_{31}$

  plus

Effect shared with other exogenous variable(s)

$$r_{12}[p_{52}+p_{54}\,(p_{42}+p_{43}p_{32})+p_{53}p_{32}]$$

The term in square brackets represents the combined direct and indirect effects of the other exogenous variable in the system.

4. The mention of "neglected topics" on p. 135 is now obsolete. Several papers in the recent sociological literature have provided examples of models incorporating unmeasured variables, measurement errors, and reciprocal causation ("feedback"); and the treatment of two-wave, two-variable panel data has been explicated from the viewpoint of path analysis.[3]

5. I am in general agreement with Blalock's comment on the paper.[4] I would perhaps stress two points more strongly, however. First, in problems involving unmeasured variables or measurement error it may not be practicable to work with (raw-score) path regressions in preference to (standardized) path coefficients. Second, the choice between the two conventions is of no great moment with respect to the formulation, testing, and estimation of models, since the coefficients may be rescaled at will. An exception to this statement may be the kind of model which includes an explicit specification concerning error variance (say, that it is constant over time); in such a case use of the standardized form may create unnecessary mathematical difficulties. Blalock is correct in observing that, for purposes of interpretation across populations, the raw-score regression form may be more useful in many cases; this is illustrated by a study of the process of stratification in the white and nonwhite populations.[5]

3. Otis Dudley Duncan, "Some Linear Models for Two-Wave, Two-Variable Panel Analysis," *Psychological Bulletin*, 72 (September, 1969): 177–182.
4. H. M. Blalock, Jr., "Path Coefficients versus Regression Coefficients," *American Journal of Sociology*, 72, (May, 1967): 675–676.
5. Otis Dudley Duncan, "Inheritance of Poverty or Inheritance of Race?" in Daniel P. Moynihan (Ed.), *On Understanding Poverty* (New York: Basic Books, 1969).

Chapter 8

CAUSAL INFERENCES, CLOSED POPULATIONS, AND MEASURES OF ASSOCIATION

H. M. BLALOCK, JR.*
University of Washington

Two of the most important traditions of quantitative research in sociology and social psychology are those of survey research and laboratory or field experiments. In the former, the explicit objective is usually that of generalizing to some specific population, whereas in the latter it is more often that of stating relationships among variables. These two objectives are not thought to be incompatible in any fundamental sense, but nevertheless we lack a clear understanding of their interrelationship.

One of the most frequent objections to laboratory experiments turns on the question of generalizability, or what Campbell and Stanley refer to as "external validity."[1] In essence, this question seems to reduce to at least two related problems: (1) that of representativeness or typicality, and (2) the possibility of interaction effects that vary with experimental conditions. In the first case, the concern would seem to be with central tendency and dispersion of single variables, that is, whether the means and standard deviations of variables in the experimental situation are sufficiently close to those of some larger population. The second involves the question of possible

Reprinted by permission of the publisher from the *American Political Science Review*, Vol. 61, pp. 130–136. Copyright 1967, The American Political Science Association.

* I am indebted to the National Science Foundation for support of this research.

1. See especially Donald T. Campbell and Julien S. Stanley, "Experimental and Quasi-experimental Designs for Research on Teaching," in N. L. Gage (ed.), *Handbook of Research on Teaching* (Chicago: Rand McNally & Company, 1963), pp. 171–246. See also Leslie Kish, "Some Statistical Problems in Research Design," *American Sociological Review*, 24 (1959), pp. 328–338.

disturbing influences introduced into the experimental setting that produce non-additive effects when combined with either the experimental variable or the premeasurement.[2] These same variables may of course be operative in larger populations. But presumably they take on different numerical values, with the result that one would infer different relationships between major independent and dependent variables in the two kinds of research settings.

As a sociologist who is only superficially acquainted with trends and developments in quantitative behavioral political science, it is my impression that, with the exception of simulation studies, the overwhelming emphasis has been on stating generalizations appropriate to specific populations rather than stating general laws of political behavior. Consistent with this has been the frequent use of correlation coefficients as measures of degree of relationship, as contrasted with the use of unstandardized regression coefficients as measures of the *nature* and form of relationships appropriate for general structural equations representing causal laws. One reason for this emphasis on particular populations is perhaps that the kinds of populations dealt with by political scientists are often of more inherent descriptive or practical importance than many of the (usually smaller) populations sampled by sociologists. I shall return to this question in discussing the Miller-Stokes study of constituency influence.

The question of whether or not one is generalizing only to specific populations or attempting to state scientific laws has created considerable confusion in the sociological literature, and I hope that political scientists will be in a position to benefit from this confusion so as to by-pass controversies such as those concerning whether or not one should make tests of statistical significance when data for the entire population are available. The purpose of the present paper is to bring this general issue into sharper focus. In doing so, I shall take a position with which many political scientists will undoubtedly disagree.

Rather than taking as the ultimate objective the goal of generalizing to specific populations, I would maintain that it is preferable to attempt to state general laws that interrelate variables in terms of hypothetical "if-then" statements. These could be of the form, "If X changes by one unit under conditions A, B, and C, then Y should change by b_{yx} units." In effect, then, I would consider generalizations to populations as means rather than ends. But given the limitations imposed by most data collection techniques, it is often necessary to carry out studies on specific populations at a single point in time, or at most several points in time. If so, then what must one assume about these populations? Since no real populations will be completely isolated

2. For a systematic discussion of the handling of various interaction effects in experimental designs see John A. Ross and Perry Smith, "Experimental Designs of the Single-Stimulus, All-or-Nothing Type," *American Sociological Review*, 30 (1965), pp. 68–80.

or "closed," what kinds of assumptions concerning less than completely closed populations can realistically be made? And what bearing does this have on choice of measures of association? Let me first consider the question of the closure of populations.

Closed populations and closed theoretical systems

A completely closed theoretical system would be one in which no variables have been omitted, and which (if mathematically formulated) would imply perfect mathematical functions with no stochastic or error terms. Obviously, such completely closed systems are impossible to find in the social sciences. Furthermore, our approximations to this ideal are not even close. The error terms one finds empirically are usually too large to be considered negligible. Therefore one is faced with the necessity of making assumptions about these errors and why they occur. Such assumptions will become quite complex whenever one is dealing with theoretical systems involving reciprocal causation, time lags, interaction terms, and the like.

Let us therefore confine our attention to simple recursive equations of the form:

$$X_1 = e_1$$
$$X_2 = b_{21}X_1 + e_2$$
$$X_3 = b_{31}X_1 + b_{32}X_2 + e_3$$
$$X_4 = b_{41}X_1 + b_{42}X_2 + b_{43}X_3 + e_4$$

One can show in this case that unbiased estimates of the regression coefficients can be obtained by assuming that the error terms in each equation are uncorrelated with each other and also with all of the *independent* variables that appear in their respective equations.[3] Thus e_2 is assumed uncorrelated with X_1 and also the remaining error terms e_i. Similarly, e_3 is unrelated to X_1 and X_2, and so forth.

What do these assumptions mean in terms of the behavior of outside variables not explicitly contained in the model? In brief, if one assumes that outside variables have a direct effect on *only one* of the explicit variables, then the assumptions can be met. Notice that an implicit variable might have an *indirect* effect on some variable through one of the remaining X_i without violating the assumptions. But if an implicit factor *directly* affects two or more explicit variables, then it will ordinarily be correlated with one of the independent variables in its equation, and the assumptions will not be met. If this is the case, least squares estimates will be biased, and one's inferences will be incorrect. Such a variable should be explicitly included in the system. At

---

3. See Herman Wold and Lars Juréen, *Demand Analysis* (New York: John Wiley & Sons, 1953), Ch. 2.

some point one must stop and make the simplifying assumption that all remaining implicit factors operate (in a major way) on only one explicit variable.

Analogously, a completely closed population is one which is subject to no outside influences including immigration or emigration. A completely closed theoretical system that implied a stable equilibrium could be tested in such a closed population by collecting data at a single point in time, provided it was assumed that stability had actually been reached.[4] But given that such completely closed populations can never be found empirically, the major problem seems to be that of specifying a satisfactory analogue to the imperfectly closed theoretical system that allows for error terms in the equations.

It seems to me that in order to state and test theoretical generalizations based on population data, one must assume that the lack of closure of the population does not violate the above assumptions regarding error terms.[5] That is, disturbances that systematically affect one variable should not affect the others in a major way. For example, migration factors that directly affect X_2 should not also affect X_1, nor should they affect X_3 or X_4 except through the operation of X_2. This means that migration processes (or other disturbances emanating from outside populations) should not affect *relationships* among the variables, though they may very well affect measures of central tendency or dispersion for *single* variables.

For example, individuals obviously migrate for economic reasons. Certain cities will have higher income or occupational levels than others, or may be more homogeneous economically than others. Individuals will of course also migrate for other reasons as well—to join relatives, or for cultural or recreational purposes. In many instances, however, it will be plausible to assume that these additional reasons are "idiosyncratic" and that, when aggregated, do not systematically distort relationships among variables. If, however, large numbers of persons move for *combinations* of reasons, then one's inferences regarding relationships among variables may very well be misleading. For example, suppose that high-income liberals move into communities containing large numbers of low-income conservatives (e.g., rural college communities). A study relating income to conservatism could lead to erroneous conclusions if based solely on this community.

---

4. There will of course be numerous dynamic models all of which predict the same stability conditions. Ideally, theories should be formulated in dynamic terms in such a way that time enters in in an essential way (as in difference equations). The approach of "comparative statics" can then be used to study equilibrium conditions. For a very readable discussion of this question see William J. Baumol, *Economic Dynamics* (New York: The Macmillan Company, 1959). See also Paul A. Samuelson, *The Foundations of Economic Analysis* (Cambridge: Harvard University Press, 1947); and Herbert A. Simon, *Models of Man* (New York: John Wiley & Sons, 1957), Chs. 6–8.

5. Of course somewhat less restrictive assumptions concerning the error terms might be used. Whatever set of assumptions are used, however, it would seem necessary to assume that the population is "closed" in the sense of meeting these assumptions.

I assume that many objections to "atypical" populations are based on this kind of concern about selective migration. Detroit is certainly not-typical of metropolitan centers with respect to income distribution. Whether or not it is considered objectionable, from the standpoint of generalizations to other populations, however, would seem to depend on whether or not Detroit is peculiar with respect to combinations of characteristics of interest to the investigator. Ideally one should define the boundaries of his population in such a way that such selective migration (by several variables) is reduced to a minimum. Thus he might prefer to use an entire metropolitan area, rather than the central city, arguing that although migration *within* the metropolitan area may be selective, this will not be the case *between* such larger units. Had he used central cities, he might have found this assumption much less plausible. For example, high-income Negroes might be more likely to remain within the city, as might also be true for certain extremely high-status families (e.g., the "Proper Bostonians").

An example: constituency influence

Before proceeding with a rather general discussion of standardized and unstandardized coefficients, I should like to introduce as a concrete example the study of constituency influence in Congress by Miller and Stokes.[6] The authors give correlational data based on a sample of 116 congressional districts and then interpret these data in terms of a causal model as indicated in Figure 8.1. The direction of influence between the representative's

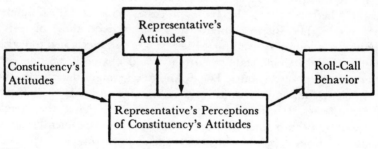

Figure 8.1.

attitudes and his *perceptions* of the constituency's attitudes is left unspecified, though the authors discuss the implications of the two limiting models in which the one or the other of the two arrows is erased. Cnudde and McCrone suggest some possible revisions of this model, based on the magnitudes of the

6. Warren E. Miller and Donald E. Stokes, "Constituency Influence in Congress," *The American Political Science Review*, 57 (1963), pp. 45–56.

coefficients.[7] In particular, they suggest that the data are compatible with a model in which (1) the arrow from constituency's attitude to representative's attitude is erased, and (2) it is assumed that the representative's perception affects his own attitudes, rather than vice versa. There is no need, here, to concern ourselves with this particular substantive issue.

The basic problem with which Miller and Stokes deal is that of measuring the relative importance of the two major paths from constituency's attitude to roll-call behavior. In the case of civil rights they conclude that the path via the representative's perceptions is more important than that via the representative's own attitudes. The measures they display in the paper are correlation coefficients, but they also make use of path coefficients (which will be discussed below). The conclusion reached is that in the case of civil rights roll-call behavior, and the least favorable assumptions regarding the importance of the representative's perceptions, the path via perceptions accounts for more than twice as much of the variance as does the path involving the representatives' own attitudes.

This is an excellent example of a study in which there is inherent interest in generalizing to a single population, since there is only one U.S. House of Representatives. Once inferences have been made from the sample of 116 districts to this total population, one might then take the position that there is no point in attempting to formulate more general "laws" of constituency influence. But there are a number of respects in which the data are not completely general. First, only a sample of political issues could be studied. Second, the study is obviously time-bound, and it might be desirable to compare results (for these same issues) over a period of time in order to ascertain whether or not the basic processes have remained unaltered. Third, one might wish to compare these results with those of legislative bodies in other countries. Had the Miller-Stokes data pertained to legislative behavior within a single state, then one would obviously be interested in comparing results across states. For example, one might determine whether the coefficients for Southern and Northern states were similar with respect to civil rights issues. If different with respect to civil rights, they might be similar with respect to other issue areas. These types of problems require one to formulate propositions more abstractly than in terms of specific populations and periods of time.

The question of the possible lack of closure of a population may not be as relevant for this type of substantive problem as would be the case in voting behavior studies. Legislative bodies are closed at least in the sense that, with minor exceptions, persons are elected for specified periods of time and do not

7. Charles F. Cnudde and Donald J. McCrone, "The Linkage Between Constituency Attitudes and Congressional Voting Behavior: A Causal Model," *The American Political Science Review*, 60 (1966), pp. 66–72.

migrate into and out of such "populations." In developing measures of constituency attitudes, one likewise need not be too concerned about lack of closure since presumably representatives are concerned about the makeup of *present* constituencies, and ordinarily assume that the distribution of attitudes will not be modified in any major way by migration. Each constituency, however, will be influenced by neighboring districts, and it will undoubtedly be necessary to make simplifying assumptions about how this influence process affects the closure of these smaller units.

With this example in mind, let us return to the question of one's choice of appropriate measures. I shall then comment briefly on why I believe that unstandardized measures would be more suitable for certain purposes for which the Miller-Stokes type of data might be used.

Standardized versus unstandardized regression coefficients

The method of "path coefficients" or "dependence coefficients" has been recommended as an important methodological tool for measuring the relative contributions to associations between pairs of variables in multivariate analyses. Raymond Boudon implies that sociologists may have failed to use such coefficients because of a certain confusion over the meaning of regression coefficients in simultaneous equations, and also because of the identification problems that may arise.[8] It is important, however, to be well aware of the major differences between standardized measures, such as correlation and path coefficients, and unstandardized regression coefficients. The former seem most appropriate for describing relationships in particular populations; the latter for comparing populations or stating general laws.[9]

It is instructive to examine the relationship between correlation and regression coefficients by conceiving of the numerical value of a correlation coefficient as a dependent variable, being a function of (1) the causal law connecting two (or more) variables, and (2) the relative amounts of variation that happen to exist in any particular population or that may be induced in experimental manipulations. Making the assumptions necessary for least squares, we may write

$$r_{xy} = b_{yx}\left(\frac{s_x}{s_y}\right)$$

8. Raymond Boudon, "A Method of Linear Causal Analysis: Dependence Analysis," *American Sociological Review*, 30 (1965), pp. 365–374. See also Sewall Wright, "Path Coefficients and Path Regressions: Alternative or Complementary Concepts?," *Biometrics*, 16 (1960), pp. 189–202; and Dudley Duncan, "Path Analysis: Sociological Examples," *American Journal of Sociology*, 72 (1966), pp. 1–16.

9. This position is basically similar to that taken by John W. Tukey in "Causation, Regression, and Path Analysis," in Oscar Kempthorne *et. al.* (eds.), *Statistics and Mathematics in Biology* (Ames, Iowa: Iowa State College Press, 1954), Chap. 3.

Let us assume that the sample size is sufficiently large that we can ignore sampling error. Similar expressions can be written in the case of three or more variables; for example:

$$r_{xy.w} = b_{yx.w} \left(\frac{s_x}{s_y} \frac{\sqrt{1 - r^2_{xw}}}{\sqrt{1 - r^2_{yw}}} \right)$$

I shall confine the discussion to the simple two-variable case, as the extension is straightforward.

The coefficient b_{yx} (or $b_{yx.w}$) represents the change in Y produced by a unit change in X and is appropriate for use in a general statement of a causal law.[10] Such a law is expressed in the hypothetical "if-then" form. There is no assertion that X has changed, or will change, by a given amount. But in order to apply or test such a law one must deal with specific populations or manipulations in particular experiments. The factor s_x/s_y, or its extensions in the multivariate case, involves *actual* variations in X and Y. Assuming that there are no measurement errors in either variable, we would presume that variation in X (e.g., constituency attitudes) is produced by factors not explicitly considered, and that variation in Y is jointly affected by X plus additional factors left out of the theoretical system. Least squares procedures will give unbiased estimates of the true regression coefficients in causal laws only if certain assumptions are met concerning the effect of variables left out.[11] Ordinarily, however, one is in no theoretical position to specify *a priori* the *amount* of actual variation produced by omitted factors in real populations. In the case of populations that are not completely closed, the existence of migration makes such assumptions even less plausible.

Thus the amount of variation in X relative to variation in Y produced by factors not considered may be taken as "accidental" from the point of view of one's theory. Of course one may take X as itself being determined by other variables, in which case variation in X may also be partly explained. But we are here considering X as "exogenous," and it is of course necessary to

10. The numerical value of b_{yx} is of course also affected by one's choice of units of measurement. Unlike the expression s_x/s_y, however, these units of measurement are interrelated by purely *a priori* or definitional operations (e.g., 100 pennies = one dollar). It is true, as McGinnis notes, that one can transform r_{xy} into b_{yx} by multiplying by a simple scalar quantity. It does not follow, however, that correlation and regression coefficients are essentially interchangeable as McGinnis implies. For this scalar quantity s_y/s_x is a function of standard deviations peculiar to each population. A reader who is given only the correlation coefficient is therefore likely to be misled in interpreting results of comparative studies. For a further discussion of this point see H. M. Blalock, *Causal Inferences in Nonexperimental Research* (Chapel Hill: University of North Carolina Press, 1964), Ch. 4. See also Robert McGinnis, "Review of *Causal Inferences in Nonexperimental Research,*" *Social Forces*, 44 (1966), pp. 584–586.

11. In particular, one must assume that the error terms in each equation have zero means and are uncorrelated with each other and with any of the independent variables that appear in their respective equations.

have some such exogenous variables in one's theoretical system. These are the "givens" that the theorist makes no effort to explain. In terms of the coefficients, he cannot account for the numerical values of the variance in exogenous variables. In this sense they are taken as accidental, and are unique to each population even where the same causal laws are operative on all populations.

Let me illustrate with a simple example. Suppose one finds stronger correlations between constituency's and representative's attitudes in the North than is true in the South. It is quite conceivable that the same laws are operative, giving the same values of b_{yx} in each region. Yet there may be more variation in constituency's attitudes in the North, and if extraneous factors operated to the same extent in both regions this would account for the larger correlation. Fortunately, the amount of variation in X can be measured and the regions compared in this respect. But uncontrolled and unknown disturbing influences cannot, and one would have no way of determining whether or not these also varied more in the North than in the South. It would therefore be more meaningful to compare the slope estimates than the respective correlations.

The same basic issues concerning standardization arise in the case of more complex causal models. As Miller and Stokes have noted, the method of path coefficients provides a simple and useful way of representing a total correlation between any two variables as a function of the causal paths that connect them. Consider, for example, the following model:

Letting p_{ij} represent the path coefficient from X_j to X_i, we can write down expressions for each of the r_{ij}. For example:

$$r_{23} = p_{21}p_{31}$$

and

$$r_{14} = p_{21}p_{42} + p_{31}p_{43}$$

These expressions can either be derived algebraically, as indicated in Boudon's paper, or they can be obtained directly by following certain rules or "algorithms" for tracing paths. The latter method has more intuitive appeal, and is easier to apply in simple models, but may lead one astray in more complex situations. The general rule is that one can trace paths by proceeding backward and then forward, or forward only, but it is not legitimate to move forward and *then* backward. Thus in the case of the paths between X_2 and X_3, one finds a path through X_1 (going back against the direction of the arrow, and then forward), but *not* through their common effect X_4 (which would require going forward and then back).

One can then attribute a certain proportion of the total correlation to each component path, thereby obtaining a measure of the relative contribution of each variable to this correlation. But why take the *correlation* between two variables as something to be explained? According to my previous argument, this should be a function of variation in exogenous variables peculiar to particular populations. Breaking up a correlation coefficient into component parts would seem to require that these parts, themselves, be peculiar to the population. This is in fact the case, as can be seen from the definition of a path coefficient.

A path coefficient p_{ij} is defined as the ratio of two quantities. The standard deviation in the dependent variable X_i is in the denominator. The numerator is essentially an adjusted standard deviation, being the standard deviation in X_i that would result if X_j retained the same amount of variation, but if all other causes of X_i (direct and indirect) remained constant. In symbols:

$$p_{ij} = \frac{s_{i \cdot j}}{s_i}$$

where $s_{i \cdot j}$ represents the standard deviation in X_i that can be attributed to X_j, with the other variables held constant. It is possible, therefore, that a path coefficient can take on a value greater than unity, though this is not likely in most realistic examples.

Notice that this definition of path coefficients, from which the simple algebraic relationships with correlations can be derived, involves a combination of the hypothetical and the real. On the one hand, the *actual* variations in both X_j and X_i are accepted as givens. On the other, we are asked to imagine what would happen if the remaining variables were held constant. This mixture of real and hypothetical poses some interesting questions. How, for example, would one retain the same variation in X_3, while holding constant X_1 which is one of its causes? To do so would require one to manipulate some *other* cause of X_3 not included in the model. It is of course possible to imagine experiments in which this could be accomplished. The real question, it seems, is: "Why combine these hypothetical manipulations with the actual variations peculiar to a given population?" Put another way, if one were interested in controlling some of the variables, why would he insist that the independent variable under study retain the same amount of variation? This might make sense if the so-called independent variables were not themselves causally interrelated, but the rationale seems to be less clearcut in more complex situations.[12]

Unstandardized regression coefficients provide direct answers to the kind of hypothetical question that I believe to be more appropriate. For example, one could ask what would be the expected change in X_4 produced by a unit change in X_1, given that X_1 affects both X_2 and X_3, and assuming that outside factors produce only random variation. Suppose, for example, that a unit change in X_1 will increase X_2 by three units, and decrease X_3 by four units. Suppose also that unit increases in X_2 and X_3 will increase X_4 by two and four units respectively. Then an increase of one unit in X_1 should increase Z_4 by $3(2) = 6$ units via X_2 and change X_4 by $(-4)(4) = -16$ units via X_3. The total expected change would then be ten units in the negative direction.

Notice that nothing is being said here about actual changes in a given population. The population data are used to *estimate* the regression coefficients, but the formulation is purely hypothetical. I have used a simple numerical example for illustrative purposes, but the general procedure is quite straightforward *provided* one assumes one-way causation and no feedback, plus the usual least squares assumptions regarding error terms. Turner and Stevens provide both an algebraic procedure and an algorithm for tracing paths similar to that given by Wright for the standardized path coefficients.[13]

Returning to the Miller-Stokes data, the reason why the path via the representative's perception was found to explain more than twice as much of the variance as the other major path was that the correlation between constituency's attitude and perception was .63, whereas that between constituency's and representatives' attitudes was only .39. The correlations between the two intervening variables and roll-call behavior were almost identical (being .82 and .77 respectively). Let us rule out the possibility of sampling error and assume that these correlations adequately describe the magnitudes of the relationships for this particular population, at this given time (1958), for civil rights issues.

Suppose, now, that additional data were available for other populations,

---

12. If interest is in generalizing to a population, it might make more sense to use a measure that does not involve any hypothetical manipulations. One may of course break down $R^2_{4.123}$ into the components r^2_{14}, $r^2_{24.1}(1-r^2_{14})$, and $r^2_{34.12}(1-R^2_{4.12})$. Since x_1, x_2, and x_3 are intercorrelated, these components cannot be directly associated with these variables. However, the exogenous causes of the X_i are assumed orthogonal in the case of simple least squares, and therefore one may—if he wishes—link the above components of $R^2_{4.123}$ with the respective error terms, given these assumptions about the causal ordering of x_1, x_2, and x_3. This of course raises the question of why one would want to associate components with exogenous variables that have not been included in the theoretical system.

13. Malcolm E. Turner and Charles D. Stevens, "The Regression Analysis of Causal Paths," *Biometrics*, 15 (1959), pp. 236–258.

time periods, or issues. To be specific, suppose one wished to compare the Miller-Stokes results with those for several different periods of time, posing the question as to whether or not basic changes in influence processes were occurring. As noted above, it is entirely possible that the basic laws, as measured by slopes, would remain unchanged whereas the relative magnitudes of the correlations could be altered. In the case of constituency attitudes, which are the starting points for both paths, an increase in the variance would be expected to increase *both* correlations with the two intervening variables. But it is quite possible that outside or exogenous factors affecting the representative's attitudes might produce a smaller variance in subsequent periods, though they might continue to create essentially random disturbances. If so, the correlation between constituency's attitude and representative's attitude would increase, perhaps to a level comparable to that between constituency's attitude and representative's perception. With reduced variation in representative's attitude, the correlation between this variable and roll-call behavior might also decrease, again with no basic changes in the slope coefficients.

The general point, of course, is that both the simpler correlation coefficients and more complex path coefficients are functions of the nature of the underlying processes *and* the relative magnitudes of disturbance terms. As long as one is dealing with a single set of data—as is true with respect to the Miller-Stokes example—the use of path coefficients will not be misleading. When one is interested in making comparisons, however, he should become sensitized to the differences between the two types of measures.

Conclusions

I suspect that one reason why both standardized and unstandardized regression coefficients have not found favor with sociologists and political scientists is a general reluctance to work with interval-scale assumptions and an understandable resistance to committing oneself to specific causal models. I would hope that we will begin to move more and more in these directions. In doing so, however, we must keep clearly in mind the distinction between working with causal laws and unstandardized coefficients, and attempting to measure relative importance of variables in specific populations. We must recognize that relative importance cannot be evaluated in the abstract: the contribution of each factor to the total variation in a dependent variable is a function of how much the various independent variables happen to vary in that given population. Since I am arguing against the advisability of generalizing to populations, at least as an ultimate objective, I must also argue that we would not be interested in these standardized measures except for descriptive or practical purposes.

Tukey has taken essentially the same position and has recommended working with unstandardized coefficients.[14] Wright has pointed out that, like the ordinary correlation coefficients, standardized path coefficients have much simpler properties than the unstandardized measures.[15] I would agree with Tukey, however, who suggests that the price of simplicity may be too high. It would seem preferable to make use of unstandardized coefficients that have some chance of being invariant from one population to the next, rather than measures that have admittedly simpler descriptive properties.

14. Tukey, *op. cit.*
15. Wright, *op. cit.*

PART III

Simultaneous-Equation Techniques

This is a difficult section involving a good many rather elusive though fundamental issues facing all of the social sciences. The literature on simultaneous-equation estimation procedures is becoming extensive but is relatively more technical than materials contained in the remaining sections of this volume. The reader who is totally unfamiliar with nonrecursive systems may therefore wish to begin with the Mason and Halter paper, which explains rather simply the main essentials of two-stage least squares as applied to the substantive example of a diffusion model. This might be followed with a second substantive paper, that by Duncan, Haller, and Portes, and then by Miller's paper applying the logic of two-stage least squares to experimental and nonexperimental designs. The reader should then be in a position to follow some of the more abstract papers by Koopmans, by Strotz and Wold, and by Fisher and Ando. The latter set of readings might best be studied in conjunction with textbook materials on simultaneous-equation estimation.[1]

Part III begins with a classic paper by Koopmans, that conceptualizes the identification problem in the context of supply and demand models and which points to the need for exogenous variables and *a priori* restrictive assumptions in order to reduce the number of unknowns relative to knowns in the general k-equation case. Koopmans is dealing with static models that require equilibrium assumptions. In these models it is generally impossible to estimate the relative effects of each variable on the others when we allow for reciprocal causation among all "endogenous" or mutually-dependent variables. The proposed resolution to the identification problem arising in the case of such static models is to introduce predetermined variables in such a way that at least $k-1$ variables have been left out of each equation that is to be identified. These variables may be truly exogenous or "independent" of

---

1. See especially Carl F. Christ, *Econometric Models and Methods* (New York: John Wiley, 1966); and J. Johnston, *Econometric Methods* (New York: McGraw-Hill, 1963).

any of the endogenous variables, or they may be lagged values of endogenous variables.

The next paper, by Strotz and Wold, states the case for recursive models involving lagged endogenous variables.[2] In brief, the authors argue that especially in instances where each equation can be linked with autonomous actors (e.g., suppliers, customers, and retailers) a model is most adequately conceived in terms of stimulus-response situations in which each party is responding (with a lag) to the actions of the others. If so, then simultaneous equations involve "specification errors" in that they fail to capture the time-lags involved. In effect, Strotz and Wold argue that adequate models will be recursive in nature and that the use of lagged endogenous variables permits one to conceptualize reciprocal causation in dynamic terms, where differences in time periods are explicitly taken into consideration. The issues raised in these first two papers are indeed fundamental ones that have implications for sociology, political science, and psychology. One of the greatest difficulties faced in these latter fields, however, is that of the appropriateness of lagged variables in instances when the time lags are unknown or not uniform. Furthermore, lagged variables involve one with difficult problems of autocorrelation of the disturbance terms.[3]

The papers by Fisher and Ando and by Fisher deal with additional practical issues that introduce further technical complications. Obviously, no model can be completely realistic. Therefore it involves specification errors of one kind or another—errors produced by faulty assumptions about omitted variables, about linearity and additivity, and about the lack of measurement errors involved. Assumptions used to identify a system (e.g., that certain coefficients are zero) are never strictly correct, and therefore the question arises as to the seriousness of the errors produced whenever these assumptions are in fact invalid. Fisher and Ando give a nontechnical discussion of an important theorem to the effect that as long as assumptions are *approximately* correct, we can count on only minor distortions in our estimates and that even our inferences for long-run dynamic models can be reasonably safe. It is important to realize, however, that assumptions that are totally unjustified empirically *will* produce misleading results. Here we see the necessity of having a reasonably sound theory prior to accurate estimation.

The paper by Fisher on instrumental variables explores the problem of

2. Wold's more recent position is a good deal more complex but seems to entail a convergence with Fisher's emphasis on block-recursive models. See H. O. A. Wold, "Mergers of Economics and Philosophy of Science," *Synthese*, *20* (1969): 427–482; H. O. A. Wold, "Non-experimental Statistical Analysis from the General Point of View of Scientific Method," *Bulletin of the International Statistical Institute*, *42*, Part I (1969); 391–424; and H. O. A. Wold, "Toward a Verdict on Macroeconomic Simultaneous Equations," *Pontificiae Academiae Scientiarum Scripta Varia*, *28* (1965); 115–185.

3. See Christ, *op. cit.*, pp. 482–487, and Johnston, *op. cit.*, pp. 178–192.

making practical decisions as to one's choice among exogenous and lagged endogenous variables in the case of macrolevel models involving large numbers of variables. A careful reading of Fisher's paper should make it abundantly clear that there will always be unmet assumptions and compromises with reality, as well as decisions that must be based on inadequate information.

A point that has been emphasized by Fisher in his paper on the choice among instrumental variables, as well as elsewhere, is that what have been referred to as "block-recursive" models afford a realistic compromise between the simplicity of the recursive models stressed by Wold and the more general linear systems of Koopmans and others. In a block-recursive system one allows for reciprocal causation *within* blocks of variables but one-way causation *between* blocks. Thus certain blocks of variables are assumed to be causally prior to others, with no feedback being permitted from the latter to the former. This kind of assumption is, of course, needed in order to treat certain variables as predetermined in any given system. Thus, if variables in Blocks A and B are assumed to be possible causes of variables in Block C, whereas the possibility of Block C variables affecting Blocks A and B is ruled out, then when one is studying the interrelationships among variables in Block C, he may utilize variables from Blocks A and B as predetermined. These variables may be truly exogenous, or they may be lagged values of variables in Block C, and Fisher discusses the relative merits of both kinds of factors. The notion of "instrumental variables" is used as a generic term to refer to any variables that can be used to help identify and estimate the parameters in the system.

Perhaps the most fundamental idea that pervades Part III, and that has been implicit in the previous sections, is that of "structural parameters" which are seen as providing the "true" causal structure of the theoretical system. In the case of recursive systems, these parameters were the b_{ij} that could be estimated in a straightforward manner by ordinary least squares. But in the more general case one is faced with the fact that there will ordinarily be indefinitely many different sets of parameter values that all imply the same empirical data. The identification problem can be conceptualized as that of recovering the true structural parameters from the emprical data, and in the case of static formulations this cannot be accomplished without the aid of untestable *a priori* assumptions. Usually, though not necessarily, these take the form of assumptions that certain of the parameters have zero values. In the special case of recursive systems, for example, half of the possible b_{ij} have been set equal to zero so as to produce a triangular slope matrix. Additionally, we also assume that the covariances of all pairs of disturbance terms e_i are zero, and these two kinds of assumptions make identification possible in the case of recursive systems.

In the general k-equation case it will always be possible to rewrite the system in terms of a mathematically equivalent set of equations referred to as a "reduced form." If we represent the endogenous variables as X_i and the predetermined variables as Z_j, each of the equations for the endogenous X_i can be written as a linear function of the Z_j alone. One may therefore estimate each X_i by using only the Z_j, and in fact these reduced forms are used in the first stage of the two-stage least-squares procedure that is discussed in several papers in this section. However, it does *not* follow that one can always estimate the true structural parameters from the estimates of the reduced-form parameters. Thus the identification problem can also be conceived as the problem of moving from the reduced-form equations to the structural equations. Whenever there are too many unknown structural parameters for this to be done, we say that the equation(s) is underidentified. Whenever there are exactly the right number and combination of unknown parameters, there may be a unique solution for the structural parameters in terms of the reduced-form parameters, in which case we say that the equation(s) is exactly identified. Whenever there are fewer unknown structural parameters than necessary for exact identification, the equation(s) will be overidentified, and there will be no *unique* way of estimating the parameters.

In the overidentified case, therefore, questions arise as to the "best" method of estimating the parameters, and there has been extensive discussion of this technical problem in the econometrics literature. In general, so-called "full information" methods that utilize information from the entire set of equations at once tend to be relatively more efficient than two-stage least squares, which deals with the equations sequentially. However, the full-information procedures seem more sensitive to specification errors that arise in instances where theoretical foundations for the model are weak. It would appear as though two-stage least squares is entirely adequate for less advanced fields such as political science and sociology, given the presence of relatively poor measurement procedures and the very tentative nature of existing theories.

Overidentified systems are especially necessary whenever *tests* of a model are being considered. In the case of recursive systems we saw that each time we erased an arrow between a pair of variables we added a prediction that a partial slope (or correlation) should be approximately zero except for sampling errors. In fact, a recursive system with no additional b_{ij} set equal to zero turns out to be exactly identified given the assumption that all covariances among disturbance terms are zero. If we set one additional $b_{ij} = 0$, this produces one empirical prediction that will not automatically be satisfied by the data. In effect, we may use all but one of the equations in Simon's procedure to estimate the parameters, considering the remaining equation as "redundant" and therefore usable for testing purposes. The more coefficients assumed equal to zero, the more such excess equations we have for testing purposes. As a general principle, it would seem as though the less sure we are of our theories the more desirable that they be highly overidentified, so that multiple predictions can be made from the excess equations. This point should be more apparent in Part IV, where we deal with identification problems brought about by the presence of unmeasured variables in a causal system.

Chapter 9

IDENTIFICATION PROBLEMS
IN ECONOMIC MODEL CONSTRUCTION

TJALLING C. KOOPMANS*
Yale University

1. Introduction

The construction of dynamic economic models has become an important
tool for the analysis of economic fluctuations and for related problems of
policy. In these models, macro-economic variables are thought of as determined by a *complete system of equations*. The meaning of the term "complete" is
discussed more fully below. At present it may suffice to describe a complete
system as one in which there are as many equations as endogenous variables,
that is, variables whose formation is to be "explained" by the equations. The
equations are usually of, at most, four kinds: equations of economic behavior,
institutional rules, technological laws of transformation, and identities. We
shall use the term structural equations to comprise all four types of equations.

Systems of structural equations may be composed entirely on the basis of
economic "theory." By this term we shall understand the combination of (a)
principles of economic behavior derived from general observation—partly
introspective, partly through interview or experience—of the motives of
economic decisions, (b) knowledge of legal and institutional rules restricting

Reprinted by permission of the author and publisher from *Econometrica*, Vol. 17, pp. 125–
143. Copyright 1949, The Econometric Society.

* I am indebted to present and former Cowles Commission staff members and to my
students for valuable critical comments regarding contents and presentation of this article.
An earlier version of this paper was presented before the Chicago Meeting of the Econometric
Society in December 1947. This article was reprinted with the addition of a sixth example in
Section 2, as Chapter II of *Studies in Econometric Method*, William C. Hood and Tjalling
C. Koopmans (Eds.), John Wiley, 1953.

individual behavior (tax schedules, price controls, reserve requirements, etc.), (c) technological knowledge, and (d) carefully constructed definitions of variables. Alternatively, a structural equation system may be determined on the dual basis of such "theory" combined with systematically collected statistical data for the relevant variables for a given period and country or other unit. In this article we shall discuss certain problems that arise out of model construction in the second case.

Where statistical data are used as one of the foundation stones on which the equation system is erected, the modern methods of statistical inference are an indispensable instrument. However, without economic "theory" as another foundation stone, it is impossible to make such statistical inference apply directly to the equations of economic behavior which are most relevant to analysis and to policy discussion. Statistical inference unsupported by economic theory applies to whatever statistical regularities and stable relationships can be discerned in the data.[1] Such purely empirical relationships when discernible are likely to be due to the presence and persistence of the underlying structural relationships, and (if so) could be deduced from a knowledge of the latter. However, the direction of this deduction cannot be reversed— from the empirical to the structural relationships—except possibly with the help of a theory which specifies the form of the structural relationships, the variables which enter into each, and any further details supported by prior observation or deduction therefrom. The more detailed these specifications are made in the model, the greater scope is thereby given to statistical inference from the data to the structural equations. We propose to study the limits to which statistical inference, from the data to the structural equations (other than definitions), is subject, and the manner in which these limits depend on the support received from economic theory.

This problem has attracted recurrent discussion in econometric literature with varying terminology and degree of abstraction. Reference is made to Pigou [16], Henry Schultz [17, especially Chapter II, Section IIIe], Frisch [4, 5], Marschak [15, especially Sections IV and V], Haavelmo [6, especially Chapter V]. An attempt to systematize the terminology and to formalize the treatment of the problem has been made over the past few years by various authors connected in one way or another with the Cowles Commission for Research in Economics. Since the purpose of this article is expository, I shall draw freely on the work by Koopmans and Rubin [14], Wald [18], Hurwicz [7, 8], Koopmans and Reiersöl [13], without specific acknowledgement in each case. We shall proceed by discussing a sequence of examples, all drawn from econometrics, rather than by a formal logical presentation, which can be found in references [14], [7] and [13].

---

1. See T. C. Koopmans [12].

2. Concepts and examples

The *first example*, already frequently discussed, is that of a competitive market for a single commodity, of which the price p and the quantity q are determined through the intersection of two rectilinear schedules, of demand and supply respectively, with instantaneous response of quantity to price in both cases. For definiteness' sake, we shall think of observations as applying to successive periods in time. We shall further assume that the slope coefficients α and γ of the demand and supply schedules respectively are constant through time, but that the levels of the two schedules are subject to not directly observable shifts from an equilibrium level. The structural equations can then be written as:

$$(1) \quad \begin{cases} (1d) & q + \alpha p + \epsilon = u \quad \text{(demand)} \\ (1s) & q + \gamma p + \eta = v \quad \text{(supply)}. \end{cases}$$

Concerning the shift variables u and v we shall assume that they are random drawings from a stable joint probability distribution with mean values equal to zero:

$$(2) \qquad \phi(u, v), \qquad \mathscr{E}u = 0, \qquad \mathscr{E}v = 0.$$

We shall introduce a few terms which we shall use with corresponding meaning in all examples. The not directly observable shift variables u, v are called *latent variables*, as distinct from the *observed variables*, p. q. We shall further distinguish *structure* and *model*. By a structure we mean the combination of a specific set of structural equations (1) (such as is obtained by giving specific numerical values to α, γ, ϵ, η) and a specific distribution function (2) of the latent variables (for instance a normal distribution with specific, numerically given, variances and covariance). By a model we mean only a specification of the form of the structural equations (for instance their linearity and a designation of the variables occurring in each equation), and of a class of functions to which the distribution function of the latent variables belongs (for instance, the class of all normal bivariate distributions with zero means). More abstractly, a model can be defined as a set of structures. For a useful analysis, the model will be chosen so as to incorporate relevant *a priori* knowledge or hypotheses as to the economic behavior to be described. For instance, the model here discussed can often be narrowed down by the usual specification of a downward sloping demand curve and an upward sloping supply curve:

$$(3) \qquad \alpha > 0, \qquad \gamma < 0.$$

Let us assume for the sake of argument that the observations are produced by a structure, to be called the "true" structure; which is contained in (permitted by) the model. In order to exclude all questions of sampling variability (which are a matter for later separate inquiry), let us further make the unrealistic assumption that the number of observations produced by this structure can be increased indefinitely. What inferences can be drawn from these observations toward the "true" structure?

A simple reflection shows that in our present example neither the "true" demand schedule nor the "true" supply schedule can be determined from any number of observations. To put the matter geometrically let each of the two identical scatter diagrams in Figure 9.1A and 9.1B represent the jointly observed values of p and q. A structure compatible with these observations can be obtained as follows: Select arbitrarily "presumptive" slope coefficients α and γ of the demand and supply schedules. Through each point $S(p, q)$ of the scatter diagrams draw two straight lines with slopes given by these coefficients. The presumptive demand and supply schedules will intersect the quantity axis at distances $-\epsilon + u$ and $-\eta + v$ from the origin, *provided* the presumptive slope coefficients α and γ are the "true" ones. We shall assume this to be the case in Figure 9.1A. In that case the values of ϵ and η can be found from the consideration that the averages of u and v in a sufficiently large sample of observations are practically equal to zero.

However, nothing in the situation considered permits us to distinguish the "true" slopes α, γ (as shown in Figure 9.1A) from any other presumptive slopes (as illustrated in Figure 9.1B). Any arbitrary set of slope coefficients α, γ (supplemented by corresponding values ϵ, η of the intercepts) represents another, statistically just as acceptable, hypothesis concerning the formation of the observed variables.

Let us formulate the same remark algebraically in preparation for further

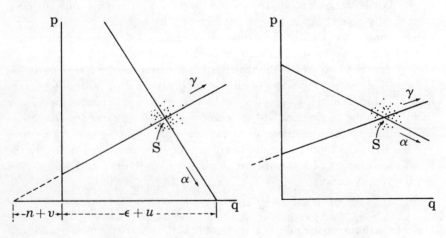

Figure 9.1A.   *Figure 9.1B.*

examples in more dimensions. Let the numerical values of the "true" parameters α, γ, ϵ, η in (1) be known to an individual who, taking delight in fraud, multiplies the demand equation (1d) by 2/3, the supply equation (1s) by 1/3, and adds the result to form an equation

(4d)
$$q + \frac{2\alpha + \gamma}{3}p + \frac{2\epsilon + \eta}{3} = u',$$

which he proclaims to be the demand equation. This equation is actually different from the "true" demand equation (1d) because (3) implies $\alpha \neq \gamma$. Similarly he multiplies the same equations by 2/5 and 3/5 respectively, say, to produce an equation

(4s)
$$q + \frac{2\alpha + 3\gamma}{5}p + \frac{2\epsilon + 3\eta}{5} = v',$$

different from the "true" supply equation (1s), but which he presents as if it were the supply equation. If our prankster takes care to select his multipliers in such a manner as not to violate the sign rules (3) imposed by the model, the deceit cannot be discovered by statistical analysis of any number of observations.[2] For the equations (4), being derived from (1), are satisfied by all data that satisfy the "true" equations (1). Moreover, being of the same form as the equations (1), the equations (4) are equally acceptable *a priori*.

Our *second example* differs from the first only in that the model specifies a supply equation containing in addition an exogenous variable. To be definite, we shall think of the supply of an agricultural product as affected by the rainfall r during a critical period of crop growth[3] or crop gathering. This variable is called exogenous to our model to express the plausible hypothesis that rainfall r, while affecting the market of the commodity concerned, is not itself affected thereby. Put in mathematical terms, this hypothesis specifies that the disturbances u and v in

(5) $\begin{cases} \text{(5d)} \qquad q + \alpha p \qquad\ + \epsilon = u \quad \text{(demand)} \\ \text{(5s)} \qquad q + \gamma p + \delta r + \eta = v \quad \text{(supply)} \end{cases}$

are statistically independent[4] of the values assumed by r.

---

2. The deceit could be discovered if the model were to specify a property (e.g., independence) of the disturbances u and v, which is not shared by $u' = (2u + v)/3$ and $v' = (2u + 3v)/5$. We have not made such a specification.

3. With respect to this example, the assumption of a linear relationship can be maintained only if we think of a certain limited range of variation in rainfall. Another difficulty with the example is that for most agricultural products, the effect of price on supply is delayed instead of instantaneous, as here assumed. A practically instantaneous effect can, however, be expected in the gathering of wild fruits of nature.

4. It is immaterial for this definition whether the exogenous variable is regarded as a given function of time—a concept perhaps applicable to a variable set by government policy—or as

It will be seen at a glance that the supply equation still cannot be determined from a sample of any size. If, starting from "true" structural equations (5) we multiply by $-1/2$ and $3/2$, say, and add the results to obtain a pretended supply equation,

$$(6s) \qquad q + \frac{3\gamma - \alpha}{2}p + \frac{3\delta}{2}r + \frac{3\eta - \epsilon}{2} = v'$$

of the same prescribed form as (5s), any data will satisfy this equation (6s) as well as they satisfy the two equations (5).

A similar reasoning can *not* be applied to the demand equation in the present model. Any attempt to construct another pretended demand equation by a linear combination involving the supply equation (5s) would introduce into that pretended demand equation the variable r which by the hypotheses underlying the model does not belong in it.

It might be thought that, if r has the properties of a random variable, its presence in the pretended demand equation might be concealed because its "contribution" cannot be distinguished from the random disturbance in that equation. To be specific, if $4/3$ and $-1/3$ are arbitrarily selected multipliers, the disturbance in the pretended demand equation might be thought to take the form

$$u' = \frac{4u - v}{3} - \frac{\delta}{3}r.$$

This, however, would violate the specification that r is exogenous and that therefore r and u' are to be statistically independent as well as r and (u, v). The relevance of the exogenous character of r to our present discussion is clearly illustrated by this remark.

Our analysis of the second example suggests (and below we shall cite a theorem establishing proof) that a sufficiently large sample does indeed contain information with regard to the parameters α, ϵ of the demand equation (it being understood that such information is conditional upon the validity of the model). It can already be seen that there must be the following exception to the foregoing statement. If in fact (although the model does not

itself a random variable determined by some other structure involving probability distributions—a concept applicable particularly to weather variables. It should further be noted that we postulate independence between r and (u, v), not between r and (p, q), although we wish to express that r "is not affected by" p and q. The meaning to be given to the latter phrase is that in other equations explaining the formation of r the variables (p, q) do not enter. Precisely this is implied in the statistical independence of r and (u, v), because (p, q) is, by virtue of (5), statistically dependent on (u, v), and any role of (p, q) in the determination of r would therefore create statistical dependence between r and (u, v). On the other hand, the postulated statistical independence between r and (u, v) is entirely compatible with the obvious influence, by virtue of (5), of r on (p, q).

require it) rainfall has no influence on supply, that is, if in the "true" structure $\delta = 0$, then any number of observations must necessarily be compatible with the model (1), and hence does not convey information with regard to either the demand equation or the supply equation.

As a *third example* we consider a model obtained from the preceding one by the inclusion in the demand equation of consumers' income i as an additional exogenous variable. We assume the exogenous character of consumers' income merely for reasons of exposition, and in full awareness of the fact that actually price and quantity on any market do affect income directly to some extent, while furthermore the disturbances u and v affecting the market under consideration may well be correlated with similar disturbances in several other markets which together have a considerably larger effect on consumers' income.

The structural equations are now

$$(7) \quad \begin{cases} (7d) & q + \alpha p + \beta i \quad\quad + \epsilon = u \quad \text{(demand)} \\ (7s) & q + \gamma p \quad\quad + \delta r + \eta = v \quad \text{(supply)}. \end{cases}$$

Since each of the two equations now excludes a variable specified for the other equation, neither of them can be replaced by a different linear combination of the two without altering its form. This suggests, and proof is cited below, that from a sufficiently large sample of observations, the demand equation can be accurately determined provided rainfall actually affects supply ($\delta \neq 0$), and the supply equation can be determined provided consumers' income actually affects demand ($\beta \neq 0$).

The *fourth example* is designed to show that situations may occur in which some but not all parameters of a structural equation can be determined from sufficiently many observations. Let the demand equation contain both this year's income i_0 and last year's income i_{-1}, but let the supply equation not contain any variable absent from the demand equation:

$$(8) \quad \begin{cases} (8d) & q + \alpha p + \beta_0 i_0 + \beta_{-1} i_{-1} + \epsilon = u \\ (8s) & q + \gamma p \quad\quad\quad\quad\quad\quad + \eta = v. \end{cases}$$

Now obviously we cannot determine either α or ϵ, because linear combinations of the equations (8) can be constructed which have the same form as (8d) but other[5] values α' and ϵ' for the coefficients α and ϵ. However, as long as (8d) enters with some nonvanishing weight into such a linear combination, the ratio β_{-1}/β_0 is not affected by the substitution of that linear combination for the "true" demand equation. Thus, if the present model is correct, the observations contain information with respect to the relative importance of

5. As regards ϵ' this is true whenever $\epsilon \neq \eta$. As regards α' it is safeguarded by (3).

present and past income to demand, whereas they are silent on the price elasticity of demand.

The *fifth example* shows that an assumption regarding the joint distribution of the disturbances u and v, where justified, may open the door to a determination of a structural equation which is otherwise indeterminate. Returning to the equation system (5) of our second example, we shall now make the model specify in addition that the disturbances u in demand and v in supply are statistically independent. Remembering our previous statement that the demand equation can already be determined without the help of such an assumption, it is clear that in attempting to construct a "pretended" supply equation, no linear combination of the "true" demand and supply equations (5), other than the "true" supply equation (5s) itself, can be found which preserves the required independence of disturbances in the two equations. Writing λ and $1 - \lambda$ for the multipliers used in forming such a linear combination, the disturbance in the pretended supply equation would be

$$(9) \qquad\qquad v' = \lambda u + (1 - \lambda)v.$$

Since u and v are by assumption independent, the disturbance v' of the pretended supply equation is independent of the disturbance u in the demand equation already found determinable, if and only if $\lambda = 0$, i.e., if the pretended supply equation coincides with the "true" one.

We emphasize again the expository character of the foregoing examples. It has already been indicated that the income variable i is not truly exogenous. By assuming it to be so, we have held down the size of the equation system underlying our discussion, and we may as a result have precluded ourselves from seeing indeterminacies that could come to light only by a study of all relationships participating in the formation of the variables involved. It will therefore be necessary to develop criteria by which indeterminacies of the coefficients of larger equation systems can be detected. Before discussing such criteria for linear systems, we shall formalize a few of the concepts used or to be used.

3. *The identification of structural parameters*

In our discussion we have used the phrase "a parameter that can be determined from a sufficient number of observations." We shall now define this concept more sharply, and give it the name *identifiability* of a parameter. Instead of reasoning, as before, from "a sufficiently large number of observations" we shall base our discussion on a hypothetical knowledge of the probability distribution of the observations, as defined more fully below. It is clear that exact knowledge of this probability distribution cannot be derived from any finite number of observations. Such knowledge is the limit approachable but not attainable by extended observation. By hypothesizing nevertheless the full availability of such knowledge, we obtain a clear separation between problems of statistical inference arising from the variability of finite samples, and problems of identification in which we explore the limits to which inference even from an infinite number of observations is subject.

A *structure* has been defined as the combination of a distribution of latent variables and a complete set of structural equations. By a *complete set of equations* we mean a set of as many equations as there are endogenous variables. Each endogenous variable may occur with or without time lags, and should occur without lag in at least one equation. Also, the set should be such as to permit unique determination of the nonlagged values of the endogenous variables from those of the lagged endogenous, the exogenous, and the latent variables. Finally, by *endogenous variables* we mean observed variables which are not exogenous, i.e., variables which are not known or assumed to be statistically independent of the latent variables, and whose occurrence in one or more equations of the set is necessary on grounds of "theory."

It follows from these definitions that, for any specific set of values of the exogenous variables, the distribution of the latent variables (i.e., one of the two components of a given structure) entails or generates, through the structural equations (i.e., the other component of the given structure), a probability distribution of the endogenous variables. The latter distribution is, of course, conditional upon the specified values of the exogenous variables for each time point of observation. This conditional distribution, regarded again as a function of all specified values of exogenous variables, shall be the hypothetical datum for our discussion of identification problems.

We shall call two structures S and S' (observationally) *equivalent* (or indistinguishable) if the two conditional distributions of endogenous variables generated by S and S' are identical for all possible values of the exogenous variables. We shall call a structure S permitted by the model (uniquely) *identifiable* within that model if there is no other equivalent structure S' contained in the model. Although the proof has not yet been completely indicated, it may be stated in illustration that in our third example almost all structures permitted by the model are identifiable. The only exceptions are those with either $\beta = 0$ or $\delta = 0$ (or both). In the first and second examples, however, no structure is identifiable, although in the second example, we have stated that the demand equation by itself is determinate. To cover such cases we shall say that a certain parameter θ of a structure S is uniquely *identifiable* within a model, if that parameter has the same value for all structures S' equivalent to S, contained in the model. Finally, a *structural equation* is said to be *identifiable* if all its parameters are identifiable.

This completes the formal definitions with which we shall operate. They can be summarized in the statement that anything is called identifiable, the knowledge of which is implied in the knowledge of the distribution of the endogenous variables, given the model (which is accepted as valid). We now proceed to a discussion of the application of this concept to linear models of the kind illustrated by our examples.

4. Identifiability criteria in linear models

In our discussion of these examples, it has been possible to conclude that a certain structural equation is not identifiable whenever we are able to construct a different equation, obtained by linear combination of some or all structural equations, which likewise meets the specifications of the model. In the opposite case, where we could show that no such different linear combination exists, we could not yet conclude definitely that the equation involved is identifiable. Could other operations than linear combination, perhaps be used to derive equations of the same form?

We shall now cite a theorem which establishes that no such other operations can exist. The theorem relates to models specifying a complete set of structural equations as defined above, and in which a given set of endogenous and exogenous variables enters linearly. Any time lags with which these variables may occur are supposed to be integral multiples of the time interval between successive observations. Furthermore the exogenous variables (considered as different variables whenever they occur with a different time lag) are assumed not to be linearly dependent, i.e., in the functional sense.[6] Finally, although simultaneous disturbances in different structural equations are permitted to be correlated, it is assumed that any disturbances operating in different time units (whether in the same or in different structural equations) are statistically independent.

Suppose the model does not specify anything beyond what has been stated. That is, no restrictions are specified yet that exclude some of the variables from specific equations. Obviously, with respect to such a broad model, not a single structural equation is identifiable. However, a theorem has been proved [14] to the effect that, given a structure S within that model, any structure S' in the model, equivalent to S, can be derived from S by replacing each equation by some linear combination of some or all equations of S.

It will be clear that this theorem remains true if the model is narrowed down by excluding certain variables from certain equations, or by other restrictions on the parameters. Thus, whenever in our examples we have

---

6. The criteria of identifiability to be stated would require amended formulation if certain identities involving endogenous variables would be such that each variable occurring in them also occurs, in some equation of the complete set, with a time lag, and if this time lag were the same for all such variables. In this case, a complication arises from linear (functional) dependence among lagged endogenous (and possibly exogenous) variables.

concluded that different linear combinations of the same form prescribed for a structural equation did not exist, we have therewith established the identifiability of that equation. More in general, the analysis of the identifiability of a structural equation in a linear model consists in a study of the possibility to produce a different equation of the same prescribed form by linear combination of all equations. If this is shown to be impossible, the equation in question is thereby proved to be identifiable. To find criteria for the identifiability of a structural equation in a linear model is therefore a straightforward mathematical problem, to which the solution has been given elsewhere [14]. Here we shall state without proof what the criteria are.

A *necessary* condition for the identifiability of a structural equation within a given linear model is that the number[7] of variables excluded from that equation (more generally: the number of linear restrictions on the parameters of that equation) be at least equal to the number (G, say) of structural equations less one. This is known as the *order condition* of identifiability. A *necessary and sufficient condition* for the identifiability of a structural equation within a linear model, restricted only by the exclusion of certain variables from certain equations, is that we can form at least one nonvanishing determinant of order $G - 1$ out of those coefficients, properly arranged, with which the variables excluded from that structural equation appear in the $G - 1$ other structural equations. This is known as the *rank condition* of identifiability.

The application of these criteria to the foregoing examples is straightforward. In all cases considered, the number of structural equations is $G = 2$. Therefore, any of the equations involved can be identifiable through exclusion of variables only if at least $G - 1 = 1$ variable is excluded from it by the model. If this is so, the equation is identifiable provided at least one of the variables so excluded occurs in the other equation with nonvanishing coefficient (a determinant of order 1 equals the value of its one and only element). For instance, the conclusion already reached at the end of the discussion of our second example is now confirmed: The identifiability of the demand equation (5d) is only then safeguarded by the exclusion of the variable r from that equation if $\delta \neq 0$, that is, if that variable not only possibly but actually occurs in the supply equation.

5. The statistical test of a priori uncertain identifiability

The example just quoted shows that the identifiability of one structural parameter, θ, say, may depend on the value of another structural parameter, η, say. In such situations, which are of frequent occurrence, the identifiability of θ cannot be settled by *a priori* reasoning from the model alone. On the

---

7. Again counting lagged variables as separate variables.

other hand, the identifiability of θ cannot escape all analysis because of possible nonidentifiability of η. As is argued more fully elsewhere [13], since the identifiability of any parameter is a property of the distribution of the observations, it is subject to some suitable statistical test, of which the degree of conclusiveness tends to certainty as the number of observations increases indefinitely. The validity of this important conclusion is not limited to linear models.

In the case of a linear model as described in Section 4, the present statement can also be demonstrated explicitly by equivalent reformulation of the rank criterion for identifiability in terms of identifiable parameters only. By the *reduced form* of a complete set of linear structural equations as described in Section 4, we mean the form obtained by solving for each of the *dependent* (i.e., nonlagged endogenous) variables, in terms of the *predetermined* (i.e., exogenous or lagged endogenous) variables, and in terms of transformed disturbances (which are linear functions of the disturbances in the original structural equations). It has been argued more fully elsewhere [14, Section 3.1.6], that the coefficients of the equations of the reduced form are parameters of the joint distribution of the observations, and as such are always identifiable.

It may be stated briefly without proof that the following rank criterion for identifiability of a given structural equation, in terms of coefficients of the reduced form, is equivalent to that stated in Section 4 above: Consider only those equations of the reduced form that solve for dependent variables, specified by the model as occurring in (strictly: as not excluded from) the structural equation in question. Let the number of the equations so obtained be H, where $H \leqslant G$. Now form the matrix II^{**} of the coefficients, in these H equations, of those predetermined variables that are excluded by the model from the structural equation involved. A necessary and sufficient condition for the identifiability of that structural equation is that the rank of II^{**} be equal to $H-1$. A direct proof of the equivalence of the two identification criteria will be published in due course.

6. Identification through disaggregation and introduction of specific explanatory variables

As a further exercise in the application of these criteria, we shall consider a question which has already been the subject of a discussion between Ezekiel [2, 3] and Klein [9, 10]. The question is whether identifiability of the investment equation can be attained by the subdivision of the investment variable into separate categories of investment. In the discussion referred to, which took place before the concepts and terminology employed in this article were developed, questions of identifiability were discussed alongside with questions regarding the merit of particular economic assumptions incorporated in the model, and with questions of the statistical method of estimating parameters that have been recognized as identifiable. In the present context, we shall avoid the latter two groups of problems and concentrate on the formal analysis of identifiability, accepting a certain model as economically valid for purposes of discussion.

As a starting point we shall consider a simple model expressing the crudest elements of Keynesian theory. The variables are, in money amounts,

$$(10) \quad \begin{cases} S & \text{savings} \\ I & \text{investment} \\ Y & \text{income} \\ Y_{-1} & \text{income lagged one year.} \end{cases}$$

The structural equations are:

$$(11) \quad \begin{cases} (11\text{id}) & S - I & = 0 \\ (11\text{S}) & S \quad - \alpha_1 Y - \alpha_2 Y_{-1} - \alpha_0 = u \\ (11\text{I}) & I - \beta_1 Y - \beta_2 Y_{-1} - \beta_0 = v. \end{cases}$$

Of these, the first is the well-known savings-investment identity arising from Keynes's definitions of these concepts.[8] The second is a behavior equation of consumers, indicating that the money amount of their savings (income not spent for consumption) is determined by present and past income, subject to a random disturbance u. The third is a behavior equation of entrepreneurs, indicating that the money amount of investment is determined by present and past income, subject to a random disturbance v.

Since the identity (11id) is fully given *a priori*, no question of identifiability arises with respect to the first equation. In both the second and third equations, only one variable is excluded which appears in another equation of the model, and no other restrictions on the coefficients are stated.[9] Hence both of these equations already fail to meet the necessary order criterion of identifiability. This could be expected because the two equations

8. These definitions include in investment all increases in inventory, including undesired inventories remaining in the hands of manufacturers or dealers as a result of falling demand. In principle, therefore, the "investment" equation should include a term or terms explaining such inventory changes. The absence of such terms from (11) and from later elaborations thereof may be taken as expressing the "theory" that for annual figures, say, such changes can be regarded as random. Alternatively, investment may be defined so as to exclude undesired inventory changes, and (11id) may be interpreted as an "equilibrium condition," expressing the randomness of such changes by replacing the zero in the right hand member by a disturbance w. The obvious need for refinement in this crude "theory" does not preclude its use for illustrative purposes.

9. The normalization requirement that the variables S and I shall have coefficients $+1$ in (11S) and (11I) respectively does not restrict the relationships involved but merely serves to give a common level to coefficients which otherwise would be subject to arbitrary proportional variation.

connect the same savings-investment variable with the same two income variables, and therefore can not be distinguished statistically.

Ezekiel attempts to obtain identifiability of the structure by a refinement of the model as a result of subdivision of aggregate investment I into the following four components:

(12a) $\begin{cases} I_1 \text{ investment in plant and equipment} \\ I_2 \text{ investment in housing} \\ I_3 \text{ temporary investment: changes in consumers' credit and in} \\ \quad \text{business inventories} \\ I_4 \text{ quasi-investment: net contributions from foreign trade and the} \\ \quad \text{government budget.} \end{cases}$

If each of these components were to be related to the same set of explanatory variables as occurs in (11), the disaggregation would be of no help toward identification. Therefore, for each of the four types of investment decisions, Ezekiel introduces a separate explanatory equation, either explicitly or by implication in his verbal comments. In attempting to formulate these explanations in terms of a complete set of behavior equations, we shall introduce two more variables:

(12b) $\begin{cases} H \text{ semi-independent cyclical component of housing investment} \\ E \text{ exogenous component of quasi-investment.} \end{cases}$

In addition, linear and quadratic functions of time are introduced as trend terms in some equations by Ezekiel. For purposes of the present discussion, we may as well disregard such trend terms, because they would help toward identification only if they could be excluded *a priori* from some of the equations while being included in others—a position advocated neither by Ezekiel nor by the present author.

With these qualifications, "Ezekiel's model" can be interpreted as follows:

(13) $\begin{cases} \text{(13id) } S - I_1 - I_2 - I_3 - I_4 & = 0 \\ \text{(13S) } S & - \alpha_1 Y - \alpha_2 Y_{-1} & - \alpha_0 = u \\ \text{(13I}_1\text{) } \quad I_1 & - \beta_1 Y - \beta_2 Y_{-1} & - \beta_0 = v_1 \\ \text{(13I}_2\text{) } \quad\quad I_2 & - \gamma_1 Y - \gamma_2 Y_{-1} - H & - \gamma_0 = v_2 \\ \text{(13I}_3\text{) } \quad\quad\quad I_3 & - \delta_1 Y + \delta_1 Y_{-1} & - \delta_0 = v_3 \\ \text{(13I}_4\text{) } \quad\quad\quad\quad I_4 - \epsilon_1 Y - \epsilon_2 Y_{-1} & - E - \epsilon_0 = v_4 \end{cases}$

(13id) is the savings-investment identity. (13S) repeats (11S), and (13I$_1$) is modeled after (11I). More specific explanations are introduced for the three remaining types of investment decisions.

Housing investment decisions I_2 are explained partly on the basis of income[10] Y, partly on the basis of a "semi-independent housing cycle" H. In Ezekiel's treatment H is not an independently observed variable, but a smooth long cycle fitted to I. We share Klein's objection [9, p. 255] to this procedure, but do not think that his proposal to substitute a linear function of time for H does justice to Ezekiel's argument. The latter definitely thinks of H as produced largely by a long-cycle mechanism peculiar to the housing market, and quotes in support of this view a study by Derksen [1] in which this mechanism is analyzed. Derksen constructs an equation explaining residential construction in terms of the rent level, the rate of change of income, the level of building cost in the recent past, and growth in the number of families; he further explains the rent level in terms of income, the number of families, and the stock of dwelling units (all of these subject to substantial time lags). The stock of dwelling units, in its turn, represents an accumulation of past construction diminished by depreciaton or demolition. Again accepting without inquiry the economic assumptions involved in these explanations, the point to be made is that H in $(13I_2)$ can be thought to represent specific observable exogenous and *past* endogenous variables.

Temporary investment I_3 is related by Ezekiel to the rate of change in income. Quasi-investment I_4 is related by him partly to income[11] (especially via government revenue, imports), partly to exogenous factors underlying exports and government expenditure where used as an instrument of policy. The variable E in $(13I_4)$ is therefore similar to H in that it can be thought to represent observable exogenous or past endogenous variables.

It cannot be said that this interpretation of the variables H and E establishes the completeness of the set of equations (13) in the sense defined above. The variable H has been found to depend on the past values of certain indubitably endogenous variables (building cost, rent level) of which the present values do not occur in the equation system (13), and which therefore remain unexplained by (13). The reader is asked to accept what could be proved explicitly: that incompleteness of this kind does not invalidate the criteria of identifiability indicated.[12]

Let us then apply our criteria of identifiability to the behavior equations in (13). In each of these, the number of excluded variables is at least 5, i.e., at least the necessary number of identifiability in a model of 6 equations. In

---

10. We have added a term with Y_{-1} because the exclusion of such a term could hardly be made the basis for a claim of identifiability.

11. We have again added a term with Y_{-1} on grounds similar to those stated with respect to $(13I_2)$.

12. Provided, as indicated in footnote 6, there is no linear functional relationship between the exogenous and lagged endogenous variables occurring in (13).

order to apply the rank criterion for the identifiability of the savings equation (13S), say, we must consider the matrix

(14)

$$
\begin{array}{cccccc}
(I_1) & (I_2) & (I_3) & (I_4) & (H) & (E) \\
\begin{bmatrix}
-1 & -1 & -1 & -1 & 0 & 0 \\
1 & 0 & 0 & 0 & 0 & 0 \\
0 & 1 & 0 & 0 & -1 & 0 \\
0 & 0 & 1 & 0 & 0 & 0 \\
0 & 0 & 0 & 1 & 0 & -1
\end{bmatrix}
\end{array}
$$

There are several ways in which a nonvanishing determinant of order 5 can be selected from this matrix. One particular way is to take the columns labeled I_1, I_2, I_3, H, E. It follows that if the present model is valid, the savings equation is indeed identifiable.

It is easily seen that the same conclusion applies to the equations explaining investment decisions of the types I_1 and I_3. Let us now inspect the rank criterion matrix for the identifiability of $(13I_2)$:

(15)

$$
\begin{array}{ccccc}
(S) & (I_1) & (I_3) & (I_4) & (E) \\
\begin{bmatrix}
1 & -1 & -1 & -1 & 0 \\
1 & 0 & 0 & 0 & 0 \\
0 & 1 & 0 & 0 & 0 \\
0 & 0 & 1 & 0 & 0 \\
0 & 0 & 0 & 1 & -1
\end{bmatrix}
\end{array}
$$

Again the determinant value of this square matrix of order 5 is different from zero. Hence the housing equation is identifiable. A similar analysis leads to the same conclusion regarding the equation $(13I_4)$ for quasi-investment.

It may be emphasized again that identifiability was attained not through the mere subdivision of total investment, but as a result of the introduction of specific explanatory variables applicable to some but not all components of investment.[13] Whenever such specific variables are available in sufficient number and variety of occurrence, on good grounds of economic theory as defined above, the door has been opened in principle to statistical inference

---

13. In fact, more specific detail was introduced than the minimum necessary to produce identifiability. Starting again from (11), identifiability can already be obtained if it is possible to break off from investment I some observable exogenous component, like public works expenditure P (supposing that to be exogenous for the sake of argument). Writing $Q = I - P$ for the remainder of investment, (11) is then modified to read

(11a)
$$
\begin{cases}
S - Q - P & = 0 \\
S & -\alpha_1 \Upsilon - \alpha_2 \Upsilon_{-1} - \alpha_0 = u \\
Q & -\beta_1 \Upsilon - \beta_2 \Upsilon_{-1} - \beta_0 = v,
\end{cases}
$$

of which each equation meets our criteria of identifiability. The intent of this remark is largely formal, because (11a) is not as defensible a "theory" as (13).

regarding behavior parameters—inference conditional upon the assumptions derived from "theory."

How wide the door has been opened, i.e., how much accuracy of estimation can be attained from given data, is of course a matter depending on many circumstances, and to be explored separately by the appropriate procedures of statistical inference.[14] In the present case, the extent to which the exclusion of H and/or E from certain equations contributes to the reliability of estimates of their parameters depends very much on whether or not there are pronounced differences in the time-paths of the three *predetermined variables* Y_{-1}, H, E, i.e., the variables determined either exogenously or in earlier time units. These time-paths represent in a way the basic patterns of movement in the economic model considered, such that the time-paths of all other variables are linear combinations of these three paths, modified by disturbances. If the three basic paths are sufficiently distinct, conditions are favorable for estimation of identifiable parameters. If there is considerable similarity between any two of them, or even if there is only a considerable multiple correlation between the three, conditions are adverse.

7. Implications of the choice of the model

It has already been stressed repeatedly that any statistical inference regarding identifiable parameters of economic behavior is conditional upon the validity of the model. This throws great weight on a correct choice of the model. We shall not attempt to make more than a few tentative remarks about the considerations governing this choice.[15]

It is an important question to what extent certain aspects of a model of the kind considered above are themselves subject to statistical test. For instance, in the model (13) we have specified linearity of each equation, independence of disturbances in successive time units, time lags which are an integral multiple of the chosen unit of time, as well as exclusions of specific variables from specific equations. It is often possible to subject one particular aspect or set of specifications of the model to a statistical test which is conditional upon the validity of the remaining specifications. This is, for instance, the case

14. We are not concerned here with an evaluation of the particular estimation procedures applied by Ezekiel.

15. In an earlier article [11] I have attempted, in a somewhat different terminology, to discuss that problem. That article needs rewriting in the light of subsequent developments in econometrics. It unnecessarily clings to the view that each structural equation represents a causal process in which one single dependent variable is determined by the action upon it of all other variables in the equation. Moreover, use of the concept of identifiability will contribute to sharper formulation and treatment of the problem of the choice of a model. However, the most serious defect of the article, in my view, cannot yet be corrected. It arises from the fact that we do not yet have a satisfactory statistical theory of choice among several alternative hypotheses.

with respect to the exclusion of any variable from any equation whenever the equation involved is identifiable even without that exclusion. However, at least *four* difficulties arise which point to the need for further fundamental research on the principles of statistical inference.

In the *first* place, on a given basis of maintained hypotheses (not subjected to test) there may be several alternative hypotheses to be tested. For instance, if there are two variables whose exclusion, either jointly or individually, from a given equation is not essential to its identifiability, it is possible to test separately (a) the exclusion of the first variable, or (b) of the second variable, or (c) of both variables simultaneously, as against (d) the exclusion of neither variable. However, instead of three separate tests, of (a) against (d), (b) against (d), and (c) against (d), we need a procedure permitting selection of one of the four alternatives (a), (b), (c), (d). An extension of current theory with regard to the testing of hypotheses, which is concerned mainly with choices between two alternatives, is therefore needed.

Secondly, if certain specifications of a model can be tested given all other specifications, it is usually possible in many different ways to choose the set of "other" specifications which is not subjected to test. It may not be possible to choose the minimum set of untested specifications in any way so that strong *a priori* confidence in the untested specifications exists. Even in such a case, it may nevertheless happen that for any choice of the set of untested specifications, the additional specifications that are confirmed by test also inspire some degree of *a priori* confidence. In such a case, the model as a whole is more firmly established than any selected minimum set of untested specifications. However, current theory of statistical inference provides no means of giving quantitative expression to such partial and indirect confirmation of anticipation by observation.

Thirdly, if the choice of the model is influenced by the same data from which the structural parameters are estimated, the estimated sampling variances of these estimated parameters do not have that direct relation to the reliability of the estimated parameters which they would have if the estimation were based on a model of which the validity is given *a priori* with certainty.

Finally, the research worker who constructs a model does not really believe that reality is exactly described by a "true" structure contained in the model. Linearity, discrete time lags, are obviously only approximations. At best, the model builder hopes to construct a model that contains a structure which approximates reality to a degree sufficient for the practical purposes of the investigation. The tests of current statistical theory are formulated as an (uncertain) choice, from two or more sets of structures (single or composite hypotheses), of that one which contains the "true" structure. Instead we need to choose the simplest possible set—in some sense—which contains a structure sufficiently approximative—in some sense—to economic reality.

8. For what purposes is identification necessary?

The question should finally be considered why it is at all desirable to postulate a structure behind the probability distribution of the variables and thus to become involved in the sometimes difficult problems of identifiability. If we regard as the main objective of scientific inquiry to make prediction possible and its reliability ascertainable, why do we need more than a knowledge of the probability distribution of the variables to permit prediction of one variable on the basis of known (or hypothetical) simultaneous or earlier values of other variables?

The answer to this question is implicit in Haavelmo's discussion of the degree of permanence of economic laws [6, see p. 30] and has been formulated explicitly by Hurwicz [8]. Knowledge of the probability distribution is in fact sufficient whenever there is no change in the structural parameters between the period of observation from which such knowledge is derived and the period to which the prediction applies. However, in many practical situations it is required to predict the values of one or more economic variables either under changes in structure that come about independently of the economist's advice, or under hypothetical changes in structural parameters that can be brought about through policy based in part on the prediction made. In the first case knowledge may, and in the second case it is likely to, be available as to the effect of such structural change on the parameters. An example of the first case is a well-established change in consumers' preferences. An example of the second case is a change in the average level or in the progression of income tax rates.

In such cases, the "new" distribution of the variables on the basis of which predictions are to be constructed can only be derived from the "old" distribution prevailing before the structural change, if the known structural change can be applied to identifiable structural parameters, i.e., parameters of which knowledge is implied in a knowledge of the "old" distribution combined with the *a priori* considerations that have entered into the model.

References

[1] DERKSEN, J. B. D., "Long Cycles in Residential Building: An Explanation." *Econometrica*, Vol. 8, April 1940, pp. 97–116.

[2] EZEKIEL, M., "Saving, Consumption and Investment," *American Economic Review*, Vol. 32, March 1942, pp. 22–49; June 1942, pp. 272–307.

[3] ———, "The Statistical Determination of the Investment Schedule," *Econometrica*, Vol. 12, January 1944, pp. 89–90.

[4] FRISCH, R., *Pitfalls in the Statistical Construction of Demand and Supply Curves*, Veröffentlichungen der Frankfurter Gesellschaft für Konjunkturforschung, Neue Folge, Heft 5, Leipzig, 1933.

[5] ———, "Statistical versus Theoretical Relations in Economic Macrodynamics," Mimeographed document prepared for a League of Nations conference concerning Tinbergen's work, 1938.

[6] HAAVELMO, T., "The Probability Approach in Econometrics," *Econometrica*, Vol. 12, Supplement, 1944, also Cowles Commission Paper, New Series, No. 4.

[7] HURWICZ, L., "Generalization of the Concept of Identification," in *Statistical Inference in Dynamic Economic Models*, Cowles Commission Monograph 10, New York, John Wiley and Sons (forthcoming).

[8] ———, "Prediction and Least-Squares," in *Statistical Inference in Dynamic Economic Models*, Cowles Commission Monograph 10, New York, John Wiley and Sons (forthcoming).

[9] KLEIN, L., "Pitfalls in the Statistical Determination of the Investment Schedule," *Econometrica*, Vol. 11, July–October 1943, pp. 246–258.

[10] ———, "The Statistical Determination of the Investment Schedule: A Reply," *Econometrica*, Vol. 12, January 1944, pp. 91–92.

[11] KOOPMANS, T. C., "The Logic of Econometric Business Cycle Research," *Journal of Political Economy*, Vol. 49, 1941, pp. 157–181.

[12] ———, "Measurement Without Theory," *The Review of Economic Statistics*, Vol. 29, No. 3, August 1947, pp. 161–172, also Cowles Commission Paper, New Series, No. 25.

[13] KOOPMANS, T. C., and REIERSOL, O., "Identification as a Problem in Inference," to be published.

[14] KOOPMANS, T. C., RUBIN, H., and LEIPNIK, R. B., "Measuring the Equation Systems of Dynamic Economics," in *Statistical Inference in Dynamic Economic Models*, Cowles Commission Monograph 10, New York, John Wiley and Sons (forthcoming).

[15] MARSCHAK, J., "Economic Interdependence and Statistical Analysis," in *Studies in Mathematical Economics and Econometrics*, in memory of Henry Schultz, Chicago, The University of Chicago Press, 1942, pp. 135–150.

[16] PIGOU, A. C., "A Method of Determining the Numerical Values of Elasticities of Demand," *Economic Journal*, Vol. 20, 1910, pp. 636–640, reprinted as Appendix II in *Economics of Welfare*.

[17] SCHULTZ, HENRY, *Theory and Measurement of Demand*, Chicago, The University of Chicago Press, 1938.

[18] WALD, A., "Note on the Identification of Economic Relations," in *Statistical Inference in Dynamic Economic Models*, Cowles Commission Monograph 10, New York, John Wiley and Sons (forthcoming).

Chapter 10

RECURSIVE VERSUS NONRECURSIVE SYSTEMS: AN ATTEMPT AT SYNTHESIS

ROBERT H. STROTZ
Northwestern University
H. O. A. WOLD
University of Uppsala

Over the past fifteen years there has been an extended discussion of the meaning and applicability of nonrecursive as distinct from recursive systems in econometrics, and throughout this discussion there has been a marked divergence of views as to the merits of the two types of models. It is not the purpose of this note to extend that controversy further, but rather to attempt a constructive statement of the relationship between the two approaches and the circumstances under which each is applicable.

We assume that the reader is generally familiar with the past discussion[1] and that it will suffice here simply to recall that a recursive, or causal-chain, system has the formal property that the coefficient matrix of the non-lagged endogenous variables is triangular (upon suitable ordering of rows and columns) whereas a nonrecursive, or interdependent, system is one for which this is not the case. While the triangularity of the coefficient matrix is a formal property of recursive models, the essential property is that each relation is provided a causal interpretation in the sense of a stimulus-response relationship. The question of whether and in what sense nonrecursive systems allow a causal interpretation is the main theme of this paper.

Reprinted by permission of the authors and publisher from *Econometrica*, Vol. 28, pp. 417–427. Copyright 1960, The Econometric Society.
1. See references appended at end. An extensive bibliography is included in [8].

1. Fundamental principles

Much controversy can, in our opinion, be resolved once there is agreement on some initial points of principle.

(1) The first thing to consider when constructing an economic model is its purpose, that is, how it is to be applied in dealing with economic facts. We want to distinguish in this connection between descriptive and explanatory models. A descriptive model simply sets forth a set of relationships which have "bound together" different variables in situations in which they have previously been observed. More generally, these relationships may be described in probability terms, certain terms in these relationships representing the "disturbances" which in fact occurred. One can in this way describe given observations as a random drawing from a joint conditional probability distribution. Methodologically, the estimation of such a distribution is an exercise in n-dimensional "curve fitting." A descriptive model is thus cognate to the notion of a vector *function* such as (in the linear case)

$$(1) \qquad\qquad\qquad Ax' = u'$$

where A is a (not necessarily square) matrix of constants, x' is a column vector of the variables in question, and u' is a vector of zeros in the exact case or of stochastic variables in the case of a probability model. Whatever the validity of such a specification, the validity of any other model obtained by applying any linear transformation is the same. If *a priori* restrictions are imposed upon the sort of distribution which is to be used for this descriptive model, this may, of course, circumscribe the acceptable transformations.

Explanatory models, by contrast, are causal. This means that each relation (equation) in the model states something about "directions of influence" among the variables. (But see Section 3(b) below.) In the case of explanatory models, then, the theorist asserts more than functional relationships among the variables; he also invests those relationships with a special interpretation, that is, with a causal interpretation. But what is a "causal interpretation" to mean?

(2) No one has monopoly rights in defining "causality." The term is in common parlance and the only meaningful challenge is that of providing an explication of it. No explication need be unique, and some may prefer never to use the word at all. For us, however, the word in common scientific and statistical-inference usage has the following general meaning.[2] z is a cause of y if, by hypothesis, it is or "would be" possible by *controlling* z indirectly to control y, at least stochastically. But it may or may not be possible by controlling y indirectly to control z. A causal relation is therefore in essence asymmetric, in that in any instance of its realization it is asymmetric. Only in special cases may it be reversible and symmetric in a causal sense. These

---

2. H. O. A. Wold has elaborated his views in [6, 7].

are the cases in which sometimes a controlled change in z may cause a change in y and at other times a controlled change in y may cause a change in z, but y and z cannot both be subjected to simultaneous controlled changes independently of one another without the causal relationship between them being violated.

The asymmetry of causation in any instance of its realization has the following probability counterpart. It may make sense to talk about the probability distribution of y as being *causally conditional* on z, but not make sense to talk about the probability distribution of z as being *causally conditional* on y. This asymmetry is classical in statistical theory. It appears in the difference between a sample statistic and a population parameter. We speak of the probability that the sample frequency of successes will be 0.5 conditional upon the population frequency being 0.4. We do not speak of the probability that the population frequency is 0.4 conditional upon the sample frequency being 0.5.[3] Thus if we wish to estimate (by the maximum likelihood method) a population parameter knowing a sample of observations, we write the likelihood function as the conditional probability distribution of the *sample*.

Suppose we were to estimate by the maximum likelihood method the nth value of a causal variable (population parameter) $z(n)$ on the basis of the nth value of a resultant variable (a sample observation) $y(n)$ by use of a regression fitted to $n-1$ previous observations in all of which z has been causal. We should use the regression of y on z—not of z on y—over the previous observations, although this point is occasionally misunderstood.[4] Causality as used here is an essential notion in the statistical inference of population parameters by the maximum likelihood method. We must hypothesize how the sample observations are *generated* (i.e., caused) in order to proceed.

The concept of causality presented here is intended to be that of the everyday usage in the laboratory and emphasizes mainly the notion of control. Now, others may present a different explication of causality. Other versions may involve strange and seemingly unnatural notions, two of which are of particular interest to us. (a) The first involves accepting simultaneously the two statements: (1) "y has the value 100 because of (by cause of) z having the value 50" and (2) "z has the value 50 because of (by cause of) y having the value of 100." (b) The second involves accepting simultaneously the two statements: (1) "z causes y in accordance with the function $y=f(z)$" and (2) "z causes y in accordance with the function $y=g(z) \neq f(z)$." Usage (a) we

3. "Probability" is used here in the "relative frequency," not in the "degree of belief" sense.
4. For what we regard as the correct treatment, see A. Mood, [2, Sec. 13.4]. For the contrary view see F. V. Waugh [5]. A qualification is needed: one must not have any constraining *a priori* knowledge about the possible values of z, or, if z is itself a random variable, about its probability distribution. The model we have in mind is given by $y=a+\beta z+u$, with u and z statistically independent. Otherwise, the likelihood function is $f(y(1), \ldots, y(n)|z(1), \ldots z(n)) \cdot g(z(n))$, rather than the f function alone, where f and g are probability density functions.

shall describe as a "causal circle" and discuss in Section 3(c). Usage (b) we describe as "bicausality" and discuss in Section 3(d).

Whether such notions of causality seem weird or not, whether or not they conform to usage in the scientific workshop, there is nothing to prevent their use in theory construction. Argument for the interpretation of causality presented by us is not an argument for "strait-jacketing" the freedom of the theorist and econometrician to use other interpretations. But we would (and will) argue that the notion of causality in economics is the one we have presented. Examples are: "Income is the cause of consumer expenditure (the consumption function)," "Price is a cause of quantity demanded," and "Price is a cause of quantity supplied." Most of the problems in assessing this claim arise in equilibrium models.

2. *The causal interpretation of a recursive system*

It was not our purpose in the previous section to provide a precise definition of "causation." The term enters our discussion essentially as a "primitive," and what efforts we have made at definition have been ostensive: we have pointed to the familiar usage of the word in the laboratory. With reference to this primitive meaning of "causation," however, we wish to define the concept of "the causal interpretability of a parameter." This is what will occupy us next.

Suppose a recursive system is written in the form

$$
\begin{aligned}
y_1 + \beta_{12}y_2 + \;\ldots\; + \beta_{1g}y_g + \beta_{1,g+1}y_{g+1} + \;\ldots\; + \beta_{1G}y_G + \sum_k \gamma_{1k}z_k &= u_1, \\
y_2 + \;\ldots\; + \beta_{2g}y_g + \beta_{2,g+1}y_{g+1} + \;\ldots\; + \beta_{2G}y_G + \sum_k \gamma_{2k}z_k &= u_2, \\
\cdots\cdots\cdots\cdots\cdots\cdots\cdots\cdots\cdots\cdots\cdots\cdots\cdots\cdots\cdots & \\
y_g + \beta_{g,g+1}y_{g+1} + \;\ldots\; + \beta_{gG}y_G + \sum_k \gamma_{gk}z_k &= u_g, \\
\cdots\cdots\cdots\cdots\cdots\cdots\cdots\cdots\cdots\cdots\cdots\cdots\cdots\cdots\cdots & \\
y_G + \sum_k \gamma_{Gk}z_k &= u_G,
\end{aligned}
$$

(2)

where the y's are causally dependent variables, the z's predetermined variables, and the u's stochastic variables statistically independent of the z's. Each u_g is assumed, moreover, to be statistically independent of y_{g+1}, $y_{g+2}, \ldots, y_G$.[5] In each equation the y variable with unit coefficient is regarded

---

5. Although Wold has imposed this specification in his definition of a causal chain system, Strotz feels it may be too restrictive and would classify causal chain systems under two headings: those that are causal chains in their stochastic form (Wold's case) and those that are causal chains only in their exact part. In the latter case the covariance matrix of the u_g's need not be diagonal. For further discussion of this, see Strotz, *infra*, p. 430, fn. 6.

as the resultant variable and the other y variables and the z's are regarded as causal variables. We now consider the possibility that we gain direct control over y_g, that is, we can manipulate y_g by use of variables other than the z's appearing in the model. In this case we now need a new model. It can be obtained, however, by a single change in the old one. We merely strike out the gth equation and reclassify y_g as an exogenous (predetermined) variable rather than as a dependent variable. The coefficients of y_g in the $G-1$ equations of the new model will be the same as they were before, namely, $\beta_{1g}, \ldots, \beta_{g-1,g}$, and zeros. It is in this sense that each non-unit coefficient in a recursive system has a causal interpretation. It describes the influence of the variable whose coefficient it is on the resultant variable, irrespective of whether the causal variable is dependent or exogenous in the system. Such a parameter has causal interpretability.

3. The causal interpretation of nonrecursive systems

We now turn our attention to nonrecursive systems. What is the possibility of causal interpretation in these systems?

(A) NO CAUSAL INTERPRETATION

It may be that no causal interpretation of a nonrecursive system is intended. The relations in the system may be asserted only to define the joint probability distribution of the dependent variables conditional upon the predetermined variables. The coefficients to be estimated are then simply parameters in the joint conditional distribution of y given z. With nothing further claimed, there is no objection to such a model or to efforts to estimate the parameters of the distribution.

(B) VECTOR CAUSALITY

It may be asserted for the *nonrecursive* model

$$(3) \qquad\qquad By' + \Gamma z' = u'$$

that the vector z *causes* the vector y. Causality in this sense goes beyond the definition of "causality" given in Wold [6, 7]. It may readily be accepted, however, as an abstract terminological extension of the more usual notion of causation and may be employed in the everyday sense of the statement, "The food supply causes the fish population." An example may be useful. Suppose z is a vector whose elements are the amounts of various fish feeds (different insects, weeds, etc.) available in a given lake, and that y is a vector whose elements are the numbers of fish of various species in the lake. The reduced form $y' = -B^{-1}\,\Gamma z' + B^{-1} u'$ would tell us specifically how the number of fish of any species depends on the availabilities of different feeds. The coefficient of any z is the partial derivative of a species population with respect to a food supply. It is to be noted, however, that the reduced form tells us nothing about the interactions among the various fish populations—it does not tell us the extent to which one species of fish feeds on another species. Those are causal relations among the y's.[6]

Suppose, in another situation, we continuously restock the lake with species g, increasing y_g by any desired amount. How will this affect the values of the other y's? If the system were recursive and we had estimates of the elements of B, we would simply strike the gth equation out of the model and regard y_g, the number of fish of species g, as exogenous—as a food supply or, when appearing with a negative coefficient, as a poison. It will be the purpose of subsections (c) and (d) to determine whether if the model is not recursive the problem can be dealt with in this same way. The nonrecursive model does, in any case, enable us to predict the effects on the y's of controlled variations in the z's.

Herbert Simon in developing a sense of causality for econometric models [3] has used this notion of vector causality. He defines causal relations among *subsets* of dependent variables by using a model recursive in these subsets. Partition y' into three subsets, that is, into three column vectors, y'_1, y'_2, and y'_3, so that $y' = (y_1, y_2, y_3)'$ and partition B conformally. Consider the system (3) in which B may be written as

$$(4) \qquad\qquad B = \begin{pmatrix} B_{11} & B_{12} & B_{13} \\ 0 & B_{22} & B_{23} \\ 0 & 0 & B_{33} \end{pmatrix}$$

consisting of nine submatrices. Then y'_3 is caused by z'; y'_2 is caused by y'_3 and z'; and y'_1 is caused by y'_2, y'_3, and z'. In the previous sentence the word "caused" is used in the sense of vector causation, and B is "block triangular." No causal relations among the variables *within* a subset are defined. Press this logic further. If each subset consists of but a single endogenous variable, and a causal sequence is established among subsets, B is triangular and the system is recursive.

If, by way of contrast with vector causality, each effect variable is given as an explicit function of only variables that are its causes, we may speak of *explicit causality*.

(c) CAUSAL CIRCLES, MUTUAL CAUSATION, AND EQUILIBRIUM CONDITIONS

By a "causal circle" we shall mean a system such as

$$(5a) \qquad\qquad p(t) = \alpha_1 + \beta_1 q(t) + \gamma_1 z_1(t) + u_1(t),$$
$$(5b) \qquad\qquad q(t) = \alpha_2 + \beta_2 p(t) + \gamma_2 z_2(t) + u_2(t),$$

6. Indeed, even though $\partial y_g / \partial z_k > 0$, this does not imply that fish species g consumes food supply k. It may be that species g consumes species h which consumes food supply k.

where $z_1(t)$ and $z_2(t)$ are exogenous and for which the following two statements are asserted: (1) In equation (5a) $q(t)$ is a cause of $p(t)$; (2) In equation (5b) $p(t)$ is a cause of $q(t)$. Causation is here used in a sense not allowed by the operative meaning that causation has in an experimental laboratory. To accept a causal circle is, in the laboratory meaning of the word "cause," to suppose that the value of one variable is determined by the value of another variable whose value cannot be determined until that of the first has been determined. To assume that the values of the two variables determine each other makes sense only in an equilibrium system, and such a system provides no explanation of how the equilibrium comes about (of change or of causal connections among the endogenous variables of the system).[7]

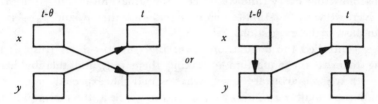

Figure 10.1.

The familiar illustration of the three balls in the bowl mutually *causing* one another's location, which has been advanced as an example of mutual causation,[8] might be considered in this connection. For the steady state (equilibrium) there are certain mutual conditions which must be satisfied; but if the balls are displaced and then roll towards equilibrium they are either in mutual contact and roll (or slide) as a single mass or the position of each can depend on the positions of the others only when the latter are lagged in time. Indeed, mutual causation in a dynamic system can have meaning only as a limit form of the arrow schemes shown in Figure 10.1 where the time lag θ is reduced towards zero.[9]

There is, however, a sense in which the coefficients of an equilibrium system may be given a causal interpretation, even though the relations in an

7. If, for example, an entrepreneur wishing to produce a given amount of product at minimum cost decides simultaneously on how much of each of two factors of production, x_1 and x_2, to employ, it might be said that his decision as to x_1 causes his decision as to x_2 and his decision as to x_2 causes his decision as to x_1. We do not believe this conforms to the "laboratory" meaning of causation and we therefore reject this usage. On this, see [1].

8. This illustration, due to Marshall, has been referred to recently by Stone [4] in this connection. Marshall spoke of mutual "determination" rather than "causation" and it is not clear whether these words are to be regarded as synonyms.

9. In equilibrium when $x(t) = x(t-\theta)$ and $y(t) = y(t-\theta)$, these structures may be collapsed into one of apparent "mutual causation," but what are simultaneous equilibrium conditions ought not to be confused with causal relations.

equilibrium system may not themselves be causal relations. Let us take first an imaginary case in ecology: the balanced aquarium. Suppose there are two species of fish in an aquarium, big, b, and small, s. Their populations are y_b and y_s. The big fish feed on the small ones and on weed type a, available in quantity x_a. The small fish feed only on weed type c, available in quantity x_c. It takes time for the big fish to catch the small ones. The model is linear and stochastic, thus:

(6a) $\qquad\qquad y_b(t) = \alpha_1 + \beta_1 y_s(t-\theta) + \gamma_1 x_a(t) + u_1(t),$

(6b) $\qquad\qquad y_s(t) = \alpha_2 + \beta_2 y_b(t-\theta) + \delta_2 x_c(t) + u_2(t).$

Suppose now that every time we observe the aquarium it is in equilibrium. Moreover, we wish to estimate two numbers—are they β_1 and β_2?—so that we can answer these questions:

If we controlled the population of the big (small) fish, y_b (resp., y_s), by adding them to the aquarium or taking them out, and thereby held y_b (resp., y_s) at some arbitrary level, what would the expected value of the population of small (resp., big) fish, y_s (resp., y_b), be at the new equilibrium level, conditional upon the values of x_a and x_c?

Suppose we next formulated the model:

(7a) $\qquad\qquad y_b(t) = \alpha_1 + \beta_1 y_s(t) + \gamma_1 x_a(t) + u_1(t),$

(7b) $\qquad\qquad y_s(t) = \alpha_2 + \beta_2 y_b(t) + \delta_2 x_b(t) + u_2(t).$

To control the population of big fish is to wipe out or invalidate relation (6a) and to regard $y_b(t-\theta)$ as exogenous. To control the population of small fish is to wipe out (6b) and to regard $y_s(t-\theta)$ as exogenous. In the absence of such intervention, we certainly cannot say that $y_s(t)$ *causes* $y_b(t)$ and that $y_b(t)$ *causes* $y_s(t)$, i.e., we cannot use model (7) as a *causal* model telling us what happens through time in the uncontrolled aquarium. Nevertheless, the values of β_1 and β_2 appearing in model (7) do tell us what a second fish population will be conditional upon our specifying (controlling, manipulating) a first fish population—provided that the aquarium is then brought back to an equilibrium situation. Equilibrium models do tell us (enable us to predict) something about equilibrium values under *control*.

A comparable example in economics might well be the cobweb model. The model is:

(8a) $\qquad\qquad p(t) = \alpha - \beta q_h(t) + \epsilon z_1(t) + u_1(t) \quad \text{(demand)},$

(8b) $\qquad\qquad q_h(t) = \gamma + \delta p(t-1) + \eta z_2(t) + u_2(t) \quad \text{(supply)},$

where $p(t)$ is price at time t, q_h is quantity harvested, z_1 and z_2 are exogenous variables, and u_1 and u_2 are stochastic shocks. This system is recursive, but if observed in equilibrium may, by use of the equilibrium condition

$$p(t-1) = p(t),$$

be written as

(9a) $p(t) = \alpha - \beta q_h(t) + \epsilon z_1(t) + u_1(t)$ (demand),

(9b) $q_h(t) = \gamma + \delta p(t) + \eta z_2(t) + u_2(t)$ (supply),

and will be subject to the same causal interpretation as given in the previous example. The question of how β and δ are best to be estimated is left open.

(D) BICAUSALITY

Suppose we confront a demand-supply model of the following sort

(10a) $q(t) = \alpha_{10} + \alpha_{11} p(t) + \alpha_{13} z_1(t) + u_1(t)$ (demand),

(10b) $q(t) = \alpha_{20} + \alpha_{21} p(t) + \alpha_{24} z_2(t) + u_2(t)$ (supply),

where $q(t)$ is quantity, $p(t)$ is price, $z_1(t)$ and $z_2(t)$ are exogenous variables, and $u_1(t)$ and $u_2(t)$ are stochastic shocks.

Now suppose this system is given the following causal interpretation: $p(t)$ causes $q(t)$ in accordance with equation (10a) and $p(t)$ also causes $q(t)$ in accordance with equation (10b). This notion of causality is certainly out of accord with the usual laboratory or control notion which we find so natural. Those who write such systems do not, however, really mean what they write, but introduce an ellipsis which is familiar to economists. What is meant is that

(11a) $q_d(t) = \alpha_{10} + \alpha_{11} p(t) + \alpha_{13} z_1(t) + u_1(t),$

(11b) $q_s(t) = \alpha_{20} + \alpha_{21} p(t) + \alpha_{24} z_2(t) + u_2(t),$

(11c) $q_d(t) = q_s(t),$

where $q_d(t)$ is quantity demanded and $q_s(t)$ is quantity supplied. This is an equilibrium model (nonrecursive), and (11c) is not an *identity*, but an *equality* which is assumed to hold in fact over the observations.[10]

A somewhat far-fetched example, but in a surer context, is the following. Suppose there are two crops, d and s, whose yield is measured in bushels, and that (over the relevant range) the yield of one, q_d, is a positive linear

---

10. Especially for one not familiar with the economist's ellipsis, difficulty may result from the careless use of symbols in this reduction. Strictly speaking, the q in (10a and b) should be either a q_d or a q_s, or an additional equation such as $q = \min(q_d, q_s)$ or $q = q_d$ should be added to model (11). Otherwise, identity (and not simply equality) of quantities demanded and supplied is technically implied.

function of rainfall, p, while the yield of the other, q_s, is a negative linear function of rainfall, and that these functions interesect within the relevant range. An amount z_1 of fertilizer 1 is applied to crop d and an amount z_2 of fertilizer 2 is applied to s. Suppose for each of N years we conduct an experiment for each crop, applying different amounts of fertilizer. Rainfall is uncontrolled. Imagine now the amazing result that each year of the experiment Nature chooses a rainfall that makes the two yields equal. We may then represent the experiment by system (11) and reduce this to system (10) simply by dropping the subscripts on q and keeping track of which equation is for which crop.

Now, while it would be remarkable for Nature to choose rainfall so as to give us this strange result, it may be not so remarkable for the market to choose price so that quantity demanded equals quantity supplied, at least approximately. This is because, while rainfall is independent of past crop yields, price may well depend on past quantities demanded and supplied, and, if the system is not subject to violent change, the price adjustment relation may work with great efficiency. Whether it will or not is, of course, an empirical question: the answer may vary from market to market and time to time; but this is a matter of realism which need not concern us here. When the equality holds the theoretical system (11) may be represented by system (10), although if (11c) holds only approximately, system (10) is one with errors in the variables.

The causal system which underlies the equilibrium model (11) is then one in which (11c) is replaced by some function such as

$$(11d) \qquad p(t) = f[q_d(t-\theta), q_s(t-\theta), p(t-\theta), z_1(t), z_2(t), z_1(t-\theta),$$
$$z_2(t-\theta)] + u_3(t)$$

and the causal (and, in this case, dynamic) model is recursive. If $p(t)$ were now to be subject to direct control, (11d) must be abandoned and $p(t)$ must be regarded as exogenous. Equations (11a) and (11b) would then answer questions regarding the causal effect of controlled variation in $p(t)$ on $q_d(t)$ and $q_s(t)$, and α_{11} and α_{12} would be causally interpretable coefficients. They are, moreover, the same coefficients which enter the "bicausal" system (10).

What is to be concluded from all this is that equilibrium systems may appear to entail "causal circles" or "bicausality," but that this is not what is intended. The causal interpretation of a coefficient in either of these types of equilibrium models is to be found in the underlying dynamic model which, *if the laboratory notion of causality is to be sustained*, will be recursive in character.[11]

11. Incidentally, differential equation systems are regarded as recursive with respect to infinitesimal time intervals. See [8].

Two major questions remain: (1) Can a stochastic shock model of the sort commonly considered—i.e., equation (1)—ever be assumed to be always in equilibrium whenever observed?[12] (2) If not, must it not be said that either there are measurement errors introduced by the assumption of equilibrium (for example, ought not (11c) be regarded as an *approximate* equality) or there is a specification error? If so, this raises questions as to appropriate estimation procedure and as to the properties of estimates that ignore these model qualifications. The subsequent paper by Strotz deals with this problem.

Our contribution ends with a paper by Wold, who gives a brief presentation of conditional causal chains, a new type of model which is designed as an extension of ordinary (pure) causal chains in the direction of independent systems.

---

12. For (11a, b, and c) to hold exactly, (11d) would need to include $u_1(t)$ and $u_2(t)$ as arguments and exclude $u_3(t)$.

References

[1] BENTZEL, R., and HANSEN, B., "On Recursiveness and Interdependency in Economic Models," *Review of Economic Studies*, 22, pp. 153–168.

[2] MOOD, A., *Introduction to the Theory of Statistics*, McGraw-Hill, 1950.

[3] SIMON, HERBERT A., "Causal Ordering and Identifiability," in Wm. C. Hood and Tjalling C. Koopmans, eds., *Studies in Econometric Method*. Wiley & Sons, 1953.

[4] STONE, RICHARD, "Discussion on Professor Wold's Paper," *Journal of the Royal Statistical Society*, Series A, 119, I, 1956, p. 51.

[5] WAUGH, FREDERICK: "Choice of the Dependent Variable in Regression," *Journal of the American Statistical Association*, 38, 22 (June, 1943), pp. 210–214.

[6] WOLD, H. O. A.: "Causality and Econometrics," *Econometrica*, 22, pp. 114 ff.

[7] ——, "On the Definition and Meaning of Causal Concepts," manuscript, submitted to *Philosophy of Science*.

[8] ——, "Ends and Means in Econometric Model Building. Basic Considerations Reviewed," in U. Grenander, ed., *Probability and Statistics* (The Harald Cramer volume), Stockholm: Almqvist & Wiksell, 1959.

[9] WOLD, H. O. A., and JURÉEN, L., *Demand Analysis*, Almqvist & Wiksell, 1952.

Chapter 11

TWO THEOREMS ON *CETERIS PARIBUS* IN THE ANALYSIS OF DYNAMIC SYSTEMS

FRANKLIN M. FISHER
ALBERT ANDO
Massachusetts Institute of Technology

Analysis of the dynamic properties of two or more interrelated systems is a recurrent problem in social science theory. A particular problem frequently arises (although it often goes unrecognized) in assessing the validity of an analysis of a system, some variables of which are causally related to other variables, which latter, in turn, are either not explicitly taken into account or are assumed constant. Examples are easy to find: economists may study the behavior of a single country's economy with only secondary regard for the rest of the world; studies of group behavior may pay only secondary attention to the other roles played by the group members in other contexts; two more examples are worked out below and others may be found in the works about to be cited. Indeed, in a larger sense, the division of social science itself (or of natural science, for that matter) into separate disciplines is an example, for the variables taken as given by one discipline are the very subject matter of another and *vice versa*. In all these examples, the very real problem is present that if variables taken as given are causally affected by the variables of the system being analyzed, or if variables assumed not to affect that system actually do affect it, the results of the analysis may have little relevance for the study of real problems.

The principal purpose of this paper is to call the attention of social scientists outside the field of mathematical economics to two related theorems in

* Reprinted by permission of the authors and publisher from the *American Political Science Review*, Vol. 56, pp. 108–113. Copyright 1962, The American Political Science Association.

this area that have recently been proved.[1] We shall not attempt a technical discussion of the theorems here but instead give a general description of them in the next section. We then present two illustrative, albeit somewhat simplified, examples of the sort of results that these theorems can be used to obtain in political science.

I

Suppose a number of variables such that at any time, t, the value of each of them is a function of the values of some or all of the same set of variables at some past time t-1.[2] Suppose further that it is possible to collect the variables into subsets such that the variables within each subset are functions only of the past values of variables in the *same* subset, but not of the past values of any variables in any *different* subset.[3] Then the system is said to be *completely decomposable* and it is obvious that it really consists of several independent systems each one of which can be analyzed separately without reference to any of the others. In the examples mentioned above, this would be the case if every country's economy were really closed so that there were no inter-country effects and if every member of a group had no other roles to play outside the group or if those other roles had no effect whatsoever on actions within the group.

While the assumption of complete decomposability (or *ceteris paribus*) is often convenient to make, it is seldom likely to be fully satisfied in practice. Thus there *are* some exports and imports affecting every country; there *are*

1. H. A. Simon and A. Ando, "Aggregation of Variables in Dynamic Systems," *Econometrica*, Vol. 29 (April, 1961), pp. 111–138 and A. Ando and F. M. Fisher, "Near-Decomposability, Partition and Aggregation, and the Relevance of Stability Discussions," in detail (forthcoming) present and prove the theorems. The relation of the sort of system involved to ordinary notions of causation is discussed in H. A. Simon, "Causal Ordering and Identifiability," ch. 3 in *Studies in Econometric Method* (W. C. Hood and T. C. Koopmans, eds., New York, 1953; Cowles Commission Monograph No. 14), reprinted as ch. 1 in H. A. Simon, *Models of Man* (New York, 1957); while the bearing of this sort of problem on the estimation of parameters in one of a set of interrelated systems is covered in F. M. Fisher, "On the Cost of Approximate Specification in Simultaneous Equation Estimation." *Econometrica*, Vol. 29 (April 1961), pp. 139–170.

2. If values in the further past are relevant, a formal redefinition can always be made to eliminate time before $t-1$, without changing anything. Simultaneous dependencies can also be treated, though, for reasons of clarity and intuitive appeal, we restrict ourselves to cases where there is some time lag somewhere in the system. Further, we could consider time as continuous without essential changes. Strictly speaking, however, the theorems under discussion are only known to hold for cases in which the relations involved are linear. Since this was written, the principal results of the theorems have been shown to hold for at least one important class of nonlinear systems in F. M. Fisher, "Decomposability, and Balanced Growth Under Constant Returns to Scale" (forthcoming).

3. Hereafter, to simplify terminology, by the term "set" instead of "subset," we mean a subset within the set of all variables in the system under consideration.

outside roles for group members, and so forth. The question thus naturally arises: What remains of the results of an analysis carried out under an assumption of complete decomposability if the system being studied is in fact embedded in a larger system which is not truly completely decomposable, so that variables assumed to be causally irrelevant do in fact matter? Of course, if the assumption of irrelevance—of complete decomposability—is a very bad one, it is unreasonable to expect much to be left or results obtained under it; but what if variables assumed irrelevant do not in fact matter very much? Is there any sense in which complete decomposability and the great simplification which it permits can be used as a good approximation, so that results obtained under it can be expected to be approximately valid when it is relaxed? This is where the first of our two theorems comes in.

Suppose that our system, instead of being completely decomposable, is in fact only *nearly* completely decomposable. In other words, suppose that the variables within each set do depend on the past values of variables outside that set but that this dependence is small relative to within-set dependencies. In such a case, the Simon-Ando theorem[4] asserts the following: carry out the analysis of the system on the assumption that it is really completely decomposable (i.e., ignore inter-set dependencies altogether). Provided that inter-set dependencies are sufficiently weak relative to intra-set ones, *in the short run* that analysis will remain approximately valid in all respects—that is, the system will behave almost as if it *were* completely decomposable.[5]

Now, if this were all, it would be useful but not very remarkable, for it would merely mean that if neglected influences are sufficiently weak they take a long time to matter much; however, the theorem does not stop here but asserts a far stronger result.

Consider the long-run behavior that the system would exhibit if it were truly completely decomposable. In particular, consider the *relative* behavior of the variables within each set (i.e., consider the long-run behavior of their ratios). Provided again that inter-set dependencies are sufficiently weak relative to intra-set ones, that same relative behavior will show up approximately in the long-run behavior of the true only *nearly* completely decomposable system. It is important to fully grasp this result. It asserts that even when influences which have been neglected have had time to make themselves fully felt, the *relative* behavior of the variables within any set will be

4. Simon and Ando, *op. cit.*

5. Here and later what is meant by "sufficiently weak" depends on what standard of approximation one wishes to impose on the results. The more closely one insists that the behavior of the system must approximate that of the corresponding completely decomposable one, the weaker must "sufficiently weak" be. What the theorem guarantees is that *whatever* standard of approximation is required (so long as it is an approximate and not an exact standard) a non-zero degree of weakness always exists which is sufficient to produce results satisfying that standard.

approximately the same as would have been the case had those influences never existed, and this despite the fact that the *absolute* behavior of the variables—their levels and rates of change—may be very different indeed. To recapitulate: if a nearly completely decomposable system is analyzed as though it were really completely decomposable, the results obtained will remain approximately valid even in the long run as regards the *relative* behavior of the variables within any one set.[6]

The detailed examples of the next section will make all this clearer; however, let us pause briefly over the examples already cited. In one variant of the international trade case, the Simon-Ando theorem asserts that if a country trades very little with the rest of the world, its short-run production of every commodity will be approximately the same as if it did not trade at all. Further, in the long run, the *ratio* in which it produces any two commodities will also be approximately the same, although the *levels* and *rates of growth* of production may be very different in the two cases. Similarly, in the group behavior case, the Simon-Ando theorem asserts that, if outside roles for group members are relatively unimportant, the short-run behavior of the group will be approximately the same as if those roles did not exist, while in the long run, the *relative* behavior of the group members *vis-à-vis* each other will also be approximately the same, even though the behavior of the group *as a whole*[7] *vis-à-vis* the rest of the world may be quite different.

Unfortunately, however, useful as completely decomposable or nearly completely decomposable systems are, the assumptions inherent in near complete decomposability are grossly unrealistic for many systems which are of great interest to social scientists. We often study systems which we do not believe, even as an approximation, to be causally uninfluenced by outside forces. In many cases, we deal with systems whose variables are believed to be influenced by outside forces but not to influence these outside variables, so that the latter may be taken as givens of the problem. This is the case of causal influences running only one way among sets of variables (although there may be "whorls" of causation within each set). Thus the economist frequently takes tastes or technology as causally influencing the variables he studies but as being causally uninfluenced by them. So too, a sociologist may

---

6. Even before the full system settles down to its ultimate behavior, variables within any one set will move proportionally, so that inter-set influences can be analyzed as influences among indices, each index representing all variables in a particular subset of the system, rather than as among the individual variables themselves. This point, while a little aside from the main drift of our discussion in the text, is useful and important and will show up in our examples below. It is true of both theorems.

7. This phrase is not used accidentally. The influence of the outside roles will eventually be on group behavior as a whole rather than on individial behavior within the group (remember that such influences are small relative to within-group forces). See the preceding footnote.

take the existing means of production as given independently of the variables he studies but as influencing the latter in a significant way.

More formally, this kind of assumption is equivalent to saying that our variables can be collected into sets *numbered* (from 1 to N, say) so that the variables in any given set are functions of their own past values *and* of the past values of the variables in any lower-numbered set but not of the past values of the variables in any higher-numbered one. This sort of system is called *decomposable*. (The reader should go back to the definition of *complete* decomposability to be sure he understands the difference.) Clearly, the dynamic behavior of any set of variables in a decomposable system can be studied taking the behavior of variables in lower-numbered sets as given and without any regard for higher-numbered sets. (Note, however, that the influence of lower-numbered sets *must* be explicitly recognized.)

Again as in the case of complete decomposability, however, the assumption of decomposability is frequently justified only as a working approximation. Thus tastes and technology are not *really* independent of the workings of the economic system; the means of production are not *really* given independently of sociological factors.[8] The question then arises as before of the validity of results obtained under such assumptions. Indeed, this question is perhaps even more important here than in the completely decomposable case, for we have already pointed out (and the examples just cited illustrate) that the very separation of social science into the social sciences is a use of the assumption of decomposability.

Fortunately, the same things are essentially true here as in the nearly completely decomposable case. For nearly decomposable systems which are not nearly completely decomposable—in other words, for systems in which *one-way* inter-set influences are too large to ignore—the Ando-Fisher theorem[9] yields substantially the same results as the Simon-Ando theorem does for the nearly completely decomposable case. Thus the economist who takes tastes and technology as influencing but uninfluenced by economic variables will find—provided that such an assumption is *nearly* correct—that his results will be approximately valid in all respects in the short run and that even in the long run, when the full effects of feedbacks in the causal structure are felt, the *internal, relative* behavior of the variables he studies will be approximately the same. The importance of this result for the usefulness of intra-disciplinary studies in an interrelated world needs no emphasis.[10]

8. Indeed, it would be odd (although not impossible) for both statements to hold exactly.

9. Ando and Fisher, *op. cit.*

10. This is not to deny, of course, the usefulness of inter-disciplinary work. The point is that the results of intra-disciplinary studies need not be vitiated because the real world is not so neatly divided as the academic one.

II

We come now to the application of these theorems to two examples in political science which we shall work out in moderate detail, although without any attempt to argue that these examples are more than illustrations.

First, let us consider an over-simple model of armament races. Suppose that at any time, the stocks of armaments of any country (as measured by the number of units of each type of weapon in its arsenal) are a function of the stocks of armaments of all countries (including itself) at some past date.[11] The influences of such past stocks may be of different kinds. Thus armaments may be higher the higher a prospective enemy's armament stocks; lower the higher the stocks of prospective allies; effects on different weapons may be different; stocks of one type of weapon may influence stocks of others positively or negatively; and so forth.

Now suppose that the world is divided into several arms races in such a way that the armaments of a country in any one arms race depend principally on those of the other countries in the same arms race and relatively little on those of countries in other arms races. (This may not be a bad approximation; one might think of the Arabs and Israelis on the one hand and the East-West arms race on the other.) The system is then nearly completely decomposable and the Simon-Ando theorem predicts the following.

From the initiation of the various arms races (since they are at least slightly interdependent they will all begin at least nominally at the same time) until some time thereafter, each arms race will proceed approximately as it would in the absence of the other races. Indeed, this will continue until after the transient effects of different starting stocks of armaments have effectively disappeared. Once this has happened, there will come a time after which the stocks of various weapons for all the countries in each arms race will grow (or shrink or fluctuate) approximately proportionally, so that the influence of any one arms race on any other may be considered as that of an aggregate "country" with one aggregate stock of weapons on another, despite the fact that the influences among the countries and weapons making up the aggregates may be quite varied. Finally, in the long run, the size and rate of growth of every country's armament stocks at any period will be determined by the rate of growth of that arms race which would

11. Again, the use of past time is not a restriction; the past date can be last year or yesterday or an hour ago. Similarly, influences in the further past can be formally subsumed under this model by redefinition. Finally, the formulation includes the case in which it is the *rate of change* rather than the *level* of the armament stocks which are dependent on past armaments. This sort of treatment of arms races originates with L. F. Richardson. See his *Arms and Insecurity* (Chicago, Quadrangle Books, 1960). Of course the stocks of armaments depend on other things such as economic resources; we are trying to keep the example as simple as possible. The functions in question are supposed to represent the strategic choices made by governments.

grow fastest in the absence of the other arms races, but the *relative* sizes of the weapon stocks within any one arms race will remain approximately the same as if no other arms races existed.

Now consider a somewhat different situation in which the world is again divided into arms races and the arms races are numbered such that armament stocks in any given country are functions of past stocks of other countries in the same arms race and of countries in lower-numbered arms races but only slightly of stocks of countries in higher-numbered arms races.[12] (This, too, may be somewhat realistic. On the one hand, the level of Pakistani armaments is affected by United States military aid; on the other hand, the level of United States armaments is hardly affected by Pakistani arms levels.) Then the system is nearly decomposable and the Ando-Fisher theorem yields results similar to those just presented in the nearly completely decomposable case. Perhaps it is worth remarking here that the theorem thus shows that a very rapid long-run rate of arms accumulation in a high-numbered arms race (say India-Pakistan or North and South Vietnam) can force the long-run rate of arms accumulation in a lower-numbered race (say U.S.-U.S.S.R.) to the same level but cannot more than negligibly affect the *relative* positions in the latter race.

For the second example, we turn to the voting strength of political parties. Suppose that there are several political parties and that the number of votes for any one party at a given time is a function of the number of votes for each party at some past time. For convenience, we shall assume a constant total population and that every individual votes for one and only one party. We shall further assume that the effect of past votes on present party strength can be represented for each party by a sum of terms, each term representing the probability of an individual who votes initially for a particular party changing his vote to the party in question, times the number of people voting for the initial party. Of course, individuals who stay in the same party are counted as going from that party to itself. It follows then that if we add the coefficients which give the probabilities of going from a particular party to all parties in existence, the sum must be unity, as every individual must end up somewhere.[13]

Thus, in equation form, let X_{1t} be the number of votes for the first party at

---

12. They need not be functions of armament stocks in *all* lower-numbered races; one will do. Similarly, not every country in the given arms race need have such links; all that is required is that at least one does, so that the system, while nearly decomposable, is not nearly *completely* decomposable. It is also possible to analyze a case in which a part of a nearly decomposable system happens to be nearly completely decomposable.

13. A discussion of this general sort of model which aggregates from the individual level is given in T. W. Anderson, "Probability Models for Analyzing Time Changes in Attitudes," Chapter 1 in *Mathematical Thinking in the Social Sciences*, P. F. Lazarsfeld, ed. (Glencoe, 1954). It would be possible to abandon the probability interpretation and to let higher strength in

time, t, X_{2t} be the number of votes for the second party at the same time, and so forth. We have (where there are n parties):

$$X_{1t} = A_{11}X_{1t-1} + A_{12}X_{2t-1} + \ldots + A_{1n}X_{nt-1}$$

(1) $\qquad X_{2t} = A_{21}X_{1t-1} + A_{22}X_{2t-1} + \ldots + A_{2n}X_{nt-1}$

$$\vdots$$

$$X_{nt} = A_{n1}X_{1t-1} + A_{n2}X_{2t-1} + \ldots + A_{nn}X_{nt-1}$$

Here, A_{11} is the probability of an individual voting for party 1 continuing to do so; A_{12} is the probability of an individual voting for party 2 changing to party 1; A_{21} is the probability of an individual voting for party 1 changing to party 2; and so forth. Clearly, all the A's must lie between zero and one, and the sum of the A's in any column must be unity.

Now consider any set of parties (a single party can count as a set). Ignore the fact that such a set may gain votes from outside itself and consider only its own internal workings. There will be in the long run a single probability that a randomly chosen individual voting for some party in the set will continue to vote for some party in the set at the next time period (he may move between parties in the set). Equivalently, without ignoring the fact that the set may gain votes from outside, we may consider the long-run probability that one of the people *originally* voting for some party in the set who has remained so voting through some particular time will continue so to vote for yet one more period; this comes to the same thing. (In either definition, we assume that every party in the set begins with a very large number of votes so that a zero vote does not become a problem save for parties which lose all their votes every time period.) We call that long-run probability the *cohesiveness* of the set. Clearly, it must lie between zero and one; the cohesiveness of any single party is the A coefficient in its own row and column (thus, for example, A_{11} is the cohesiveness of the first party taken alone); and the cohesiveness of all parties taken together is unity (since nobody can leave the system as a whole). In general, the cohesiveness of a set lies between the smallest and the largest probability of an individual voting for any given party in the set staying put or changing to another party in the same set (this latter probability is given by the sum of the A's in the

---

one party lead to lower strength in another, but this would lead to an example without some of the nice features of the present one. It would also be possible to build in other influences on party voting strength. Again, we are striving for an illuminating example rather than for a full-blown "realistic" theory. The assumption that every individual votes for some party is innocuous, since we can count all those not voting for any formal party as voting for a party of their own, the "Non-such" Party.

column corresponding to the party in question and in the rows corresponding to all parties in the set including the initial one).[14]

Now suppose that the parties can be divided into sets such that the probability of an individual moving between sets is small relative to the probability of his remaining in the same set. Clearly, each set then has cohesiveness close to unity. The system is then nearly completely decomposable and the Simon-Ando theorem yields the following results:

Begin with any distribution of voting chosen at random. In the short run, the voting strength of each party will behave approximately as it would if there were no movements between sets of parties whatsoever. Moreover, there will come a time after which the ratio of the votes for any party to the votes for any other party in the same set will remain approximately constant. Thereafter, each set of parties can be treated as a single party for purposes of analyzing inter-set movements, with the cohesiveness of the set acting as the probability of remaining therein. Finally, even in the long run, the equilibrium distribution of relative voting strength *within* each set of parties will be approximately the same as if there were no inter-set movements although the absolute number of votes involved may be quite different.

In this example, however, the more interesting case is that of near decomposability. Let us first consider what a truly decomposable system would be. This would occur if the parties could be divided into sets where the sets are numbered (from 1 to N, say) in such a way that nobody voting for a party in any set ever changes to a party in a lower-numbered set but such that there are non-negligible movements into higher numbered sets. Thus anybody in set N stays there; anybody in set $N-1$ either stays there or moves to set N; anybody in set $N-2$ either stays there, moves to set $N-1$, or moves to set N; and so forth. (Note that set N has cohesiveness 1; no other single set has cohesiveness 1, but set N and set $N-1$ together, set N, set $N-1$, and set $N-2$ together, and so forth all have cohesiveness 1.) The sets are thus "nested," in the sense that all inter-set movements go toward the center which consists of set N.

Now suppose that all sets begin with a very large number of votes (so that the fact that the lower-numbered sets will eventually lose all their votes is not a difficulty). Consider any set. A time will come such that thereafter the *relative* strength of the parties in that set is determined primarily by their tendency to attract voters from parties in the set with the highest cohesiveness

14. *Technical footnote*. Precisely, cohesiveness is given by the largest characteristic root of the submatrix of A's corresponding to the parties in the set. See F. M. Fisher, "An Alternate Proof and Extension of Solow's Theorem on Nonnegative Square Matrices," *Econometrica*, Vol. 30 (July, 1962) forthcoming. The fact that the root lies between the largest and smallest column sums is well known—see R. M. Solow, "On the Structure of Linear Models," *Econometrica*, Vol. 21 (January, 1952), pp. 29–46.

among those sets that are not higher numbered than the set in question. (In the case of set N or of set 1, this is the set in question itself; in any other case, it need not be.) This is a reasonable result, because as time goes on the parties in the sets with the greatest cohesiveness will acquire more and more votes, so that, given the probabilities of any *single* voter moving among the sets, what happens to these sets becomes of increasing importance to all those sets of parties that acquire voters from them.

We now alter the assumptions and suppose that although the dominant inter-set movements are to higher-numbered sets, there are small movements to lower-numbered ones. (This may not be too unrealistic. We might think of set N as the major parties; there may be a far higher tendency to move into or stay in them than there is to move out.) The system is now only nearly decomposable and the Ando-Fisher theorem yields the following results:

Begin with any distribution of voting chosen at random. In the short run, the actual number of votes for each party will behave approximately as it would if the only inter-set movements were to higher-numbered sets. Moreover, there will come a time after which the *relative* distribution of voting among the parties within any set will remain approximately the same as would have been the case in the truly decomposable case earlier described. After this time, inter-set movements can be analyzed without regard for the voting distribution within the various sets. Finally these *relative* intra-set distributions will be approximately maintained even in the long run, although the absolute number of votes eventually cast for the parties in each set will depend almost wholly on the tendency of that set as a whole to gain voters from set N (which by this time is far larger than any other set).

Note that this result implies that an analysis of the *relative* strength of "minor" parties can proceed without explicit account of the tendency of such parties to gain voters from or even to lose voters to major ones, despite the fact that the latter tendency is large. So far as *relative* voting strength is concerned, all that matters are the various tendencies of the minor parties to lose voters to and gain voters from each other (and even some of these may be negligible). Even wide differences in tendencies to lose voters to (or gain them from) major parties need not be explicitly taken into account, provided only that the former tendencies are very strong relative to the latter, a rather surprising result.[15]

15. We are perhaps making this result sound a bit more paradoxical than it is. Different tendencies to lose voters to major parties do in fact matter and get taken into account in an implicit fashion. Since every party's voters end up *somewhere* (the sum of the A's in any column is one), a minor party with a high propensity to lose voters to major ones will have—*other things being equal*—a lower propensity to retain voters than a minor party with a lower propensity to lose voters to major ones. This will show up in considering their relative strength in isolation; however, it can be nullified by other tendencies if other things are *not* equal.

Chapter 12

THE APPLICATION OF A SYSTEM OF SIMULTANEOUS EQUATIONS TO AN INNOVATION DIFFUSION MODEL

ROBERT MASON
ALBERT N. HALTER*
Oregon State University

Systems of interdependent simultaneous equations have been used extensively to describe social behavior in the field of economics, or, more specifically, in econometrics. A system of equations in the social sciences is usually considered a nonexperimental model, i.e., a model for which data came from a nonexperimental setting such as time-series or cross-sectional studies. Two problems which arise when using a system of simultaneous equations in a nonexperimental setting are (1) identification and (2) estimation. The problem of identification has been given extensive treatment in the econometric literature and has recently been introduced into the literature of sociology by Blalock[1] and Boudon.[2]

A logical next step is to consider the estimation problem in the context of building behavioral theory. Since econometrics has pioneered in the development of estimation procedures for determining coefficients in systems of

Reprinted from *Social Forces*, Vol. 47. (December 1968) pp. 182–195, by permission of the authors and the publisher (Copyright, 1968, Social Forces.)

* The authors wish to thank Dr. Norman McKown, Director of Institutional Research at Oregon State University, for his critical reading and comments on earlier drafts of this paper. Published as Technical Paper 2459, Oregon Agricultural Experiment Station.

1. Hubert M. Blalock, Jr., "The Identification Problem and Theory Building: The Case of Status Inconsistency," *American Sociological Review*, 31 (February 1966), pp. 52–61.

2. Raymond Boudon, "A Method of Linear Causal Analysis: Dependence Analysis," *American Sociological Review*, 30 (June 1965), pp. 365–374.

simultaneous equations, a reasonable starting place for other behavioral sciences is to consider these developments and their applicability to their own problems. The purpose of this paper is to show the results of applying the Theil-Basmann method (two-stage least-squares) to a system of simultaneous equations involving both sociological and economic variables. In this paper, first, the identification problem is reviewed. Then the logic of the two-stage estimation procedure is presented. Finally, a specific model concerning the diffusion of technical innovations is formulated and tested.

Review of identification problem

Blalock[3] has shown how the identification problem arises in attempting to specify a system of equations (model) to describe status inconsistency. One of the models had the following three equations:

$$Y = b_1 X_1 + b_2 X_2 + b_3 W + e_y$$

$$W = b_4 Z + e_w$$

$$Z = f(X_1 - kX_2) \text{ where}$$

Y is votes for liberal candidates; X_1 is income; X_2 is education; W represents the strain factor; Z stands for status inconsistency; b_1, b_2, b_3, and b_4 are coefficients to be estimated from some data; and k is a known parameter. The error terms, e_y and e_w are assumed to account for variables which are excluded from the equations and are assumed uncorrelated with one another. In order for the coefficients in a given equation to be called identifiable, Blalock states that "the number of variables excluded from this equation must be at least equal to one less than the number of equations."[4] Applying this counting rule to each of the equations in the above system, we find: (1) the first equation has only the variable Z excluded, thus it would need another variable such as a V in the second equation to identify it; (2) the second equation is identified since it has two variables, X_1 and X_2 excluded, which is equal to one less than the number of equations; (3) the third equation is an exact mathematical relation without an error term and hence the the identification question is not relevant. The first equation is said to be underidentified and the second, exactly identified.

Coefficients in individual equations in a system can be estimated by ordinary least-squares regression techniques, provided the equation is just identified. If a model contains one or more underidentified equations, then certain alterations must be made before the coefficients can be estimated. Blalock

3. Blalock, *loc. cit.*

4. An equivalent form of this counting rule can be expressed as "the number of endogenous variables appearing in any given equation cannot be greater than one more than the number of exogenous variables left out of this equation."

has noted that by bringing into the second equation another exogenous variable (i.e., one that is not to be explained within the system), one that would not logically appear in the first equation, the equation for Y can be identified. This adding of a variable would not affect the identification of the second equation.

Another case of identification is where an equation is overidentified.[5] For example, if the first equation contained another variable such as age, X_3, which did not appear in the equation for W, then the second equation would be overidentified. By the counting rule the second equation would have three variables excluded, which is equal to the number of equations. The case of overidentification would seem to be the most prevalent case in behavioral science theory construction; that is, one is more likely to think of more variables to include in an explanation than to attempt to rely on a parsimonious interpretation.

Underidentification is a more serious hurdle than overidentification. Alterations must be made in the model to remove the former. One does not need to remove the latter before estimation of the coefficients, but use of ordinary least-squares regression is not recommended.[6] Work in statistical techniques compatible with the overidentification problem has advanced rapidly since Haavelmo's contribution in 1943.[7] The Cowles Commission has sponsored further research in the development of limited-information–maximum-likelihood techniques for estimating the coefficients of a single equation.[8] Recently a new technique has been developed, attributed to both Theil[9] and Basmann,[10] which is closely related to the limited-information approach but is computationally more simple. This technique is frequently called the Theil-Basmann or two-stage least-squares technique of estimation. Although the complete mathematical and statistical justification for this technique is beyond the scope of this paper, the technique would seem of sufficient importance that the steps in its application should be described and applied to a specific model, viz., the diffusion of technical innovations.

5. Identified means that the equation is either exactly or overidentified. Not identified means the equation is underidentified.

6. Least-squares regression applied to an over-identified equation will lead to estimates of the coefficients that are biased and inconsistent. In addition, such estimates are less efficient than those obtained by alternative procedures. See Stefan Valavanis, *Econometrics, An Introduction in Maximum Likelihood Methods* (New York: McGraw-Hill Book Co., 1959).

7. T. Haavelmo, "The Statistical Implications of a System of Simultaneous Equations," *Econometrica*, 11 (1943), pp. 1–12.

8. See for example, T. C. Koopmans (ed.), *Statistical Inference in Dynamic Economic Models* (New York: John Wiley & Sons, 1950); and W. C. Hood and T. C. Koopmans (eds.), *Studies in Econometric Method* (New York: John Wiley & Sons, 1953).

9. H. Theil, *Estimation and Simultaneous Correlation in Complete Equation Systems* (The Hague: Central Plan Bureau, 1953).

10. R. L. Basmann, "A Generalized Classical Method of Linear Estimation of Coefficients in a Structural Equation," *Econometrica*, 25 (1957), pp. 77–84.

Two-stage least-squares estimation

First, assume the following system of equations with endogenous and exogenous variables and error terms.[11] (The meaning of the variables will be discussed in the next section.)

$$Y_1 = c_1 + a_{11}Y_2 + a_{12}Y_4 + b_{11}X_2 + b_{12}X_4 + b_{13}X_5 + e_1 \tag{1}$$

$$Y_2 = c_2 + a_{21}Y_1 + a_{22}Y_4 + b_{21}X_1 + b_{22}X_2 + b_{23}X_7 + e_2 \tag{2}$$

$$Y_3 = c_3 + a_{31}Y_1 + a_{32}Y_2 + b_{31}X_6 + e_3 \tag{3}$$

$$Y_4 = c_4 + a_{41}Y_3 + b_{41}X_1 - b_{42}X_3 + b_{43}X_4 + e_4 \tag{4}$$

This system is first transformed into reduced form equations:

$$Y_1 = c'_1 + z_{11}X_1 + z_{12}X_2 - z_{13}X_3 + z_{14}X_4 + z_{15}X_5 + z_{16}X_6 + z_{17}X_7 + v_1 \tag{5}$$

$$Y_2 = c'_2 + z_{21}X_1 + z_{22}X_2 - z_{23}X_3 + z_{24}X_4 + z_{25}X_5 + z_{26}X_6 + z_{27}X_7 + v_2 \tag{6}$$

$$Y_3 = c'_3 + z_{31}X_1 + z_{32}X_2 - z_{33}X_3 + z_{34}X_4 + z_{35}X_5 + z_{36}X_6 + z_{37}X_7 + v_3 \tag{7}$$

$$Y_4 = c'_4 + z_{41}X_1 + z_{42}X_2 - z_{43}X_3 + z_{44}X_4 + z_{45}X_5 + z_{46}X_6 + z_{47}X_7 + v_4 \tag{8}$$

where each endogenous variable (Y_i) is expressed as a function of all the exogenous variables $(X_1, \ldots, X_7)$. Since each equation contains only one endogenous variable, the coefficients in each of these equations can be estimated by ordinary least-squares regression.[12] This is the first stage of the two-stage least-squares procedure.

Having estimated the coefficients in the reduced-form equations, the next step is to obtain estimated values for the endogenous variables Y_1, Y_2, Y_3, and Y_4, using these coefficients and the observed values for the exogenous variables, $X_1, \ldots, X_7$. Using these new values of the endogenous variables, $\hat{Y}_1$, $\hat{Y}_2$, $\hat{Y}_3$, and $\hat{Y}_4$, and the same observed values of the exogenous variables on the right-hand side, one then estimates the coefficients in the original system (equations (1), (2), (3), and (4)) by ordinary least-squares regression. That is, each equation is estimated separately in the following set of equations:

$$Y_1 = c_1 + a_{11}\hat{Y}_2 + a_{12}\hat{Y}_4 + b_{11}X_2 + b_{12}X_4 + b_{13}X_5 + e_1 \tag{9}$$

$$Y_2 = c_2 + a_{21}\hat{Y}_1 + a_{22}\hat{Y}_4 + b_{21}X_1 + b_{22}X_2 + b_{23}X_7 + e_2 \tag{10}$$

$$Y_3 = c_3 + a_{31}\hat{Y}_1 + a_{32}\hat{Y}_2 + b_{31}X_6 + e_3 \tag{11}$$

$$Y_4 = c_4 + a_{41}\hat{Y}_3 + b_{41}X_1 - b_{42}X_3 + b_{43}X_4 + e_4 \tag{12}$$

11. Error terms can cover a multitude of sins. These include omission of possible variables or equations, imperfect specification of relationships, and errors of measurement. For application of the two-stage procedure it is assumed that error is due to omission of variables and not to errors of measurement. For a discussion of assumptions concerning the error term, see Valavanis, *op. cit.*, pp. 5–6, 9–18.

12. For a simple presentation of the two-stage least-squares procedure in matrix notation, see T. D. Wallace and G. G. Judge, *Discussion of the Theil-Basmann Method for Estimating Equations in a Simultaneous System* (Stillwater, Oklahoma: Agricultural Experiment Station, Processed Series P-301, 1958).

In order to distinguish these estimates from those obtained from the reduced-form equations—(5), (6), (7), and (8)—they will be indicated as $\widehat{\widehat{Y}}_1$, $\widehat{\widehat{Y}}_2$, $\widehat{\widehat{Y}}_3$, and $\widehat{\widehat{Y}}_4$, and referred to as structural equations elsewhere in this paper. The coefficients estimated by this procedure are still biased, but are consistent and more efficient than if ordinary least-squares had been applied. Significance of coefficients is usually tested by the usual methods, including Student's t. Reservations must be attached to interpretations of multiple correlation coefficients of the structural equations.[13]

Specification of the diffusion model

To illustrate the application of the two-stage technique a diffusion model is specified. The model is composed of both sociological and economic variables that have a bearing on the diffusion of technical innovations. The model is thus not only a vehicle for illustrating the estimation procedure, but also illustrates how a system of interdependent equations can be justified and tested. Once the coefficients in the model are estimated, the important task of interpretation and prediction can be undertaken.

When one begins to construct a model there usually are more explanatory or exogenous variables available than there are equations. The problem comes in selecting not only the variables to include in the interdependent system (endogenous variables) but also those that will serve as explanatory or predictor (exogenous) variables. The diffusion model was developed in part from already existing theory and in part from established empirical relationships.

As a starting point, the "accounting scheme" of Katz, Levin, and Hamilton[14] was employed. With their approach, a set of component elements was formulated as key variables in the diffusion process. Their process was characterized as (1) acceptance, (2) over time, (3) of some specific item—an idea or practice, (4) by an adopting unit—individual, group, etc., linked (5) to specific channels of communication, (6) to a social structure, and (7) to a given system of values or culture. As they point out, there is a growing interest in exploring the effects of social structures in which adopting units are linked. They also note that the field will be advanced if effects of other channels of communication, including the mass media, on these structures can be determined. We would like to add here that effects of economic variables—such as level of production—also can impinge on a social structure just as the adoption or acceptance of an innovation can have implications for production. It might prove fruitful to consider such an economic variable in the model under consideration.

---

13. R. L. Basmann, "Letter to the Editor," *Econometrica*, 30 (1962), pp. 824–826.
14. Elihu Katz, Martin L. Levin, and Herbert Hamilton, "Traditions of Research on the Diffusion of Innovation," *American Sociological Review*, 28 (April 1963), pp. 237–252.

SPECIFICATION OF ENDOGENOUS VARIABLES

The following variables will be considered: (1) adoption, (2) social structure, and (3) production.

1. *Adoption.* Considering the Katz *et al.*, scheme, it is stipulated at the outset that acceptance or the "sustained use" of an innovation, by individuals in a single-occupation category, represents the definition of the adoption variable. There is a considerable body of evidence, particularly in agricultural economics,[15] which suggests the hypothesis that when other attributes are taken into account, the relationship between adoption of agricultural innovations and production is positive. The adoption of innovations derived from research findings of the biological sciences also suggests a basis for increased production.[16]

2. *Social Structure.* Many diffusion researchers classify individuals in terms of social influence and prestige, and there are both conceptual and empirical bases for postulating that an individual's position in one hierarchy is related to his position in the other, but is not identical with it. Merton[17] states that an individual's position in a local interpersonal influence-structure may be related to his position in other hierarchies and, conversely, his position in the class, power, or prestige hierarchies contributes to the potential for interpersonal influence, but does not determine the extent to which it occurs. Influence is considered persuasive and is supported by the giving or withholding of attitudinal sanctions of approval or disapproval. Assuming that an individual has access to some channel of communication, he still must possess other attributes in order to exert influence. Research on persuasion effects has clearly established that the attributes of the apparent source of a message contribute to the effectiveness of the message. The messages of an individual with prestige, for example, tend to carry weight, and the possession of prestige can be conceived as a base for influence.[18] Prestige is the valuation of a

15. Theodore W. Schultz, *Transforming Traditional Agriculture* (New Haven: Yale University Press, 1964), pp. 110–144.

16. This is not to say that farmers are better off from an income standpoint when they adopt. Increased output, if the new technology is widely adopted, will depress prices by a greater percentage than the increase in production—assuming a free market, i.e., no outside force sets the price at a fixed level. Despite this, however, an individual farmer's failure to adopt an innovation will result in even lower income, since he acquires no production advantage and receives all the price disadvantages.

17. Robert K. Merton, "Patterns of Influence: Local and Cosmopolitan Influentials," in *Social Theory and Social Structure* (Glencoe, Illinois: The Free Press, 1957), pp. 387–420.

18. Empirical support for a positive relationship between influence and prestige variables has been reported by Lionberger and Coughenour, and by Rogers. See Herbert F. Lionberger and C. Milton Coughenour, *Social Structure and Diffusion of Farm Information* (Columbia, Missouri: Agricultural Experiment Station Research Bulletin 631, 1957); Herbert F. Lionberger, "Community Prestige and the Choices of Sources of Farm Information," *Public Opinion Quarterly*, 23 (1959), pp. 111–118; and Everett M. Rogers, *Diffusion of Innovations* (New York: The Free Press, 1962).

particular position that an individual occupies within a social system. Status refers to the ordinal position in a hierarchy of rankings. Thus, an interdependent relationship between an individual's influence and prestige is postulated —one serves as a basis for the occurrence of the other and vice versa.

But the effects of influence and prestige, while interdependent, also may be related to the adoption of innovations as well. That is, those high in influence or prestige tend to adopt innovations more than those low in these attributes, assuming community norms support innovation. Individuals with these attributes often possess the characteristics that contribute to innovation: viz., greater formal education; greater use of the channels of mass communication, particularly the printed word; more social contacts outside their communities; and higher incomes with commensurate styles of life.[19]

3. *Production.* Production is defined as an entrepreneurial function. Among individuals who exercise the entrepreneurial role are single-proprietorships, such as small retail firms and individual farmers. Thus, it is assumed that all decisions concerning production are centered in the individual, including decisions involving risk. Production is measured in terms of output, total product, or output per unit of some fixed input.

Control of economic resources has been emphasized as a basis of influence in society, as Cartwright[20] has recently pointed out in an excellent summary on the matter. In short, an individual gains the ability to exercise influence by occupying positions which control economic resources, and presumably, the production from these resources as well. Considering only individuals in a single-occupation category who perform an entrepreneurial function, it seems reasonable to expect that level of production will be positively associated with level of social influence. High-producing farmers, for example, living in a community in which production is commonly valued, should be expected to wield more influence among farmer-peers than low-producing farmers. The possession of control of valued resources (land, equipment, for example) is postulated to represent a basis for influence. Those individuals who manage these resources so that their efforts are visible and valued—such as high producers—should also be influential.

Moreover, from a functional point of view, production also may be a basis for prestige. Even when one is concerned with only individuals in a single-occupation category, the prestige of one position may be higher than that of another to the extent that the individual occupying the position has been

19. Again, Lionberger and Rogers have offered empirical support concerning the positive relationship between influence, prestige, and adoption variables. See Lionberger and Coughenour, *op. cit.*, and Rogers, *op. cit.*, pp. 289–292.

20. Dorwin Cartwright, "Influence, Leadership, Control," in James C. Marsh (ed.), *Handbook of Organizations* (Chicago: Rand McNally & Co., 1965), pp. 1–47.

perceived by others as having made a larger contribution to the function, i.e., production in this case.[21]

This concludes the specification of endogenous variables in the interdependent system. The empirical relationships expected to be found among these variables are summarized as follows:

$$Y_1 = f(Y_2, Y_4), \tag{13}$$

$$Y_2 = g(Y_1, Y_4), \tag{14}$$

$$Y_3 = h(Y_1, Y_2), \tag{15}$$

$$Y_4 = l(Y_3). \tag{16}$$

where Y_1 is an individual's social-influence score,

Y_2 is an individual's prestige score,

Y_3 is an individual's innovation-adoption score,

Y_4 is an individual's level of production.

SPECIFICATION OF EXOGENOUS VARIABLES

Explanatory or exogenous (predictor) variables are assumed to be outside the interdependent system. They represent crucial operational requirements for analyzing the system empirically, as has already been noted. Furthermore, the specification of these variables and their relationship to endogenous variables can, in itself, represent derivations from existing theory, or, in the absence of such theory, from known empirical associations. The set of predictors for each endogenous variable will be discussed in the order that these variables were presented in the previous section.

1. *Adoption.* The adoption of innovations by individuals requires information or knowledge about these innovations. This information may come from many sources, but the effects of one type of source have been clearly established as providing a link between the use of this source of information and the adoption of the innovations it is promoting. This source, which Rogers[22] calls a "change agent," is a professional who attempts to influence adoption decisions in the direction he feels is desirable. In education they

---

21. Mason and Gross, who tested a functional education-prestige hypothesis among Massachusetts school superintendents, did not find empirical support and concluded that a highly visible variable, salary, is a more important determinant of prestige. However, if level of production is highly visible, the functional hypothesis should receive empirical support. See Ward S. Mason and Neal Gross, "Intra-occupational Prestige Differentiation: The School Superintendency," *American Sociological Review*, 20 (June 1955), pp. 326–331.

22. Rogers, *op. cit.*, p. 254.

may be school counselors; in medicine or health fields, they are physicians or public health workers; in agriculture, they are county agents or commercial field men.[23]

2. *Social Structure.* Three variables are postulated as predictors of social influences. One, as suggested in the discussion on production, is the control of economic resources necessary for production, such as land, machinery, etc. In other words, those who exercise such control gain the ability to exercise social influence. A second variable is the utilization of the mass media—particularly the mass media commensurate with the individual's area of influence such as public affairs, health, etc. The development of the "two-step" hypothesis which states that "ideas often flow from radio and print to opinion leaders and from these to less active sections of the population" has a bearing here.[24] Assuming that the terms "influential" and "opinion leader" represent identical attributes, one would predict that influentials expose themselves more to pertinent forms of mass media than those less influential.

The third variable is level of education. Education effects are assumed to provide a person with greater knowledge and skills. The knowledge acquired, of whatever quality, can only expand a person's total world of reality. Each increment of schooling adds to the individual's competence through the acquisition of knowledge and incidental skills. Moreover, the advancement into college or university training is taken to reflect the potential of better performance compared to those who are screened from higher education. This acquisition of competence through formal training is postulated as a contributor to social influence and one would predict a positive relationship between level of education and level of influence.[25]

Three variables are postulated as predictors of an individual's prestige. One of these is, again, level of education. Education effects are pervasive and may be positively related to prestige. Formal recognition of the acquisition of knowledge and skills has consequences that may have a greater effect than the learning of content only. Each additional diploma or degree leads to an inculcation of the appropriate ideology or pattern of tastes, attitudes,

23. Whatever the profession, there is considerable empirical support, as Rogers has summarized, to suggest that the use made of the information provided by these professionals is positively associated with the adoption of innovations they are promoting. See Rogers, *op. cit.*, pp. 254–267.

24. See for example, Paul Lazarsfeld, Bernard Berelson, and Hazel Gaudet, *The People's Choice* (New York: Columbia University Press, 1944); Elihu Katz and Paul Lazarsfeld, *Personal Influence* (Glencoe, Illinois: The Free Press, 1955); Herbert Menzel and Elihu Katz, "Social Relations and Innovation in the Medical Profession: The Epidemiology of a New Drug," *Public Opinion Quarterly*, 19 (1955), pp. 337–352; and Elihu Katz, "The Two-Step Flow of Communication: An Up-to-Date Report on an Hypothesis," *Public Opinion Quarterly*, 21 (1957), pp. 61–78.

25. Katz has summarized empirical support for such a relationship. Katz, *loc. cit.*, p. 74.

and values, as Sanford[26] has noted. Such skills provide the basis for appropriate behaviors associated with a status position. It is assumed that each position carries with it a set of appropriate learned behaviors. Given this, level of education is postulated as one mechanism for the learning of these behaviors, particularly for those of higher status.

Utilization of the mass media is a second variable that provides a basis for prestige. As Lazarsfeld and Merton[27] have pointed out, one function of the mass media is to confer recognition on people which in turn may affect their status. The social standing of a person is enhanced when he commands favorable attention in the mass media. Such recognition testifies that he has "arrived," that he is important enough to be singled out from the mass for public notice. This publicity does not go unnoticed among those who are in positions of high status, and these individuals monitor the appropriate mass media for the cues of status conferral upon themselves, their peers, and others.

A final base for prestige is type of residence. The type of dwelling, according to Barber,[28] is a likely symbol for social class position in all societies. This is because the home is the place where many important consumption, socialization, educational or social activities are conducted, i.e., where one is more likely to associate intimately and equally with one's peers. Since it is assumed that a status position carries with it a set of appropriate, learned behaviors, the house where these behaviors occur—its style, size, and surroundings—may indicate the status of the owner as well.

3. *Production.* Three exogenous variables are hypothesized as predictors of production. One of these is type of residence. Assuming that production is a primary source for income and wealth, high-producing individuals are likely to afford the type of residence commensurate with their economic position. Another base for production, as noted earlier, is the control of resources. The control of land, for example, is positively associated with production, according to a recent agricultural census.[29] Moreover, age of the operator has been repeatedly shown to be negatively associated with production by the same source. Thus, the three exogenous variables in the production equation are type of residence, control of land, and age of operator.

26. Nevitt Sanford (ed.), *The American College* (New York: John Wiley & Sons, 1962), p. 34.

27. Paul F. Lazarsfeld and Robert K. Merton, "Mass Communication, Popular Taste and Organized Social Action," in Lyman Bryson (ed.), *The Communication of Ideas* (New York: Harper & Bros., 1948), pp. 95–118.

28. Bernard Barber, *Social Stratification* (New York: Harcourt, Brace & Co., 1957), pp. 144–146.

29. U.S. Bureau of the Census, *U.S. Census of Agriculture: Oregon* (Washington, D. C.: Government Printing Office, 1964), Vol. I, Part 47. See also G. B. Davis and D. Curtis Mumford, *Farm Organization and Financial Progress in the Willamette Valley* (Corvallis, Oregon: Agricultural Experiment Station Bulletin 444, 1947), pp. 52–54.

Combined with the relationships postulated among the endogenous variables, the complete system can be described by the following relations:

$$Y_1 = f(Y_2, Y_4; X_2, X_4, X_5), \tag{17}$$

$$Y_2 = g(Y_1, Y_4; X_1, X_2, X_7), \tag{18}$$

$$Y_3 = h(Y_1, Y_2; X_6), \tag{19}$$

$$Y_4 = l(Y_3; X_1, X_3, X_4). \tag{20}$$

where Y_1 to Y_4 refer to variables in relations (13) to (16), and

X_1 is an individual's type of residence,

X_2 is an individual's educational level,

X_3 is an individual's age,

X_4 is an individual's level of control over production resources,

X_5 is an individual's level of exposure to mass media appropriate for the exercise of influence,

X_6 is an individual's level of use of technological information sources, and

X_7 is an individual's level of exposure to mass media appropriate for recognition.

Using the counting rule described earlier, all equations in the system postulated are overidentified. The next step is to secure the appropriate operational measures for these variables and to obtain sufficient data to test the model empirically.[30]

Operational measures and sources of data

An agricultural setting afforded an opportunity to empirically test the hypothesized system. Such a setting contains (1) individuals, (2) in a social structure, (3) who adopt innovations that conceivably lead to (4) increased production. The agricultural setting in this case was among full-time farmers in an Oregon community in which virtually all raised ryegrass seed as their primary source of income.

A personal interview survey and examination of records available at the county assessor's and other governmental offices were the principal means of securing data. With the survey, each respondent was interviewed twice. The first interview provided data for identifying full-time farmers, measuring

30. As used here, "test" refers to the procedure by which variables in the equations meet some predetermined level of statistical significance and in which the signs of the coefficients are compared to those hypothesized. Furthermore, to accept a model subsequent to a test, a necessary condition is that any variable excluded for reasons of lack of significance or incorrect sign must result in an identified system of equations.

interpersonal influence, media exposure, and demographic characteristics. The second interview provided data on sources of information used. A total of 195 schedules was completed for the first interview, 154 for the second—a 79 percent completion rate. The operational measures employed are described in the order in which the variables were presented earlier. Measurement of endogenous variables will be discussed first, then measurement of exogenous variables.

MEASUREMENT OF ENDOGENOUS VARIABLES

Adoption. The agricultural area selected suffered from soil drainage and fertility problems and innovations were selected that, in part, enabled a farmer to cope with these problems. Moreover, the innovations selected required the involvement of some governmental agency and unequivocal adoption data were available from these agencies. The innovations were: use of a soil test, installation of tile drainage, completion of land leveling, and joining a community drainage project. Adoption data were subjected to a scalogram analysis and items met the minimum requirements for a scale.[31] Scale scores represented a measure of the adoption variable.

Social Structure. Two variables are involved as aspects of the community social structure—social influence and prestige. Three methods were employed to develop items to measure social influence: (1) sociometric choice, (2) self-detection, and (3) rating by a judge.[32]

Scores from each type of measure were subjected to a scalogram analysis.[33] Nondichotomized scale scores were employed as the measure of social influence.

The prestige rating technique described by Ellis[34] was employed, in part, to develop an operational measure of prestige. This required procedures for

31. Coefficient of Reproducibility, *.95*; Coefficient of Scalability (items), *.71*; Coefficient of Scalability (individuals), *.60.*

32. The sociometric item employed was, "May I ask the name of three or four people in this community whom you consider to be your best friends?" A modification of the items developed by Berelson *et al.* was used as a method for self-detection of influence. (See Bernard R. Berelson, Paul F. Lazarsfeld, and William N. McPhee, *Voting, A Study of Opinion Formation in a Presidential Campaign* [Chicago: University of Chicago Press, 1954], pp. 109–115.) Two types of items were employed: one set covering farming matters, the other covering activities in the political realm. Scores were summed for each set and each sum represented an item for subsequent development of the influence measure. The local county extension agent, who had known the respondents for more than 15 years, ranked each according to a definition of influence: the relative ability of a respondent to affect, through persuasion, the opinions or behavior of other farmers in the study area.

33. Coefficient of Reproducibility, *.94*; Coefficient of Scalability (items), *.82*; Coefficient of Scalability (individuals), *.78*; Spearman-Brown split-half (odd-even) reliability coefficient, *.84.*

34. Robert A. Ellis, "The Prestige-Rating Technique in Community Stratification Research," in R. N. Adams and J. J. Preiss (eds.), *Human Organization Research* (Homewood, Illinois: Dorsey Press, 1960), pp. 324–337.

(1) selecting ratees and raters,[35] (2) the rating technique,[36] and (3) combining rating scores into a prestige measure.[37]

Production. Total pounds of cleaned rye-grass seed produced by each individual was the measure of production employed. These data were obtained from the Oregon Department of Agriculture, which had gathered the information from warehouse receipts for the production year the personal interview survey was completed. The Department was conducting a referendum among grass seed growers concerning the establishment of a growers' commission which required production information.

MEASUREMENT OF EXOGENOUS VARIABLES

Adoption. One exogenous variable was postulated as a predictor for adoption of innovations. This variable was the level of use of technical information sources. Two such sources were available for three of the innovations promoted in the area (soil test, land leveling, tile drainage). These were the county extension agent and soil scientists at Oregon State University. In addition, a third source was available for the innovation of joining a community drainage project, the local Soil Conservation Service technician.

35. All individuals—heads of households—sampled in the study area (195 in total) were selected as ratees. Eight raters were selected that had the following characteristics in common: (a) were beyond the age of adolescence but not senile; (b) possessed the characteristic cultural values of the community; (c) had been long-time residents of the area; (d) occupied strategic positions in the community that afforded each a wide range of interaction with other residents; and (e) were willing to cooperate.

36. Names of ratees were typed on eight sets of cards and the cards in each set randomized, one set for each rater. The interviewer first placed seven blank sheets of white paper side by side before each rater in separate and independent judging sessions. Cards on which the words "High Social Standing in the Community" or "Low Social Standing in the Community" were printed served as verbal stimuli that anchored each end of the 7-point scale. The rater was instructed to judge each individual according to his social standing in the community. The cards with each ratee's name were given to the rater, one at a time, and he placed the card face down on one of the seven sheets of white paper. If a rater was unable to make a rating, the interviewer put down an "unable to rate" card and instructed the rater to place the ratee's card face down on this new card. After judging had been completed, the interviewer asked the rater to divide the "unable to rate" deck on the basis of difficulty to rate or lack of knowledge about the ratee. In all cases, the raters said they were unable to rate because they didn't know the ratee. Following the judging session each rater was asked, through a series of standardized open-ended items, to describe the criteria employed for his rating.

37. Cards from each of the several piles for each rater were scored from one to seven, with those in the extreme positive category receiving a score of "7". Scores were arranged in a rater by ratee matrix, converted to standard scores so that scores across raters were comparable. Scores for each ratee were summed and averaged. This score represented the prestige value for each ratee. Where a rater had been unable to rate, a dummy score, the ratee's average, was used. Analysis of variance of the standard scores in the rater by ratee matrix was completed as a preliminary step for estimating the reliability of the prestige measure, following the procedure McNemar has described. (Quinn McNemar, *Psychological Statistics* [New York: John Wiley & Sons, 1962], pp. 296–301.) The reliability estimate, $1 - 1/F$, equaled 0.76 in this study. One degree of freedom was subtracted from the error term for each dummy value employed in the rater by ratee matrix.

This source was added to the other two (county agent, State College scientist) for this practice. Each item contained a source, an innovation, and a set of response alternatives and had the same basic construction.[38] Response scores were summed across all nine items to form a technical information use measure.

Social Structure. Three exogenous variables were postulated as predictors of social influence; three of prestige as well. For social influence, these variables were the control of economic resources necessary for production, use of certain forms of the mass media, and level of education.

Control of land, necessary for production, was selected as the measure of resource control. For this study, the number of cropland acres owned per individual, available from the local tax assessor, was the operational measure employed for control of land.[39]

An agricultural setting suggests that mass media exposure appropriate to that sphere provides an adequate subject matter for examining the mass media information-seeking behavior of influentials in the study area. New ideas about farming, for example, come from magazines, and respondents could subscribe to at least four national and regional magazines in this field. The number of subscriptions to these magazines by each individual was employed as the measure of mass media exposure.

Level of education was measured by the response to a single item employed in the personal interview survey.

Two exogenous variables, in addition to level of education, were postulated as predictors of prestige. These were type of residence and exposure to mass media appropriate for recognition.

All respondents resided in single-family dwelling units. This provided a comparable base that would not be found in an urban setting, i.e., an admixture of single- and multiple-family dwelling units, and permitted the use of the market value of the house as a measure of type of residence for the purpose of this study. Such market value data were obtained from the county tax assessor.[40]

38. For example, "How much have you talked to someone at State College about a community drainage project—a lot, quite a bit, a little, or not at all?" Ascending or descending order of responses was determined randomly.

39. The selection of cropland ownership is straightforward. The grass seed industry in Oregon mechanized rapidly following World War II. With mechanization came the demand for more land, commensurate for the operation of an economic farm unit. The pattern of part ownership soon developed in the study area in which some individuals who already owned a block of land rented rather than purchased additional property. Those unable to mechanize and therefore unable to function as an economic farm unit, found it to their advantage to rent and to derive income from rent and from off-farm employment. Thus, a highly positive relationship has developed between ownership and renting. Because of this high association, ownership of cropland in the area is considered a valid measue of control of land.

40. Oregon law requires that county assessors must employ as appraisers only certified professionals who have passed appropriate state civil service commission examinations. These appraisers, in the judgment of professionals on the faculty of Oregon State University, can be expected to estimate the market value of a house within five percent of its true cash value.

Weekly newspapers provided the mass media channel appropriate for recognition in the study area. Four such newspapers, with widely overlapping circulations, were available and the number of subscriptions to these newspapers, by respondents, was the operational measure of mass media exposure for recognition purposes.

Production. One exogenous variable, in addition to two already described (control of resources and type of residence) was postulated as a predictor of production. This was the individual's age, and was measured by response to a single item employed in the personal interview survey.

PRELIMINARY ANALYSIS

Scatter diagrams were plotted between each exogenous and endogenous variable prior to the analysis by two-stage least-squares. The purpose of such diagrams was to ascertain visually the order of polynomial of fitting the data. From this inspection, all reduced-form equations were first written to include both the linear and quadratic forms of each exogenous variable. The quadratic term was significant and was utilized in the reduced-form and the structural equations for three of these variables. These were level of education, age, and mass media exposure for recognition. All other variables were linear.

Results and discussion

Multiple correlation coefficients and zero-order correlation coefficients between each endogenous and exogenous variable are given in Table 12.1.

Table 12.1. Multiple correlation coefficients and zero-order correlations between each exogenous and each endogenous variable*

Exogenous variables	Endogenous variables			
	Social influence (Y_1)	Prestige (Y_2)	Innovation adoption (Y_3)	Production (Y_4)
Market value of house (X_1)	.389	.196	.223	.341
Education (X_2)	.470	.364	.333	.185
Age (X_3)	−.238	−.181	−.165	−.223
Number cropland acres owned (X_4)	.188	.021	.277	.649
Number farm magazine subscriptions (X_5)	.188	.073	.183	.112
Use of technical information sources (X_6)	.455	.319	.482	.367
Number weekly newspaper subscriptions (X_7)	.128	.239	.108	.039
Multiple correlation coefficient................	.611	.463	.541	.719

* $p_{.05} = .159$; $p_{.01} = .208$

One can note that the correlations between the exogenous and endogenous variables are as hypothesized in relations (17), (18), (19), and (20). For example, Level of Education (X_2), Ownership of Cropland (X_4), and Number of Farm Magazine Subscriptions (X_5) are all significantly related to Social Influence (Y_1) Some exogenous variables, however, are significantly related to endogenous variables other than the ones predicted. As an example, Use of Technical Information Sources (X_6) is significantly related to the other endogenous variables (Y_1, Y_2, Y_4) as well as to the predicted variable, Innovation Adoption (Y_3). These correlations should not be misinterpreted, since the test of the model is made on its structural form and not on its reduced form.[41] The structural form of the model is shown in equations (21), (22), (23), and (24) with the estimated coefficients as given by the two-stage technique. (Numbers under the coefficients are Student's t values: (*) denotes $.05 < p < .10$; (**) $.01 < p < .05$; and (***) $p < .01$, one-tailed test.)

$$\hat{Y}_1 = -4.239 + (.315)\hat{Y}_2 + (.514 \times 10^{-5})\hat{Y}_4 + (.063)X_2 -$$
$$\qquad (2.803)^{***}(1.894)^{**} \qquad\quad (1.376)^{*}$$
$$\qquad\qquad\qquad (.950 \times 10^{-3})X_4 + (.409)X_5 \quad (21)$$
$$\qquad\qquad\qquad (-.712) \qquad\quad (1.478)^{*}$$

$$\hat{Y}_2 = 31.423 + (1.558)\hat{Y}_1 - (.321 \times 10^{-5})\hat{Y}_4 - (.877 \times 10^{-4})X_1 +$$
$$\qquad (2.568)^{***} \ (-.867) \qquad\qquad (-.584)$$
$$\qquad\qquad\qquad (.060)X_2 + (.467)X_7 \quad (22)$$
$$\qquad\qquad\qquad (.487) \qquad\ (2.037)^{**}$$

$$\hat{Y}_3 = -.588 + (.185)\hat{Y}_1 - (.023)\hat{Y}_2 + (.047)X_6 \qquad\qquad (23)$$
$$\qquad (2.63)^{***} \ (-.596) \quad (2.423)^{***}$$

$$\hat{Y}_4 = 103705.400 + (92887.630)\hat{Y}_3 + (5.696)X_1 -$$
$$\qquad (2.431)^{***} \qquad\quad (1.739)^{**}$$
$$\qquad\qquad\qquad (1714.761)X_3 + (371.178)X_4 \quad (24)$$
$$\qquad\qquad\qquad (-2.748)^{***} \quad (7.910)^{***}$$

The postulated and empirically supported relationships of the model are shown in Figure 12.1.

In equation (21), Prestige $(\hat{Y}_2)$, Production $(\hat{Y}_4)$, Level of Education (X_2), and Number of Farm Magazine Subscriptions (X_5) are all significantly related to Social Influence $(\hat{Y}_1)$.[42] Number of Cropland Acres Owned (X_4)

41. Certain coefficients are assumed to be zero in the structural form of the model, which implies that exogenous variables with zero coefficients are hypothesized to have no influence on the endogenous variables.

42. It should be noted that X_2, X_3, and X_7 represent the square of the measure of level of education, age, and number of weekly newspaper subscriptions respectively.

is not related, suggesting that the basis for influence in this case is production, not control of resources. Such control is an important predictor of production (equation (24)), which in turn is a significant predictor of influence. Furthermore, the hypothesis concerning exposure to mass media by influentials is supported, as are the hypotheses about prestige and education effects.

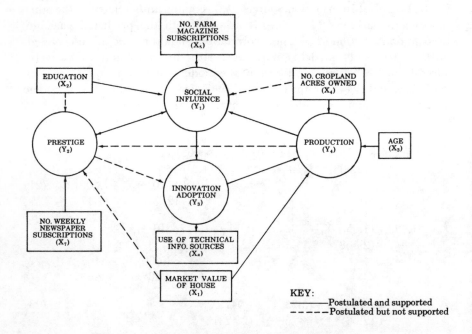

Figure 12.1. *Diagram of the innovation diffusion model.*

In equation (22) both Social Influence $(\hat{Y}_1)$ and Number of Weekly Newspaper Subscriptions (X_7) are significantly related to Prestige $(\hat{Y}_2)$, while Production $(\hat{Y}_4)$, Market Value of the House (X_1), and Level of Education (X_2) are not. Level of education does not have a direct effect on prestige, although education is a predictor of influence and influence is, in turn, a predictor of prestige. The same may be said for production effects. This cannot be said, however, for the variable of market value of the house. While this exogenous variable is a predictor of production (see equation (24)), production is not significantly related to prestige. An examination of responses to the open-ended questions given by the raters concerning the criteria they employed in judging the social standing of respondents revealed that none dealt with level of agricultural production or type of residence in any way.[43] Assuming that the pursuit of high production levels rquires considerable outlays of scarce resources, such as the individual's time and money, an alternative hypothesis is suggested that those high in production may not necessarily be high in prestige, i.e., that production is not a basis for prestige. Moreover, while type of residence may be a predictor of production (for reasons cited earlier), it would not necessarily predict prestige when house type is measured solely in terms of market value. There appears to be nothing in the notion of prestige as operationalized by the raters (the quality of interpersonal relations) which suggests that a relationship to market value of a house would be found.[44] Exposure to mass media appropriate for recognition as a basis for prestige is straightforward and is supported by the data. Similarly, the interdependence between influence and prestige is straightforward and is supported empirically, too.

In equation (23) Social Influence $(\hat{Y}_1)$ and Use of Technical Information Sources (X_6) are related to Innovation Adoption $(\hat{Y}_3)$ while Prestige $(\hat{Y}_2)$ is not. Prestige may be construed not to have a direct effect on innovation adoption. It serves, however, as a base for influence which in turn is related to adoption.

In equation (24) Innovation Adoption $(\hat{Y}_3)$, Market Value of the House (X_1), Age (X_3), and Number of Cropland Acres Owned (X_4) are all significantly related to Production $(\hat{Y}_4)$ in the predicted direction.

On the basis of the t values one could reformulate the model by excluding the variables with low t values. The equations in that case would still be overidentified. However, to make the most meaningful test of the new model would require acquisition of a new set of data.

SOME IMPLICATIONS OF THE MODEL

An established proposition concerning the behavior of influentials is that they are more likely than those less influential to expose themselves to mass communications, especially to those channels and messages likely to deal with topics in their sphere or spheres of influence. As well, this selective exposure contributes to the fulfillment of the influential role. While the findings of this study do not contradict this proposition, they do suggest that the information influentials seek is used for more than the enhancement of their opinion

---

43. Rather, respondents were judged on the perceived quality of their interpersonal relations with others in the community. Attributes such as "willingness to work with others for the betterment of the community," "generous with their time and money," "honesty and integrity in their dealings with neighbors," "ability to cooperate with others," and "active in civic affairs," were cited.

44. Type of residence, however, may be a basis for influence. The variable of Market Value of the House (X_1) correlated highest with influence, and, when added to equation (21), was significant at the *.07* level ($t = 1.875$), two-tailed test. Significance levels of other terms in the equation ($\hat{Y}_2$, $\hat{Y}_4$, X_2, X_4, and X_5) were not increased.

leadership role. Influentials in this study, compared to those less influential, adopt significant innovations which contribute, in turn, to increased production. Decisions leading to the adoption of innovations may require considerable information from many sources, including the mass media. While influentials may (or may not) pass on information to those who are less influential, there is considerable evidence which suggests that this information is used for the pursuit of purely economic goals. Thus, influentials appear to play a key role in the agricultural production process, a role distinct—but not independent—from their prestige and other attributes of social position. The fact that they are more productive, compared to those less influential, enhances their influence position and undoubtedly has implications for their capital position as well.

The importance of the influential can be noted when the model is used to predict the consequences of changing the level of a variable. For example, if an increase in agricultural production is a desired goal, how does one go about increasing production in an area comparable to one in which this study was conducted? That is, which variables must be manipulated? An examination of the important variables in equation (24) suggests that individuals who adopt innovations and who also control resources are likely to be high producers. Those who adopt innovations, according to equation (23), are influentials who utilize technological sources of information. And influentials (equation (21)) are those who are well educated, who expose themselves to relevant mass media channels, and who are prestigious in their community. A starting point for increasing production would appear to be knowledge of the influentials.

Conclusions

The purpose of this study was to describe the logic of, and to utilize, the Theil-Basmann two-stage estimation procedure for systems of simultaneous equations. Using behavioral data, the methodology appears to have promise for explaining or accounting for the effects of interdependent systems involving sociological and economic variables.

Specifically, variables relating to the diffusion of technical innovations were found to represent an interdependent system—a system in which the relationships among endogenous variables were examined and the effects of a set of exogenous variables were tested. The methodology is recommended for analysis of other kinds of interdependent systems in behavioral areas which heretofore have yielded less with less powerful techniques.

Chapter 13

PEER INFLUENCES ON ASPIRATIONS:
A REINTERPRETATION

Otis Dudley Duncan
University of Michigan
Archibald O. Haller
University of Wisconsin
Alejandro Portes[1]
University of Wisconsin

The hypothesis that interaction with peers influences levels of educational and occupational aspirations of adolescents, enunciated by Haller and Butterworth in 1960,[2] has proved to be an intriguing one, to judge by the attention given it subsequently. Without mentioning the several studies of "school climates," wherein the hypothesis is more or less assumed to be correct in order to interpret ostensible "school effects," we may refer to studies specifically directed to tests of the hypothesis itself or one of several closely related hypotheses which have also been subjected to scrutiny.[3]

To summarize our present knowledge: (1) The supposition that homophily with respect to socioeconomic characteristics is generated by socioeconomic segregation of school populations was considered by Rhodes,

Reprinted by permission of the authors and publisher from the *American Journal of Sociology*, Vol. 74, pp. 119–137, and Vol. 75, pp. 1042–1046. Copyright 1968 and 1970, The University of Chicago Press.

1. This is a report from Project 5-0074 (EO-191), "Socioeconomic Background and Occupational Achievement: Extensions of a Basic Model," carried out under Contract OE-5-85-072 with the U.S. Office of Education. The assistance in computation of Ruthe C. Sweet is gratefully acknowledged.

2. A. O. Haller and C. E. Butterworth, "Peer Influences on Levels of Occupational and Educational Aspiration," *Social Forces*, XXXVIII (May, 1960), 289–295.
3. C. Norman Alexander, Jr., and Ernest Q. Campbell, "Peer Influences on Adolescent Educational Aspirations and Attainments," *American Sociological Review*, XXIX (August, 1964), 568–575; Ernest Q. Campbell and C. Norman Alexander, "'Structural Effects and Interpersonal Relationships," *American Journal of Sociology*, LXXI (November, 1965), 284–289; M. Richard Cramer, "The Relationship between Educational and Occupational Plans of High School Students" (presented at the 1967 meeting of the Southern Sociological Society).

Reiss, and Duncan,[4] who were able to show that a minor part of the observed homophily is due to school segregation, the greater part to assortative choices of friends within schools. (2) In their study, Haller and Butterworth were concerned to eliminate socioeconomic homophily as a complete explanation of similarity in aspirations of friends. Hence, they considered peer-pairs whose members were alike in social class background and with respect to level of parental aspiration for their sons, as well as in measured intelligence. They showed that a positive intraclass correlation of close friends' aspirations held within such homogeneous pairs. (3) Invoking balance theory, Alexander and Campbell observed that agreement between friends' plans and desires to attend college was greater when the friendship choice was reciprocated than when it was not.[5] (4) In a second analysis, the same writers showed that "structural effects" of school socioeconomic composition were mediated by individual status effects, in that the former disappeared when the latter were taken into account: "Given knowledge of an individual's immediate interpersonal influences, the characteristics of the total collectivity provide no additional contribution to the prediction of his [college plans]."[6] (5) While Cramer notes an appreciable frequency of extreme incongruity between educational plans and occupational aspirations, the correlation between the two variables is relatively high, and too high to be explained fully by the operation of background factors as common causes.[7]

That "structural effects" are no large part of the explanation of similarity in friends' aspirations is easily demonstrated by an even more straightforward method than that used by Campbell and Alexander. For illustration, consider the correlation of .4986 between educational plans and friend's plans obtained by William H. Sewell (unpublished) for an all-Wisconsin sample of 4,386 boys who were high school seniors in 1957. Sewell found a correlation of .3364 between respondent's plans and the percentage of students in his class planning to go to college and similarly a correlation of .3327 between friend's plans and percentage going. (This is formally the same as the correlation ratio of individual plans on school.) Hence, if "structural effects" explained the correlation between friends, the latter would have been (.3364) (.3327) = .1119, which falls short of the observed correlation by .3867. Stated otherwise, the average within-school correlation between plans and friend's plans was .4354 (closely comparable to figures cited below for boys in a single school district).

4. Albert Lewis Rhodes, Albert J. Reiss, Jr., and Otis Dudley Duncan, "Occupational Segregation in a Metropolitan School System," *American Journal of Sociology*, LXX (May, 1965), 682–694, and LXXI (July, 1965), 131.
5. Alexander and Campbell, *op. cit.*
6. Campbell and Alexander, *op. cit.*, p. 288.
7. Cramer, *op. cit.*

The evidence is clear, therefore, that neither status homophily nor similarity in aspirations of friends is close to being adequately explained by school "structural effects" or school segregation. Yet the latter factors are important enough that they must be taken into account in estimating the impact of peer interaction on the formation of aspirations. By limiting the inquiry to a single school (or, alternatively, by looking at average within-school relationships), one can eliminate these factors from the analysis.

There remains the question of how to estimate the magnitude of peer influence, a problem not tackled directly in the studies cited, where the authors were content to stop with the detection of significant relationships indicating that a non-spurious correlation between aspirations (or plans) and friend's aspirations actually exists. The estimation (as distinct from detection) of such effects appears to be a particular instance of a generic problem for which explicit explanatory models have not yet been proposed. The purpose of this report is to suggest the possibilities in one kind of model. The purpose is realized with a presentation of some possible reinterpretations of the data originally collected and analyzed by Haller and Butterworth in the paper already cited.

Data

The original sample consisted of all seventeen-year-old boys in school in Lenawee County (Michigan) during the spring of 1957, interviews and test data being secured for 442 persons. For 329 of these boys, data were included in the same sample for at least one person listed as a best friend. Whether the friendship was reciprocated is not considered in this analysis. Some of the friends are, of course, included among the 329 respondents identified by this procedure, but others are not. It is important to note that the data on social and psychological characteristics as well as aspirations were obtained directly from the friend and not via the respondent's report on his friend.

The five variables to be considered are briefly enumerated (for lengthier descriptions, see the original publication):[8] *Level of occupational aspiration* is the score on Haller and Miller's Occupational Aspiration Scale. *Level of educational aspiration* is a composite score based on several questions about the number of years of college or university training the respondent planned to complete. *Socioeconomic status (SES)* is measured by Sewell's socioeconomic status scale, which includes items of parental educational attainment as well as material possessions in the home. *Intelligence* refers to raw scores on Cattell's Test of G Culture Free. *Parental aspirations* are indexed by a composite score

8. See also Archibald O. Haller and Irwin W. Miller, *The Occupational Aspiration Scale: Theory, Structure and Correlates* (Technical Bulletin 288 [East Lansing: Agricultural Experiment Station, Michigan State University, 1963]).

from the answers to questions asked about the degree to which parents "encouraged" the respondent to have high levels of achievement. The distribution of each of these variables was normalized as a preliminary step to all further calculations.

The intercorrelations of these variables are presented in Table 13.1. For comparison, the same table includes the correlations derived from the complete data on all 442 boys. It appears that the correlations either for friends or for respondents are fairly representative of those obtaining within the whole population.

Models

It is easy to demonstrate that neither socioeconomic homophily nor friendship assortment by intelligence, nor the combination of the two, suffices to account for the correlation between respondent's and friend's aspirations. For example, the correlation between the two occupational aspirations is given in Table 13.1 as .42. In a multiple regression of respondent's occupational aspiration on friend's occupational aspiration, with the intelligence, parental aspiration, and SES of both boys included as additional independent variables, the standardized net regression coefficient (β coefficient) is a highly significant .26. If the regression is turned around, with friend's aspiration as the dependent variable and respondent's aspiration as one of the seven independent variables, its coefficient is .24.

While these results demonstrate that there is a net relationship between

Table 13.1. Observed correlations for 329 respondents and their best friends (above diagonal), and "synthetic" correlations, including observed correlations for 442 respondents (below diagonal)

Variable	Symbol	X_a	X_b	X_c	Y_1	Y_2	X_d	X_e	X_f	Y_3	Y_4
Respondent:											
Intelligence	X_a	....	.1839	.2220	.4105	.4043	.3355	.1021	.1861	.2598	.2903
Parental aspiration	X_b	.16*	....	.0489	.2137	.2742	.0782	.1147	.0186	.0839	.1124
Family SES	X_c	.23*	.09*	....	.3240	.4047	.2302	.0931	.2707	.2786	.3054
Occupational aspiration	Y_1	.45*	.22*	.37*	....	.6247	.2995	.0760	.2930	.4216	.3269
Educational aspiration ..	Y_2	.41*	.29*	.41*	.64*	....	.2863	.0702	.2407	.3275	.3669
Best friend:											
Intelligence	X_d	.34	.09	.21	.28	.29	....	.2087	.2950	.5007	.5191
Parental aspiration	X_e	.09	.11	.06	.08	.09	.16*	....	—.0438	.1988	.2784
Family SES	X_f	.21	.06	.27	.29	.27	.23*	.09*	....	.3607	.4105
Occupational aspiration	Y_3	.28	.08	.29	.42	.33	.45*	.22*	.37*	....	.6404
Educational aspiration.	Y_4	.29	.09	.27	.33	.37	.41*	.29*	.41*	.64*	....

* Observed correlations for 442 respondents; remaining correlations below diagonal are obtained by averaging correlations above diagonal, as explained in the text.

respondent's and friend's aspirations with homophily taken into account, the method by which these regression coefficients are estimated is not acceptable if we postulate both a causal influence of friend's on respondent's aspiration and vice versa. If friend's aspiration influences respondent's, it is illogical to use a model in which the latter is an explanatory variable in accounting for the former without reckoning with the reciprocal influence of the former upon the latter. Given that only one observation is made upon each aspiration, presumably at a stage when both have become relatively crystallized, we must think of the two dependent variables as being simultaneously determined, each being influenced by the other as well as by the remaining variables in the model.

Some exposition of simultaneous models, or models incorporating reciprocal influences, appears in the literature on path analysis.[9] Models of this type have been extensively considered in econometrics.[10] It is clear from the discussion in both these contexts that straightforward regression of one dependent variable upon a set of predictor variables does not yield the proper estimate of the effect of a variable which is simultaneously being determined within the model. Our interpretation here is presented in the framework of path analysis, but takes advantage of some of the approaches developed in econometrics. The reader is referred to a previous discussion of path analysis in sociological research,[11] with the warning that some of the simplified algorithms for path diagrams stated there apply only to simple recursive systems and not to simultaneous systems. This paper, then, affords an introduction to and illustration of the treatment of such systems in a path framework. Emphasis is placed on explicit statement of the equations and specifications of the model and the derivations that may be made therefrom to secure equations from which estimates may be calculated.

A just-identified model

Several models will be presented for didactic purposes before we arrive at one that represents a reasonably firm though tentative interpretation. Model I

9. Sewall Wright, "The Treatment of Reciprocal Interaction, with or without Lag, in Path Analysis," *Biometrics*, XVI (September, 1960), 423–445.

10. J. Johnston, *Econometric Methods* (New York: McGraw-Hill Book Co., 1963), chap. ix; Arthur S. Goldberger, *Econometric Theory* (New York: John Wiley & Sons, 1964), chap. vii; E. Malinvaud, *Statistical Methods of Econometrics* (Chicago: Rand McNally & Co., 1966), Part V; R. L. Basmann, "An Expository Note on Estimation of Simultaneous Structural Equations," *Biometrics*, XVI (September, 1960), 464–480. For a more elementary presentation, Mordecai Ezekiel and Karl A. Fox, *Methods of Correlation and Regression Analysis* (3d ed.; New York: John Wiley & Sons, 1959), chap. xxiv. See also Everett R. Dempster, "The Question of Stability with Positive Feedback," *Biometrics*, XVI (September, 1960), 481–483.

11. Otis Dudley Duncan, "Path Analysis: Sociological Examples," *American Journal of Sociology*, LXXII (July, 1966), 1–16.

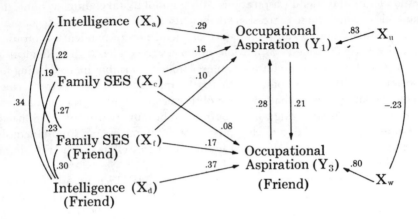

Figure 13.1. *Model I.*

(Fig. 13.1) represents occupational aspiration as depending directly on intelligence, family SES, friend's family SES, friend's occupational aspiration, and unspecified residual factors (or "disturbance," in the econometrician's parlance). The crucial assumption of the model is that occupational aspiration does *not* depend *directly* on friend's intelligence. Occupational aspiration does, however, depend directly on friend's family SES, an assumption that seems plausible enough if we consider the possibility that members of the friend's family as well as one's own may afford role models.

Three classes of variables are distinguished. The variables to the left, denoted by X's with letter subscripts taken from the first part of the alphabet, are "predetermined variables" with respect to this model. (The same variables might, of course, occur in a different role in some other model.) The Y's, with numerical subscripts, are the "endogenous variables," determined within the model, sometimes also called "jointly dependent variables." The X's with letter subscripts drawn from the end of the alphabet are "disturbances," standing for the residue of factors influencing aspiration but not explicitly measured.

The essential specification for all models of this type is that the disturbances are uncorrelated with the predetermined variables, though not (of course) with the endogenous variables and not necessarily with each other. Thus $r_{au}=r_{cu}=r_{fu}=r_{du}=r_{aw}=r_{cw}=r_{fw}=r_{dw}=0$. (We use r_{au} as a more economical notation for $r_{X_a X_u}$, etc.)

The intercorrelations of the predetermined variables are represented by the curved lines connecting them; similarly, there is a correlation between the two disturbances represented by a curved line. (The arrowheads at both ends of such curved lines, which are conventional in path diagrams, are omitted here to suggest that one must not rely on the usual algorithm for reading compound paths from the diagram when the system is non-recursive.)

While the diagram, on the conventions understood for reading it, specifies the model adequately, it is essential that the model also be stated explicitly in equations. Model I comprises two equations:

$$Y_1 = p_{1a}X_a + p_{1c}X_c + p_{1f}X_f + p_{13}Y_3 + p_{1u}X_u$$

and (Model I)

$$Y_3 = p_{3d}X_d + p_{3f}X_f + p_{3c}X_c + p_{31}Y_1 + p_{3w}X_w.$$

To these equations must be attached the earlier stipulation that disturbances are uncorrelated with predetermined variables.

To calculate estimates of the path coefficients, we must derive equations that yield a solution for them. To do this, we take advantage of the condition concerning the zero correlation of the predetermined variables and disturbances. Consider the first equation of the Model I. Multiply both sides of the equation by X_a, sum both sides over sample observations, and divide both sides by N, the number of sample observations. This yields

$$\frac{\Sigma Y_1 X_a}{N} = p_{1a}\frac{\Sigma X_a X_a}{N} + p_{1c}\frac{\Sigma X_c X_a}{N} + p_{1f}\frac{\Sigma X_f X_a}{N} + p_{13}\frac{\Sigma Y_3 X_a}{N} + p_{1u}\frac{\Sigma X_u X_a}{N}.$$

Since we are dealing with standardized variables (zero mean, unit variance), an expression like $\Sigma Y_1 X_a / N$ simplifies immediately to r_{1a} while $\Sigma X_a X_a / N = 1$. Note especially that $\Sigma X_u X_a / N = r_{ua} = 0$, on the specification already stated. We proceed to multiply the first equation through by each of the four predetermined variables and to simplify the results as just indicated. This work yields the following set of four equations:

$$r_{1a} = p_{1a} + p_{1c}r_{ac} + p_{1f}r_{af} + p_{13}r_{3a},$$
$$r_{1c} = p_{1a}r_{ac} + p_{1c} + p_{1f}r_{cf} + p_{13}r_{3c},$$
$$r_{1f} = p_{1a}r_{af} + p_{1c}r_{cf} + p_{1f} + p_{13}r_{3f},$$
$$r_{1d} = p_{1a}r_{ad} + p_{1c}r_{cd} + p_{1f}r_{df} + p_{13}r_{3d}.$$

Or, in matrix form,

$$\begin{pmatrix} 1 & r_{ac} & r_{af} & r_{3a} \\ r_{ac} & 1 & r_{cf} & r_{3c} \\ r_{af} & r_{cf} & 1 & r_{3f} \\ r_{ad} & r_{cd} & r_{df} & r_{3d} \end{pmatrix} \begin{pmatrix} p_{1a} \\ p_{1c} \\ p_{1f} \\ p_{13} \end{pmatrix} = \begin{pmatrix} r_{1a} \\ r_{1c} \\ r_{1f} \\ r_{1d} \end{pmatrix}.$$

It will be noted that the square matrix on the left is not symmetric, unlike the case of the normal equations in conventional regression. Nevertheless, it will almost always be possible to invert this matrix (barring excessive collinearity among the predetermined variables) and thus to solve the four equations for the four unknown path coefficients, all the correlations on both the left- and right-hand sides of the equations being given in the data.

That we have exactly four equations to solve for four unknowns is essentially what is meant by saying that the model, or, more particularly, the relation in which Y_1 figures as the dependent variable, is "just identified." (The same holds, in this model, for the relation in which Y_3 is the dependent variable, but it need not always be the case that the situation in regard to identifiability is the same with respect to all relations in the model.) The econometricians have much more elegant ways of analyzing identifiability, but what it comes down to in cases like the one at hand is this; Y_1 depends on four variables explicitly (leaving aside the disturbance term), and there is just the same number of *predetermined* variables in the model. If there were four explanatory variables for Y_1 but fewer predetermined variables in the model, then the relation for Y_1 would be "underidentified"; that is, we could not derive a sufficient number of equations to yield a unique solution for the estimated paths leading to Y_1 (at least, not without some alteration in the specification of the model). On the other hand, if there are more predetermined variables than there are explanatory variables occurring in the model's equation for Y_1, this relation would be "overidentified" (examples of over-identification are given below).

The same procedure can be followed to secure equations from which we may solve for the paths leading to Y_3; that is, the second equation of the model is multiplied through, in turn, by each of the four predetermined variables, and the results are simplified to yield four equations in known correlations and four unknown path coefficients.

The method just presented yields exactly the same results as does the method of "indirect least squares," which is applicable to just-identified relations in a model. Computationally, however, it is a considerable simplification over indirect least squares, as has been noted in at least one textbook of econometrics.[12]

Some tedious but straightforward work remains if we are to calculate residual paths and the correlation between disturbances. We now multiply through each of the model equations by each of the endogenous variables and by each of the disturbance variables. This yields eight equations, which take the following form upon simplification:

$$r_{11} = 1 = p_{1a}r_{1a} + p_{1c}r_{1c} + p_{1f}r_{1f} + p_{13}r_{13} + p_{1u}r_{1u};$$
$$r_{13} = p_{1a}r_{3a} + p_{1c}r_{3c} + p_{1f}r_{3f} + p_{13} + p_{1u}r_{3u};$$
$$r_{33} = 1 = p_{3d}r_{3d} + p_{3f}r_{3f} + p_{3c}r_{3c} + p_{31}r_{13} + p_{3w}r_{3w};$$

12. Goldberger, *op. cit.*, p. 348.

$$r_{13} = p_{3d}r_{1d} + p_{3f}r_{1f} + p_{3c}r_{1c} + p_{31} + p_{3w}r_{1w};$$

$$r_{1u} = p_{13}r_{3u} + p_{1u}; \text{ hence } p_{1u}{}^2 = p_{1u}r_{1u} - p_{13}p_{1u}r_{3u};$$

$$r_{3w} = p_{31}r_{1w} + p_{3w}; \text{ hence } p_{3w}{}^2 = p_{3w}r_{3w} - p_{31}p_{3w}r_{1w};$$

$$r_{3u} = p_{31}r_{1u} + p_{3w}r_{uw};$$

$$r_{1w} = p_{13}r_{3w} + p_{1u}r_{uw}.$$

A convenient solution routine is to compute $p_{1u}r_{1u}$ from the first equation (all other terms in it now being known), $p_{1u}r_{3u}$ from the second, $p_{3w}r_{3w}$ from the third, and $p_{3w}r_{1w}$ from the fourth. The values thus obtained can be substituted into the fifth and sixth equations to compute p_{1u} and p_{3w}, and it is then possible to obtain r_{1u}, r_{3w}, r_{3u}, and r_{1w} by a back solution. Either of the last two equations can then be used to obtain r_{uw}; if both are used, one has a partial check on the arithmetic.

Although it is advisable to retain a generous number of decimal places in the initial correlations and all intermediate calculations, the results are not likely to be meaningful for more than two places; the rounded estimates are shown in Figure 13.1.

Model I was also used with educational aspiration in place of occupational aspiration; that is, Y_2 replaced Y_1 and Y_4 replaced Y_3, with the predetermined variables and specifications remaining unchanged. For comparison, the results are as follows:

$$p_{2a} = .27 \quad p_{4c} = .04, \quad p_{2v} = .84,$$

$$p_{2c} = .26, \quad p_{4f} = .22, \quad p_{4z} = .79,$$

$$p_{2f} = .02, \quad p_{4d} = .36, \quad r_{vz} = -.38,$$

$$p_{24} = .25, \quad p_{42} = .29,$$

where X_v and X_z are the disturbances for Y_2 and Y_4, respectively.

The two sets of results are similar in most respects. Intelligence and family SES are appreciable influences on aspiration, while the influence of friend's family SES is barely detectable. The reciprocal paths of influence of friend's aspiration on respondent's aspiration, and vice versa, are around .2 or .3, by no means a negligible value. In both sets of results, consistent estimates are obtained only by acknowledging a rather substantial negative correlation between the disturbances of the two aspiration variables. If the analyst feels uncomfortable with the size of this correlation, as one may well feel in the absence of any evident rationalization of it, he may be inclined to reject the model even though the remaining estimates are reasonable.

Several things could be awry. Perhaps it is mistaken to argue that friend's intelligence can have no direct influence on one's aspiration (even though insertion of an additional path for this variable in Model I will render it underidentified). Perhaps there is a variable (such as "ambition," introduced into Model IV) omitted from the model with respect to which there is pronounced homophily and which is a significant cause of aspiration. In this event, the paths between the aspiration variables are probably overestimated, and the residual correlation is forced to compensate for this. In the present state of theory in social psychology, we are not likely to have firm grounds for asserting the validity of a model on grounds completely independent of the data for a given problem. Hence, it would seem that the best we can do is propose reasonable models, consider their plausibility, and, where indicated, undertake the construction of alternative ones (or await the work of a critic who may do so). Several alternatives to Model I were in fact attempted which yielded even less satisfactory results, but this does not prove that still another alternative could not be plausibly proposed.

An overidentified model

One such alternative is instructive, both as an example of estimation procedure when one is confronted with overidentification and as an indication of the sensitivity of the results to what may appear to be minor modifications of the model. In Model II (Fig. 13.2), we delete the path from friend's family SES to aspiration (and vice versa), suspecting on the basis of results with Model I that this variable is not very consequential. With this deletion, the equations are:

$$Y_1 = p_{1a}X_a + p_{1c}X_c + p_{13}Y_3 + p_{1u}X_u$$

and   (Model II)

$$Y_3 = p_{3d}X_d + p_{3f}X_f + p_{31}Y_1 + p_{3w}X_w.$$

In the presence of overidentification, we cannot proceed as before to translate the foregoing specification about the model directly into a set of equations for estimating the model's parameters from a set of sample data. If we were to require that all four predetermined variables be uncorrelated with each residual variable *in the sample data*, we would be led to an inconsistency. From the first equation of the model, for example, requiring $r_{au} = r_{cu} = r_{fu} = r_{du} = 0$ would imply that there are four equations (one each for r_{1a}, r_{1c}, r_{1f}, and r_{1d}) involving just three unknowns (p_{1a}, p_{1c}, and p_{13}). The solution obtained from any three of these equations will not, in general, satisfy the fourth. Indirect least squares, or the equivalent procedure described above, is not available as a method of estimation.

In this situation we derive a set of estimating equations that are implied by the econometrician's method of "two-stage least squares." (The proof of the equivalence of our procedure to 2SLS, though elementary, is omitted.) We

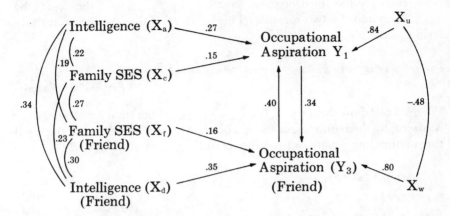

Figure 13.2. *Model II.*

begin by computing the "first stage regression" of each dependent variable on all the predetermined variables, obtaining the regression equations:

$$\hat{Y}_1 = \beta_{1a.cfd} X_a + \beta_{1c.afd} X_c + \beta_{1f.acd} X_f + \beta_{1d.acf} X_d$$

and

$$\hat{Y}_3 = \beta_{3a.cfd} X_a + \beta_{3c.afd} X_c + \beta_{3f.acd} X_f + \beta_{3d.acf} X_d$$

where the β-coefficients are the ordinary regression coefficients in standard form computed from the sample data. These β-coefficients are of interest in connection with the "reduced form" of the model, as is pointed out in a subsequent section of the paper; but their immediate use is the one noted in the next paragraph.

The 2SLS method entails the following restrictions on the correlations between predetermined variables and residuals *in the sample*: $r_{au} = r_{cu} = r_{fw} = r_{dw} = 0$; $\beta_{3f.acd} r_{fu} + \beta_{3d.acf} r_{du} = 0$; and $\beta_{1a.cfd} r_{aw} + \beta_{1c.afd} r_{cw} = 0$. Note that neither r_{fu} nor r_{du}, individually, is zero, but their weighted sum is forced to be zero, the weights being those that obtain as a consequence of the 2SLS method. A parallel statement holds for r_{aw} and r_{cw}.

Let us multiply through the first equation of Model II, in turn, by each of the predetermined variables. We obtain:

$$r_{1a} = p_{1a} + p_{1c} r_{ac} + p_{13} r_{3a}$$

$$r_{1c} = p_{1a} r_{ac} + p_{1c} + p_{13} r_{3c}$$

$$r_{1f} = p_{1a} r_{af} + p_{1c} r_{cf} + p_{13} r_{3f} + p_{1u} r_{fu}$$

$$r_{1d} = p_{1a} r_{ad} + p_{1c} r_{cd} + p_{13} r_{3d} \times p_{1u} r_{du}$$

Now, multiply the third of these equations by $\beta_{3f.acd}$ and the fourth by $\beta_{3d.acf}$ and add the two together. This yields (omitting the secondary subscripts of the β's)

$$\beta_{3f}r_{1f}+\beta_{3d}r_{1d}=p_{1a}(\beta_{3f}r_{af}+\beta_{3d}r_{ad})+p_{1c}(\beta_{3f}r_{cf}+\beta_{3d}r_{cd})$$
$$+p_{13}(\beta_{3f}r_{3f}+\beta_{3d}r_{3d}).$$

We need not show the term $p_{1u}(\beta_{3f}r_{fu}+\beta_{3d}r_{du})$ on the right hand side, since it is zero, by the requirement stated above. We can similarly write the set of three estimating equations from the second equation of the model:

$$r_{3f}=p_{3d}r_{df}+p_{3f}+p_{31}r_{1f}$$
$$r_{3d}=p_{3d}+p_{3f}r_{df}+p_{31}r_{1d}$$
$$\beta_{1a}r_{3a}+\beta_{1c}r_{3c}=p_{3d}(\beta_{1a}r_{ad}+\beta_{1c}r_{cd})+p_{3f}(\beta_{1a}r_{af}+\beta_{1c}r_{cf})$$
$$+p_{31}(\beta_{1a}r_{1a}+\beta_{1c}r_{1c})$$

The solutions of the two sets of estimating equations are shown as the path coefficients in Figure 13.2. The solutions for the residual paths (p_{1u} and p_{3w}) and for the correlation between residuals (r_{uw}) are obtained by a routine like that described in the previous section. The equations to be solved are the following:

$$r_{11}=1=p_{1a}r_{1a}+p_{1c}r_{1c}+p_{13}r_{13}+p_{1u}r_{1u}$$
$$r_{13}=p_{1a}r_{3a}+p_{1c}r_{3c}+p_{13}+p_{1u}r_{3u}$$
$$r_{33}=1=p_{3d}r_{3d}+p_{3f}r_{3f}+p_{31}r_{13}+p_{3w}r_{3w}$$
$$r_{13}=p_{3d}r_{1d}+p_{3f}r_{1f}+p_{31}+p_{3w}r_{1w}$$
$$r_{1u}=p_{13}r_{3u}+p_{1u}$$
$$r_{3w}=p_{31}r_{1w}+p_{3w}$$
$$r_{1w}=p_{1a}r_{aw}+p_{1c}r_{cw}+p_{13}r_{3w}+p_{1u}r_{uw}$$
$$r_{3u}=p_{3d}r_{du}+p_{3f}r_{fu}+p_{31}r_{1u}+p_{3w}r_{uw}$$

Note that the last two of these equations include the four non-zero correlations of predetermined variables with residuals. Their values are obtained from the respective estimating equations that contain them. For example, from the equation for r_{1f} given earlier, we obtain $r_{fu}=(r_{1f}-p_{1a}r_{af}-p_{1c}r_{cf}-p_{13}r_{3f})/p_{1u}$. From equations like these, we find

$$r_{fu}=.0665$$
$$r_{du}=-.0340$$
$$r_{aw}=-.0346$$
$$r_{cu}=.0551$$

These small values do not seriously call into question the assumption of the model that all the correlations between predetermined variables and disturbances *in the universe* are zero. No such assumption is made in regard to the correlation between disturbances, so that we are prepared to find that r_{uw} differs from zero. Nevertheless, the substantial negative correlation, $r_{uw} = -.48$, seems difficult to interpret in substantive terms.

If we neglect the correlations of predetermined variables with residuals, we can compute a set of "implied correlations" that depend only on the path coefficients and the intercorrelations of the predetermined variables. Deviations of the implied correlations from the corresponding observed correlations provide another perspective on the "goodness of fit" of the model. For the implied correlation, r'_{1f}, for example, we have $r'_{1f} = p_{1a}r_{af} + p_{1c}r_{cf} + p_{13}r_{3f}$. Shown below are the implied correlations that are constrained to equal their observed counterparts.

$$r'_{1f} = .2371 \ (-.0559) \qquad r'_{3a} = .2876 \ (.0278)$$

$$r'_{1d} = .3281 \ (.0286) \qquad r'_{3c} = .2342 \ (-.0444)$$

Deviations from observed values are in parentheses. These deviations appear (with signs reversed) in the numerators of formulas of the type already illustrated for calculating the correlations of predetermined variables with sample residuals. Were these deviations to be sizable, we should be inclined to call the model into question.

A block-recursive model

Both models discussed thus far are "simultaneous" models in that the endogenous variables are jointly determined by the model within a single period of observation. In simple recursive models, by contrast, we assume that the endogenous variables are successively determined, and the specification is altered to exclude correlation of the disturbances among themselves. The latter specification (zero intercorrelation of disturbances) is common to the Simon-Blalock procedure of causal analysis and to the examples of stratification models given in a previous publication on path analysis.[13] There is no apparent reason, however, why features of both types of model cannot be combined in a single construction. (The term "construction" might well be preferred to "model" in contexts like the present one, to emphasize that we are indeed "construing" the data to mean what our interpretation via a diagram or system of equations represents them to mean.)

13. Hubert M. Blalock, Jr., *Causal Inferences in Non-experimental Research* (Chapel Hill: University of North Carolina Press, 1964); Herbert A. Simon, *Models of Man* (New York: John Wiley & Sons, 1957), chap. ii; Duncan, *op. cit.*

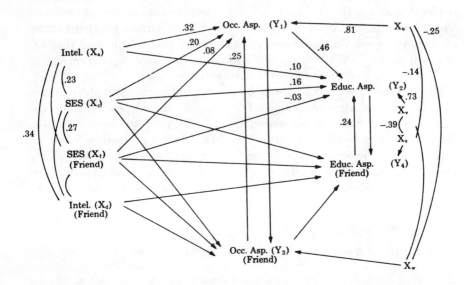

Figure 13.3. *Model III.*

In Model III (Fig. 13.3), we reason as though respondents and their friends "first" make up their minds what occupations they would like to pursue, and "then," on the basis of the occupational choice and other considerations, "decide" what educational preparation they may need. That such a construction is at best an oversimplification may be evident from introspection. This model, like the preceding ones, serves primarily a didactic purpose.

In the first sector of the model, occupational aspirations Y_1 and Y_3 are simultaneous endogenous variables and the specification is exactly the same as for Model I. We then assume that with respect to educational aspiration (Y_2 and Y_4) the predetermined variables include not only X_a, X_c, X_f, and X_d but also Y_1 and Y_3. Hence the specification $r_{1v} = r_{3z} = r_{uv} = r_{wz} = 0$; but r_{uz}, r_{vw}, r_{uw}, r_{vz}, r_{3v}, and r_{1z} are not necessarily zero. The equations of the model are

$$Y_1 = p_{1a}X_a + p_{1c}X_c + p_{1f}X_f + p_{13}Y_3 + p_{1u}X_u,$$

$$Y_3 = p_{3d}X_d + p_{3f}X_f + p_{3c}X_c + p_{31}Y_1 + p_{3w}X_w,$$

$$\text{(Model III)}$$

$$Y_2 = p_{2a}X_a + p_{2c}X_c + p_{2f}X_f + p_{21}Y_1 + p_{24}Y_4 + p_{2v}X_v,$$

$$Y_4 = p_{4d}X_d + p_{4f}X_f + p_{4c}X_c + p_{43}Y_3 + p_{42}Y_2 + p_{4z}X_z.$$

In estimating the parameters of this model, we have engaged in a preliminary manipulation of the data which has nothing to do with the properties of the model but which is suggested by the somewhat artificial design of the data matrix. From the original correlation matrix in Table 13.1, we constructed a "synthetic" correlation matrix which was forced to be symmetrical in variables pertaining to respondent and friend. The intercorrelations of educational aspiration, occupational aspiration, family SES, and intelligence were assumed to be the same for respondents and friends, and the values thereof were assumed to be those observed in the entire original sample of 442 boys. The correlation between friend and respondent on each of these variables was retained from the data on the 329 pairs. The "cross-correlations" between friend and respondents were averaged; thus, for example, in the synthetic correlation matrix $r_{1a} = r_{3d}$ and each is the average of r_{1a} and r_{3d} as initially computed. The synthetic matrix is shown below the diagonal in Table 13.1. Given the symmetry of the data and the model, it is necessary to carry out computations for estimating only the path coefficients in the first and third equations.

Estimates for the first equation are obtained in the same way as described for Model I, and, indeed, the results differ from those in Model I only slightly. The third equation (for Y_2) is just identified, in virtue of the specification $r_{1v} = 0$. Thus we can multiply this equation through by Y_1, X_a, X_c, X_f, and X_d in turn and simplify to obtain five equations in the five unknown path coefficients and known correlations. The calculation of residual paths for all equations proceeds along the lines already illustrated for Model I.

From the perspective of the hypothesis that orients this study, the most interesting estimates are those for the reciprocal paths for aspirations: $p_{13} = p_{31} = .25$ and $p_{24} = p_{42} = .24$. The paths from predetermined to endogenous variables seem reasonable, except perhaps for the negative though small value of $p_{2f}(=p_{4c})$, $-.03$. That family SES has an apparently larger influence on educational aspiration than does intelligence may be explained by two considerations: intelligence has a sizable influence on occupational aspiration, which, in this model, intervenes between the latter and educational aspiration; and the family SES scale is heavily weighted by parental educational attainment.

In short, the model gives satisfactory estimates on the whole, if we are prepared to accept the excessively rationalistic assumption that occupational decisions precede educational decisions (both being measured well before the actual decision point), and if we are prepared to overlook the substantial negative correlations between disturbances, $r_{uw} = -.25$ and $r_{vz} = -.39$. Dissatisfaction with our ability to rationalize the latter motivated one more alternative construction on these data.

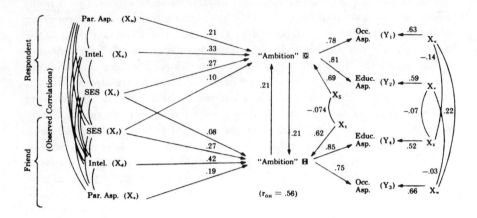

Figure 13.4. *Model IV.*

A composite model

The approach taken in Model IV (Fig. 13.4) was suggested by a remark of Turner and Stevens, who called attention to the possibility of constructions including aspects of both factor analysis and causal modeling.[14] The analogy with factor analysis here consists in the postulation of an unobserved variable, called "ambition" for lack of a better term, that underlies both educational and occupational aspiration. There are perhaps two justifications for such a postulate. First, both aspiration variables are probably rather unreliable relative to the other variables in the model, and it might be advisable to follow a procedure that reduces the attenuation introduced by measurement error before proceeding to a causal interpretation. Second, on a purely introspective basis it seems likely that many boys do not make a neat concep-tual separation of educational and occupational aspirations, nor do they make plans for schooling and job choices in any fixed order. The argument here is just the opposite of the one that would have to be used to justify the precedence of occupational aspiration with respect to educational aspiration in Model III. If the reader likes, he may identify "ambition" with general level of aspiration, as the latter was conceptualized in the classic literature on the subject.[15] Our procedure would then suggest that level of aspiration can only be manifested in and recognized by orientations toward particular

14. Malcolm E. Turner and Charles D. Stevens, "The Regression Analysis of Causal Paths," *Biometrics,* XV (June, 1959), 236–258.
15. K. Lewin, Tamara Dembo, L. Festinger, and Pauline S. Sears, "Level of Aspiration," in J. McV. Hunt (ed.), *Personality and the Behavior Disorders* (New York: Ronald Press, 1944), I, 333–378.

goals, such as educational attainment or occupational achievement. We are, in effect, using verbalized educational and occupational aspirations as *indicators* of the construct, level of aspiration or "ambition."

Although the approach taken to the construction of hypothetical "ambition" variables is suggested by factor analysis, the actual procedure is an ad hoc one that depends on various heuristic considerations rather than on one of the standard factor models. Lest this arouse undue anxiety, we observe that the classic factor models, in their time, were similarly motivated by heuristic concerns. That they have become frozen into a canonical procedure taken over by investigators of problems whose structures are quite different from those of the pioneers is perhaps a commentary on the relative potence of propensities to imitate and to innovate in research. Certainly, after Wright's illuminating contrast between the interpretive and the purely mathematical approaches to factor analysis,[16] we need no longer feel constrained to follow a single routine that someone has ventured to dub "objective" or "optimal."

We begin, as usual, by writing the entire set of equations which are graphically represented in the path diagram of Model IV:

$$Y_1 = p_{1G}G + p_{1u}X_u,$$
$$Y_2 = p_{2G}G + p_{2v}X_v,$$
$$Y_3 = p_{3H}H + p_{3w}X_w,$$
$$Y_4 = p_{4H}H + p_{4z}X_z, \quad \text{(Model IV)}$$
$$G = p_{Gb}X_b + p_{Ga}X_a + p_{Gc}X_c + p_{Gf}X_f + p_{GH}H + p_{Gs}X_s,$$
$$H = p_{He}X_e + p_{Hd}X_d + p_{Hf}X_f + p_{Hc}X_c + p_{HG}G + p_{Ht}X_t.$$

The last two equations contain the substance of the model. G and H are the simultaneous endogenous variables, $X_a, \ldots, X_f$ are the predetermined variables, and X_s and X_t are the disturbances, which need not be uncorrelated with each other although both are uncorrelated with all predetermined variables. Each relation is overidentified, since each includes only five explanatory variables while there are six predetermined variables in the model. We shall again employ the version of two-stage least squares illustrated for Model II when we come to the estimation of the path coefficients in these two equations.

Before proceeding to this task, we must first construct the two hypothetical endogenous variables by deriving their correlations with the predetermined variables, making use of the intercorrelations of the aspiration scores. Hence, attention will be focused first on the right-hand portion of the diagram.

16. Sewall Wright, "The Interpretation of Multivariate Systems," in O. Kempthorne *et al.* (eds.), *Statistics and Mathematics in Biology* (Ames: Iowa State College Press, 1954), chap. ii, especially pp. 27–32.

The factor model employed here says that the correlation between a boy's educational and occupational aspirations is completely accounted for by his "ambition." The correlation between the aspirations of friends is substantially accounted for by the correlation of their respective values on "ambition," but the model allows for some between-friend correlation of specific elements in the two aspiration scores. Hence, the specifications $r_{uv}=r_{wz}=0$; but r_{uz}, r_{vw}, r_{vz}, and r_{uw} are not necessarily zero. There are six known correlations among the aspiration variables, $Y_1, \ldots, Y_4$, and we have four equations of complete determination, stipulating that each aspiration variable is completely determined by the appropriate "ambition" variable and the residual. These ten conditions, however, do not suffice to estimate the paths in the first four equations of Model IV, inasmuch as we must estimate the four paths from "ambition" to aspiration, the four residual paths, four intercorrelations of residuals, and the unknown correlation between the two "ambition" variables, to wit, r_{GH}, for a total of thirteen unknowns. This portion of the model, by itself, is underidentified. Underidentification is, of course, the typical situation in factor analysis, which the analyst gets around by imposing various mathematical constraints on the solution. Here we invoke, instead, the "external" information provided by the predetermined variables as a constraint on the solution.

We begin by noting that the six correlations among the aspiration variables can be written as follows (obtained by "multiplying through" each of the first four equations in the model by the other aspiration variables):

$$r_{12}=p_{1G}p_{2G}=r_{1G}r_{2G},$$
$$r_{34}=p_{3H}p_{4H}=r_{3H}r_{4H},$$
$$r_{13}=p_{1G}p_{3H}r_{GH}+p_{1u}p_{3w}r_{uw},$$
$$r_{24}=p_{2G}p_{4H}r_{GH}+p_{2v}p_{4z}r_{vz},$$
$$r_{14}=p_{1G}p_{4H}r_{GH}+p_{1u}p_{4z}r_{uz},$$
$$r_{23}=p_{2G}p_{3H}r_{GH}+p_{2v}p_{3w}r_{vw}.$$

Bringing the predetermined variables into the picture, we note that $r_{1a}=p_{1G}r_{aG}$ and $r_{2a}=p_{2G}r_{aG}$. From these it would follow that $p_{1G}/p_{2G}=r_{1a}/r_{2a}$; but we can equally well compute $p_{1G}/p_{2G}=r_{1b}/r_{2b}$, and so on. As a compromise among the six possible estimates of this ratio, we take

$$p_{1G}/p_{2G}=\sum_i r_{1i}\Big/\sum_i r_{2i},$$

where $i=a, \ldots, f$. Given this ratio p_{1G}/p_{2G} and the previously noted $r_{12}=p_{1G}p_{2G}$, we can solve at once for p_{1G} and p_{2G}. A similar procedure yields p_{3H} and p_{4H}.

Now, if we disregard correlations among the residual factors of the Y's, we may compute the implied correlations,

$$r'_{13} = p_{1G}p_{3H}r_{GH},$$
$$r'_{24} = p_{2G}p_{4H}r_{GH},$$
$$r'_{14} = p_{1G}p_{4H}r_{GH},$$
$$r'_{23} = p_{2G}p_{3H}r_{GH}.$$

Let $\delta_1 = r_{13} - r'_{13}$, $\delta_2 = r_{24} - r'_{24}$, $\delta_3 = r_{14} - r'_{14}$, $\delta_4 = r_{23} - r'_{23}$, and $S = \Sigma\delta^2$. We wish to select r_{GH} so that S is at its minimum. Finding dS/dr_{GH}, setting it equal to zero, and rearranging, we obtain

$$r_{GH} = \frac{r_{13}p_{1G}p_{3H} + r_{24}p_{2G}p_{4H} + r_{14}p_{1G}p_{4H} + r_{23}p_{2G}p_{3H}}{(p_{1G}p_{3H})^2 + (p_{2G}p_{4H})^2 + (p_{1G}p_{4H})^2 + (p_{2G}p_{3H})^2}.$$

The path coefficients in this expression have already been estimated and the correlations are known; hence r_{GH} is easily calculated as .56, which is the hypothetical correlation between "ambition" of respondent and "ambition" of friend. It is a materially higher value than any of the observed correlations between aspiration scores. This is the most important result of the work done to this point. We complete this phase of the calculations by computing residual paths for the aspiration variables, using formulas like $p_{1u}^2 = 1 - p_{1G}^2$, which are obvious from the model equations. Finally, we may return to the identities stated for the intercorrelations among the Y's with enough information in hand to solve the last four equations for r_{uw}, r_{vz}, r_{uz}, and r_{vw}, respectively.

One more step is necessary before we can begin the estimation of the last two model equations. As already noted, $r_{1a} = p_{1G}r_{aG}$ and $r_{2a} = p_{2G}r_{aG}$. Since r_{1a} and r_{2a} are known and we now have estimates of p_{1G} and p_{2G}, we obtain two solutions for r_{aG}. These are not the same, so we strike a simple average of the two and follow an analogous procedure to secure correlations of G and H with all the predetermined variables.

By this sequence of estimates and approximations, we have arrived at a complete correlation matrix for variables G, H, and X_a, ..., X_f. Coefficients in the last two equations of Model IV are now estimated by the two-stage least-squares procedure already illustrated for Model II. The estimating equations are derived by multiplying through the last two equations of Model IV (those involving G and H) by each of the six predetermined variables, imposing the following restrictions on the sample correlations between residuals and predetermined variables, in conformity with the 2SLS principle of estimation: $r_{bs} = r_{as} = r_{cs} = r_{fs} = r_{ct} = r_{ft} = r_{dt} = r_{et} = \beta_H d^r ds + \beta_{He}r_{es} = \beta_{Gb}r_{bt} + \beta_{Ga}r_{at} = 0$.
The solutions for the residual paths and for the non-zero correlations of

predetermined variables and residuals are accomplished by the routine that was illustrated for Model II. We find

$$r_{ds} = .0291$$
$$r_{es} = -.0683$$
$$r_{bt} = -.0122$$
$$r_{at} = .0079$$

Neglecting these residual correlations we have the following implied values for correlations that are not forced to equal their observed values (deviations from the latter are shown in parentheses):

$$r'_{Gd} = .3508 \ (-.0201)$$
$$r'_{Ge} = .1397 \ (.0471)$$
$$r'_{Hb} = .1293 \ (.0076)$$
$$r'_{Ha} = .3383 \ (-.0049)$$

None of these results casts doubt on the credibility of the model, which seems acceptable, moreover, in regard to the reasonable magnitudes of the path coefficients and the small size of the correlation between residuals ($r_{st} = -.074$, as shown in Figure 13.4). We may, as a final indication of goodness of fit, compute all the correlations involving the aspiration variables that are implied by the path coefficients, neglecting correlations involving residuals (except for r_{st}). Typical formulas for this purpose are:

$$r'_{1a} = p_{1G} r_{Ga}$$
$$r'_{1d} = p_{1G} r'_{Gd}$$
$$r'_{14} = p_{1G} r_{GH} p_{4H}$$

The implied correlations and their deviations from observed correlations are shown in Table 13.2. The deviations of the implied from the observed correlations are analogous to the "residual correlations" obtained after extracting the "meaningful" factors in a factor analysis. They may be attributed to sampling error, if this seems reasonable. If not, they afford material for an investigator who wishes to essay a more convincing interpretation than that afforded by Model IV.

Concerning the reduced form

In all the discussion thus far we have considered only what the econometricians call the "structural form" of the models. For some purposes, it is instructive also to pay attention to the "reduced form." Returning to the last two equations of Model IV, which constitute the substance of that model,

Table 13.2. Correlations implied by Model IV between aspiration variables and other variables in the model

Variable	Variable (see stub)			
	Y_1	Y_2	Y_4	Y_3
Respondent:				
Parental aspiration (X_b)	.2388(.0251)	.2482(−.0260)	.1104(−.0020)	.0969(.0130)
Intelligence (X_a)	.3997(−.0108)	.4155(.0112)	.2889(−.0014)	.2537(−.0061)
Family SES (X_c)	.3567(.0327)	.3707(−.0340)	.3114(.0060)	.2734(−.0052)
Friend:				
Family SES (X_f)	.2623(−.0307)	.2726(.0319)	.4106(.0001)	.3605(−.0002)
Intelligence (X_d)	.2719(−.0276)	.2826(−.0037)	.5447(.0256)	.4783(−.0214)
Parental aspiration (X_e)	.1083(.0323)	.1126(.0424)	.2524(−.0260)	.2216(.0228)
Respondent:				
Occupational aspiration (Y_1) .	....	.6247*	.3738(.0469)	.3283(−.0933)
Educational aspiration (Y_2)...	....	....	.3885(.0216)	.3412(.0137)
Friend:				
Educational aspiration (Y_4) ..	....	....	....	.6404*
Occupational aspiration (Y_3)..	....	....	....	....

NOTE. Deviations from observed correlations are in parentheses.
* Model permits no deviation of implied from observed correlation. (Deviations from the other observed intercorrelations among the Y's occur if residual intercorrelations are neglected.)

let us substitute the expression for H given in the last equation into the next-to-last equation. We obtain a result that can be put into the form

$$G = \alpha_a X_a + \alpha_b X_b + \alpha_c X_c + \alpha_d X_d + \alpha_e X_e + \alpha_f X_f + \alpha_s X_s + \alpha_t X_t.$$

Similarly, substituting the fifth equation into the sixth, we obtain

$$H = \beta_a X_a + \beta_b X_b + \beta_c X_c + \beta_d X_d + \beta_e X_e + \beta_f X_f + \beta_s X_s + \beta_t X_t.$$

Let $\gamma = 1/(1 - p_{GH}p_{HG})$. Then the constants in the two foregoing reduced-form equations are defined as follows:

$$\alpha_a = p_{Ga}\gamma, \quad \alpha_b = p_{Gb}\gamma, \quad \alpha_c = (p_{Gc} + p_{GH}p_{Hc})\gamma, \quad \alpha_d = p_{GH}p_{Hd}\gamma, \quad \alpha_e = p_{GH}p_{He}\gamma,$$
$$\alpha_f = (p_{Gf} + p_{GH}p_{Hf})\gamma, \quad \alpha_s = p_{Gs}\gamma, \quad \alpha_t = p_{GH}p_{Ht}\gamma,$$
$$\beta_a = p_{HG}p_{Ga}\gamma, \quad \beta_b = p_{HG}p_{Gb}\gamma, \quad \beta_c = (p_{Hc} + p_{HG}p_{Gc})\gamma, \quad \beta_d = p_{Hd}\gamma, \quad \beta_e = p_{He}\gamma,$$
$$\beta_f = (p_{Hf} + p_{HG}p_{Gf})\gamma, \quad \beta_s = p_{HG}p_{Gs}\gamma, \quad \beta_t = p_{Ht}\gamma.$$

Each reduced-form equation represents one endogenous variable as a linear combination of all the predetermined variables and the disturbances. The coefficients in this linear combination are not, however, linear combinations of the coefficients of the structural form.

Since X_s and X_t are specified to be uncorrelated with the predetermined variables, the coefficients $\alpha_a, \ldots, \alpha_f$ can be estimated by the ordinary regression of G on $X_a, \ldots, X_f$ and the β's from the regression of H on the same six variables. (These regressions have already been computed for the first stage of the two-stage estimation procedure.)

It may be observed that $\alpha_d/\beta_d = p_{GH}$; but $\alpha_e/\beta_e = p_{GH}$, also. If we use our first-stage regression estimates of the α's and β's, the former implies $p_{GH} = .2891$ while the second yields $-.0838$. Similarly, estimating p_{HG} from β_a/α_a and β_b/α_b yields two inconsistent answers, .2338 and .1722, respectively. These inconsistencies present the problem of overidentification in an especially striking fashion. Had the equations in Model IV both been just identified, such inconsistencies would not have arisen. Indeed, the method of "indirect least squares," alluded to earlier as a technique for estimating coefficients in a just-identified system, consists precisely in estimating the reduced-form coefficients first and then deriving therefrom the estimates of coefficients in the structural equations of the model.

Although the overidentification means that the reduced-form coefficients do not yield unique estimates of the structural coefficients, we may still be interested in the reduced form of the model. To begin with, having obtained the structural coefficients by the two-stage procedure, we may compute the implied values of the reduced-form coefficients from them. Table 13.3 shows the reduced-form coefficients of Model IV, both as estimated from the first-stage

Table 13.3. Reduced-form coefficients for Model IV

		Dependent variable			
		Set (A)		Set (B)	
Independent Variable	*Symbol*	G	H	G	H
Respondent:					
Intelligence.............	X_a	.3378	.0790	.3418	.0725
Parental aspiration	X_b	.2199	.0379	.2169	.0460
Family SES.............	X_c	.3056	.1426	.2919	.1396
Best Friend:					
Intelligence.............	X_d	.1291	.4464	.0913	.4399
Parental aspiration	X_e	−.0159	.1900	.0418	.2016
Family SES.............	X_f	.1499	.3034	.1585	.2942

NOTE. Set (A), as estimated in first-stage regression; set (B), as computed from structural coefficients estimated in two-stage regression.

regressions and as computed from the structural coefficients. For the most part, the discrepancies appear small, although it is these very discrepancies that preclude the indirect least-squares approach.

Apart from computation and estimation, the reduced-form coefficients, as defined in terms of the structural coefficients, have some conceptual or interpretive significance, for their definitions indicate something of the "mechanisms" through which the predetermined variables influence the endogenous variables. Consider

$$\alpha_a = \frac{p_{Ga}}{1 - p_{GH}p_{HG}} = \frac{.3267}{.9560} = .34.$$

The form of this expression indicates that X_a influences G directly, via p_{Ga}, and that this influence is slightly amplified, to the extent of $1/(.956) = 1.046$, by the reciprocal action of respondent's and friend's "ambition." A more complex mechanism is suggested by

$$\alpha_c = \frac{p_{Gc} + p_{GH}p_{Hc}}{1 - p_{GH}p_{HG}} = \frac{.2749 + (.2074)(.0785)}{.956} = .29.$$

In this case, there is not only the direct effect, p_{Gc}, but also a compound or indirect effect of X_c on G, via H, as represented by $p_{GH}p_{Hc} = .0163$, while the sum of the two is amplified by the reciprocation. The third type of mechanism is exemplified by

$$\alpha_d = \frac{p_{GH}p_{Hd}}{1 - p_{GH}p_{HG}} = \frac{(.2074)(.4205)}{.956} = .09.$$

Here the influence of X_d on G is entirely indirect, via H, with the same factor of amplification as in the previous examples. Indeed, it is the assumption that some of the predetermined variables influence the endogenous variables only indirectly that permits the model to be identified in the first place. (Econometricians somewhat confusingly call both just-identified and over-identified models or equations "identified.")

The formulas for the reduced-form coefficients, of course, merely reflect the assumptions built into the model. But if the assumptions are accepted, it is of interest to include in the interpretation some evaluation of the relative importance of the various mechanisms that the model implicitly postulates.

Evaluation and discussion

Closing remarks are confined to comments on the rationale and results of Model IV. Some deficiencies of the earlier models have already been mentioned, and others that merit emphasis are shared by them with Model IV.

To recapitulate, the study was concerned with the hypothesis that adolescent boys influence each other in forming their occupational and educational aspirations. The earlier analysis of Haller and Butterworth had demonstrated that some correlation between the aspirations of boys in a peer group remained even if the groups were confined to those homogeneous on background factors presumed to give rise to aspirations. The present analysis accepts a different task: not that of hypothesis testing, but that of *estimation* in the context of an *explicit causal interpretation* of the influences on aspiration. The estimates are meaningful only to the extent that the initial study design is adequate to the purposes of identifying determinants of aspiration and of ascertaining the patterns of homophily operative in a relevant population.

The first question, then, is posed by a limitation on the design noted by the authors of the original study: with these data we cannot rule out the possibility that friendships are formed partially on the basis of common interests in educational and occupational goals. If this be the case, then all the estimates attempted here are beside the point, because we have treated aspirations as outcomes of the background characteristics of the respondent and his friend (treated as "predetermined variables") and of their respective influences on each other. As was also noted in the earlier paper, a longitudinal design would be required to eliminate the possibility of assortment on the basis of aspirations (although it is not entirely clear how the requisite causal inferences would be made, even if the design were longitudinal). The results here are, therefore, in the same provisional status as those of the predecessor study. If assortment on the basis of aspirations proved to be important, our estimates of the mutual influence of friends on each other's aspirations are not merely wrong; they become irrelevant.

Supposing, however, that friendship assortment occurs primarily on the basis of social and personal characteristics other than aspirations (though possibly, as the models suggest, on the basis of factors affecting aspirations); then we must reckon with the further question of whether the effects of such characteristics are adequately accounted for. Percentages of "explained" variance in the jointly dependent variables of simultaneous models are not readily computed as they are for ordinary multiple regressions. From the size of the path coefficients for the disturbances, however, we might be prone to assume that some relevant background characteristics are omitted. Still, it is not obvious what they might be, since most studies of status achievement and aspirations have focused on variables much like those used here. Strictly speaking, the disturbance in a model represents all variables that operate "accidentally" or randomly with respect to the influence of predetermined variables. Retrospective introspection certainly suggests that many accidental experiences, not necessarily shared with one's best friend, may have an impact on the formation of aspirations. Again, the results must be left in provisional form: if further investigation discloses major background factors inducing high or low aspirations, and if there is significant homophily with respect to these factors, incorporation of such factors into constructions like Model IV may well result in drastic reduction of the paths representing reciprocal influence of respondent's and friend's aspirations.

Looking more specifically at the results with Model IV, we may note that some of the asymmetry between respondent and friend that seemed implausible in Models I and II has disappeared in the more elaborate model. Except that friend's "ambition" seems to be more heavily influenced by his intelligence than is the case for respondent's "ambition," the results for the two boys are much alike. It is only a coincidence that $p_{GH} = p_{HG}$ when the results are rounded to two decimal places. But either of these coefficients at a value of roughly .2 seems like a reasonable estimate of the influence of a friend's aspirations upon one's own. This estimate does not differ greatly from those for Models I and III, but is on the conservative side by comparison with them. Recalling that the correlation between H and G, the two constructed "ambition" variables, came out as .56, the .21 value for p_{GH} and p_{HG} suggests that a significant part of the explanation for resemblance between aspirations of peers is due to mutual influence, but a goodly part of it is also due to the way in which peers come to associate (assortatively with respect to background characteristics) in the first place—bearing in mind the reservation already stated concerning the cogency of this interpretation.

The result that p_{GH} is very nearly the same as p_{HG} may be regarded as somewhat anomalous. In Model III the two reciprocal paths were forced to be equal, but in Models I and II, where this was not the case, the influence of friend on ego appeared to be somewhat stronger than that of ego on friend. This is perhaps what we should expect, given that the friendship pairs analyzed here are not defined by mutual choices but by the unilateral choice of the respondent. We know (or can presume) that friend is a significant other for ego, but we cannot be sure that the converse is true. Clearly, the whole matter of the extent to which an individual's dispositions are influenced by significant others should be further explored in research designed to include measures of degree of significance of those others, estimated independently of the dependent variable under study.

Of the discrepancies between observed correlations and those implied by the model, only the one of $-.09$ for r_{13}, between the two friends' occupational aspirations, seems interesting (this discrepancy appears in a different guise as $r_{uw} = .22$). The model may seem to fail to represent quite adequately some specific aspect of similarity of friend's occupational choices. It need not be argued, however, that the model underestimates mutual influence of friends' occupational aspirations. If friends encounter the same role models, apart from their families, this could induce some similarity in their cognitive and affective orientations to the world of work.

A final reservation will be stated, although others may well occur to the reader. The parental aspiration variable is based on the respondents' reports of their parents' attitudes. Hence this variable may well be contaminated to some degree by the dependent variables which it supposedly helps to explain. Fortunately, the study design precludes a similar contamination of the data on friend's aspirations.

The reader may well be appalled at all the apparatus brought into play in an attempt to demonstrate the reasonableness of what he already knew— even though he has been privileged to witness only a small part of the trial and error going into the construction of Model IV. The rejoinder to such a possible criticism would surely be that if a hypothesis is worth considering at all, it should be worthwhile to do some hard work to estimate its significance. On the purely conceptual level, it may suffice to recognize peer-group influence on aspiration as an actual process and to reason from that in a qualitative way to some of its consequences. Ultimately, however, we shall want to know, of the factors and processes that operate in the real world, which ones do how much of the work. Constructions like those exhibited in this paper not only offer one approach to the rendering of relevant estimates, but also present interpretations in such a form that their weaknesses—and those of the theories giving rise to them—are fairly evident. If the results of more of our research could be cast into this form, we would begin to understand better how much we do and do not know.

Chapter 14

THE CHOICE OF INSTRUMENTAL VARIABLES IN THE ESTIMATION OF ECONOMY-WIDE ECONOMETRIC MODELS

FRANKLIN M. FISHER[1]
Massachusetts Institute of Technology

1. Introduction

This paper is concerned with an important class of problems encountered in the estimation of economy-wide econometric models. The essential characteristics of such models for our purposes are three. They are dynamic, including lagged endogenous variables as essential parts of the system. They are large and nearly self-contained so that they include relatively few truly exogenous variables. Finally, they are essentially interdependent in that their dynamic structure is indecomposable.

Because an economy-wide model tends to be large, it is frequently impossible to estimate its reduced form by unrestricted least squares, since the number of exogenous and lagged endogenous variables is greater than the number of available observations. In addition, as will be brought out below,

Reprinted by permission of the author and publisher from the *International Economic Review*, Vol. 6, pp. 245–274. Copyright 1965, Kansai Economic Federation.

1. This paper which forms part of a longer contribution to *The Brookings-SSRC Quarterly Econometric Model of the United States*, J. Duesenberry, G. Fromm, E. Kuh, and L. R. Klein, eds., to be published by North-Holland Publishing Co., 1965, a volume describing the Social Science Research Council model of the United States economy, was largely written during my tenure of a National Science Foundation Postdoctoral Fellowship at the Econometric Institute of the Netherlands School of Economics. I am indebted to T. J. Rothenberg for helpful conversations and to L. R. Klein and E. Kuh for criticism of earlier drafts, but retain responsibility for any errors.

in the presence of serial correlation in the residuals, such estimation will not be consistent given that there are lagged endogenous variables. It is therefore usually necessary to use some form of instrumental variables method.

While there are a number of essentially equivalent ways of describing such methods, for our purposes we may think of estimation by instrumental variables as consisting of choosing a list of variables to be treated as instruments and then estimating a given equation by two-stage least squares, treating all non-instrumental variables in the equation as endogenous and using the instruments as though they were the only exogenous variables in the system. In other words, all noninstrumental variables on the right-hand side of the given equation are replaced by values calculated from their regressions on the instruments and the equation then estimated by ordinary least squares.[2] Note that there is no reason why the instrumental variables so used need be the same for every equation. We shall argue below that it is positively desirable that they be different.

We shall be concerned with the choice of instrumental variables to be used in such a procedure. Our discussion is in two parts. First we consider the choice of an eligible list of instruments, the criterion for eligibility being near zero correlation in the probability limit with the disturbance term from the given equation. In this connection, we pay particular attention to the eligibility of lagged endogenous variables. Since the eligible list will generally be too long for every variable on it to be used, we then consider how one should go about selecting from it the instrumental variables which will actually be employed. The latter discussion is essentially independent of the way in which the eligible list is constructed and is therefore of more general application than the model discussed in selecting an eligible list.

2. The model to be estimated

We suppose that the model to be estimated is

$$(2.1) \qquad y_t = Ay_t + By_{t-1} + Cz_t + u_t,$$

where u_t is an m-component column vector of disturbances; y_t is an m-component column vector of current endogenous variables; z_t is an n-component column vector of exogenous variables (known at least to be uncorrelated in the probability limit with all current and past disturbances); A, B, and C are constant matrices to be estimated; and $(I - A)$ is nonsingular, while A has zeros everywhere on its principal diagonal. The assumption that there are no terms in $y_{t-\theta}$ for $\theta > 1$ involves no loss of generality in the present discussion,

---

2. Other k-class estimators such as limited-information, maximum-likelihood also have their analogous instrumental variable estimators; essentially the same treatment would apply to them.

since it can always be accomplished by redefinition of y_t and expansion of the equation system and will be used only for convenience in dealing with the solution of (2.1) regarded as a system of stochastic difference equations.

To examine the correlations among the disturbance terms and the current and lagged endogenous variables, we solve the system for y_t, obtaining

$$(2.2) \qquad y_t = (I-A)^{-1}By_{t-1} + (I-A)^{-1}Cz_t + (I-A)^{-1}u_t.$$

Denote $(I-A)^{-1}$ by D. Assuming that DB is stable, we have[3]

$$(2.3) \qquad y_t = \sum_{\theta=0}^{\infty} (DB)^{\theta}(DCz_{t-\theta} + Du_{t-\theta}).$$

Denoting the covariance matrix of u_t and $y_{t-\theta}$ by $W(\theta)$ with columns corresponding to elements of u_t and rows corresponding to elements of $y_{t-\theta}$, and that of u_t and $u_{t-\theta}$ by $V(\theta)$ (which is assumed to be independent of t), with columns corresponding to u_t and rows to $u_{t-\theta}$,

$$(2.4) \qquad W(0) = \sum_{\theta=0}^{\infty} (DB)^{\theta}(DV(\theta)).$$

Similarly,

$$(2.5) \qquad W(1) = \sum_{\theta=1}^{\infty} (DB)^{\theta-1}(DV(\theta)).$$

Unless one is willing to assume $V(\theta) = 0$ for all $\theta > 0$ (no serial correlation) or to make other assumptions thereon, and on D and B, lagged endogenous variables will generally be correlated with current disturbances.

3. *Near-consistency, block-recursive systems and the choice of eligible instrumental variables*

3.1 INTRODUCTION
In this section we discuss the choice of an eligible list of predetermined instruments. Until further notice then we discuss only whether and under what circumstances a given single variable ought to be treated as predetermined.

In general, we desire two things of a variable which is to be treated as predetermined in the estimation of a given equation. First, it should be uncorrelated in the probability limit with the disturbance from that equation; second, it should closely causally influence the variables which appear in that

---

3. We shall not discuss the assumption of the stability of DB in any detail at this point. If it is not stable, then it suffices to assume that the model begins with non-stochastic initial conditions. Obviously, if stability fails, the question of serial correlation in the disturbances becomes of even greater importance than if stability holds. We shall return to this and shall discuss the question of stability in general in a later section.

equation and should do so independently of the other predetermined variables.[4] If the first criterion is not satisfied, treating the variable as predetermined results in inconsistency; if the second fails, such treatment does not
aid much in estimation—it does not reduce variances. In practice, these
requirements may frequently not be consistent, and one has to compromise
between them. The closer the causal connection, the higher may be the
forbidden correlation. Thus, in one limit, the use of ordinary least squares
which treats all variables on the right-hand side of the equation as predetermined perfectly satisfies the second but not the first criterion. In the
other limit, the use of instrumental variables which do not directly or indirectly causally influence any variable in the model perfectly meets the
first requirement but not the second.[5] In general, one is frequently faced
with the necessity of weakening the first requirement to one of low rather than
of zero correlation and accepting indirect rather than direct causal relations
between instruments and included variables. (Such a compromise may result
in different instruments for different equations when a limited-information
estimator is used; this will be the case below.)

In the present section, we discuss the circumstances under which zero or
low inconsistencies can be expected, leaving explicit use of the causal criterion
to the next section.

Now, two sets of candidates for treatment as instrumental variables are
obviously present. The first of these consists of those variables which one is
willing to assume truly exogenous to the entire system and the lagged values
thereof; the second consists of the lagged endogenous variables. The dynamic
and causal structure of the system may well provide a third set, however, and
may cast light on the appropriateness of the use of lagged endogenous variables; to a discussion of this we now turn.

3.2. THE THEORY OF BLOCK-RECURSIVE SYSTEMS

A generalization of the recursive systems introduced by Wold[6] is provided by
what I have elsewhere termed "block-recursive systems".[7] In general, such
systems have similar properties to those of recursive systems when the model
is thought of as subdivided into sets of current endogenous variables and
corresponding equations (which we shall call sectors) rather than into single
endogenous variables and their corresponding equations.

    4. It should therefore be relatively uncorrelated with the other variables used as instru-
ments so that lack of collinearity is not really a separate criterion. We shall return to this in
the next section.
    5. If only such variables are available for use (or if an insufficient number of more interesting
ones are) then the equation in question is underidentified and even asymptotic variances are
infinite.
    6. See Wold and Juréen [17], Wold [19] and other writings.
    7. Fisher [8].

Formally, we ask whether it is possible to partition the vectors of variables and of disturbances and the corresponding matrices (renumbering variables and equations, if necessary) to secure a system with certain properties. In such partitionings, the I-th subvector of a given vector x will be denoted as x^I. Similarly, the submatrix of a given matrix M which occurs in the I-th row and J-th column of submatrices of that matrix will be denoted by M^{IJ}. Thus

$$(3.1) \qquad M = \begin{bmatrix} M^{11} & M^{12} \ldots M^{1N} \\ M^{21} & M^{22} \ldots M^{2N} \\ \cdot & \cdot \\ \cdot & \cdot \\ \cdot & \cdot \\ M^{N1} & M^{N2} \ldots M^{NN} \end{bmatrix} ; x = \begin{bmatrix} x^1 \\ x^2 \\ \cdot \\ \cdot \\ \cdot \\ x^N \end{bmatrix}.$$

We shall always assume the diagonal blocks, M^{II}, to be square.

If when written in this way, the matrix M has the property that $M^{IJ}=0$ for all $I=1, \ldots, N$ and $J>I$, the matrix will be called *block-triangular*. If $M^{IJ}=0$ for all $I=1, \ldots, N$ $J \neq I$, the matrix will be called *block-diagonal*.[8]

Now consider the system (2.1). Suppose that there exists a partition of that system (with $N>1$) such that

(BR. 1) A is block-triangular;

(BR. 2) $V(0)$ is block-diagonal;

(BR. 3) $V(\theta)=0$ for all $\theta>0$.[9]

In this case, it is easy to show that the *current* endogenous variables of any given sector are uncorrelated in probability with the current disturbances of any higher-numbered sector. Such variables may thus be consistently treated as predetermined instruments in the estimation of the equations of such higher-numbered sectors.

To establish the proposition in question, observe that by (BR. 3)

$$(3.2) \qquad\qquad W(0) = DV(0).$$

By (BR. 1), however, $D=(I-A)^{-1}$ is block-triangular, while $V(0)$ is block-diagonal by (BR. 2). It follows that their product is block-triangular with the same partitioning. Thus

$$(3.3) \qquad\qquad W(0)^{IJ}=0 \qquad\qquad \text{for all } I, J=1, \ldots, N \text{ and } J>I,$$

but this is equivalent to the proposition in question.

As can also be done in the special case of recursive systems, assumption

---

8. Block-triangularity and block-diagonality are the respective canonical forms of decomposability and complete decomposability.

9. (BR. 1) and (BR. 2) are generalizations of the corresponding assumption for recursive systems. See Wold [19, pp. 358–359].

(BR. 3) can be replaced by a somewhat different assumption. (BR. 3*) B is block-triangular with the same partitioning as A, as is $V(\theta)$ for all $\theta > 0$. Further, either all B^{II} or all $V(\theta)^{II}(\theta > 0)$ are zero $(I = 1, \ldots, N)$.

To see that this suffices, observe that in this case every term in (2.4) will be block-triangular.

Note, however, that whereas (BR. 1)–(BR. 3) patently suffice to give $W(1) = 0$ and thus show that lagged endogenous variables are uncorrelated with current disturbances, this is not the case when (BR. 3) is replaced by (BR. 3*). As in the similar case for recursive systems, what is implied by (BR. 1), (BR. 2) and (BR. 3*) in this regard is that $W(1)$ is also block-triangular with zero matrices on the principal diagonal so that lagged endogenous variables are uncorrelated with the current disturbances of the same or *higher*-numbered blocks, but not necessarily with those of *lower*-numbered ones.

If A and B are both block-triangular with the same partitioning, then the matrix DB is also block-triangular and the system of difference equations given by (2.2) is decomposable. In this case, what occurs in higher-numbered sectors *never* influences what occurs in lower-numbered ones, so that there is, in any case, no point in using current or lagged endogenous variables as instruments in lower-numbered sectors. This is an unlikely circumstance to encounter in an economy-wide model in any essential way, but it may occur for partitionings which split off a small group of equations from the rest of the model. If it does not occur, then (BR. 3) is generally necessary for the block-triangularity of $W(0)$. Indeed unless either (BR. 3) or the first statement of (BR. 3*) holds, *no* $W(0)^{IJ}$ can generally be expected to be zero if $B \neq 0$.

To see this, observe that (2.4) implies that $W(0)$ cannot generally be expected to have any zero submatrices unless every term in the sum which is not wholly zero has a zero submatrix in the same place. This cannot happen unless every matrix involved is either block-diagonal or block-triangular. Hence, if $V(\theta) \neq 0$ for all $\theta > 0$, all such $V(\theta)$ must at least be block-triangular, as must B.[10]

3.3. BLOCK-RECURSIVE ASSUMPTIONS IN ECONOMY-WIDE MODELS

Unfortunately, while block-triangularity of A is not an unreasonable circumstance to expect to encounter in practice the assumptions on the disturbances involved in (BR. 2) and (BR. 3) or (BR. 3*) seem rather unrealistic

---

10. Of course, this does not show that (BR. 3) or (BR. 3*) is necessary, since counterexamples may easily be produced in which different non-zero terms in (2.4) just cancel out. The point is that this cannot be assumed to occur in practice. To put it another way, since such cancellation cannot be known to occur, it clearly occurs only on a set of measure zero in the parameter space. Thus (BR. 3) or (BR. 3*) is necessary with probability 1.

in economy-wide models.[11] Thus, it does not seem reasonable to assume that the omitted effects which form the disturbances in two different sectors have no common elements; nor does it seem plausible to assume either that there is no serial correlation of disturbances or that the dynamic system involved is decomposable.

Note, however, that these assumptions may be better approximations than in the case of recursive systems. Thus one may be more willing to assume no correlation between contemporaneous disturbances in two different aggregate sectors than between disturbances in any two single equations. A similar assumption may be even more attractive when the disturbances in question are from different time periods, as will be seen below. Thus also, the dynamic system may be thought *close* to decomposability when broad sectors are in view and feedbacks within sectors explicitly allowed. If such assumptions are approximately satisfied, then the inconsistencies involved in the use of current and lagged endogenous variables, as predetermined in higher-numbered sectors, will be small.[12]

Nevertheless, the assumption of no correlation between contemporaneous disturbances from different sectors, the assumption of no serial correlation in the disturbances and the assumption of decomposability of the dynamic system all seem rather strong ones to make. If none of these assumptions is in fact even approximately made, then the use of current endogenous variables as instruments in higher-numbered sectors leads to not negligible inconsistencies. We shall show, however, that this need not be true of the use of some *lagged* endogenous variables in higher-numbered sectors under fairly plausible assumptions as to the process generating the disturbances. We thus turn to the question of the use of lagged endogenous variables, assuming that A is known to be at least nearly block-triangular.

3.4. REASONABLE PROPERTIES OF THE DISTURBANCES

The problems which we have been discussing largely turn on the presence of common omitted variables in different equations and on the serial correlation properties of the disturbances. It seems appropriate to proceed by setting up an explicit model of the process generating the disturbances in terms of such omitted variables and such serial correlation.

We shall assume that the disturbances to any equation are made up of three sets of effects. The first of these will consist of the effects of elements common to more than one sector—in general, common to all sectors. The second will consist of the effects of elements common to more than one

11. It is encountered in preliminary versions of the SSRC model. C. Holt and D. Steward have developed a computer program for organizing a model in block-triangular form.

12. See Fisher [8]. The theorems involved are generalizations of the Proximity Theorem of Wold for recursive systems. See H. Wold and P. Faxér [18].

equation in the sector in which the given equation occurs. The third will consist of effects specific to the given equation.

Thus, let the number of equations in the I-th sector be n_1. We write

$$(3.4) \qquad u_t{}^I = \phi^I e_t + \psi^I v_t{}^I + w_t{}^I \qquad\qquad (I = 1, \ldots, \mathcal{N})$$

where

$$(3.5) \qquad e_t = \begin{bmatrix} e_{1t} \\ \cdot \\ \cdot \\ \cdot \\ e_{Kt} \end{bmatrix}$$

is a vector of implicit disturbances whose effects are common (in principle) to all equations in the model and ϕ^I is an $n_I \times K$ constant matrix;

$$(3.6) \qquad v_t{}^I = \begin{bmatrix} v_{1t}{}^I \\ \cdot \\ \cdot \\ \cdot \\ v_{H_I t}{}^I \end{bmatrix}$$

is a vector of implicit disturbances, whose effects are common (in principle) to all equations in the I-th sector but not to equations in other sectors; ψ^I is an $n_I \times H_I$ constant matrix; and

$$(3.7) \qquad w_t{}^I = \begin{bmatrix} w_{1t}{}^I \\ \cdot \\ \cdot \\ \cdot \\ w_{n_I t}{}^I \end{bmatrix}$$

is a vector of implicit disturbances, the effect of each of which is specific to a given equation in the I-th sector.

Define

$$(3.8) \qquad \phi = \begin{bmatrix} \phi^1 \\ \cdot \\ \cdot \\ \cdot \\ \phi^N \end{bmatrix};$$

$$(3.9) \qquad v_t = \begin{bmatrix} v_t{}^1 \\ \cdot \\ \cdot \\ \cdot \\ v_t{}^N \end{bmatrix};$$

$$(3.10) \qquad \psi = \begin{bmatrix} \psi^1 & 0 & \ldots & 0 \\ 0 & \psi^2 & \ldots & 0 \\ \cdot & \cdot & & \cdot \\ \cdot & \cdot & & \cdot \\ \cdot & \cdot & & \cdot \\ 0 & 0 & \ldots & \psi^N \end{bmatrix};$$

and

$$(3.11) \qquad w_t = \begin{bmatrix} w_t{}^1 \\ w_t{}^2 \\ \cdot \\ \cdot \\ \cdot \\ w_t{}^N \end{bmatrix}.$$

Then (3.4) may be rewritten more compactly as

$$(3.12) \qquad u_t = \phi e_t + \psi v_t + w_t.$$

We shall refer to the elements of e_t, v_t and w_t as *economy-wide, sector* and *equation* implicit disturbances, respectively, noting that whether an economy-wide or sector implicit disturbance actually affects a given equation depends on the relevant rows of ϕ and ψ, respectively. (The unqualified term "disturbance" will be reserved for the elements of u_t.)

All elements of e_t, v_t and w_t are composites of unobservables; it is hardly restrictive to assume that

(A. 1) Every element of e_t, v_t or w_t is uncorrelated in probability with all present or past values of any *other* element of any of these vectors. The vectors can always be redefined to accomplish this.

We shall assume that each element of each of these implicit disturbance vectors obeys a (different) first-order auto-regressive scheme.[13] Thus

$$(3.13) \qquad e_t = \Lambda_e e_{t-1} + e_t{}^*,$$

$$(3.14) \qquad v_t = \Lambda_v v_{t-1} + v_t{}^*,$$

$$(3.15) \qquad w_t = \Lambda_w w_{t-1} + w_t{}^*,$$

where Λ_e, Λ_v and Λ_w are diagonal matrices of appropriate dimension and $e_t{}^*$, $v_t{}^*$ and $w_t{}^*$ are vectors of non-auto-correlated random variables. Assuming that the variance of each element of e_t, v_t and w_t is constant through time, the diagonal elements of Λ_e, Λ_v and Λ_w are first-order auto-correlation coefficients and are thus each less than one in absolute value.

Now let Δ_e, Δ_v and Δ_w be the diagonal variance-covariance matrices of the elements of e_t, v_t and w_t, respectively. In view of (A.1) and (3.13)–(3.15), it is easy to show that (3.12) implies

$$(3.16) \qquad V(\theta) = \phi \Lambda_e{}^\theta \Delta_e \phi' + \psi \Lambda_v{}^\theta \Delta_v \psi' + \Lambda_w{}^\theta \Delta_w \qquad (\theta \geqq 0).$$

Evidently, $V(\theta)$ will be non-zero unless some other assumptions are imposed. Consider, however, the question of whether $V(\theta)$ will be block-diagonal.

---

13. Auto-regressive relations of higher orders could be considered in principle, but this would rather complicate the analysis. We shall thus assume that first-order relationships are sufficiently good approximations. If higher-order relationships are involved, there is no essential change in the qualitative results.

Since all the Λ and Δ matrices are diagonal, and since ψ is itself block-diagonal by (3.10), we have

$$(3.17) \qquad V(\theta)^{IJ} = \phi^I \Lambda_e^{\theta} \Delta_e \phi^{J\prime} \qquad (\theta \geqq 0;\ I,\ \mathcal{J},\ = 1,\ \ldots,\ N;\ \mathcal{J} \neq I).$$

Thus the off-diagonal blocks of $V(\theta)$ depend only on the properties of the economy-wide disturbances.

This result is perhaps worth emphasizing. When applied to $\theta = 0$, it merely states formally what we have said previously, that contemporaneous disturbances from the equations of the model which occur in different sectors cannot be assumed uncorrelated if there are common elements in each of them, that is, implicit disturbance elements affecting both sectors. When applied to $\theta > 0$, however, the result is at least slightly less obvious. Here it states that despite the fact that contemporaneous disturbances from different sectors may be highly correlated, and despite the fact that every disturbance may be highly auto-correlated, a given disturbance will *not* be correlated with a lagged disturbance from another sector unless the economy-wide implicit disturbances are themselves auto-correlated. To put it another way, the presence of economy-wide implicit disturbances and the presence of substantial serial correlation do not prevent us from taking $V(\theta)$ as block-diagonal for $\theta > 0$, provided that the serial correlation is entirely confined to the sector and equation implicit disturbances.

Is it then reasonable to assume that the serial correlation is so confined? I think it is reasonable in the context of a carefully constructed economy-wide model. Any such model inevitably omits variables the effects of which are not confined within sectors. Effects which are highly auto-correlated, however, are effects which are relatively systematic over time. In an inevitably aggregate and approximate economy-wide model, there are likely to be such systematic effects influencing individual equations and even whole sectors. Systematic effects which spread over more than one sector, however, seem substantially less likely to occur, especially when we recall that the limits of a sector in our sense are likely to be rather wide.[14] Variables which give rise to such effects are not likely to be omitted variables whose influence lies in the disturbance terms. Rather they are likely to be explicitly included in the model, if at all possible. If not, if they relate to the occurrence of a war, for example, and are thus hard to specify explicitly, the time periods in which they are most important are likely to be omitted from the analysis. In short, systematic behavior of the disturbances is an indication of incomplete specification. Such incompleteness is much less likely to occur as regards effects which are widespread than as regards effects which are relatively narrowly confined, especially since the former are less likely to be made up of

14. As they are in the SSRC model.

many small effects.[15] (Recall that an economy-wide implicit disturbance is one which affects more than one sector *directly*, not simply one whose effects are transmitted through the dynamic causal structure of the explicit model.) It thus does not seem unreasonable to assume that

(3.18) $$\Lambda_e = 0$$

and therefore

(3.19) $$V(\theta)^{IJ} = 0 \qquad (\theta > 0;\ I,\ J = 1,\ \ldots,\ N;\ J \neq I)$$

as good approximations.

3.5. IMPLICATIONS FOR THE USE OF LAGGED ENDOGENOUS VARIABLES

Of course, assuming (3.19) to hold is not sufficient to yield consistency when lagged endogenous variables are treated as predetermined. We have already seen that unless $V(\theta) = 0$, the decomposability of the dynamic system must be assumed in addition to (3.19) to secure such consistency. We argued above, however, that such decomposability was rather unlikely in an interconnected economy, although the fact that (3.19) is likely to hold approximately makes it important to look for *near*-decomposability and thus secure *near*-consistency.[16]

Even if such near-decomposability of the dynamic system does not occur, however, (3.19) has interesting consequences for the treatment of lagged endogenous variables as predetermined.

Consider the expression for $W(1)$ given in equation (2.5). Writing out the first few terms of the sum, we obtain

(3.20) $$W(1) = DV(1) + DBDV(2) + (DB)^2DV(3) + \ldots .$$

Since D is block-triangular and $V(1)$ block-diagonal by (3.19), the first term in this expansion is also block-triangular. Hence even if the dynamic system is not decomposable, endogenous variables lagged one period are approximately uncorrelated in the probability limit with disturbances in *higher*-numbered sectors (but not in the same or lower-numbered sectors), to the extent that the right-hand terms in (3.20) other than the first can be ignored.

In what sense is it legitimate, then, to assume that such terms can in fact be

15. A similar argument obviously implies that sector implicit disturbances are less likely to be serially correlated than are equation implicit disturbances. The analysis of the effects of this on $V(\theta)$ and the subsequent discussion is left to the reader. The assumption of no serial correlation in the sector implicit disturbances seems considerably more dangerous than that being discussed in the text.

16. Near-decomposability of a dynamic system has a number of interesting consequences in addition to this. See A. Ando, F. M. Fisher and H. A. Simon [3], especially Ando and Fisher [2].

ignored? Assume that the matrix DB is similar to a diagonal matrix, so that there exists a non-singular matrix P such that

(3.21) $DB = PHP^{-1}$,

where H is diagonal and has for diagonal elements the latent roots of DB.[17] Let

(3.22) $\Lambda = \begin{bmatrix} \Lambda_e & 0 & 0 \\ 0 & \Lambda_v & 0 \\ 0 & 0 & \Lambda_w \end{bmatrix}$,

(3.23) $\Delta = \begin{bmatrix} \Delta_e & 0 & 0 \\ 0 & \Delta_v & 0 \\ 0 & 0 & \Delta_w \end{bmatrix}$,

(3.24) $Q = [\phi \vdots \psi \vdots I]$

Then every such term can be written as

(3.25) $(DB)^{\theta-1} DV(\theta) = PH^{\theta-1}P^{-1}DQ\Lambda^{\theta}\Delta Q'$ $(\theta > 1)$.

We know that every diagonal element of the diagonal matrix Λ is less than unity in absolute value (indeed, we are assuming that some of the diagonal elements are zero). Moreover, *if we are prepared to maintain the stability assumption on DB* which was slipped in some time ago, every diagonal element of the diagonal matrix H will also be less than unity in absolute value. It follows that every element of every term in the expansion of $W(1)$ other than the first is composed of a sum of terms, each of which involves at least the product of a factor less than unity and the square of another such factor. There is clearly a reasonable sense in which one may be prepared to take such terms as negligible, at least when compared with the non-zero elements of the first term in the expansion for $W(1)$ which involve only the diagonal elements of Λ to the first power. If one is willing to do this, then one is saying that the use of endogenous variables lagged one period as instruments in higher-numbered sectors involves only negligible inconsistency, at least as compared with the use of the same variables as instruments in their own or lower-numbered sectors.

There may be considerable difficulties in accepting such a judgment, however. In the first place, it is well to be aware that there are two different statements involved. It is one thing to say that the effects in question are negligible compared to others and quite another to say that they are negligible in a more absolute sense. If one accepts the stability assumption, then there certainly is a value of θ beyond which further terms in the expansion of $W(1)$ are negligible by any given standard. These may not be all terms after

17. The assumption involved is, of course, very weak and is made for ease of exposition.

the first, however; we shall discuss the case in which there are nonnegligible terms after the first below.

Second (a minor point but one worth observing), even our conclusion about *relative* importance *need* not hold although other assumptions are granted. While it is true that as θ becomes large the right-hand side of (3.25) approaches zero, such approach need not be monotonic. To put it another way, every element of the matrix involved is a sum of terms. Each such term involves a diagonal element of Λ to the θ and a diagonal element of H to the $\theta - 1$. If all such diagonal elements are less than unity in absolute value, then the absolute value of each separate term approaches zero monotonically as θ increases; this need not be true of the *sum* of those terms, however, and it is easy to construct counter-examples. Nevertheless, there is a sense in which it seems appropriate to assume the terms in the expansion for $W(1)$ to be negligible for θ greater than some value, perhaps for $\theta > 1$.

All this, however, has leaned a bit heavily on the stability of DB. If that matrix has a latent root greater than unity in absolute value, then part of the reason for assuming that the right-hand side of (3.25) is negligible even for high values of θ has disappeared. Of course, the diagonal elements of Λ are known to be less than unity in absolute value, so that the infinite sum involved in $W(1)$ may still converge. However, such convergence is likely to be slow in an unstable case and may not occur at all, so that the effects of serial correlation are even more serious than in the stable case. Clearly, the stability assumption requires additional discussion at this point.

The usual reason for assuming stability of the dynamic model being estimated is one of convenience or of lack of knowledge of other cases. Since the unstable case tends to lead to unbounded moment matrices, the usual proofs of consistency of the limited-information estimators tend to break down in that circumstance. Indeed, maximum-likelihood estimators are presently known to be consistent only in the stable case and in rather special unstable cases.[18] It is therefore customary to assume stability in discussions of this sort. For present purposes, even if limited-information estimators are consistent in unstable cases and even if the Generalized Proximity Theorems which guarantee small inconsistencies for sufficiently good approximations also hold, the approximations which we are now discussing are relatively unlikely to be good ones in such cases.[19] Even if the existence of $W(1)$ is secured by assuming that the dynamic process (2.1) begins with non-stochastic initial conditions at some finite time in the past (and even this does not

18. For example, if *all* latent roots are greater than unity in absolute value. See T. W. Anderson [1]. J. D. Sargan has privately informed me that he has constructed a proof of consistency for the general case. The classic paper in this area is that of H. B. Mann and A. Wald [12].

19. See F. M. Fisher [8].

suffice for the existence of the probability limit), the effects of serial correlation will not die out (or will die out only slowly) as we consider longer and longer lags. The conclusion seems inescapable that if the model is thought to be unstable (and the more so, the more unstable it is), the use of lagged endogenous variables as instruments *anywhere* in an indecomposable dynamic system with serially correlated disturbances is likely to lead to large inconsistencies at least for all but very high lags. The lower the serial correlation and the closer the model to stability, the less dangerous is such use.

Is the stability assumption a realistic one for economy-wide models then? I think it is. Remember that what is at issue is not the ability of the economy to grow, but its ability to grow (or to have explosive cycles) with no help from the exogenous variables and no impulses from the random disturbances. Since the exogenous variables generally include population growth, and since technological change is generally either treated as a disturbance or as an effect which is exogenous in some way, this is by no means a hard assumption to accept. While there are growth and cycle models in economic theory which involve explosive systems, such models generally bound the explosive oscillations or growth by ceilings or floors which would be constant if the exogenous sources of growth were constant.[20] The system *as a whole* in such models is not unstable in the presence of constant exogenous variables and the absence of random shocks.[21] We shall thus continue to make the stability assumption.

Even when the stability assumption is made, however, it may not be the case, as we have seen, that one is willing to take the expression in (3.25) as negligible for all $\theta > 1$. In particular, this will be the case if serial correlation is thought to be very high so that the diagonal elements of Λ are close to unity in absolute value. In such cases, one will not be willing to assume that the use of endogenous variables lagged *one* period as instruments in higher-numbered sectors leads to only negligible inconsistencies. Accordingly, we must generalize our discussion.

Fortunately, this is easy. There clearly does exist a smallest $\theta^* > 0$ such that for all $\theta > \theta^*$ even the diagonal blocks of $V(\theta^*)$ are negligible on any given standard. Consider $W(\theta^*)$, the covariance matrix of the elements of u_t and those of $y_{t-\theta^*}$ with the columns corresponding to elements of u_t and the rows to elements of $y_{t-\theta^*}$. Clearly,

$$(3.26) \quad \begin{aligned} W(\theta^*) &= DV(\theta^*) + \sum_{\theta=\theta^*+1}^{\infty} (DB)^{\theta-\theta^*} DV(\theta) \\ &= DV(\theta^*) + \sum_{\theta=\theta^*+1}^{\infty} FH^{\theta-\theta^*} P^{-1} DQ\Lambda^{\theta} Q'. \end{aligned}$$

20. See, for example, J. R. Hicks [10] and R. F. Harrod [9].
21. Whether a linear model is a good approximation if such models are realistic is another matter.

Since D is block-triangular and $V(\theta^*)$ block-diagonal by (3.19), the product, $DV(\theta^*)$, is also block-triangular. Considering $W(\theta^*)^{IJ}$ for $J > I$, it is apparent that the covariances of endogenous variables lagged θ^* periods and current disturbances from *higher-numbered sectors* are made up of only negligible terms. Not only is $V(\theta)$ negligible by assumption for $\theta > \theta^*$, but also every such term involves at least one power of H, which by assumption is diagonal and has diagonal elements less than unity in absolute value.

Note, however, that a similar statement is clearly false as regards the covariances of endogenous variables lagged θ^* periods and current disturbances *from the same or lower-numbered sectors*. Such covariances involve the non-zero diagonal blocks of $V(\theta^*)$ in an essential way. It follows that the order of inconsistency so to speak, involved in using endogenous variables lagged a given number of periods as instruments, is less if such variables are used in higher-numbered sectors than if they are used in the same or lower-numbered sectors. To put it another way, the minimum lag with which it is reasonably safe to use endogenous variables as instruments is at least one less for use in higher-numbered than for use in the same or lower-numbered sectors.

As a matter of fact, our result is a bit stronger than this. It is apparent from (3.26) that the use of endogenous variables lagged θ^* periods as instruments in higher-numbered sectors involves covariances of the order of $\Lambda^{\theta^*+1}H$. Even the use of endogenous variables lagged $\theta^* + 1$ periods as instruments in the same or lower-numbered sectors, however, involves covariances of the order of only Λ^{θ^*+1}. No positive power of H is involved in the first term of the expansion for the latter covariances. Since H is diagonal with diagonal elements less than unity in absolute value, the difference between the minimum lag with which it is safe to use endogenous variables as instruments in the same or lower-numbered sectors and the corresponding lag for use in higher-numbered ones may be even greater than one. This point will be stronger the more stable one believes the dynamic system to be. It arises because the effects of serial correlation in sector and equation implicit disturbances are direct in the case of lagged endogenous variables used in the same or lower-numbered sectors and are passed through a damped dynamic system in the case of lagged endogenous variables used in higher-numbered sectors.[22]

To sum up: so far as inconsistency is concerned, it is likely to be safer to use endogenous variables with a given lag as instruments in higher-numbered sectors than to use them in the same or lower-numbered sectors. For the

---

22. All this is subject to the minor reservation discussed above concerning sums each term of which approaches zero monotonically. In practice, one tends to ignore such reservations in the absence of specific information as to which way they point.

latter use, the endogenous variables should be lagged by at least one more period to achieve the same level of consistency.[23]

Now, it may be thought that this result is a rather poor return for all the effort we have put into securing it. While one can certainly conceive of stronger results, the usefulness of the present one should not be underestimated. We remarked at the beginning of this section that one important *desideratum* of an instrumental variable was a close causal connection with the variables appearing in the equation to be estimated. In general, economy-wide (and most other) econometric models have the property that variables with low lags are often (but not always) more closely related to variables to be explained than are variables with high ones. There may therefore be a considerable gain in efficiency in the use of recent rather than relatively remote endogenous variables as instruments, and it is important to know that in certain reasonable contexts this may be done without increasing the likely level of resulting inconsistency. We now turn to the discussion of the causal criterion for instrumental variables.

4. Causality and rules for the use of eligible instrumental variables

4.1. THE CAUSAL CRITERION FOR INSTRUMENTAL VARIABLES

We stated above that a good instrumental variable should directly or indirectly causally influence the variables in the equation to be estimated in a way independent of the other instrumental variables, and that the more direct such influence is, the better. This statement requires some discussion. As far as the limiting example of an instrument completely unrelated to the variables of the model is concerned, the lesson to be drawn might equally well be that instrumental variables must be correlated in the probability limit with at least one of the included variables. While it is easy to see that *some* causal connection must therefore exist, the question naturally arises why it must be one in which the instrumental variables cause the included ones. If correlation is all that matters, surely the causal link might be reversed or both variables influenced by a common third one.

This is not the case. Consider first the situation in which the proposed instrumental variable is caused in part by variables included in the model. To the extent that this is the case, no advantage is obtained by using the proposed instrumental variable over using the included variables themselves. Obviously, the included variables are more highly correlated with themselves than with the proposed instrument. Further, correlation with the disturbance

---

23. The reader should be aware of the parallel between this result and the similar result for the use of *current* endogenous variables which emerges when (BR. 1)–(BR. 3) are assumed. Essentially, we have replaced (BR. 2) with (3.19) and have dropped (BR. 3).

will be maintained if the proposed instrument is used. To the extent that the proposed instrument is caused by variables unrelated to the included variables, correlation with the disturbances will go down, but so also will correlation with the included variables.

The situation is similar if the proposed instrumental variable and one or more of the included ones are caused in part by a third variable. In this case, it is obviously more efficient to use that third variable itself as an instrument, and, if this is done, no further advantage attaches to the use of the proposed instrumental variable in addition. (The only exception to this occurs if data on the jointly causing variable are not available. In such a case the proposed instrument could be used to advantage.)

In general then, an instrumental variable should be known to cause the included variables in the equation, at least indirectly. The closer such a causal connection is the better. As can easily be seen from our discussion of block-recursive systems, however, the closer is that connection in many cases, the greater the danger of inconsistency through high correlations with the relevant disturbances. In such systems, for example, current endogenous variables in low-numbered sectors directly cause current endogenous variables in high-numbered sectors, while the same endogenous variables lagged are likely to be safer in terms of inconsistency but are also likely to be more remote causes.[24] The value of the result derived at the end of the last section is that it provides a case in which one set of instrumental variables is likely to dominate another set on both criteria.

4.2. AVAILABLE INSTRUMENTS AND MULTICOLLINEARITY

There is obviously one set of variables which has optimal properties on several counts. These are the exogenous variables explicitly included in the model. Such variables are (by assumption) uncorrelated in the probability limit with the disturbances, and are also in close causal connection to the current variables in any equation; indeed, they *are* some of those variables in some cases.[25] In the happy event that such exogenous variables are adequate in number, that their variance-covariance matrix is non-singular, and that no lagged endogenous variables appear, there is no need to seek further for instrumental variables to use.

Unfortunately, this is unlikely to be the case in an economy-wide econometric model. Such models tend to be almost self-contained with relatively few truly exogenous variables entering at relatively few places. This is especially the case if government policies obey regular rules, follow signals from

24. On causation in general and in decomposable systems (or our block-recursive systems) in particular, see H. A. Simon [13].
25. They may not cause all such variables even indirectly if the dynamic system is decomposable. Such cases are automatically treated in the rules given below.

the economy and are therefore partly endogenous for purposes of estimation.[26] In estimating any equation, all variables not used as instruments (except the variable explained by the equation) must be replaced by a linear combination of instruments and the dependent variable regressed on such linear combinations. If the second stage of this procedure is not to involve inversion of a singular matrix, then (counting instrumental variables appearing in the equation) there must be at least as many instruments used as there are parameters to be estimated. Further, the linear combinations employed must not be perfectly correlated. Current exogenous variables are simply not generally sufficient to meet this requirement in economy-wide models. Moreover, they do not cause lagged endogenous variables which are likely to be present in a dynamic system.

Clearly, however, if the system is dynamic, it will be possible to use *lagged* exogenous variables as well as current ones. Such use may be especially helpful if lagged endogenous variables are to be treated as endogenous and replaced by linear combinations of instruments which can be taken as causing them in part. Indeed, if lagged endogenous variables *are* to be taken as endogenous, then exclusive use of current exogenous variables as instruments will not satisfy the causal criterion for instrumental variables already discussed. Since we have already seen that lagged endogenous variables should be used as instruments only with caution, it follows that lagged exogenous variables may well provide a welcome addition to the collection of available instruments.

Unfortunately, this also is unlikely to suffice. While it is true that one can always secure a sufficient number of instruments by using exogenous variables with larger and larger lags, such a procedure runs into several difficulties. In the first place, since rather long lags may be required, there may be a serious curtailment of available observations at the beginning of the time period to be used. Second, exogenous variables in the relatively distant past will be relatively indirect causes of even the lagged endogenous variables appearing in the equation to be estimated; it follows that their use will fail the causal criteria given, and that it may be better to accept some inconsistency by using endogenous variables with lower lags. Finally, after going only a few periods back, the chances are high in practice that adding an exogenous variable with a still higher lag adds a variable which is very highly correlated with the instruments already included, and therefore adds little independent causal information.[27] While the use of lagged exogenous variables is therefore highly desirable, it may not be of sufficient practical help to allow the search for instrumental variables to end.

---

26. This is to be sharply distinguished from the question of whether governmentally controlled variables can be used as *policy* as opposed to estimation instruments.

27. This is especially likely if the exogenous variables are ones such as population which are mainly trends.

Whatever collection of current exogenous, lagged exogenous and (none, some, or all) lagged endogenous variables are used, however, the multi-collinearity difficulty just encountered tends to arise. Some method must be found for dealing with it.

One set of interesting suggestions in this area has been provided by Kloek and Mennes.[28] Essentially, they propose using principal component analysis in various ways on the set of eligible instruments in order to secure orthogonal linear combinations. The endogenous variables are then replaced by their regressions on these linear combinations (possibly together with the eligible instruments actually appearing in the equation to be estimated), and the dependent variable regressed on these surrogates and the instruments appearing in the equation. Variants of this proposal are also examined.

This suggestion has the clear merit of avoiding multicollinearity, as it is designed to do. However, it may eliminate such multicollinearity in an undesirable way. If multicollinearity is present in a regression equation, at least one of the variables therein is adding little causal information to that already contained in the other variables. In replacing a given endogenous variable with its regression on a set of instruments, therefore, the prime reason for avoiding multicollinearity is that the addition of an instrument which is collinear with the included ones adds little causal information while using up a degree of freedom. The elimination of such multicollinearity should thus proceed in such a way as to conserve causal information. The Kloek-Mennes proposals may result in orthogonal combinations of instruments which are not particularly closely causally related to the included endogenous variables. Thus such proposals may well be inferior to a procedure which eliminates multicollinearity by eliminating instruments which contribute relatively little to the causal explanation of the endogenous variable to be replaced.[29] Clearly, this may involve using different sets of instruments in the replacement of different endogenous variables. Proposals along these lines are given below.

4.3. RULES FOR THE USE OF ELIGIBLE INSTRUMENTAL
VARIABLES

We have several times pointed out that the causal criterion and that of no correlation with the given disturbance may be inconsistent and that one may only be able to satisfy one more closely by sacrificing the other to a greater extent. In principle, a fully satisfactory treatment of the use of instrumental variables in economy-wide models would involve a full-scale Bayesian analysis of the losses and gains from any particular action. Such an

---

28. K. Kloek and L. B. M. Mennes [11].

29. This seems to have been one of the outcomes of experimentation with different forms of principal component analysis in practice. See L. D. Taylor [16].

analysis is clearly beyond the scope of the present paper, although any recommended procedure clearly has some judgment of probable losses behind it, however vague such judgment may be.

We shall proceed by assuming that the no-correlation criterion has been used to secure a set of eligible instrumental variables whose use is judged to involve only tolerable inconsistencies in the estimation of a given equation. Note that the set may be different for different equations. Within that set are current and lagged exogenous variables and lagged endogenous variables sufficiently far in the past that the effects of serial correlation are judged to be negligible over the time period involved. As shown in the preceding section, the time period will generally be shorter for endogenous variables in sectors lower-numbered than that in which the equation to be estimated appears than for endogenous variables in the same or higher-numbered sectors.[30] Clearly, other things being equal, the use of current and lagged exogenous variables is preferable to the use of lagged endogenous variables and the use of lagged endogenous variables from lower-numbered sectors is preferable to the use of endogenous variables with the same (or possibly even a slightly greater) lag from the same or higher-numbered sectors than that in which the equation to be estimated occurs. We shall suggest ways of modifying the use of the causal criterion to take account of this. For convenience we shall refer to all the eligible instrumental variables as predetermined and to all other variables as endogenous.

We shall assume that each endogenous variable is associated with a particular structural equation (either in current or lagged form) in which it appears on the left-hand side with a coefficient of unity. This is not an unreasonable assumption, as such normalization rules are generally present in model building, each variable of the model being naturally associated with that particular endogenous variable which is determined by the decision-makers whose behavior is represented by the equation. The normalization rules are in a real sense part of the specification of the model, and the model is not completely specified unless every endogenous variable appears (at least implicitly) in exactly one equation in normalized form. For example, it is not enough to have price equating supply and demand, equations should also be present which explain price quotations by sellers and buyers and which describe the equilibrating process. (For most purposes, of course, such additional equations can remain in the back of the model builders' mind; however, the rules for choosing instrumental variables about to be discussed may require that they be made explicit.) For another example, it is always clear which equation is the "consumption function," even though consumption is one of a set of jointly-determined variables whose values are

---

30. It will not have escaped the reader's notice that very little guidance has been given as to the determination of the absolute magnitude of that time period.

determined by the system as a whole.[31] The fact that one may not be certain as to the proper normalization rules to use in a given case should be taken as a statement of uncertainty as to proper specification and not as a statement that no proper normalization rules exist.

We are now ready to discuss the procedure recommended for selecting instrumental variables from the eligible list. Consider any particular endogenous variable in the equation to be estimated, other than the one explained by that equation. That right-hand endogenous variable will be termed of *zero causal order*. Consider the *structural* equation (either in its original form or with all variables lagged) that explains that variable. The variables other than the explained one appearing therein will be called of *first causal order*. Next, consider the structural equations explaining the *first causal order* endogenous variables.[32] All variables appearing in those equations will be called of *second causal order* with the exception of the *zero causal order* variable and those endogenous variables of first causal order the equations for which have already been considered. Note that a given predetermined variable may be of more than one causal order. Take now those structural equations explaining endogenous variables of second causal order. All variables appearing in such equations will be called of *third causal order* except for the *endogenous* ones of lower causal order, and so forth. (Any predetermined variables never reached in this procedure are dropped from the eligible set while dealing with the given zero causal order variable.)

The result of this procedure is to use the *a priori* structural information available to subdivide the set of predetermined variables according to closeness of causal relation to a given endogenous variable in the equation to be estimated. Thus, predetermined variables of first causal order are known to cause that endogenous variable directly; predetermined variables of second causal order are known directly to cause other variables which directly cause the given endogenous variable, and so forth. Note again that a given predetermined variable can be of more than one causal order, so that the subdivision need not result in disjunct sets of predetermined variables.

We now provide a complete ordering of the predetermined variables relative to the given endogenous variable of zero causal order.[33] Let p be the

31. This argument is, of course, closely related to that of R. H. Strotz and H. Wold [14] in which simultaneity is the approximate or equilibrium version of a system with very small time lags. For an illuminating discussion which bears directly on our discussion, see R. L. Basmann [5] and [6] and cf. Strotz and Wold [15]. The issue of whether normalization rules are in fact given in practice is of some consequence in the choice of two-stage least squares or limited-information, maximum-likelihood. See G. C. Chow [7].

32. Observe that endogenous variables appearing in the equation to be estimated other than the particular one with which we begin may be of positive causal order. This includes the endogenous variable to be explained by the equation to be estimated.

33. I am indebted to J. C. G. Boot for aid in the construction of the following formal description.

largest number of different causal orders to which any predetermined variable belongs. To each predetermined variable we assign a p-component vector. The first component of that vector is the lowest numbered causal order to which the given predetermined variable belongs; the second component is the next lowest causal order to which it belongs and so forth. Vectors corresponding to variables belonging to less than p different causal orders have infinity in the unused places. Thus, for example, if $p = 5$, a predetermined variable of first, second and eighth causal order will be assigned the vector: $(1, 2, 8, \infty, \infty)$. The vectors are now ordered lexicographically. That is, any vector, say f, is assigned a number, $\beta(f)$, so that for any two vectors, say f and h

$$\begin{aligned} &\beta(f) > \beta(h) \text{ if and only if either } f_1 > h_1 \text{ or for some} \\ &j(1 < j \leqq p) \, f_i = h_i \ (i = 1, \ldots, j-1) \text{ and } f_j > h_j. \end{aligned}$$

(4.1)

The predetermined variables are then ordered in ascending order of their corresponding β-numbers. This will be called the β-ordering.

Thus predetermined variables of first causal order are assigned lower numbers than predetermined variables of only higher causal orders; predetermined variables of first and second causal order are assigned lower numbers than predetermined variables of first and only causal orders higher than second (or of no higher causal order) and so forth.[34]

The procedure just described gives an *a priori* preference order on the set of instrumental variables relative to a given zero causal order endogenous variable. This order is in terms of closeness to causal relation. Alternatively, one may wish to modify that order to take further account of the danger of inconsistency. This may be done by deciding that current and lagged exogenous variables of a given causal order are always to be preferred to lagged endogenous variables of no lower causal order, and that lagged endogenous variables from sectors with lower numbers than that of the equation to be estimated are always to be preferred to endogenous variables with the same lag and causal order from the same or higher-numbered sectors. One might even go further and decide that *all* current and lagged exogenous variables of finite causal order are to be preferred to *any* lagged endogenous variable.

However the preference ordering is decided upon, its existence allows us to use *a posteriori* information to choose a set of instruments for the zero causal order endogenous variable in the way about to be described. Once that set

34. This is only one way of constructing such an order. If there is specific *a priori* reason to believe that a given instrument is important in influencing the variable to be replaced (for example, if it is known to enter in several different ways with big coefficients) then it should be given a low number. In the absence of such specific information the order given in the text seems a natural way of organizing the structural information.

has been chosen, that endogenous variable is replaced by its regression on the instruments in the set and the equation in question estimated by least squares regression of the left-hand endogenous variable on the resulting right-hand variables.[35]

We use *a posteriori* information in combination with the *a priori* preference ordering in the following manner. Suppose that there are T observations in the sample. Regress the zero causal order endogenous variable on the first $T-2$ instruments in the preference ordering (a regression with one degree of freedom). Now drop the least preferred of these instruments from the regression. Observe whether the multiple correlation of the regression drops significantly as a result. (The standard here may be the significance level of R^2 or simply its value corrected for degrees of freedom.) If correlation does drop significantly, then the $T-2$nd instrument contributes significantly to the causation of the zero order endogenous variable even in the presence of all instruments which are *a priori* more closely related to that variable than it is. It should therefore be retained. If correlation does not drop significantly, then the variable in question adds nothing and should be omitted.

Now proceed to the $T-3$rd instrument. If the $T-2$nd instrument was retained at the previous step, reintroduce it; if not, leave it out. Observe whether omitting the $T-3$rd instrument reduces the multiple correlation significantly. If so, retain it, if not, omit it and proceed to the next lower-numbered instrument.

Continue in this way. At every step, a given instrument is tested to see whether it contributes significantly to multiple correlation in the presence of all instruments which are *a priori* preferred to it and all other instruments which have already passed the test. When all instruments have been so tested, the ones remaining are the ones to be used.

4.4. DISCUSSION OF THE RULES

The point of this procedure (or the variants described below) is to replace the right-hand endogenous variables in the equation to be estimated by their regression-calculated values, using instruments which satisfy the causal criterion as well as possible while keeping inconsistency at a tolerable level. Certain features require discussion.

In the first place, multicollinearity at this stage of the proceedings is automatically taken care of in a way consistent with the causal criterion. If some set of instruments is highly collinear, then that member of the set which is least preferred on *a priori* grounds will fail to reduce correlation significantly when it is tested as just described. It will then be omitted and the procedure guarantees that it will be the *least* preferred member of the set which is so

---

35. An important modification of this procedure is described below.

treated. If the β-ordering is used, this will be the one most distantly structurally related to the endogenous variable to be replaced. Multicollinearity
will be tolerated where it should be, namely, where despite its presence each
instrument in the collinear set adds significant causal information.

Second, it is evident that the procedure described has the property that no
variable will be omitted simply because it is highly correlated with other
variables already dropped. If two variables add significantly to correlation
when both are present but fail to add anything when introduced separately,
then the first one to be tested will not be dropped from the regression, as
omitting it in the presence of the other instrument will significantly reduce
correlation.[36] While it is true that variables may be dropped because of correlation with variables less preferred than the $T-2$nd, which are never tested,
the exclusion of the latter variables seems to be a relatively weak reliance on
a priori information.

This brings us to the next point. Clearly, it is possible in principle that
instruments less preferred than the $T-2$nd would in fact pass the correlation
test described if that test were performed after some lower-numbered
instruments were tested and dropped. Similarly, an instrument dropped at an
early stage might pass the test in the absence of variables *later* dropped because
of the increased number of degrees of freedom. One could, of course, repeat
the entire procedure in order to test every previously dropped variable after
each decision to omit; it seems preferable, however, to rely on the *a priori*
preference ordering in practice and to insist that instruments which come
late in the β-ordering pass a more stringent empirical test than those which
come early. The rationale behind the β-ordering is the belief that it is the
earlier instruments in that order which contribute most of the causal information, so that it seems quite appropriate to calculate the degrees of freedom
for testing a given instrument by subtracting the number of its place in the
order from the total number of observations (and allowing for the constant
term).[37]

Turning to another issue, it may be objected that there is no guarantee
that the suggested procedures will result in a non-singular moment matrix to
be inverted at the last stage. That is, there may be some set of endogenous
variables to be replaced whose regressions together involve less than r
predetermined variables. Alternatively, counting the instruments included
in the equation to be estimated there may not be as many instruments used
in the final stage as there are parameters to be estimated. This can happen,

36. This property was missing in the procedure suggested in an earlier draft of this paper in
which variables were added in ascending order of preference and retained if they added
significantly to correlation. I am indebted to Albert Ando for helpful discussions on this point.
37. Admittedly, this argument loses some of its force when applied to the modifications of
the β-order given above.

of course, although it is perhaps relatively unlikely. If it does occur, then it is a sign that the equation in question is unidentifiable from the sample available, and that the causal information contained in the sample is insufficient to allow estimation of the equation without relaxing the inconsistency requirements. To put it another way, it can be argued that to rectify this situation by the introduction in the first-stage regressions of variables failing the causal test as described is an *ad hoc* device which adds no causal information. While such variables may in fact appear in such regressions with non-zero coefficients in the probability limit, their use in the sample adds nothing to the quality of the estimates save the ability to secure numbers and disguise the problem.

Of course, such an argument is a bit too strong. Whether a variable adds significantly to correlation is a question of what one means by significance. The problem is thus a continuous rather than a discrete one and should be treated as such. For the criterion of significance used, in some sense, the equation in question cannot be estimated from the sample in the circumstance described; it may be estimable with a less stringent significance criterion. In practice, if the significance requirements are relaxed, the moment matrix to be inverted will pass from singularity to near-singularity, and estimated asymptotic standard errors will be large rather than infinite. The general point is that if multicollinearity cannot be sufficiently eliminated using causal information, little is to be gained by eliminating it by introducing more or less irrelevant variables.

A somewhat related point is that the use of different variables as instruments in the regressions for different endogenous variables in the same equation may result in a situation in which the longest lag involved in one such regression is greater than that involved in others. If data are available only from an initial date, this means that using the regressions, as estimated, involves eliminating some observations at the beginning of the period that would be retained if the longest-lagged instrument were dropped. In this case, some balance must be struck between the gain in efficiency from extra observations and the loss from disregarding causal information if the lagged instrument in question is dropped. It is hard to give a precise guide as to how this should be done. (My personal preference would be for retaining the instrument in most cases.) Such circumstances will fortunately be relatively infrequent as the periods of data collection generally begin further than those of estimation, at least in models of developed economies. Further, the reduction in available observations attendant on the use of an instrument with a large lag renders it unlikely that the introduction of that instrument adds significantly to correlation.

Finally, the use of different instruments in the regressions replacing different endogenous variables in the equation to be estimated reintroduces the problem of inconsistency. When the equation to be estimated is rewritten with calculated values replacing some or all of the variables, the residual term includes not only the original structural disturbance but also a linear combination of the residuals from the regression equations used in such replacement. When the equation is then estimated by regressing the left-hand variable on the calculated right-hand ones and the instruments explicitly appearing, consistency requires not only zero correlation in the probability limit between the original disturbance and all the variables used in the final regression but also zero correlation in the probability limit between the residuals from the earlier-stage regression equations and all such variables. If the same set of instruments is used when replacing every right-hand endogenous variable, and if that set includes the instruments explicitly in the equation, the latter requirement presents no problem since the normal equations or ordinary least squares imply that such correlations are zero even in the sample.[38] When different instruments are used in the replacement of different variables, however, or when the instruments so used do not include those explicitly in the equation, the danger of inconsistency from this source does arise.

There are several ways of handling this without sacrificing the major benefits of our procedures. One way is simply to argue that these procedures are designed to include in the regression for any right-hand endogenous variable any instrument which is correlated with the residuals from that regression, computed without that instrument. The excluded instruments are either those which are known *a priori* not to be direct or indirect causes of the variable to be replaced, or those which fail to add significantly to the correlation of the regression in question. The former instruments are known *a priori* not to appear in equations explaining the variable to be replaced and cannot be correlated in the probability limit with the residual from the regression unless both they and the replaced variable are affected by some third variable not included in that regression.[39] Such a third variable cannot be endogenous, however, since in that case the excluded instruments in question would also be endogenous; moreover, our procedure is designed to include explicitly any instrument significantly affecting the variable to be replaced. Any such third variable must therefore be omitted from the model, and it *may* not be stretching things too far to disregard correlations between residuals and excluded instruments stemming from such a source.

As for instruments which are indirectly causally related to the endogenous variable involved but which fail to add significantly to the correlation of the

---

38. This is the case when the reduced form equations are used, for example, as in the classic version of two-stage least squares.

39. If they were non-negligibly caused by the replaced variable itself, they would be endogenous, contrary to assumption.

regression in question, these cannot be significantly correlated with the *sample* residual from that regression. One can therefore argue that the evidence is against their being significantly correlated with that residual in the probability limit.

Such an argument can clearly be pushed too far, however. If there are strong *a priori* reasons to believe that the excluded instruments should be included in view of the causal structure of the model, one may not want to reject correlation in the probability limit because multicollinearity (for the long continuance of which there may be no structural reason). leads to insignificant correlation in the sample. A modified course of action then is to include in the regression for any replaced variable any instrument which one believes *a priori* to be important in that regression *and* which appears either in the equation to be estimated or in the regression for any other replaced variable, as computed by the procedures described above.[40] Clearly, not much is lost by doing this since the added variables will not contribute much to the equation in the sample.

Alternatively, one may go the whole way toward guarding against inconsistency from the source under discussion and include in the regression for any replaced variable all instruments which appear in the equation to be estimated or in the regression for any other replaced variable, as computed by the described procedures, whether or not such instrument is thought *a priori* to be important in explaining the replaced variable. This alternative clearly eliminates the danger under discussion. It may, however, reintroduce multicollinearity and may involve a serious departure from the causal criterion if *a priori* non-causal instruments are thus included. Nevertheless, it does retain the merit that every instrumental variable used is either explicitly included in the equation or contributes significantly to the causal explanation of at least one variable so included. In practice, there may not be a great deal of difference between these alternatives, and the last one described may then be optimal (unless it is unavailable because of the degrees of freedom required).

Whatever variant of our procedures is thought best in practice, they all have the merit of using information on the dynamic and causal structure of the model in securing estimates. The use of such information in some way is vital in the estimation of economy-wide econometric models where the ideal conditions for which most estimators are designed are unlikely to be encountered in practice.[41]

---

40. Omitting instruments which do *not* so appear does not cause inconsistency.

41. The use of the causal structure of the model itself to choose instrumental variables as described in the text is closely akin to the methods used by H. Barger and L. R. Klein to estimate a system with triangular matrix of coefficients of current endogenous variables. See [4].

272 *Causal models in the social sciences*

References

[1] ANDERSON, T. W., "On Asymptotic Distributions of Estimates of Parameters of Stochastic Difference Equations," *Annals of Mathematical Statistics*, XXX (September, 1959), 676–687.

[2] ANDO, A., and FISHER, F. M., "Near-Decomposability, Partition and Aggregation, and the Relevance of Stability Discussions," *International Economic Review*, IV (January, 1963), 53–67; reprinted as Chapter 3 of [3].

[3] ANDO, A., FISHER, F. M:, and SIMON, H. A., *Essays on the Structure of Social Science Models*, (Cambridge, Massachusetts: M.I.T. Press, 1963).

[4] BARGER, H., and KLEIN, L. R., "A Quarterly Model for the United States Economy," *Journal of the American Statistical Association*, XLIX (September, 1954), 413–437.

[5] BASMANN, R. L., "The Causal Interpretation of Non-Triangular Systems of Economic Relations," *Econometrica*, XXXI (July, 1963), 439–448.

[6] ———, "On the Causal Interpretation of Non-Triangular Systems of Economic Relations: A Rejoinder," *Econometrica*, XXXI (July, 1963), 451–453.

[7] CHOW, G. C., "A Comparison of Alternative Estimators for Simultaneous Equations," IBM Research Report, RC-781, 1962.

[8] FISHER, F. M., "On the Cost of Approximate Specification in Simultaneous Equation Estimation," *Econometrica*, XXIX (April, 1961), 139–170; reprinted as Chapter 2 of [3].

[9] HARROD, R. F., *Towards a Dynamic Economics*, (London: Macmillan, 1948).

[10] HICKS, J. R., *A Contribution to the Theory of the Trade Cycle*, (Oxford: Clarendon, 1950).

[11] KLOEK, T., and MENNES, L. B. M., "Simultaneous Equation Estimation Based on Principal Components of Predetermined Variables," *Econometrica*, XXVIII (January, 1960), 45–61.

[12] MANN, H. B., and WALD, A., "On the Statistical Treatment of Linear Stochastic Difference Equations," *Econometrica*, XI (July–October, 1943), 173–220.

[13] SIMON, H. A., "Causal Ordering and Identifiability," Chapter 3 in *Studies in Econometric Method*, ed. Wm. C. Hood and T. C. Koopmans, Cowles Commission Monograph 14, (New York: John Wiley, 1953); reprinted as Chapter 1 of H. A. Simon, *Models of Man*, (New York: John Wiley, 1957) and as Chapter 1 of [3].

[14] STROTZ, R. H., and WOLD, H., "Recursive vs. Nonrecursive Systems: An Attempt at Synthesis," *Econometrica*, XXVIII (April, 1960), 417–427.

[15] ———, "The Causal Interpretability of Structural Parameters: A Reply," *Econometrica*, XXXI (July, 1963), 449–450.

[16] TAYLOR, L. D., "The Principal-Component-Instrumental-Variable Approach to the Estimation of Systems of Simultaneous Equations," mimeographed and unpublished paper, (1963), and Ph.D. Thesis by same title, Harvard University, Cambridge, (1962).

[17] WOLD, H., and JURÉEN, L., *Demand Analysis*, (New York: John Wiley, 1953).

[18] WOLD, H., and FAXÉR, P., "On the Specification Error in Regression Analysis," *Annals of Mathematical Statistics*, XXVIII (March, 1957), 265–267.

[19] WOLD, H., "Ends and Means in Econometric Model Building," *Probability and Statistics*, ed. U. Grenander, The Harald Cramér Volume, (New York: John Wiley, 1960), 354–434.

Chapter 15

LOGIC OF CAUSAL ANALYSIS: FROM EXPERIMENTAL TO NONEXPERIMENTAL DESIGNS

ALDEN DYKSTRA MILLER
Boston University

In recent years sociologists have more and more frequently felt compelled to make causal inferences in the course of their research. Unfortunately the discipline as a whole has not had access to a methodology that would permit such inferences in the general case where there is reciprocal causation and where unmeasured confounding influences abound. Appropriate methods have been known to exist, but have seemed to be mysteriously shrouded, available only to those on the frontiers of statistical science. Yet actually the necessary analytical apparatus has been available in other disciplines and taught at the advanced undergraduate and beginning graduate levels. The logic can be grasped without extensive training in mathematics or statistics by advanced undergraduate majors in sociology.

It is our purpose here to present a part of this logic[1] in nontechnical terms, assuming only an elementary understanding of what a multiple regression equation is. For convenience we will begin with an experimental design and describe the logic involved in terms of two-stage least squares, sometimes called generalized classical linear estimation. This particular estimator, or

---

Paper prepared especially for *Causal Models in the Social Sciences*.

1. The identification problem, the problem of showing that it is possible to estimate the coefficients of a model, is discussed quite fully in Franklin M. Fisher, *The Identification Problem in Econometrics* (New York: McGraw-Hill, 1966), and more simply in Carl Christ, *Econometric Models and Methods* (New York: John Wiley, 1966), pp. 298–346; Arthur S. Goldberger, *Econometric Theory* (New York: John Wiley, 1964), pp. 306–318; J. Johnston, *Econometric Methods* (New York: McGraw-Hill, 1963), pp. 240–252.

technique for solving for causal effects, is one technique from one major class of techniques that might be used. It may be thought of as differing from other techniques in that major class only in the way in which it responds to sampling error and errors in assumptions.[2] The logic will then be extended from experimental to nonexperimental designs. The object of our discussion may be understood as a generally understandable and applicable approach for putting existing theory into interaction with data in order to extend theory.

1. An experiment concerning a single measured cause of prejudice

Consider an imaginary experiment with a heavy debt to Miller and Bugelski.[3] It would be an attempt to discover the effect of frustration on prejudice, if any, and would thus constitute a test of one application of frustration-aggression theory. Subjects are subjected to experiences intended to produce frustration, which in turn is expected to produce prejudice. We might, following Miller and Bugelski, have subjects take an impossibly difficult test and miss bank night at the weekly movie, if we thought such experiences would be appropriately frustrating. We could measure frustration in a questionnaire or interview by tapping the degree to which such goals as maintaining a positive self image and getting to the movie were experienced as important and blocked. We could measure prejudice by tapping negative attitudes and stereotypes toward minority groups.

How might we proceed? It is usual in an experiment to have an experimental group and a control group, with subjects randomly assigned into one or the other. The two groups are then made to differ on the presumed causal or independent variable, and tested to see whether they differ on the caused or dependent variable. We would make the two groups differ in frustrtion and assess the difference that resulted in prejudice. Sometimes this basic design is elaborated to include measurements on the dependent variable both before and after the experimental and control groups are made to differ on the independent variable. Then we could conceptualize the making of the two groups to differ on the independent variable as a change in the independent variable, a change that occurs systematically only in the experimental group, and conceptualize the effect for which we are looking as

2. Franklin M. Fisher, *op. cit.*, pp. 52–56; Carl Christ, *op. cit.*, pp. 347–494; J. Johnston, *op. cit.*, pp. 231–274; Arthur S. Goldberger, *op. cit.*, pp. 288–380; E. Malinvaud, *Statistical Methods of Econometrics* (Chicago: Rand McNally, 1966), pp. 497–613; Herman O. A. Wold, "Forecasting by the Chain Principle," in Herman O. A. Wold (Ed.), *Econometric Model Building, Essays on the Causal Chain Approach* (Amsterdam: North Holland Publishing Company, 1964), pp. 25–33.

3. Neal E. Miller and Richard Bugelski, "Minor Studies of Agression: II. The Influence of Frustrations Imposed by the In-Group on Attitudes Expressed Toward Out-Groups," *Journal of Psychology*, 25 (1948): 437–442.

a change in the dependent variable, where we are checking to see whether the experimental group changed in a manner different from the manner in which the control group may have changed.

We would have the subjects in our experimental group take the test and miss bank night, while the subjects in the control group would be exempted from such treatment. After checking to see that we had actually produced more frustration in the experimental group than in the control group, we would ascertain the effect of frustration on prejudice, either by simply noting the difference between the experimental and control groups in final prejudice level or by noting any systematic change in prejudice level in the experimental group, where that change was different from any change that took place in the control group.

What is the core idea in the design of such an experiment? What makes it convincing as a test of a causal proposition? It is not the fact of manipulation *per se*. Consider a rather informal version of the experiment we are describing, where the experimenter relies on the idea of manipulation to make his case. He frustrates whom he chooses and observes that they are prejudiced more than other people. He finds himself open to attack as a second Chanticleer on the ground that he may have chosen to frustrate those who have characteristics that would lead them to be prejudiced anyway or on the ground that he may have tended to frustrate people who were already prejudiced.

Instead of the fact of manipulation *per se*, a major part of the key is randomization, the random assignment to experimental and control groups. Then the manipulation coupled with this assignment becomes simply another variable that causes frustration, one which, because of its random character, (subjects having been assigned randomly to categories differentially subjected to manipulation), can be assumed to be unrelated, except for chance, to alternative causes of prejudice besides frustration. The fact of control, manipulation of the subjects by the experimenter, accomplishes only one thing: it makes it fairly easy to locate or, rather, create, a cause of frustration that is not related to other causes of prejudice.

It is also very important for the experimenter to be able to convince those who read his report that the manipulation could not have caused prejudice directly, thus competing with frustration as a possible cause of prejudice, but there is nothing built into the procedure of the experiment to guarantee that.

The experimenter makes use of this notion of random control, together with a bald assumption to the effect that the manipulation does not cause prejudice directly, in the following argument:

If the manipulation, a cause of frustration, was unrelated to any unmeasured causes of prejudice and did not cause prejudice directly, it could be related to prejudice only by way of a causal link between frustration and prejudice. Therefore, if the experimental and control groups differed on prejudice or on change in prejudice, it must have been because of differences in frustration, or changes in frustration.

Suppose we designate level of frustration as X, level of prejudice as Y, and the presence or absence of experiences intended by the experimenter to be frustrating as Z. Alternatively we could designate *change* in frustration as X, *change* in prejudice as Y, and *change* in the presence or absence of experiences intended to be frustrating as Z. In either case, if:

(1) Z, a cause of X, does not cause Y except through X
(2) Z is unrelated to any unmeasured causes of Y that do not operate solely through X

then any empirical association between Z and Y must be due to the effects of X on Y, since X is the only possible link between Z and Y (see Fig. 15.1). The argument would hold regardless of what other causes of prejudice there might be and regardless of what other causes of frustration there might be, including prejudice itself. *The two assumptions stated above, not the fact of manipulation* per se, *are the core of the experimental logic.*

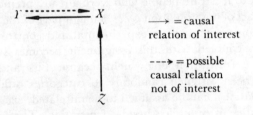

Figure 15.1. (*unmeasured variables omitted for simplicity*)

We could, following out this argument a little further, assess the exact nature of the effect of frustration, X, on prejudice, Y, by computing the regression coefficient of Y on expected values of X given Z, the manipulation, using ordinary least squares. Let us see first exactly how this would be done, and then look to the logic of its validity as a way to assess degree of causal effect.

First we need the expected values of X, given Z. We regress X on Z by ordinary least squares and end up with the regression equation:

$$X = a + bZ$$

This is the first stage of two-stage least squares. For each case, we take this equation and the value of Z associated with the case and calculate the predicted (expected) value of X. Denoting the predicted value of X as $\hat{X}$, we then regress Y on $\hat{X}$ using ordinary least squares and end up with a regression equation:

$$Y = c + d\hat{X}$$

which is the second stage of two-stage least squares. The regression coefficient d represents the effect of X on Y, the increase in Y because of a unit increase in X.

Why would such a procedure give us the causal effect of X on Y? What is the sense in the procedure? The main problem in causal inference from the association of two variables is the possibility that at the same time the independent variable, X, is high, some unmeasured, possibly unthought of, cause of Y is also high, so that we mistakenly impute the effect of the unmeasured cause to X. Thus, if X is frustration, Y is prejudice, and an unmeasured cause of prejudice is the norms one has been taught with respect to intergroup relations, we would be in difficulty if it turned out that those who were very frustrated were also frequently people who had learned norms of intergroup relations in childhood that, quite aside from any connection with frustration, made prejudice a matter of course. Such norms might be part of a social structure that created severe frustration. People who were high on frustration might then be high on prejudice just because they had been taught to be prejudiced, not because they were frustrated. The solution, obviously, is to create analytically a situation where the value a person has on the independent variable, frustration, is unrelated to the values he may have on other, unmeasured causes of the dependent variable, such as norms. What we do in the laboratory is simply to determine each subject's value of Z by chance, in the randomization process, so that except for chance it will *not* be related to the offending unmeasured causes of Y. We also assume, without proof, that Z does not itself directly affect Y. We then use Z, the manipulation, to isolate a certain part of the variation in X, frustration, that we are sure is unrelated to unmeasured causes of Y, prejudice. We can do this by predicting X from Z and using the predicted values of X as variation in X not related to unmeasured causes of Y, as above. If Z is unrelated to unmeasured causes of Y, then the predicted values of X must be also, since the predicted values of X are an exact linear function of the values of Z.

In effect we simply translate Z into X units. We have these experiences, failing an impossible test and missing a movie, that we think may cause prejudice, but only by way of causing frustration, which in turn causes prejudice. Our procedure is to express these experiences, to measure them if you will, in terms of units of frustration produced by them. To ascertain the effect of frustration, X, on prejudice, Y, we ask what effect an experience producing X units of frustration has on prejudice. In the laboratory we might interpret this as meaning that we try to predict prejudice from that variation in frustration that *we* produced *in a random pattern*, so as to be unrelated to other causes of prejudice, such as learned norms of intergroup relations. We exclude from consideration all other variation in frustration, on the ground that it just might be related to some other causes of prejudice, such as learned norms of intergroup relations.

Note particularly that we do not have to assume that X, frustration, was not caused by Y. We use only variation in X that was ultimately caused by Z. The remaining variation in X, variation that we do not use, may have been caused by anything, including Y. Actually, the variation in X that we do use, that predicted by Z, may be partially caused by Y also. But the variation in Y that would have caused it would be variation in Y that had been caused in the first place by variation in X produced by Z. It would thus be variation ultimately caused by Z. It would not be variation in Y produced by the unmeasured causes of Y. The critical point is that the variation in X, on which we regress Y, not be confounded with variation in unmeasured causes of Y. The fact that it may have been produced in part by Y is not itself important. Y had to be caused by something, and if the variation we use in X is unrelated to other causes of Y, then our prediction of Y from that variation is representative of a causal relationship, the effect of X on Y. Note carefully that if X did not cause Y, we could not predict Y from variation in X *that was unrelated to unmeasured causes of Y.*[4] The regression coefficient of Y on such variation in X would equal zero.

Neither do we have to assume that the manipulation of Z, in our experiment the subjection to experience intended to be frustrating, completely determined the value of X in each and every subject. We simply estimate by

---

4. An alternative but related line of argument is to note that algebraically it can be shown that the slope of Y on $\hat{X}$ is the same as the slope of $\hat{Y}$ on $\hat{X}$, where both slopes are least squares coefficients and $\hat{Y}$ is the expected value of Y given Z. Since $\hat{Y}$ is completely determined by $\hat{X}$, we make use of the fact that a relation without error may be estimated consistently, regardless of the presence or absence of feedback, by least squares, provided that there is not a singular matrix of regressors involved (Fisher, *op. cit.*, pp. 87–88). The more technically inclined reader, incidentally, may enjoy applying this principle (of identification and consistent estimation by least squares of determinate relations where the regressors are not confounded) to nonstochastic versions of the models discussed in this paper. He will find that a number of them actually depend on the presence of errors for identification. Practically, sociologists do not seem to be on the verge of trouble stemming from that fact except in a few areas such as status inconsistency or mobility research where definitional relationships are involved, since most sociological relations do involve error. Such problems, when they do occur, can generally be solved by enlarging the model to include more exogenous variables and considering the confounded independent variables as endogenous. Of course, it is also true that some models that are not identified when they have error are identified when they do not. Nonstochastic models are not discussed in this paper because of the rarity of their occurrence in current sociological research. They can be dealt with, however, in terms of the framework discussed in this paper.

regression what effect it did have and use the variation in X corresponding to that effect. We do not have to throw out cases that did not respond to Z exactly as we expected them to, as is sometimes done in experimental work. In fact, we would want to avoid throwing out cases as such a procedure would, as is well known, destroy the randomness of the allocation to experimental and control groups, and might result in Z, which is in effect the distinction between the experimental group and the control group, being related to unmeasured causes of Y.

We do have to assume that Z is not caused by either X or Y. If we did not, we would necessarily violate the assumption already made that Z is unrelated to the unmeasured causes of Y. If Y caused Z, then the influence of the unmeasured causes of Y would be fed right into Z. If X caused Z, and had been caused by Y, or was related to unmeasured causes of Y, then the influence of the unmeasured causes of Y would again be fed right into Z. Thus the assumption that Z is not caused by X or Y flows by necessity from the assumption that Z is not related to the unmeasured causes of Y.[5]

Let us look more closely at how we might go about making all these assumptions plausible in an experiment. The assumption that Z is unrelated to the unmeasured causes of Y is assured except for chance by randomizing values on Z. Frequently that means nothing more than random allocation of subjects to experimental and control groups, as in our present, imaginary experiment. The other major assumption, that Z does not affect Y except through X, that is that the experiences do not cause prejudice except by producing frustration, is a completely unsupported assumption in the model as it stands, with one Z. It is one that the experimenter must assert as a given. Whether his colleagues believe him depends on the plausibility of a bald

5. We might point out that when significance is assessed with an F test in experimental design, the explained and unexplained variances are frequently derived from the regression of Y on Z, where Z is the distinction between the control group and the experimental group. A more powerful test, taking advantage of more variance in X, might be constructed, and usually is in econometrics, by computing the variance of the predicted values in Y where the prediction is from the observed values of X, using the regression coefficient obtained in two stage least squares, or a similar estimator. The variance of those predicted values is the variance in Y explained by X. The variance of the residuals from those predicted values is the variance in Y unexplained by X. These two variances are used in constructing an F test or t test (Carl Christ, *op. cit.*, pp. 503–520). It should be noted that should these variances be used to compute a measure of association, such a measure would be like a Beta weight rather than like a correlation coefficient, in that it could take values beyond the bounds of $+1$ and -1, since the unexplained variance, reflecting the effects of unmeasured causes of Y, is not assumed to be unrelated to X, but only to the Z's. The measure would be the square root of the ratio of the explained variance to the total observed variance. The total observed variance is not equal to the simple sum of the explained and unexplained variances, but rather to that sum plus twice the geometric mean of the variances times the correlation between them. The quantity is most easily obtained by simply computing the variance of Y Note also, that as long as *linear effects only* are estimated, the term "uncorrelated" would be sufficient in place of the term "unrelated" in the above discussion and throughout this article.

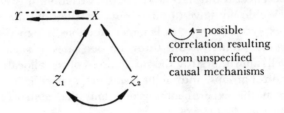

Figure 15.2.

assertion, possibly supported in some way by previous research which in turn was based on other, similar, bald assertions.

The assertion that Y is not directly caused by Z must stand unaided *unless* the researcher elects to use more than one Z (see Fig. 15.2) and make certain tests for the consistency of the several sets of resulting assumptions, one with another. We have, following Miller and Bugelski, said we would subject those of our subjects in the experimental group to the experience of failing an impossible test and missing bank night at the local movie. Unfortunately, if these two supposedly frustrating experiences always occur together, they are for all practical purposes a single experience. If the two experiences are introduced in such a manner as to be distinguishable, however, *some* subjects failing the impossible test not missing the movie and *some* subjects missing the movie not failing the test, then a partial test of the assumptions that the Z's did not affect Y directly, and were unrelated to unmeasured causes of Y, would be possible. The steps of the procedure can be stated:

(1) solve by ordinary least squares for the b in the equation $Y = a + b\hat{X}$ where $\hat{X} = c + dZ_1 + eZ_2$, coefficients estimated by least squares regression of X on Z_1 and Z_2

(2) solve by ordinary least squares the equation:

$$(Y - bX) = f + gZ_1 + hZ_2$$

where g and h should be found to equal zero.

The logic is quite simply that if the Z's operate on Y only through X, and are not related to unmeasured causes of Y, then if the effect of X is removed, all the variation explainable by the Z's should also have been removed.[6] *If* we had assumed that Z_1 was not directly a cause of Y and was unrelated to unmeasured causes of Y, we could have solved for b, the effect of X on Y, using only Z_1. Then, subtracting the effect of X from Y, any relation between

6. Carl Christ, *op. cit.*, pp. 531–542; J. Johnston, *op. cit.*, p. 263.

Z_2 and the remaining variation in Y would be evidence that Z_2 either caused Y directly or was related to unmeasured causes of Y. If we had assumed that Z_2 was not directly a cause of Y and was unrelated to unmeasured causes of Y, we could have solved alternatively for the effect of X on Y using only Z_2. Then, subtracting the effect of X from Y, any relation between Z_1 and the remaining variation in Y would be evidence that Z_1 either caused Y directly or was related to unmeasured causes of Y. In either case, the Z used to solve for the effect of X on Y would be unrelated to the remaining variation in Y (after the effect of X had been subtracted out) because the effect of X was solved for by regressing Y on an exact linear function of the Z, so that any separate effect of the Z, not through X, would not be distinguishable.

Using *both* Z's to get the effect of X on Y yields a kind of average of what would have been obtained using each separately. The procedure actually suggested is thus a way of symmetrically combining the tests that would follow from estimating the effect of X on Y using either Z and testing the assumptions about the other. The test is thus quite simply a test of the *consistency* of assuming that *both* Z's are not direct causes of Y and are unrelated to unmeasured causes of Y. It is quite possible to be consistent but wrong. Still, if the two Z's are not merely different measures of the same thing, the test strongly supports the assumptions about both Z's, even though not constituting proof. The more Z's used, obviously, the more compelling the support. In our experimental design with randomization, one assumption is, of course, satisfied except for chance by the process of randomization of the Z's. Thus, except for chance, failure of the design to pass this test would mean that the assumption that the Z's are not direct causes of Y is the one at fault.[7]

2. *Nonexperimental analysis*

In nonexperimental research we have exactly the same picture as in experimental research, except that the Z's are not conditions we have ourselves imposed in a random fashion, which makes the assumption that the Z's are unrelated to unmeasured causes of Y more of a substantive assumption, and except for the fact that the analysis may become more complicated, including more variables, in order to support that now more substantive assumption.

Lacking the device of randomization, what sort of picture of the world we are studying must we assume? The general model has been called block recursive. The idea is of blocks, or categories, of variables where the blocks are numbered in such a way, and variables allocated to the blocks in such a way, that we can say that while variables in lower numbered blocks may cause variables in higher numbered blocks, variables in higher numbered

---

7. Significance tests are also available for the test of the consistency of the assumptions about the Z's (Carl Christ, *op. cit.*, pp. 531–542).

blocks are not causes of variables in lower numbered blocks. Further, variables in lower numbered blocks are not related to unmeasured causes of variables in higher numbered blocks. Then we must be able to choose variables from lower numbered blocks that are causes of some variables in higher numbered blocks but not of other variables in those blocks, these chosen variables to act as the Z's did in our discussion in the preceding section. Nothing is said about the relationships among variables within the same block. Such variables may be reciprocally related, or even spuriously related.

How realistic is such a conception of the world? How could we employ such a model of reality if we happen to believe that ultimately everything causes everything else to some degree? Consider a case where we have selected two variables out of an infinity of variables, these two being whether or not Mr. Jones insists on drinking milk and the success of the war effort of the nation wherein Mr. Jones resides. If the war effort is stepped up so as to be successful, Mr. Jones's supply of milk may be cut off and he may be compelled to stop drinking milk. On the other hand, if Mr. Jones and all other milk drinkers refuse to abide by the law and insist on getting their milk and drinking it, the war effort may fail. There is thus a reciprocal relationship between Mr. Jones's milk drinking and the war effort. But consider the effect of Mr. Jones's drinking milk, independently of the effect of all other dissident citizens' drinking milk. Mr. Jones's drinking milk—by itself—has so little effect on the war effort as to be negligible. It takes the concerted action of thousands and thousands of milk drinkers to affect the war effort significantly enough to be measured. If Y refers to the war effort and X_1 refers to Mr. Jones's drinking milk, other X's referring to milk drinking by other persons, then Y affects X_1, and X_1 affects Y, but the effect of X_1 on Y is so small that it can be ignored, unless it is related to the other X's. In such a case Y could be taken for the purpose of a research project to be a cause of X_1 but uncaused by X_1.

Unless the world is a lot simpler than this example, which is simple enough, the idea that everything ultimately affects everything else should not prevent us from mapping the world into the block recursive form for a particular research project. We should always be able to identify some variables that will serve as appropriate Z's with respect to the X's and Y's in which we are centrally interested.

A recently published empirical analysis using such a rationale is Scanzoni's study of aspiration and the need for achievement.[8] Aspiration is for us the Y, need for achievement the X, and childrearing practices known to produce need for achievement, the Z (see Fig. 15.3a). Each variable *could* have been defined as a change, alternatively, although at considerable inconvenience

---

8. John Scanzoni, "Socialization, Achievement, and Achievement Values," *American Sociological Review, 32* (1967): 449–456.

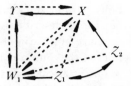

Figure 15.3*a*.   *Figure* 15.3*b*.   *Figure* 15.3*c*.

given the nature of the variables. Scanzoni assumes implicitly that the child-rearing practices in question have no effect on aspirations except through need for achievement, and that they are unrelated to all unspecified causes of aspiration. His test of the effect of need achievement on aspirations is simply to relate aspirations to the childrearing practices, need achievement not being measured in the study, its relationship to child rearing practices being documented from the literature. Not having need for achievement as a measured variable meant that a regression coefficient showing the effect of need achievement on aspiration could not be calculated. However, the existence or nonexistence of a relationship between the childrearing practices and aspirations would reflect respectively the existence or nonexistence of an effect of need for achievement on aspiration. No assumption was needed regarding the effect of the aspiration on need for achievement.

Suppose that the X, need for achievement, had been measured, and that there had also arisen a question regarding the assumption that Z, childrearing practices, affected aspirations only through need for achievement. Or suppose that someone questioned the assumption that Z, childrearing practices, was not related to unmeasured causes of Y, aspirations. What would be the simplest way to handle the problem?

The first thing would probably be to introduce additional Z's into the model and to test the consistency of the assumptions about their relationships to Y and the unmeasured causes of Y. If this test showed the assumptions to be inconsistent, we would have to agree that the assumptions were wrong, and alter the model.

One possibility would be to find a different Z, for which the necessary assumptions did in fact seem plausible. A perhaps more realistic strategy might be to try to figure out *how* the original Z affected Y aside from acting through X, or *what* unmeasured causes of Y were related to Z. It is with the latter approaches that the model becomes a little more complicated. The additional links besides X connecting Z to Y must be included in the analysis, as must some *measure* of the to this point *un*measured causes of Y that are thought to be related to Z.

Let us first attend to the matter of Z affecting Y over and above its effect through X. Any causal relationship can be broken down into intervening links by more detailed specification of the causal mechanism. Thus we should be able to describe the effect of Z on Y not through X by introducing W_1, a measure of a variable thought to constitute a link between Z and Y in addition to the link already constituted by X. Thus, we say that childrearing practices affect aspirations by way of need for achievement and also by way of W_1. W_1 might be belief in the moral necessity of high aspirations. If W_1 is not thought to be caused by either X or Y (see Fig. 15.3b) or to be in any other way related to unmeasured causes of Y, we can simply regress Y on the W_1 and the expected value of X, given Z and W_1. W_1 is thought of as being in the same block of the block recursive system as Z, and hence there is no need for any assumption regarding the nature of the causal connection between Z and W_1. W_1 can be treated as just another Z. Since W_1, like Z, is assumed to be uncaused by X or Y, and unrelated to additional unmeasured causes of Y, we can use its observed value in the regression estimation procedure, rather than substituting an expected value as we did with X. Notice that W_1 is included among the givens for the expected values of X. This means that $\hat{X}$ includes variation coming from W_1, so that effects of W_1 passing through X instead of affecting Y directly, will be controlled out of our estimate of the direct effect of W_1 on Y by the second stage of two-stage least squares.

In such a case, to test the consistency of our assumptions, given several Z's as causes of X but not Y and unrelated to unmeasured causes of Y, we would regress $(Y-bX)$ on W *and the several Z's*, where b is the effect of X on Y, and, as before, check to see that the coefficients of the Z's were equal to or close to zero. Thus

(1) $Y = a + b\hat{X} + cW_1$ by least squares
   where $\hat{X} = d + eZ_1 + fZ_2 + gW_1$, coefficients estimated by least squares
   regression of X on Z_1 and Z_2, and W_1

(2) $(Y - bX) = h + iW_1 + jZ_1 + kZ_2$, where j and k should equal zero.

Suppose that we cannot assume that W_1 is not caused by X or Y? If it is caused by Y, either directly or through X (see Fig. 15.3c), it will be related to all unmeasured causes of Y. We will then need to regress Y on the expected value of W_1 given our original Z, now called Z_1, and some other Z, say Z_2, and on the expected value of X, given Z_2 and our original Z, now called Z_1. Thus

$$Y = a + b\hat{X} + c\hat{W}_1 \text{ where } \hat{X} = d + eZ_1 + fZ_2 \text{ and } \hat{W}_1 = g + hZ_1 + iZ_2$$

and where all coefficients are estimated by ordinary least squares.

What of the other problem, where Z is simply thought to be related to some unmeasured cause of Y? In effect we have already solved that problem, because the case where Z causes Y through other channels than X is simply a routine example of that problem. We simply introduce the previously un-measured variable, W_2, and treat it exactly as we did W_1, introducing its observed value if it is not caused by X or Y, and is not related to unmeasured causes of Y, introducing an expected value if it is.

It will have been noticed that when we introduce expected values of W_1 or W_2, we introduce them given an additional Z. This is because if we intro-duced the expected values of X and W_1 given Z_1 in the same equation, they would be perfectly related to each other, both being exact linear functions of Z_1, which would prevent our being able to distinguish the effects of the two variables, X and W_1, unless we had an assumption on which we were willing to rely concerning the relative effects of the two variables on Y. In general, then, how many Z's do we have to round up to estimate a causal model? We need as many Z's assumed not to cause Y as we have independent variables thought likely to be caused by Y or likely to be related to unmeasured variables causing Y—that is, as many variables as we have included among the possible causes of Y that are classified as in the same block as Y in the block recursive system. In effect, for each variable that may be a cause of Y, for which we cannot assume independence of the unmeasured causes of Y, either because of common cause or because of reciprocal effects, we need a Z that is a cause of that variable but not directly a cause of Y.

Thus far we have been concerned with the estimation of single equations—that is, ascertaining the effects of certain variables on one particular depen-dent variable, in spite of spuriousness or reciprocal causation. In practice we would often be concerned with a whole system of equations representing the interdependence of an entire set of mutually dependent variables. The logic we have been discussing is suited to this kind of problem. It is referred to as a "limited information" estimator, or a single equation estimator because it attacks such a system of equations, one equation at a time. The advantage is that errors in assumptions, sampling, or measurement have less comprehen-sive effects. Only errors affecting information actually required to estimate a particular equation affect the estimation of that equation. In full information techniques, which estimate entire systems of equations in one operation, errors in any part of the system are more likely to ramify through the entire set of equations. It is a matter of choosing how many baskets to put one's eggs in. The advantage of the single basket, a full information estimator, is that parts of the error terms can be eliminated, for greater reliability and accuracy of results.

The strategy of applying the single equation estimator we have been dis-cussing to the problem of a set of simultaneous equations is no more compli-cated than the single equation problems we have been discussing. One merely considers each equation in the set as if one really had no interest in the

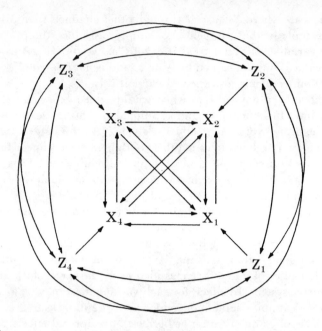

Figure 15.4*a.*

others except as a source of assumptions aiding in the solution of the equation at hand. Frequently the same Z's can be used in estimating several equations, so that the number of such variables we have to dig up does not necessarily increase drastically with the number of equations. If we had four X's and each X caused every other X, we would require four Z's (see Fig. 15.4a). There are four equations involved. In the first equation, X_1 is dependent on Z_1, X_2, X_3, and X_4. It is regressed on the observed values of Z_1 and the predicted values of X_2, X_3, and X_4 given Z_1, Z_2, Z_3 and Z_4. In the second equation, X_2 is dependent on Z_2, X_1, X_3, and X_4. It is regressed on the observed value of Z_2 and the predicted values of X_1, X_3, and X_4 given Z_1, Z_2, Z_3, and Z_4. In the third equation, X_3 is dependent upon Z_3, X_1, X_2, and X_4. It is regressed on the observed value of Z_3 and the predicted values of X_1, X_2, and

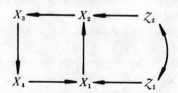

Figure 15.4*b.*

X_4 given Z_1, Z_2, Z_3, and Z_4. In the fourth and last equation, X_4 is dependent on Z_4, X_1, X_2, and X_3. It is regressed on the observed value of Z_4 and the predicted values of X_1, X_2, and X_3 given Z_1, Z_2, Z_3, and Z_4.

If not every X causes every other X, even though there are still feedback loops in the model the picture gets even simpler, as we do not need all four Z's. Suppose X_1 causes X_2, which causes X_3, which causes X_4, which causes X_1. Each X is caused directly by only one other X, though indirectly by all other X's. To estimate all four causal links in this circle of causation, we need a minimum of two Z's with certain specific relationships to the X's. Suppose Z_1 causes X_1 but no other X and is not related to unmeasured causes of any other X. Suppose Z_2 causes X_2 but no other X and is not related to unmeasured causes of any other X (see Fig. 15.4b). Then we can ascertain the effect of X_1 on X_2 by regressing X_2 on Z_2 and the expected values of X_1 given Z_1 and Z_2. We must include Z_2 because it is a cause of X_2 that may be related to Z_1. We can ascertain the effects of X_2 on X_3 by regressing X_3 on the expected values of X_2 given Z_2, or given Z_1 and Z_2, since Z_1 is related to X_3 only through X_2, by way of X_1. We can ascertain the effect of X_3 on X_4 by regressing X_4 on the expected values of X_3 given Z_2, since Z_2 is related to X_4 only through X_3 by way of X_2, or similarly on the expected values of X_3 given Z_1 and Z_2. Finally we can ascertain the effect of X_4 on X_1 by regressing X_1 on Z_1 and the expected values of X_4 given Z_2 and Z_1. Introduction of additional Z's would allow us to test the consistency of all of the assumptions about the relationships of the Z's to the X's and to the unmeasured causes of the X's.

It should be noted that, if one wanted to know the effect of Z_1 on X_2 and was unconcerned with the fact that X_1 was part of the mechanism by way of which Z_1 affected X_2, one could simply regress X_2 on Z_1 and Z_2. Since the Z's are assumed to be unrelated to unmeasured variables affecting the X's, such a procedure would not cause any difficulty. If we had wanted to speak, in an earlier section, of the effect of various experiences (Z) on prejudice (Y), not being concerned with whether the effect was by way of frustration, we could have simply regressed prejudice, Y, on experiences, Z. Such a development is called a "simple recursive" system, in contrast to the block recursive system. No block, beyond the first, contains more than one measured variable. The difference in results is simply that intervening mechanisms are not specified.

3. Interpretation with respect to time

It is frequently suggested that the measurement of all variables at the same point in time, and at only one point in time, gets the researcher into the awkward position of having to assume instantaneous causation and equilibrium in order to measure any causal effects at all. The problem stems from the attempt to predict a variable from a contemporaneous value of another variable and to interpret the result as a causal effect.

Consider the matter of equilibrium, where the effects of two variables on each other balance in such a way that the system is maintained without long-run change. Does measuring all variables at the same point in time compel us to make some sort of equilibrium assumption? Let us take the two variables X and Y, and suppose that each causes the other. We will estimate the effect of X on Y by regressing Y on Z_2 and the expected value of X given Z_1 and Z_2, and the effect of Y on X by regressing X on Z_1 and the expected value of Y given Z_2 and Z_1, where Z_1 does not cause Y directly and is not related to unmeasured causes of Y, and Z_2 does not cause X directly and is not related to unmeasured causes of X (see Fig. 15.5). Our estimate of the

Figure 15.5.

effect of X on Y is thus dependent on the observed association between Z_1 and X and between Z_1 and Y, controlling Z_2. These observed relationships place no logical constraint on the corresponding relationships between Z_2 and X and between Z_2 and Y, controlling Z_1, on the basis of which the effect of Y on X is estimated. There is thus no reason why this strategy should necessarily yield an estimate that describes a system as being in equilibrium, even if all variables are measured at the same point in time.

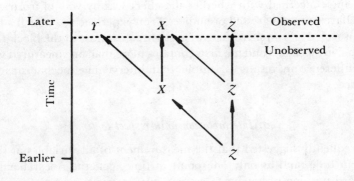

Figure 15.6.

Measuring all the variables at one point in time does not constrain us to assume that all effects are instantaneous either, if we are willing to accept "arbitrarily close" approximations of effect over time. If we are assessing the effect of X on Y, assuming Z is a cause of X but not of Y, and is unrelated to unmeasured causes of Y, then the only way Z could be related to Y would be for X at some point of time, not necessarily the present, to have caused Y (see Fig. 15.6). The b that we estimate by regressing Y on the expected value of X given Z in the present will approximate the b reflecting the effect of X on Y over time to the degree that the values of X in the present approximate the values of X at the point in the past when the relevant values of X occurred that affect Y in the present, or to the degree that changes in X have been nearly random with respect to Z. Bothersome changes in X are those brought about by changes in Z or related variables and those brought about by feedbacks of X on itself, through Y or other variables. Both of these kinds of change in X are bothersome because they will be related to Z. All "bothersome" changes in X that an investigator considers likely should be thought through in the effort to anticipate their effect on the estimated b. If such changes in X are slight relative to the original variance of X, there is no great problem. If such changes are major, it is desirable not only to anticipate their effects on the estimated b, but to compensate for them. If the changes in X come from Z, the b will be attenuated. If the changes are from a feedback loop that increases the variation of X, then the estimated b will again be attenuated, while if the variation in X has been decreased by a feedback loop, the estimated b will be too large. If a feedback has reflected X, then the sign of the estimated b will be reversed.

Frequently, but certainly not always, the researcher will have at least general knowledge of the existence of such processes to the extent that they have brought about major change. Fortunately, the changes referred to here as "bothersome" are likely to be minimal in many situations. Remember also that the presence or absence of an effect of X on Y, as opposed to its size and direction, is not in doubt. If Z is related to Y, so that any effect of any kind is estimated, X must have had some effect of some kind on Y. The problem is in pinning down the exact nature of that effect.

It should be remembered, of course, that any effects that are not in equilibrium necessarily mean that the effects are at least partly over time rather than instantaneous. If all effects were instantaneous, all changes would be over in an instant and the system would reach equilibrium or fluctuate with infinite speed for all of infinity. Practically, lack of equilibrium means over time change, i.e., delayed effect, and caution must be used, as suggested above, in interpreting such effects inferred from cross sectional data without time lags.

These principles apply to both experimental and nonexperimental designs.

4. Exploitation of time in the use of causal variables from preceding blocks

It has been suggested, and seems valid at first glance, that a terribly simple approach would be the use of explicit time order in measurement, both in experimental and in nonexperimental designs. One would simply measure all variables at two points in time and regress each of the variables in turn, measured at the later time, on all the variables measured at the earlier time. The argument would be simply that the variable measured earlier could not have been caused by the value of the variables observed at a later time, since things do not cause other things that precede them. The earlier value could be thought of as being a preceding block in the block recursive system. Thus we might measure X and Y at two points in time, denoting the measurement of X at the earlier time as X_1 and the measurement of X at the later time as X_2, and denoting the measurement of Y at the earlier time as Y_1 and the measurement of Y at the later time by Y_2. We simply regress the observed value of Y_2 on the observed value of X_1, and regress the observed value of X_2 on the observed value of Y_1 and conclude that we have neatly assessed the effect of X on Y and of Y on X (see Fig. 15.7).

Figure 15.7.

Unfortunately, it is quite possible, however, for the regression of Y_2 on X_1 to reflect the effect of Y on X, rather than the effect of X on Y. The problem is serial correlation of Y with itself through time, or serial correlation of unmeasured causes of Y with themselves over time. If Y at some prior time caused X_1 and also caused Y_2, it is obvious that the regression of Y_2 on X_1 would reflect the effect of Y on X (Y_1 on X_1 and Y_1 on Y_2) rather than the effect of X on Y (see Fig. 15.8). Similarly, if an unmeasured variable caused Y at an earlier time which in turn caused X_1, and if this same unmeasured

Figure 15.8.

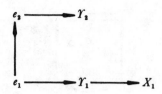

Figure 15.9.

variable caused itself at a later time, and in turn caused Y_2, then, again, the regression of Y_2 on X_1 would reflect the effect of Y on X (see Fig. 15.9).

In the case of Y being serially correlated with itself, all we would have to do is control Y_1, at the expense, however, of omitting from our estimate any immediate effect of X on Y, perhaps not usually such a serious loss, but enough to reverse the direction of relationship in some cases where the effect of X on Y is immediate and temporary. What would be picked up would be the fading of the temporary effect, which would be interpreted as the effect itself. In the case of the serially correlated unmeasured causes of Y the problem becomes more massive. Techniques for handling the problem, which we will not describe here, involve adding and subtracting exact mathematical equations from each other to generate new equations that contain the wanted regression parameters but not the unwanted serially correlated errors, these new equations being the ones finally solved by ordinary least squares.[9] Such a solution requires that all variables be measured at four different points in time and that it be assumed that the same causal relationship obtains over the entire period of time involved. Use of time order and ordinary least squares is thus expensive in that it requires a great deal of data. It also is cumbersome in that the most practically workable of the techniques referred to may be sluggish, and in extreme cases totally ineffective, in dealing with the difficulty.

One last possibility that suggests itself must be disposed of. Suppose that we defined X_1, X_2, Y_1 and Y_2 as immediately above and, in order to assess the immediate or nearly immediate effects of X on Y and of Y on X, took the regression of Y_2 on Y_1 and the expected value of X_2 given X_1 and Y_1 and the regression of X_2 on X_1 and the expected value of Y_2 given Y_1 and X_1. Following the logic of the first two sections of this paper, we would assume that X_1 caused X_2 but did not cause Y_2 except through X_2 and Y_1, and that Y_1 caused Y_2 but did not cause X_2 except through Y_2 and X_1 (see Fig. 15.10). Further we would assume that X_1 was unrelated to all unmeasured causes of Y_2 and that Y_1 was unrelated to all unmeasured causes of X_2.

9. Carl Christ, *op. cit.*, pp. 481–494; Arthur S. Goldberger, *op. cit.*, pp. 231–248; J. Johnston, *op. cit.*, pp. 177–200; E. Malinvaud, *op. cit.*, pp. 420–496.

Figure 15.10.

Obviously this solution, like the one above, is faulty on the count that serial correlation of unmeasured causes of X and Y will result in X_1 being related to unmeasured causes of Y_2, and Y_1 being related to unmeasured causes of X_2 as above. But this is a minor objection if we are willing to measure X and Y at four different points in time and assume that the relationship between X and Y is the same over the entire period of time involved. At least, it is minor compared to a perhaps less obvious point. The assumption that X_1 causes X_2 and does not cause Y_2 except through X_2 and Y_1 is not consistent with the assumption that Y_1 causes Y_2 but does not cause X_2 except through Y_2 and X_1, unless it is also assumed that the effect of X on Y and of Y on X occurs only when the data is being gathered, and not in between data gatherings. Suppose that it occurred at a time in between the two measurements we have been discussing and that we designate X at this point $X_{1\frac{1}{2}}$ and Y at the same time as $Y_{1\frac{1}{2}}$. Then X_1 causes $X_{1\frac{1}{2}}$ which causes $Y_{1\frac{1}{2}}$ which causes Y_2, which in other words means that X_1 causes Y_2 through other links than merely X_2 and Y_1. The same principle obtains for the effect of Y on X. Y_1 causes $Y_{1\frac{1}{2}}$ which causes $X_{1\frac{1}{2}}$ which causes X_2, which means that Y_1 causes X_2 by other links than merely Y_2 and X_1, contrary to our necessary assumption (see Fig. 15.11a and 15.11b).

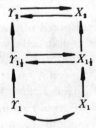

Figure 15.11a.   *Figure* 15.11b.

It would, of course, be perfectly legitimate to regress Y_2 on the expected value of X_1 given Z, where, as usual, we assume Z to be a cause of X_1 but to be related to Y_2 only through X_1, and to be unrelated to unmeasured causes of Y_2, therefore, of course, not caused by Y_2 and not caused by X_1 (see Fig. 15.12). Such a procedure would give us the effect of X on Y over the specified time interval and would avoid the bias due to serial correlation. This is, in fact, probably the most workable solution, and is merely the two-stage least-squares procedure we have been discussing all along, now with time intervals

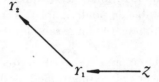

Figure 15.12.

built into the data so that over time effects and disequilibrium analyses will be perfectly straightforward. This procedure is appropriate for estimating difference equations which may be transformed into differential equations— avoiding the usual difficulties with autocorrelated errors and similar problems encountered in solving for the coefficients of such equations. The procedure is not, however, an exploitation of time to provide a short cut and avoid assumptions. The existence of such a short cut seems doubtful at best.

5. Conclusion

We began by pointing out that one would expect strong similarities between the mechanics of causal inference in experimental and nonexperimental settings. We found that such was, in fact, the case and that consistency tests of assumptions in experimental and nonexperimental research, together with ways of complicating nonexperimental designs to make the necessary assumptions tenable, make it not only theoretically possible but practically feasible to apply the same basic analysis to both kinds of research.

It may be added here that the approach described, two-stage least squares, is what is referred to in the statistical literature as a "consistent" estimator. That means that as the sample size is increased toward infinity, the estimates approach the population parameters. Two-stage least squares does have some sampling error problems on small samples, however.

When one more Z is used than is required for estimation, the results will be approximately unbiased.[10] The word "approximately" is necessary because of a technical problem in defining the expectation mathematically. On large sample analysis of the kind common in sociology there should be no problem in any case. But with very small samples, such as ten or twenty

10. Carl Christ, *op. cit.*, p. 470.

cases, one begins to worry a little about bias, if one happens *not* to be using exactly one extra Z. The problem in that case becomes analogous to the bias of the common chi-square statistics on small samples, except that by using exactly one extra Z the problem can be bypassed.

It should also be pointed out that two-stage least-squares estimates have larger sampling variances than do ordinary least-squares estimates. This loss of efficiency, which is considerable on small samples, is the price paid for the gain of having a consistent estimate. On large samples the price would seem to be a small one indeed.

While the capabilities of the approach described are very great, it must be stressed that it is not a means of getting something for nothing. It is a technique for putting existing theory into interaction with data in order to extend theory. In no case is it possible to determine causal relationships on the basis of data alone. However, the fact that the technique allows for consistency checks on assumptions does make trial and error on the basis of minimal theory a feasible procedure.

PART IV

The Causal Approach to Measurement Error

The discussions in this and the final section are much more tentative and exploratory than those of the previous sections. In part, this is because sociologists and political scientists are just beginning to be concerned about the implications of measurement errors and other kinds of complications for their analysis procedures. Many of our most important theoretical concepts are only indirectly measured, and there is relatively little consensus on either theoretical or operational definitions. Psychologists, as well, have been plagued by the indirectness of their measurement procedures but have often been able to utilize relatively simple assumptions in order to relate indicators to their unmeasured constructs. Most of the papers in this section ultimately derive from the work of psychologists and represent exploratory efforts to apply path analysis and causal modeling approaches to measurement errors, while allowing for somewhat more complex models than have generally been considered in the psychology literature.

Before turning to the multiple-indicator approaches utilized in the papers of this section, it should be noted that whenever one is willing to make relatively strong *a priori* theoretical assumptions about the model, other approaches can be utilized. If one can obtain independent estimates of measurement error variances, or ratios of measurement error variances to variances in true values, rather straightforward corrections can be applied. Likewise, one may utilize instrumental variables that are assumed not to appear in a given equation in order to obtain consistent slope estimates that are approximately unbiased in the case of large samples. However, these procedures appear to be relatively more sensitive to specification errors than ordinary least squares and seem less useful in exploratory analyses.[1]

1. See J. Johnston, *Econometric Methods* (New York: McGraw-Hill, 1963), chap. 6; and H. M. Blalock, Caryll S. Wells, and Lewis F. Carter, "Statistical Estimation in the Presence of Random Measurement Error," in Edgar Borgatta (Ed.), *Sociological Methodology* 1970 (San Francisco: Jossey-Bass, 1970), Chap. 5.

Whenever there are multiple measures of each variable there may be sufficient empirical information to produce overidentified systems, provided relatively simple assumptions can be made about sources of random and nonrandom measurement errors. As a general rule, the more indicators one has and the simpler his assumptions, the greater the number of excess equations that will be available to test the compatibility of the data with the model. There will always be a number of alternative models that are consistent with any given set of data, but one may proceed by rejecting inadequate models. Having tentatively settled on a particular model, one may then estimate path coefficients, though it may not be possible to estimate unstandardized coefficients.

The simplest models involving multiple indicators obviously stem from the literature on factor analysis and related approaches, but they afford a somewhat different perspective that permits the introduction of various kinds of complications involving different sources of nonrandom errors. The general strategy suggested is to construct "auxiliary theories" that explicitly link each indicator variable with the unmeasured variables of interest.[2] In factor analysis the unmeasured variables or "factors" are taken as causes of the indicators, and each indicator is taken as an endogenous variable that is a function of the unmeasured factors alone, plus a unique disturbance term. If the indicators are represented as I_i and the factors as F_j we in effect have a set of reduced-form equations of the type

$$I_i = b_{i1}F_1 + b_{i2}F_2 + \ldots + b_{ik}F_k + u_i$$

where we assume that none of the indicators appears in any of the equations for the remaining indicators. In other words, we rule out any direct causation among the indicators. In many sociological and political science applications, however, this simple model is obviously inappropriate and we need a more complex auxiliary theory.

The notion of an auxiliary theory implies that we construct causal models linking indicators and unmeasured variables, just as though there were no fundamental difference between the two. We then examine the situation to see if, using only the measured variables, we have available enough empirical information to estimate all of the path or regression coefficients in the system. Usually the system will be underidentified, and we must then consider the nature of the simplifications that will be necessary to achieve identification and to produce excess equations that can be utilized for testing purposes.

In the opening paper in Part IV, Costner begins with a very simple model

2. See H. M. Blalock, "The Measurement Problem: A Gap Between the Languages of Theory and Research," in H. M. Blalock, and Ann B. Blalock (Eds.), *Methodology in Social Research* (New York: McGraw-Hill, 1968), chap. 1.

involving only two indicators of X and two of Y, assuming strictly random measurement error and a recursive context in which X affects Y. With a total of four measures there are six correlations that can be obtained from the data and these may be used to estimate the five path coefficients of the model. The excess equation can then provide a test criterion in this overidentified system. The principle can be extended in a number of directions, as Costner and others have shown. First, it can be extended to the general k-equation case, provided there are at least two measures of each variable, and it may also be utilized in connection with certain kinds of simple causal chains when there is a single measure for the intervening variables. If additional indicators of each variable are used, the system becomes highly overidentified so that multiple tests can be made. This also permits one to introduce certain relatively simple kinds of nonrandom measurement errors in some of the indicators, as demonstrated in the papers by Costner, by Althauser, Heberlein, and Scott, and by Werts, Linn, and Jöreskog.

Essentially the same kind of argument can be applied to temporal data, where one has measures at two or more points in time. Heise shows that with single measures it will be necessary to utilize at least three points in time in order to handle random measurement errors, but it can also be shown that two measures at each of two time periods will suffice. Furthermore if one has two measures at three time points, or three measures at two time periods, certain kinds of nonrandom measurement errors can be estimated.[3] The papers by Wiley and Wiley and by Althauser, Heberlein, and Scott develop further elaborations on the Costner and Heise approaches, while introducing additional cautions regarding the underlying assumptions. The contribution by Werts, Linn, and Jöreskog involves a synthesis of the path-analytic and factor-analytic approaches. My own paper deals with a somewhat different kind of model; namely, one in which some of the indicator variables are taken as causes rather than effects of the unmeasured variables.

These rather abstract papers suffer because of the lack of realistic applications of this relatively new approach. In many instances, one is confronted with situations where a wide variety of indicators are available but where little is known about their theoretical linkages with the unmeasured concepts, which are often only very vaguely defined. Initially there must be a great deal of exploratory work involving *ex post facto* decisions as to which indicators to retain and which to discard. Van Valey's application of Costner's suggested procedure provides an interesting illustration of the kinds of practical decisions one must face whenever the number of indicators becomes large, and whenever the data depart to varying degrees from the predictions of one's model. Similarly, the paper by Sullivan involves a practical strategy utilizing

---

3. H. M. Blalock, "Estimating Measurement Error Using Multiple Indicators and Several Points in Time," *American Sociological Review*, 35 (February, 1970): 101–111.

multiple-partial controlling techniques as an alternative to the multiple-indicator approach. In many instances one will be dealing with blocks of highly intercorrelated variables, with no clear idea as to the causal connections within these blocks. Therefore it will not be possible to utilize the very simple kinds of auxiliary theories discussed by Costner, Heise, and myself. Nor will it be practical to use each indicator separately because of the multiplicity of tests and estimates.

In this section we shall encounter some of the most formidable problems facing the social sciences, where there are myriads of indicators available but only rudimentary theories enabling one to link these indicators with a smaller number of theoretical constructs. Until recently, we have in effect followed the dictum that intercorrelated indicators are more or less interchangeable. But as we attempt to make our theories more precise, it will become crucial that we pay close attention to the measurement process. As a step in this direction we must learn to make our assumptions as explicit as possible.

Chapter 16

THEORY, DEDUCTION, AND RULES OF CORRESPONDENCE

HERBERT L. COSTNER*
University of Washington

The requirement that scientific theories include both abstract concepts and concrete implications, and that the two be logically connected, has been treated rather casually by sociologists. Traditionally, sociological theorists have focused on abstractions with loose and ill-defined implications about matters of fact. More recently, some sociological formulations have shifted to the opposite extreme, stating only connections between measures without any attempt to make more abstract claims. Either of these modes of theory construction is costly, sacrificing either the clarity of empirical implications or the integrating potential of abstract concepts. Although the literature of the philosophy of science has provided us with terms for referring to the gap between abstract conceptions and concrete events—*rules of correspondence, epistemic correlations, operational definitions,* and *indicators of abstract dimensions*— these terms do little more than remind us that the gap is there. They do not provide clear guidelines for bridging the gap and suggest no criteria for determining the adequacy of the more or less arbitrarily devised connections between abstract and empirical levels. Clearly, the empirical testing of abstract theories must remain somewhat loose until some strategies for dealing with this problem are devised. To the degree that rules of correspondence

Reprinted by permission of the author and publisher from the *American Journal of Sociology,* Vol. 75, pp. 245–263. Copyright 1969, The University of Chicago Press.

* Revised version of paper presented at the meeting of the American Sociological Association, Boston, Massachusetts, August 26–29, 1968. I wish to thank Hubert M. Blalock, Jr., Otis Dudley Duncan, Jack P. Gibbs, Arthur S. Goldberger, and Karl F. Schuessler for helpful comments on an earlier version of this paper.

are weak and subject to distorting errors, deductions about matters of fact must be regarded as uncertain and possibly misleading.

This general problem is explored in the present paper, not as a problem in semantics—which is the common way of treating it—but as a special problem in theory construction. The general strategy to be employed consists of including the rules of correspondence as an auxiliary part of the theory. The auxiliary theory will thus consist of statements connecting abstract dimensions and their empirical indicators, statements which will be treated like other theoretical propositions. The implications that may then be deduced allow, under certain conditions, two different kinds of decisions to be made empirically. First, one may determine whether particular indicators are inadequate for testing the implications of a specific abstract formulation because of artifactual measurement error. Second, if the indicators are not found inadequate, one may determine whether the abstract formulation itself is tenable. Although the second kind of decision—the tenability of the abstract formulation itself—is the crucial decision in the final analysis, some decision on the adequacy of the indicators is a prerequisite.

This attempt to treat the problem of rules of correspondence in a formal way builds quite explicitly on the work of others and owes much to their lead. It represents an extension of their work rather than a major departure from their approach. Blalock (1968), following Northrop, has argued convincingly for the necessity of two languages—a theoretical and an operational language—and has suggested that the connections between the two be expressed in an auxiliary theory. I will follow Blalock in representing the auxiliary theory in the form of an explicit causal model. Siegel and Hodge (1968), building on the work of Blalock, Duncan, and Wright, have utilized causal models representing auxiliary theories to investigate the effects of measurement error on the correlation between selected variables. Their detailed work, along with that of Blalock, sets the tone for the present discussion.

We will begin with a discussion of specific desiderata that auxiliary theories should help to achieve, illustrating the problems encountered with simple models incorporating highly simplified auxiliary theories. We will then move to a discussion of auxiliary theories more nearly adequate to the tasks outlined in the earlier discussion.

We consider first a relatively simple model proposing a one-way causal relation between two abstract variables; it may be summarized in the proposition that a change in X leads to a change in Y, but not the reverse, and may be represented graphically by an arrow from X to Y. An auxiliary theory providing one indicator for each of the abstract variables is added. We assume that the indicators are "reflectors" of the abstract variables, that is, that a change in the abstract variable will lead to a change in its own indicator, and we represent these connections with arrows from abstract variable to indicator.[1] The model representing the basic theoretical proposition and the auxiliary theory is shown in Figure 16.1. Associated with each of the three arrows in this causal diagram is a coefficient representing the regression of one variable on another, assuming all variables to be in the form of standard measures. These coefficients may take any value from -1 to 1. Arrows from unspecified sources are added in the graphic representation of the model to represent variation not accounted for in the model; specifically, when the coefficients a, b, and c are less than unity in absolute value, these additional arrows may be assigned values such that all of the variance is "accounted for" either by the model or by unspecified sources. In this model we make the usual assumption for causal models that there are no common sources of error variance, or, referring to the algebraic representation of the model, following Simon (1959), that all error terms are uncorrelated.

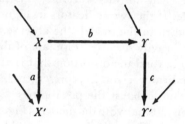

Figure 16.1. *Two-variable model with one indicator for each variable.*

Ideally, we would be able to estimate the magnitudes of the three unknown coefficients in the model. In this case, however, we have only one observed correlation, $r_{X'Y'}$, and although the model implies that this correlation is a function of the three unknown coefficients ($r_{X'Y'} = abc$, where a, b, and c are path coefficients as shown in Fig. 16.1), this single equation in three unknowns does not provide unique solutions for the coefficients without further assumptions. Assuming knowledge only of the signs of the epistemic coefficients a and c, which is not an unreasonable assumption, it is possible to draw a conclusion about only the sign of the coefficient between abstract variables, b, from knowledge of the sign of the observed correlation, $r_{X'Y'}$. But this is a weak deduction at best and would have limited utility in making further deductions if this miniature model were to be incorporated as a unit

1. In experimental studies the indicators of independent variables may be treated as "producers" rather than "reflectors" of the abstract variables, and the connection would be represented by arrows from indicator to abstract variable. Somewhat different problems are presented by the experimental case, which is not discussed in this paper.

into a more complex model involving several abstract variables. Our usual procedure in "testing" causal models with only one indicator for each abstract variable is to take the correlation between indicators as the correlation between the corresponding abstract variables. In so doing we are, in effect, assuming that the epistemic coefficients are either 1 or else very high and subject only to minor random errors. If both epistemic coefficients are less than unity—and they should usually be assumed to be so—$r_{x'y'}$ will be a biased estimate of the coefficient between abstract variables, underestimating that coefficient to the degree that the product of the epistemic coefficients is less than unity. Such bias of typically unknown degree in the estimates of the abstract coefficients seriously hampers efforts to test certain implications of more complex models, although the disadvantage of this conservative bias is not made immediately evident by the very simple model of Figure 16.1.

There is, however, the possibility of another kind of error more pernicious than random errors of measurement. With an auxiliary theory that provides only one indicator for each abstract variable, this more pernicious error remains unrecognizable. If the two indicators in Figure 16.1 have common sources of error not shown in the model, the observed correlation between indicators may yield a heavily distorted estimate of the coefficient between abstract variables even beyond the distortion that is attributable to random error. This kind of indicator error is represented by the two models in Figure 16.2, which do not exhaust the possibilities. Each of the models in Figure 16.2 represents an alternative to the model of Figure 16.1, alternatives in which the error terms for the Figure 16.1 model would be correlated, contrary to assumption. The pernicious character of this kind of measurement error is that if it is present we may be grossly misled, and, with only one indicator for each abstract variable, its presence cannot be readily recognized. Even if such error is suspected, its influence cannot be disentangled from the influence of the causal connections explicitly represented in the other parts of the model.

The traditional language of measurement error includes no term for this specific kind. The measurement error represented in the models of Figure 16.2

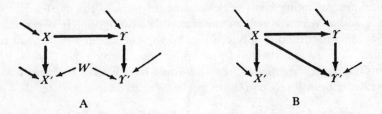

A   B

Figure 16.2. *Two-variable model with one indicator for each variable and differential bias.*

is not *constant error* as we ordinarily think of it, that is, an identical quantity added to or subtracted from every measure; such constant error would be uncorrelated with any other variable and hence of no consequence in a causal model. Neither is it *random error*. And it is not *correlated error* in its usual meaning—that is, error magnitudes correlated with the magnitude of the true value. The measurement error in the models of Figure 16.2 is a *differential constant error*, that is, an error that would be constant over repeated measurement for a given case but variable over cases so that this constant error is correlated with another indicator in the model. The general notion of such differential constant error, or *differential bias*, as I shall call it, is quite familiar, although a general term for designating it is not. For example, when arrests are used as an indicator of the incidence of crime in different areas of the city, the abstract correlation between social class and crime, thus measured, is presumably exaggerated because of differential bias. The economic characteristics of areas affect not only the incidence of crime but also the degree of error in arrests as an indicator of the incidence of crime. Figure 16.2B represents this general kind of circumstance in abstract form, that is, the independent variable has an effect on the indicator of the dependent variable both through the dependent variable and directly. A different kind of differential bias is represented in Figure 16.2A. For example, when two abstract variables are measured by responses to verbal statements and both sets of responses are affected by "social desirability" response sets, the correlation between the errors in the two indicators will lead to a distorted estimate of the correlation between the two abstract variables because of this additional common source of variation in the indicators. Differential bias, then, is not a new idea, although this particular way of representing it in the form of unwanted connections between indicators in a causal model may not be familiar. Unlike random error, differential bias does not necessarily lead to an underestimation, on the average, of the correlation between the abstract variables, and its effects cannot be taken into account by utilizing such familiar devices as sampling distributions or a "correction for attenuation," which are based on the assumption of random errors. Ideally, auxiliary theories would be so constructed that differential bias, if present, would be recognizable empirically. This is evidently not the case with such simple auxiliary theories as those represented in Figures 16.1 and 16.2.

Now we consider a slightly more complex model in which three abstract variables are linked in a causal sequence, with one indicator for each. The model is shown in Figure 16.3.[2] Reference to this model will allow consideration of still another problem, in testing the implications of causal models, that formal auxiliary theories would, ideally, help to resolve.

2. A precisely parallel problem is encountered if the model is changed by reversing the arrow between X and Y, that is, if the relationship between X and Z is spurious.

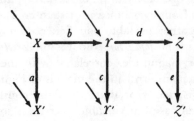

Figure 16.3. *Three-variable model with one indicator for each variable.*

With epistemic coefficients a, c, and e of 1, this model would imply that $r_{X'Z'}$, $r_{X'Y'}$, and $r_{Y'Z'}$ are nonzero and that $r_{X'Z'} = r_{X'Y'}r_{Y'Z'}$. The empirical tenability of this implication would provide the clue as to whether additional causal connections between abstract variables X and Z should be added to the model. But with epistemic coefficients less than unity in absolute value, this implication will not, in general, be true. In fact, with epistemic coefficients less than unity in absolute value, and with only one indicator for each abstract variable, it is not at all clear how a decision on this implication of the model can be made empirically except by some rather casual rule of thumb. Blalock (1961, pp. 148–155) has shown that random error in the measurement of the intervening variable is especially troublesome in this regard, whereas random error in the measurement of the other two variables is much less critical. But an auxiliary theory, ideally, would go further and allow a test of the implications of the abstract model on the abstract plane, uncomplicated by measurement error; the extension to still more complex models would then be relatively straightforward. This is not possible with the auxiliary theory represented in Figure 16.3, even in the absence of any differential bias; the presence of differential bias would complicate the matter still further.

We have now enumerated and illustrated very briefly three desiderata that should ideally be accomplishable by utilizing an auxiliary theory formally representing the connections between abstract variables and their indicators. First, it should be possible to arrive at an estimate for each of the unknown coefficients, including the epistemic coefficients. Second, it should be possible to recognize differential bias, if present, and thereby recognize the inappropriateness of particular indicators in the test of a specific formulation. And third, it should be possible to test the implications of the causal connections incorporated on the abstract plane of the model, without resorting to the grossly oversimplified assumption that the epistemic coefficients are so close to unity as to be of no concern.

We can achieve these desiderata quite adequately if our auxiliary theory provides at least three indicators for each abstract variable in the model; we achieve them somewhat less completely if our auxiliary theory provides only two indicators for each abstract variable, provided the model on the abstract plane is not unduly complicated. For simplicity, we concentrate here on models that propose only one path between each pair of abstract variables. The general line of reasoning should apply to more complex models, provided they are identifiable (on the identification problem, see Fisher 1966). We consider first auxiliary models that provide only two indicators for each abstract variable and then proceed to consider models providing three indicators.

Two-indicator models

Figure 16.4 represents the model identical, on the abstract plane, with the model of Figure 16.1, but now with an auxiliary theory that provides two indicators for each abstract variable. We assume that the correlation between all pairs of indicators is known; hence, instead of one observed correla-

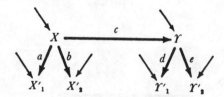

Figure 16.4. *Two-variable model with two indicators for each variable.*

tion as in Figure 16.1, we now have six observed correlations. With the assumption of uncorrelated error terms, each of these six observed correlations may be expressed as a function of the five unknown coefficients as follows:

$$r_{X'_1 X'_2} = ab, \tag{1}$$

$$r_{Y'_1 Y'_2} = de, \tag{2}$$

$$r_{X'_1 Y'_1} = acd, \tag{3}$$

$$r_{X'_1 Y'_2} = ace, \tag{4}$$

$$r_{X_2' Y'_1} = bcd, \tag{5}$$

$$r_{X'_2 Y'_2} = bce. \tag{6}$$

These six equations allow an empirically testable deduction that serves as a clue to the presence of certain kinds of differential bias. It is evident that the model implies nonzero r's and

$$(r_{X'_1Y'_1})(r_{X'_2Y'_2}) = (r_{X'_1Y'_2})(r_{X'_2Y'_1}). \tag{7}$$

This may be shown by substituting the equivalents for these correlations in terms of unknown coefficients, which yields

$$(acd)(bce) = (ace)(bcd), \tag{8}$$

$$abc^2de = abc^2de. \tag{9}$$

If differential bias is present, as illustrated in Figure 16.5A, equation (7) will not hold. In Figure 16.5A, we have

$$r_{X'_1Y'_1} = acd, \tag{3'}$$

$$r_{X'_1Y'_2} = ace, \tag{4'}$$

$$r_{X'_2Y'_1} = bcd + fg, \tag{5'}$$

$$r_{X'_2Y'_2} = bce, \tag{6'}$$

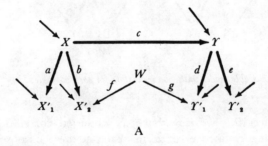

A

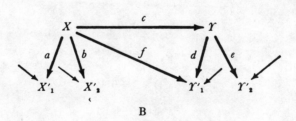

B

Figure 16.5. *Two-variable models with two indicators for each variable and differential bias.*

and

$$r_{X'_1Y'_1}r_{X'_2Y'_2} \neq r_{X'_1Y'_1}r_{X'_2Y'_1}, \tag{10}$$

since

$$(acd)(bce) \neq (ace)(bcd + fg). \tag{11}$$

In general, when differential bias provides an additional source of common variance between two and only two indicators, or when different amounts of additional common variance between different pairs of indicators are supplied by differential bias, equation (7) will not hold. However, equation (7) *will* hold for the kind of differential bias illustrated in Figure 16.5B. In figure 16.5B, we have

$$r_{X'_1Y'_1} = acd + af, \tag{3''}$$

$$r_{X'_1Y'_2} = ace, \tag{4''}$$

$$r_{X'_2Y'_1} = bcd + bf, \tag{5''}$$

$$r_{X'_2Y'_2} = bce; \tag{6''}$$

and equation (7) holds, that is,

$$(r_{X'_1Y'_1})(r_{X'_2Y'_2}) = (r_{X'_1Y'_2})(r_{X'_2Y'_1}),$$

since

$$(acd + af)(bce) = (ace)(bcd + bf),$$
$$abc^2de + abcef = abc^2de + abcef.$$

For two-indicator models, equation (7), which we will call the "consistency criterion" for two-indicator models, is thus a necessary, but not a sufficient, condition for the absence of differential bias. If this equation holds exactly, the two estimates for a given path coefficient will be identical; otherwise the two estimates for a given coefficient will be unequal. Failure of the data to satisfy this equation, at least approximately, indicates that, in some respect, the indicators provided in the auxiliary theory are not appropriate for testing the abstract model. With only two indicators for each abstract variable, no test that is sufficient for ruling out all kinds of differential bias has been devised. But if equation (7) holds, unique estimates for each coefficient in the model may be computed, and the other desiderata previously outlined may be fulfilled in a relatively straightforward fashion. We return to Figure 16.4 for a discussion of these other desiderata.

The six equations generated by the model of Figure 16.4 [i.e., equations (1), (2), (3), (4), (5), and (6)] yield two estimates for each unknown coefficient; these two estimates will be identical if equation (7) is exactly satisfied. Alternatively, the satisfaction of the consistency criterion uses one of the six equations, leaving five equations in five unknowns which may be solved to yield unique solutions for the unknown coefficients. The solutions[3] are:

$$c^2 = \frac{(r_{X'_1 Y'_2})(r_{X'_2 Y'_1})}{(r_{X'_1 X'_2})(r_{Y'_1 Y'_2})} = \frac{(r_{X'_1 Y'_1})(r_{X'_2 Y'_2})}{(r_{X'_1 X'_2})(r_{Y'_1 Y'_2})}, \tag{12}$$

$$a^2 = (r_{X'_1 X'_2})\frac{(r_{X'_1 Y'_2})}{(r_{X'_2 Y'_2})} = (r_{X'_1 X'_2})\frac{(r_{X'_1 Y'_1})}{(r_{X'_2 Y'_1})}, \tag{13}$$

$$b^2 = (r_{X'_1 X'_2})\frac{(r_{X'_2 Y'_2})}{(r_{X'_1 Y'_2})} = (r_{X'_1 X'_2})\frac{(r_{X'_2 Y'_1})}{(r_{X'_1 Y'_1})}, \tag{14}$$

$$d^2 = (r_{Y'_1 Y'_2})\frac{(r_{X'_2 Y'_1})}{(r_{X'_2 Y'_2})} = (r_{Y'_1 Y'_2})\frac{(r_{X'_1 Y'_1})}{(r_{X'_1 Y'_2})}, \tag{15}$$

$$e^2 = (r_{Y'_1 Y'_2})\frac{(r_{X'_2 Y'_2})}{(r_{X'_2 Y'_1})} = (r_{Y'_1 Y'_2})\frac{(r_{X'_1 Y'_2})}{(r_{X'_1 Y'_1})}. \tag{16}$$

The potentiality for obtaining empirical esimates for each of the unknown coefficients of the model fulfills another of the desiderata for auxiliary theories outlined above. The possibility of deriving estimates for the epistemic coefficients bears comment, especially since they may be given more importance than they properly deserve. It is not the case that such empirically estimated epistemic coefficients provide a solution to the "semantic problem" frequently alluded to in discussing the problem of devising appropriate indicators. The empirically estimated epistemic coefficients estimate the correlation

3. The solutions, stated in terms of squares, leave the signs of the corresponding path coefficients formally ambiguous. First, it should be noted that it is empirically possible for the squares representing these solutions to be negative—an outcome clearly inconsistent with the implications of the model and therefore requiring a modification in it. Assuming that all squares representing solutions are positive, the determination of the signs of the coefficients is still ambiguous, since either the positive or the negative root could be taken. Furthermore, different patterns of signs in the path coefficients may yield an identical pattern of signs in the observed correlations. For example, if all indicators are inverse indicators of their respective abstract variables, the pattern of signs among the observed correlations would be identical to that obtaining if all indicators are direct indicators of their respective abstract variables. This ambiguity must be resolved by making *a priori* assumptions about the signs of the epistemic coefficients, that is, assumptions as to whether each indicator is a direct or an inverse indicator of its abstract variable. With these assumptions, the sign of the path coefficients connecting abstract variables is no longer ambiguous; that is, the sign of that path is the same as the sign of the observed correlation between two direct indicators or two inverse indicators and opposite to the sign of the observed correlation between a direct and an inverse indicator. Assumptions about the signs of the epistemic coefficients must, of course, be consistent with the observed correlations between indicators of the same abstract variable; for example, if two indicators of the same abstract variable are negatively correlated with each other, both cannot be assumed to be direct indicators of that variable and both cannot be assumed to be inverse indicators of that variable.

between each specific indicator and the abstract variable that is assigned a particular role in the model on the abstract plane; they have no bearing whatsoever on the appropriateness, in terms of conventional meanings, of the terms that are attached to the abstract variables. The epistemic coefficients thus do not provide a solution to the semantic aspects of the problem of indicator validity. They provide only an estimate of the degree to which extraneous factors and random error influence an indicator's service as indicator of an abstract variable that takes its meaning both from the role it is assigned in the abstract model and from the total set of indicators that are provided for it in the auxiliary theory.

We now move to the third of the desiderata for auxiliary theories outlined above. Ideally, we have noted, an auxiliary theory would allow a test of the implications of causal models on the abstract plane, uncomplicated by problems of measurement error. Figure 16.6 represents an abstract model in

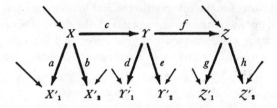

Figure 16.6. *Three-variable model with two indicators for each variable.*

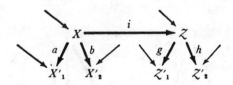

Figure 16.7. *The model of figure* 16.6 *with the intervening variable omitted.*

which such an implication on the abstract plane emerges, and reference to that figure will facilitate discussion. For easy reference, Figure 16.7 presents the model represented in Figure 16.6 with the intervening variable omitted. It should be clear from the preceding discussion that the consistency criterion must, in this instance, be satisfied in three different ways, that is, with respect to that segment of the model involving X and Y and their indicators, Y and Z and their indicators, and X and Z and their indicators. If the consistency

criterion is not satisfied in any one of these three tests, some of the indicators
are subject to differential bias and hence not appropriate to test the abstract
model as a whole. If the consistency criterion is satisfied in all three of these
tests, it should be evident that we could proceed to derive a solution for each
of the three coefficients between abstract variables, c, f, and i. Such solutions
are based on equations analogous to equation (12) for c^2. With solutions for
the coefficients between abstract variables, it is no longer necessary to work
with the directly observed correlations in testing the implications of the model
on the abstract plane. The solutions for the coefficients on the abstract plane
may be used instead. Thus the implication of the model in Figure 16.6 is
that

$$cf = i. \tag{17}$$

This, rather than any equation involving the directly observed correlations,
provides a test for the abstract model. A high degree of random measurement
error in the indicators for the intervening variable no longer has such serious
implications as it does when one must work with the directly observed correlations, although such random measurement error will increase the random
variation in the solutions for unknown coefficients involving that intervening
variable, that is, c and f.

Three-indicator models

Figure 16.8 represents the model identical, on the abstract plane, with the
model of Figure 16.1, but now with an auxiliary theory that provides three
indicators for each abstract variable. Again we assume that the correlation

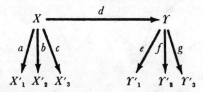

Figure 16.8. *Two-variable model with three indicators for each variable.*

between all pairs of indicators is known; hence we have fifteen observed
correlations, three between indicators of X, three between indicators of Y,
and nine between indicators of X and Y. There are two general ways to
proceed to obtain estimates of the unknown coefficients in this model, and
each procedure provides different clues to the presence of differential bias.
On the one hand, we may take the indicators for each abstract variable in

pairs and proceed exactly as in the two-indicator case with the nine two-indicator models thus formed. On the other hand, we may take advantage of the fact that with three indicators for each abstract variable, the epistemic coefficients may be estimated utilizing only that fragment of the model which constitutes the auxiliary theory for that abstract variable. Using the solutions thus obtained, we may then proceed to obtain additional estimates of the coefficient linking the abstract variables. If the model is uncomplicated by any kind of differential bias, the several estimates derived by the two procedures for each coefficient should all be identical except for random error; inconsistencies will serve as clues to differential bias, as elaborated below.

We first consider the procedure of forming nine two-indicator models from the single three-indicator model. One such two-indicator model may be formed from each set of pairs of indicators for each abstract variable, that is, X'_1 and X'_2 combined with Y'_1 and Y'_2, X'_1 and X'_3 combined with Y'_1 and Y'_2, etc. In a manner analogous to that described above, we obtain a consistency-criterion equation for each of the nine two-indicator models, each analogous to equation (7) above. These nine consistency-criterion equations will have the form

$$\left(r_{X'_h Y'_i}\right)\left(r_{X'_j Y'_k}\right) = \left(r_{X'_h Y'_k}\right)\left(r_{X'_j Y'_i}\right). \tag{18}$$

where $h, i, j,$ and k each assume the values 1, 2, and 3 subject to the restriction that $h \neq j$ and $i \neq k$.[4]

As before, the failure of any one of these equations to be satisfied indicates the presence of differential bias of the type illustrated in Figure 16.9A, and the specific consistency-criterion equations that fail to hold will locate the indicators having a common source of variance not represented in the original model. For Figure 16.9A, for example, showing a common source of variance between X'_3 and Y'_1, all consistency-criterion equations involving both of these indicators would fail to hold. For the model of Figure 16.9A all the remaining consistency-criterion equations should be true except for random measurement error.

Each of the nine two-indicator models which can be formed from a single three-indicator model will yield two estimates of the abstract coefficient, d, for a total of eighteen such estimates. For example, in a manner analogous to that for obtaining equation (12) above, we obtain

$$d^2 = \frac{\left(r_{X'_1 Y'_2}\right)\left(r_{X'_2 Y'_1}\right)}{\left(r_{X'_1 X'_2}\right)\left(r_{Y'_1 Y'_2}\right)} = \frac{\left(r_{X'_1 Y'_1}\right)\left(r_{X'_2 Y'_2}\right)}{\left(r_{X'_1 X'_2}\right)\left(r_{Y'_1 Y'_2}\right)} \tag{19}$$

4. Although thirty-six such equations may be formed, only nine are distinct, since the order of the *r*'s on a given side of the equality sign is irrelevant. Thus, for example, $(r_{X'_1 Y'_2})(r_{X'_2 Y'_3}) = (r_{X'_1 Y'_3})(r_{X'_2 Y'_2})$ is the same equation as $(r_{X'_2 Y'_2})(r_{X'_1 Y'_3}) = (r_{X'_2 Y'_3})(r_{X'_1 Y'_2})$.

from the two-indicator model involving X'_1, X'_2, Y'_1, and Y'_2. These two estimates will be identical if the corresponding consistency-criterion equation holds, that is, if $(r_{X'_1 Y'_2})(r_{X'_2 Y'_1}) = (r_{X'_1 Y'_1})(r_{X'_2 Y'_2})$. Eight additional pairs of estimates for d^2 may be analogously obtained. All have the form

$$d^2 = \frac{(r_{X'_h Y'_i})(r_{X'_j Y'_k})}{(r_{X'_h X'_j})(r_{Y'_i Y'_k})} = \frac{(r_{X'_h Y'_k})(r_{X'_j Y'_i})}{(r_{X'_h X'_j})(r_{Y'_i Y'_k})} \tag{20}$$

where h, i, j, and k each assume the values 1, 2, and 3 subject to the restriction that $h \neq j$ and $i \neq k$.

Although the satisfaction of the nine consistency-criterion equations implies that each pair of such estimates should be equal, the satisfaction of these consistency-criterion equations is not, in itself, sufficient to imply that equality obtains between pairs. As previously noted in the discussion of two-indicator models, the satisfaction of such consistency-criterion equations is not sufficient to imply the absence of differential bias of the kind illustrated in Figure 16.9B, even though differential bias of the kind illustrated in Figure 16.9A will lead to the failure of some of these equations to hold. An additional criterion can be specified for three-indicator models which, if satisfied, will be sufficient to imply the absence of the kind of differential bias illustrated in Figure 16.9B. This requires that we obtain additional estimates of the abstract coefficient, d, by a different route.

Referring once again to Figure 16.8 and assuming no common sources of variance between the indicators X'_1, X'_2, and X'_3 except their common dependence on the abstract variable, X, we may express the correlations between these three indicators in terms of epistemic coefficients as follows:

$$r_{X'_1 X'_2} = ab, \tag{21}$$

$$r_{X'_1 X'_3} = ac, \tag{22}$$

$$r_{X'_2 X'_3} = bc. \tag{23}$$

By simple algebra we obtain the following estimates for the squares of each of these epistemic coefficients:

$$a^2 = \frac{(r_{X'_1 X'_2})(r_{X'_1 X'_3})}{r_{X'_2 X'_3}}, \tag{24}$$

$$b^2 = \frac{(r_{X'_1 X'_2})(r_{X'_2 X'_3})}{r_{X'_1 X'_3}}, \tag{25}$$

$$c^2 = \frac{(r_{X'_1 X'_3})(r_{X'_2 X'_3})}{r_{X'_1 X'_2}}. \tag{26}$$

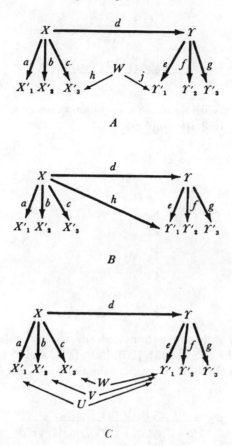

Figure 16.9. *Two-variable models with three indicators for each variable and differential bias.*

In an analogous manner, we obtain the following equations for the correlations between Y indicators:

$$r_{Y'_1 Y'_2} = ef, \qquad (27)$$

$$r_{Y'_1 Y'_3} = eg, \qquad (28)$$

$$r_{Y'_2 Y'_3} = fg. \qquad (29)$$

And the following estimates for the squares of the epistemic coefficients for Y may be obtained as simple algebraic solutions of the three equations above:

$$e^2 = \frac{(r_{Y'_1 Y'_2})(r_{Y'_1 Y'_3})}{r_{Y'_2 Y'_3}}, \qquad (30)$$

$$f^2 = \frac{(r_{Y'_2 Y'_3})(r_{Y'_1 Y'_2})}{r_{Y'_1 Y'_3}},$$ (31)

$$g^2 = \frac{(r_{Y'_1 Y'_3})(r_{Y'_2 Y'_3})}{r_{Y'_1 Y'_2}}.$$ (32)

We note further that, with the same assumption of uncorrelated error terms, the model of Figure 16.8 also implies

$$r_{X'_1 Y'_1} = ade,$$ (33)

$$r_{X'_1 Y'_2} = adf,$$ (34)

$$r_{X'_1 Y'_3} = adg,$$ (35)

$$r_{X'_2 Y'_1} = bde,$$ (36)

$$r_{X'_2 Y'_2} = bdf,$$ (37)

$$r_{X'_2 Y'_3} = bdg,$$ (38)

$$r_{X'_3 Y'_1} = cde,$$ (39)

$$r_{X'_3 Y'_2} = cdf,$$ (40)

$$r_{X'_3 Y'_3} = cdg.$$ (41)

Squaring both sides of these equations and substituting in them the solutions given above (equations [24], [25], [26], [30], [31], and [32]) for the epistemic coefficients, we obtain nine additional estimates for d^2. All will have the form

$$d^2 = \frac{(r^2_{X'_h Y'_i})(r_{X'_j X'_k})(r_{Y'_m Y'_n})}{(r_{X'_h X'_j})(r_{X'_h X'_k})(r_{Y'_i Y'_m})(r_{Y'_i Y'_n})}$$ (42)

where h, i, j, k, m, and n each assume the values 1, 2, and 3, subject to the restriction that $h \neq j \neq k$ and $i \neq m \neq n$.

In the absence of differential bias (i.e., as in the model of Fig. 16.8) all nine estimates of d^2 should be identical, except for random measurement error. The model of Figure 16.9A, on the other hand, involves differential bias and will not yield identical estimates. That model yields a set of nine equations identical with equations (33)–(41), except that equation (39) will be

$$r_{X'_3 Y'_1} = cde + hj,$$ (39')

and the one estimate of d^2 based on $r_{X'_3 Y'_1}$ will be an overestimate if hj is positive, that is,

$$d^2 < \frac{(r^2_{X'_3 Y'_1})(r_{X'_1 X'_2})(r_{Y'_2 Y'_3})}{(r_{X'_1 X'_3})(r_{X'_2 X'_3})(r_{Y'_1 Y'_3})(r_{Y'_1 Y'_2})}$$ (43)

As previously noted, the presence of differential bias of the type represented in Figure 16.9A would also have been indicated by the fact that certain of the consistency-criterion equations (having the form of equation [18]) would fail to hold. However, the consistency of the nine estimates for d^2 given by equations having the form of equation (42) will also be sensitive to the presence of differential bias of the type represented in Figure 16.9B. In the model of Figure 16.9B

$$r_{X'_1 Y'_1} = ade + ah, \qquad (33')$$

$$r_{X'_2 Y'_1} = bde + bh, \qquad (36')$$

and

$$r_{X'_3 Y'_1} = cde + ch. \qquad (39'')$$

Estimates of d^2 having the form of equation (42) and based on $r_{X'_1 Y'_1}$, $r_{X'_2 Y'_1}$, or $r_{X'_3 Y'_1}$ will be overestimates if the paths a, b, c, and h are all positive. Thus these three estimates would diverge from the other six in the same direction but not necessarily to the same degree.

We have now defined two types of consistency criteria for three-indicator models. The first consists of a set of nine equations of the form of equation (18) which are analogous to equation (7) for the two-indicator model. Failure of any one of these equations to hold indicates the presence of differential bias of the type illustrated in Figure 16.9A. The second type of consistency criteria for three-indicator models consists of a set of nine estimates of d^2 having the form of equation (42). The failure of all of these estimates to be equal to each other indicates the presence of differential bias, either of the type represented in Figure 16.9A or in Figure 16.9B. More specifically, the divergence of a single estimate in this set of nine from the remaining estimates indicates the presence of differential bias of the type represented in Figure 16.9A, that is, extraneous common variance between one indicator of X and one indicator of Y. The divergence (not necessarily equal divergence) of three of these estimates of d^2, each of which is based on a single Y indicator, would indicate the presence of differential bias of the type represented in Figure 16.9B if the consistency-criterion equations of the form of equation (18) were all satisfied but would indicate the type of differential bias suggested by Figure 16.9C if the consistency-criterion equations involving Y'_1 were not satisfied. The three-indicator model thus allows a test for a type of differential bias not possible with the two-indicator model by introducing an additional consistency criterion, namely, that all nine estimates of d^2 given by equations having the form of equation (42) be identical.

We may go one step further with the three-indicator model. We have been concerned above with differential bias, that is, a source of common variance extraneous to the model between at least one indicator of X and at least one indicator of Y. There is another kind of nonrandom measurement error which can also distort the estimates of the abstract coefficient (d in the model of Figure 16.8). This is a source of common variance between the indicators of the same abstract variable other than their common dependence on that abstract variable. This is illustrated in Figure 16.10. In the model of Figure 16.10, X'_1 and X'_2 have common variance both because of their common dependence on X and because of their common dependence on W. The correlation $r_{X'_1 X'_2}$ will therefore be larger than would be the case without this extraneous common variance, assuming, for simplicity, that all coefficients are positive. As a consequence, all estimates of d^2 having the term $r_{X'_1 X'_2}$ in the numerator would be overestimates of d^2, while all estimates having that term in the denominator would be underestimates. The three-indicator model yields twenty-seven estimates of d^2 [i.e., eighteen estimates having the form of equation (20) and an additional nine estimates having the form of equation (42)]. Twelve of these estimates have $r_{X'_1 X'_2}$ in the denominators and will be underestimates (assuming a, b, h, and j all positive), three

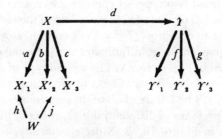

Figure 16.10. *Two-variable model with three indicators for each variable and with an extraneous source of common variance between two indicators of the same variable.*

have that term in the numerators and will be overestimates, while the remaining twelve do not include that term and will not be affected. Clearly, different types of nonrandom measurement error will result in different patterns of divergence among the twenty-seven estimates of d^2 given by the three-indicator model and thus allow the pattern of inconsistency among estimates to be used as a clue, not only to the presence of differential bias, but also to the nature of whatever nonrandom measurement error may be operating. Certain complex combinations of different types of nonrandom error, however, would probably defy an attempt to discern the pattern.

If all the above-named consistency conditions for the three-indicator model are satisfied, it will be possible to derive estimates for all the coefficients and to test the implications of the model on the abstract plane in a manner analogous to that represented in equation (17) above.

Discussion

Since the various consistency conditions outlined above are crucial for obtaining unique estimates of the unobservable coefficients in abstract causal models, some brief elaboration of these conditions may be appropriate. The consistency conditions defined here serve to underscore the points made in several insightful discussions of the utility of multiple indicators in testing abstract propositions (Curtis and Jackson 1962; Lazarsfeld 1959; Webb *et al.* 1966, chap. 1). Let it be noted, however, that the consistency criteria here defined do *not* require that all correlations between different pairs of indicators be identical; rather, the criteria require that certain products of correlations shall be identical or that several estimates of a single abstract coefficient shall be consistent. These criteria may be met even though all observed correlations between X and Y indicators are quite different from each other. The expectation that all correlations between different pairs of indicators be identical is unnecessarily restrictive; it assumes, in effect, that all epistemic coefficients between a given abstract variable and its indicators are identical, that is, that all indicators of a given variable are equally good indicators, which is contrary to our common thinking about the uneven quality of indicators.

It may be reasonably asked what is meant when we say that the consistency criterion is satisfied. Do we mean that the two sides of equation (7) are exactly identical, that they are approximately identical, or that they should not differ to a degree that is statistically significant at the commonly utilized levels of significance? If all measures are made on the same set of cases, no variation between the two sides of equation (7) should be attributable to variation between samples of cases, and since random measurement error has been explicitly taken into account in the model, it may appear that such error would not contribute to variation between the two sides of equation (7). While it is true that measurement error has been taken into account in one sense, it has not been taken into account in a way that rules out its effect in producing variation between the two sides of equation (7). In effect, equation (7) asserts the equality of two estimates of the same abstract coefficient, c. But both estimates are subject to sampling variability to the degree that the epistemic coefficients (a, b, d, and e) are less than unity. What we mean, then, when we say that the consistency criterion is satisfied is that the two sides of equation (7) do not differ from each other to a statistically significant degree. This is formally identical to the vanishing of the "tetrad difference" in the classic Spearman factor analysis, and the standard error of the "tetrad difference" is known (Holzinger 1930, p. 6). Satisfying the additional consistency criteria in the three-indicator model presents an additional statistical inference problem, the solution to which does not appear to be found in the factor analysis literature.

If the consistency criterion is satisfied in a particular model or segment of a model, there may be a temptation to interpret it as a validation test for the indicators. The consistency criterion is not a validation of indicators; the absence of differential bias for a given set of indicators in the context of one specific model is no guarantee that differential bias for some of those same indicators will be absent in the context of a different model—or even in another segment of the same complex model. The satisfaction of the consistency criterion is a feature of the model or a segment thereof; it is not a feature of the indicators themselves that can be transferred with them to other models.

The general conclusion to be reached from this discussion is that, although causal models are strictly untestable with a single indicator for each abstract variable unless one assumes very slight measurement error, an auxiliary theory providing multiple indicators for each of the abstract variables will, assuming the consistency criteria are met, allow a test of the implications of the abstract causal model and provide, in addition, estimates of the epistemic coefficients involved in the auxiliary theory itself. A crucial matter in the whole enterprise, however, is the satisfaction of the consistency criteria as a guard against differential bias, and we may find that certain causal models are simply not testable with certain indicators because differential bias is present.

The general strategy of devising and utilizing auxiliary theories that has been outlined in this paper, with the crucial role it assigns to the intercorrelation between different indicators of a single abstract variable, is probably inappropriate as a guide for dealing with formulations at the highest levels of abstraction. The ties between very highly abstract concepts and the empirical world appear to take a form that is different from that assumed in this discussion. Specifically, highly abstract concepts are frequently designed to encompass a variety of different forms of a given phenomenon that are not necessarily intercorrelated with each other. There is no reason to assume *a priori*, for example, that all of the many forms of deviant behavior are intercorrelated. Similarly, frustrations are many and varied, and the degree to which one suffers frustration in one guise is no clue to the degree of frustration of another kind. The admission of uncorrelated indicators for a given abstract variable renders the strategy discussed in this paper inapplicable. The problems associated with detailing the connections between such highly abstract concepts, their uncorrelated subforms, and the indicators of each subform—and doing so in a way that allows an unambiguous empirical test of the theory at the highest level of abstraction—will undoubtedly require a more complex and intricate kind of auxiliary theory than the relatively simple type employed in the present discussion. Some progress toward the development of these more complex and intricate auxiliary theories would help provide a needed integration of high levels of abstraction and testable deductions in sociological theory.

References

BLALOCK, HUBERT M., Jr. 1961. *Causal Inferences in Nonexperimental Research.* Chapel Hill: University of North Carolina Press.

———. 1968. "The Measurement Problem: A Gap between the Languages of Theory and Research." In *Methodology in Social Research*, edited by H. M. Blalock and A. Blalock. New York: McGraw-Hill.

CURTIS, RICHARD F., and JACKSON, ELTON F. 1962. "Multiple Indicators in Survey Research." *American Journal of Sociology* 68 (September): 195–204.

FISHER, FRANKLIN M. 1966. *The Identification Problem in Econometrics.* New York: McGraw-Hill.

HOLZINGER, KARL JOHN. 1930. *Statistical Resumé of the Spearman Two-Factor Theory.* Chicago: University of Chicago Press.

LAZARSFELD, PAUL F. 1959. "Problems in Methodology." In *Sociology Today: Problems and Prospects*, edited by R. K. Merton *et al.* New York: Basic Books.

SIEGEL, PAUL M., and HODGE, ROBERT W. 1968. "A Causal Approach to the Study of Measurement Error." In *Methodology in Social Research*, edited by H. M. Blalock and A. Blalock. New York: McGraw-Hill.

SIMON, HERBERT A. 1959. "Spurious Correlation: A Causal Interpretation." In *Models of Man*, Herbert A. Simon, New York: Wiley.

WEBB, EUGENE T., CAMPBELL, DONALD T., SCHWARTZ, RICHARD D., and SECHREST, LEE. 1966. *Unobtrusive Measures: Nonreactive Research in the Social Sciences.* Chicago: Rand McNally.

Chapter 17

ON THE EVALUATION OF SIMPLE MODELS
CONTAINING MULTIPLE INDICATORS
OF UNMEASURED VARIABLES

THOMAS L. VAN VALEY
Colorado State University

Costner (1969) has demonstrated that multiple indicators can be used empirically to test the assumption of randomness of error and, additionally, to provide estimates of both the true relationships and the existing degree of measurement error (that is, if the data do, in fact, satisfy the test criteria). Blalock (1969) discusses Costner's procedure and extends the argument to recursive systems in general. As these treatments are ample, we will quickly turn to the evaluation of our model.

The simple model presented below should suffice for the explanation of the procedure used in estimating the required P_i. The estimates may be calculated by combining pairs of cross correlations in the following manner, where the pairs of estimates of the P_i *should* be equal, or nearly so:[1]

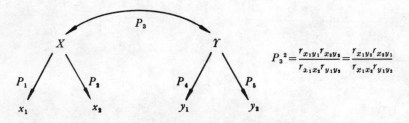

$$P_3{}^2 = \frac{r_{x_1y_1}r_{x_2y_2}}{r_{a_1x_2}r_{y_1y_2}} = \frac{r_{x_1y_2}r_{x_2y_1}}{r_{x_1x_2}r_{y_1y_2}}$$

Paper prepared especially for *Causal Models in the Social Sciences.*

1. When there are additional indicators of the unmeasured variables, further tests of the model(s) are possible. See Costner (1969) for a computing formula and more detailed explanation. It should also be noted that in this simple case, $P_3 = r_{xy}$, and therefore the procedure allows us to estimate the *correlation* between X and Y.

When the pairs of estimates are not substantially in agreement, the possibility of nonrandom measurement error should be entertained.

The model we are presenting herein involves the historically concomitant processes of urbanization, industrialization, and the development of facilities for transportation and communication. The unit of analysis is the county, and the sample (taken from the *County and City Data Book: 1960*) includes at least a majority from each of the following eight states in the Deep South: Alabama, Florida, Georgia, Mississippi, North Carolina, South Carolina, Tennessee, and Virginia. (We considered all other states "border" or non-Southern and therefore excluded them.)

Four indicators were used to measure urbanization: (1) population per square mile; (2) per cent of the population classified as urban; (3) per cent of the population classified as rural-farm; and (4) the amount of land in farms as a per cent of all land. Industrialization, our second variable, also has four indicator-measures:[2] (1) the amount of *primary* economic activity (i.e., the number of persons employed in agriculture and construction); (2) the amount of *secondary* economic activity (the number of persons employed in the manufacture of durable and nondurable goods); (3) the amount of *tertiary* activity (the number of persons employed in trade and finance); and (4) the amount of *quaternary* activity (the number of persons employed in education and public administration). Finally, for the transportation-communication variable, we used five indicators: (1) the per cent of the labor force that worked out of the county of residence; (2) the number of persons employed in transportation and communication; (3) the per cent of occupied dwelling units with a television set; (4) the per cent of occupied dwelling units with two or more automobiles; and (5) the per cent of farms with a telephone. The detailed model is causally represented below:[3]

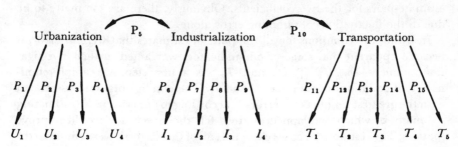

2. These four indicators, as well as the second indicator for transportation-communication, all refer to the actual numbers of people. We realize that there is no standardization for size and that this may have significance for any substantive conclusions to be drawn from our data. However, it should not affect the application of the methods being reported herein.

3. The curved arrows in this figure indicate the ambiguity of the causal relations. More-

Before we proceed with the evaluation of our model, we should introduce several cautions. First, the procedure clearly involves *ex post facto* decisions. While this *may* not involve any difficulty, depending on the general research design, the user should be aware of the fact. One possibility for handling such a problem (though it has not yet been carried out on the present data) might be to divide the sample in half and evaluate the model on only one part, retaining the second half for a test. This, of course, would require a very large data-set.

A second caution, common to virtually all "tests," is the fact that any decision rule is highly arbitrary. Yet, though this is admittedly an unhappy circumstance, until we know more about both the technique and our model, it is necessary. For our own analysis, we have used a difference between the r's of .15 as the maximum acceptable spread between the two elements of each estimate pair.

Third, concepts such as urbanization, industrialization, and transportation-communication are probably configurations or "syndromes" of several, less general variables, whose relationships are only poorly understood. This of course, allows for considerable "slippage" in fitting any set of data.

Finally, we have assumed that sampling errors are minimal. These are difficult to estimate, especially given some of the above considerations, and consequently it would be well to confine the procedure to large samples and reasonably large correlations.

Table 17.1 contains the 36 possible pairs of estimates for the P_5 coefficient. Given our decision rule (15 points maximum allowable divergence), *14* of these are in error. For them we have not calculated an average estimate. In addition, though because of space considerations they could not be included in this paper, of the 60 possible pairs of estimates for the P_{10} coefficient, *35* more exceeded the cutting point. This left us with only 47 out of 96 possible estimate-pairs for the two coefficients. Obviously, there are too many to be due to the fluctuations of sampling error alone.

In listing the equations for all the pairs of estimates that were in error, it became apparent that some of our indicators warranted further investigation; namely, U_1, U_4, I_1, T_1, and T_2. As a first step, we simply eliminated all equations containing U_4 and I_1. These indicators were associated with the greatest numbers of "errors" (according to our criteria) in estimating P_5, many of which overlapped, and we felt their exclusion would improve matters. The results were as we expected; all of the "errors" were eliminated.[4]

---

over, as the figure is for illustrative purposes, the P_5 and P_{10} coefficients have been included but not the P_{16} coefficient for the direct urbanization-transportation relation. The causal diagrams to follow will be modified to include this path.

4. We might caution the reader at this point that although this procedure does seem to be highly effective, the indiscriminate exclusion of indicators very rapidly reduces the number of estimate-pairs that are possible for a given P_i. This in turn would seem to raise some doubts about the reliability of the remaining estimates.

Table 17.1. Estimates of the P_5 Coefficient

Indicators involved	$\dfrac{r_{x_i y_k}\, r_{x_j y_l}}{r_{x_i x_j}\, r_{y_k y_l}}$	$\dfrac{r_{x_j y_k}\, r_{x_i y_l}}{r_{x_i x_j}\, r_{y_k y_l}}$	Average estimate
$U_1 U_2\ I_1 I_2$	.9266	.9850	.9558
$I_2 I_3$	.9118	.9313	.9216
$I_3 I_4$	.9079	.8904	.8992
$I_1 I_3$	.8169	.8871	.8520
$I_1 I_4$	.8838	.9413	.9126
$I_2 I_4$	.9803	.9821	.9812
$U_1 U_3\ I_1 I_2$	.9596	.6210	....
$I_2 I_3$	.8824	.9647	.9236
$I_3 I_4$	.8952	.8617	.8785
$I_1 I_3$	.9906	.5594	....
$I_1 I_4$	.8713	.5933	....
$I_2 I_4$	.9667	1.0174	.9921
$U_1 U_4\ I_1 I_2$	.9142	.4490	....
$I_2 I_3$	.9898	.9186	.9542
$I_3 I_4$	.9815	.9669	.9742
$I_1 I_3$	.8870	.4041	....
$I_1 I_4$	.9556	.4294	....
$I_2 I_4$	1.0599	.9691	1.0145
$U_2 U_3\ I_1 I_2$	.7541	.4589	....
$I_2 I_3$	.6522	.6979	.6751
$I_3 I_4$	.6475	.6355	.6415
$I_1 I_3$	.6210	.4046	....
$I_1 I_4$	.6845	.4377	....
$I_2 I_4$	.7143	.7504	.7324
$U_2 U_4\ I_1 I_2$	3.3478	1.5590	....
$I_2 I_3$	3.4335	3.1181	....
$I_3 I_4$	3.3333	3.3469	3.3401
$I_1 I_3$	3.2659	1.3719	....
$I_1 I_4$	3.5229	1.4848	....
$I_2 I_4$	3.6835	3.3610	....
$U_3 U_4\ I_1 I_2$	.2539	.1922	.2231
$I_2 I_3$	.4243	.3603	.3923
$I_3 I_4$	.3851	.3941	.3896
$I_1 I_3$	.2462	.1588	.2025
$I_1 I_4$	.2650	.1750	.2200
$I_2 I_4$	.4542	.3947	.4245

Similar results occurred with the estimates of P_{10} when we excluded all equations involving T_1. However, we were left with one errant indicator, T_2 (all of the errors associated with U_1 were eliminated when U_4 and I_1 were taken out). Following a hunch, we compared the intercorrelations among the indicators appearing in the equations for the few remaining doubtful estimates. The result was a strong relationship between our last doubtful indicator, T_2, and one of our "good" indicators, I_4. Since, as the reader may remember, T_2 refers to the number of persons employed in Transportation and Communication, there are ample theoretical grounds for including it in with the I_4 indicator, which refers to the degree of Quaternary economic activity. Therefore, we added T_2 to I_4 to create a new indicator, I_4^*.

Given the above considerations with respect to our indicators, we recomputed all the pairs of estimates on the basis of the modified model. The result was no "errors," as defined by our decision rule. This model and the estimates of the relevant path coefficients are given below:

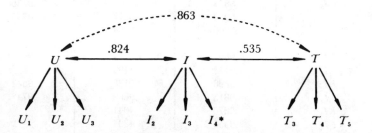

It was evident from the range of the average estimates in Table 17.1 (0.2025 to 3.3401) that a second decision rule would be advisable with respect to the comparisons across indicators. This time we decided to recompute the coefficient over a field defined by the mean of the average estimates plus-or-minus 15 points, throwing out all estimates outside the field. When we applied this new procedure to the modified model described above, only the P_5 estimate was affected, and this by the deletion of a single estimate-pair $(U_2 U_3, I_3 I_4^*)$. This adjusted value of P_5 was .851, only slightly larger than the earlier estimate.[5]

Canonical correlation analysis

"Canonical correlation analysis is a procedure for studying the inter-correlations between two sets of variables measured on the same subjects. These variables are predictors in one set and criteria in the other set. The canonical correlation gives the maximum correlation between linear functions of the two sets of variables" (IBM, 1966, p. 26). In other words, given two sets of variables (or indicators), X_i and Y_i, this computerized technique is a means by which the degree of relationship between the two *sets* of variables

5. When the two decision rules were applied in the reverse order, the estimate for the P_5 coefficient was .959. Moreover, we were not able to isolate any of the indicators which might have caused the difficulty.

can be estimated. In fact, as it is the process by which the appropriate weights are estimated, it is the general case of the more familiar multiple correlation, in which a set of independent variables operate on a single dependent variable instead of a set of them.

The results of the canonical analysis, and the model on which it was performed, are given in the causal diagram below. Note especially the degree of similarity between the coefficients produced by the canonical analysis and the previous results obtained from the path analysis.

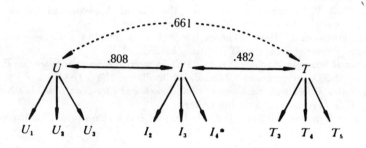

Summary and conclusions

For the present paper, two techniques—path analysis and canonical analysis—were applied to a body of real data related to the processes of urbanization, industrialization, and the development of facilities for transportation and communication. The implications of our analyses reach far beyond the data. We have briefly examined two very sophisticated (for the social sciences) statistical techniques and found a high degree of complementarity. This alone is significant, for were we in the practical setting and relying on more commonly used methods, say partial or multiple correlation analysis, the end result would have been misleading at best. As it were, path analysis and, at present, to an unknown extent, canonical analysis provide a useful set of tools for the examination, refinement, and then re-examination of our data and our theoretical models.

This paper has also pointed up, by way of example, a note of caution which Blalock (1964) among others has expressed: that a high correlation between two independent variables, by allowing considerable sampling error, makes it difficult to choose reliably among alternative models. This word of caution, it would seem, could as well be applied to high correlations among indicators. The case of the unmeasured variables themselves, on the other hand, is not so clear. The fact of inference from the level of the indicator to the level of the unmeasured variable introduces the possibility of still further complicating factors, in addition to those resulting from the matters discussed above. Further work, perhaps in the area of computer simulation, may allow us to specify some of the effects of such complicating factors, thereby shedding some light on the complex relationships that are involved.

References

BLALOCK, HUBERT M., Jr. 1964. *Causal Inferences in Nonexperimental Research*. Chapel Hill: University of North Carolina Press.
————. 1969. "Multiple Indicators and the Causal Approach to Measurement Error," *American Journal of Sociology, 75* (Sept.): 264–272.
COSTNER, HERBERT L. 1969. "Theory, Deduction, and Rules of Correspondence," *American Journal of Sociology, 75* (Sept.): 245–263.
International Business Machines (IBM). 1966. *System/360, Scientific Subroutine Package, (360A-CM-03X), Programmer's Manual*. White Plains, N.Y.: IBM.
United States Bureau of the Census. 1960. *County and City Data Book*. Washington, D.C.: U.S. Government Printing Office.
VAN VALEY, THOMAS L. 1969. "Industrialization and Urbanization." (Mimeo.)

Chapter 18

MULTIPLE INDICATORS AND
COMPLEX CAUSAL MODELS

John L. Sullivan
Iowa State University

Several authors have recently pointed out the usefulness of multiple indicators. Curtis and Jackson [1] argue that the use of each indicator separately has certain advantages over combining them into an index. It increases the number of predictions made by a particular model, enables the careful researcher to determine the existence of an unknown spurious cause, increases confidence in the validity of the indicators, and guides conceptual reformulation. Other authors, such as Siegel and Hodge [2], Costner [3] and Blalock [4] have illustrated the use of multiple indicators to determine the existence and nature of measurement error. The present paper addresses itself to the former use of multiple indicators, extends the implications of Curtis and Jackson to a more general model and introduces a method which deals with the problems arising as a result of this extension.

A common problem encountered in testing complex causal models is the selection of indicators. A common solution is the selection of one indicator (from among perhaps three or four) that seems "on its face" to best represent the construct we wish to measure. This involves a loss of information and accuracy, as the two or three indicators that are thrown out are likely to have some validity and their addition may produce a more correct representation of the construct. A second solution is that of combining the three or four indicators into an index, in an attempt to represent the construct more accurately than any one (even the "best") of the indicators could possibly do. This seems preferable, yet as Curtis and Jackson note, this has certain costs involved as well. Thus their argument in favor of using each indicator

Paper prepared especially for *Causal Models in the Social Sciences*.

separately. As will be noted later, factor analysis is not deemed an acceptable solution to the problem.

Extension to the general model

The use of each indicator separately has certain practical limitations whenever we are dealing with a large number of variables, hence an even larger number of indicators. The number of tests of the predictions, without even attempting to assess the assumptions of the model, quickly becomes unmanageable. In Figure 18.1, for example, six predictions are made, but

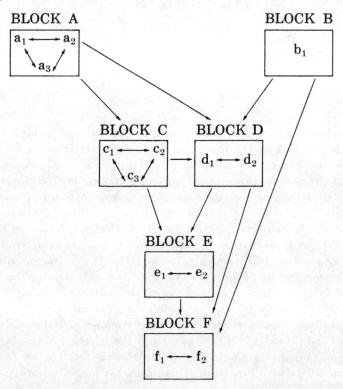

Predictions	Number of tests
1. $r_{AB}=0$	3
2. $r_{BC}=0$	3
3. $r_{BE \cdot D}=0$	4
4. $r_{CF \cdot DE}=0$	24
5. $r_{AE \cdot CD}=0$	36
6. $r_{AF \cdot CD}=0$	36

Figure 18.1. *Causal model with multiple indicators.*

there are 106 tests of these predictions, a number that would increase rapidly with every additional indicator. If one wishes to check the correlational assumptions of the model, the number of tests becomes even more unmanageable.

Must we, then, lose the advantages of multiple indicators precisely in those situations where we need them the most? As our models become more complex and meaningful, must we fall back upon selecting the "best" indicator? Hopefully, the answer is no. As a sensible compromise, I would suggest the use of multiple-partial correlation coefficients to test complex causal models. This involves using the indicators of the dependent[1] variable separately, but allowing the indicators of the independent and the control variables to operate as a block.[2] Thus we have more tests of each prediction (the same number as the number of indicators of the dependent variable in each test) but also a more accurate representation of the theoretical constructs. For example, in Figure 18.1, the prediction that $r_{AE \cdot CD} = 0$ now has two rather than 36 tests: $r_{e_1(a_1a_2a_3) \cdot (c_1c_2c_3d_1d_2)} = 0$ and $r_{e_2(a_1a_2a_3) \cdot (c_1c_2c_3d_1d_2)} = 0$. That is, we allow all of the indicators of the control variables to wipe out as much variation as they can in the dependent variable, and then see how much of the remaining variation is explained by all of the indicators of the independent variable. One could argue that "of course, any partial will drop to or near zero if we allow so many variables to first wipe out variation in the dependent variable." However, I propose that one also use this method to check the assumptions upon which the model is based, thus looking for non-zero multiple-partials. For example, the model in Figure 18.1 assumes causal connections between D and E, D and F, and E and F. If this is true, then D and F ought to be related, even controlling for E. Therefore the following two "tests" or "checks" of that assumption can be made: $r_{f_1(d_1d_2) \cdot (e_1e_2)} \neq 0$ and $r_{f_2(d_1d_2) \cdot (e_1e_2)} \neq 0$. Standard F-tests can be used to determine whether the multiple-partial is significantly greater than zero.

An empirical illustration

A brief example of this technique follows, more as an illustration of its use than as a test of this particular model. Table 18.1 lists the constructs and the indicators corresponding to Figure 18.1. The unit of analysis is the state, with an N of 35, as there were 35 states with senatorial elections in 1966, and one

---

1. "Dependent" is used advisedly in this case. It is a dependent variable only in terms of one particular test of the model, not in terms of the entire model.

2. Of course, the use of this procedure means that the empirical equations for each test of a single prediction will differ. The weights given to various indicators shift because the slope coefficients shift as the various indicators of the "dependent" variable are used. Since we are interested in the "total direct effects" of one block of variables on another block, this probably is not a serious problem, although our estimates will vary.

Table 18.1. Constructs and indicators of Figure 18.1

BLOCK A. RESOURCES
  a_1 % home ownership
  a_2 median income
  a_3 % white collar occupation

BLOCK B. HETEROGENEITY
  b_1 weighted sum of the standard deviations (by congressional district) of a_1, a_2, c_1, c_3, d_1, % urban and % foreign stock

BLOCK C. SOPHISTICATION OF ELECTORATE
  c_1 % with a college education
  c_2 median education
  c_3 % functionally illiterate

BLOCK D. DISCRIMINATION
  d_1 % Negro
  d_2 difference between the ratio of home ownership/renter occupied dwellings for whites vs. nonwhites

BLOCK E. PARTY COMPETITION
  e_1 % for presidential candidate who carried the state in 1960
  e_2 mean difference, winner's % vs. loser's % of the vote, by congressional district

BLOCK F. ELECTORAL CHOICE
  f_1 senatorial challenger vs. incumbent attitudinal differences on issues, 1966[3]
  f_2 mean attitudinal differences on issues, challenger vs. incumbent, by congressional district

---

of the constructs, electoral choice, is dependent upon questionnaires administered in that election. The results of the tests of the predictions and assumptions of the model are presented in Tables 18.2 and 18.3. The small N implies large sampling errors, hence these results are merely suggestive.

Table 18.2 lists the six predictions and the fourteen tests of these predictions. All fourteen tests are successful at the .01 level of confidence. This makes it difficult to reject the null hypothesis that the correlation is equal to zero. If the .05 level of confidence is used, two of the thirteen tests are unsuccessful, whereas approximately one is expected to be unsuccessful by chance.

Fifteen of the 33 tests of the nine assumptions are not met at the .01 level. Again, however, with such a small N the .01 confidence level is highly rigorous. If the .05 level is substituted, 22 of these tests are successful while eleven are unsuccessful. Of these eleven, five occur as the only unsuccessful

3. From a 16-point scale developed from questionnaires given to all candidates in the 1966 Congressional and Senatorial elections by NBC. See Robert O'Connor and John Sullivan, *Systemic Determinism or Popular Choice?*, unpublished mimeo, University of North Carolina.

Table 18.2. Predictions

	.05 level	.01 level
1. $r_{AB}=0$		
(1) $r_{a_1b_1}=.13$	NS	NS
(2) $r_{a_2b_1}=-.14$	NS	NS
(3) $r_{a_3b_1}=.27$	NS	NS
2. $r_{BC}=0$		
(1) $r_{c_1b_1}=.12$	NS	NS
(2) $r_{c_2b_1}=-.25$	NS	NS
(3) $r_{c_3b_1}=-.13$	NS	NS
3. $r_{BE \cdot D}=0$		
(1) $r_{e_1(b_1) \cdot (d_1d_2)}=.10$	NS	NS
(2) $r_{e_2(b_1) \cdot (d_1d_2)}=.16$	NS	NS
4. $r_{CF \cdot DE}=0$		
(1) $r_{f_1(c_1c_2c_3) \cdot (d_1d_2e_1e_2)}=.14$	NS	NS
(2) $r_{f_2(c_1c_2c_3) \cdot (d_1d_2e_1e_2)}=.32$	NS	NS
5. $r_{AE \cdot CD}=0$		
(1) $r_{e_1(a_1a_2a_3) \cdot (c_1c_2c_3d_1d_2)}=.18$	NS	NS
(2) $r_{e_2(a_1a_2a_3) \cdot (c_1c_2c_3d_1d_2)}=.43$	SIGN	NS
6. $r_{AF \cdot CD}=0$		
(1) $r_{f_1(a_1a_2a_3) \cdot (c_1c_2c_3d_1d_2)}=.28$	NS	NS
(2) $r_{f_2(a_1a_2a_3) \cdot (c_1c_2c_3d_1d_2)}=.46$	SIGN	NS

test of a certain assumption, whereas four occur in the six tests of assumption three, and the other two are the only two tests of assumption two. It appears that these two assumptions may in fact be false.

The model assumes that a high degree of sophistication causes a low degree of discrimination. Four of the six "tests" of this assumption indicate that the data do not fit. However, two of the three tests using % Negro as an indicator of discrimination indicate that sophistication and discrimination are very strongly related. The failure of the three tests using the difference between the ratio of home ownership/renter occupied dwellings for whites vs. non-whites as an indicator of discrimination may reflect its inadequacy as an indicator. This method allows us to explore and explain such inconsistencies. In any case, the size of the correlations for the two successful tests indicates that the arrow from sophistication to discrimination in Figure 18.1 should not be removed until further evidence is presented.

The model also assumes that a high degree of heterogeneity causes a low degree of discrimination. As Table 18.3 indicates, this assumes that $r_{BD} \neq 0$ and both tests of that assumption are unsuccessful. However, the relationship

Table 18.3. Assumptions

		.05 level	.01 level
1.	$r_{AC} \neq 0$		
	(1) $r_{a_1c_1} = .61$	SIGN	SIGN
	(2) $r_{a_1c_2} = .74$	SIGN	SIGN
	(3) $r_{a_1c_3} = -.74$	SIGN	SIGN
	(4) $r_{a_2c_1} = .10$	NS	NS
	(5) $r_{a_2c_2} = .55$	SIGN	SIGN
	(6) $r_{a_2c_3} = -.63$	SIGN	SIGN
	(7) $r_{a_3c_1} = .76$	SIGN	SIGN
	(8) $r_{a_3c_2} = .71$	SIGN	SIGN
	(9) $r_{a_3c_3} = -.62$	SIGN	SIGN
2.	$r_{BD} \neq 0$		
	(1) $r_{b_1d_1} = .33$	NS	NS
	(2) $r_{b_1d_2} = .17$	NS	NS
3.	$r_{CD} \neq 0$		
	(1) $r_{c_1d_1} = -.29$	NS	NS
	(2) $r_{c_1d_2} = 0$	NS	NS
	(3) $r_{c_2d_1} = -.78$	SIGN	SIGN
	(4) $r_{c_2d_2} = .08$	NS	NS
	(5) $r_{c_3d_1} = .93$	SIGN	SIGN
	(6) $r_{c_3d_2} = -.13$	NS	NS
4.	$r_{DE} \neq 0$		
	(1) $r_{d_1e_1} = -.46$	SIGN	SIGN
	(2) $r_{d_1e_2} = .65$	SIGN	SIGN
	(3) $r_{d_2e_1} = -.47$	SIGN	SIGN
	(4) $r_{d_2e_2} = -.03$	NS	NS
5.	$r_{EF} \neq 0$		
	(1) $r_{e_1f_1} = .46$	SIGN	SIGN
	(2) $r_{e_1f_2} = .22$	NS	NS
	(3) $r_{e_2f_1} = -.65$	SIGN	SIGN
	(4) $r_{e_2f_2} = -.79$	SIGN	SIGN
6.	$r_{AD \cdot C} \neq 0$		
	(1) $r_{d_1(a_1a_2a_3) \cdot (c_1c_2c_3)} = .37$	SIGN	NS
	(2) $r_{d_2(a_1a_2a_3) \cdot (c_1c_2c_3)} = .70$	SIGN	SIGN
7.	$r_{BF \cdot DE} \neq 0$		
	(1) $r_{f_1(b_1) \cdot (d_1d_2e_1e_2)} = .43$	SIGN	NS
	(2) $r_{f_2(b_1) \cdot (d_1d_2e_1e_2)} = .34$	NS	NS
8.	$r_{CE \cdot D} \neq 0$		
	(1) $r_{e_1(c_1c_2c_3) \cdot (d_1d_2)} = .27$	NS	NS
	(2) $r_{e_2(c_1c_2c_3) \cdot (d_1d_2)} = .39$	SIGN	NS
9.	$r_{DF \cdot E} \neq 0$		
	(1) $r_{f_1(d_1d_2) \cdot (e_1e_2)} = .55$	SIGN	SIGN
	(2) $r_{f_2(d_1d_2) \cdot (e_1e_2)} = .42$	SIGN	NS

between the index of heterogeneity and % Negro appears to be significantly nonlinear.[4] In spite of that fact, $r_{b_1 d_1} = .33$. Using an unrestricted model and relating the index to % Negro, an $E^2 = .56$ ($E = .75$) is obtained. That is, over half of the variance in % Negro is "explained" by the index, if the assumption of linearity is removed. Further research may specify the exact form of this relationship, but for present purposes it is sufficient to demonstrate that it exists.

Conclusion

The use of multiple-partial correlation coefficients allows the researcher to make ample use of multiple indicators while at the same time retaining a manageable number of predictions. The result is better measurement of underlying constructs and parsimony in evaluating a specific model. It has other advantages. Unlike factor analysis, the indicators may be causally related to one another apart from the spuriousness produced by the assumption that both (or all) indicators are at least partially caused by the underlying factors. No assumptions about the causal interrelations of any one block of indicators need to be made. They may take any form, including reciprocal causation, as indicated in Figure 18.1. We do not have to know which variables in Block A affect which variables in Block C, but we do assume that no variables in Block C affect Block A. That is, we assume a block recursive system, and attempt to assess relationships between, but not within, the blocks. This is a common situation, especially in macrolevel studies. This procedure also forces the decision of which ᵢ .dicators "indicate" which construct to be made on theoretical rather than empirical grounds. This forces clearer conceptualization, avoids the false impression .hat empirical techniques can do our theory building for us, and results in a more valid representation of the constructs.

As Curtis and Jackson note, different indicators of the same construct need not be highly associated with one another and may in fact be negatively

---

4. The use of causal modeling assumes linearity and no interaction. Using the .01 level of confidence, three of 69 tests for linearity are significantly nonlinear. One is between % Negro and % home ownership, and is only one of six tests among indicators of the constructs discrimination and resources. Another is between % college educated and % home ownership, one of nine tests among indicators of sophistication and resources. The last is one of two tests among the indicators of heterogeneity and discrimination. Only in the latter case is theoretical nonlinearity suspected.

The assumption of no interaction was also tested, using the .01 level of confidence. There are 187 tests, of which only 10 show significant interaction. Five of the ten interactions involve only one of between eight to eighteen tests among indicators of the theoretical constructs involved. Hence theoretical interaction is highly doubtful. The remaining five show the possibility of interaction between resources and discrimination, *vis à vis* choice, and sophistication and discrimination *vis à vis* party competition. The former involves 3 of 12, the latter 2 of 12, tests.

associated. They may explain different portions of the variance in the construct, having little common variance. This makes empirical determination (on the basis of the degree of association among indicators) of which indicators represent the same construct at best tenuous, at worst misleading, antitheoretical and a deterrent to our goals and purposes as social scientists.

References

1. CURTIS, RICHARD F., and JACKSON, ELTON F., "Multiple Indicators in Survey Research," *American Journal of Sociology, 68* (September, 1962): 195–204.
2. SIEGEL, PAUL M., and HODGE, ROBERT W., "A Causal Approach to the Study of Measurement Error," in H. M. Blalock, and Ann B. Blalock (Eds.), *Methodology in Social Research* (New York: McGraw-Hill, 1968), chap. 2.
3. COSTNER, HERBERT L., "Theory, Deduction and Rules of Correspondence," *American Journal of Sociology, 75,* (September, 1969): 245–263.
4. BLALOCK, H. M., Jr., "Multiple Indicators and the Causal Approach to Measurement Error," *American Journal of Sociology, 75* (September, 1969): 264–272.

Chapter 19

CAUSAL MODELS INVOLVING
UNMEASURED VARIABLES
IN STIMULUS-RESPONSE SITUATIONS

H. M. BLALOCK, JR.
University of Washington

We are rapidly accumulating an extensive literature dealing with causal approaches to the handling of measurement error, but most of this deals with situations where indicators are taken as effects rather than causes of the unmeasured variables. The papers by Costner, Heise, Van Valey, and Wiley and Wiley in this part of this book all illustrate this approach. These models are especially appropriate whenever one is dealing with two or more postulated internal states of individuals (e.g., attitudes, values, or motives) that are being inferred on the basis of responses of one kind or another.

The paper by Miller in Part III points to another important kind of causal situation, though without dealing with the complications produced by imperfect measurement. Specifically, Miller has explicated the rationale for making causal inferences in experimental and nonexperimental situations in which the fundamental independent variable of interest (X) is manipulated by varying one or more of its causes (Z_i), under the assumption that these exogenous Z_i do not appear in the equation for the dependent variable Y. If the Z_i affect Y through any variables other than X, these latter variables must be explicitly introduced into the model. Miller shows that basically the same rationale applies to nonexperimental designs where it has not been possible to manipulate the Z_i independently of other sources of variation in X or Y.

Paper prepared especially for *Causal Models in the Social Sciences*.

Miller also implies that X may sometimes be *measured* in terms of one or more of its causes Z_i. Thus, if one is attempting to manipulate frustration (X) in order to study aggression or prejudice (Y), one may not have obtained an independent measure of frustration, but he may merely assume that X varies with Z. For example, if the manipulation involves withholding food or sleep, the amount of frustration (or hunger or fatigue) may be taken as proportional to the duration of the period within which food or sleep has been withheld. Similarly, an investigator may attempt to induce frustration by insulting his subjects to varying degrees but without attempting to measure degree of frustration more directly. As Miller points out, it may be to one's advantage to have multiple manipulations in such instances so that there is some degree of insurance that the several Z_i are not all related to Y via unknown mechanisms in violation of the basic assumptions. If we take Y as indirectly measured by several indicators assumed to be effects of Y, we may diagram this very simple model as in Figure 19.1.

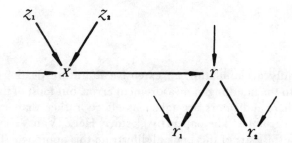

Figure 19.1.

The purpose of this paper is to explore the implications of models of this type by developing elaborations of various kinds.[1] These elaborations will involve the addition of effect measures of X and possible disturbances between measures taken to be causes and effects of X and the dependent variable Y. For simplicity, however, we shall always assume that Y is measured by two effect indicators subject only to random errors.

This particular kind of model arises very frequently in political science, psychology, and sociology. The stimulus-response (S-R) tradition in psychology has sometimes though not always involved a rather extreme form of operationalism in which the causal connections involving the unmeasured intervening variables have been conceived in terms of an impenetrable "black

---

1. Land has independently reached essentially the same conclusions as those to be elaborated in the present paper. Land's models involve the single unmeasured variable X, measured by both causes and effects. See Kenneth Land, "On the Estimation of Path Coefficients for Unmeasured Variables from Correlations among Observed Variables," *Social Forces*, **48** (June, 1970): pp. 506–511.

box." Stimuli have been conceived as having more or less direct effects on responses or at least researchers have proceeded as though this were the case. But a similar tradition also prevails within political science and sociology, though it may have not been recognized as such. Many so-called "background" variables such as race, sex, occupation of father, religion, community, region, and even "age" are basically crude indicators of stimuli that are thought to influence behavior. But the intervening psychological mechanisms may not be spelled out, particularly in empirical research. Usually, one tries out various combinations of background factors to see which predict most satisfactorily to behavior or attitudes, with no serious effort being made to spell out the causal mechanisms involved. It is hoped that the orientation made possible by the explicit introduction of unmeasured variables into a causal model will help to overcome some of the shortcomings produced by this type of rather atheoretical research.

Model I. All indicators of X are causes of X

Let us begin very simply with Model IA of Figure 19.2, which is basically the same as the model of Figure 19.1 except that the notation has been made

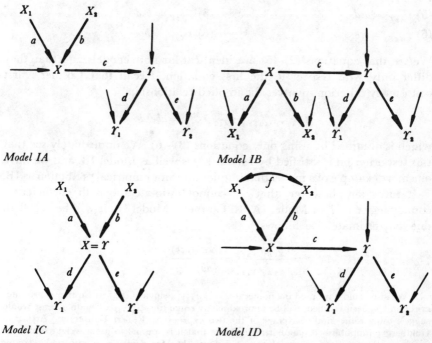

Model IA

Model IB

Model IC

Model ID

Figure 19.2.

to coincide with that of Costner's Figure 16.4, which is here reproduced (without the primes) as Model IB of our Figure 19.2. We have relabeled the causes of X as X_1 and X_2 in order to emphasize that these causes of X are being used as measures of X. In Models IA and IB of Figure 19.2 we are assuming that other sources that produce variation in X, Y, and the two measures Y_1 and Y_2 have aggregate effects that are approximately random. This is implied by the side arrows that have not been connected with the other variables in the system. In Model IA the absence of an arrow linking the two causes of X implies that $r_{X_1 X_2} = 0$, except for sampling error. The path coefficients, here all total correlations, have been labeled a, b, c, d, and e (following Costner) in both diagrams.

The equations linking the measured correlations to the unknown path coefficients are as follows:

Model IA	Model IB (Costner's Model)
(1) $r_{X_1 X_2} = 0$	(1) $r_{X_1 X_2} = ab$
(2) $r_{Y_1 Y_2} = de$	(2) $r_{Y_1 Y_2} = de$
(3) $r_{X_1 Y_1} = acd$	(3) $r_{X_1 Y_1} = acd$
(4) $r_{X_1 Y_2} = ace$	(4) $r_{X_1 Y_2} = ace$
(5) $r_{X_2 Y_1} = bcd$	(5) $r_{X_2 Y_1} = bcd$
(6) $r_{X_2 Y_2} = bce$	(6) $r_{X_2 Y_2} = bce$

We see that equations (2)–(5) are identical for both models and that they differ only with respect to the first equation. Recall that Costner's first consistency criterion involves the implied relationship

$$r_{X_1 Y_1} r_{X_2 Y_2} = r_{X_1 Y_2} r_{X_2 Y_1} = abc^2 de$$

which is obtained by using only equations (3)–(6). We immediately see that this test criterion is satisfied by Model IA as well as Model IB, and we have one more example of a model that implies the same empirical prediction as IB.

It turns out, however, that we cannot estimate the path coefficient c connecting X to Y in Model IA. In Costner's Model IB, it will be recalled, one may estimate c^2 as follows:[2]

$$c^2 = \frac{r_{X_1 Y_1} r_{X_2 Y_2}}{r_{X_1 X_2} r_{Y_1 Y_2}} = \frac{(acd)(bce)}{(ab)(de)}$$

2. We also could have used the numerator $r_{X_1 Y_2} r_{X_2 Y_1}$, which, if the first Costner consistency criterion has been satisfied, will be approximately equal to $r_{X_1 Y_1} r_{X_2 Y_2}$. Common sense would suggest using some kind of average of the two expressions. Robert Hauser and Arthur S. Goldberger (unpublished manuscript) indicate that it is optimal to use a weighted average involving the standard errors of the coefficients, but for exploratory research a simple arithmetic mean should suffice.

Notice that this procedure involves dividing by $r_{X_1 X_2}$, which is taken to be zero in Model IA. The basic problem is that there is no way to isolate c in any of the equations (3)–(6), and in Model IA we cannot obtain a separate expression for the product ab, as is possible in Model IB. Looking at the matter another way, in Model IA we really only have five equations and five unknowns, since the first equation is completely trivial (though of course not automatically satisfied by the data). But among these five equations is one redundant equation, which may be used as a test criterion but which means that the five equations are not completely independent. Therefore we shall not be in a position to solve for all of the unknowns, and in particular we cannot solve for c.

Another way of seeing this is to note that if X and Y were identical, so that $c = 1$, we would have Model IC of Figure 19.2, which implies a set of predictions that do not involve c but that could not be distinguished empirically from those of Model IA.[3] In fact, we could have replaced Model IA by any number of alternative models involving a series of unmeasured variables interrelating X and Y, and none of these models could have been distinguished empirically from Model IA. We have here another example of the identification problem, one stemming from the existence of unmeasured variables in a recursive system.

Of course, the simple Model IA could be distinguished empirically from IB by the absence of a correlation between the two causal variables X_1 and X_2. In nonexperimental situations we generally expect such stimulus variables to be intercorrelated as in Model ID of Figure 19.2. For example, if X_1 were race and if X_2 were occupation of father, with X being the conceptual variable "exposure to educational discrimination," we would anticipate a correlation between the two indicators of X, as represented by the curved arrow in Model ID. The equations for Model ID are somewhat more complex and are as follows:

(1) $r_{X_1 X_2} = f$ (4) $r_{X_1 Y_2} = ce(a + bf)$

(2) $r_{Y_1 Y_2} = de$ (5) $r_{X_2 Y_1} = cd(b + af)$

(3) $r_{X_1 Y_1} = cd(a + bf)$ (6) $r_{X_2 Y_2} = ce(b + af)$

Again, the first Costner consistency criterion is satisfied since

$$r_{X_1 Y_1} r_{X_2 Y_2} = r_{X_1 Y_2} r_{X_2 Y_1} = c^2 de(a + bf)(b + af)$$

The coefficient f is given directly by the correlation between X_1 and X_2, and we may solve for d and e by obtaining the ratio d/e by dividing (3) by (4) or

3. These predictions are as follows: $r_{X_1 X_2} = 0$; $r_{Y_1 Y_2} = de$; $r_{X_1 Y_1} = ad$; $r_{X_1 Y_2} = ae$; $r_{X_2 Y_1} = bd$; and $r_{X_2 Y_2} = be$.

by dividing (5) by (6). Multiplying either of these ratios (which should be identical except for sampling error) by de we can obtain an expression for d^2. A similar expression for e^2 can likewise be obtained. But we shall not be able to use the remaining equations to disentangle c from a and b. If we were to use the estimate appropriate for Costner's Model IB we would obtain the result

$$\frac{r_{X_1 Y_1} r_{X_2 Y_2}}{r_{X_1 X_2} r_{Y_1 Y_2}} = \frac{c^2 de(a+bf)(b+af)}{def} = c^2 \frac{(a+bf)(b+af)}{f}$$

which is certainly not equal to c^2. Furthermore, Models IB and ID could not be distinguished on purely empirical grounds unless the temporal sequences linking X to X_1 and X_2 could be used to reject one or the other model. The implication is that if one cannot decide whether the indicators are causes or effects of X, he should not attempt to estimate the path coefficient c linking X to Y.

Model II. A single cause and single effect of X

Having failed to estimate the effects of X on Y when both measures of X are taken as causes, let us next examine a very simple model involving a single cause of X and a single effect that are not linked by any path other than through X. This model, Model IIA, is represented in Figure 19.3. It can readily be seen that the equations for Model IIA are identical with those for Costner's Model IB. Therefore we may utilize the same test for compatibility of the data with the model, and we may also legitimately estimate c^2 using the equation

$$\frac{r_{X_1 Y_1} r_{X_2 Y_2}}{r_{X_1 X_2} r_{Y_1 Y_2}} = \frac{(acd)(bce)}{(ab)(de)} = c^2$$

Thus if we are able to locate a single indicator of X that is assumed to be an effect of X, we may utilize this second indicator in conjunction with the indicator causing X to estimate all of the coefficients in this very simple model.[4]

Let us next see what complications are introduced if we allow for two kinds of disturbances involving X_2, namely (1) the possibility that X_1 affects X_2 by some additional path f not involving X and (2) the possibility that X_2 is linked to Y by a path other than that through X. The first of these possibilities is represented as Model IIB and the second as Models IIC and IID.

---

4. The method of instrumental variables may also be used in this particular model, though it is somewhat more sensitive to specification error than is ordinary least squares in instances where there may be an additional path from X_1 to Y. See H. M. Blalock, Caryll S. Wells, and Lewis F. Carter, "Statistical Estimation in the Presence of Random Measurement Error," in Edgar F. Borgatta and George Bohrnstedt (Eds.), *Sociological Methodology* 1970 (San Francisco: Jossey-Bass, 1970), chap. 5.

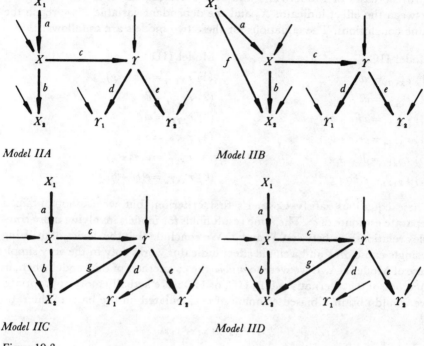

Model IIA   *Model IIB*

Model IIC   *Model IID*

Figure 19.3.

In the case of Model IIB, where there is an additional path f from X_1 to X_2, we have the following six equations involving six unknowns:

(1) $r_{X_1 X_2} = ab + f$ (4) $r_{X_1 Y_2} = ace$

(2) $r_{Y_1 Y_2} = de$ (5) $r_{X_2 Y_1} = cd(b + af)$

(3) $r_{X_1 Y_1} = acd$ (6) $r_{X_2 Y_2} = ce(b + af)$

Once again it turns out that Costner's first consistency criterion is satisfied since

$$r_{X_1 Y_1} r_{X_2 Y_2} = r_{X_1 Y_2} r_{X_2 Y_1} = ac^2 de(b + af)$$

but for familiar reasons we cannot disentangle c from a, b, and f. If we were to try to estimate c^2 utilizing the same function of the correlations appropriate for Models IB and IIA we would obtain the result

$$\frac{r_{X_1 Y_1} r_{X_2 Y_2}}{r_{X_1 X_2} r_{Y_1 Y_2}} = \frac{ac^2 de(b + af)}{(ab + f)(de)} = c^2 \frac{ab + a^2 f}{ab + f}$$

which would approximate c^2 if f were very small or if a^2 were almost unity, but which would otherwise not be an appropriate estimate.

In the cases of Models IIC and IID involving direct causal linkages g between the effect indicator X_2 and the dependent variable Y we reach the same conclusions. The equations for these two models are as follows:

Model IIC

(1) $r_{X_1 X_2} = ab$

(2) $r_{Y_1 Y_2} = de$

(3) $r_{X_1 Y_1} = ad(c + bg)$

(4) $r_{X_1 Y_2} = ae(c + bg)$

(5) $r_{X_2 Y_1} = d(bc + g)$

(6) $r_{X_2 Y_2} = e(bc + g)$

Model IID

(1) $r_{X_1 X_2} = a(b + cg)$

(2) $r_{Y_1 Y_2} = de$

(3) $r_{X_1 Y_1} = acd$

(4) $r_{X_1 Y_2} = ace$

(5) $r_{X_2 Y_1} = d(bc + g)$

(6) $r_{X_2 Y_2} = e(bc + g)$

These equations satisfy Costner's first criterion, but we cannot obtain a separate estimate of c^2. The same result holds for models involving more complex relationships between X_2 and Y. We conclude that the device of utilizing a single cause of X and a single effect indicator works only in the very simple case of Model IIA. If we were to *assume* the correctness of this model when, in fact, one of the alternatives IIB, IIC, or IID were actually more appropriate, we would obtain a biased estimate of c^2 calculated on the basis of the ratio

$$r_{X_1 Y_1} r_{X_2 Y_2} / r_{X_1 X_2} r_{Y_1 Y_2}.$$

These results are comparable to those obtained by Costner for nonrandom errors in instances where there are only two indicators of each variable, and the obvious suggestion is to introduce additional indicators. Let us therefore turn to a comparison of the relative merits of using one effect and two causal indicators of X versus using one causal and two effect indicators.

Model III. Two causes, one effect of X

In Model IIB we considered the case where there is one cause and one effect indicator connected by an additional path f. Let us modify this model by adding another cause indicator X_3 that is permitted to be correlated with X_1 as in Model III in Figure 19.4. The equations for this model are as follows:

(1) $r_{X_1 X_2} = f + b(a + gh)$

(2) $r_{X_1 X_3} = g$

(3) $r_{X_2 X_3} = bh + g(ab + f)$

(4) $r_{Y_1 Y_2} = de$

(5) $r_{X_1 Y_1} = cd(a + gh)$

(6) $r_{X_1 Y_2} = ce(a + gh)$

(7) $r_{X_2 Y_1} = cd[b + f(a + gh)]$

(8) $r_{X_2 Y_2} = ce[b + f(a + gh)]$

(9) $r_{X_3 Y_1} = cd(h + ag)$

(10) $r_{X_3 Y_2} = ce(h + ag)$

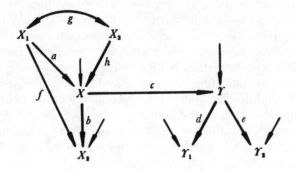

Model III

Figure 19.4.

We encounter exactly the same difficulty; although the test criterion is satisfied we cannot estimate c^2. Suppose we now set $g=0$, meaning that we have been able to find a second cause of X (namely, X_3) that is completely unrelated to X_2 except through X. It might now be expected that we could solve for c^2, just as we did in the case of Model IIA where there was no link between the indicators of X except through X itself. But even where $g=0$, and where we ignore the indicator X_1, we discover that we cannot estimate c^2 utilizing the simple Costner estimate since

$$\frac{r_{X_2 Y_1} r_{X_3 Y_2}}{r_{X_2 X_3} r_{Y_1 Y_2}} = \frac{cd(b+af)ceh}{(bh)(de)} = c^2[1+af/b]$$

Of course if $f=0$, in addition, then we have the very simple model for which there is no link between X_2 and either cause of X (except through X) and estimation of c^2 becomes possible. In fact, if $f=0$ with $g\neq 0$ we can also estimate c^2 as would be expected.

The important point is that if the effect indicator X_2 is linked with *any* causal indicator of X by any path other than through X we are in difficulty. This is an extremely significant problem if we keep in mind that, in any particular application, a causal variable such as X_1 may be unknown to the investigator. The implication is that with a single effect indicator we cannot rely on multiple indicators that are causes of X unless we make the extreme assumption that the effect indicator is unrelated to all such variables except through X.

Model IV. Two effects, one cause of X

Having found difficulties with each of the preceding models let us turn to the situation where we have more than one effect indicator. As we would certainly anticipate by now, the situation will prove hopeless if all such effect indicators are linked in unknown ways either to the causal indicator(s) of X or to Y or its indicators. Our basic hope in using multiple effect indicators is that there may be one or more such indicators that are *not* so linked to the other variables in the system. But if this were in fact the case, how would we tell which effect indicators have the desirable properties and which do not? If we use multiple effect indicators, and if all but one or two give almost identical results, then *perhaps* we can muster some faith that, having removed the indicators that yield different results, the remaining indicators have the desired properties. This is essentially the strategy followed in Van Valey's application of Costner's procedure.

If we let X_3 be a second effect indicator of X, it can be shown that if X_3 is linked to X_1 via an additional path it will once more be impossible to isolate c^2 from the remaining unknown coefficients. Let us therefore confine our attention to Model IVA in Figure 19.5, where the causal indicator X_1 is linked to X_2 via the path f but is not linked to X_3 except through X. The equations for this model are as follows:

(1) $r_{X_1 X_2} = ab + f$ (6) $r_{X_1 Y_2} = ace$

(2) $r_{X_1 X_3} = ag$ (7) $r_{X_2 Y_1} = cd(b + af)$

(3) $r_{X_2 X_3} = g(b + af)$ (8) $r_{X_2 Y_2} = ce(b + af)$

(4) $r_{Y_1 Y_2} = de$ (9) $r_{X_3 Y_1} = cdg$

(5) $r_{X_1 Y_1} = acd$ (10) $r_{X_3 Y_2} = ceg$

In applying Costner's first criterion we can of course utilize all three pairings of the X_i, namely (X_1, X_2), (X_1, X_3), and (X_2, X_3). It can immediately be seen that this consistency criterion should be satisfied, except for sampling errors, in all three pairings. However, if we then estimate c^2 using the three pairings, as we might do if we made the erroneous assumption that $f = 0$, we would obtain the following results:

$$\frac{r_{X_1 Y_1} r_{X_2 Y_2}}{r_{X_1 X_2} r_{Y_1 Y_2}} = \frac{(acd)(ce)(b + af)}{(ab + f)(de)} = c^2 \frac{ab + a^2 f}{ab + f}$$

$$\frac{r_{X_1 Y_1} r_{X_3 Y_2}}{r_{X_1 X_3} r_{Y_1 Y_2}} = \frac{(acd)(ceg)}{(ag)(de)} = c^2$$

$$\frac{r_{X_2 Y_1} r_{X_3 Y_2}}{r_{X_2 X_3} r_{Y_1 Y_2}} = \frac{cd(b + af)(ceg)}{g(b + af)(de)} = c^2$$

We see that two of the three possible pairings give the correct estimate, whereas the pairing involving (X_1, X_2) does not (as we previously saw in the

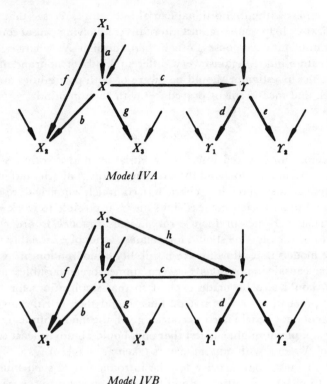

Model IVA

Model IVB

Figure 19.5.

case of Model IIB). *If* we were willing to assume that only one of the effect indicators is linked with X_1, then we could infer which of the two has the nonzero link by looking for the estimate that differs from the remaining two. Of course the more indicators that appear in the role of effect indicators, the more faith we would have in this procedure. It should be emphasized, however, that it will *always* be necessary to make a number of *a priori* simplifying assumptions that are inherently untestable. The more indicators we have in relation to the number of unmeasured variables, the more tests of compatibility between the model and the data we can make.

Finally, we must return to a point made by Miller that it will be advisable to utilize multiple causal indicators, as well as multiple effect indicators, to guard against alternatives involving linkages of one or more of these variables with Y. In Model IVB we have complicated Model IVA by adding a path h from X_1 to Y, and it can easily be shown that this again makes it impossible to isolate the path c. In this particular model, the compound path $(c + ah)$ will replace c, but since the existence of h may be unknown, it will be difficult to discover the bias without additional causal indicators. We see that multiple causal indicators help guard against alternatives involving causal connections between stimuli and responses, other than through X, whereas multiple effect indicators guard against very different kinds of nonrandom errors. Obviously, the investigator should be aware of both possibilities and design his research and measurement procedures with each in mind.

Concluding remarks

In introducing unmeasured intervening variables into a stimulus-response setup, one is attempting to avoid the extreme operational orientation that, in many practical instances, has characterized much empirical research in sociology and other social sciences. This makes it possible to work explicitly with constructs and measurement errors in causal models in order to guide one's research. Ideally, one should formulate a series of reasonably plausible alternative models that allow for the possibility of nonrandom measurement errors. The causal connections between unmeasured variables and their indicators should also be made explicit so that implications for tests and estimating procedures can be noted. This should then tell the investigator what pieces of data he will need to collect, given the models under consideration. For example, it might suggest that one should obtain at least two effect measures of X along with any indicators taken as causes of X.

But we obviously pay a price for the introduction of such unmeasured variables. In effect, we introduce additional unknowns into the system and are likely to encounter identification problems as a result. Discussions of the identification problem in the econometrics literature have centered around the k-equation system, where we have seen that there must be at least $k - 1$ restrictions on the parameters for any equation that is to be identified. Such discussions usually presume that all variables have been perfectly measured, however. The kinds of identification problems presently under consideration are basically similar to those encountered in factor analysis, where the underlying factors are taken as unknowns. Nevertheless, we can profit from the discussions of identification in the econometrics literature, where one essential strategy is that of introducing exogenous variables into the causal system.

If one thinks in terms of models of the type discussed by Costner, where all indicators are effect variables, then additional causal indicators such as X_1 may be considered as exogenous variables that are presumed to affect X but not Y. Similarly, one might attempt to locate causal indicators of Y that are assumed unrelated to X or any of its indicators. In models involving additional unmeasured variables, a similar strategy of locating both causal indicators and effect indicators would also apply. In general, the more complex and numerous the linkages among the unmeasured variables, the simpler the required assumptions about the indicators and the more numerous these indicators must be in order to avoid identification problems.

It would be helpful to develop necessary and sufficient conditions for the general model involving unmeasured as well as measured variables, but in the absence of such general criteria, one can readily investigate the properties of specific models that seem most appropriate in a given context. Obviously it would also be useful to attempt to catalog the various kinds of causal models that are most likely to be utilized in different substantive areas, so that investigators can be alerted to a wide range of possible complications and ways of coping with each. It is undoubtedly unwise to expect too much of this kind of model-building enterprise, which can only sensitize one to his untested assumptions rather than doing away with them completely. But this approach does have the very great advantage of bringing these assumptions into the open, where they can be studied and modified if necessary.

Chapter 20

SEPARATING RELIABILITY AND STABILITY IN TEST-RETEST CORRELATION

DAVID R. HEISE*
City University of New York (Queens)

The theory of measurements traditionally has been the province of psychometricians. Sociologists certainly can benefit from the large and excellent literature in that field (e.g., Lord and Novick, 1968). However, the problems in psychological and sociological measurement are not always the same, and psychometric solutions sometimes may be less useful than techniques tailored more directly to sociometric dilemmas. Measuring reliability appears to be a case in point. The psychometricians have grounded much of their reliability theory on the idea of a test in which there are multiple items and for which there may be equivalent forms. The resulting techniques of assessing reliability (internal consistency measures, crossform correlations) may be only of peripheral interest when key variables can be measured practically only by a single question. In this case, which is a frequent sociological situation, it is more appropriate to turn to test-retest correlations to assess reliabilities.

Unfortunately, a simple test-retest correlation may not measure true reliability because it is affected by temporal instability in a variable as well as by errors of measurement. Consider the hypothetical case of a test which measures without error, and whose true reliability, therefore, is 1.00. Suppose persons are evaluated with the test at time 1 and time 2, and the measurement

Reprinted by permission of the author and publisher from the *American Sociological Review*, Vol. 34, pp. 93–101. Copyright 1969, The American Sociological Association.

* The author is grateful to George Bohrnstedt and to the *Review*'s referees for their helpful comments on earlier drafts of this paper. Edgar F. Borgatta kindly provided data from a study in progress for one of the empirical examples.

interval is sufficiently long so that some shifts in the measured attribute occur during the measurement interval. Then, because of the shifts in true scores—i.e., because some persons increase in value and others decrease— the distribution of individuals at time 2 will not coincide exactly with the distribution at time 1. It follows that the correlation between the two testings will be less than 1.00, and we would conclude that we have a test with reliability less than 1.00 even though this is contrary to the initial assumption.

One may attempt to reduce the effect of temporal instability on test-retest correlations by reducing the time interval between measurements, thereby reducing the amount of shifting which can occur in true scores. However, an immediate test-retest may not be practical with many measures. Further, this procedure often raises the problem of respondents recalling their first answer so that the second assessment is not independent of the first.

It would be desirable, therefore, to have a general procedure for analyzing test-retest correlations so that the effects of measurement errors and true-score instability could be separated analytically. Coleman (1968) has demonstrated that such a separation is possible if one gathers data at three points in time rather than two. This paper interprets Coleman's insight in terms of traditional statistics used in tests and measurements.

The analysis below is carried out using path analysis, a quantitative procedure for analyzing relations between variables, developed by the biologist, Sewall Wright (1934). The rules of path analysis are not presented since a number of expository articles on the topic are available elsewhere (Turner and Stevens, 1959; Duncan, 1966; Heise, 1968; Boudon, 1968). Path analysis has been applied previously to reliability problems by Wright (1934) and by Siegel and Hodge (1968), and Blalock (1963) has employed a similar approach. Part of the discussion here is drawn from these sources.

Path analysis of measurements

Suppose we have a test or index which measures a variable x. Conceptually, we can distinguish between the true variable x and the obtained measurement x' as two different variables related by the fact that the value on x determines to some degree the value we find on the measurement, x'. In this case we are making the customary assumption that $x' = x + e$, where e is a random variable representing errors of measurement and the correlation between errors and true values (i.e., between x and e) is zero. The relationship between x and x' can be represented in a path diagram as illustrated in Figure 20.1. This diagram indicates that x' is determined both by x and by the random variable e. The parameter, $p_{x'x}$, is a number which indicates the amount of relationship between x and x'. It is related to the traditional reliability coefficient, as will be seen below. The coefficient, p_{xe}, indicates the extent to which variations in x' are a function of errors. It is not an independent unknown since, once p_{xx} is known, we can determine how much variance in x' is *not* determined by x, and the value of p_{xe} is set accordingly.

$$x \xrightarrow{\quad p_{x'x} \quad} x' \xleftarrow{\quad p_{xe} \quad} e$$

Figure 20.1.

Let us first consider how path analysis can be applied to analyze reliability coefficients based on parallel forms, a traditional psychometric topic. Because we now have two tests, we have a total of three substantive variables to consider: x and observed-score variables, x'_1 and x'_2. In addition, of course, there are two random error variables, e_1 and e_2, which are assumed to be uncorrelated. The path diagram for this situation is given in Figure 20.2.

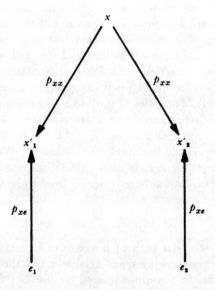

Figure 20.2.

Notice that the amount of determination of test scores by x is represented as identical for both tests (p_{xx}). This follows from the customary assumption that the parallel forms are completely equivalent.

From Figure 20.2 and the rules of path analysis, one finds that the relationship between p_{xx} and the reliability coefficient, r_{12}, is $r_{12} = p^2_{xx}$. Thus, the reliability measure, p_{xx}, which appears in the path analysis, is the square root of the traditional reliability coefficient.

Wright (1934) has shown how the correction for attenuation can be derived from a path analysis of measurements, and this demonstration is reproduced here to further illustrate the meaningfulness of path analysis in measurement problems.

We now have two true variables, x and y, plus two tests for measuring each of these, x'_1 and x'_2, and y'_1 and y'_2. The variables x and y are correlated, and our goal is to estimate the true correlation, r_{xy}, from correlations among the test variables. The path diagram for this situation is given in Figure 20.3.

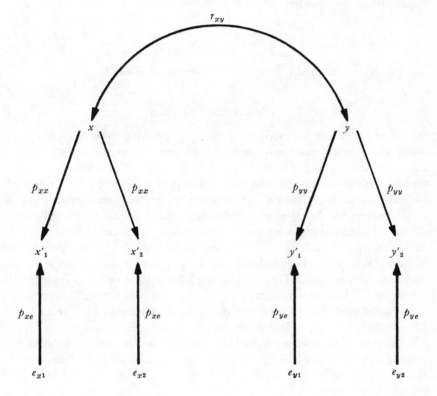

Figure 20.3.

As empirical information, we have the reliabilities of the tests, $r_{x'_1 x'_2}$ and $r_{y'_1 y'_2}$, and the correlations between one of the x' forms with one of the y' forms, say, $r_{x'_1 y'_1}$. Following the rules of path analysis, we can write:

$$r_{x'_1 y'_1} = p_{xx} r_{xy} p_{yy}$$
$$r_{x'_1 x'_2} = p^2_{xx} \tag{1}$$
$$r_{y'_1 y'_2} = p^2_{yy}$$

These equations can be algebraically manipulated to:

$$r_{xy} = \frac{r_{x'_1 y'_1}}{p_{xx} p_{yy}}$$

$$p_{xx} = \sqrt{r_{x'_1 x'_2}} \tag{2}$$

$$p_{yy} = \sqrt{r_{y'_1 y'_2}}$$

Substituting, we obtain:

$$r_{xy} = \frac{r_{x'_1 y'_1}}{\sqrt{r_{x'_1 x'_2}} \sqrt{r_{y'_1 y'_2}}} \tag{3}$$

which is the traditional correction-for-attenuation formula.

The test-retest situation

Suppose we measure x imperfectly at time 1. Following the convention established above, we then have two substantive variables of interest: x_1, the true scores at time 1, and x'_1, the empirical measurements with errors. Now suppose we measure again with the same test or index at time 2. Again, we have two variables, x_2 and x'_2. Here x_1 and x_2 are distinguished as separate variables since the distribution of individuals at the two times generally is not the same: some changes have occurred during the measurement interval. However, x_1 and x_2 are correlated and, in addition, we know that x_1 preceded x_2; hence, it is reasonable to say that x_1 in part determines x_2, but x_2 does not determine x_1. The path analysis for this situation is indicated in Figure 20.4. The new variable, u_2, in this diagram represents the aggregation of variables that have affected or disturbed x during the interval from 1 to 2. The coefficient, p_{xu_2}, indicates the extent of such disturbances; p_{xu_2} is like p_{xe} in that it is defined as a residual and so does not constitute an independent unknown in the system. The path coefficient, p_{21}, is a measure of the stability of x over time, since it indicates the degree to which x_1 determines x_2 over the given interval.

A careful examination of the diagram reveals the several assumptions that are being made at this point. First, we are assuming the relationship between the true variable and the index is constant over time: both paths, $x_1 \rightarrow x'_1$ and $x_2 \rightarrow x'_2$, are labeled p_{xx}. Second, the assumption that errors are uncorrelated with true scores is indicated by the absence of curved lines connecting e's with x's. Third, it is assumed that measurement errors at different times are uncorrelated: a curved line does not connect e_1 and e_2. Fourth, it is assumed that disturbances in x that develop between times 1 and 2 are uncorrelated with the initial values of x so that no curved line connects x_1 and

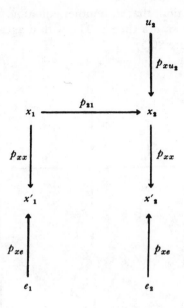

Figure 20.4.

u_2. Also, it may be noted that the rate of change in the true scores is presumed to be approximately constant within the measurement interval.

Following the rules of path analysis, the test-retest correlation can be analyzed as follows (where r_{12} indicates the true correlation between the *measured* variables, x'_1 and x'_2):

$$r_{12} = p_{xx}p_{21}p_{xx} = p^2{}_{xx}p_{21} \qquad (4)$$

The relationship between reliability coefficient and path coefficient, that was mentioned above, i.e., $r_{xx} = p^2{}_{xx}$, can be true in this case only if $p_{21} = 1.00$. But this would imply that the variable x remains completely stable over time. Allowing that this is not so (i.e., p_{21} is less than 1.00), we see that the test-retest correlation is not simply the square of the reliability parameter, p_{xx}.

What we would like to do, then, is to find the actual value of p_{xx}. Then we could square it, obtaining a reliability coefficient which is comparable to other reliability coefficients in that it is uncontaminated by the temporal instability of variable x. This reliability coefficient would have the value we theoretically would obtain by a test-retest correlation in which the retest came instantly after the first test.

Equation 4 expresses an observed correlation as a function of two unknowns, p_{xx} and p_{21}. Because there are *two* unknowns, we cannot turn this equation around and solve for p_{xx}. So, if we are to estimate the value of p_{xx}, we need more information, that is, another equation. This can be obtained by making another retest at a time 3. The path diagram for the three-wave testing is given in Figure 20.5.

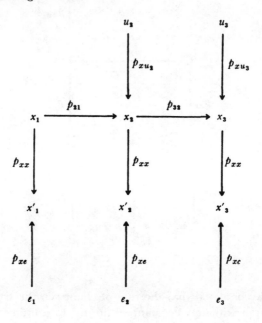

Figure 20.5.

From the diagram it can be seen that a third unknown (p_{32}) arises by adding another retest, if we maintain the assumptions stated above, and further require that disturbances at times 2 and 3 are uncorrelated. Now, however, the additional testing allows us to write two new equations so that we have three equations and three unknowns. (Again, the r's represent the true correlations between *measured* variables.)

$$r_{12}=p_{xx}p_{21}p_{xx}=p^2{}_{xx}p_{21}$$
$$r_{23}=p_{xx}p_{32}p_{xx}=p^2{}_{xx}p_{32} \quad\quad (5)$$
$$r_{13}=p_{xx}p_{21}p_{32}p_{xx}=p^2{}_{xx}p_{21}p_{32}$$

The first two of these equations can be manipulated as follows:

$$p_{21}=\frac{r_{12}}{p^2{}_{xx}}$$

$$p_{32}=\frac{r_{23}}{p^2{}_{xx}} \quad\quad (6)$$

Substituting these results into the last of equations 5:

$$r_{13} = p^2{}_{xx} \frac{r_{12}}{p^2{}_{xx}} \frac{r_{23}}{p^2{}_{xx}} = \frac{r_{12}r_{23}}{p^2{}_{xx}} \qquad (7)$$

or

$$p^2{}_{xx} = \frac{r_{12}r_{23}}{r_{13}} \qquad (8)$$

It is the square of p_{xx} that corresponds to a customary reliability coefficient, so that equation 8 indicates the formula for a new measure of reliability based on test-retest data but free of temporal change effects.

$$r_{xx} = \frac{r_{12}r_{23}}{r_{13}} \qquad (9)$$

The symbols in formula 9 are meant to designate true correlations in the population of interest. When one substitutes empirical correlations based on samples, an estimate of the true reliability is obtained, and the estimate of course is subject to sampling variability.

Stability coefficients

Once the reliability coefficient is available, it is possible to correct the test-retest correlations for attenuation and thereby obtain stability coefficients measuring the amount of change that occurred during a given interval. In fact, if interest centers on the stability coefficients, they can be obtained without calculating r_{xx} first. Let the stability coefficient for a given interval be s; this is the correlation between true scores at one time with true scores at another time. From Figure 20.5 and the rules of path analysis, it follows that:

$$\begin{aligned} s_{12} &= p_{21} \\ s_{23} &= p_{32} \\ s_{13} &= p_{21}p_{32} \end{aligned} \qquad (10)$$

Now, equations 6 and 8 can be solved directly for p_{21} and p_{32}.

$$\begin{aligned} p_{21} &= r_{12}/p^2{}_{xx} = r_{12}r_{13}/r_{12}r_{23} = r_{13}/r_{23} \\ p_{32} &= r_{23}/p^2{}_{xx} = r_{23}r_{13}/r_{12}r_{23} = r_{13}/r_{12} \end{aligned} \qquad (11)$$

Hence:

$$\begin{aligned} s_{12} &= r_{13}/r_{23} \\ s_{23} &= r_{13}/r_{12} \\ s_{13} &= r_{13}{}^2/r_{12}r_{23} \end{aligned} \qquad (12)$$

Empirical examples

Correlations between IQ measures of children passing through third, sixth, and ninth grades have been presented by Crowther (1965). At each level, the instrument employed was the California Test of Mental Maturity, and a measurement was the total score over all subscales. The test involves different forms for different levels, but this does not affect the analysis if it is assumed that the reliabilities and validities are the same for all forms.

Observed correlations between testings were as follows:

$$r_{12} = .56; \; r_{23} = .65; \; r_{13} = .52$$

Then, by formula 9:

$$r_{xx} = .70$$

By formulas 12:

$$s_{12} = .80; \; s_{23} = .93; \; s_{13} = .74$$

The corrected coefficient, r_{xx}, is considerably higher than the test-retest correlations computed over a three-year interval. The r_{xx} compares well with, but is slightly lower than, the reported reliability based on parallel forms: the test-publisher reports that between-form correlations range from .72 to .81 at different age levels (Stanley, 1965). The values of the stability coefficients indicate that IQ is less stable between third and sixth grades than between sixth and ninth; further, only a little more than half of the ninth grade IQ variance is shared with the third grade variance. Although these values may seem low for what often is thought of as a "permanent" trait, notice that the stability coefficients are substantially higher than the raw test-retest correlations. If one were to overlook measurement error, he might seriously underestimate the stability of IQ.

A longitudinal study of college students (unpublished) by Edgar F. Borgatta provides another illustration. In this study, measurement 1 was made when the students were first semester freshmen; measurement 2, when they were second semester freshmen; and measurement 3, when they were second semester sophomores. The question of interest asked students how often they attended religious services. The test-retest correlations for males and females were:

$$r_{12} = .71, .73$$
$$r_{23} = .80, .78$$
$$r_{13} = .60, .62$$

from which it follows that:

$$r_{xx} = .95 \text{ for males}$$
$$r_{xx} = .92 \text{ for females}$$

Again, the corrected reliabilities are substantially above the raw test-retest values, indicating the importance of making the correction.

The stability coefficients for these data are:

$$s_{12} = .75; .79$$
$$s_{23} = .85; .85$$
$$s_{13} = .64; .67$$

These figures indicate that patterns of church attendance change at a relatively rapid rate during the first few months on campus.

Freedman, Coombs, and Bumpass (1965) reported the following test-retest correlations obtained in a longitudinal study in which the key variable was expectations about family size.

$$r_{12} = .81$$
$$r_{23} = .85$$
$$r_{13} = .78$$

From these figures one can estimate the reliability of their measure as .88, and the stability coefficients as:

$$s_{12} = .92$$
$$s_{23} = .96$$
$$s_{13} = .88$$

These reliability and stability coefficients suggest that a sizable proportion of the flux in family size expectations is a matter of ambiguity in measurement rather than due to actual changes of mind.

Restrictions

Formulas 9 and 12 provide estimates of the reliability and stability coefficients under the following assumptions: (a) determination of the index by the underlying variable is constant over time; (b) the rate of instability in the underlying variable is constant between adjacent measurement times; (c) measurement errors are uncorrelated with true scores; (d) measurement errors at different times are uncorrelated with each other; and (e) disturbances at times 2 and 3 are uncorrelated with each other or with the true scores at time 1. Both (a) and (c) are standard metric assumptions, and (b) can usually be managed by adjusting the test-retest intervals. The problems posed by (d) and (e) are discussed below.

Assumption (d) requires that errors be serially uncorrelated. The assumption may be violated when respondents recall earlier answers and try to be consistent in their responses. In such a case, distortions occurring in early measurements will tend to be reproduced over time. If errors are serially correlated, the model in Figure 20.5 must be replaced by the one in Figure 20.6. In this model the error terms are connected by curved lines indicating they are correlated.

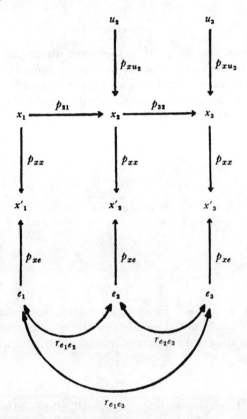

Figure 20.6.

With three waves of testing, there are three empirical correlations available for defining equations. However, it can be seen from Figure 20.6 that the model now has six independent unknowns $(p_{xx}, p_{21}, p_{32}, r_{e_1e_2}, r_{e_2e_3}, r_{e_1e_3})$, and so there is not enough information to identify the parameters. Furthermore, adding additional waves of observations does not solve this problem since every new wave continues to add new unknowns. For example, obtaining a fourth wave would yield six test-retest correlations, but there would be a total of ten unknowns to identify (those in Figure 20.6 plus p_{43}, $r_{e_3e_4}$, $r_{e_2e_4}$, and $r_{e_1e_4}$). One might suppose that a different solution to this problem could be obtained by equalizing the measurement intervals and then assuming that the stability coefficients and the serial correlations in errors do not change over time. This would reduce the number of unknowns in Figure 20.6 to four (p_{xx}, p_x, $r_{e_1e_2}$, and $r_{e_1e_3}$, where $p_x = p_{21} = p_{32}$ and $r_{e_1e_2} = r_{e_2e_3}$). Although it is impossible to identify these four unknowns from three waves of testing, it might seem that now additional retests could help, since each retest will add only one new unknown, i.e., the correlation between errors at time 1 and at the last testing. This is not so, however, since with the constant-parameters model each additional testing adds only one *new* empirical piece of information—the correlation between the first and last tests. All of the other additional correlations are merely replications of those already obtained. For example, the correlation r_{34} would be only another estimate of the true correlation between two adjacent testings, thus serving as a replication on r_{12} and r_{23}. With each additional retest adding a new unknown and only one new piece of information, it is clear that a constant-parameters model also is unsolvable, whatever the number of retests. In general, then, when measurement errors are serially correlated, it is impossible to obtain enough information to solve for reliability and stability coefficients.

Assumption (e) requires that disturbances in the underlying variable, x, are uncorrelated over time and that these disturbances are uncorrelated with the

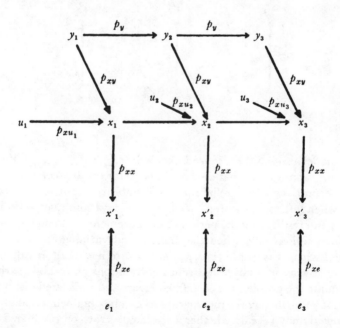

Figure 20.7.

initial values of x. This assumption would be violated if there is some un-measured variable, y, that has stability over time and unilaterally affects x, as indicated in Figure 20.7.

This situation would necessitate the model in Figure 20.8. This model has six unknowns $(p_{xx}, p_{21}, p_{32}, r_{1u_2}, r_{1u_3}, r_{u_2u_3})$ and is unsolvable. Adding a fourth wave of observations adds three test-retest correlations, but the

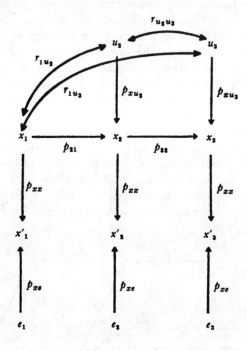

Figure 20.8.

required model also has three more unknowns $(r_{1u_4}, r_{u_2u_4}, r_{u_3u_4})$. Obviously, the situation is parallel to that discussed above for serially-correlated errors, and, in general, accurate reliability and stability coefficients cannot be obtained when some unmeasured variable is having a continuous effect on the variable of interest during the period of measurements. Of course, the problem becomes serious only when the unmeasured variable has a substantial impact and when it is stable (i.e., p_{xy} and p_y are not small in value).

There is no way to analyze test-retest correlations on a single variable so as to eliminate the problems of correlated errors and correlated disturbances. However, if a fourth wave of measurements can be obtained, an analysis can be conducted that reveals whether correlated errors or correlated distur-bances are interfering with reliability and stability estimates. To derive this

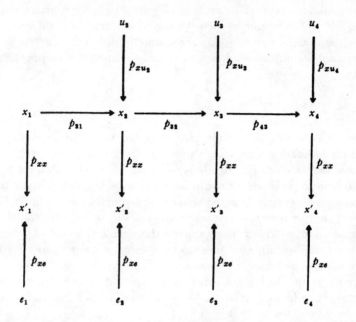

Figure 20.9.

procedure, we assume that the model in Figure 20.9 holds; then the following equations would be appropriate according to formulas 8 and 11 (we obtain p_{43} by treating measurements 2 through 4 as a separate set of test-retests).

$$p_{x'x}^2 = \frac{r_{12}r_{23}}{r_{13}}$$

(13)

$$p_{21} = \frac{r_{13}}{r_{23}} \quad p_{32} = \frac{r_{13}}{r_{12}} \quad p_{43} = \frac{r_{24}}{r_{23}}$$

The correlation r_{14} then can be predicted as follows:

$$r_{14} = p_{x'x}^2 p_{21} p_{32} p_{43}$$

$$r_{14} = \left(\frac{r_{12}r_{23}}{r_{13}}\right)\left(\frac{r_{13}}{r_{23}}\right)\left(\frac{r_{13}}{r_{12}}\right)\left(\frac{r_{24}}{r_{23}}\right)$$

(14)

$$r_{14} = \frac{r_{13}r_{24}}{r_{23}}$$

or:

$$r_{14}r_{23} = r_{13}r_{24}$$

(15)

In actual practice it is unlikely that the left and right terms of 15 will be exactly equal. However, if the model in Figure 20.5 is appropriate and one is working with a large sample, then the two products should differ very little. If the left and right terms of (15) are distinctly different, one has evidence that required assumptions are not met, and the model is inappropriate for the data.

Summary

Following Coleman's lead and using path analysis, formulas have been derived for estimating a measure's reliability and a variable's stability from test-retest correlations. The reliability estimate does not require a test with multiple items or two equivalent measures; hence, the reliability of a single question or observation can be determined. Furthermore, the reliability coefficient, unlike a simple test-retest correlation, is not attenuated in size because of changes which occur during the testing interval. The formulas depend on these assumptions: measurement errors are not serially correlated, and no unmeasured variable has a significant continuous impact on the measured variable during the measurement period. The legitimacy of these assumptions can be examined if a fourth wave of measurements is obtained.

References

BLALOCK, H. M., Jr. 1963. "Making causal inferences for unmeasured variables from correlations among indicators," *American Journal of Sociology*, 69: pp. 53–62.

BOUDON, R. 1968. "A new look at correlation analysis," in H. M. Blalock, Jr., and A. B. Blalock (eds.), *Methodology in Social Research* (New York: McGraw-Hill), pp. 199–235.

COLEMAN, J. S. 1968. "The mathematical study of change," in H. M. Blalock, Jr., and A. B. Blalock (eds.), *Methodology in Social Research* (New York: McGraw-Hill), pp. 428–478.

CROWTHER, BETTY. 1965. "A Sociological Analysis of Academic Achievement Correlates," unpublished Ph.D. dissertation (Madison: University of Wisconsin, Department of Sociology).

DUNCAN, O. D. 1966. "Path Analysis: sociological examples," *American Journal of Sociology*, 72: pp. 1–16.

FREEDMAN, R., COOMBS, L. G., and BUMPASS, L. 1965. "Stability and change in expectations about family size: a longitudinal study," *Demography*, 2: pp. 250–275.

HEISE, D. R. 1968. "Problems in path analysis and causal inference," in E. F. Borgatta, (ed.), *Sociological Methodology* (Jossey-Bass, in press).

LORD, F. M., and NOVICK, M. R. 1968. *Statistical Theories of Mental Test Scores* (Reading, Mass.: Addison-Wesley).

SIEGEL, P. M., and HODGE, R. W. 1968. "A causal approach to the study of measurement error," in H. M. Blalock, Jr., and A. B. Blalock (eds.), *Methodology in Social Research* (New York: McGraw-Hill), pp. 28–59.

STANLEY, J. C. 1965. "Review of California short-form test of mental maturity, 1963 revision," in O. K. Buros (ed.), *The Sixth Mental Measurements Yearbook* (Highland Park, N. J.: Gryphon Press), pp. 694–697.

TURNER, M. E., and STEVENS, C. D. 1959. "The regression analysis of causal paths," *Biometrics*, 15: pp. 236–258.

WRIGHT, S. 1934. "The method of path coefficients," *Annals of Mathematical Statistics*, 5: pp. 161–215.

Chapter 21

THE ESTIMATION OF MEASUREMENT
ERROR IN PANEL DATA

DAVID E. WILEY
University of Chicago
JAMES A. WILEY*
University of Illinois, Chicago Circle

In general, there are three ways of dealing with the problem of measurement error in path analyses of social and psychological data. Correction of parameter estimates for the attenuating effects of random error of measurement may be accomplished (1) by the use of *a priori* estimates of measurement error, (2) by designing into studies alternate measures of the same construct, or (3) by repeated measurements on the same population over time. This paper considers models for the estimation of measurement error in the latter case.

Taking his lead from Coleman (1968), Heise (1969) has formulated a path analysis model for the assessment of reliability when a variable is observed at three or more points in time. A consequence of this model is a simple formula for reliability uncontaminated by instability in the true scores. One of the several assumptions necessary to the empirical validity of Heise's model, i.e., the assumption that the reliability of the measured scores is stable over time, is argued to be doubtful.

Measurement models

It is useful to distinguish between a *causal model*, describing the structure of causal relations between "true scores," and a *measurement model*, which

Reprinted by permission of the authors and publisher from the *American Sociological Review*, Vol. 35, pp. 112–117. Copyright 1970, The American Sociological Association.
* The authors would like to acknowledge the helpful comments of the referee.

describes the relationship between measured scores and true scores (Blalock, 1968). Models for empirical phenomena may be evaluated with respect to their formal mathematical properties or with respect to their correspondence with the phenomenon. The argument in support of the measurement model proposed in this paper is based on the assumption that it is a more adequate representation of the empirical conditions of measurement than models heretofore proposed.

Consider the usual linear decomposition of a measured score into true score and error components.

$$x = \xi + \epsilon \tag{1}$$

Here x is the measured score, ξ the true score, and ϵ the error of measurement. If the true score and error components are independent, the variance of the measured scores (i.e., the total variance) is simply the sum of the true score variance and the measurement error variance.[1]

$$V(x) = V(\xi) + V(\epsilon) \tag{2}$$

The reliability of the measured score x, here denoted ρ^2, is defined as the ratio of the true score variance to total variance.

$$\rho^2 = \frac{V(\xi)}{V(\xi) + V(\epsilon)} \tag{3}$$

The classical definition of reliability is the square of the correlation between the observed and true scores (Lord and Novick, 1968:61), Equation (3) is equivalent to this definition under the stated assumptions.

Error variance is best conceived as a property of the measuring instrument itself and not of the population to which it is administered. On the other hand, the true score variance is more realistically considered as a property of the population. Thus the specification of stable reliability will normally require assumptions about populations as well as assumptions about the measuring instrument.

Reliability will remain constant under two different conditions. Both true score variance and error variance may change such that the ratio given in Equation (3) remains constant. This appears to be unlikely. Second, both true score and error variance may be constant. In this case, in addition to the assumption of constant error variance, the specification of constant reliability requires either the measurement of a stable trait or some form of aggregate equilibrium for the true score distribution. In Heise's paper ". . . the rate of

---

1. We adopt the following notational convention: $V(x_i)$ denotes the population variance of x_i; $C(x_i x_j)$ denotes the population covariance of x_i and x_j; and $\rho(x_i x_j)$, the population correlation of x_i and x_j. The symbol " $\wedge$ " over any of these symbols denotes an estimate of a population quantity based on a sample.

change in the true scores is presumed to be approximately constant within the measurement interval" (Heise, 1969:96). If the rate of change in the true scores is *absolutely* constant in the interval $(0, t)$, i.e., if $d\xi_i/dt = k$ where ξ_i represents the true score of individual i, then $\xi_{it} = kt + \xi_{io}$ for all i. Hence the true score at time t is equal to the true score at time 0 plus a constant function of the time interval. Such a change process does produce constant true score variance. However, it would require that the path coefficient relating pairs of times be unity, and that there be no differential changes for individuals. Thus the stability coefficient, defined as the correlation between the true scores at two points in time, will always be unity. In this case there would be no need to formulate a model which separates stability and reliability in panel data.

Given the implausibility of stable true score variance for most cases of practical interest, we are forced to conclude that most indicators cannot be characterized by a unique reliability. For example, any social process which tends to increase concensus (e.g., selective migration, increased interaction) results in a reduction of the true variability in attitudes without necessarily affecting the characteristics of the measuring instrument. Thus, the reliability of the instrument will tend to decrease. Even in completely stable situations, where reliability information, together with the total variance, is equivalent to information concerning the variance of the measurement error, this variance is probably a better index of the accuracy of the instrument's characterization of an individual's score, since the standard error of measurement is proportional to the width of the confidence interval for an individual's true score.

Similarly, comparisons across populations can be expected to yield widely varying reliabilities for the same indicator. An increase in reliability can always be obtained by conducting measurements on a more heterogeneous population (Lord and Novick, 1968:199).

It is clear that the specification of constant error variance avoids excessively strong assumptions about populations inherent in the specification of constant reliability. In the most general case neither assumption is valid. However, stable error variance will hold approximately while reliability is subject to considerable fluctuation. And if the characterization of stable error variance is faulty, then the characterization of stable reliability will almost always be in error.

A lag-1 model with constant error variance

A path diagram for a lag-1 model in three waves of observation is given in Figure 21.1. Here x_i is the measured score at time i, ξ_i is the true score, θ_i is the random shock, ϵ_i is the measurement error, and the α_{ji} are lagged

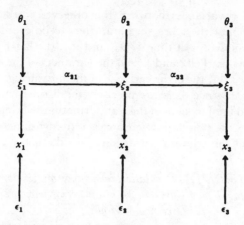

Figure 21.1.

Note: The α_{ji} are *not* path coefficients. They are path regression coefficients relating the true scores.

causal parameters linking the true scores at times j and i. It is assumed that (i) the measurement errors are uncorrelated with the true scores, (ii) the measurement errors are serially uncorrelated, (iii) the random shocks are serially uncorrelated, (iv) the error variance is homogeneous $[V(\epsilon_1) = V(\epsilon_2) = V(\epsilon_3) = V(\epsilon)]$, and (v) the system is lag-1 (i.e., α_{31} is identically equal to zero). Two sets of equations describe the model. First, we write a set of structural equations specifying the causal relations among the true scores.

$$\xi_1 = \theta_1$$
$$\xi_2 = \alpha_{21}\theta_1 + \theta_2 \qquad (4)$$
$$\xi_3 = \alpha_{32}(\alpha_{21}\theta_1 + \theta_2) + \theta_3$$

A set of measurement equations linking the measured and true scores is given in (5):

$$x_1 = \xi_1 + \epsilon_1$$
$$x_2 = \xi_2 + \epsilon_2 \qquad (5)$$
$$x_3 = \xi_3 + \epsilon_3$$

Substitution of the expressions for the true scores given in (4) into (5) generates a new set of equations (6) from which the structure of the covariances between the measured variables can be deduced.

$$x_1 = \theta_1 + \epsilon_1$$
$$x_2 = \alpha_{21}\theta_1 + \theta_2 + \epsilon_2 \qquad (6)$$
$$x_3 = \alpha_{32}(\alpha_{21}\theta_1 + \theta_2) + \theta_3 + \epsilon_3$$

The matrix of covariances between the observed variables is given in Table 21.1. Note that there are six parameters to be estimated: $V(\theta_1)$, the variance of the true scores at time 1; α_{21} and α_{32}, the lag-1 path regressions linking the true scores; $V(\theta_2)$ and $V(\theta_3)$, the variances of the shocks at times 2 and 3; and finally $V(\epsilon)$, the error variance of the measuring instrument. The model is *just identified* since there are precisely six distinct entries in the covariance matrix, and the Jacobian of the transformation relating the parameters to be estimated to the population variances and covariances is non-zero for non-zero values of the relevant parameters (Wald, 1950).

Table 21.1. Population covariance matrix for lag-1 model assuming constant error variance for three waves of observations

$$V(x_1) = V(\theta_1) + V(\epsilon)$$
$$C(x_1x_2) = \alpha_{21}V(\theta_1)$$
$$C(x_1x_3) = \alpha_{21}\alpha_{32}V(\theta_1)$$
$$V(x_2) = \alpha^2{}_{21}V(\theta_1) + V(\theta_2) + V(\epsilon)$$
$$C(x_2x_3) = \alpha_{32}[\alpha^2{}_{21}V(\theta_1) + V(\theta_2)]$$
$$V(x_3) = \alpha^2{}_{32}[\alpha^2{}_{21}V(\theta_1) + V(\theta_2)] + V(\theta_3) + V(\epsilon)$$

Estimators for the parameters of this model are presented in Table 21.2. In this case estimators are obtained by recursive solution of the six equations given in Table 21.1. Expressions for these estimators solely in terms of observed variances and covariances can be obtained by successive substitution.

Under reasonable distributional assumptions, the estimators specified above will be consistent. Under the assumption of normality, since the

Table 21.2. Parameters and estimators for lag-1 model assuming constant error variance

Parameter	Estimator
α_{32}	$\hat{C}(x_1x_3)/\hat{C}(x_1x_2)$
$V(\epsilon)$	$\hat{V}(x_2) - [\hat{C}(x_2x_3)/\hat{\alpha}_{32}]$
$V(\theta_1)$	$\hat{V}(x_1) - \hat{V}(\epsilon)$
α_{21}	$\hat{C}(x_1x_2)/\hat{V}(\theta_1)$
$V(\theta_2)$	$\hat{V}(x_2) - [\hat{\alpha}_{21}\hat{C}(x_1x_2) + \hat{V}(\epsilon)]$
$V(\theta_3)$	$\hat{V}(x_3) - [\hat{\alpha}_{32}\hat{C}(x_2x_3) + \hat{V}(\epsilon)]$

Note: The estimators are given in the appropriate recursive order.

estimates will reproduce the sample covariance matrix exactly, they will thus maximize the likelihood function. Therefore, under these conditions the estimators will be efficient.

Reliability and stability

Since this model imposes no restrictions on the variance of the true scores, for three waves of observations there are three reliabilities to be estimated, not one. The expressions for the reliabilities below are derived directly from the definition of reliability given previously.

$$\rho^2_1 = V(\theta_1)/[V(\theta_1) + V(\epsilon)] \tag{7}$$
$$\rho^2_2 = [\alpha^2_{21} V(\theta_1) + V(\theta_2)]/[\alpha^2_{21} V(\theta_1) + V(\theta_2) + V(\epsilon)]$$
$$\rho^2_3 = \{\alpha^2_{32}[\alpha^2_{21} V(\theta_1) + V(\theta_2)] + V(\theta_3)\}/\{\alpha^2_{32}[\alpha^2_{21} V(\theta_1) + V(\theta_2)] +$$
$$V(\theta_3) + V(\epsilon)\}$$

It may be demonstrated that Heise's formula for reliability $\dfrac{\rho(x_1x_2)\rho(x_2x_3)}{\rho(x_1x_3)}$ is, given the assumptions of the present model, the reliability of the instrument at time 2.

We define the stability coefficient γ_{ij} as the correlation between the true scores at times i and j. For the three wave model the three stability coefficients are given as follows:

$$\gamma_{12} = \alpha_{21} \frac{\sqrt{V(\theta_1)}}{\sqrt{\alpha^2_{21} V(\theta_1) + V(\theta_2)}} \tag{8}$$

$$\gamma_{23} = \alpha_{32} \frac{\sqrt{\alpha^2_{21} V(\theta_1) + V(\theta_2)}}{\sqrt{\alpha^2_{32}(\alpha^2_{21} V(\theta_1) + V(\theta_2)) + V(\theta_3)}}$$

$$\gamma_{13} = \alpha_{21}\alpha_{32} \frac{\sqrt{V(\theta_1)}}{\sqrt{\alpha^2_{32}(\alpha^2_{21} V(\theta_1) + V(\theta_2)) + V(\theta_3)}}$$

Note that $\gamma_{13} = \gamma_{12}\gamma_{23}$.

It can be shown that Heise's measures of stability S_{ij} have the structure:

$$S_{12} = \rho_{13}/\rho_{23} = \gamma_{12}\frac{\rho_1}{\rho_2}$$

$$S_{23} = \rho_{13}/\rho_{12} = \gamma_{23}\frac{\rho_3}{\rho_2} \tag{9}$$

$$S_{13} = \rho^2_{13}/\rho_{12}\rho_{23} = \gamma_{13}\frac{\rho_1\rho_3}{\rho^2_2}$$

where ρ_i is the square root of the reliability at time i.

It is clear from this result that $S_{ij} = \gamma_{ij}$ for all i,j, if, and only if, the reliabilities are homogeneous. Since this is an implausible assumption, we conclude that the S_{ij} are contaminated by heterogeneity in the reliabilities.

The γ_{ij} may be regarded as path coefficients relating the true scores across time. However, in this case, they cannot be derived directly from the correlations between the observed variables, since under the stable error variance model the standardization of the observed variables results in a loss of relevant information.

An application of the model

As an illustration we apply the lag-1 model, assuming homogeneous error variance, to repeated observations on reported earnings. Covariances between reported earnings for three successive years are given in Cutright (1969). These covariances are based on reported earnings from a sample of

Table 21.3. Sample covariances and correlations for reported earnings in three successive years

Covariance matrix* with correlations in parenthesis

	X_1	X_2	X_3
X_1: 1962 earnings	11.495	....	....
X_2: 1963 earnings	10.106 (.827)	12.995	....
X_3: 1964 earnings	10.455 (.778)	11.808 (.827)	15.708

* Multiply entries by 10^6 to obtain sample covariances.

6,222 white males for the years 1962–1964. The sample covariance and correlation matrices are presented in Table 21.3. Estimates of the six parameters of the model are given below:

$$\hat{\alpha}_{32} = 1.035$$
$$\hat{\alpha}_{21} = 1.019$$
$$\hat{V}(\epsilon) = 1.581 \times 10^6$$
$$\hat{V}(\theta_1) = 9.914 \times 10^6$$
$$\hat{V}(\theta_2) = 1.116 \times 10^6$$
$$\hat{V}(\theta_3) = 1.906 \times 10^6$$

The estimated reliability and stability coefficients under Heise's model and the model formulated in this paper are presented in Table 21.4.

Table 21.4. Estimated reliability and stability coefficients under assumptions of stable reliability versus stable error variance

	Stable reliability	Stable error variance
A. Reliability		
Time 1	.878	.862
Time 2	.878	.878
Time 3	.878	.899
B. Stability		
Times 1 and 2	.941	.950
Times 2 and 3	.941	.930
Times 1 and 3	.886	.884

Note that the reliabilities under the second model increase regularly with time; this is a necessary consequence of the increasing variability of true income. For these data, Heise's measures underestimate the stability of true income between 1962 and 1963 and overestimate the stability of true income between 1963 and 1964. The small differences between the two models are due to the relatively close spacing of the observations. An increase in the time interval between measurements should lead to more dramatic differences between the models.

The effects of standardization

An important implication of the previous discussion is that the choice between standardized and unstandardized forms of a model is not trivial. In fact, the difference between the two models considered herein is strongly related to the distinction between path coefficients and path regressions.

Each standardized parameter is a function of more than one unstandardized parameter. In general, *if two or more of the unstandardized parameters of a model are equal, the corresponding standardized parameters will be unequal because they are not related to the unstandardized parameters by an equivalent transformation.*

For example, while it is possible to impose the condition of equal reliability in a standardized model (as Heise does), this model cannot in general satisfy the constraint of equal error variance in the corresponding unstandardized model. Similarly, stability in the path coefficients of a standardized model is not in general compatible with stability in the path regression coefficients of an unstandardized model. This is the reason that quantitatively different results (see above) are obtained when the two models are applied to the same data.

The distinction between path analysis and path regression analysis is crucial where one is attempting to compare the parameters of several populations. This case is fully discussed by Blalock (1967b). The distinction is equally important for models characterizing stable processes or where stability is assumed in order to achieve identifiability. In this case it will generally be more appropriate to assume stability in the unstandardized parameters.

Discussion

The preceding discussion has assumed that the system is lag-1. This assumption is not a trivial one. If, in fact, the degree of lag is higher than that, the parameters are not identifiable for only three time points. Under the assumption of stability of measurement error variance, it is possible to fit a model with a lag degree 2 less than the number of time points. Since the degree of lag is unlikely to be too high for most systems, it seems possible to fit a reasonable model if enough time points are available. It is then possible to test empirically the assumption of homogeneous error variance if the degree of lag in the model is small in comparison to the number of time points. We have argued that homogeneity of error variance is a more plausible assumption than homogeneous reliability.

In spite of repeated warnings (Tukey, 1954; Turner and Stevens, 1959; Blalock, 1967a and 1967b) most sociological applications of linear models are confined to standardized systems (e.g., Duncan, 1966; Blau and Duncan, 1967; Duncan *et al.*, 1968; Sewell *et al.*, 1969). The convenience of path analysis algorithms and the apparent ease of translation from standardized to unstandardized systems (Wright, 1960) probably accounts for this tendency. We have demonstrated above that the structure of the model considered in this paper is *not* invariant under standardization. In particular, homogeneity of error variance is not preserved under transformation to a standardized system. These considerations are also relevant for more complex longitudinal models, where it may be desirable to assume *a priori* that certain causal parameters are stable. The corresponding standardized parameters will generally be heterogeneous.

References

BLALOCK, H. M., Jr. 1967a. "Path coefficients versus regression coefficients." *American Journal of Sociology* 72: 675–676.
———. 1967b. "Causal inference, closed populations, and measures of association." *American Political Science Review* 61 (March): 130–136.
———. 1968. "The measurement problem: a gap between the languages of theory and

research." Pp. 5–27 in H. M. Blalock, Jr., and A. B. Blalock (eds.), *Methodology in Social Research*. New York: McGraw-Hill.

BLAU, PETER M., and DUNCAN, OTIS DUDLEY. 1967. *The American Occupational Structure*. New York: Wiley.

COLEMAN, J. S. 1968. "The mathematical study of change." Pp. 428–478 in H. M. Blalock, and A. B. Blalock (eds.), *Methodology in Social Research*. New York: McGraw-Hill.

CUTRIGHT, PHILLIPS. 1969. *Achievement, Military Service, and Earnings*. Forthcoming.

DUNCAN, OTIS DUDLEY. 1966. "Path analysis: sociological examples." *American Journal of Sociology* 72 (July): 1–16.

DUNCAN, OTIS DUDLEY, HALLER, ARCHIBALD O., and PORTES, ALEJANDRO. 1968. "Peer influences on aspirations: a reinterpretation." *American Journal of Sociology* 74 (September): 119–137.

HEISE, DAVID R. 1969. "Separating reliability and stability in test-retest correlation." *American Sociological Review* 34 (February): 93–101.

LORD, FREDERICK M., and NOVICK, MELVIN R. 1968. *Statistical Theories of Mental Test Scores*. Reading, Mass.: Addison-Wesley.

SEWELL, WILLIAM H., HALLER, ARCHIBALD O., and PORTES, ALEJANDRO. 1969. "The educational and early occupational attainment process." *American Sociological Review* 34 (February): 82–91.

TUKEY, JOHN W. 1954. "Causation, regression, and path analysis." Pp. 35–66 in O. Kempthorne, *et al.* (eds.), *Statistics and Mathematics in Biology*. Ames: Iowa State College Press.

TURNER, M. E., and STEVENS, C. D. 1959. "The regression analysis of causal paths." *Biometrics* 15 (June): 236–258.

WALD, A. 1950. "Note on the identification of economic relations." Pp. 238–244 in Koopmans, T. C. (ed.), *Cowles Commission Monograph No. 10*, New York: Wiley.

WRIGHT, SEWALL. 1960. "Path coefficients and regression coefficients: alternative or complementary concepts?" *Biometrics* 16 (June): 189–202.

Chapter 22

A CAUSAL ASSESSMENT OF VALIDITY: THE AUGMENTED MULTITRAIT-MULTIMETHOD MATRIX

ROBERT P. ALTHAUSER
Princeton University

THOMAS A. HEBERLEIN
University of Wisconsin

ROBERT A. SCOTT*
Princeton University

The methodological literature of sociology is replete with various demarcations between the "reliability" and "validity" of measures (Goode and Hatt 1952; Kerlinger, 1965; Selltiz et al., 1967). In research where causal models are composed not only of underlying concepts or variables but of their imperfect measures as well, yet another, perhaps more encompassing, demarcation offers itself. In causal modeling, the influence of underlying concepts and random error on individual measures of these concepts is a matter of the reliability of measures. In contrast, questions of validity arise when non-substantive (extraneous or methodological) variables influence the measures of two or more variables in a model.

Campbell and Fiske (1959) have presented a way of gaging the influence of different procedures of measurement or data collection on measures. They proposed a series of comparisons of correlations among measures of two or more concepts by two or more methods. An example of the matrix of these correlations is shown in Figure 22.1 for two concepts X and Y and two methods of data collection common to survey research, interviews, and questionnaires. A causal model consistent with Campbell and Fiske's

* Revision of the second part of a paper read at the September, 1969 meeting of the American Sociological Association, entitled "Reliability and Validity, Methods of Data Collection and the Multitrait-Multimethod Matrix." For helpful comments on previous versions of this paper, we wish to thank Charles Werts.

Method		Interview		Questionnaire	
Measures of		$X\ (X_I)$	$Y\ (Y_I)$	$X'\ (X_Q)$	$Y'\ (Y_Q)$
Interview	X (X_1)				
	Y (Y_I)	m_{yx} $r_{X_I Y_I}$			
Questionnaire	X' (X_Q)	$v_{x'x}$ $r_{X_Q X_I}$	$h_{x'y}$ $r_{X_Q Y_I}$		
	Y' (Y_Q)	$h_{y'x}$ $r_{X_I Y_Q}$	$v_{y'y}$ $r_{Y_Q Y_I}$	$m_{y'x'}$ $r_{X_Q Y_Q}$	

Figure 22.1. A multitrait-multimethod matrix of correlations among measures of two concepts obtained by two methods (interviews, questionnaires).

assumptions about the ways in which method influence measures of X and Y is shown in Figure 22.2.

This paper develops some modifications in Campbell and Fiske's approach to the assessment of validity. These are proposed in light of certain difficulties in the inferences to be made from their comparisons of correlations (as

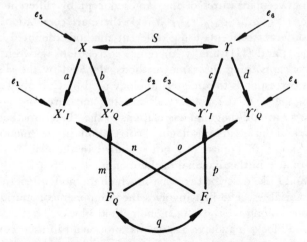

Figure 22.2. A causal model of two correlated measures in the multitrait-multimethod matrix.

discussed in Althauser and Heberlein, 1970) and in other nonideal aspects
of their conceptualization of these procedures. As a remedy, certain changes
in the underlying model of the matrix are made, resulting in "augmented"
multitrait-multimethod matrices of two types. The first, dealing with the
general effect of methods and of reactive measurement, is known as the
"collapsed" augmented matrix. The second, which encompasses both
specific methods' factors and their interaction with other variables is termed
a "full" augmented matrix. Working from these two modified matrices and
their underlying models, the procedures which may be used to assess the
validity (and reliability) of measures are set forth.

The multitrait-multimethod matrix

Campbell and Fiske (1959) recommended two major criteria for establishing
the validity of a measure. A test should demonstrate (1) convergent validity;
i.e., show a high correlation with another measure of the same trait; and (2)
discriminant validity; i.e., show low correlations with other tests from which
they were intended to differ. To demonstrate convergent and discriminant
validity and to obtain some idea of the impact of method variance, Campbell
and Fiske proposed the multitrait-multimethod matrix in which the same
set of traits is measured by two or more methods.

A generic form of the matrix is presented in Figure 22.1. Correlations are
designated in two ways—using the notation for the correlation coefficient,
e.g., $r_{X'_I X'_Q}$, and using a notation (the v's, h's, m's) designed to differentiate between three different types of correlations in the matrix: (I) There are
correlations between measures of the same concept by different methods,
denoted by the v's (e.g., $r_{X'_I X'_Q}$, $r_{Y'_I Y'_Q}$): (II) there are correlations between
measures of different concepts using different methods, denoted by the h's
$(r_{X'_I Y'_Q}, r_{X'_Q Y'_I})$; and (III) finally, there are correlations between measures
of different concepts using the same methods, denoted by the m's $(r_{X'_I Y'_I}$,
$r_{X'_Q Y'_Q})$. This corresponds to some terminology used by Campbell and Fiske
in designating parts of the matrix: v's are the measures of "convergent
validity"; the h's are off-diagonal correlations in the "heteromethod" blocks
of the matrix; and the m's are off-diagonal correlations in the "monomethod"
blocks.[1] Not shown in Figure 22.1 but included in the original work are
reliability estimates in the diagonal of the monomethod blocks.

Campbell and Fiske describe two ways in which methods affect the correlations among variables. The first involves the component of spuriousness in
the correlations among measures in monomethod blocks. That is, measures
in monomethod blocks may have a spurious component in their correlations

1. More precisely, the "heterotrait-heteromethod" and "heterotrait-monomethod"
triangles of each block.

because the same method was used to obtain these measures. This can be referred to as "common methods variance." In factor analytic terms, we posit the operation of individual methods' factors specific to each method used to gather data, e.g., a questionnaire or interview factor.

The second way in which methods affect correlations is that different specific methods may not be independent. This "methods covariance" will appear as a component of the correlations in the heteromethod blocks (i.e., the *v*'s and *h*'s). This lack of independence may also be conceptualized as a "general methods factor" by viewing different methods as categories of such a factor.

There are four steps in the assessment of convergent and discriminant validity:

Convergent validity is established when the correlations between measures of the same underlying concept using different methods are sizable. No specific degree of correlation is mentioned, but the correlations—the *v*'s —should be greater than the other correlations and, we might surmise, at least statistically significant. Assuming we observe sizable *v*'s, the inference we are to make is that different methods of measurement do not affect the association between measures of the same concept.

To establish "discriminant validity," three comparisons of correlations are proposed:

First, the correlations between measures of the *same* concept using *different* methods should be greater than the correlations between measures of *different* concepts using these same set of *different* methods. This requires a comparison of the measures of convergent validity (the *v*'s) as found in the diagonals of the heteromethod blocks with the off-diagonal correlations within the blocks (the *h*'s). If each *v* in a given row and column of a heteromethod block is clearly greater in size than the *h*'s in the same row or column of that block, this desideratum is met (e.g., when $v_{x'x}$ is greater than $h_{y'x}$, $h_{x'y}$).

Since this comparison considers only correlations within the heteromethod block, methods' effects of the second type—the relative lack of independence of methods—operate equally on both types of correlations. What we are examining is the difference between correlations of measures of the same traits (which should be high) and correlations between measures of different traits (which should be low, since the underlying traits are different).

Second, *different* concepts measured by the *same* method should not correlate more highly than do measures of the *same* concept using *different* measures. Otherwise, we could be tempted to attribute such a higher correlation to the sameness of method rather than the sameness of the concepts being measured. Correlations between different concepts measured by the same methods are symbolized by the *m*'s, the off-diagonal correlations in the two monomethod blocks. If the v's in a given row and column are approached or surpassed in size by the m's in the same row or column, it could indeed be due to the commonality of methods (or "common methods variance") absent in the heteromethod blocks.

As with the first comparison, we expect a positive difference between high correlations of same-trait measures and low correlations of measures of different traits. In addition, the first type of methods' effect can inflate the m's and diminish the difference between the v's and m's. The second type of methods' effect—the non-independence of specific methods—can affect the same difference by inflating (or diminishing) the v's. In addition, if the concepts or traits underlying different measures, say X'_Q and Y'_Q are *really* not the same, then we expect the measures will "discriminate" and show low correlations with other measures "from which they were intended to differ." (Campbell and Fiske, 1959:81). So in this comparison, the question of whether one or both types of methods' effects are present is confounded with the question of whether a measure (say X'_Q) has shown a low correlation with other measures (e.g., Y'_Q).

The very same mixture of confounded questions appears in the third proposed comparison of correlations. Regardless of the methods used, the same pattern of off-diagonal correlations (h's, m's) should hold. This would reflect an underlying matrix of substantive or "true" correlations between concepts that is maintained in spite of possible methods' effects of either type. If the same pattern of relative sizes among corresponding h's and m's is observed, this desideratum is met.

Some problems

There are a number of problems with Campbell and Fiske's approach. To begin with, these procedures in examining the correlations of this matrix comprise a structure of inferences about the effects of underlying concepts and methods on measures. At many points this inference structure has been found not viable (Althauser and Heberlein, 1970). This can be established either by a formal discussion of the procedures—making reference to the causal model that underlies the matrix (Figure 22.2)—or by less formal discussion.

The causal model shown in Figure 22.2 portrays the relationships among two underlying concepts X and Y, two measures of each concept (X'_I, X'_Q, Y'_I, Y'_Q) and two methods factors F_Q and F_I, where X'_I denotes a measure of X using interview data, Y'_Q a measure of Y using questionnaire data, F_Q represents a questionnaire factor, and so on. The "true" or substantive relationship between the two underlying concepts (or traits) is labeled "S." The epistemic paths between each concept and its two measures are denoted by "a", "b", "c", and "d".

The specific methods paths for questionnaire and interview factors are denoted by "*m*", "*o*," and "*n*," "*p*," respectively. The correlation "*q*" denotes the extent to which the independence of these two methods is absent. Error terms $e_1 \ldots e_4$ are shown affecting each measure and terms e_5 and e_6 are shown affecting the underlying concepts X and Y. The model assumes that these terms are correlated neither with each other nor with measures or concepts other than the one to which they are assigned.

Note that X, Y, F_I and F_Q are all unmeasured variables. F_I and F_Q are best conceived of as symbols for extraneous variables that are peculiar to each method of collecting data. For example, the respondents' need for acceptance or approval, his willingness to confide confidential information, his need for achievement as expressed in his "performance" as a respondent, or his sensitivity to the researcher's expectations are all extraneous variables that may be differentially represented in the methods factors.

Based on this causal model, a path analysis of the correlations being compared in the first and third assessments of discriminant validity reveals that one must assume away an instance of what we are trying to assess: the presence of methods' effect. That is, it has been shown that the desiderata in the first and third comparisons would be met, *even when* the effects of two specific methods factors (F_I and F_Q in Figure 22.2) are *sizable and equal.*

The assessment of convergent validity is similarly troubled. In effect, we must assume that the second type of methods' effect—a lack of independence of methods—does not operate. Otherwise, the size of the *v*'s may be inflated or diminished to an unknown extent.

Only the second comparison of correlations in the assessment of discriminant validity is viable, providing we make two assumptions: (1) that the epistemic paths are equal and of like sign and (2) that the methods' effects are of like sign.

There are, in addition, other questions about Campbell and Fiske's approach. Most of these can be raised by making reference to the causal model in Figure 22.2.

As reflected in the notation of the measures, X'_I, Y'_Q, etc., each measure is a "trait-method unit." That is, Campbell and Fiske have chosen to deliberately confound the effects of traits and methods on measures. This has several questionable consequences.

1. We must assume that there is essentially simultaneous measurement of all measures. If the same respondents or subjects are studied by the different methods, this is, of course, impossible: first one, then the other method must be administered.

2. As a consequence of 1, reactive effects of initial upon subsequent measurement may exist. That is, if subject X is measured using method A and remeasured using method B, the latter measures may be affected by the

former or initial measures regardless of the particular methods A and B that are used.

3. When traits and methods are confounded, it is less plausible to assume that the epistemic paths are equal (as required in the application of the second measure of discriminant validity) than when they are not so confounded.

4. When traits and methods are confounded, both the main effects of traits and methods and the interaction of methods and traits are likewise confounded. Thus the additive and nonadditive effects of methods cannot be distinguished, yet there are many conceivable types of interactions worth our attention.

For example, if we allow for reactive effects, then there might be an interaction between methods and the reactive effects of initial upon subsequent measurement. An initial measure of political orientation may affect a subsequent measure of the same concept, depending on the particular combination of methods used to make each measurement. Or there may be an interaction of methods and epistemic paths. A given item measuring political orientation might be superior to another measure depending on the combination of methods used. Or there may be an interaction between the underlying concept and reactive effects. Initial measures of certain kinds of variables may be more likely to have a reactive effect on subsequent measures than initial measures of other kinds of variables. Other types of interactions are conceivable but more complex. For example, there may be higher order interactions that could appear in differences between the interaction effects attending the different variables (X's, Y's) in a given correlation.

5. Finally, there is a severe problem of how to estimate and deal with reliability within the Campbell and Fiske approach. Reliability in most respects is underplayed in this approach, perhaps because of the ambiguity in placing reliability estimates along side of correlations in the same matrix. Ignoring sampling error, which is discussed elsewhere (Heberlein, 1969), a reliability coefficient is often thought of as an estimate of stability rather than as purely an estimate of measurement error. Instability of observed scores may be produced by either an actual change in true scores between tests or through a lack of equivalence between forms of tests. For both of these reasons, the reliability coefficient underestimates the true reliability defined as the degree of measurement error.

Guttman (1945) and Johnson (1950) have pointed out that a split-half correlation underestimates reliability and is inappropriate to use when correcting correlations for attenuation due to measurement error. Cronbach's alpha (1951) is also a measure of reliability based on the internal consistency of items, and it makes use of more information than a split-half correlation.

However, according to Lord and Novick (1968), even alpha is merely a lower bound for reliability. Its values will tend to be too low unless one has items that are parallel or at least tau-equivalent, in which case it is an unbiased estimate.

Johnson has shown that "lack of equivalence in comparable forms has a tendency to lower the magnitude of reliability coefficients, but has no tendency to lower the magnitude of observed trait coefficients" (p. 115). Johnson concluded that the most appropriate reliability estimate to use when correcting for attenuation in correlations is a test-retest correlation, with the time between retesting being the same length as the interval between administration of the two tests which yield the trait coefficients.

Actually, the effect of instability in true scores can be accounted for in test-retest data, providing one has three waves of testing (Heise, 1969). Heise demonstrated that a test-retest correlation corrected for stability is substantially higher than the usual test-retest correlations. This indicates that the usual test-retest correlations also tend to underestimate reliability.

Two augmented matrices

In light of all these problems with the matrix as originally proposed, we would like to offer a modification in the procedures just discussed and in the underlying causal model. At the very least, we hope that the changes to be described represent a partial solution to many of the problems discussed above. At the same time, we will see that by limiting ourselves to two measures per underlying concept, our modified procedures will be somewhat awkward and circumspect.

The modifications we have in mind take the form of two "new" multitrait-multimethod matrices, each with an underlying model. The first we call the "collapsed" form of the modified or "augmented" matrix. Combinations of specific methods and the interaction of methods with other variables are ignored. The focus is on the additive effects of methods and reactive effects. The second we call the "full" matrix, because it encompasses the effects of specific methods and interactions. We designate the overall modification as an "augmented matrix" (or matrices) because consideration of both the order of measurement and combinations of methods enlarges the scope of the original approach.

The "collapsed" matrix

The causal model underlying the first of these two augmented matrices is shown in Figure 22.3. As before, there is a substantive path S between X and

Y, epistemic paths (a_1, a_2, c_1, c_2) from X and Y to initial and subsequent measures of X and Y ($X'_1, Y'_1; X'_2, Y'_2$), and paths from a methods' variable to these measures (f_1, f_2, h_1, h_2). In addition, we include the reactive effect of an initial measure of X and Y upon the subsequent measures (paths s and t). The residuals of each of the measures and of the underlying concepts are assumed uncorrelated. It may also be reasonable to assume in certain cases that epistemic and methods paths to both measures of each respective concept are respectively equal (i.e., $a_1 = a_2$; $f_1 = f_2$, etc.), now that measures do not confound traits and methods, but we will not yet assume these equalities.

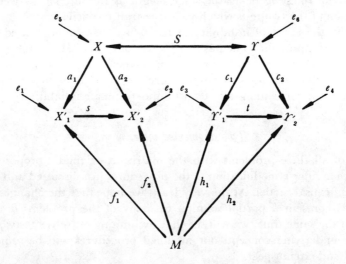

Figure 22.3. *A causal model of two correlated measures in the collapsed, augmented matrix.*

With traits and methods no longer confounded, we can conceive of methods as a variate like the other variables in the model. Methods become, in effect, a dummy variable, composed of no more than two categories (e.g., interviews and questionnaires, in the illustrations to follow). Studies of more than two methods must be subdivided into studies of pairs of methods, on this approach.

Other contrasts between this model and the previously discussed model can be drawn. We do not assume simultaneous measurement but distinguish between an "initial" and a "subsequent" measure. We can thereby take into account the reactive effects of the order of measurement. Reliability can be estimated directly from the correlations in the matrix, as will be shown later. Note should also be taken of the fact that this is *not* a test-retest model. We assume that there is a fairly brief lapse of time between the initial and final measurement, and that the rate of change of the measures over this lapse of time is negligible.

With four distinct measures there are six possible correlations among measures. Their placement in the tabular presentation of the "collapsed" matrix is shown in Figure 22.4. The four correlations in the block in the upper right of the table are correlations between successive measures (initial and subsequent) of X and Y. Two of these are on the diagonal $(r_{X'_1 X'_2}, r_{Y'_1 Y'_2})$ and are correlations between measures of the same concept. The other two are correlations $(r_{X'_1 Y'_2}, r_{X'_2 Y'_1})$ between successive measures of different concepts. The correlations in the upper left $(r_{X'_1 Y'_1})$ and the lower right $(r_{X'_2 Y'_2})$ blocks are correlations between different measures made at the same point in the order of measurement—either correlations among initial or among subsequent measures.

Order of Measurement	Measures	First Measure		Subsequent Measure	
		X'_1	Y'_1	X'_2	Y'_2
Initial Measure	X'_1			$r_{X'_1 X'_2}$	$r_{X'_1 Y'_2}$
	Y'_1	$r_{Y'_1 X'_1}$		$r_{Y'_1 X'_2}$	$r_{Y'_1 Y'_2}$
Subsequent Measure	X'_2				
	Y'_2		$r_{Y'_2 X'_2}$		

Figure 22.4. A collapsed augmented matrix of correlations among initial and subsequent measures of two concepts obtained by two methods.

Correlations from some sociological data illustrating this (and the "full" matrix to follow) are shown in Table 22.1. The example is drawn from interview and questionnaire data gathered by undergraduate students participating in a class survey of fellow students. Each of several concepts—social class identification, political orientation and liberalism—were measured twice, either by a repetition of the same item (as with Class) or by two differently worded items[2] (Political Orientation, Liberalism). The initial measurement of each concept is distinguished from the second or subsequent

2. The wording of the items was as follows:
Class (1 and 2)—"To which of these four classes do you believe your family belongs: 1—upper, 2—middle, 3—working, 4—lower?"
Pol. Or. 1—"Which one of the following categories most accurately reflects your general

Table 22.1. Correlation matrix illustrating the collapsed (augmented)
multitrait-multimethod matrix

Order of Measurement	Initial			Subsequent		
Measures:	Class 1	Pol. Or .1	Lib. 1.	Class 2	Pol. Or. 2	Lib. 2
Initial						
Class 1	....	....	....	.97*	−.10	−.08
Pol. Or. 1	−.09	....	....	−.09	.50*	.47*
Lib. 1	.00	.27*	....	.00	.29*	.37*
Subsequent						
Class 2	....	....	....	....	....	....
Pol. Or. 2	....	(N=227)	....	−.10	....	....
Lib. 2	....	....	....	−.08	.35*	....

* Significant at the .01 level.

measurement by the number 1 or 2 following the abbreviations of the concepts (i.e., Class 1, Pol. Or. 2, Lib. 2, etc.).

There are at least two possible approaches to the assessment of the validity
of measures using these correlations. Both require a path analysis of the correlations, which can be expressed in terms of path coefficients as follows:

Correlations between successive measures of the same concept:

(1) $r_{X'_1 X'_2} = a_1 a_2 + f_1 f_2 + s$

(2) $r_{Y'_1 Y'_2} = c_1 c_2 + h_1 h_2 + t$

Correlations between successive measures of different concepts:

(3) $r_{X'_1 Y'_2} = a_1 S c_2 + a_1 S c_1 t + f_1 h_2 + f_1 h_1 t = a_1 S (c_2 + c_1 t) + f_1 (h_2 + h_1 t)$

(4) $r_{X'_2 Y'_1} = a_2 S c_1 + s a_1 S c_1 + f_2 h_1 + s f_1 h_1 = S c_1 (a_2 + s a_1) + h_1 (f_2 + s f_1)$

political orientation: 1—radical leftist, 2—very liberal, 3—somewhat liberal, 4—middle-of-
the-roader, 5—somewhat conservative, 6—very conservative, 7—radical rightist?"

Pol. Or. 2—"On a seven-point scale of general political orientations, where do you believe
you fall?"

Radical leftist   Radical rightist
1   2   3   4   5   6   7

Lib. 1—"To what extent do you feel that Negroes should be given an equal opportunity to
better themselves?: 1—to a very great extent, 2—to quite an extent, 3—to some extent,
4—to a slight extent, 5—to no extent."

Lib. 2—"To what extent would you favor the passage of Federal legislation that would
assure Negroes that they would not be kept away from living in residential areas from which
they are now systematically excluded?" (Response categories the same as for Lib. 1.)

Correlations among initial and subsequent measures of different concepts:

(5) $r_{X'_1Y'_1} = a_1Sc_1 + f_1h_1$

(6) $r_{X'_2Y'_2} = a_2Sc_2 + sa_1Sc_2 + sa_1Sc_1t + a_2Sc_1t + f_2h_2 + sf_1h_2 + sf_1h_1t + f_2h_1t$

$\qquad = Sc_2(a_2 + sa_1) + Sc_1t(a_2 + sa_1) + f_2(h_2 + th_1) + f_1s(h_2 + h_1t)$

$\qquad = S(a_2 + sa_1)(c_2 + c_1t) + (f_2 + e_1s)(h_2 + th_1)$

The first assessment of validity focuses on the reactive effects as expressed in the paths s and t. If we are willing in a given research situation to make some assumptions about epistemic and methods' paths being equal, it is possible to estimate these paths from the correlations. For example, if we consider the difference between a correlation between successive measures of different concepts and a correlation between initial measures of these same concepts:

(7) $r_{X'_1Y'_2} - r_{X'_1Y'_1} = a_1S(c_2 + c_1t) + f_1(h_2 + h_1t) - (a_1Sc_1 + f_1h_1)$

$\qquad = a_1Sc_2 + a_1Sc_1(t-1) + f_1h_2 + f_1h_1(t-1)$

If $c_1 = c_2 = c$, and $h_1 = h_2 = h$, then equation 7 becomes:

(8) $r_{X'_1Y'_2} - r_{X'_1Y'_1} = t(a_1Sc + f_1h)$

Since $r_{X'_1Y'_1} = (a_1Sc + f_1h)$, given the same assumptions, we can solve for the path t:

(9) $t = \dfrac{r_{X'_1Y'_2} - r_{X'_1Y'_1}}{r_{X'_1Y'_1}}$

If we likewise assume that $a_1 = a_2 = a$ and $f_1 = f_2 = f$, we can solve for the path s:

(10) $s = \dfrac{r_{X'_2Y'_1} - r_{X'_1Y'_1}}{r_{X'_1Y'_1}}$

In general, we must be able to assume that the epistemic and methods paths to the measures whose reactive effects we wish to estimate are equal.

In the general case where the matrix is composed of measures of three or more concepts, there will be more than one estimate of the reactive effects of the initial upon the subsequent measure of each concept. Thus, for Class, we can estimate the reactive effects of Class 1 upon Class 2 in the model where Class and Pol. Or. are correlated, and in the model where Class and Liberalism are correlated. The procedure consistent with the above formula is to take the correlations in the successive measures blocks (e.g., the Class 2— Pol. Or. 1, and Class 2—Lib. 1 correlations) and subtract from them the corresponding correlations in the initial measures' blocks (i.e., Class 1— Pol. Or. 1, Class 1—Lib. 1, respectively), then divide by the latter correlations. In the illustrative data shown in Table 22.1, this yields the following estimates of the reactive effects for measures of Class: .00 and .00; for Political

Orientation: $+.11$, $+.07$ and for Liberalism: $-.11$, $+.74$. The latter estimate is obviously too large, suggesting a serious reactive effect, but the estimates are suspiciously inconsistent as well. The dependence of these estimates
on the model must be remembered. As we will see from the next approach to
assessing validity, there is reason to doubt the validity of the second measure
of Liberalism. In general, a meaningful interpretation of these estimates
turns on the results of this following approach.

The other approach to the study of this matrix and its underlying model
is to test the model (in Fig. 22.3). However, a direct test of this model is
impossible; in fact, we cannot even identify the estimates of all the unknown
paths, with the exception of s and t as shown above. We have six observed
correlations to use in solving for seven unknown paths. A necessary but not
sufficient condition for estimating these paths is that we have as many knowns
—correlations here—as unknown paths. Hence we cannot identify the paths
in this model.

However, we can consider a simpler, overidentified model as shown in
Figure 22.5. It assumes random measurement error and we can test this
assumption (Costner, 1969; Blalock, 1969). In particular, we can test the
model against the alternative of the model which underlies the collapsed
matrix.

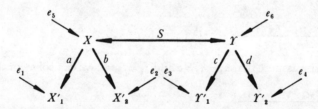

Figure 22.5. An overidentified causal model of measures of two underlying concepts,
X and Y.

Starting with the overidentified model, we can deduce the following equality, which Costner called the "consistency criterion":

$$(11) \quad (r_{X'_1 Y'_2})(r_{X'_2 Y'_1}) = (r_{X'_1 Y'_1})(r_{X'_2 Y'_2})$$

This criterion can be first used to test the overidentified model. In theory, the
criterion should hold. If, empirically, it *does* hold, we have failed to reject the
model against certain alternative models for which the criterion should not,
in theory, have held. On the other hand, there are other alternative models
for which the model should have also held, in theory, and against these our

test of the overidentified model has no power. That is, we cannot distinguish between the overidentified model above and this latter group of hypothetical alternatives. Any one of them might be the "best" model, but we cannot decipher which one that is.

We can illustrate the above principles by first considering the model underlying the collapsed matrix. We can substitute our expressions for the correlations from equations 3, 4, 5 and 6 into equation 11 above, in order to see if the consistency criterion should hold for this model.

$$(12) \quad [a_1 S(c_2 + tc_1) + f_1(h_2 + th_1)][Sc_1(a_2 + sa_1) + h_1(f_2 + sf_1)]$$
$$\neq [(a_2 Sc_1 + f_1 h_1)][(S)[(a_2 + sa_1)(c_2 + tc_1) + (f_2 + sf_1)(h_2 + th_1)]]$$

As might be suspected, we see that the consistency criterion would not, in theory, hold if the alternative model were correct. If the observed correlations are now substituted into equation 11 and the criterion (or equality) empirically holds, we can reject this alternative model and any other for which the criterion would not in theory hold. If, in contrast, the criterion does not empirically hold, we could reject the basic overidentified model, but without any indication of which among many plausible alternative models is more appropriate.

However, what if we think it would be reasonable to assume certain epistemic or methods paths equal? For example, the initial and subsequent measures of X might be identical in content (as they were for measures of Class). There is no apparent reason why the epistemic paths to X'_1 and X'_2 should differ. Of course, if the content of repeated measures of another concept Y are not identical (as they were for Political Orientation and Liberalism), then such assumptions may not seem warranted.

If we are in a position to assume certain methods or epistemic paths equal, then the unhappy result may be that, in theory, the criterion *will* hold. Whether the criterion will or will not hold depends on which combination of assumptions is made. Thus, it can be shown that the criterion will hold for models similar to those in Figure 22.3, where both sets of epistemic and methods paths are assumed equal (i.e., $a_1 = a_2 = a$; $c_1 = c_2 = c$; $f_1 = f_2 = f$; $h_1 = h_2 = h$). It will also hold when any three of these equalities are assumed, or when the epistemic and methods' paths leading to one or the other of the pairs of measures of one of the concepts are assumed equal (i.e., $a_1 = a_2$, $f_1 = f_2$ or $c_1 = c_2$, $h_1 = h_2$).

In the event that a researcher makes these combinations of assumptions, he will be effectively unable to test the basic, overidentified model against the particular alternative of the model underlying the collapsed matrix. That is, he will not be able to distinguish between these two models. To avoid this dilemma, nonidentical items purporting to measure the same concept could be used, making unlikely the equality of epistemic and methods paths and hence making any assumption of equality unplausible.

It can also be shown that the criterion will *not* hold in theory, where only one of the four equalities just considered is assumed, or where the equalities for both pairs of methods or epistemic paths are assumed to hold.

If we consider a second, alternative model, similar to the first except that no reactive effects are postulated (see Figure 22.6A), the same results follow. The criterion in theory *will* hold if the epistemic and methods paths to just one of the two sets of measures are assumed equal, or if any three or all four of the pairs of epistemic or methods paths are assumed equal. It will *not* hold, again, if only one of the four pairs are equal, or if both pairs of methods or of epistemic paths are assumed to be equal.

There are other conceivable alternative models. The methods variable might affect only one of the two measures of each concept (Fig. 22.6B), in which case the criterion will not hold (with or without reactive effects included in the model). If the methods' variable affects both measures of only one concept, however, the criterion will hold, as it will if only reactive effects (and no method's effects) are postulated in a model (Figs. 22.6C, 6D).

Clearly the utility of our approach will be limited when certain epistemic or methods' paths are assumed to be equal. The remedy is either to use differently worded or constructed measures of the same concept so that such assumptions are unwarranted, or (following Costner, 1969) increase the number of measures of each concept to three thereby facilitating the distinction between the overidentified model and the alternatives previously confounded with that model.

An example

Let us apply the second procedure above to the illustration in Table 22.1. We will be testing three, overidentified models against the distinguishable alternatives just enumerated: a model identical to that shown in Figure 22.5 where the two variables are Class and Political Orientation; a model where the variables are Class and Liberalism, and one where the variables are Political Orientation and Liberalism.

Substituting the appropriate correlations into equation 10, for each model. we have:

Model: Class—Political Orientation
$$(-.09)(-.10) = (-.09)(-.10)$$

Model: Class—Liberalism
$$(.00) \quad (.00) = \quad (.00)(-.08)$$

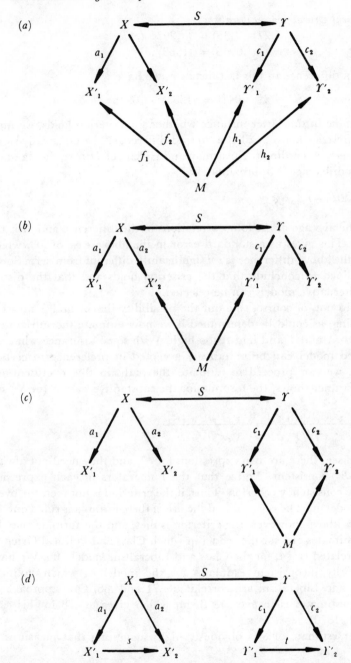

Figure 22.6. (A–D) Some alternative models.

Model: *Political Orientation—Liberalism*

$$(.27) \quad (.35) = \quad (.29) \quad (.47)$$
$$(.0945) = (.1363)$$

Forming a difference in this last instance, we have

$$.0418 = (.1363) - (.0945)$$

To determine in this latter instance whether the criterion holds, we must see if the difference above, called a "tetrad difference," is statistically significant from zero. According to Spearman and Holzinger (1924), the standard error of this difference is approximately:[3]

$$(13) \quad \sigma_{\text{dif}} = 2r(1 - r)/\sqrt{N}$$

where r is the average of the four correlations in the difference and N is the sample size. This gives us a standard error in the above case of .03, which means that the above difference is *not* significantly different from zero. So we may be inclined to conclude that the criterion holds and that the distinguishable alternative models can be rejected.

This would not, of course, rule out the possibility that X and Y measure the same thing, as could be determined if we now estimate the substantive path between X and Y and find it too high. With some assurances that the overidentified model can be tentatively accepted in preference to certain alternatives, we can proceed to estimate the paths in this overidentified model. As Costner shows, the formula for the substantive path S (or S^2) is:

$$(14) \quad S^2 = \frac{(r_{X'_1 Y'_1})(r_{X'_2 Y'_2})}{(r_{X'_1 X'_2})(r_{Y'_1 Y'_2})} = \frac{(r_{X'_1 Y'_2})(r_{X'_2 Y'_1})}{(r_{X'_1 X'_2})(r_{Y'_1 Y'_2})}$$

As we can see, there are two expressions for S^2, and they need not always be empirically consistent. Notice that the numerators of each expression comprise the consistency criterion. Thus, if the criterion is not met, the overidentified model must be rejected and the use of these formula is ruled out. In the examples above, however, the criterion is met, and the formula may be used. The estimates of S for the model in which Class and Political Orientation are correlated is .14, for the Class and Liberalism model, .00. We have two empirically inconsistent estimates for the model in which Political Orientation and Liberalism are correlated: .71 and .86. One approach to inconsistent estimates is to average them, which gives us .78 in this case (Goldberger, 1970).

This latter estimate of S is obviously high, suggesting that measures of

---

3. This holds unless both N and r are small, when slight differences in the thousands digit appear between this approximation and the true formula.

Political Orientation and Liberalism measure the "same thing." Inspection of Table 22.1 suggests that this result is due more to the second measure of Liberalism, Lib. 2, than to Lib. 1, since the correlation between Political Orientation 1 and Liberalism 2 is a high .47, while the correlation between Lib. 1 and Pol. Or. 2 is a more modest .29. On this basis, then, we would conclude that at least some of our measures of Political Orientation and Liberalism do not discriminate and hence, lack "discriminant validity."

There is a problem, however, with the use of Costner's "consistency criterion." "Tetrad differences" composed of small (roughly less than .30)[4] correlations will rarely be significantly different from zero, whatever their individual values. The differences between the products of correlations this size are simply too small for the tests of the overidentified model to have any power against the alternative models. Only if the average size of the correlations being multiplied are larger than those shown in Table 22.1 can a test for a model acquire reasonable power.

There are two ways to "increase" this average of correlations. The first is carefully to select pairs or larger groups of measures that, from theoretical reasoning, should be strongly interrelated. They may turn out to be so highly correlated as to lead us to conclude that they are measures of the "same thing," i.e., that certain measures might be better conceptualized as measures of the *same* underlying concept rather than of *two* distinct underlying concepts. This situation is illustrated below with respect to measures of Political Orientation and Liberalism, as we have seen. What is important to show in a validity study, in summary, is that by using various methods of measurement, traits which might be expected to be related on theoretical grounds are empirically distinct.

---

4. The reader may be puzzled about the value, .30. Why not .20 or .40? We arrived at this as a rule of thumb after calculating a great many tetrad differences and checking for their significance. A more systematic determination would be to graph for values of r (the average of the four correlations in the difference), the values of one and two standard errors of the tetrad difference. We would then superimpose on this graph sets of random normal distributions of tetrad differences of the form, $(a_1 a_2 - b_1 b_2)$, with separate distributions of differences centered about successive values of r (i.e., .10, .20 and .30, etc.).

To simplify the generation of differences, we would assume that both values of a (a_1 and a_2) are less than r, while both values of b are greater than r. Each distribution of differences would be further subject to specified lower limits in the value of the a's and upper limits on the value of the b's. For example, for $r = .20$, we would generate a random normal distribution of twenty differences subject to the constraint that a_1 and a_2 lie between .10 and .20 and that the b's lie between .20 and .30.

Having superimposed several distributions of tetrad differences centered about various values of r onto the graph of the one and two standard errors, we could determine by rough inspection what proportion of these differences would be greater than, say, two standard errors.

In lieu of this procedure, we have plotted the maximum values of the tetrad differences that would be generated by the above procedure. It appears from the resulting graph that the estimate of .30 is still reasonable, though if anything a little too low.

The second approach which makes use of the estimates of the paths in the overidentified model is tó provisionally correct the correlations in the matrix for attenuation. One of the assumptions made in this model is that the errors are uncorrelated. This assumption is also the basis of the correction for attenuation. Until we have satisfactorily tested the overidentified model, and in particular this assumption, however, our correction for attenuation can only be provisional.

This correction is illustrated in Table 22.2. The most straightforward way of obtaining the necessary estimates of reliability, considering the literature

Table 22.2. Correlation matrix for the collapsed (augmented)
matrix corrected for attenuation

Order of Measurement	Initial			Subsequent		
Measures:	Class 1	Pol. Or. 1	Lib. 1	Class 2	Pol. Or. 2	Lib. 2
Initial						
Class 1	. . . .	. . . .	. . . .	1.00	−.14	−.23
Pol. Or. 1.	−.13	. . . .	. . . .	−.13	1.00	1.10*
Lib. 1	.00	.63	. . . .	.00	.67	1.00
Subsequent						
Class 2	. . . .	. . . .	. . . .	. . . .	. . . .	. . . .
Pol. Or. 2.	. . . .	. . . .	. . . .	−.14	. . . .	. . . .
Lib. 2	. . . .	. . . .	. . . .	−.13	.81	. . . .

* See footnote 6.

on reliability reviewed earlier, is to provisionally estimate the paths in the overidentified model. Once we have these estimates, we can estimate the reliability of our measures. The formula for the four epistemic paths in the overidentified model (see Fig. 22.5) are shown below (from Costner, 1969).[5]

$$(15) \quad a^2 = (r_{x'_1 x'_2}) \frac{(r_{x'_1 Y'_2})}{(r_{x'_2 Y'_2})} = (r_{x'_1 x'_2}) \frac{(r_{x'_1 Y'_1})}{(r_{x'_2 Y'_1})}$$

$$(16) \quad b^2 = (r_{x'_1 x'_2}) \frac{(r_{x'_2 Y'_2})}{(r_{x'_1 Y'_2})} = (r_{x'_1 x'_2}) \frac{(r_{x'_2 Y'_1})}{(r_{x'_1 Y'_1})}$$

5. The reader should take note of Costner's footnote 4 (1969) before using these formulas. Furthermore, anything more than a provisional calculation of these epistemic paths using these formulas should depend on (1) the results of the tests of the overidentified model, as described above, and (2) on the sample size and hence probable sampling error. Even when the overidentified model survives rejection, as it does in the case of the correlation of Class and Political Orientation, the estimates of epistemic paths can in some instances be greater than

(17) $\quad c^2 = \left(r_{Y'_1 Y'_2}\right)\dfrac{\left(r_{X'_2 Y'_1}\right)}{\left(r_{X'_2 Y'_2}\right)} = \left(r_{Y'_1 Y'_2}\right)\dfrac{\left(r_{X'_1 Y'_1}\right)}{\left(r_{X'_1 Y'_2}\right)}$

(18) $\quad d^2 = \left(r_{Y'_1 Y'_2}\right)\dfrac{\left(r_{X'_2 Y'_2}\right)}{\left(r_{X'_2 Y'_1}\right)} = \left(r_{Y'_1 Y'_2}\right)\dfrac{\left(r_{X'_1 Y'_2}\right)}{\left(r_{X'_1 Y'_1}\right)}$

The reliability of X' and Y' in terms of these paths is:

(19) $\quad R_{XX'} = ab$ and

(20) $\quad R_{YY'} = cd$

Substituting the above expressions for a, b, c, and d, we see that

(21) $\quad R_{XX'} = r_{X'_1 X'_2}$

(22) $\quad R_{YY'} = r_{Y'_1 Y'_2}$

Thus, our estimates of reliability are nothing but the v's in the multitrait-multimethod matrix (Werts and Linn, 1969).

We can now proceed to correct our correlations for attenuation (see Table 22.2). For example, the expression for the disattenuated value of $r_{X'_1 Y'_2}{}^*$ is

(23) $\quad r_{X'_1 Y'_2}{}^* = r_{X'_1 Y'_2} / \sqrt{R_{XX'} R_{YY'}}$

If we let $X = $ Class and $Y = $ Political Orientation, we correct the correlation between Class 1 and Pol. Or. 1 as follows:

(24) $\quad -.13 = -.09 / \sqrt{(.97)(.50)}$

In a similar fashion, the remaining correlations in Table 22.1 have been corrected. Notice that the average size of the disattenuated correlations is larger than the size of the unattenuated correlations.[6]

---

one. While it is possible for a path coefficient to legitimately assume a value greater than 1.00, such a result in this context is a reflection of the small off-diagonal correlations. These are often statistically insignificant and subject to such sampling fluctuations as to undermine their interpretation. To make a meaningful interpretation of epistemic paths possible, one must attempt to include in the matrix measures of concepts that are expected to be at least modestly related to one another. Correlations in the off-diagonals of the matrix will then be larger, and more likely significant, and the estimates of epistemic paths more likely to be stable and less than one.

6. When an off-diagonal correlation, e.g., the one for Pol. Or. 1—Lib. 2 is larger than the approximate average of the reliability estimates for the two measures, the correction for attenuation will produce disattenuated correlations greater than one. We can view these disattenuated correlations greater than 1 as the result of mistakenly assuming that the overidentified model is "correct" and that there is no correlated error due to methods or other factors. This mistaken assumption is, however, formally discerned using the consistency criterion rather than from the fact that the correlations provisionally corrected for attenuation are greater than 1.00.

If we now check our previous conclusion that the consistency criterion was satisfied for the model correlating Political Orientation and Liberalism, we find that the tetrad difference of correlations is:

(25) $(.63)(.81) = (.67)(1.00)$

Forming a difference, we have

$(.51) - (.67) = -.16$

The standard error of this difference using equation 12 is .023. Quite clearly, this difference *is* significantly different from zero. We now must formally conclude that at least one of the measures involved does not discriminate. As we saw previously, it appears that the measure, Lib. 2, dealing with open housing, does not discriminate itself from the political orientation measures and might be better thought of as a third measure of political orientation.

The "full" matrix

The causal model underlying the second of the two augmented matrices is not easily portrayed. As we can see from an illustration of the full matrix in Table 22.3, we have now allowed for the possibility of interaction between methods and other variables. Rather than show this interaction directly (following Boudon, 1968, and showing paths bisecting paths), we think it would be better "understood" that the epistemic paths and reactive paths in the model we finally set down may have different values for each of the four combinations of methods. Thought of in this manner, we might use as our model Figure 22.5 and proceed as before to estimate its paths.

Could we assume, however, that the errors of such a model are uncorrelated? Not likely, for while methods as a general factor no longer operates on measures, individual methods may—producing what may otherwise appear as correlated errors. In the monomethod blocks, for example, errors attached to the measures might be correlated because of a single underlying method; in the heteromethod blocks, because of two underlying methods that lack complete independence of each other.

So different models, understood to reflect possible interaction as well as the influence of individual methods, are necessary for the monomethod and heteromethod blocks of the full matrix (see Figs. 22.7 and 22.8). (Note that the latter model is a replica of the model for the original matrix.)

The first step in assessing the full matrix is to compare the values in each of these four blocks with the values in the collapsed matrix. This comparison may, fortunately, suggest the absence of interaction or of specific methods' effects of greater or lesser size than that possessed by the general methods

Table 22.3. Illustration of a full (augmented) matrix

Method		Interview						Questionnaire					
		Initial			Subsequent			Initial			Subsequent		
Order of measurement	Measures:	Class 1	Pol. Or. 1	Lib. 1	Class 2	Pol. Or. 2	Lib. 2	Class 1	Pol. Or. 1	Lib. 1	Class 2	Pol. Or. 2	Lib. 2
INTERVIEW Initial	Class 1	.....	.....	.....	1.00	−.24	−.10	.....	.....	.....	.96*	−.24	−.11
	Pol. Or. 1	−.14	.....	.....	−.14	.40*	.44*	.....	.....	.....	.01	.71*	.49*
	Lib. 1	.00	.36	.....	.00	.33	.32	.....	.....	.28	−.06	.36	.51*
Subsequent	Class 2	.....	(N=56)	.....	.....	.....	.....	.....	(N=50)	.....	.....	.....	.....
	Pol. Or. 2	.....	.....	.....	−.24	.....	.....	.....	.....	.....	−.25	.....	.....
	Lib. 2	.....	.....	.....	−.10	.16	.....	.....	.....	.....	−.12	.58*	.....
QUESTIONNAIRE Initial	Class 1	.....	.....	.....	.94*	.00	−.14	.....	.....	.....	1.00*	.00	−.10
	Pol. Or. 1	−.01	.....	.....	−.01	.54*	.42*	.....	.....	.37	−.24	.44*	.54*
	Lib. 1	+.17	.07	.....	.11	.20	.24	.....	.....	.....	−.07	.30	.42*
Subsequent	Class 2	.....	(N=63)	.....	.....	.....	.....	.....	(N=57)	.....	.....	.....	.....
	Pol. Or. 2	.....	.....	.....	.00	.....	.....	.....	.....	.....	.00	.....	.....
	Lib. 2	.....	.....	.....	−.10	.45*	.....	.....	.....	.....	−.10	.27	.....

* Significant at the .01 level.

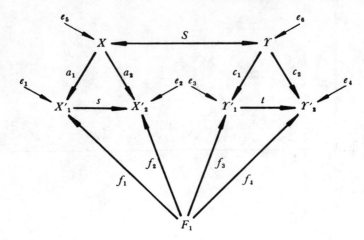

Figure 22.7. *A causal model of two correlated measures in a monomethod block of the full augmented matrix.*

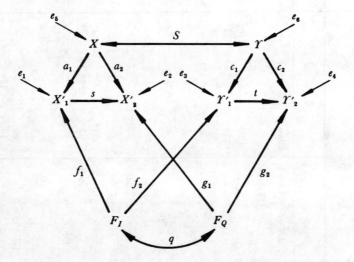

Figure 22.8. *A causal model of two correlated measures in a heteromethod block of the full augmented matrix.*

variable in the collapsed matrix. Note, however, that such specific methods effects and interaction are confounded here; we cannot discern their *respective* influences. If there is a great deal of discrepancy evident in these comparisons, we can safely conclude that interaction or methods effects are present. If there is little discrepancy, we can take little comfort from that fact, because there may be certain combinations of methods paths and interaction effects that produce a zero or near zero difference. Note also that this comparison is complicated by the reduction of sample size in the blocks of the full matrix as compared with the size of the collapsed matrix.

A second step possible only in the monomethod blocks is to estimate the reactive effects among measures. The procedure is the same as discussed before. This estimate may differ, both from those in other monomethod blocks and from the estimate made in the collapsed matrix. This may reflect either the interaction of methods and reactive effects or the differences between the effects of a general methods factor and specific methods factor for that particular monomethod block.

The final and most basic step is the use of Costner's consistency criterion. Since the models for the monomethod and heteromethod blocks differ, the test of an overidentified model (Fig. 22.5 again) against the alternatives posed by the models will not be equally powerful.

MONOMETHOD BLOCKS

Because the model for the monomethod blocks of the full matrix (Fig. 22.7) is structurally identical to the model for the collapsed matrix, the previous discussion of the collapsed matrix applies and need not be repeated. The only difference in the models is that the specific method factor replaces the general methods factor.

HETEROMETHOD BLOCKS

The power of a test of the overidentified model (Fig. 22.5) againt the alternative of the model for the heteromethod blocks (Fig. 22.8) is slightly greater than in the case of the monomethod blocks. In the case where there are no reactive effects, it can be shown (Althauser and Heberlein, 1970) that the criterion will be met only if two conditions are satisfied: q, the correlation between specific methods, is ± 1 and $c/d = \pm p/o$ and $a/b = \pm n/m$. If methods are carefully selected, the possibility that $q = \pm 1$ can be ruled out. If reactive effects are not zero, the criterion will not be met.

Application of these procedures to the full matrix must be tempered, of course, by the results of previous analysis of the collapsed matrix. Thus, looking at Table 22.3, we are not surprised to find a similar pattern of Pol. Or. $1 = \text{Lib. 2}$ correlations. Only in the upper right block (Interview-Questionnaire combination) is the consistency criterion satisfied (after provisional correction for attenuation); in the other three blocks, it is not met as in the collapsed matrix. Beyond finding patterns here that parallel the collapsed matrix, one can informally examine corresponding correlations in the four blocks for pronounced deviations from the collapsed matrix or from each other. Unfortunately, there will be many possible but confounded explanations for most patterns; and the smaller sample size within blocks will increase sampling error, further complicating such informal comparisons.

Our example in Table 22.2 is not entirely suitable for such comparisons, since the inadequacy of the Lib. 2 measures of Liberalism dominate the patterns within blocks, and the average sample size of about 57 is perhaps too small to sufficiently dampen sampling error. Nonetheless, we are theoretically able to distinguish the additive effects of a general methods factor in the collapsed matrix from the combination of interaction and specific methods factors in this full matrix.

Summary and discussion

Working from causal models of intercorrelated measures of different concepts, we have proposed a modification in the model underlying Campbell and Fiske's "multitrait-multimethod matrix." The principle change is in not confounding methods and traits in measures, and in measuring indicators of underlying concepts with both (in the case of two) methods. This has led us to two augmented multitrait-multimethod matrices: a collapsed matrix focusing primarily on reactive effects and the additive effects of a general methods factor; and a full matrix portraying the non-additive effects of methods and the effects of individual methods. The principal device for assessing the presence of validity (or the verity of an assumption that only random errors of measurement are present in the models) of measures has been Costner's "consistency criterion." The criterion is deduced from a simpler, overidentified model showing no methods or reactive effects, and then it is theoretically determined whether alternative models comprised of the models underlying the matrices will meet the criterion or not. If they should not, theoretically, and do not, empirically, then we can reject them in favor of the overidentified model.

Because some alternative models *are* distinguishable from the overidentified model while others *are not*, the use of the consistency criterion in these cases where there are two measures/concept is awkward. It requires the full use of one's theory—"main" and "auxiliary" and circumspection in the conclusions drawn. It is a matter of opinion only, but it seems to us that when you have three measures/concept and follow Costner's procedure (1969), you choose a cumbersome but interpretatively sounder procedure over a less cumbersome but interpretatively more awkward and incomplete procedure as just outlined. This may appear to some as an "even trade-off," but what may tip the balance in the direction of attempts like ours is the impracticality and cost of taking three measures of each concept whose validity we are concerned with. We doubt that the behavior of researchers will easily or quickly adapt to the advantages of taking three measures. If this bears out, then either the procedure above or some alternative approaches yet to be developed will have to serve in our assessments of the validity of our measures.

References

ALTHAUSER, ROBERT P., and HEBERLEIN, THOMAS A. 1970. "A Causal Assessment of Validity and the Multitrait-Multimethod Matrix," in Edgar Borgatta (Ed.), *Sociological Methodology* 1970. San Francisco : Jossey-Bass, Inc., pp. 151–169.

BLALOCK, H. M., Jr. 1969. "Multiple Indicators and the Causal Approach to Measurement Errors," *American Journal of Sociology*, pp. 264–272.

BOUDON, RAYMOND. 1968. "A New Look at Correlation Analysis," in H. M. Blalock, Jr., and A. B. Blalock (Eds.), *Methodology in Social Research*. New York: McGraw-Hill, pp. 199–235.

CAMPBELL, DONALD T., and FISKE, DONALD W. 1959. "Convergent and Discriminant Validation by the Multitrait-Multimethod Matrix," *Psychological Bulletin*, 56: 81–105.

COSTNER, HERBERT L. 1969. "Theory, Deduction and Rules of Correspondence," *American Journal of Sociology*, 75: 245–263.

CRONBACH, L. J. 1951. "Coefficient Alpha and the Internal Structure of Tests," *Psychometrika*, 16: 297–334.

GOLDBERGER, ARTHUR S. 1970. "On Boudon's Method of Linear Causal Analysis," *American Sociological Review*, 35 (February): 97–101.

GOODE, WILLIAM, and HATT, PAUL. 1952. *Methods in Social Research*. New York: McGraw-Hill.

GUTTMAN, L. A. 1945. "A Basis for Analyzing Test-Retest Reliability," *Psychometrika*, 10: 255–282.

HEBERLEIN, THOMAS A. 1969. "The Correction for Attenuation and the Multitrait-Multimethod Matrix: Some Prospects and Pitfalls," University of Wisconsin, M.A. thesis.

HEISE, DAVID. 1969. "Separating Reliability and Stability in Test-Retest Correlation," *American Sociological Review*, 34: 93–101.

JOHNSON, H. C. 1950. "Test Reliability and Correction for Attenuation," *Psychometrika*, 15: 115–119.

KERLINGER, FRED. 1965. *Foundations of Behavioral Research*. New York: Holt, Rinehart, and Winston.

LORD, FREDERICK M., and NOVICK, M. R. 1968. *Statistical Theories of Mental Test Scores*. Reading, Mass.: Addison-Wesley.

SELLTIZ, CLAIRE, JAHODA, MARIE, DEUTSCH, MORTON, and COOK, STUART W. 1967. *Research Methods in Social Relations*. New York: Holt, Rinehart, and Winston.

SPEARMAN, C., and HOLZINGER, K. 1924. "The Sampling Error in the Theory of Two Factors," *British Journal of Psychology*, 15: 17–19.

WERTS, CHARLES E., and LINN, ROBERT L. 1970. "Cautions in Applying Various Procedures for Determining the Reliability and Validity of Multiple-Item Scales," *American Sociological Review*, 35: 757–759.

Chapter 23

ESTIMATING THE PARAMETERS OF PATH MODELS INVOLVING UNMEASURED VARIABLES

CHARLES E. WERTS
ROBERT L. LINN
KARL G. JÖRESKOG
Educational Testing Service

Costner (1969), Blalock (1969), and Heise (1969) have demonstrated the application of path analysis to problems involving multiple indicators of underlying constructs. In this type of problem the researcher is frequently called on to deal with overidentified systems, e.g., Costner has demonstrated the use of the "consistency criterion" (Spearman tetrad difference) as a test of the fit of the data to the hypothetical model in simple two construct systems with two independent measures of each construct. The purpose of this note is to discuss the use of a general method for factor analysis (Jöreskog, 1969a) to obtain a single "best fit" estimate of each parameter and an overall goodness of fit test for the consistency of the data with the model. Factor analysis is a special case of Jöreskog's (1970) general method for the analysis of covariance structures that could be used instead of the confirmatory factor analysis procedure discussed in this paper.

I. Using confirmatory factor analysis to obtain estimates for path models

Jöreskog's confirmatory factor analysis procedures allow the investigator to fix some parameters (called "fixed") of the model and estimate the others (called "free"). This procedure can be illustrated with the problem depicted in Figure 23.1 in which three measures X_0, X_1 and X_2 of mathematics achievement (T_1) are administered at time 1 and two of these measures X_3 and X_4

Paper prepared especially for *Causal Models in the Social Sciences* are repeated at a later time 2 (T_2). Thus X_1 and X_3 are obtained from the same test as are X_2 and X_4 and the corresponding errors of measurement are assumed to be correlated for this reason. Suppose the researcher wants to estimate the reliabilities of the tests and the correlation between T_1 and T_2. In order to analyze this model the path analyst would write the following equations involving the correlation among variables and path coefficients (b^*):

$$\rho_{01} = b^*_{X_0 T_1} b^*_{X_1 T_1},$$

$$\rho_{02} = b^*_{X_0 T_1} b^*_{X_2 T_1},$$

$$\rho_{12} = b^*_{X_1 T_1} b^*_{X_2 T_1},$$

$$\rho_{03} = b^*_{X_0 T_1} \rho_{T_1 T_2} b^*_{X_3 T_2},$$

$$\rho_{04} = b^*_{X_0 T_1} \rho_{T_1 T_2} b^*_{X_4 T_2}, \tag{1}$$

$$\rho_{13} = b^*_{X_1 T_1} \rho_{T_1 T_2} b^*_{X_3 T_2} + b^*_{X_1 e_1} \rho_{e_1 e_3} b^*_{X_3 e_3},$$

$$\rho_{14} = b^*_{X_1 T_1} \rho_{T_1 T_2} b^*_{X_4 T_2},$$

$$\rho_{23} = b^*_{X_2 T_1} \rho_{T_1 T_2} b^*_{X_3 T_2},$$

$$\rho_{24} = b^*_{X_2 T_1} \rho_{T_1 T_2} b^*_{X_4 T_2} + b^*_{X_2 e_2} \rho_{e_2 e_4} b^*_{X_4 e_4},$$

and $\quad \rho_{34} = b^*_{X_3 T_2} b^*_{X_4 T_2};$

where $b^*_{X_1 e_1} = \sqrt{1 - (b^*_{X_1 T_1})^2},$

$\qquad b^*_{X_2 e_2} = \sqrt{1 - (b^*_{X_2 T_2})^2},$

$\qquad b^*_{X_3 e_3} = \sqrt{1 - (b^*_{X_3 T_2})^2},$ and

$\qquad b^*_{X_4 e_4} = \sqrt{1 - (b^*_{X_4 T_2})^2}.$

From the perspective of structural analysis these equations can only be useful for exploring the identification question. If each of the path coefficients can be expressed as a function of the correlations in at least one way, then the system is identifiable. The factor analyst who is dealing with this type of problem prefers to explore the identification question in matrix form (Jöreskog, 1969a, p. 186), checking to see if there is a "unique" solution for each parameter, i.e., if all linear transformations of the factors that leave the fixed parameters unchanged also leave the free parameters unchanged. In Jöreskog's approach, finding all possible solutions of these path equations (as in Costner, 1969) has no purpose (except for possibly exploring the identification question). All that is required is that the fundamental structural equations from which the path equations derive be stated in matrix form. To formulate the above model in terms of Jöreskog's general model, one has to write a structural equation for each observed variable. Each equation relates an observed variable to some unobserved variables. In Figure 23.1, there are seven unobserved variables all together, namely, the two true

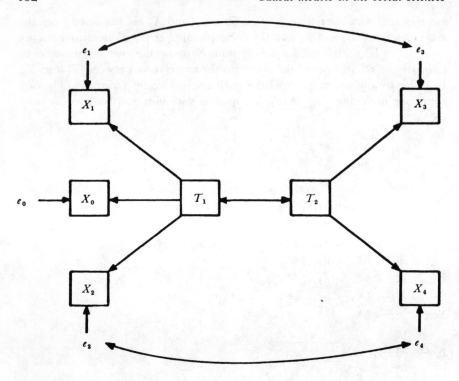

Figure 23.1.

scores T_1 and T_2 and the five error scores e_0, e_1, e_2, e_3 and e_4. For a given observed variable X_i there are as many terms in the equation for X_i as there are arrows pointing to X_i in the graph. It is convenient to regard each variable as being measured as deviations from its mean so that mean values can be excluded in the equations. The equations corresponding to Figure 23.1 are

$$\left.\begin{array}{l} X_0 = \beta_0 T_1 + e_0 \\ X_1 = \beta_1 T_1 + e_1 \\ X_2 = \beta_2 T_1 + e_2 \\ X_3 = \beta_3 T_2 + e_3 \\ X_4 = \beta_4 T_2 + e_4 \end{array}\right\}, \tag{2}$$

The error terms are assumed to be uncorrelated with T_1 and T_2. The path equations (1) may be derived from equations (2) using the procedure given by Duncan (1966). If the error terms were all mutually uncorrelated, the equations (2) would represent a factor analysis model with two oblique factors and certain factor loadings specified to be zero (Jöreskog, 1969a) or as a model for two sets of congeneric tests (Jöreskog, 1969c). However, when some error terms are correlated it is necessary to formulate the model differently. Equations (2) may be written in matrix form as

$$
\begin{pmatrix} X_0 \\ X_1 \\ X_2 \\ X_3 \\ X_4 \end{pmatrix} = \begin{bmatrix} \beta_0 & 0 & 1 & 0 & 0 & 0 & 0 \\ \beta_1 & 0 & 0 & 1 & 0 & 0 & 0 \\ \beta_2 & 0 & 0 & 0 & 1 & 0 & 0 \\ 0 & \beta_3 & 0 & 0 & 0 & 1 & 0 \\ 0 & \beta_4 & 0 & 0 & 0 & 0 & 1 \end{bmatrix} \begin{pmatrix} T_1 \\ T_2 \\ e_0 \\ e_1 \\ e_2 \\ e_3 \\ e_4 \end{pmatrix} \tag{3}
$$

It was assumed that e_0, e_1 and e_2 are uncorrelated and so also e_3 and e_4 but that e_1 is correlated with e_3 and e_2 is correlated with e_4. The variance-covariance matrix of $(T_1, T_2, e_0, e_1, e_2, e_3, e_4)$ is therefore of the form

$$
\Phi = \begin{bmatrix} 1 & & & & & & \\ \rho_{T_1 T_2} & 1 & & & & & \\ 0 & 0 & \sigma^2_{e_0} & & \text{symmetric} & & \\ 0 & 0 & 0 & \sigma^2_{e_1} & & & \\ 0 & 0 & 0 & 0 & \sigma^2_{e_2} & & \\ 0 & 0 & 0 & \sigma_{e_1 e_3} & 0 & \sigma^2_{e_3} & \\ 0 & 0 & 0 & 0 & \sigma_{e_2 e_4} & 0 & \sigma^2_{e_4} \end{bmatrix} \tag{4}
$$

The ones in the diagonal of this matrix indicate that the variances of T_1 and T_2 were for convenience standardized to unit variance and the error variances in the diagonal indicate that these variances are "free parameters" to be estimated by the program. The off diagonal zeros indicate that the corresponding factors are assumed uncorrelated; the remaining off diagonal covariances ($\rho_{T_1 T_2}$, $\sigma_{e_1 e_3}$, $\sigma_{e_2 e_4}$) between the correlated factors being estimated ("free parameters") by the program. The covariance between T_1 and T_2 is a correlation because of the standardization. The basic input into Jöreskog's computer program is the identification of fixed and free parameters defined by equations (3) and (4) and the sample variance-covariance matrix or correlation matrix (see Jöreskog, Gruvaeus, and van Thillo, 1970).

From (3) and (4) the population variance-covariance matrix (Σ) of the observed scores ($X_0, X_1, \ldots X_4$) is

$$
\Sigma = \Lambda \Phi \Lambda' \tag{5}
$$

where Λ is the 5×7 matrix of factor loadings from equation (3), Λ' is the transpose of this matrix and Φ is the matrix in (4). This is a special case of Jöreskog's (1969a) confirmatory factor analysis model with five observed scores, seven factors and no residual factors. In this model there are thirteen parameters to be estimated from the data, namely the five

β_i, the five variances $\sigma^2_{e_i}$, the correlation $\rho_{T_1T_2}$ and the two covariances $\sigma_{e_1e_3}$ and $\sigma_{e_2e_4}$. However, there are fifteen (five population variances plus ten population covariances) independent elements in Σ, so that (5) represents a system of fifteen equations in thirteen unknowns. In practice, the population matrix Σ is not available and the parameters have to be estimated from a sample variance-covariance matrix. Two different methods of estimation may be used: the least-squares method and the maximum likelihood method (see Jöreskog, Gruvaeus, and van Thillo, 1970). The maximum likelihood method is based on the assumption that the observed variables have a multivariate normal distribution and with this method a chi-square statistic will be obtained for testing the goodness of fit of the model. Approximate standard errors may also be obtained for each estimated parameter. The least-squares method does not depend on any distributional assumptions but with this method, no goodness of fit statistic is available.

A question that arises in the analysis of models of this kind is: When is it appropriate to standardize the observed variables and use the sample correlation matrix instead of the sample variance-covariance matrix? Standardization is convenient when the units of measurement are arbitrary or irrelevant but should not be done unless the model is scale-free. A model is said to be scale-free if a change in the unit of measurement in one or more of the observed variables can be appropriately absorbed by a corresponding change in the parameters. The model (5) is scale free. For example, it is seen that if we use aX_1 and bX_3 instead of X_1 and X_3, the new parameters β^*_1, β^*_3, $\sigma^2_{e_1}{}^*$, $\sigma^2_{e_3}{}^*$ and $\sigma_{e_1e_3}{}^*$ will be $a\beta_1$, $b\beta_3$, $a^2\sigma^2_{e_1}$, $b^2\sigma^2_{e_3}$ and $ab\sigma_{e_1e_3}$, so that one can get the new estimates from the old with a knowledge about the scale-factors a and b. However, if it is assumed that two or more of the X_i are parallel or tau-equivalent, each of these measures cannot be standardized separately. Standardization can only be done to a common metric for the variables that are assumed to be equivalent.

II. Cautions concerning correlated errors

For the example in Figure 23.1, the model may be phrased in terms of the multitrait-multimethod approach (Campbell and Fiske, 1959) by postulating the existence of one method (M) factor for each of the repeated tests. The structural equations would then be:

$$X_0 = \beta_0 T_1 + e'_0$$
$$X_1 = \beta_1 T_1 + \alpha_1 M_1 + e'_1$$
$$X_2 = \beta_2 T_1 + \alpha_2 M_2 + e'_2 \tag{6}$$
$$X_3 = \beta_3 T_2 + \alpha_3 M_1 + e'_3$$
$$X_4 = \beta_4 T_2 + \alpha_4 M_2 + e'_4$$

where the e'_i are assumed to be mutually uncorrelated and uncorrelated with the T_i or M_i.

It can be shown that α_1, α_2, α_3, and α_4 cannot be separately identified but only the products $(\alpha_1)(\alpha_3)$ and $(\alpha_2)(\alpha_4)$ can be identified. This problem might be handled assuming $\alpha_1 = \alpha_3 = \alpha'$ and $\alpha_2 = \alpha_4 = \alpha''$. Given this assumption (6) can be written

$$
\begin{pmatrix} X_0 \\ X_1 \\ X_2 \\ X_3 \\ X_4 \end{pmatrix} = \begin{bmatrix} \beta_0 & 0 & 0 & 0 \\ \beta_1 & 0 & \alpha' & 0 \\ \beta_2 & 0 & 0 & \alpha'' \\ 0 & \beta_3 & \alpha' & 0 \\ 0 & \beta_4 & 0 & \alpha'' \end{bmatrix} \begin{pmatrix} T_1 \\ T_2 \\ M_1 \\ M_2 \end{pmatrix} + \begin{bmatrix} e'_0 \\ e'_1 \\ e'_2 \\ e'_3 \\ e'_4 \end{bmatrix} \tag{7}
$$

In matrix notation (7) is written as

$$ X = \Lambda F + e' $$

where F is the vector of factors and e' is the vector of residuals. The variance-covariance matrix of the factors is assumed to be

$$
\Phi = \begin{bmatrix} 1 & \rho_{T_1 T_2} & 0 & 0 \\ \rho_{T_1 T_2} & 1 & 0 & 0 \\ 0 & 0 & 1 & 0 \\ 0 & 0 & 0 & 1 \end{bmatrix}
$$

The population variance-covariance matrix is then:

$$ \Sigma = \Lambda \Phi \Lambda' + \psi^2 \tag{8} $$

where ψ^2 is a diagonal matrix of residual variances, i.e., indicating residual terms.

Models (5) and (8) are equivalent. Both have thirteen independent parameters and there is a one-to-one correspondence between the parameters of each model. The purpose of discussing a multitrait-multimethod formulation of the problem is because the assumption that the methods factors are independent of each other and the trait factors must be made explicitly. Hopefully, the investigator will be reminded that such assumptions must be substantively justified. Unless some theoretical specifications are made about the nature of the methods factors, there is no way of considering the reasonableness of the assumptions. If, for example, the methods factor resulted from memory for the items from the first occasion to the second, then the "method" or memory factor in the first test might well be associated with the "method" or memory factor on the second test, the degree of association depending perhaps on the similarity of item formats. Furthermore, a memory factor might well be associated with the mathematics achievement factor (i.e., "trait" in Campbell and Fiske's language) since memory ability may influence mathematics achievement. On close examination the investigator may discover that a "methods" factor may be really just another "trait" factor. For these reasons we strongly recommend against the common practice of drawing correlated error terms on path diagrams without explicit substantive justification. Researchers should try to specify exactly what influences they believe underlie the correlated errors and consider whether such influences may be reasonably assumed to be independent of the true trait factors on which the study has focused.

An important question in multitrait-multimethod models is whether two traits in fact differ. The correlation between T_1 and T_2 is a measure of trait similarity but there are no rules for knowing how high this correlation should be before the traits are considered to be essentially the same trait for theoretical purposes. If the researcher wishes a significance test of whether $\rho_{T_1 T_2} = 1$, then the procedure given by Jöreskog (1969c, pp. 14–17) can be used.

III. Unstandardized path analysis

It can be observed that in dealing with the unmeasured variable problem, Costner (1969), Blalock (1968), and Heise (1969) have typically made assumptions involving correlations, e.g., Heise assumed that reliability remained constant over time. Path analysis may also be performed using unstandardized regression coefficients and assumptions may be made at this level. For example, suppose that in the model depicted in Figure 23.1 that no third measure (X_0) at time 1 was available, which would mean that the model was underidentified (six known versus seven unknown parameters). If the researcher were willing to assume that X_1 and X_2 had the same units of measurement and were measures of the same factor, this would correspond to the assumption that the corresponding unstandardized regression weights were equal, i.e., $B_{X_1 T_1} = B_{X_2 T_1}$ or $R_{X_1 T_1} \sigma_{X_1} = R_{X_2 T_1} \sigma_{X_2}$. The assumption means that the covariance of X_1 with T_1 equals the covariance of X_2 with T_1 and that the corresponding path coefficients are:

$$b^*_{X_1 T_1} = \sqrt{R_{12}(\sigma_2 \div \sigma_1)},$$

and

$$b^*_{X_2 T_1} = \sqrt{R_{12}(\sigma_1 \div \sigma_2)},$$

where $\sigma_i^2 = $ variance of X_i.

Given these coefficients the other unknown coefficients may be computed. In the particular case of repeated tests, it is often more plausible to assume the units of measurement for the same test over time stay constant (e.g., $B_{X_1 T_1} = B_{X_3 T_2}$), although the reliabilities may change (e.g., $R_{X_1 T_1} \neq R_{X_3 T_2}$). This assumption allows one to compute the total regression of T_2 on T_1 as follows:

1. From path analysis of the model in Figure 23.1 (X_0 excluded):

$$R_{23} = b*_{X_2 T_1} R_{T_1 T_2} b*_{X_3 T_2},$$
$$R_{12} = b*_{X_1 T_1} b*_{X_2 T_1}.$$

2. By substitution:

$$R_{23} = \left(\frac{R_{12}}{b*_{X_1 T_1}} \right) R_{T_1 T_2} b*_{X_3 T_2}.$$

3. Substituting in the unstandardized weights

$$b*_{X_1 T_1} = \frac{B_{X_1 T_1} \sigma_{T_1}}{\sigma_1} \text{ and } b*_{X_3 T_2} = \frac{B_{X_3 T_2} \sigma_{T_2}}{\sigma_3} :$$

$$R_{23} = R_{12} \left(\frac{\sigma_1}{B_{X_1 T_1} \sigma_{T_1}} \right) (R_{T_1 T_2}) \left(\frac{B_{X_3 T_2} \sigma_{T_2}}{\sigma_3} \right).$$

4. Since $B_{T_2 T_1} = R_{T_1 T_2} (\sigma_{T_2}/\sigma_{T_1})$, the assumption that $B_{X_1 T_1} = B_{X_3 T_2}$ substituted into step 3 implies that $R_{23} = R_{12} \left(\frac{\sigma_1}{\sigma_3} \right) B_{T_2 T_1}$,

or $B_{T_2 T_1} = \frac{\sigma_{23}}{\sigma_{12}}$.

5. Path analysis also yields the correlation of T_1 and T_2 as:

$$R_{T_1 T_2} = \sqrt{\frac{R_{14} R_{23}}{R_{12} R_{34}}} = \sqrt{\frac{\sigma_{14} \sigma_{23}}{\sigma_{12} \sigma_{34}}}.$$

6. Therefore the ratio of the true variances is:

$$\frac{\sigma_{T_2}}{\sigma_{T_1}} = \frac{B_{T_2 T_1}}{R_{T_1 T_2}} = \frac{\sigma_{23}}{\sigma_{12}} \sqrt{\frac{\sigma_{12} \sigma_{34}}{\sigma_{14} \sigma_{23}}},$$

or $\frac{\sigma_{T_2}}{\sigma_{T_1}} = \sqrt{\frac{\sigma_{23} \sigma_{34}}{\sigma_{12} \sigma_{14}}}.$

When assumptions are to be made at the units of measurement level, it may be simpler for purposes of studying the identification question to write the path equations in terms of covariances and unstandardized regression weights, e.g., the equation for Figure 23.1 (X_0 excluded) would be:

$$\sigma_{14} = B_{X_1 T_1} \sigma_{T_1 T_2} B_{X_4 T_2} = B_{X_1 T_1} B_{T_2 T_1} B_{X_4 T_2} \sigma^2_{T_1},$$
$$\sigma_{23} = B_{X_2 T_1} \sigma_{T_1 T_2} B_{X_3 T_2} = B_{X_2 T_1} B_{T_2 T_1} B_{X_4 T_2} \sigma^2_{T_1},$$
$$\sigma_{12} = B_{X_1 T_1} B_{X_2 T_1} \sigma^2_{T_1}, \text{ and}$$
$$\sigma_{34} = B_{X_3 T_2} B_{X_4 T_2} \sigma^2_{T_2}.$$

The purpose in presenting the algebra of unstandardized systems is that the user of Jöreskog's program needs to understand the consequences of various assumptions and the question of identifiability needs to be explored prior to actual computations. Thus the user must know that assuming $B_{X_1 T_1} = B_{X_2 T_1}$ leads to the identification of the corresponding path coefficients in the Figure 23.1 model (excluding X_0), whereas the assumption that $B_{X_1 T_1} = B_{X_3 T_2}$ does not identify the corresponding path coefficients but fixes the ratio of the variance in T_2 to the variance in T_1. In the former case it is permissible to standardize both T_1 and T_2, whereas in the latter case only one of these factors should be standardized (e.g., if T_1 is standardized then the program estimates the true unstandardized regression weight $B_{T_2 T_1}$).

The assumption that $B_{X_1 T_1} = B_{X_3 T_2}$ is basic to longitudinal growth studies since growth implies a change with time along a particular dimension. If this assumption is inserted into the model in Figure 23.1 (i.e., in equation (2) $\beta_1 = \beta_3$) and only T_1 is standardized, it becomes directly possible to estimate the true correlation of status with gain from estimates generated by the model:

$$\hat{R}_{(T_1)(T_2 - T_1)} = \frac{\hat{\sigma}_{T_1 T_2} - 1}{\sqrt{\hat{\sigma}^2_{T_2} + 1 - 2\,\hat{\sigma}_{T_1 T_2}}}$$

where $\hat{\sigma}_{T_1 T_2}$ is the estimated covariance of T_1 and T_2,

and $\hat{\sigma}^2_{T_2}$ is the estimated variance of T_2.

If the problem is to estimate the true gain for each person, it is helpful to define a change factor Δ defined as $T_2 = T_1 + \Delta$.
Equations (2) now become

$$X_0 = \beta_0 T_1 + e_0$$
$$X_1 = \beta_1 T_1 + e_1$$
$$X_2 = \beta_2 T_1 + e_2$$
$$X_3 = \beta_3 T_1 + \beta_3 \Delta + e_3$$
$$X_4 = \beta_4 T_1 + \beta_4 \Delta + e_4.$$

In essence Δ has replaced T_2 and estimating true gain involves the familiar problem of estimating factor scores. Jöreskog (1969b) gives additional details in applying his general model to growth studies.

References

BLALOCK, H. M., Jr. 1969. "Multiple Indicators and the Causal Approach to Measurement Error," *American Journal of Sociology*, 75: 264–272.

CAMPBELL, D. T., and FISKE, D. W. 1959· "Convergent and Discriminant Validation by the Multitrait-Multimethod Matrix," *Psychological Bulletin*, 56: 81–105.

DUNCAN, O. D. 1966. "Path Analysis: Sociological Examples," *American Journal of Sociology, 72:* 1–16.

GUTTMAN, L. A. 1955. "A Generalized Simplex for Factor Analysis," *Psychometrika, 20:* 173–192.

HEISE, D. R. 1959. "Separating Reliability and Stability in Test-Retest Correlation," *American Sociological Review, 34:* 93–101.

JÖRESKOG, K. G. 1969a. "A General Approach to Confirmatory Maximum Likelihood Factor Analysis," *Psychometrika, 34* (June): 183–202.

——— 1969b. "Factoring the Multitest-Multioccasion Correlation Matrix," Research Bulletin 69–62. Princeton, N. J.: Educational Testing Service, July.

——— 1969c. "Statistical Analysis of Sets of Congeneric Tests," Research Bulletin 69–97. Princeton, N.J.: Educational Testing Service, December.

——— 1970. "A General Method for Analysis of Covariance Structures," *Biometrika, 57:* 239–251.

JÖRESKOG, K. G., GRUVAEUS, G. T., and VAN THILLO, M. 1970. "ACOVS—A General Computer Program for Analysis of Covariance Structures," Research Bulletin 70–15. Princeton, N.J.: Educational Testing Service, February.

PART V

Other Complications

This concluding section continues a discussion of further complications that frequently occur in social research. The first two papers by Wilson and by Boyle deal with ordinal measurement, which is perhaps more common than interval and ratio measurement in all of the social sciences except economics. There have been numerous discussions of ordinal measures of association. Many of these have involved attempts to give operational meanings to these measures and to deal with the vexing problem of how one handles the numerous ties that occur in the case of ordered categories. Wilson in effect concludes that it will be extremely difficult if not impossible to utilize such measures in causal models. This is not only because of difficulties with respect to interpretation, but more fundamentally because ordinal measures are defined in terms of predictions about ordered pairs that involve comparisons across cases or replications, whereas the rationale behind causal modeling procedures requires conceptualization of processes that are internal to each case.

Clearly, if ordinal measures and procedures are to be incorporated within the causal modeling literature, there must be some fundamental rethinking of our basic concepts. This does not mean, however, that the various ordinal measures and partialing techniques cannot be used in exploratory research, or that they may not behave in such a way as to lead to correct inferences. But it does seem to imply that whenever ordinal procedures are used it will be exceedingly difficult to evaluate exactly how serious the distortions are likely to be. Wilson concludes with an argument that undoubtedly will have occurred to the reader of the previous section—that we must take measurement problems much more seriously than we have in the past and that we are rarely able to correct for weak measurement in the analysis stage of research.

Boyle's paper suggests an alternative to the use of ordinal measures of association, namely the extension of dummy-variable analysis in such a way that the ordering among categories is preserved. It is well known that since dichotomies can be considered as special cases of interval scales, one may break up a nominal scale consisting of k categories into a series of $k-1$ dichotomies, using ordinary least-squares regression analysis on these so-called "dummy variables." Boyle shows how this very simple idea can be utilized in conjunction with path analysis and knowledge of the ordering among categories to provide useful insights within the causal-modeling framework. He also applies the procedure in exploratory fashion to some empirical data for which the dependent variable consists of ordered categories.

Althauser is concerned with the very important notion of statistical interaction, which is conventionally handled in regression analyses by introducing cross-product terms into the equations. He points out that this procedure can lead to some rather serious problems of multicollinearity because of the high correlations among the supposedly "independent" variables that are functionally interrelated. This is the only paper in the volume that deals with problems of multicollinearity, which Althauser notes arise quite frequently whenever one is dealing with several variables from within the same block of variables. In fact, he shows how the cross-product terms can be considered as special cases of a problem that has been discussed in a more general context by Gordon, namely that of "redundancy" in the use of indicator variables.[1] Whenever such redundancy is evident, some sort of combined index or a procedure such as suggested by Sullivan would seem preferable to a multiple-indicators approach unless the within-block causal structure can be clearly specified. Obviously, we have just begun to scratch the surface in discussing the implications of complications of this nature.

The final paper by Hannan represents a summary and synthesis of the very extensive literature on aggregation that has appeared in the econometrics literature and that has had certain parallels within the sociological literature (where the focus has been more on disaggregation, however). Clearly, most of our macrolevel analyses are very much affected by choices of units of analysis (e.g., states or counties versus nations, census tracts versus blocks), and we often lack definitive theories to serve as guidelines in making these choices. If one is to expect "consistency" across several levels of aggregation, it is necessary to assume relatively simple linear models as well as homogeneity of the causal processes (as measured by the slope coefficients) across the categories into which the individual elements have been grouped. In many practical situations involving aggregation, as when persons are grouped according to their geographic proximity to each other, we often lack an adequate understanding of the relationship between the criterion used for grouping (e.g., proximity within a single county) and the other

1. See Robert A. Gordon, "Issues in Multiple Regression, "*Americal Journal of Sociology*, *73*, (1968): 592–616.

variables in the theoretical system. If we are to crystallize our thinking across levels of analysis it will obviously become necessary to deal more systematically with the problems discussed in Hannan's paper.

The papers in this final section should make it abundantly clear that there is nothing rigid or closed about the causal approach to modeling and formalization and that many diverse methodological problems can be conceptualized in causal terms. But although the approach itself is flexible, all specific applications point to the fact that the construction of really testable theories, as well as the estimation of the parameters in these theories, is an exceedingly difficult task. More often than not, realistic theories will contain too many unknowns for solution, so that compromises involving simplifying assumptions must be built in at numerous points. When one adds to this the fact that the collection of adequate data is both expensive and time-consuming, so that any given analysis will necessarily involve a number of unmeasured variables, it becomes obvious that the road ahead will be difficult indeed. Nevertheless, it is highly desirable to construct tentative theories that can be evaluated with partly inadequate data, so that a cumulative process can be set in motion. If we merely hide our assumptions and fail to face up to the complexities of theory construction and data analysis, this may increase our sense of accomplishment and reduce our personal anxieties, but it will not resolve our methodological problems. In short, there are many more chapters to be written.

Chapter 24

CRITIQUE OF ORDINAL VARIABLES

Thomas P. Wilson*
University of California, Santa Barbara

A recurrent methodological theme in sociology has been the effort to formulate theoretical ideas in mathematical terms. Although some attention has been given to the mathematical description of structural patterns (e.g., Davis and Leinhardt, 1968; Oeser and Harary, 1962, 1964), and discrete phenomena (Coleman, 1964a, 1964b), the major emphasis recently has been on formulating substantive models employing systems of real variables (e.g., Berger, et al., 1966; Blalock, 1969a; Boudon, 1965; Coleman, 1968; Stinchcombe, 1968). The virtues of mathematical methods in theoretical work are well known: clarity, precision, capacity to analyze complex relations, and the like.

However, the power and elegance of mathematical methods also impose stringent requirements on the empirical measurement of variables entering into theoretical models, and the measurement problems become particularly acute in the case of models formulated in terms of real variables. As Blalock (1965, 1969c) has emphasized, uncontrolled or inadequately assessed random measurement error can seriously weaken conclusions concerning the fit between a model and the data, and when undetermined measurement error is nonrandom, the situation is nearly hopeless. The purpose of this paper is to show, first, that the level of measurement is no less important: when the variables in a model are conceptualized as real numbers, measurement must be at least at the interval level, and when only ordinal measurements are possible, only very weak conclusions, if any, can be drawn from the data relative to a proposed model. Second, it will be shown that the formal properties

Reprinted with minor revisions by permission of the author and publisher from *Social Forces*, Vol. 49 (in press). Copyright 1971, The University of North Carolina Press.

* I wish to thank Morris F. Friedell and Bruce C. Straits for discussing the argument with me and for their useful comments on earlier versions of the manuscript.

of strictly ordinal variables are too weak to permit their use in the formulation of theoretical propositions about substantive phenomena.

In the past two decades, apparently only Simon (1957, Part II) has attempted to come to grips in a serious way with the limitations of ordinal measurement. Drawing on econometric methods, he has shown that under certain circumstances even with ordinal measurement some inferences can be made concerning the behavior of systems expressed in terms of differential and difference equations, but these inferences are relatively weak and require strong faith in the causal structure posited in the model. More frequently in sociological research, the causal structure itself is uncertain, and what one is seeking is evidence concerning the usefulness of some particular set of assumptions about the causal structure. This, for example, is the paradigm situation in path analysis studies. Other authors (Labovitz, 1970; Labovitz and Lubeck, 1969, p. 4; Gold, 1969, p. 43; Boyle, 1970) have questioned the importance of the level of actual measurement and have argued for the use of interval-level statistical techniques even when the data are clearly at best ordinal. While this position may be somewhat defensible with univariate data, it will be shown below to be untenable in a strict sense when more than one variable is involved.

Some attempts have also been made to apply the causal model idea using ordinal variables, notably by Leik and Gove (1969). However, their discussion appears to confuse an asymmetric causal relation formulated in a theoretical model with the question of statistical prediction (p. 698), and they treat ordinal measurement as simply a weak or crude form of interval measurement. As a consequence, they do not explore the problems of formulating a causal model in strictly ordinal terms, and their notion of an asymmetric causal relation depends implicitly on the assumption of interval variables for its formulation (specifically, they rely on Costner and Leik, 1964, who use Simon's 1957 additive model), without addressing the question of how a model stated in terms of interval variables can be related to data measured at best at the ordinal level. But the problems connected with these questions are precisely those that render ordinal measurement unsuitable for the empirical investigation of mathematically formulated theoretical models. [1]

This paper, then, is a critique of the use of ordinal variables in empirical research oriented to the development and modification of explanatory theories formulated in mathematical, axiomatic, or deductive form. The main thesis is essentially equivalent to that argued by McGinnis (1969): the task of developing valid, reliable interval measurement is not a technical detail that can be postponed indefinitely while the main efforts in sociological research are devoted to substantive theory construction; rather it is the central

1. Throughout this paper we are excluding structural and discrete-process models.

theoretical and methodological problem in scientifically oriented sociology.

Before proceeding to the main argument, it will be well to make clear the characteristics of ordinal variables that are the source of the methodological problems of concern here. An ordinal variable can be viewed as a set of mutually exclusive and exhaustive categories such that the categories can be put into a definite fixed sequence but, for whatever reason, it is impossible to justify assigning a specific metric invariant to within an affine transformation.[2] In fact, if x is an ordinal variable, then any one-one transformation, T, is allowable that satisfies one of the following conditions: (1) for all i, j, if $x_i < x_j$ then $T(x_i) < T(x_j)$, or alternatively (2) for all i, j, if $x_i < x_j$ then $T(x_i) > T(x_j)$. We may call such a function an "ordinal transformation."[3]

Consider, for example, an attitude index composed of dichotomous questions that fit together to form a Guttman scale.[4] Such an index is an ordinal variable with categories arranged from "low" to "high." It is clear that any sequence of numerals can be assigned to these categories so long as the order of the numbers preserves the order of the categories. Moreover, the categories cannot be treated as a discrete interval variable by assigning the numerals 0, 1, 2, . . ., as can the number of children in a family. For if the index is a discrete variable, then it should be impossible to find additional categories lying between any two of those already present. However, it is in principle always possible to add another question to the index that would have precisely the effect of creating a new category between two of those in the original scale, and such items could be added indefinitely.[5]

2. An affine transformation is of the form $A(x) = k + Lx$. Such transformations are often called "linear" because the graph of such a function is a straight line. Strictly speaking, however, a linear transformation is defined by the conditions (1) $L(x+y) = L(x) + L(y)$ and (2) $L(ax) = aL(x)$, where a is a constant. Hence, an affine transformation is linear if and only if $k = 0$.

3. In view of some persistent confusions (e.g., Labovitz, 1968, p. 543), it is perhaps necessary to point out that the maximal level of measurement of a variable is not up to the researcher's discretion. Thus, a scale is not an interval scale merely because the researcher chooses to regard it as such so as to avail himself of certain mathematical procedures. Rather, if a variable is to be treated as interval-level, the researcher must show that the assigned metric represents observable properties of the phenomena that would be misrepresented by a nonaffine ordinal transformation of the scale. Otherwise, all conclusions dependent on the assigned metric can be regarded by an unsympathetic critic as artifacts of the researcher's coding procedure, and the researcher has no defense through recourse to the data. That is to say, in order to claim interval-level measurement in a strict sense, the researcher must show that a nonaffine ordinal transformation of the scale misrepresents the data. For further discussion, the reader is referred to the standard literature on the subject, beginning of course with Norman Campbell's excellent statement in 1921.

4. The discussion below applies to other commonly used methods of scale construction as well, and the Guttman scale example is used only for clarity of exposition.

5. It follows that "ordinal measurement" does not yield ordinal numbers in the technical mathematical sense, since the finite ordinal numbers satisfy Peano's axioms (Kelley, 1955, pp. 266–272), which forbid the kind of indefinite subdivision just demonstrated as possible with ordinal measurement. From this it also follows that Spearman's rho is not applicable to strictly ordinal variables but rather is a product-moment measure for discrete interval variables.

The transformation conditions (1) or (2), together with the conceptual possibility of infinite subdivision, mean that the basic statements concerning ordinal variables upon which statistical operations can be based are necessarily propositions about pairs of cases rather than propositions that locate individual cases in particular categories, for the latter have no significance except in terms of statements about pairs. The methodological difficulties discussed below result from the transformational freedom allowable with ordinal variables and from the necessity to treat ordinal propositions as statements about pairs of cases.

Interval models and ordinal measurement

Current theoretical and causal models formulated in mathematical terms almost uniformly take interval-level measurement for granted, and the propositions in such models typically express the values of certain variables as functions of other variables.[6] When the level of empirical measurement is in fact interval, then, identification problems aside, the parameters of the model can be estimated by various curve-fitting and regression-analysis procedures directly from the data. However, when the measurements are at best ordinal, then it is obviously impossible to obtain numerical estimates of the parameters, and one must instead attempt to make other kinds of inferences connecting the model and the data. We shall now show that the limitation to ordinal measurement virtually precludes any serious inferences concerning the fit between a model and the data.

We will demonstrate this through a series of examples, each focused on a different aspect of the relation between the data and a mathematically formulated model: the form of the functional relations posited in the model (e.g., additive versus multiplicative); the causal structure of the model (e.g., which of the path coefficients vanish); and finally the use of causal models in coping with random measurement error.

INTERACTION EFFECTS AND ORDINAL VARIABLES

The first point to be made is the simplest: restriction to the ordinal level of measurement makes it impossible to decide between additive and multiplicative models. The issue is important substantively, since, as Blalock (1969a, pp. 156–157) notes,

> in a fairly common kind of theoretical situation, one assumes that a given phenomenon is most likely when two (or more) factors are both present, but that it is

6. For the purposes of this discussion it is assumed that if an abstract theory is being employed to describe some given empirical situation, then the relevant boundary conditions have been determined and any functional equations (e.g., differential or difference equations) have been solved to yield specific functions for the problem at hand.

unlikely whenever one of these factors is absent. In terms of continuous variables, this is to assume that Y values will be large only when both X_1 and X_2 are high, but that Y scores will be small if either X_1 or X_2 approaches zero, even where the other is quite large.

Consider, for example, the data in Table 24.1, where the entries are not cell frequencies but rather the mean Y scores of the cases having the various combinations of X_1 and X_2 values.[7] It is clear that these data do not fit an additive model, but instead strongly support the hypothesis of a substantial interaction effect between X_1 and X_2, which can be expressed by the model $Y = 1 + 1.7X_1 + 1.7X_2 + 3X_1X_2$.

Table 24.1. Mean Y scores, by scores in X_1 and X_2

| | | X_1 | |
X_2	0	1	*differences*
0	1	2.7	1.7
1	2.7	7.4	4.7
differences	1.7	4.7	

Suppose, however, that the measurements on Y were at best ordinal. In that case, any scale values could have been assigned in the coding procedure just so long as they preserved relative order. In particular, one could have assigned values that turned out to be the natural logarithms of $46.6Y$, where Y is the scale value employed in Table 24.1, and 46.6 is a constant factor introduced to simplify the results. Calling this alternative scale Y', and recalculating the means, the data would appear as in Table 24.2. It is evident that the data now fit the additive model $Y' = 3 + X_1 + X_2$. Thus, the interaction effect between the two variables has disappeared, and if one had begun with the kind of theoretical supposition quoted from Blalock above, one would have

7. The data are, of course, hypothetical and were generated in the following manner. Let $Y(k) = (1/46.6)e^k$, where $e = 2.718 \ldots$ is the base of the natural logarithms, and k is an index that can take on arbitrary values. For each combination of values of X_1 and X_2, a sample of five individuals was assumed. The scores for the individuals were computed by assigning each individual a value for the index k and then computing $Y(k)$ from the above formula. The values of k were assigned as follows. For $X_1 = X_2 = 0$, the index values were $k = 1, 2, \ldots,$ 5. For $X_1 = 0$ and $X_2 = 1$, the index values were $2, 3, \ldots, 6$. For $X_1 = X_2 = 1$, the index values were $3, 4, \ldots, 7$. And, for $X_1 = 1$, $X_2 = 0$, the values were $2, 3, \ldots, 6$. The figures in Table 24.1 result from taking the means of the four sets of scores generated this way. The figures in Table 24.2 result from transforming the same sets of scores by the relation $Y'(k) = Log_e$ $[46.6Y(k)] = k$ and again computing means.

to reject the model. The difficulty, of course, is that there is no way to choose between Y, on the one hand, and its logarithmic variant Y', on the other. Either measurement procedure represents the original data equally well under the limitations of ordinal measurement. Consequently, the decision about a presumably critical theoretical matter—whether the phenomenon exhibits the kind of acceleration pattern described by Blalock—depends on

Table 24.2. Mean Y' scores, by scores in
X_1 and X_2

	X_1		
X_2	0	1	*differences*
0	3	4	1
1	4	5	1
differences	1	1	

which coding procedure we adopt, i.e., whether we believe that it is Y or Y' that "really measures" the dependent variable. In short, if the measurement problem is taken seriously, no decision can be made on the basis of the data as to the functional form of the relation between the underlying variables.

THE STABILITY OF PARTIAL r

One of the most common applications of mathematical formulations in current sociological research is the use of explicit path models to represent the causal structure of a theory. The question of whether the path model adequately fits the data is, of course, complex, but a major burden of the argument is carried by determining which path coefficients are large and which are sufficiently small as to be negligible or attributable to random error. If, then, the level of measurement is at best ordinal, the utility of path analysis as a technique depends on the stability of the path coefficients under ordinal transformations, for if the relative magnitudes of path coefficients depend on how one transforms the scales, then nothing can be concluded from the data concerning the causal structure among the underlying variables. That there is little room for optimism on this score will be shown by examining the simplest case, the stability of the partial correlation under ordinal transformations.

Consider the simple causal model $X_1 \leftarrow F \rightarrow X_2$. In this case, F is assumed to be normally distributed with unit variance and zero mean, and the variables X_1 and X_2 have been normalized to have unit variances also. Algebraically, the model is represented by the equations

$$X_1 = a_1 F + e_1$$

$$X_2 = a_2 F + e_2$$

where e_1 and e_2 are normally distributed with zero means, variances $s_1^2 = 1 - a_1^2$ and $s_2^2 = 1 - a_2^2$, and are assumed to be uncorrelated with each other and with F. Under these assumptions, we have $E(X_1 F) = a_1$, $E(F X_2) = a_2$, and $E(X_1 X_2) = a_1 a_2$. Hence $r_{X_1 X_2 \cdot F} = 0$. Suppose we now impose an ordinal transformation on the X_i of the form $X'_i = v_i X_i^3$, where v_i is chosen so that X'_i has unit variance. The question is whether $r_{X'_1 X'_2 \cdot F}$ vanishes. Intuitively, of course, there is no reason at all to suppose that it does, and in fact direct calculation yields $r_{X'_1 X'_2} - r_{X'_1 F} r_{X'_2 F} = 6 v_1 v_2 a_1^3 a_2^3$.

In this example, as in the previous one, a critical theoretical issue—in the present case, whether X_1 and X_2 are spuriously related—cannot be resolved by an appeal to the data so long as measurement is limited to the ordinal level. At best, advocates of different positions in the matter are locked in an argument over what are the "real" measures of the underlying variables, the X_i or the X'_i. Such an argument is, of course, meaningless or, more precisely, unresolvable in principle so long as measurement is at best ordinal.

THE TREATMENT OF RANDOM ERROR

Path analysis provides a useful strategy for isolating relations between underlying variables in the face of random measurement error (e.g., Siegel and Hodge, 1968; Costner, 1969; Blalock, 1969b). Essentially, the strategy relies on having multiple indicators of each variable such that each indicator is correlated directly with only one underlying variable. A simple example is given in the following model.

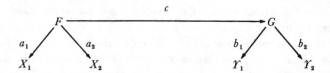

A critical step in applying the method is to verify that in fact X_1 is not directly related to G, and so on. Treating the model as a variant of a two-factor factor-analysis situation, it is evident that this is the case when the tetrad difference $r_{X_1 Y_1} r_{X_2 Y_2} - r_{X_1 Y_2} r_{X_2 Y_1}$ vanishes. However, when the correlations are expressed in terms of the path coefficients, it is readily seen that this tetrad difference vanishes if and only if the partial correlation between X_1 and Y_1 controlling for F vanishes. But, as was shown above, the vanishing of such partial correlations is by no means invariant under ordinal transformations in the measured variables X_1 and Y_1. As a consequence, this essential test in applying the technique cannot be performed, or rather, its results are completely dependent on how the variables were originally coded. To the extent, then, that one has confidence in only the ordinal properties of the coding procedures, the results are entirely ambiguous.

IMPLICATIONS

The major import of these results is that the interpretation of data relative to an interval-variable model will be ambiguous so long as measurement is limited to the ordinal level. In particular, any attempt to check a model stated in terms of interval variables against data available only at the ordinal level will be inconclusive, for virtually any conclusion purportedly based on the data can be reversed by performing entirely legitimate ordinal transformations on the measured variables. This indeterminacy is extremely serious from a scientific point of view, for it means that one cannot decide between alternative theories by appealing to the data. It is clear, then, that if interval-variable models are to be taken seriously in other than a metaphorical or heuristic sense, the problem of establishing valid and reliable interval-level measures must be addressed and solved.

This conclusion is not altered by suggestions that in some situations it may make little practical difference what scoring procedure is used (e.g., Labovitz, 1970; Boyle, 1970). For, in any given situation, one would have to show that the scoring procedure actually employed makes little difference in the particular situation at hand in order to justify faith in the conclusions of an analysis of that situation. Such a demonstration, however, requires either knowing the "real" underlying variable (in which case valid, reliable interval measurement is already possible, and one would not generally settle for an ordinal substitute) or knowing that the situation in question falls into a class of situations for which the scoring procedure is known to be essentially irrelevant (which requires a strong substantive theory, itself based on valid, reliable interval measurement). Thus, to show that a few particular examples of ordinal transformations make little difference in certain statistics (e.g., Labovitz, 1970) is beside the point, since there is no way of knowing whether an actual situation involves one of the "safe" examples.[8] Or for Boyle (1970) to show

---

8. It should be noted that Labovitz explicitly attempts to restrict his discussion to tests of significance and to exclude measures of association (1967, p. 158; 1968, p. 544). However, the general argument developed here appears to apply to both descriptive and test statistics. In the first place, in the interval-level case, test statistics such as F tend to be functions of sample size, degrees of freedom, and a descriptive measure such as r^2 or the correlation ratio. If one keeps the sample size and degrees of freedom constant, and varies the descriptive measure by means of ordinal transformations on the scales, the value of F will vary as well, and, depending on the transformation, F may exceed or be less than any particular critical

that in one example an "effects proportional" assignment of metric does not change path coefficients much from an "equal interval" assumption does not entitle him to conclude that his results "clearly support the contention that it will not *usually* be dangerous to assume an interval scale based on categories" (p. 478). On the contrary, there is no *a priori* reason to suppose that an effects-proportional metric is any closer to some imagined "true" scale than, say, a monotonic polynomial, logarithmic, or exponential transformation that radically changes the causal structure.[9] Instead of arguments such as these, what is required in the absence of interval measurement is demonstration that conclusions are invariant under ordinal transformations if there is to be any rigorous justification of claims to having confronted a model with data.

Ordinal variables and theoretical models

In view of the preceding results and the fact that at present few sociological variables are adequately measurable at the interval level, an interim strategy might be to accept the ordinal level as such and attempt to construct theoretical models explicitly in terms of ordinal rather than interval variables, thereby insuring invariance under ordinal transformations. However, there are two difficulties with this strategy, one technical and the other more profound, that suggest that little can be expected from such an approach.

LIMITATIONS OF ORDINAL DESCRIPTION

A principal consequence of the weak character of ordinal measurement is the poverty of the formal techniques by which ordinal variables can be manipulated.[10] Of particular importance in this regard are the ways in which information concerning one variable can be used to predict another variable, since a model employed for this purpose is, in effect, a description of the relation between the two variables, and it is such relations that are the central concern of both empirical investigation and theoretical explanation.

Characteristics of prediction models. Much of the recent work on ordinal statistics has been devoted to interpreting ordinal association in terms of prediction and error (Davis, 1963; Somers, 1968; Wilson, 1969; Leik and

---

value. Second, as Labovitz himself notes (1967, p. 158), violation of more than one statistical assumption often causes serious trouble even with highly "robust" statistics. But, unless the actual underlying variable is known, there is no way to check on how many assumptions have been violated.

9. Moreover, Boyle's analysis of the general problem (1970, p. 462) is incorrect since it depends on computing means and variances, both of which can be radically altered by arbitrary ordinal transformations.

10. It should be reemphasized here that ordinal variables do not take ordinal numbers as values, but rather are constructs that inherently require statements to be in terms of pairs of cases rather than about the locations of individual cases.

Gove, 1969). One of the strong arguments in favor of such a strategy is its success in the case of interval variables. However, it is important to note certain properties of prediction models for interval variables that do not carry over to the ordinal case.

In general, a *prediction model* consists of an independent variable, a dependent variable, specification of what characteristic of the dependent variable is to be predicted, a definition of error, and two prediction rules:

(I) for predicting the dependent variable in the absence of information about the independent variable;

(II) for predicting the dependent variable using information about the independent variable.

Such a model yields a convenient measure of association between the two variables called the "proportional reduction in error," or PRE, by the formula

$$\text{PRE} = \frac{\text{Error by rule (I)} - \text{Error by rule (II)}.}{\text{Error by rule (I)}}$$

In the case of interval variables, the standard model for predicting a dependent variable, y, from an independent variable, x, is to specify a function, say f (for example, in the bivariate additive case, $f(x) = a + bx$), and to predict that when the independent variable takes on a particular value, x_0, the dependent variable assumes the value $f(x_0)$. Generally, the function f is chosen to yield predictions that, in a well-defined sense, are the "best possible." In this section, the notion of best possible prediction will be explicated and the difficulties that arise in attempting to extend this notion to ordinal variables will be examined.

Three properties of interval-variable prediction models contribute to the sense in which they yield the best possible predictions. First, the prediction rules depend only on certain statistics of the joint density of the dependent and independent variables (e.g., regression coefficients, within-category means). Thus, in order to make a prediction about a particular case, it is necessary to know only the values for that case on the independent variables, and no information whatever is required concerning the value of the dependent variable for that case. A model based on rules of this sort will be called *totally predictive*. Second, the expected value of the predictions from the model coincides with the average over the sample of the characteristic being predicted. For want of a better term, such rules may be called *accurate in the average*.[11] Third, a prediction model in any particular situation can be

11. The term "unbiased" is avoided here since it is generally used to refer to the relation between a population parameter and the expected value of a sample estimator of that parameter. Here attention is confined to the description of a sample, and the question of biased estimation of a population parameter is not relevant.

obtained by finding those accurate-in-the-average prediction rules that minimize the expected error of prediction. Rules that minimize error will be termed *minimum-error* rules. Since the prediction rules for interval variables are accurate-in-the-average rules that minimize error, it makes considerable sense to measure the degree of association in terms of the proportional reduction in error.

With ordinal variables the situation is quite otherwise. The prediction rules for ordinal variables, instead of dealing with a single case, predict the order properties of a pair of cases, such as whether the pair is tied, concordant, or discordant on the dependent variable. This fact profoundly alters the character of ordinal prediction models.

To begin with, most of the prediction models proposed in the literature for ordinal variables, indeed, are totally predictive. The major exception is Davis's (1963) model for gamma, which requires that no prediction be made when there is a tie on either variable, and consequently, before a prediction can be made about a particular pair, one must know whether or not it is tied on the dependent variable.

Second, however, the prediction rules proposed for gamma, d_{yx}, and d'_{yx} predict more concordant pairs (or discordant pairs of the association is negative) than exist in the data. Thus, in the sense defined here, these rules are not accurate in the average. The rules Wilson (1969) used for tau, however, are accurate in the average.

Third, the totally predictive models uniformly fail to minimize error. This fact was noted explicitly for Wilson's model for tau, but it is also true in the case of Somers' model for d_{yx} and Leik and Gove's for d'_{yx}: since, for these measures, ties are admitted as data, it is meaningful to predict a tie, and in general one should do so whenever this leads to less expected error.

It is clear that the prediction models for ordinal variables proposed in the literature fail in various respects to have the properties that make the notion of prediction such a powerful tool in the case of interval variables. This might indicate merely that the models proposed thus far have not been sufficiently ingenious. Unfortunately, we will now see that this is not the case.

The negative PRE theorem. Our task here is to show that the failure of ordinal prediction models to exhibit the three characteristics of interval models is not accidental but rather a reflection of the weak character of ordinal measurement. To accomplish this we will demonstrate that if an ordinal prediction model is constructed that has these three properties, the resulting measure of association is unacceptable. To this end, we shall prove the following result:

Theorem. For any ordinal prediction model that is (1) totally predictive, (2) accurate in the average, and (3) minimum error, there exists bivariate densities for which PRE is negative, irrespective of how error is defined.

Proof: any reasonable definition of error for a totally predictive model can be expressed as

$$\text{error} = \begin{cases} 0 \text{ if the prediction is correct} \\ \epsilon \text{ if the prediction is incorrect and there is a tie in either the actual} \\ \quad \text{pair or the prediction} \\ \delta \text{ if the prediction is incorrect and no ties are involved} \end{cases}$$

where ϵ and δ are arbitrarily chosen but fixed positive numbers. Consider now Table 24.3. After some fairly lengthy computations,[12] we find that the prediction rules satisfying conditions (1)–(3) for these data are as follows.

(I) (prediction without use of x)
    predict a tie in all pairs.

(II) (prediction using x)
    (a) If the pair is tied on x, predict a tie on y.
    (b) If the pair is not tied on x, predict concordance with probability d_{yx} and a tie with probability $1-d_{yx}$, where d_{yx} is Somers' asymmetric measure of association, which is positive for Table 24.3.

Calculation of the expected errors then yields
    error by rule (I) $=0.444 \ \epsilon$
    error by rule (II) $=0.444 \epsilon + 0.12(\delta/4)$.
Hence, PRE $= -0.133 \ (\delta/4\epsilon)$.

Thus, no matter how the definition of error is arranged, the attempt to satisfy simultaneously conditions (1)–(3) results in a negative value of PRE for Table 24.3, which amounts to asserting that the use of additional information results in less adequate prediction. This is surely an inadmissible property for a rational prediction model.

In view of this result, an obvious strategy is to relax condition (2), accuracy in the average, since perhaps the concept of expected value is itself suspect when dealing with ordinal variables. However, when this condition is relaxed other difficulties appear. In particular, for Table 24.3, the prediction rules satisfying (1) and (3), but not (2), are the same in rule (I) and rule (II): predict a tie in all cases. This means, however, that PRE is zero, even though there are four times as many concordant as discordant pairs (note that gamma is substantial and both d_{yx} and tau are relatively large). But, conventionally, a difference between the numbers of concordant and discordant pairs has always been taken as evidence of an ordinal association between the variables.

12. The details are available on request.

*Table 24.3. Hypothetical Data Exhibiting
Negative PRE*

	x		
y	Low	High	Total
High	20	40	60
Low	20	10	30
Total	40	50	90

γ = 0.600
d_{yx} = 0.300, d_{xy} = 0.333
τ = 0.316
u_x = 0.494 (= proportion of pairs untied on x)
u_y = 0.444 (= proportion of pairs untied on y)
w_{yx} = 0.389 (= proportion of pairs untied on y among those tied on x)
e_{yx} = 0.500 (= proportion of pairs untied on y among those not tied on x)

Thus, relaxing condition (2) leads to a measure of association that is zero in situations that by conventional standards exhibit association.

It is evident, then, that the mathematical properties of ordinal statistics are inherently less satisfactory than those of interval statistics, and as a consequence, theoretical models stated in terms of ordinal variables will necessarily be less powerful and interesting. Acknowledging these essentially technical limitations, one might still seek to develop models of ordinal association and construct ordinal theories on the grounds that a complete parallel between interval and ordinal variables should not be anticipated, and that a useful, systematic treatment of ordinal variables can be developed independently of an analogy with interval variables. However, there is a deeper objection to the use of ordinal variables in theoretical models, to which we now turn.

THEORETICAL MODELS AND LEVELS OF MEASUREMENT

The propositions entering into current theoretical or causal models express the values of certain variables as functions of other variables. Clearly, in the case of interval-level measurement, such propositions are identical in form with what have been called here "prediction rules." Such is not the case for ordinal variables, however, and in fact it appears that ordinal variables cannot be used to express substantive theoretical propositions.

We have seen that the prediction rules for ordinal variables are not expressed in a form in which the value for an individual case on the dependent variable is a function of the values for that case on the independent variables. Rather, ordinal predictions are necessarily predictions about the relative order of two cases on the dependent variable, and these predictions are based on the relative orders of the two cases on the independent variables. However, a strong argument can be advanced that theoretical propositions of the type considered in this paper inevitably have the form of a function relating specific values of one variable to specific values of others.

Consider a hypothetical example. Suppose one found that, with other factors held constant, highly cohesive groups had higher levels of conformity to group norms than did less cohesive groups, but that both cohesiveness and level of conformity were measured at best at the ordinal level. The logically precise statement of the finding, then, is that if group A is more cohesive than group B, then group A has a higher level of conformity than group B, and if A and B have the same level of cohesiveness, they have the same level of conformity. However, a theoretical model of the processes leading to this effect is not likely to consist of some mechanism that operates between group A and group B to produce a difference in conformity between them on the basis of a difference in cohesiveness. Rather, one would look to mechanisms in the interaction processes within each group separately that would produce a given level of conformity in each group resulting from its particular degree of cohesiveness. But then one is conceiving of the level of conformity in a particular group as a function of its degree of cohesiveness when other variables are held constant.

It should be evident that this argument is quite general. The central point is that whatever we take to be the system to which the theory applies, the theory makes predictions about each such system without reference to the states of other systems. Should the definition of "system" be expanded to consist of an ensemble of the original systems interrelated in some specified way, then the statistical procedures considered here are no longer relevant unless we obtain a sample of such ensembles. And then the above argument applies all over again. Consequently, a construct, such as the notion of an ordinal variable, that requires comparisons between systems for its fundamental meaning cannot be used in a theory that deals with each system separately. Ordinal variables, then, are inherently too weak for formulating theoretical propositions of the kind considered here.

Discussion

The main results of this investigation are, first, that the ordinal level of measurement prohibits all but the weakest inferences concerning the fit between data and a theoretical model formulated in terms of interval variables, and second, that ordinal variables themselves cannot figure directly in the formulation of substantive theoretical models. These conclusions have two important implications for sociological investigation.

First, it will be noted that the discussion thus far has been from an essentially "hard science" perspective, in which theoretical statements, inferences, and measurements tend to be interpreted literally. In terms of these austere criteria, there is no escaping the conclusion that the problem of finding valid and reliable interval measures of sociological variables is the most important methodological and theoretical issue confronting sociology. Thus, to the extent that sociology seeks to proceed on the basis of canons of theoretical and methodological rigor paralleling those in the natural sciences, the measurement problem is paramount and commands the first priority in research and theoretical efforts.

Second, however, the problem is an extremely complex and difficult one, and substantive sociological research will continue even though solutions are not readily forthcoming. Moreover, there seems little doubt that mathematically formulated techniques, for example path analysis, will be used increasingly in substantive sociological research. Although such interval-level techniques cannot be taken literally when applied to ordinal data, they can nevertheless perform an important heuristic and metaphorical function in the interpretation of social phenomena. Thus, for example, in this perspective Boyle's (1970) proposals for the use of path analysis with ordinal data suggest useful interpretive techniques for examining a particular body of data, even though no serious claim to having "tested" a more generally applicable model or theory can be sustained. Similarly, though strictly ordinal statistics have serious general limitations, they can be extremely useful for interpreting a given set of data.[13] However, when employed this way, the results of statistical analyses must be interpreted with considerable judgment and caution, with due allowance by the researcher for what he knows about the phenomenon through other sources of evidence. This approach permits, if not forces, the researcher to evaluate his interpretations through a number of empirical procedures, no one of which is immune from severe criticism in terms of strictly scientific standards, but taken together permit a plausible story to be told (cf. Webb *et al.*, 1966). The limitation of this approach, of course, is that a variety of interpretations can always be put on the available evidence, and no sharp empirical choices between alternatives can be made so long as the measurement problem remains unsolved. It is better, however, for one to have a realistically modest estimate of the power of his methods, and to present his conclusions in that perspective, than to lay claim to greater rigor than can be achieved in practice. To borrow from Quine (1960), whistling in the dark is not the method of true scholarship, whether in sociology, high energy physics, or philosophy.

13. For suggestive discussion, see Davis (1963), Somers (1962, 1968), Wilson (1968), Leik and Gove (1969), Morris (1970).

References

BERGER, JOSEPH, MORRIS ZELDITCH, Jr., and BO ANDERSON. 1966. _Sociological Theories in Progress_. Boston: Houghton Mifflin.

BLALOCK, HUBERT M., Jr. 1965. "Some implications of random measurement error for causal inferences." _American Journal of Sociology_, 71 (July): 37–47.

――. 1969a. _Theory Construction: From Verbal to Mathematical Formulations_. Englewood Cliffs, N.J.: Prentice-Hall.

――. 1969b. "Multiple indicators and the causal approach to measurement error." _American Journal of Sociology_, 75 (September): 264–272.

――. 1969c. "The future of sociological research: measurement errors and their implications." Presented at the American Sociological Association annual meeting.

BOUDON, RAYMOND. 1965. "A method of linear causal analysis." _American Sociological Review_, 30 (June): 365–374.

BOYLE, RICHARD P. 1970. "Path analysis and ordinal data." _American Journal of Sociology_, 75 (January) (No. 4 Part 1): 461–480.

CAMPBELL, NORMAN. 1921. _What is Science?_ New York: Dover.

COLEMAN, JAMES S. 1964a. _Introduction to Mathematical Sociology_. New York: Free Press.

――. 1964b. _Models of Change and Response Uncertainty_. Englewood Cliffs, N.J.: Prentice-Hall.

――. 1968. "The mathematical study of change." In Hubert M. Blalock, Jr. and Ann B. Blalock (Eds.), _Methodology in Social Research_. New York. McGraw-Hill.

COSTNER, HERBERT L. 1969. "Theory, deduction, and rules of correspondence." _American Journal of Sociology_, 75 (September): 245–263.

COSTNER, HERBERT L., and LEIK, ROBERT K. 1964. "Deductions from 'axiomatic theory.'" _American Sociological Review_, 29 (December): 819–835.

DAVIS, JAMES A. 1963. "Notes on gamma: interpretations, computation, partials, multiples." Unpublished ms.

DAVIS, JAMES A., and LEINHARDT, SAMUEL. 1968. "The structure of positive interpersonal relations in small groups." Presented at the American Sociological Association annual meeting.

GOLD, DAVID. 1969. "Statistical tests and substantive significance." _American Sociologist_, 4 (February): 42–46.

KELLEY, JOHN L. 1955. _General Topology_. New York: Van Nostrand.

LABOVITZ, SANFORD. 1967. "Some observations on measurement and statistics." _Social Forces_, 46 (December): 151–160.

――. 1968. "Reply to Champion and Morris." _Social Forces_, 46 (June): 543–544.

――. 1970. "The assignment of numbers to rank order categories." _American Sociological Review_, 35 (June): 515–524.

LABOVITZ, SANFORD, and LUBECK, STEVEN G. 1969. "Issues of social measurement." _Et al._, 2 (Summer): 1–4.

LEIK, ROBERT K., and GOVE, WALTER R. 1969. "The conception and measurement of asymmetric monotonic relationships in sociology." _American Journal of Sociology_, 74 (May): 696–709.

McGINNIS, ROBERT. 1969. "Measurement and sociological theory." _Et al._, 2 (Summer): 7–9.

MORRIS, RAYMOND N. 1970. "Multiple correlation and ordinally scaled data." _Social Forces_, 48 (March): 299–311.

OESER, O. A., and HARARY, FRANK. 1962. "A mathematical model for structural role theory I." _Human Relations_, 15 (May): 89–110.

———. 1964. "A mathematical model for structural role theory II." *Human Relations,* *17* (February): 3–17.

QUINE, WILLARD VAN ORMAN. 1960. *Word and Object.* Cambridge, Mass.: MIT Press.

SIEGEL, PAUL M., and HODGE, ROBERT W. 1968. "A causal approach to the study of measurement error." In Hubert M. Blalock, Jr., and Ann B. Blalock (Eds.), *Methodology in Social Research.* New York: McGraw-Hill.

SIMON, HERBERT A. 1957. *Models of Man.* New York: John Wiley.

SOMERS, ROBERT H. 1962. "A new asymmetric measure of association." *American Sociological Review, 27* (December): 799–811.

———. 1968. "On the measurement of associations." *American Sociological Review, 33* (April): 291–292.

STINCHCOMBE, ARTHUR L. 1968. *Constructing Social Theories.* New York: Harcourt, Brace and World.

WEBB, EUGENE J., CAMPBELL, DONALD T., SCHWARTZ, RICHARD D., and SECHREST, LEE. 1966. *Unobtrusive Measures.* Chicago: Rand McNally.

WILSON, THOMAS P. 1968. "Measures of association for ordinal hypotheses." Presented at the American Sociological Association annual meeting.

———. 1969. "A proportional-reduction-in-error interpretation for Kendall's tau-b." *Social Forces, 47* (March): 340–342.

Chapter 25

PATH ANALYSIS AND ORDINAL DATA

RICHARD P. BOYLE*
University of California, Los Angeles

The recent introduction of path analysis to sociology is an event of almost revolutionary importance (Boudon 1965; Duncan 1966; Borgatta 1968, chaps. 1 and 3). In company with other advances in techniques related to multiple-regression analysis (see Coleman 1964, chaps. 4–6), we now have available procedures which are more powerful statistically, and also more directly relevant to sociological theory. Rather than leaving data analysis and theory construction as two separate steps, these techniques provide a model in terms of which the theory is expressed, and then directly evaluate the model through the statistical procedures. That path analysis can provide these models for a wide range of traditional verbal sociological theories has been shown most lucidly by Stinchcombe (1968, chap. 3 and appendix). While the potential benefits are exciting, however, there are also barriers to the realization of these benefits. My concern is with the fact that path analysis assumes that all variables have been measured in terms of an interval scale.

For some years there has been a strong tradition in sociology emphasizing the scientific purity of nonparametric statistics. It is relatively easy to poke holes in or cast doubts on any *a priori* rationale for assuming equal intervals, and hence it is safest to avoid this altogether. This fundamental ambiguity often seems to be resolved through custom and peer-group support. Thus there seems some tendency for path analysis to be restricted to areas such as

Reprinted by permission of the author and publisher from the *American Journal of Sociology*, Vol. 75, pp. 461–480. Copyright 1970, The University of Chicago Press.
* I would like to thank Professor George A. Miller for his cooperation in making available the data presented here, and for his assistance in carrying out the analysis.

stratification, mobility, and demography, where equal-interval assumptions are familiar (if perhaps no more certain). However, this leaves many other areas of sociology in which path analysis *could* be used by researchers who are either more courageous or more foolish. The philosophy underlying this paper is that all sciences have to work out their measurement problems as they go, either finding better ways of calibrating or gaining more confidence in old ways. Accordingly, the proper procedure is to proceed, but proceed cautiously, which means being prepared to learn from experience.

To facilitate proceeding while learning from experience, this paper presents three approaches to the problem of interval assumptions in path analysis. First, a formal investigation discusses what can go wrong if a "true" equal-interval scale is distorted into unequal intervals. Second, the use of "dummy variables" in path analysis is elaborated, since dummy variables avoid any assumptions about intervals. Third, an empirical comparison is made of results obtained from path analysis with dummy variables, of path analysis with equal intervals assumed, and of nonparametric analysis, when these techniques are applied to one set of real data.

Statistical consequences of scaling distortions

Consider the typical situation in which one has collected data on a variable X in terms of categories. These categories are assumed to be ordered, but there is no *a priori* basis for an assumption that they represent equal intervals along some underlying true scale of X. If the assumed intervals (the categories) do not correspond with the true intervals, then the consequence is equivalent to bunching together intervals in some places, and spreading them out in others—an irregular transformation of the true X scale. If the true regression of Y on X is linear, then the consequence of applying this irregular transformation will be to turn a straight regression line into a zigzag of line segments. If a new regression line is fitted on the basis of the "assumed" intervals, the result would be some more or less crude approximation of the zigzag line, as in Figure 25.1.

Since both the true regression line and the corresponding zigzag line are unknown, the real problem is to start with the assumed regression line and work backward, trying to get some idea about how crude the approximation is. A useful first step toward this goal is to consider what the zigzag line might look like. If we draw in line segments connecting the category means, we get a zigzag line which will approximate the true zigzag, and the closeness of the approximation will depend on the standard errors of the category means. That is, if the true intervals were known, and the true regression was perfectly linear, the category means would be close to the true regression line, with the expectation of "closeness" depending on their standard

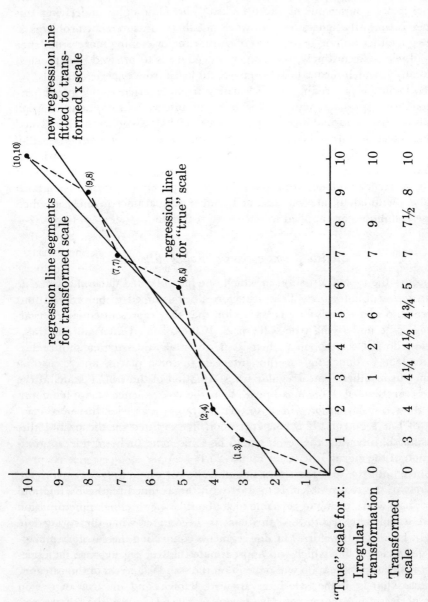

"True" scale for x:	0	1	2	3	4	5	6	7	8	9	10
Irregular transformation	0		1	1	2		6	7	9		10
Transformed scale	0	3	4	4¼	4½	4¾	5	7	7½	8	10

Figure 25.1. Consequence for a regression line of assuming equal intervals for an irregular transformation of the true interval scale.

error. Therefore, we can approximate the true zigzag regression line by using the category means of the X variable, and we can make inferences about how good this approximation is by looking at the standard errors of the category means.

If the standard errors of the category means are small, and the zigs and zags quite pronounced, then this is intuitively reasonable evidence that the assumed equal-interval scale deviates from the hypothetical true scale. Since the zigzag line does *not* involve any assumptions about intervals, it can be used as a basis for comparison. That is, if someone proceeds boldly to assume that his categories represent equal intervals, in what ways might his results be distorted depending on the extent of zigzaginess? The situation is somewhat different for correlation coefficients and regression coefficients.

The correlation coefficient is, with adjustments, a measure of how close the data fall to the regression line. This can be decomposed into variation around the category means, and variation of the category means around the regression line. A measure which is appropriate for the zigzag line is the correlation ratio, which utilizes only the first kind of variation. Since the correlation coefficient adds to this the second kind of variation, the correlation coefficient will always be smaller than the correlation ratio. Further, under the intuitive assumption that the zigzag line will almost always be a closer approximation to the true regression line, it follows that correlation coefficients computed in terms of an arbitrary equal-interval assumption will be *conservative* estimates of the true correlation. The important question, however, is under what situations will it be slightly conservative, and under what situations will it be very conservative?

The more pronounced the zigs and zags, the more variation contributed by the departure of the category means from the regression line. Therefore, the worse the assumed equal-interval scale, the more conservative the correlation coefficients. But the variation of the category means around the regression line is important only *relative to* the variation around the category means. If there is a great deal of variation around category means, proportionally the effect of the zigs and zags may not be very large. Conversely, if the data fall very close to the category means, so that the correlation ratio is close to 1.0, then only a slight amount of zigging and zagging may produce appreciable distortion. Since most sociological research works with rather low-order correlations, this suggests that the dangers of assuming equal intervals are, in addition to being conservative, not likely to be huge. Recent work by Labovitz (1967) supports this by showing that in most cases the distortion is minor.

Regression coefficients, on the other hand, measure the *slope* of the regression line. Since the regression line will try to come as close as possible to the category means, one may envisage a regression line drawn through a zigzag line in such a way as to best approximate it (see Fig. 25.1). Since the concern is not with how close fitting this best approximation is but simply with the *slope* of the approximation, it follows that it is not the *amount* of zigzaginess which will distort the regression line but rather the *pattern* which it forms. That is, if the zigging and zagging is randomly erratic (which means that the errors made by assuming equal intervals are random distortions of the true interval scale), then the slope of the estimated regression line will not be distorted at all. In fact, distortion in the slope of the line can occur only because either (1) categories in some portion of the line are disproportionately large and the line segments connecting the means of these categories have similar slopes which are also very different from the slopes of the true regression line (more simply, if the distribution of the sample weights the zigs more than the zags); or, (2) if the zigzag line forms a special kind of pattern, such as an S-shape (as in Fig. 25.1). In sum, the distortions in regression coefficients can be in either direction (conservative or "radical"), but these distortions are not so likely to occur at all since they depend on a coincidence of errors rather than on the magnitude of error. Furthermore, it seems even less likely that these coincidences will produce really drastic distortions of the sort which will lead to different substantive interpretations of the analysis.

Nevertheless, distortions are still *possible*, and this is bad in two ways. First, and most simply, even rare instances of distortion are not tolerable when they can be avoided. Second, if sociology is to become a less-crude science, our tolerance limits must shrink; better measurement must be part of this progress. Both as a check on what we are doing now, and as an instrument for finding out how to do it better, attention to the calibration of interval scales is a necessity. The preceding discussion suggests some way of doing this. Rather than assume that our categories represent equal intervals, one possibility would be to recalibrate the scale so the intervals are proportional to the "effects" of each category, that is, to work backward from the zigzag line to the true scale. This approach is conventional in covariance analysis. However, if we are studying a system of several variables, so a variable may act on more than one dependent variable, we immediately run into the possibility that the effect-proportional scale implied by one dependent variable may not be the same as the one implied by another dependent variable. The difference may be due to measurement errors, or it may mean that the effects on one or both dependent variables are nonlinear, which is certainly plausible. What we need is a way of dissecting the system which avoids as long as possible *any* assumptions about interval scaling. The use of dummy variables provides one way of approximating this.

Dummy variables and path analysis

Decomposition of an ordinal variable into dummy variables is rather analogous to translating a decimal number system into binary.[1] All of the original information is retained, but the simpler vocabulary requires longer sentences. Dummy variables are dichotomous, with the categories coded "0" and "1". To decompose a trichotomous variable, which may have been coded 0, 1, and 2, we need two of these dichotomous dummy variables. In order to retain the *ordinal* property of the categories, dummy variables are constructed as shown in Table 25.1.[2] If we know a subject's score on the two dummy variables, we know exactly his score on the original, parent variable X. Furthermore, if we are interested in the regression on X of some dependent variable Y, we could also study the *multiple* regression of this pair of dummy variables on Y.

A regression coefficient tells us the expected increase in Y for an increase of one unit in the independent variable, with other independent variables controlled. For the pair of dummy variables in Table 25.1, controlling for D_2 while looking at the effects of D_1 means that we are going to compare only

Table 25.1. Two alternative methods for decomposing a trichotomous parent variable into dichotomous dummy variables

Parent variable X	Translation to dummy variables			
	Decomposition I		Decomposition II	
	D_1	D_2	D'_1	D'_2
2	1	1	1	0
1	0	1	0	1
0	0	0	0	0

subjects who are identical on D_2, that is, subjects who are 1 on D_2 (because there are no subjects who are 0 on D_2 but different, and hence comparable, on D_1). Therefore, the regression coefficient for D_1 will estimate only that increase in Y which should be expected from an increase on the parent variable X from 1 to 2. Similarly, the coefficient for D_2 will estimate only the effect of an increase in X from 0 to 1. The two dummy variables thus separate out the effects of first moving from the lower to the middle category,

1. For a discussion of dummy variables see Daniel B. Suits (1957) and Richard P. Boyle (1966).
2. Dummy variables can also be constructed so that only nominal scale information about the categories is retained, and this method is frequently employed (see Suits 1957).

and then from the middle to the upper category of X. These are exactly the slopes of the two line segments in the zigzag regression line of X on Y discussed earlier.

Decomposition to dummy variables therefore allows us to estimate the slopes of the zigzag regression line. When there are several independent variables, each can be replaced by its own dummy variables, and in this way multiple-regression analysis can avoid equal-interval assumptions. Since the basic procedures of path analysis can be used with path-regression coefficients, it is also possible to replace all polytomous variables in a path system with dummy variables, and proceed in exactly the same way. While the basic procedure is straightforward, there are certain aspects of the application which introduce some new features, and these should be discussed at greater length. However, it will be useful to have a specific example available to illustrate this discussion. Applying path analysis to data originally reported by George A. Miller (1967) will provide this example.

THE MILLER STUDY

Miller's study of work alienation among scientists and engineers in a large industrial organization provides a good example of both the potential and the problems of using path analysis, for several reasons. First, the data come from a questionnaire survey of a fairly small sample ($N = 419$). Second, the fairly large system of eight variables all consist of ordered categories—three of the variables were dichotomous, five were trichotomous. Rather than assume that the categories represent an interval scale, his analysis consisted of extensive cross-tabulation, with the gamma-statistic computed for each partial table. Given the size of the sample, this technique severely restricted how far he could go with multivariate analysis. Therefore, although his theoretical framework assumes causal relations, the analysis was not able to fully assess the causal dynamics of the system.[3]

The causal system implied by Miller's article is shown in Figure 25.2. Scientists and engineers (X_7) with either M.A.'s or Ph.D.'s (X_8) are recruited

---

3. Miller's original hypothesis (1967, p. 757) predicted both the existence of bivariate relations and interaction effects accompanying them. Specifically, he predicted that the relations would be stronger for Ph.D.'s and for scientists than for M.A.'s and engineers. While his findings generally supported the interaction hypothesis, pronounced interaction was only discovered when scientists and engineers were compared on the effects of supervisory type and company encouragement. This poses a problem, since path analysis assumes only additive effects. The justification for proceeding with an additive model here is that (1) the complications of supervisory type concerned only the difference between "participatory" and "laissez faire" supervisory types, and this distinction is removed later on when dummy variables and effect-proportional scales are used; (2) although company encouragement should be treated in terms of an interaction model, its effects here are so slight that it is unlikely to make much difference; (3) similar substantive interpretations are generated here from the additive model, and since the purpose of this analysis is illustrative only, use of an interactive path model would be an unnecessarily complicated digression.

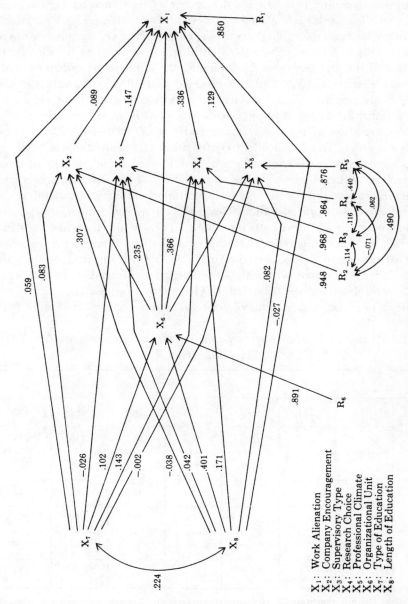

X₁: Work Alienation
X₂: Company Encouragement
X₃: Supervisory Type
X₄: Research Choice
X₅: Professional Climate
X₆: Organizational Unit
X₇: Type of Education
X₈: Length of Education

Figure 25.2. Path analysis of Miller data, using path coefficients.

into the company and assigned to either the aerospace group or the basic science research laboratory (X_6), divisions which differ from each other in goals and structure. It is assumed that a man's educational background can have an effect on his job assignment. Beyond these three primary variables, there are four variables (X_{2-5}) describing characteristics of the job in terms of its control-incentive structure (CIS), which are assumed to be potentially caused by the first three variables. Finally, the ultimate dependent variable is work alienation, (X_1), and it is assumed that all other variables in the system are possible causes of alienation. Path coefficients (not regression coefficients) are attached to the arrows, since this is more conventional.

Interpretation of this path system starts most naturally with the four CIS variables. The independent contribution of research choice (.336) is much greater than the effect of any other CIS variable on alienation, to an extent not anticipated by Miller's bivariate analysis. In comparison, the other three variables seem relatively unimportant for understanding the direct causes of work alienation. However, among these three, supervisory type emerges as the next most important (.147), while it was the least important in Miller's analysis. That this should happen is not surprising when the pattern of zero-order correlations in Table 25.2 are examined. Supervisory type is less correlated with either the background variables or the other CIS variables than are these latter. The relative independence of supervisory type is also evident in the correlations between residuals in Figure 25.2.

Table 25.2. Matrix of zero-order correlations between variables in Miller study

	2	3	4	5	6	7	8
1	.267	.251	.477	.404	.284	.163	.170
2		.011	.290	.566	.310	.146	.114
3			.239	.184	.247	.038	.138
4				.590	.464	.226	.352
5					.477	.119	.274
6						.232	.433
7							.224

NOTE. 1, work alienation; 2, company encouragement; 3, supervisory type; 4, research choice; 5, professional climate; 6, organizational unit; 7, type of education; 8, length of education.

This is a finding of some importance, since of the four CIS variables, supervisory type alone seems to refer to control, while the other three more strictly indicate incentive. Apparently, control and incentive structures are distinct not only conceptually, but also in their occurrence and in their effects.

The four CIS variables are assumed to mediate the effects of organizational unit on alienation, and in fact they do this so well that *all* of the total effect of organizational unit on alienation is accounted for. Evaluation of the paths from organizational unit to alienation is shown in Table 25.3. Half of

Table 25.3. Path contributions to the effects of the primary variables using path coefficients

Path	Effects	
A. Organizational unit		
Direct effect		.000
Paths via:		
Company encouragement	(.307) (.089) =	.027
Supervisory type	(.235) (.147) =	.035
Research choice	(.366) (.336) =	.123
Professional climate	(.442) (.129) =	.057
Total effect		.242
B. Type of education		
Direct effect		.059
Paths via:		
Organizational unit	(.143) (.242) =	.035
Company encouragement	(.083) (.089) =	.007
Supervisory type	(−.026) (.147) =	−.004
Research choice	(.102) (.336) =	.034
Professional climate	(−.002) (.129) =	.000
Total effect		.131
C. Length of education		
Direct effect		−.027
Paths via:		
Organizational unit	(.401) (.242) =	.097
Company encouragement	(−.038) (.089) =	−.003
Supervisory type	(.042) (.147) =	.006
Research choice	(.171) (.336) =	.057
Professional climate	(.082) (.129) =	.011
Total effect		.141

the total effect is explained by the fact that professionals in the basic science laboratory are given more research choice; the remainder comes from the other three CIS variables, especially professional climate. Thus path analysis provides an apparently perfect explanation for the lower work alienation in the basic science laboratory.

Remaining to be interpreted are the relatively moderate total effects of the two ultimate independent variables, length and type of education. In Table 25.3 it is evident that type of education (engineer or scientist) produces almost half (.06) of its total effect (.13) *directly*, without any mediation by the intervening variables. Of the remainder, the indirect paths show that this is accounted for by the greater propensity of scientists to be assigned to the basic science laboratory and, separately from this, to be granted greater freedom of research choice. Length of education, on the other hand, shows strong indirect paths through organizational unit (.10) and through research choice (.06). The remaining, direct, effect is slightly negative, indicating that if anything, Ph.D.'s who do not get the preferential assignment to the basic science laboratory and who are not given freedom over choice of research resent it more than do M.A.'s.

These findings support Miller's substantive conclusion that engineers, either because of recruitment or socialization, are not responsive to the same organizational variables as scientists—they continue to be more alienated from their work even when organizational variables are controlled. On the other hand, these findings also indicate that *length* of education, by itself (and Miller could not control for both simultaneously) can be satisfactorily understood in terms of the different organizational careers of M.A.'s and Ph.D.'s.

While path analysis has thus allowed us to ask questions and obtain answers which Miller could not do given his statistical technique, we now come back to the basic question of whether or not these apparently important findings can be trusted. Equal-interval scales were assumed for the five trichotomous variables, but this is a completely arbitrary assumption. Following the rationale developed earlier, the same form of path analysis will now be carried out using dummy variables to replace these trichotomies. In the process of doing this, some special features of the procedure will be explicated.

A path analysis with dummy variables

One unresolved problem in the literature on dummy variable-regression analysis concerns the use of dummy variables to represent a *dependent* variable (Coleman 1964, pp. 237–238; Boyle 1966, p. 848). This problem cannot be avoided in the present case, both because work alienation is trichotomous, and because the four intervening CIS variables are trichotomous. In fact, however, a completely workable solution is very simple.

Consider the abbreviated path system for the Miller data shown in Figure 25.3. Alienation is first represented by two dummy variables, A_1 and A_2, and these are *separate* variables. Hence A_1 and A_2 merely represent two alternative ways of dichotomizing alienation, and the path-regression coefficients tell us what we would have gotten if we had chosen each cutting point. But these cutting points are also the interval steps of the parent variable, and between them A_1 and A_2 completely determine alienation. That is, an increase of one unit in A_1 means an increase of one unit in alienation. Therefore, in Figure 25.3 the arrows from A_1 and A_2 to X_1 (alienation) are assigned coefficients of 1.0.

Carrying out the operations of path analysis means that the effects of, say, X_7 (type of education) on A_1 and A_2 are summed to get the total direct

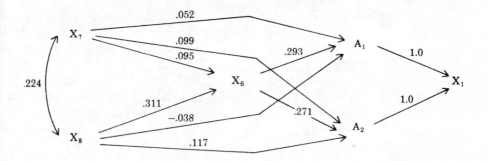

Calculation of path effects:	Paths through dummy variables:			Effect assuming Equal intervals
	A_1	A_2	Total (A_1+A_2)	
Organizational Unit (X_6)	.293	.271	.564	.564
Type of education (X_7)				
directly through A_1 and A_2	.052	.099	.151	.151
via organizational unit	.028	.026	.054	.054
total effect	.080	.125	.205	.205
Length of education (X_8)				
directly through A_1 and A_2	−.038	.117	.079	.079
via organizational unit	.091	.084	.175	.175
total effect	.053	.201	.254	.266

Figure 25.3. *Path-regression analysis of type and length of education and organizational unit on alienation using dummy variables to represent alienation.*

effect. But, as the last column in Figure 25.4 shows, *this sum is exactly what we get assuming equal intervals for alienation*. Therefore, applying path analysis operations to dependent dummy variables gives the same results as assuming equal intervals for that dependent variable, so that in one sense introducing the dummy variables is completely redundant. However, something new has been added. Comparing the effects on the two dummy variables provides an estimation of whether these effects are uniform along the categories of alienation, or whether the resistance of alienation to being effected is greater at one

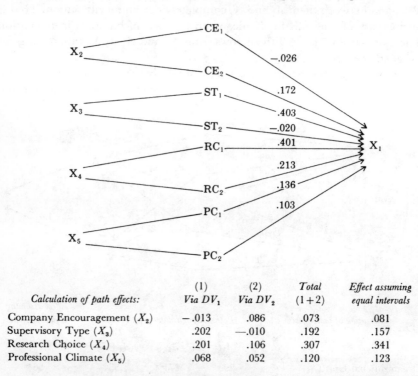

Calculation of path effects:	(1) Via DV_1	(2) Via DV_2	Total $(1+2)$	Effect assuming equal intervals
Company Encouragement (X_2)	−.013	.086	.073	.081
Supervisory Type (X_3)	.202	−.010	.192	.157
Research Choice (X_4)	.201	.106	.307	.341
Professional Climate (X_5)	.068	.052	.120	.123

Figure 25.4. *Path-regression analysis of the effects of the CIS variables on alienation when represented by dummy variables.*

end of the continuum than at the other. If the latter appears to be true, then we could recalibrate the scale for alienation by assigning more intervals to the resistant portion and fewer intervals to the less-resistant portion, and with this new scale, the standardized path coefficients for the system might change. However, since there will usually be more than one variable acting on the dummy dependent variables, such a recalibration procedure will be clear only when each of these variables implies the same recalibration. This can be avoided, of course, if the operation of combining paths is not performed, and this level hence provides the best check on the original equal-intervals analysis. But the Miller data also illustrate what is involved if one tries to move beyond this.

In Figure 25.3, the effects on A_1 and A_2 of X_6 and X_7 seem to be relatively uniform, while X_8 produces much greater effects on A_2 than on A_1. Thus it would be reasonable to leave the alienation categories as an equal-interval scale, while noting that the effect of length of education on alienation seems curvilinear, which could be handled by using a nonlinear operator. While more complicated, this would represent scientific progress, and demonstrates one way in which the workings of the system can be made more precise. In the present case, however, the effects are quite small no matter how the analysis is done, so the extra effort does not seem worthwhile.

The situation is rather different, however, for a polytomous *intervening* variable. Here any differential effects *on* the dummy variables are multiplied by any differential effects *of* each dummy variable. In order to understand the implications of this, it will be useful to start with a consideration of dummy variables simply as independent variables—for example, the effects of the four CIS variables on alienation. These are shown in Figure 25.4 with an equal-intervals scale for alienation, and with X_6, X_7, and X_8 controlled. As before, the translation to dummy variables completely determines them, and taking account of the difference in units, the effect of each CIS variable on its dummies is .50. Then applying path operations to get the total effect of, say, research choice (RC) means, in essence, taking the arithmetic mean of the effects of RC_1 and RC_2. But since these coefficients are actually the slopes of the zigzag regression line of research choice on alienation, this averaging procedure is equivalent to *making* the zigzag line straight by altering the interval scale for company encouragement. This follows from the earlier discussion of zigzag regression lines. Thus the operation of adding together paths through dummy variables *implicitly* assumes an effect-proportional interval scale for the parent independent variable.

One consequence of this is that we will not necessarily get the same results for an independent variable when we assume equal intervals and when we use dummy variables. This is evident in Figure 25.4, where the estimated effects of the CIS variables on alienation are compared using both methods. At the same time, while the two sets of estimates are not the same, they also do not differ very markedly, which is in line with the arguments of the first section.

However, assessing the effects of the CIS variables is only a small part of the total system. Assessing the way the CIS dummy variables mediate the effects of organizational unit and type and length of education means that indirect path effects are calculated by multiplying together the effects *on* and the effects *of* each dummy variable. In order to estimate the net effect of, say, organizational unit on alienation by way of research choice, we need to add together the paths through RC_1 and RC_2. It has already been established that summing the effects *on* a pair of dummy variables gives the same results as assuming an equal-interval scale for the parent variable. But now these dummy variables in turn have effects on a third variable, and it was also shown that summing *these* effects is the same as assuming an effect-proportional scale for the parent (intervening) variable. What actually happens when these two pieces of information are put together is shown in Figure 25.5.

The causal relationship between organizational unit and alienation by way of research choice is shown in Figure 25.5 in three ways, in order to demonstrate the equivalence between their logic and results. First, the paths are shown directly through the dummy variables to alienation, and the

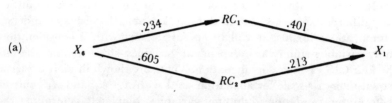

Total effect $= (.234)(.401) + (.605)(.213) = .224$

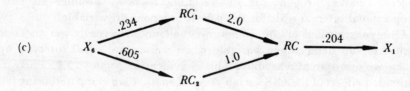

Total effect $= (1.075)(.204) = .219$

(c)

Total effect $= (.234)(2.0)(.204) + (.605)(1.0)(.204) = .219$

Figure 25.5. *Path-regression analysis of the effect of organizational unit on alienation mediated by research choice: (a) replacing research choice with dummy variables, (b) assuming an effect-proportional interval scale, (0,2,3) for research choice (RC'), and (c) assuming that the dummy variables determine RC', which in turn causes X_1.*

estimate of total effect is calculated according to path operations. Second, the argument that this use of dummy variables implicitly assumes an effect-proportional interval scale is demonstrated by assigning to research choice a scale (RC') which is approximately effect proportional. Since the effects of RC_1 and RC_2 (.401 and .213, respectively) are roughly in the ratio 2:1, the scale assigned to research choice was 0, 2, and 3 for its three categories. A path-regression analysis was carried out using RC', and the resulting estimate of total effect (.219) is almost the same as the first estimate (.224). Finally, to show that these two procedures are in fact logically interchangeable, the third diagram (Fig. 25.5) mixes the two. First, the effects of organizational unit on RC_1 and RC_2 are taken from the dummy-variable analysis. Then, the effects of RC_1 and RC_2 on RC' now correspond to the interval scores assigned to each category under RC'. Third, the effect of RC' on alienation is taken from the second diagram. This path system therefore explicates the logic behind the first diagram, and in fact the resulting estimate (.219) differs only slightly, due to the approximate nature of the RC' scale.

In sum, using dummy variables as dependent variables does not alter the results of a path-regression analysis, although it supplies information which might lead to rescaling and hence a change in standardized path coefficients. Using dummy variables as independent variables automatically assumes interval scales which are proportional to effects, and this can alter both kinds of coefficients. Finally, using dummy variables to represent intervening variables combines both of the above statements, and hence again has the consequence of building in interval scales which are proportional to effects. It must be remembered that this automatic assumption occurs only when paths are combined through addition—until that point there are truly no assumptions about interval scale, and this can be especially useful for a microscopic analysis of what is going on in the system. When the path operations are performed, the results are useful as a comparison with, or check on, the results obtained from assuming equal intervals. This is not to assert that effect-proportional scales are the true scale; at this point in the development of our science, it seems better to consider them as one alternative. But precisely because they are a very different alternative with a foundation quite removed from the foundation for assuming equal-intervals scales, they provide a very good test of whether or not the results of a particular analysis are sensitive to scale assumptions or relatively stable over both intervals scales. This test will now be applied to the remainder of the Miller data path analysis.

MILLER DATA COMPLETED

When dummy variables are used to replace the four CIS variables in the Miller data, and when alienation is retained as a trichotomy with an equal-interval scale (for reasons developed earlier), the resulting path system is shown in Figure 25.6. Applying path operations to this system provides results which can be more easily compared with the previous equal-interval results, and this is shown in the first two columns of Table 25.4. In the third column, analogous results are given for an analysis in which effect-proportional interval scales were assumed for these CIS variables (that is, interval scales roughly proportional to the effects of their dummy variables on alienation). All of the results in the first three columns are based on path-regression coefficients, since that is the rationale developed for employing dummy variables.

The dummy-variable results are quite similar to the equal-interval results, which supports the earlier conclusion that assuming equal intervals will usually not introduce much distortion into a path-regression analysis. The greatest disparity concerns the direct effect of organizational unit on alienation. Where this is essentially zero under the equal-intervals assumption, with dummy variables it increases to .096. Thus the dummy-variable analysis states that the CIS variables do not do such a perfect job of accounting for the total effect of organizational unit as the earlier analysis implied. But even this is a relatively technical difference, and it seems clear that no significant differences in theoretical interpretation arise. The results for effect-proportional scales are almost exactly the same as the dummy-variable results, which of course they should be. Finally, note that the multiple correlation (R) has been slightly improved by using the effect-proportional scales (from .527 to .548), indicating a closer fit of the model to the data.

The fourth and fifth columns of Table 25.4 compare the results for equal intervals and effect-proportional intervals when path coefficients are used. There are essentially no differences between these two columns, certainly none which would justify calling the equal-intervals assumption dangerous or misleading. The largest difference (.04) is in the direct effect of organizational unit on alienation, which was noted during the path-regression analysis—and now the difference is even smaller. As one empirical test of the consequences for path analysis of assuming equal intervals for ordinal data, these results clearly support the contention that it will not *usually* be dangerous to assume an interval scale based on categories.

Concluding remarks

The purpose of this paper was to accelerate the diffusion of path analysis by attempting to allay the fears of many sociologists about assuming any kind of interval scale for their data. This was done first through a theoretical analysis of what *could* go wrong, and second by outlining a procedure for checking on the consequences of the interval assumptions. The theoretical

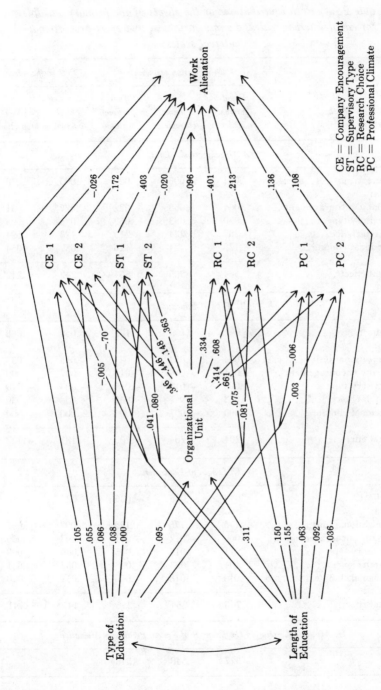

Figure 25.6. Path-regression analysis using dummy variables to replace the control-incentive structure variables (regression bs). For all dummy variables, 1 one contrasts the medium with the low category, 2 contrasts the high with the medium.

CE = Company Encouragement
ST = Supervisory Type
RC = Research Choice
PC = Professional Climate

*Table 25.4. Path contributions of the effects of the primary variables
for equal-interval scales, dummy variables, and effect-proportional
interval scales*

Path	Path-regression coefficients			Path coefficients	
	Equal-interval scales	Dummy variables	Effect-proportional scales	Equal interval	Effect-proportional
A. Organizational Unit					
Direct effect...............	.001	.096	.088	.000	.038
Paths via:					
Company encouragement ...	.064	.068	.072	.027	.031
Supervisory type	.080	.053	.059	.035	.025
Research choice............	.287	.224	.219	.123	.094
Professional climate	.132	.124	.126	.057	.054
Total effect	.564	.565	.564	.242	.242
B. Type of Education					
Direct effect...............	.092	.105	.105	.059	.068
Path via:					
Organizational unit	.054	.054	.054	.035	.035
Company encouragement ...	.011	.014	.014	.007	.009
Supervisory type	−.006	−.015	−.015	−.004	−.010
Research choice	.053	.047	.047	.034	.030
Professional climate	.000	−.001	.000	.000	.000
Total effect	.204	.204	.205	.131	.132
C. Length of Education					
Direct effect...............	−.049	−.036	−.036	−.027	−.020
Paths via:					
Organizational unit	.175	.175	.175	.097	.097
Company encouragement ...	.006	−.012	−.011	−.003	−.006
Supervisory type	.011	.016	.016	.006	.009
Research choice............	.104	.093	.093	.057	.051
Professional climate........	.019	.018	.018	.011	.010
Total effect	.266	.254	.255	.141	.141
D. Multiple Correlation Coefficient R of System Predicting Alienation					
	.527	.548	.548		

analysis concluded that regression and path coefficients are generally quite stable no matter what the interval scale, because appreciable distortion depends not on the magnitude of error, but on special coincidences between more than one kind of error. The procedure for checking on whether or not such coincidences occur consists of using dummy variables in the path analysis. This introduces no new computational complexities, and requires no initial assumption about interval scales. Application of this procedure to actual data supported the contention that interval-scale assumptions are not of crucial importance in path or regression analysis.

Aside from encouraging the use of path analysis with ordinal data, the use of dummy variables constitutes an important tool for the improvement of measurement in sociology. By dissecting the complex dynamics of a system into microscopic bits, dummy-variable analysis provides a basis for calibration in terms of the internal consistency of the system. Used in this way, the potential measurement advantages go far beyond the question of whether a particular statistical technique is sufficiently robust to withstand a lot of abuse from scaling assumptions. Along the same line, dummy-variable analysis can facilitate the discovery and specification of curvilinear relations; but this raises some very general questions about where path analysis can lead sociology.

Path analysis provides a theoretical model specified as a system of simultaneous equations which are linear, additive, and, usually, recursive. The frontier opened up by path analysis is therefore the specification of sociological theory as systems of more complicated simultaneous equations. Any sociological thinking, whether or not it is labeled "theory," which conceptualizes phenomena in terms of "variables" and relations between variables, can be and in fact *ought to be* directed toward this kind of expression. The difficulties lie not so much in the mathematics as in the muddiness of most sociological thinking. Clear thinking is not necessarily correct thinking —in fact it runs a better chance of being shown false. Path analysis is an important step in an important direction precisely because it forces systematic and explicit theoretical work. This paper will have justified itself if henceforth it becomes less easy for sociologists to use "ordinal data" as an excuse for theoretical laziness.

References

BORGATTA, EDGAR. (Ed.) 1968. *Sociology Methodology*. Vol. 1. New York: Knopf.

BOUDON, RAYMOND. 1965. "A Method of Linear Causal Analysis." *American Sociological Review* 30 (June): 365–374.

BOYLE, RICHARD. 1966. "Causal Theory and Statistical Measures of Effect: A Convergence." *American Sociological Review* 31 (December): 843–851.

COLEMAN, JAMES S. 1964. *Introduction to Mathematical Sociology*. New York: Free Press.
DUNCAN, OTIS DUDLEY. 1966. "Path Analysis: Sociological Examples." *American Journal of Sociology* 72 (July): 1–16.
LABOVITZ, SANFORD. 1967. "Some Observations on Measurements and Statistics." *Social Forces* 56 (December): 151–160.
MILLER, GEORGE A. 1967. "Professionals in Bureaucracy: Alienation among Industrial Scientists and Engineers." *American Sociological Review* 31 (December): 843–851.
STINCHCOMBE, ARTHUR. 1968. *Constructing Social Theory*. New York: Harcourt, Brace, & World.
SUITS, DANIEL B. 1957. "Use of Dummy Variables in Regression Equations." *Journal of American Statistical Association* 25 (December.): 548–551

Chapter 26

MULTICOLLINEARITY AND NON-ADDITIVE REGRESSION MODELS

ROBERT P. ALTHAUSER*

Princeton University

For many statisticians and economists, multicollinearity is known as a statistical problem that arises when the correlations between independent variables are extremely high (> .85). The standard error of regression coefficients become very large and estimates of these coefficients become quite unstable (Farrar and Glauber, 1967). Blalock (1963) and Gordon (1968) have pointed out, however, that lesser degrees of multicollinearity can pose problems for the substantive interpretation of regression coefficients. Working with "real" data these problems can remain obscure, eluding many practicing social scientists versed in correlation and regression techniques. With carefully constructed hypothetical data, however, the problems become more transparent.

A common procedure in the study of statistical interaction with regression analysis is to include multiplicative terms in one's model:

(1) $Y = b_{y1}X_1 + b_{y2}X_2 + b_{y3}X_3$, where $X_3 = X_1X_2$

The substantive issue frequently addressed by such analysis is whether one theory that implies an additive model is superior to another implying a non-additive model. For example, Jackson and Burke (1965) sought to test the theory of status inconsistency put forth by Lenski (1954, 1956, 1964) by

Paper prepared especially for *Causal Models in the Social Sciences*.

* I wish to acknowledge the assistance of John Balkcom, whose programming produced the data that prompted this paper. I am also indebted to Robert Gordon, Charles Werts and Albert Beaton for their helpful comments.

comparing an additive model of individual status components with a non-additive model containing multiplicative interaction terms. The regression coefficients for the latter would be as large or larger than those for the individual status components if "status inconsistents" tend to be more politically liberal or to have more "psychosomatic stress symptoms" (Jackson, 1962) than "status consistents." Likewise, Gockel (1969) sought to determine if individual status variables (in an additive model) or religious affiliation (in a nonadditive model) better predicted income. There are other examples like this to be found (Blalock, 1965; Lane, 1968).

As we will attempt to show below, the correlations between the individual X's in the equation above and the product term, X_1X_2, appear to undermine the substantive interpretation of estimated regression coefficients. These correlations, r_{23} (and r_{13}), unlike the usual correlation coefficient, are affected in part by the size (and difference) in the sample means of X_1 and X_2. The resulting pattern of multicollinearity among X_1, X_2 and X_3 will either depress or (less likely) inflate the regression estimates for the interaction or product term relative to those estimates for the individual terms. Which outcome occurs depends on the size of the correlation r_{12} and r_{23} (as well as r_{13}, which is similar to r_{23} for our purposes and will not be additionally treated below).

The size of r_{23}

We will first derive an expression for the correlation between an individual variable like X_2 and the product term X_1X_2, which displays the effect of the means of variables X_1 and X_2. It is best to approach the size and difference of these means by comparing X_1 and X_2, not to each other, but to other variables, say X_1 and X_2 with means of zero. We will do this by decomposing the individual X's as follows:

(2) $X_1 = X_1 + a$, where X_1 is independently $N(o, \sigma_1)$
           and X_1 is independently $N(a, \sigma_1)$

(3) $X_2 = X_2 + b$, where X_2 is independently $N(o, \sigma_2)$ and
           X_2 is independently $N(b, \sigma_2)$.

(Another way of looking at this is to consider X_1 and X_2 as transformed variables resulting from adding "constants" a and b to the variables X_1 and X_2, respectively).

The correlation between either of the individual X's, say X_2, and the product term, is, of course

(4) $r_{23} = \text{cov}(X_2X_3)/\sigma_2\,\sigma_3$

where the standard deviation of X_3 (or $X_1 X_2$) is σ_3. In the appendix following this paper, we have continued the derivations for the numerator and denominator of this correlation. Some results of this effort will be summarized below.

Taking the standard deviation of X_3 first, we find that (from equation 4 in the appendix):

(A4) $\quad \sqrt{\text{var } X_3} = \sqrt{\sigma_3^2 + a^2 \sigma_2^2 + b^2 \sigma_1^2}$

(where $E(X_1) = a$, $E(X_2) = b$ and $\sigma_3 = \text{var } X_3$).

The derivation of the numerator, the covariance term, is more complex. We find that

(A15) $\quad \text{cov}(X_2 X_3) = \text{cov}(X_2 X_3) + b \text{ cov}(X_1 X_2) + a \text{ var } X_2$

and the expression for the correlation r_{23} becomes

(A17) $\quad r_{23} = \dfrac{\text{cov}(X_2 X_3) + b \text{ cov } (X_1 X_2) + a \text{ var } X_2}{\sigma_2 \sqrt{\sigma_3^2 + a^2 \sigma_2^2 + b^2 \sigma_1^2}}$

To obtain a clearer picture of the dependence of this correlation on a and b, we simplified the above expressions for the covariance by considering the special case where the correlation between the two individual variables, r_{12}, is zero. As a result,

(A16) $\quad \text{cov}(X_2 X_3) = a \text{ var } X_2$ and

(A18) $\quad r_{23} \qquad = \dfrac{a \text{ var } X_2}{\sigma_2 \sqrt{\sigma_3^2 + a^2 \sigma_2^2 + b^2 \sigma_1^2}}$

As a final simplification, we assumed that $\sigma_1^2 = \sigma_2^2 = 1$, whereupon

(A23) $\quad r_{23} \qquad = \dfrac{a}{\sqrt{(1 + a^2 + b^2)}}$

Using this expression for the correlation between X_2 and X_3 as well as the expression above for the standard deviation of X_3, we have graphed each of these as functions of a and b (see Fig. 26.1 and 2). It is apparent that in this rather simplified case, the size of the correlation of X_2 and X_3 can be quite large for certain combinations of a and b, modest for others, and virtually zero for $a = 0$. The plot for the covariance of X_2 and X_3 is not shown, but would appear as a series of horizontal lines, with y-intercepts $= a$. The "explanation" of the pattern of values for the correlation therefore turns on the standard deviation of the product term. This term is primarily a function

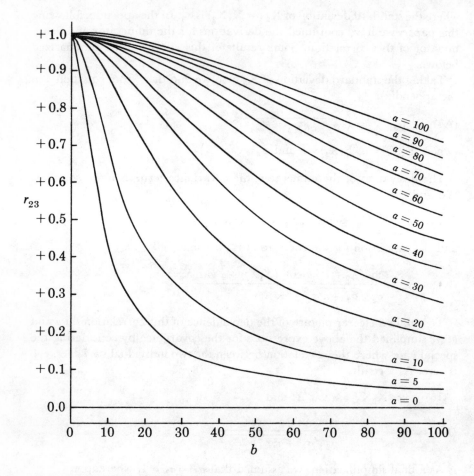

Figure 26.1. *Correlation between* X_2 *and* X_3 *for values of* a *and* b, *in the case where*

$$r_{23} = \frac{a}{(1+a^2+b^2)^{\frac{1}{2}}}; \; cov(X_2 X_3) = cov(X_1 X_2) = 0; \; var\ X_1 = var\ X_2 = 1.$$

of a and b, but for small values of either, the "1" in the expression has its effect in the curving of the lines toward the perpendicular of the y axis.

As can be seen from equation A17, the correlations for any given value of a and b will become larger in the more general case when $r_{12} \neq 0$. The numerator will swell from the contributions of $cov(X_2 X_3)$ and $cov\ (X_1 X_2)$. Yet, even in this general case, the correlation of X_2 and X_3 remains, in part, a function of the means of X_1 and X_2 (a and b). The same holds, of course, for r_{13}.

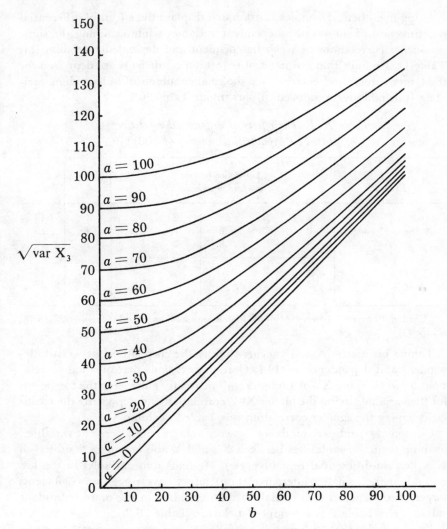

Figure 26.2. $\sqrt{\operatorname{var} X_3}$ *as a function of* a, b, *where* $\sqrt{\operatorname{var} X_3} = \sqrt{1 + a^2 + b^2}$.

Implication for nonadditive regression models

To understand the implications of the foregoing for the interpretation of the regression coefficients in equation A1, a brief review of Gordon's findings and terminology will be useful. Gordon distinguishes between the "redundancy" of variables, which refers to the high correlations between independent variables, and "repetitiveness," which refers to the number of redundant variables (1968, p. 596).

Using hypothetical samples Gordon first displays the effects of differential repetitiveness of subsets of independent variables while assuming the same zero-order correlations between independent and dependent variables (his Table 1). He finds that estimates of regression coefficients are depressed for the larger subsets and enlarged for the smaller subsets of independent variables (this table is reproduced in part in our Table 26.1).

Table 26.1. The effects of differential repetitiveness
(Based on hypothetical samples of 100) *

Example	Correlation between independent variables					r_{yi}	b_{yi}
Matrix A:	. .	.8	.8	.2	.2	.6	.19
Subsets of 3 and 2	.8	. .	.8	.2	.2	.6	.19
	.8	. .	.8	.2	.2	.6	.19
	.2	.2	.2	. .	.8	.6	.27
	.2	.2	.2	.8	. .	.6	.27

* Gordon, Robert A., 'Issues in Multiple Regression, *American Journal of Sociology*, 73(1968), p.597.

Taking his matrix A and varying slightly the correlations between independent and dependent variables, Gordon next finds that unequal correlations between Y and X's of a subset result in greatly enhancing the coefficient for the variable having the higher X–Y correlation and depressing the coefficient having the smaller correlation (his Table 2, column 4).

Gordon also studies redundancy between subsets of independent variables, assuming equal correlations between X's and Y and equal sized subsets of X's (i.e., no differential repetitiveness). He finds that variables in the less redundant (i.e., smaller intercorrelation) subset have regression coefficients larger (and standard errors smaller) than variables in the more redundant subset. (His Table 3 is reproduced below in Table 26.2.)

He concludes that differential redundancy and repetitiveness can cause misleading interpretations of any comparisons of the relative importance of variables on the basis of partial regression coefficients. The problem is one of interpretation: "It is hard to imagine any substantive importance that could be attached to the small differences between correlations" which "can create large variations among . . . regression coefficients" (1968, p. 612).

In the light of Gordon's work, let us consider the problem that collinearity between the individual X's and the product terms poses for the interpretation of regression coefficients in nonadditive models. Suppose we are estimating the coefficients in equation 1 (the corresponding causal model is

Table 26.2. The effects of two levels of unequal redundancy at three levels of between-subset correlations in a four variable matrix (all correlations with the dependent variable have been set equal to .60)*

Correlations within each two-variable subset	Correlations between subsets, $r_{13}=r_{14}=r_{23}=r_{24}$		
	.2	.5	.6
	Regression coefficients, $b_{yi}=b_{y2};\ b_{y3}=b_{y4}$		
Subset I: $r_{12}=.7$	.288	.234	.222
Subset II: $r_{34}=.8$	.264	.204	.180
Difference	.024	.030	.042
Subset I: $r_{12}=.7$ ·	.288	.246	.228
Subset II: $r_{34}=.9$	.252	.192	.156
Difference	.036	.054	.072

* Gordon, Robert A., "Issues in Multiple Regression." *American Journal of Sociology*, 73(1968), p. 601.

shown in Figure 26.3). We will make a series of assumptions to clarify the effect of this collinearity: (1) the variances of X_1 and X_2 will be assumed equal to 1; (2) the correlations of X_1, X_2 and X_3 with Y will be assumed equal (taking the cases where $r_{yx}=.6$ and $.3$); and (3) the correlations between X_1 and X_3 (r_{13}) and X_2 and X_3 (r_{23}) will be assumed equal. We will also (4) assume at first that $r_{12}=0$ and later consider the more general case where $r_{12}\neq0$.

The appropriate path equations for this hypothetical model are written below (all b's are standardized regression coefficients):

(5) $r_{y1}=\quad b_{y1}+r_{12}b_{y2}+r_{13}b_{y3}$

(6) $r_{y2}=r_{12}b_{y1}+\quad b_{y2}+r_{23}b_{y3}$

(7) $r_{y3}=r_{13}b_{y1}+r_{23}b_{y2}+\quad b_{y3}$

Since, in this example, $r_{13}=r_{23}$, it is easy to prove that $b_{y1}=b_{y2}$. If we let $r_{y1}=r_{y2}=r_{y3}=r_{yx}$, and let $b_{y1}=b_{y2}=b_A$, $b_{y3}=b_3$, and let $r_{13}=r_{23}=r_{3A}$, equations 6 and 7 can be rewritten and solved for b_A and b_3:

(8) $r_{yx}=b_A(1+r_{12})+b_3r_{3A}$

(9) $r_{yx}=2r_{3A}b_A+b_3$

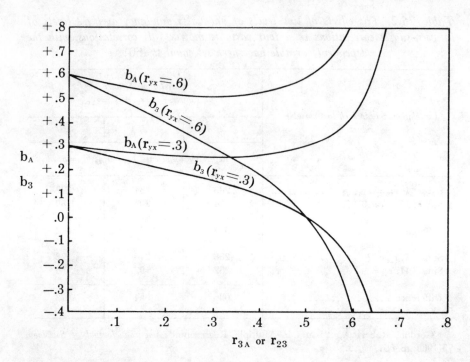

Figure 26.3a. Regression Estimates b_3, b_A as a function of r_{3A}, for $r_{12} = .0$,
$r_{yx} = .6$ *and* $.3$ ($r_{3A} = .0$ *to* $.8$).

$$(10) \quad b_A = \frac{r_{yx}(1 - r_{3A})}{(1 + r_{12} - 2r_{3A}{}^2)}$$

$$(11) \quad b_3 = \frac{r_{yx}(1 + r_{12} - 2r_{3A})}{(1 + r_{12} - 2r_{3A}{}^2)}$$

Special case: $r_{12} = 0$

In Figures 26.3a and 26.3b we have graphed the resulting values of b_A and b_3 for a range of values of r_{3A}, assuming $r_{12} = 0$, with $r_{yx} = .60$. Similar values for $r_{yx} = .30$ are shown below the lines plotted for $r_{yx} = .60$. From these two examples we can see the separate effects on the two regression coefficients of increasing collinearity r_{3A} and decreasing correlation r_{yx}.[1]

We can see from Figure 26.3a that estimates of b_A are fairly constant for

---

1. The estimates for the beta's approach infinity (plus and minus) when r_{3A} approaches the square root of $(1 + r_{12})/2$, at which point the denominators of both estimates equal zero.

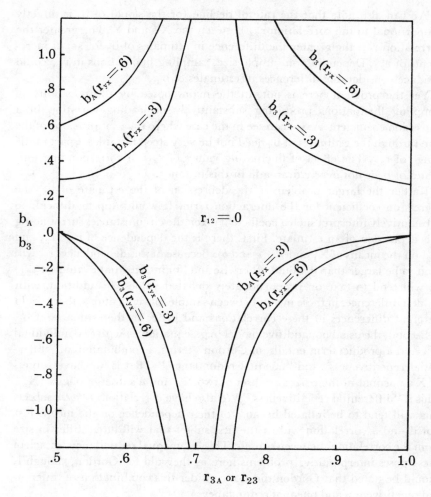

Figure 26.3b. Regression Estimates b_A, b_3 for $r_{12} = .0$, $r_{yx} = .6$ and .3
($r_{3A} = .5$ to 1.0).

values of r_{3A} from .0 to .5 (though distributed in a flattened U-shape), while estimates for b_3 decline and approach zero. Then as b_A approaches plus infinity as r_{3A} increases, b_3 approaches minus infinity. For even higher values of r_{3A} (see Figure 26.3b), estimates of b_3 are greater than for b_A. If we lower the uniform correlation between the X's and Y to .30, estimates for both coefficients decline in size, but the relationships between r_{3A} and these regression estimates are essentially unchanged.

We can also note that the rate of decline (or the slope) of b_3 is directly proportional to the correlation r_{yx} between the X's and Y. The greater the correlation r_{yx}, the greater the difference in estimates of b_3 for small increments of r_{3A}. Depending on sample size, sampling fluctuations in r_{3A} could produce considerable differences in estimates of b_3.

Yet the problem here is not, in the main, posed by the possibility of sampling fluctuations producing substantively misleading variation in a regression coefficient. As we can see in the case where $r_{yx} = .3$, the slope of the line through the estimates of b_3 need not be very steep for at least part of the range of r_{3A}. The effect of fluctuating values of r_{3A} on corresponding estimates of b_3 is not overly dramatic in this instance.

Rather the larger problem is the depression of the estimate of b_3, the regression coefficient for the interaction term. It would appear difficult to substantively interpret such a coefficient given the circumstances surrounding this depression of an estimate. First, there is the dependence of r_{3A} (r_{23} and r_{13}) on the means of X_1 and X_2 (a and b). Because of this dependence, r_{23} will tend to be larger than it would otherwise and (for intermediate values of r_{3A}) b_3 will tend to take on proportionately deflated values. In addition, with modest differences in these means between samples or replications, there could be great differences in these correlations and hence in the estimates of b_3.

Second, the usual nonadditive model (e.g., equation 1) with two individual X's and a product term entails, in Gordon's terms, a combination of "differential repetitiveness" and "unequal redundancy." That is, we have subsets of X's unequal in their size: a subset of two X's and a subset of one X (X_3). This is "differential repetitiveness." We also have correlations *between* subsets that will tend to be inflated because of their dependence on the means just noted and a correlation within the first subset that will often differ in size from the correlations between subsets. This is "unequal redundancy." Each of these poses interpretative problems here as they did for Gordon, though it should be noted that Gordon did not consider this combination of differential repetitiveness and unequal redundancy.

Of course, we see from the graph in Figure 26.3a that the differences in estimates of b_3 and b_A can be eliminated by working with variables in terms of deviation units (i.e., both a and $b = 0$). We can see that the estimates of b_3 and b_A in this instance will be equal. However, this will not hold in the more general case when $r_{12} \neq 0$, to which we turn next.

General case: $r_{12} \neq 0$

When X_1 is correlated with X_2, the means of these X's control the size of r_{23} (r_{3A}) only in part, and using variables in the form of deviation units from the means cannot therefore force this correlation to zero. First, the size of r_{23}

will be even larger for a positive r_{12} than for $r_{12}=0$, for any given values of the means, a and b. That is, r_{23} (or r_{13}) is not independent of r_{12} and hence, will tend to be larger than r_{12} (see equation A15). This means that the appropriate points of reference in the graph of estimates for this general case (Figs. 26.4a and 4b) are more toward the middle and upper part of the range of r_{3A}. Second, the lines drawn through values of b_3 and b_A (still assuming $r_{3A}=r_{13}=r_{23}$) intersect at points other than the y—intercept. By equating the expressions for b_3 and b_A, it can be seen that this is the point where $r_{12}=r_{3A}$. The greater the positive r_{12}, the further the point of intersection moves to the right. This means that for values of r_{3A} less than r_{12}, the

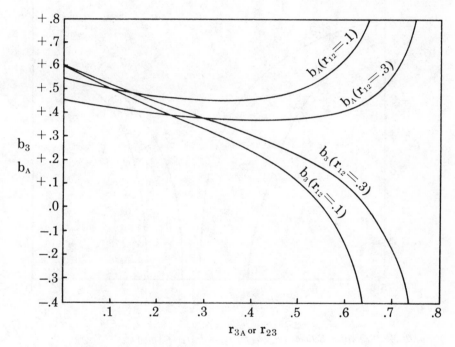

Figure 26.4a. Regression Coefficients b_3, b_A as a function of r_{3A}, for $r_{yx}=.6$,
$r_{12}=.1$ and $.3$ ($r_{3A}=.0$ to $.8$).

coefficient b_3 will be greater than b_A. Considering the first result, however, the more probable values of r_{3A} will be moderate to large, and the coefficient for the interaction term will remain smaller than those for individual terms.

In Figures 26.4a and 26.4b, we have calculated estimates for the two regression estimates for the case where $r_{yx}=.60$ and $r_{12}=.1$ and then $.3$. As can be seen, the lines for b_3 and b_A cross for values of $r_{3A}=.1$ and $.3$, respectively.

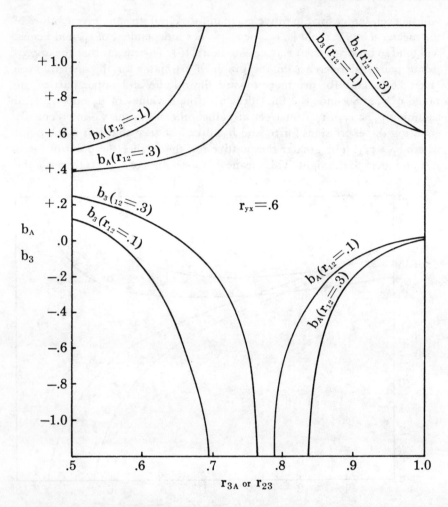

Figure 26.4b. Regression Estimates b_A, b_3 for $r_{yx} = .6$, $r_{12} = .1$ and .3
($r_{3A} = .5$ to 1.0).

Other cases

Thus far we have assumed that $\sigma_1{}^2 = \sigma_2{}^2 = 1$, that the correlations between Y and the X_1 are equal and that the individual X's are identically correlated with the product term ($r_{13} = r_{23} = r_{3A}$). We can consider the effects on the previous findings of waiving each assumption in turn. However, these touches of "realism" do not alter these findings.

$\sigma_1{}^2 = \sigma_2{}^2$

In general we would not assume that $\sigma_1{}^2 = \sigma_2{}^2 = 1$. In that case, assuming that X_1 and X_2 are independent, the variance of X_3 would be equal to the product of the variances of X_1 and X_2 and the ratio of the standard deviation of Y to that of X will differ for each X_1. Hence the ratio will be smaller for the interaction term, since $\sigma_3 > \sigma_1$, σ_2, and $\sigma_y/\sigma_3 < \sigma_y/\sigma_1$, σ_y/σ_2. The net result of waiving this assumption is that the unstandardized coefficient for the interaction term (b'_3) will be much smaller, relative to its standardized counterpart b_3, than will b'_A relative to b_A.

UNEQUAL CORRELATIONS BETWEEN Y AND X_1

As might be expected, assigning to r_{y1} a value slightly different from the other two correlations, r_{y2} and r_{y3}, has its effect on b_{y1}. For example, this coefficient is diminished slightly if $r_{y1} = .55$ while the other two correlations remain at .60. In the same manner, b_{y3} is diminished if $r_{y3} = .55$ while the others remain at .60. Despite these and other variations in the correlations between Y and X_1, there is no alteration in the previously found depression of b_{y3} relative to either b_{y2} or b_{y1}.

$r_{23} \neq r_{13}$

We can also vary r_{23} and r_{13} about previously assumed (and equal) values of $r_{3A} = r_{23} = r_{13}$. Thus, where r_{3A} had equalled .1, .2, .4, and .6, we set r_{13} below (.0, .1 etc.) each of these values and r_{23} above (i.e., .2, .3, etc), such that the absolute differences between these values and the intermediate correlations r_{3A} were the same. The result was not surprising—coefficients of b_{y1} tended to be larger than b_{y2} since X_1 had the smaller correlation with X_3. Again, the previous finding of depressed estimates for b_{y3} remained unchanged.

Discussion

In the general case where $r_{12} \neq 0$, we have seen that the correlation r_{23} depends upon the means of X_1 and X_2 (*a* and *b*) and the size of a positive r_{23} tends to be larger than a positive r_{12} as a common result. From this dependence and the emerging pattern of intercorrelations among X's we have found that the size of the interaction regression coefficient tends (with some exceptions) to be depressed relative to the coefficients for the individual terms. In addition, sampling fluctuations in the values of r_{23} over certain parts of its range will produce great fluctuations in the regression estimates of both individual and interaction terms.

Both the depression of b_3 and these possible fluctuations of estimates pose severe problems for the substantive interpretation of the regression estimates in such models as these. Substantive interpretation of these betas seems as fickle when estimates so depend on the means of the individual variables as when, as for Gordon, small differences between correlations create striking differences in estimates. Findings based on these coefficients are alleged to reflect only the adequacy of a model *vis-à-vis* the empirical world. Yet we now see that the empirical processes on which we have data are only partly reflected in the correlation matrix from which we obtain our estimates. These findings have unfortunate implications for the usual test of the interaction or non-additive as opposed to the additive model. As described elsewhere (Draper and Smith, 1966; Lane, 1968), this is an F-test to determine if the sums of squares added by the interaction term is significantly large, and hence to see if the term should be included and the non-additive model accepted.

Here the appropriate F would be:

$$F = \frac{(R^2_{NA} - R^2_A)/1}{(1 - R^2_{NA})/(N-4)}$$

where R^2_{NA} is the multiple correlation coefficient in the nonadditive model, and R^2_A the coefficient in the additive model.

The numerator and denominator are each functions of the regression coefficients (e.g., $R^2_{YX_i} = \Sigma_i b_{YX_i} r_{YX_i}$). In particular, when the coefficient for the interaction term is depressed, the regression sums of squares and multiple R square for the non-additive model will be smaller than otherwise, making the denominator larger and the difference in the numerator smaller. This reduces the size of the ratio overall. Thus, in certain instances a depressed b_3 could lead to a rejection of the interaction model.

It would appear, in short, that including multiplicative terms in regression models is not an appropriate way of assessing the presence of interaction among our independent variables. This is not altogether an original finding. Similar problems plague correlations between per capita measures and nation size, or between other types of rates and variables that are individual components of these rates (Tufte, 1969a, 1969b).

The discussion above has considered only the simplest sort of nonadditive model. More common are equations (Lane, 1968; Jackson and Burke, 1965) with several multiplicative terms. It is also common for such equations to be comprised of dummy variables, at least in part. The causal models implied and the correlation matrices for the X's are thus somewhat more complex than those considered above.

While a complete treatment of more complex nonadditive models is beyond the scope of this paper, it can be briefly argued that the above findings hold when the above approach is extended to such models. Let us consider a model such as shown in Figure 26.5, described by the equation:

(12) $\quad Y = b_1 X_1 + b_2 X_2 + b_3 X_3 + b_4 X_4 + b_5 X_5 + b_6 X_6,$

where $X_4 = X_1 X_2$, $X_5 = X_1 X_3$ and $X_6 = X_2 X_3$, and $X_1 = X_1 + a$, $X_2 = X_2 + b$, and $X_3 = X_3 + c$.

Equations for the paths from X_1, X_2 or X_3 will contain correlations among these X's and between them and the product terms. In this respect, one change over the former model (equation 1) is the number of such inter-correlations: two within the first subset of individual X's instead of one; three between the subsets of individual and product terms instead of two. What is unchanged is the dependence of the correlations *between* subsets (i.e., r_{14}, r_{24}, r_{15}, r_{35}, r_{26}, r_{36}) on the means of X_1, X_2, and X_3 (let these be a, b, and c) and on the other correlations within the first subset. Hence the former correlations will again tend to be larger than the latter correlations. So far, the same resultant—the larger size of the individual terms' coefficients relative to the product terms' coefficients for much of the range of the between subset correlations—is in the offing.

As can be seen in the lower right quadrant of the illustrative correlation matrix (Fig. 26.5), there are now some intercorrelations among product terms to deal with. The question immediately arises, are these *also* dependent on the means of the individual X's and on their intercorrelations. It can be shown that this is so. Without going through the complete derivation here, the expression for one of these intercorrelations, r_{45}, derived under the same conditions as the expression for r_{23} in equation 23 (var $X_i = 1$ and $E(X_i) = 0$ for i = 1, 2, 3; and cov $(X_1 X_2) =$ cov $(X_1 X_3) = \mathrm{cov}(X_2 X_3) = 0$) is

(13) $\quad r_{45} = \dfrac{b\,c}{\sqrt{(1 + a^2 + b^2)(1 + a^2 + c^2)}}$

Comparing this with equation A23, we see that if all the individual X's had the same mean $(a = b = c)$, then $r_{45} = r_{23}^2$. In general this will not exactly hold, but it does seem that correlations among product terms are roughly squares of corresponding correlations among individual terms.

We can sketch the results of a path analysis estimation of the betas for the individual and product terms, using the model in Figure 26.5. Let all the correlations between the X's and Y, $r_{yx} = .70$, the correlations (r_A) among individual terms be equal and zero $(r_A = r_{12} = r_{23} = r_{13} = 0)$, the correlations (r_B) between subsets of the individual and product terms be equal $(r_B = r_{14} = r_{15} = r_{24} = r_{26} = r_{34} = r_{36})$ and the correlations (r_C) among product terms be equal $(r_C = r_{45} = r_{46} = r_{56})$. Since $r_A = 0$, it turns out that there will be equal

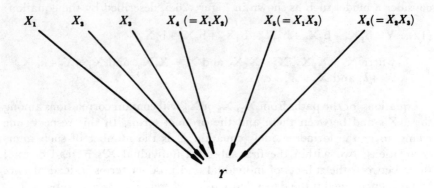

A. Causal model

	X_1	X_2	X_3	X_4	X_5	X_6
X_1	..					
X_2	r_A	..				
X_3	r_A	r_A	..			
X_4	r_B	r_B	r_D	..		
X_5	r_B	r_D	r_B	r_C	..	
X_6	r_D	r_B	r_B	r_C	r_C	..

B. Correlation matrix

Figure 26.5. *Causal Model and Correlation Matrix for*
$$Y = b_1 X_1 + b_2 X_2 + b_3 X_3 + b_4 X_4 + b_5 X_5 + b_6 X_6.$$

and zero correlations (r_D) between individual X's and the product terms not comprised of those X's ($r_D = r_{34} = r_{25} = r_{16}$).

The (more general) path equations for the model are:

(14) $r_{y1} = \quad b_{y1} + r_A b_{y2} + r_A b_{y3} + r_B b_{y4} + r_B b_{y5} + r_D b_{y6}$

(15) $r_{y2} = r_A b_{y1} + \quad b_{y2} + r_A b_{y3} + r_B b_{y4} + r_D b_{y5} + r_B b_{y6}$

(16) $r_{y3} = r_A b_{y1} + r_A b_{y2} + \quad b_{y3} + r_D b_{y4} + r_B b_{y5} + r_B b_{y6}$

(17) $r_{y4} = r_B b_{y1} + r_B b_{y2} + r_D b_{y3} + \quad b_{y4} + r_C b_{y5} + r_C b_{y6}$

(18) $r_{y5} = r_B b_{y1} + r_D b_{y2} + r_B b_{y3} + r_C b_{y4} + \quad b_{y5} + r_C b_{y6}$

(19) $r_{y6} = r_D b_{y1} + r_B b_{y2} + r_B b_{y3} + r_C b_{y4} + r_C\, b_{y5} + \quad b_{y6}$

As before, $b_{y1} = b_{y2} = b_{y3} = b_A$ and $b_{y4} = b_{y5} = b_{y6} = b_C$, as a result of our assumptions above.[2] Hence, solving these equations for b_A and b_3 (assuming $r_A = r_D = 0$), we get

(20) $b_C = \dfrac{r_{yx}(1 - 2r_B)}{(1 + 2r_C - 4r_B{}^2)}$ and $b_A = \dfrac{r_{yx}(1 + 2r_C - 2r_B)}{(1 + 2r_C - 4r_B{}^2)}$

The pattern of estimates for a full range of values of r_B (and, following equation 13, $r_C = r_B{}^2$) is very similar to that in Figures 26.3 and 26.4. Hence the same conclusions reached earlier apply here as well. Of course, the inter-correlations among individual X's will not, in general, be zero, though in some cases the average of these intercorrelations might be zero. For a slightly more general case in which $r_A = .10$, $r_D = .15$[3] $r_{yx} = .6$ and varying values of r_B (and $r_C = r_B{}^2$), a very similar pattern of estimates is again observed. In the completely general case, neither will $r_{12} = r_{13} = r_{23}$ nor will $b_{y1} = b_{y2} = b_{y3}$. The above findings should still apply in the main, however, with the respective average of beta estimates for the individual and product terms reflecting the means of the individual X's and the average levels of the sets of correlations previously assumed equal (r_A, r_B, r_C, r_D).

References

BLALOCK, H. M., Jr. 1963. "Correlated Independent Variables: The Problem of Multicollinearity." *American Journal of Sociology*, 42: 233–237.

———. 1965. "Theory Building and the Concept of Interaction." *American Sociological Review*, 30: 374–381.

BRUNK, H. D. 1960. *An Introduction to Mathematical Statistics*. Boston: Ginn.

DRAPER, N., and SMITH, H. 1966. *Applied Regression Analysis*. New York: Wiley.

FARRAR, DONALD E., and GLAUBER, ROBERT R. 1967. "Multicollinearity in Regression Analysis: The Problem Revisited." *Review of Economics and Statistics*, 49: 92–107.

GOCKEL, GALEN. 1969. "Income and Religious Affiliation: A Regression Analysis." *American Journal of Sociology*, 74: 632–646.

GORDON, ROBERT A. 1968. "Issues in Multiple Regression." *American Journal of Sociology*, 73: 592–616.

2. This can be shown by using determinants and Cramer's Rule to solve for the paths. By interchanging certain rows and columns, it can be shown that the respective determinants used to solve for the betas in each subset are identical.

3. The value of the intercorrelations within the subset of product terms was suggested by an expression (not shown) for one of the correlations signified by r_D, r_{16}, assuming equal means of X_1, X_2, and X_3, $a = b = c$.

JACKSON, ELTON, and BURKE, PETER. 1965. "Status and Symptoms of Stress: Additive and Interaction Effects." *American Sociological Review, 30*: 556–564.

LANE, ANGELA. 1968. "Occupational Mobility in Six Cities." *American Sociological Review, 33*: 740–749.

LENSKI, GERHARD. 1954. "Status Crystallization: A Non-Vertical Dimension." *American Sociological Review, 19*: 405–413.

———. 1956. "Social Participation and Status Crystallization." *American Sociological Review, 21*: 458–464.

———. 1964. "Comment." *Public Opinion Quarterly, 28*: 326–330.

TUFTE, EDWARD R. 1969a. "Improving Data Analysis in Political Science." *World Politics, 21* (July, 1969): 641–654.

———. 1969b. "A Note of Caution in Using Variables That Have Common Elements." *Public Opinion Quarterly, 33* (Winter): 622–625.

Appendix

STANDARD DEVIATION OF X_3

The derivation of the standard deviation is as follows.

(A1) $\sqrt{\text{var } X_3} = \sqrt{\text{var }(X_1 X_2)} = \sqrt{\text{var }(X_1 + a)(X_2 + b)}$

(A2) $= \sqrt{\text{var }(X_1 X_2 + aX_2 + bX_1 + ab)}$

(A3) $= \sqrt{\text{var } X_1 X_2 + a^2 \text{ var } X_2 + b^2 \text{ var } X_1}$

(A4) $= \sqrt{\sigma_3{}^2 + a^2\sigma_2{}^2 + b^2\sigma_1{}^2}$ where $\sigma_3 = \sqrt{\text{var } X_3}$

COVARIANCE OF $X_2 X_3$

The covariance of one of the independent variables, X_2 and the product term, X_3 $(= X_1 X_2)$ is as follows.

(A5) $\text{cov}(X_2 X_3) = E(X_2 X_3) - [E(X_2)\ E(X_3)]$

$= E(X_2 X_3) - [E(X_2)\ E(X_1 X_2)]$

Since $X_1 = X_1 + a$ and $X_2 = X_2 + b$, equation A5 can be written as

(A6) $= E(X_2 + b)^2\ (X_1 + a) - E(X_2 + b)\ [E(X_1 + a)(X_2 + b)]$

$= E(X_2{}^2 + 2bX_2 + b^2)(X_1 + a) - E(X_2 + b)[E(X_1 + a)$

$(X_2 + b)]$

(A7) $= E(X_1 X_2{}^2 + 2bX_1 X_2 + b^2 X_1{}^2 + aX_2{}^2 + 2abX_2{}^2 + ab^2)$

$- E(X_2 + b)[E(X_1 X_2 + aX_2 + bX_1 + ab)]$

(A8) $= E(X_1 X_2{}^2) + 2bE(X_1 X_2) + b^2 E(X_1) + a\ E(X_2{}^2)$

$+ 2ab\ E(X_2) + a\ b^2 - [E(X_2) + b][E(X_1 X_2) + a\ E(X_2)$

$+ bE(X_1) + a\ b]$

For the remainder of this derivation, we will confine ourselves to the case where $E(X_1) = E(X_2) = 0$. Several terms in equation (A8) drop out and we are left with:

$$(A9) \qquad = E(X_1X_2{}^2) + 2bE(X_1X_2) + aE(X_2{}^2) + ab^2 - b[E(X_1X_2) + ab]$$

$$(A10) \qquad = E(X_1X_2{}^2) + 2bE(X_1X_2) + aE(X_2{}^2) - bE(X_1X_2)$$

$$(A11) \qquad = E(X_1X_2{}^2) + bE(X_1X_2) + aE(X_2{}^2)$$

Since $E(X_2) = 0$ and $E(X_1) = 0$, we know that

$$(A12) \quad \text{var } X_2 = E(X_2{}^2) - [E(X_2)]^2 = E(X_2{}^2) \text{ and that}$$

$$(A13) \quad \text{cov } (X_1X_2) = E(X_1X_2) - [E(X_1)\ E(X_2)] = E(X_1X_2).$$

Since $E(X_1X_2{}^2) = E(X_2X_3)$ we also know that

$$(A14) \qquad E(X_2X_3) = E(X_2X_3) - [E(X_2)\ E(X_3)] = \text{cov } (X_2X_3)$$

Equation (A11) is therefore equivalent to

$$(A15) \quad \text{cov } (X_2X_3) = \text{cov } (X_2X_3) + b \text{ cov } (X_1X_2) + a \text{ var } X_2$$

In the special case where X_1 and X_2 are independent of each other, i.e., when the $\text{cov}(X_1X_2) = 0$, the $\text{cov}(X_2X_3) = 0$. (Since they are independent, X_1 will also be independent of $X_2{}^2$ (Brunk, 1960, p. 80). Hence, with $E(X_1) = 0$, $E(X_1X_2{}^2) = [E(X_1)\ E(X_2{}^2)] = 0$.) In this special case, equation (A15) becomes

$$(A16) \quad \text{cov } (X_2X_3) = a \text{ var } X_2$$

CORRELATION OF X_2 AND X_3

We will continue to assume that $E(X_1) = E(X_2) = 0$.
From equations (A15) and (A4) we have

$$(A17) \qquad r_{23} = \text{cov } (X_2X_3)/\sigma_2\sigma_3$$

$$= \frac{\text{cov } (X_2X_3) + b \text{ cov } X_1X_2 + a \text{ var } X_2}{\sigma_2\sqrt{\sigma_3{}^2 + a^2\sigma_2{}^2 + b^2\sigma_1{}^2}}$$

In the special case where $r_{12} = \text{cov } (X_1X_2) = 0$, this correlation becomes

$$(A18) \qquad = \frac{a \text{ var } X_2}{\sigma_2\sqrt{\sigma_3{}^2 + a^2\sigma_2{}^2 + b^2\sigma_1{}^2}}$$

One final simplification of the above expression is possible if we assume that the var $X_1 = $ var $X_2 = 1$. With this and previous assumptions,

(A19)   var $X_3 = 1$.

To show this we first need a general expression for var X_3:

(A20)   var $X_3 = E(X_3{}^2) - [E(X_3)]^2 = E(X_1 X_2)^2 - [E(X_1 X_2)]^2$
$$= E(X_1{}^2 X_2{}^2) - [E(X_1)\ E(X_2)]^2 = E(X_1{}^2 X_2{}^2).$$

Because X_1 and X_2 are independent, their squares are independent (Brunk, 1960, p. 80), and

(A21) $E(X_1{}^2 X_2{}^2) = [E(X_1)^2\ E(X_2)^2]$.

Since in general, var $Y = E(Y)^2 - [E(Y)]^2$, $E(Y)^2 = $ var $Y + [E(Y)]^2$. Hence we can write equation (A21) as

(A22) $E(X_1{}^2 X_2{}^2) = [\text{var } X_1 + (E(X_1))^2][\text{var } X_2 + (E(X_2))^2]$
$$= (\text{var } X_1)(\text{var } X_2).$$

Assuming that these variances each equal 1, we have the result in equation (A19).

Therefore the expression for r_{23} in equation (A18) can be further simplified under these assumptions:

(A23) $$r_{23} = \frac{a}{\sqrt{1 + a^2 + b^2}}$$

Chapter 27

PROBLEMS OF AGGREGATION

Michael T. Hannan*
Stanford University

The thrust of the majority of papers in this volume is to demonstrate the advantages of regression-based linear causal models for theory testing and construction in the social sciences. As has already been discussed, such approaches to making causal inferences from nonexperimental data place a number of constraints on the analyst. In particular, he must make explicit most of the assumptions underlying both his model and analysis operations. Among other things, he must close the theoretical model and make assumptions about the influences of outside variables, distinguish between measured and unmeasured variables, and specify the relations between theoretical constructs and indicators. All such constraints seem likely to improve the quality of nonexperimental research and enhance the possibilities of cumulation in the social sciences.

It is crucial in any discussion of these techniques to keep in mind the restrictiveness of the assumptions justifying their use. Given the state of theory and data in the nonexperimental social sciences, it is highly unlikely that all of the assumptions underlying any one of the techniques will be met in any substantively interesting application. In other words, complications are almost certain to arise when substantive specialists employ the proposed techniques. The advocacy of the use of linear causal model-testing procedures demands an examination of the impact of those complications that are thought to be most likely to arise in specific areas of application. A number of the econometricians and biometricians who have pioneered in the development of linear causal analysis have devoted considerable attention to complications.

Paper prepared especially for *Causal Models in the Social Sciences*.
* I would like to acknowledge the helpful comments of H. M. Blalock, Jr., Allan Mazur, John Meyer, and Francesca Cancian on an earlier draft and the editorial and typing assistance of the Laboratory for Social Research, Stanford University.

Among the complications that have received the most attention are errors in variables (including measurement error), errors of specification, multicollinearity, identification problems, problems of autocorrelation, the introduction of unmeasured variables, and changes in units of analysis.

As sociologists increasingly make use of the techniques under discussion, they will undoubtedly encounter many of the same complications found in economic and biological applications. In such cases we should be quick to seek out and adopt formulations that have proved fruitful in other disciplines, if such formulations exist. It seems likely, however, that as a consequence of differing theoretical predispositions and problem foci, sociologists will also face some complications not previously addressed in other fields. In this case we may be able to modify procedures created to handle quite different problems, or we may have to begin *de nouveau*. I would suspect that most of the complications sociologists will face will turn out to be analogous to those arising in quite different applications in other fields, with a component specific or unique to sociological research designs. If this proves to be the case, a useful set of methodological tasks would involve: (1) the identification of complications most likely to lead to faulty inference in the sociological applications of linear causal techniques: (2) a search for problem formulations that have been created to identify (and hopefully, to resolve) the same or analogous complications in other disciplines; and (3) critically evaluating the feasibility and fruitfulness of employing such formulations in sociological designs.

This is not to suggest some new line of methodological inquiry. Sociologists have been engaged in such a process almost continually since they became aware of the model-testing strategies. A notable early example is Blalock's (1964, chaps. 4 and 5) discussion of complications likely to arise in sociological applications of what has come to be known as the Simon-Blalock technique. In this paper I am attempting to continue and expand on a discussion presented there concerning the effects of changes in units or levels of analysis. In this case I will attempt to borrow quite heavily from a highly technical body of literature in economics. Much of the focus will be on reformulating mathematical and statistical arguments in causal terms more familiar to sociologists and in trying to demonstrate that an explicit causal perspective elucidates some issues that tend to be hidden in the technical complexity of the original arguments.

Sociologists are undoubtedly more familiar with that aspect of the problem of changing units labeled *disaggregation*. The attention of the discipline was forcefully directed to the problem of disaggregation by W. S. Robinson's (1950) discussion of the "ecological fallacy." He demonstrated the wide potential divergence between measures of association computed on individual level data and those computed on aggregate data. The ecological fallacy, then, consists of inferring individual relationships from calculated aggregate relationships. Sociologists are just becoming aware of the issues involved in the converse problem of *aggregation*. Much of the relevant commentary on past and present positions in the social sciences on aggregation and disaggregation is summarized in an excellent symposium collection of quantitative ecological analysis (Doggan and Rokkan, 1969), which will almost certainly stimulate additional thinking on the issues.

The available discussions of the issues tend in large measure to stress fallacious technique. Thus, we see reference to the ecological fallacy, the individualistic fallacy (arising in the aggregation of individual units) and the more inclusive term: the fallacy of the wrong level (Galtung, 1967). I agree that at some point in the development of a methodology it is useful to stress possible fallacies. But, it seems that once a complication has been brought to the attention of a discipline, a continued stress on fallacies *per se* may tend to stifle research rather than improve research practice or extend the range of research possibilities.[1] The establishment of a more sophisticated methodology would seem to require movement from such categorical thinking to a consideration of likely magnitude of errors and consequent faulty inference associated with specified procedures under a variety of situations. This seems particularly true with respect to some of the problems involved in changing units of analysis. Robinson's (1950) paper was directed at discouraging what he saw as faulty research practice. It has become clear, however, that the problems of changing units of analysis in research designs do not arise solely as a consequence of poorly conceived research. There are a number of situations in which the researcher has no choice but to compromise his design by employing data gathered on the "wrong" level or to abandon an interesting and perhaps important line of investigation.

In other words, problems of aggregation and disaggregation arise largely as a consequence of *missing data*. There are, no doubt, contemporary examples of the uncritical shifting of units which Robinson criticized. This is not the focus of this analysis, however. An early and still important example of missing data problems is presented by Durkheim's analysis of suicide. His analysis presents a clear example of the problem of disaggregation of empirical relations. Doggan and Rokkan (1969, pp. 5–6) suggest a wide variety of situations in which missing data problems are likely to arise:

> There may be data for *individuals* across a range of areal units but no way of identifying the characteristics of the proximal community contexts of their behavior (for an ecological analysis). This is frequently the case in secondary analysis of nationwide sample surveys; for reasons of secrecy, or economy, or sloppy administration, there may no longer be any possibility of allocating individual respondents to any known set of primary sampling units.

1. A forceful statement of this position is presented by Allardt (1969).

The contrary situation is even more frequent: no individual data are at hand, but *aggregate* distributions have been established for territorial units at different levels. This is the case for a wide variety of official statistics: the primary individual data have either been kept secret from the outset, as in elections or referenda, or cannot be made available for administrative or economic reasons, as will often be the case for census data, school grades, tax records, criminal statistics.

Problems of missing data are likely to be particularly acute in historical or "backward-looking" longitudinal research.[2] Here the researcher does not have the option of collecting the appropriate data; he must work with what is available or abandon the project.

To this point I have been considering changes of units or levels within a single design. Another aspect of the problem of changing units has received relatively little attention. This involves the problem of comparing research results (e.g., path coefficients, partial regression coefficients, etc.) of studies formulated on different levels of analysis employing the "same" models. In such attempts at comparison it becomes crucial to find a way to separate out the effects that are due to aggregation or disaggregation bias (to be defined below) from "true" differences at different levels. The Doggan and Rokkan collection evidences increasing interest in this issue stimulated by an interest in cross-national comparisons of results at different levels and the beginnings of data-banks that will facilitate such comparisons. Allardt (1969; p. 45), for example, evidences this concern:

> The real issue in methodological discussions of today does not seem to be the ecological fallacy but the techniques used in analyzing data from many levels of social organization.

This is another example of a concern with the effects of changing units of analysis that is not concerned with poor research technique but with extending the range of possibilities of existing methods.

The aggregation-disaggregation issues involved in comparing research results from different levels are not so obvious when the results are stated in verbal form. The same seems to be true when the results are stated in more or less descriptive form using percentage differences or coefficients of association. This perhaps explains the relative lack of attention paid to this issue. However, as attention shifts to comparing regression coefficients and similar measures and to mathematical formulations, I would expect the complications I will outline in this paper to become potentially more troublesome.

2. Linz (1969) presents an excellent discussion of some of the cross-level analysis problems faced in such research. We will see below that time-series or longitudinal research is subject to peculiar aggregation-disaggregation problems.

1. The consistency formulation

There are a number of perspectives from which sociologists might address the issue of changing levels of analysis. At the most abstract level there is an admixture of theoretical and methodological issues. Although the distinction between theoretical and methodological concerns is often arbitrary and artificial, a paper of this nature cannot hope to address both sides of the issues. For this reason I will not address the many theoretical issues involved in this problem. Let it suffice to say that the import of the technical results will depend largely on the reader's position on the question of "theoretical scope" (to use Wagner's [1964] term). Elsewhere (Hannan, 1970) I have developed a distinction suggested by Wagner between a *homology approach*, which supports the free translation of theoretical propositions across levels of analysis, and an *inconsistency position*, which rejects such a notion. I would suspect that most sociologists would reject both extreme positions and place themselves somewhere in the middle of the continuum suggested by the terms. At any rate, readers whose positions are closer to the inconsistency end of the continuum are likely to be tempted to reject aggregation and disaggregation out of hand. But it is not as simple as this. It appears that even some of those social scientists who on the theoretical level would reject the homology assumption make simplifying assumptions either in gathering data (e.g., using simple random samples in an attempt to obtain "structural" information) or in making abstract theoretical statements (e.g., constructing mathematical models that are assumed to hold for more than one level) that imply homology. In any case, the seriousness with which the reader views the conclusion that changes in levels of analysis, especially in longitudinal research, tend to produce "artificial" changes in statistical parameter estimates will depend largely on the degree to which he thinks this is natural and appropriate (due to the presence of an ontological gap between levels, "emergent properties," etc.).

The earliest concerns with problems of aggregation and disaggregation, at least in economics, arose in the context of exact or deterministic models. A number of early discussions raised serious issues of lack of consistency between analogous macro- and micro-functions when both were composed of exact relationships. Our concern is more directed at stochastic models. The statistical estimation aspects of the problem of changing units followed logically from the deterministic results. Sociologists focused from the beginning on coefficients of association, while economists have tended to restrict their attention (with a few notable exceptions discussed below) to regression estimates. In both disciplines methodological concern seems to have been aroused when it was found that aggregation and disaggregation produced results that could not be accounted for by the homology model. This is implied in the sociological literature and made explicit in the economic discussions. The economists who early examined the issue formulated an operational analog of the homology model labeled the *consistency criterion*. This was crucial since it provided a criterion against which to evaluate the effects of actually changing levels with empirical data on the statistical estimates on the level of interest. That is, this formulation permitted the identification of *aggregation-disaggregation bias*. The consistency criterion allows one to identify the changes in estimates that are due solely to aggregation-disaggregation. In other words, if the model specifies that the properties of models at different levels are identical, then any deviation at different levels can be attributed to the biasing effect of changing units. This is precisely how the problem was formulated for sociologists by Robinson (1950) and for economists by Klein (1946), May (1946), and Theil (1954).

Let us focus on the economists' formulation. We are concerned with three kinds of relationships: *microrelations*, composed of microvariables, *macrorelations*, composed of macrovariables and formed by analogy with the micromodel, and *aggregation relations*, which define macrovariables in terms of "corresponding" microvariables.[3] For a simple three variable recursive model we can represent the situation as in Figure 27.1. Here X_1, X_2 and X_3 are microvariables, X'_1, X'_2 and X'_3 are the corresponding macrovariables.

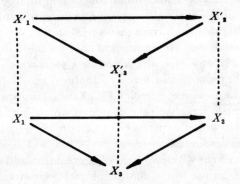

Figure 27.1.

We draw dashed lines from microvariables to corresponding macrovariables to indicate a systematic functional relationship to which we do not attach any causal significance. All of the other relations expressed in the model can be thought of as causal.

Before addressing the analytic issues raised by this formulation, I will

3. This is the appropriate formulation for considering problems of aggregation. A concern with disaggregation would have us begin with a macromodel, a micromodel formed by analogy with the macromodel, and a set of disaggregation relations.

present two examples, one from economics and one from sociology. Both are meant to be suggestive and illustrative rather than to be serious substantive models. Allen (1956) suggests the following situation. Suppose we had a well-established micro demand function that stated that the individual household's demand for tea was a function of household income, the price of tea, and the prices of several related commodities. By analogy we might construct a macromodel in which the aggregate demand for tea was a function of national income, the price of tea, and a general price index. The aggregation relations are obvious, the macro demand variable is the sum of the individual household demands, national income is the sum of all the incomes of households, etc.

A sociologist might be more interested in a model like the following. Consider a micromodel that takes the individual academic achievement (ae_i) as a function of student's parents' education (pe_i), father's occupation (fo_i) and student's measured academic aptitude (a_i):

$$ae_i = f_i(pe_i, fo_i, a_i) \tag{1}$$
$$(i = 1, \ldots, N).$$

The subscripting of the symbol denoting the function indicates that we are not requiring that all individuals "behave" alike with respect to changes in the explanatory variables. The question of whether or not all individuals in the sample do behave alike with respect to the variables included in the model becomes a significant issue in the discussion of aggreagtion in k-variable models (below). Second, consider a macromodel formed by analogy to the micromodel:

$$AE = F(PE, FO, A). \tag{2}$$

This model can be assumed to hold for classes, homerooms, entire schools, etc. Finally, we must define the functional relations between microvariables and macrovariables:

$$
\begin{aligned}
AE &= g(ae_1, \ldots, ae_n), \\
PE &= h(pe_1, \ldots, pe_n), \\
FO &= l(fo_1, \ldots, fo_n), \\
A &= m(a_1, \ldots, a_n).
\end{aligned}
\tag{3}
$$

These relations might express the macrovariables as the arithmetic means of the (scaled) microvariables for each homeroom, or on the other hand, we might define the macrovariables as distribution or dispersion measures of the corresponding microvariables, etc. For the present time we do not specify anything about the form of the three kinds of relations except to note that "noncorresponding" microvariables do not enter into the function defining macrovariables. In Figure 27.1 this is indicated by the absence of a dashed line drawn connecting any macrovariable with any noncorresponding microvariable.

Now that we have considered examples of the three kinds of relations, we can consider the issue of consistency. In any analysis of aggregation and disaggregation we must concern ourselves with the interrelations of all three kinds of relationships. The analytic problem arises as a result of the functional dependence of the macrovariables on the microvariables. This functional dependence (expressed in the aggregation relations) produces more relationships than can be chosen independently as inspection of Figure 27.1 would suggest.

Such a situation raises the possibility that the relations may be defined in such a way as to be inconsistent with each other. Although the parallels are not completely clear, this seems much like the situation of overidentification of models, which allows the possibility that the model be inconsistent with certain sets of data. Here the possibility that the three kinds of relations may be defined in ways such that, when the three are taken together, inconsistencies arise, motivates the study of the conditions under which they will be consistent. The economists have defined consistency very concretely. Green (1964, p. 35), for example, states the following:

> Consistency means that a knowledge of the "macro-relations" . . . and of the value of the aggregate independent variables would lead to the same value of the aggregate dependent variable as a knowledge of the micro-relations and the values of the individual independent variables.

Perhaps reference to a specific simple model will help clarify the meaning of this definition. What does it require of the model drawn in Figure 27.1? We are concerned with the equality of two different methods for generating predicted values of the macro dependent variable, X'_3 in this case. The first is the straightforward regression (since I have defined the model as a linear recursive one) of observed values of X'_3 on X'_1 and X'_2. We will denote the resulting prediction $\hat{X}'_3$. The second method involves obtaining predicted values of X_{3i} for all microunits using the microregressions and then aggregating the X_{3i} according to the aggregation rule (relation) defining X'_3. We will denote this value $\hat{X}''_3$. By the definition presented above, aggregation will be consistent for this model if and only if $\hat{X}'_3 = \hat{X}''_3$. If this equality does not hold, the difference $\hat{X}'_3 - \hat{X}''_3$ is said to be due to the presence of *aggregation bias* in the macroparameters. We will be able to show below what such bias terms are likely to be. It is the presence of varying magnitudes of aggregation bias in parameter estimates that I am proposing as one potential complication in the testing and evaluating of causal models.

Returning to the general statement of the problem of consistency, we can define any two of the three relations and analyze the restrictions that the third must meet for aggregation to be consistent. Since we are dealing with aggregation, we expect the micromodel to be well defined. Two broad strategies thus present themselves.[4] First, we can define the micromodel and an analogous macromodel and attempt to find the class of aggregation relations that will produce consistent aggregation. This approach has been suggested by Klein (1946) and Theil (1954). A second approach would be to define the micromodel and employ some widely used or theoretically appropriate aggregation relations and then search for consistent macromodels. This approach has been advocated by May (1946). This presentation will pursue the first course simply because the available statistical literature follows Theil's strategy.

To this point I have framed the problem in terms of aggregation. Sociologists are more familiar with the problems of disaggregation. However, examination of the sociological analyses of the disaggregation problem shows that the problem of aggregation must be dealt with (at least implicitly) before conclusions about disaggregation can be drawn. In this paper I will restrict myself to the logically prior problem of aggregation. Elsewhere (Hannan, 1970), I have summarized the existing literature on disaggregation and related the problem to what is being considered here.

2. Aggregation bias as measurement error?

Before moving on to the more technical analysis of aggregation bias, we should examine the implications of the close similarity of the problem of aggregation and conventional treatments of measurement error. One of the central aspects of this formulation of the aggregation problem is the requirement that corresponding microvariables and macrovariables be functionally related. That is, we require that there be unambiguous rules that assign unique values to the macrovariables on the basis of the values taken by the corresponding microvariables. First of all, how much does this restrict the generality of this analysis? Consistency as defined here is meaningful only when the macrovariables are all mathematical transformations of corresponding microvariables. Thus, we can restate the above question to ask how often sociologists use macrovariables of this nature.

Lazarsfeld and Menzel (1961) in a well-known discussion of the properties of measures at different levels of analysis label these kinds of macrovariables *analytical*. They are distinguished primarily from *global* macrovariables, which

---

4. This oversimplifies the variety of approaches adopted at one time or another. A useful classification of such approaches together with an up-to-date bibliography from the economics literature is found in Nataf (1969).

are defined without reference to the properties of the microunits that comprise the aggregate or collectivity. Analytical variables are typically means, proportions, standard deviations, etc. Examples of global variables usually characterize a collectivity on the basis of presence or absence of a characteristic like money as a medium of exchange or achievement motive in folk tales. However, Lazarsfeld and Menzel also characterize density measures as global variables.

It is my impression that the macrovariables employed in sociological research are more frequently analytical than global. In fact, one of the most pressing measurement problems facing the discipline is precisely a general inability to construct macro- or "structural" measures that mirror the meaning of macrotheories, i.e., measures that are more than simple transformations of individual properties or behaviors. If this assessment is accurate, the empirical problems of changing units in sociological research when macrovariables are analytical does not involve rare or special cases but may represent the modal case.

Unfortunately, this analysis will not help clarify the fundamental measurement problem mentioned above. Still, the aggregation problem as developed to this point seems to have much in common with conventional treatments of measurement error. As I have already pointed out, problems of aggregation-disaggregation arise in sociology primarily as a consequence of absence of data at the level of interest. If we consider the observed macrovariables as imperfect measures of "structural" variables (e.g., measured per capita income as an imperfect measure of "true" per capita income), we can conceptualize the intersection of the issues of measurement error and aggregation bias in a rather straightforward way.

Consider the more complicated model drawn in Figure 27.2. Here we introduce a set of theoretical macrovariables, $\bar{X}_1$, $\bar{X}_2$, and $\bar{X}_3$. We now consider the aggregated microvalues (what we are calling the macrovalues) to be measured values of the theoretical macrovariables. Following current practice in causal analyses of measurement error, we assume that the measured values are produced by the joint action of the "true" values and a number of other influences (e.g., response set, coding error, censorship, etc.) lumped together as measurement error. Thus, in this model we have causal arrows drawn from macro theoretical variables to corresponding measured variables, as well as arrows from the symbols e_1, e_2, e_3 representing the measurement error terms. Note that for purposes of simplicity we are assuming that the micromodel is perfectly measured. We wouldn't, of course, expect this in any application. But the presence of measurement error in the micromodel is not relevant to this brief excursus.

We can use the model drawn in Figure 27.2 to point out the main difference between the two concerns. In considering measurement issues we are by

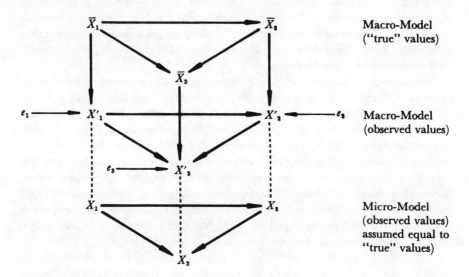

Figure 27.2.

definition dealing with the correspondence between observed and unmeasured values (in this example, $\bar{X}_1$ and X'_1, etc.). In aggregation analyses we must concern ourselves with measured quantities at two levels of aggregation. Further, we do not usually specify a causal relation between corresponding microvariables and macrovariables. Despite this fundamental difference, there remain numerous similarities between the two concerns. And Theil (1961) has suggested that it might prove useful to consider measurement error and aggregation bias as two special cases of *specification error*.[5] The reader who wishes to pursue this formal similarity is urged to consult this provocative but rather technically difficult work.

3. Aggregation bias: The bivariate case

Sociologists have tended to confine their attention *vis-à-vis* problems of changing units to relationships between two variables. Thus, we will start with this case and later discover that the bivariate case is rather a special case in the sense that some of the most troublesome problems of aggregation

5. The term specification error refers to any difference between the assumptions of a statistical model and the real properties it is assumed to represent. Below, in discussing Grunfeld and Griliches' (1960) paper, we use the term in a more restrictive sense to refer to the omission of variables from regression functions that have some independent explanatory (in the statistical sense of prediction) power.

do not arise. The attention of sociologists has been generally even further restricted to problems concerning changes in obtained coefficients of correlation. I will begin with the problems arising in grouping or aggregation affecting correlation coefficients and then consider the same problem with respect to regression coefficients.

It was noticed as early as 1939 (Thorndike) that measures of association increased with the grouping of units into aggregates. Gehkle and Biehel (1934) reported similar results. It was not until 1950 (Robinson; Yule and Kendall) that the problem received analytical treatments. Robinson presented an example that is useful as a point of reference. In the 1934 census he found that the individual correlation between race and literacy was .20. However, the correlation computed on state marginals (per cent white, per cent literate, etc.) was .77, and the same statistic computed on the eight census district marginals was .94. As in this case, it often appears that when micro-observations are grouped on areal basis, that measures of association increase as a monotonic function of the level of aggregation.

There have been a number of explanations offered for this phenomenon. It is useful to briefly consider each in turn, since they begin to shed some light on the general problem of aggregation.

Yule and Kendall (1950) proposed that the problem was one of *modifiable units*:

> This example serves to bring out an important distincton between two different types of data to which correlation analysis may be applied. The difficulty does not arise when we are considering the relationship, say, between heights of fathers and sons. The ultimate unit in this case . . . is a unique non-modifiable unit.
>
> On the other hand, our geographical areas . . . are modifiable units, and necessarily so. . . . A similar effect arises whenever we attempt to measure concomitant variation extending over continuous regions of space or time (Yule and Kendall, 1950, p. 312).

This distinction has *intuitive* appeal and seems to convey something of the difficulty involved in attempting to shift levels with empirical data. However, I am not convinced that this is a useful practical distinction. As Galtung (1967, p. 45) correctly notes, individuals, which in most sociological analyses of the problem are seen as the unique nonmodifiable units, can be considered as boundaries for a variety of subunits, such as psychological svndromes, status behaviors, behaviors in a time sequence, etc. Even the most elementary familiarity with social psychology (not to mention behavioral and physiological psychology) suffices to make this point. It would seem that even single behavioral acts are modifiable according to the measurement procedure employed to record it. Yet, in defense of Yule and Kendall, I think their point is clear: Units that are grouped on some areal or temporal criterion are liable to be highly arbitrary aggregates. It would seem to make sense to begin to discuss degrees of modifiability of data sets. Granting this, nothing specific in this perspective helps us understand the technical problem.

Yule and Kendall did not content themselves with pointing to the modifiability problem but also suggested a more specific explanation. They pointed to the effect of the presence of random components in variables on correlation coefficients. This attenuation effect has become well known to sociologists in the context of the effects of random measurement error. They suggest that by the effect of "a sampling effect"—which, unfortunately, is not clearly discussed—the correlation coefficient increases with grouping. In a later chapter on sampling, they discuss "dependent sampling," sampling from a population in which values of the variables sampled are highly correlated. Consider the development they present. We have two variables x and y, each of which is composed of a "true" component and a random component:

$$x = x' + e$$
$$y = y' + f$$

We assume a causal connection between x' and y', but assume that e and f are uncorrelated with x' and y' and with each other. In this case, we can easily show that:

$$\text{var } x = \text{var } x' + \text{var } e$$
$$\text{var } y = \text{var } y' + \text{var } f$$
$$\text{cov }(x, y) = \text{cov }(x', y')$$

We can further demonstrate that the correlation between x and y (the observed values) that we denote by r is related to the correlation of the "true" components, r', as follows:

$$r = \frac{r'}{\sqrt{1 + \dfrac{\text{var } e}{\text{var } x'}} \sqrt{1 + \dfrac{\text{var } f}{\text{var } y'}}} \tag{4}$$

Since variances are by definition nonnegative, we can see that r' cannot be less than r. To the extent to which r is less than r', we say that the correlation between the true values has been *attenuated* by the presence of random components.

The impact on these correlations of aggregation is easiest to show using the case in which the aggregates are simple sums.[6] We must ask what happens to the variances of the true components and the random components as units

6. The extension to other linear combinations of microvalues is trivial. But, as we will see below, we cannot easily handle nonlinear aggregation relations.

are grouped and sums taken (since it is ratios of such quantities that determine the attenuation effect). Consider a pair of random variables x_1 and x_2. An elementary result gives us:

$$\text{var } (x_1 + x_2) = \text{var } x_1 + \text{var } x_2 + 2 \text{ cov } (x_1, x_2).$$

The extension to the k-variable case is straightforward. This result tells us that the variance of a sum of random variables depends on the sign of the covariance term (which can take on either positive or negative values). Since we have assumed that e and f are to be distributed randomly in the population, we would expect the covariance terms for sums of e's and f's to be approximately zero, and, as a result, for each random component the variance of the sum of random variables will be approximately equal to the sum of the variance of the random variables entering the sum. This would also be true of the systematic variables x' and y' if their values were distributed randomly in space or time, i.e., if they were not systematically related to the aggregation or grouping criterion.[7] Yule and Kendall invoke the assumption (or, perhaps, empirical law) that adjacent units in any spatial or temporal distribution tend to be alike on most variables relative to the heterogeneity of any larger population, i.e., homogeneous units tend to cluster. As a result, areal or temporal aggregation will tend to group positively intercorrelated values[8] of x' and of y'. This is usually called the *clustering effect*.

In areal or temporal aggregation, then, the usual case will be that the variance of the sums (recalling the restriction to summation aggregation relations) will be greater than the sums of the variances. It is in this sense that:

> systematic effects represented by x' and y' will be cumulative, whereas the random effects represented by e and f will tend to cancel out—the larger the number of units we have, the less, relatively speaking, will their total be affected by erratic fluctuations (Yule and Kendall, 1950, p. 314).

As Yule and Kendall point out, the denominator in (4) will be reduced in such a situation as we increase the size of the groupings and thus if r' is a constant, r will continually increase towards its ceiling of 1.0.

The reader who consults the work cited above will find that a number of issues that underlie Yule and Kendall's presentation but that remained

---

7. This statement relies on Blalock's formulation, which will be treated below. Earlier analyses like the one considered here tended to restrict attention to areal proximity grouping and did not make clear that it is the presence of a systematic connection between the values of the variables and the grouping procedure that produces this inflation effect.

8. Here and elsewhere in this paper we will use the term intercorrelation of values of a variable to mean one of two things. If we have data at a single point in time, this will refer to a high positive intraclass correlation. If we have observations at numerous points in time, this will refer to a serial correlation of the variables.

implicit were introduced explicitly in the above presentation. These modifications are suggested by the analyses that have been motivated by the analysis of covariance analog suggested by areal or temporal aggregation. If area or time period is taken as the nominal covariable, the importance of the clustering effect becomes obvious. Robinson (1950) was the first to make this demonstration. I will briefly summarize the argument, since excellent treatments are available (particularly Duncan, Cuzzort and Duncan, 1961, and Alker, 1969). The following discussion and the necessary formulas presented in Table 27.1 are adapted from Alker's comprehensive analysis.[9]

The theorems employed in the analysis of covariance all begin with a decomposition like the following:

$$(X_i - X.) = (X_i - X._r) + (X._r - X.),\tag{5}$$

which simply states that the difference between a unit's value and the grand mean can be expressed as the sum of the difference between the unit's value and its subgroup (or regional) mean and the difference between the subgroup mean and the grand mean. By multiplying expression (5) by a comparable expression for the ith unit's Y value and taking expectations, we arrive at the "fundamental theorem" of the analysis of covariance:

$$C_{XY} = WC_{XY} + BC_{XY}.\tag{6}$$

This tells us that the covariance of X and Y for some N units can be represented as the sum of a within-region covariance and a between-region (or "ecological") covariance. As the definitional formulas of Table 27.1 make clear, the within-region covariance is a population weighted sum over all regions of the covariance of individual X and Y values within each region, and the ecological covariance is a population weighted average product of regional deviations in X and Y. We can prove that the two components on the righthand side of (6) are independent.

Our aim is to transform (6) into an expression in correlation coefficients. We can do this by successively dividing (6) by three standard deviation terms ($\sqrt{C_{XX}C_{YY}}$, $\sqrt{WC_{XX}WC_{YY}}$, $\sqrt{BC_{XX}BC_{YY}}$) to obtain correlational expressions as follows:

$$R_{XY} = \frac{WC_{XY} + BC_{XY}}{\sqrt{C_{XX}C_{YY}}} = \frac{WC_{XY}}{\sqrt{WC_{XX}WC_{YY}}} \cdot \sqrt{\frac{WC_{XX}WC_{YY}}{C_{XX}C_{YY}}}$$

$$+ \frac{BC_{XY}}{\sqrt{BC_{XX}BC_{YY}}} \cdot \sqrt{\frac{BC_{XX}BC_{YY}}{C_{XX}C_{YY}}}$$

9. I am restricting this analysis to areal aggregation. Alker concisely illustrates the formal similarity between temporal and areal aggregation by adding a subscript denoting time period of observation to each entry in Table 27.1 and then aggregating both across time periods and across units.

Table 27.1. Statistical elements of covariance theorems

A1.	X_{ir}, Y_{ir}	X (or Y) value for unit i in region r.
A2.	$X._r, Y._r$ $\quad \dfrac{1}{N_r} \sum\limits_{i=1}^{N_r} X_{ir}; \dfrac{1}{N_r} \sum\limits_{i=1}^{N_r} Y_{ir}$ Where N_r is the number of units in region r.	Average X (or Y) value for units i in region r.
A3.	$X., Y.$ $\quad \dfrac{1}{N} \sum\limits_{i=1}^{N} \sum\limits_{r=1}^{R} X_{ir}$, etc.	Average X (or Y) value for all units in all regions.
B1.	$C_{XX} \quad \dfrac{1}{N} \sum\limits_{i=1}^{N} (X_{ir} - X.)^2$ (similar term defined for Y)	Universal variance of X.
B2.	$C_{XY} \quad \dfrac{1}{N} \sum\limits_{i=1}^{N} (X_{ir} - X.)(Y_{ir} - Y.)$	Universal covariance of X and Y.
B3.	$WC_{XX} \quad \dfrac{1}{N} \sum\limits_{i=1}^{N} (X_{ir} - X._r)^2$ (similar term defined for Y)	Within-group variance of X.
B4.	$WC_{XY} \quad \dfrac{1}{N} \sum\limits_{i=1}^{N} (X_{ir} - X._r)(Y_{ir} - Y._r)$	Within-group covariance of X and Y.
B5.	$BC_{XX} \quad \dfrac{1}{R} \sum\limits_{r=1}^{R} (X._r - X.)^2$ (similar term defined for Y)	Between-group ("Ecological") variance of X.
B6.	$BC_{XY} \quad \dfrac{1}{R} \sum\limits_{r=1}^{R} (X._r - X.)(Y._r - Y.)$	Between-group covariance of X and Y.
C1.	$E^2{}_{XR} \quad \dfrac{BC_{XX}}{C_{XX}}$	Correlation ratio of X and R.
C2.	$E^2{}_{YR} \quad \dfrac{BC_{YY}}{C_{YY}}$	Correlation ratio of Y and R.
D1.	$R_{XY} \quad \dfrac{C_{XY}}{\sqrt{C_{XX}C_{YY}}}$	Universal correlation between X and Y.
D2.	$WR_{XY} \quad \dfrac{WC_{XY}}{\sqrt{WC_{XX}WC_{YY}}}$	Within-group correlation of X and Y.
D3.	$BR_{XY} \quad \dfrac{BC_{XY}}{\sqrt{BC_{XX}BC_{YY}}}$	Between-group ("Ecological") correlation of X and Y.

Noting that $WC_{XX}=C_{XX}-BC_{XX}$, and $WC_{YY}=C_{YY}-BC_{YY}$, and using the definitions of the correlation ratios, we arrive at the following result:

$$R_{XY}=WR_{XY}\sqrt{1-E^2{}_{YR}}\ \sqrt{1-E^2{}_{XR}}+BR_{XY}E_{YR}E_{XR}. \qquad (7)$$

Robinson (1950) employed a slightly different version of (7):

$$BR_{XY}=R_{XY}/E_{XR}E_{YR}-WR_{XY}\sqrt{1-E^2{}_{XR}}\ \sqrt{1-E^2{}_{YR}}/E_{XR}E_{YR} \qquad (8)$$

From this, Robinson deduced what I will call the *consistency condition for correlation coefficients*:

$$WR_{XY}=R_{XY}(1-E_{XY}E_{YR})/\sqrt{1-E^2{}_{XR}}\ \sqrt{1-E^2{}_{YR}}\ \text{or}\ WR_{XY}=kR_{XY} \qquad (9)$$

The individual or micro and the macro or "ecological" correlations are equal only if this identity holds. The minimum value of the quantity represented by k in the abbreviated expression is unity. This is the case in which the within-area correlations are all exactly equal to the individual (total) correlation. But Robinson argues that an examination of expression (9) shows that the inflation effect depends on the number of subareas employed and on the level (inclusiveness) of aggregation.

As smaller areas are consolidated, two things happen. First, the within-areas correlation increases as a result of increasing heterogeneity of subareas. This effect tends to diminish the ecological correlation, since the proportion of variance accounted for by an area is equal to $1-WR^2{}_{XY}$. Second, the values of the correlation ratios, E_{XR} and E_{YR}, decrease as a consequence of the decrease in the heterogeneity of the values of X and Y in the subareas. This tends to increase the ecological correlation. But Robinson (1950, pp. 356–357) argues:

> these two tendencies are of unequal importance. Investigation of [our (8)] with respect to the changes in the values of E_{XR}, E_{YR}, and WR_{XY} indicates that the influence of the changes of the E's is considerably more important than the influence of changes in the value of WR_{XY}. The net effect of changes in the E's and WR_{XY} taken together is to increase the numerical value of the ecological correlation as consolidation takes place.

What is crucial is that grouping units somehow changes variation in the variables of interest. The narrow focus on areal aggregation (the "ecological fallacy") deflected attention from the more general problem of aggregation. Exactly how grouping or aggregation affects variation in such variables became much clearer when Blalock (1964) raised the issue in the context of linear causal analysis.

Before shifting to an explicitly causal treatment, we can, following Grunfeld and Griliches (1960), more precisely specify the dependence of the inflation of correlation coefficients on clustering. Grunfeld and Griliches prefer to speak of a *synchronization effect*, defined as follows:

> The higher the correlation between the independent variables of different individuals or behavior units, *certibus paribus*, the higher the R^2 of the aggregate equation relative to the R^2's of the micro-equation (Grunfeld and Griliches, 1960, p. 4).

This term may be preferable to clustering effect, since the latter term suggests a concern only with areal aggregation.

Grunfeld and Griliches did not introduce the grouping criterion explicitly into their analysis, but rather employed a simple regression model: $y_i(t) = bx_i(t) + u_i(t)$. Both variables are assumed to be measured as deviations about their means, and the t in parentheses denotes the time period of observation. The aim is to demonstrate that the inflation effect depends on the intercorrelations of the observed values of the explanatory variables and of the disturbance term. Note that we have in this model a time series of observations for all microunits. We can thus compute product-moment correlations of arrays of microvalues for pairs of microunits.[10] Grunfeld and Griliches assume that such correlations for values of the explanatory variable and disturbance term, ρ_x and ρ_u respectively, are constant for all pairs of microunits. If we make two more simplifying assumptions: that all microunits can be represented by a micromodel with constant coefficient (i.e., $b_i = b_j$ for all i, j),[11] and that the variances S^2_{xi} and S^2_{ui} are constants, we can arrive at the following result:[12]

$$\frac{R^2 \text{macro}}{R^2 \text{micro}} = \frac{b^2 S^2_{xi} + S^2_{ui}}{b^2 S^2_{xi} + S^2_{ui} \left[\dfrac{1 + (\mathcal{N} - 1)\rho_u}{1 + (\mathcal{N} - 1)\rho_x} \right]}, \tag{10}$$

where $\mathcal{N}$ is the number of micro-units.

It is clear from (10) that the inflation of correlation coefficients with aggregation depends on the relative magnitude of the two synchronization coefficients, ρ_x and ρ_u. All that is required for such inflation is that ρ_x be larger in magnitude than ρ_u. An important contribution of this analysis is the demonstration that the inflation effect is dependent on the completeness of the micromodel. In a perfectly specified micromodel,[13] we would expect

---

10. Grunfeld and Griliches (1960, Appendix E) develop the parallel result for the case where we have a set of microvalues at a single point in time. In this case the appropriate measure of synchronization is the intraclass correlation coefficient.

11. In Section 4 we will develop the significance of this restriction. Simply, if this condition does not hold, we would observe a peculiar type of "time series aggregation bias."

12. Grunfeld and Griliches systematically relax these assumptions in a series of appendices which demonstrate that this general result is not contradicted.

13. Here we are using the term specification error in the narrow sense: failure to include one or more causally important variables in the micromodel.

the disturbance term to be composed of a large number of "random shocks." As a consequence, we would expect ρ_u to be approximately equal to zero. In such a case, even a very slight positive synchronization of values of the explanatory variable would produce inflation of the macrocoefficient of determination. The point is that the size of the coefficient ρ_u depends on the size of the specification error in the general case. This will become clearer in the analysis motivated by causal modeling considerations.

By now it has become clear that we must concern ourselves with the effects of aggregation on the variation in the variables of interest. Blalock (1964) has made this issue explicit and has made it the focus of his concern with the problem of changing units. He argues:

> in shifting from one unit of analysis to another we are very likely to affect the manner in which outside and potentially disturbing influences are operating on the dependent and independent variables under consideration (Blalock, 1964, p. 98).

The way in which this is likely to occur is that variation in X or Y or both may be manipulated in such a way that their affects become confounded with the effects of other variables. The key insight is that the effect of shifting levels on the behavior of correlation and regression coefficients depends on the manner in which units have been put together. If we explicitly consider the aggregation or grouping criterion as a variable in the system, we can see that the effect of a given kind of grouping on the variation of other variables in the system depends on the systematic connections between the grouping criterion and each other variable in the system. We have already noted, for example, that grouping by area of residence will maximize variation in most social variables (i.e., will increase between-group variation relative to within-group variation). As Blalock points out, however, we seldom have precise information on the connections between the aggregation criterion and the variables in the model.

In order to gain some insight into the likely effects of several grouping procedures on bivariate relations, Blalock examined four types of groupings: random grouping, grouping that maximizes variation in X, grouping that maximizes variation in Y, and grouping by physical propinquity. The first three are artificial groupings, the fourth corresponds to the case we have been concerned with so far. Figures 27.3, 4, and 5 illustrate the situation modeled in each of the first three gouping procedures. Figure 27.3 represents random grouping—the situation in which the grouping criterion is not systematically connected with any variable in the model. Blalock's manipulation of county level data showed that both correlation and regression coefficients remained fairly stable across a series of more and more inclusive groupings. Those fluctuations that did arise are attributed by Blalock to sampling error.[14]

14. But see the discussion of Cramer's analysis below.

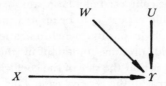

Figure 27.3.

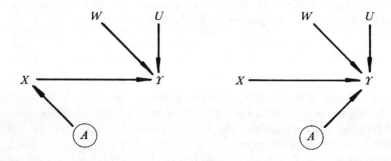

Figure 27.4.   *Figure* 27.5.

The second procedure, grouping so as to maximize variation in X (Fig. 27.4) is essentially random with respect to those independent causal factors that are not systematically related to X (W and U in our example). As a result, this type of grouping will increase the between-group variation in X relative to that in these other variables. This will lessen the "nuisance" effect of such variables, meaning that X will "explain" a larger proportion of the variation in Y. This effect should increase with the level of grouping (as more consolidation takes place, the systematic effects of A will increase the between-group variation relative to the within-group variation in X). This argument could be rephrased in terms of the clustering effect, since the effect of A is to group positively correlated[15] values of X. The data support this argument; r_{xy} increases consistently (monotonically) with the level of grouping. However, we would not expect that the reduction of nuisance effects would change the nature of the relationship between X and Y. In this case, the slope b_{yx} remained remarkably constant across levels of aggregation. But the reverse slope (which is not of direct interest since we are taking Y as

15. Since this analysis is cross-sectional, this comment refers to increasing intraclass correlations.

dependent in the model) increase with grouping. Blalock notes that this is a mathematical artifact, since $r^2_{xy} = b_{yx}b_{xy}$ and r^2_{xy} increases as b_{yx} remains constant.

The third procedure, grouping that maximizes variation in Y (Fig. 5), produces symmetrical results. We find that r^2_{xy} increases with grouping (this is expected since the correlation coefficient is symmetric with respect to X and Y). In this case it is the slope b_{xy} that remains nearly constant, so that b_{yx} (the slope of interest) increases with level of grouping. This is a serious complication and can be explained causally by noting that maximizing variation in Y confounds variation in Y due to X, with that due to other factors such as W and U. If, for example, all three causal factors are related positively to Y, then grouping units with high Y values will very likely group units which have high X, W and U values. As Blalock notes (1964, p. 108), "Almost any variable that is even slightly related to Y initially becomes a good predictor of Y under such a grouping procedure because of the fact that its effects are being confounded with those of the other variables related to Y."

The fourth procedure is closer to what concerns us in this paper, i.e., it is empirically a more likely case. Blalock's proximity grouping appeared to be somewhat intermediate between procedures one and two. However, in any instance it is an empirical question whether or not proximity (including temporal proximity) grouping will have more effect on X or Y. I have implied above that most of the variables of interest to social scientists are likely to be found clustered to some degree. If this is the case, a more realistic model is probably more like that presented in Figure 27.6, which is a composite of the

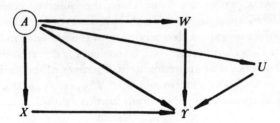

Figure 27.6.

models of Figures 27.4 and 5 with additional arrows drawn from A to the other causal factors. The issue then becomes which of these relations are the strongest. In Blalock's proximity grouping, it is apparently the case that the relation of A to X is stronger than the relations from A to W, U and Y.

The model drawn in Figure 27.6 raises an extremely interesting issue: namely, the possibility of the grouping criterion producing a spurious relationship between X and Y. Consider the models drawn in Figure 27.7.

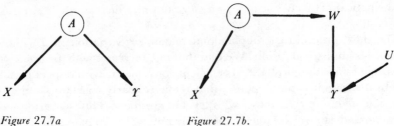

Figure 27.7a   Figure 27.7b.

Here we would expect to find no relationship between X and Y at the micro-level; but at the macrolevel such a relationship could appear as a result of the grouping process. This somewhat obvious possibility has not been discussed in the aggregation-disaggregation literature. Alker (1969) has raised this issue and suggests that the literature on ecological correlations would have developed quite differently if those who addressed the problem had considered the issue of spurious relations. Alker illustrates this possibility using Robinson's race-literacy example. Here the individual level correlation was .20 and the correlation computed on the eight census district marginals was .95. Without exception, the previous analyses of the ecological fallacy problem took the observed individual correlation as a "pure" datum. The individual level correlation was implicitly considered a substantively interesting and reliable benchmark against which to compare aggregation-disaggregation effects.

Alker suggests a perspective from which this observed correlation of .20 can be considered spurious. Due to the presence of the clustering or synchronization effect we expect that a portion of the variance in both X (being nonwhite) and Y (being illiterate) will be ecologially determined. Suppose we had reason to suspect that approximately a quarter of the variation in each variable was ecologically determined, i.e., $E^2_{XR} = E^2_{YR} = .25$. The correlational version of the covariance theorem for this example is as follows:

$$.20 = WR_{XY} \sqrt{1 - E^2_{XR}} \ \sqrt{1 - E^2_{YR}} + .95 \ E_{XR}E_{YR}.$$

Substituting the values assumed for the correlation ratios, we obtain,

$$.20 = .75 WR_{XY} + .24,$$

from which we deduce $WR_{XY} = -.05$. Thus, in a sense, the grouping criterion (which Alker suggests was operating as level of industrialization and/or urbanization) "partials out" the correlation between X and Y. If we had three interval variables, this situation would be exactly analogous to the basic three-variable prediction equation of the Simon-Blalock strategy, $R_{XY.R} \cong 0$.

This presentation is meant to be heuristic. We cannot, of course, differentiate the three-variable model drawn in Figure 27.7A from a number of alternative three-variable models. Further, situations in which thé grouping criterion is operating as a confounding variable in this sense can be identified only in the context of a theoretical formulation that relates the microvariables to the grouping variable (e.g., level of industrialization). Alker argues convincingly that this analysis problem points to the need for crosslevel theories.

Before moving to that discussion of aggregation of k-variable models, I would like to briefly mention an important result bearing on the previous discussion that to this point has not been mentioned in the sociological literature.[16] Cramer (1964) has addressed himself to the effects of various kinds of grouping procedures on bivariate correlation and regression coefficients. With respect to the former, his analysis provides an alternative procedure for demonstrating that the inflation of correlation coefficients depends on the degree of consolidation. If we hold the number of microunits constant, we can group units into successively larger and more inclusive aggregates. I am (following Robinson) referring to this process as consolidation. Blalock, for instance, grouped units in pairs, fives, tens, and, finally, fifteens. When a variation in a variable is being maximized in grouping, one places those units that are most alike on X-values in the same group. As consolidation increases both between-group and within-group variation increases. Between-group variation increases because the means diverge further and further apart. Within-group variation increases because fives will be less homogeneous than pairs, etc. This is essentially the analysis problem Robinson discussed in the framework of the analysis of covariance. The demonstration of the effect of clustering (which is here produced by the grouping criterion) suggests that the increase in between-group variation is more important than the increase in within-group variation. Cramer offers an alternative method of demonstrating that the inflation effect is a monotonic increasing function of the level of consolidation for any fixed number of microunits. Similarly, the inflation effect also increases monotonically with the number of microunits employed in the grouping.

It is the discussion of the effects of grouping on the regression estimates that bears on an issue not previously addressed. Restricting himself to Blalock's types 1 and 2 grouping procedures, Cramer proves that for a simple bivariate model[17] the regression computed on the aggregates gives an

16. I would like to thank Arthur S. Goldberger for recommending this paper, which for some reason seems to have been overlooked in the economics literature as well.

17. The development of the argument is somewhat laborious and will not be attempted here. The reader is referred to the original paper. A less mathematically demanding version is presented in Hannan (1970, chap. 2).

unbiased estimate of the population slope parameter.[18] However, the aggregate slope is less efficient than the slope computed on the microdata. For the simple bivariate case, the loss of efficiency can be expressed as a ratio of the between-group sum of squares of X to the total sums in X.

For random grouping, Cramer shows that the reduction of efficiency is an increasing function of the level of consolidation. Blalock's data conform to this observation. The case of grouping that maximizes variation in X is more problematic, as discussed above. Cramer's formulation demonstrates that as the between-group sums of squares in X relative to the within-group sums of squares increases, the efficiency of the estimator increases. Blalock's data show no variation in the slope b_{yx} with this type of grouping across several levels of consolidation. What we would need for comparison would be a grouping procedure that did not perfectly maximize variation in X as Blalock did. He suggests that his proximity grouping approximated this situation, i.e., combined the features of random grouping and grouping that maximizes X. We see that b_{yx} increasingly deviated from the true values with increasing consolidation. This, then, is an additional argument for the need of precisely specifying the relationship between the grouping criterion and the variables in the model. The ideal case seems to be that in which A (the grouping criterion) is not related to Y or to any other causes of Y, but is related to X in such a way that grouping results in great increases in the between-group variation in X.

4. Aggregation bias: The K-variable case

The approach presented in the last section can be extended to apply to more complex models. The potentially most troublesome models are those in which the grouping criterion is systematically related to a number of variables in the model. In such cases we are likely to encounter some combination of maximizing variation in dependent variables, controlling for prior variables in causal chains, and spurious macrorelations. General statements are difficult here as verbal statements very quickly become inadequate as the potential difficulties become more numerous and complex. However, a special aggregation complication arises when we have time-series observations on k-variable models that have been extensively developed by a number of econometricians. I would like to develop the argument briefly here. After considering this special case of aggregation bias, I will attempt to relate it to the causal concerns already expressed.

Before considering the time-series problem I should note that there is a

---

18. He does not mention the possible complications introduced by inadvertent manipulation of the dependent variable in aggregation.

rather extensive literature in economics dealing with the consistency conditions for *deterministic* k-variable micromodels (where as above we allow each microunit to be represented in a separate model). A series of theorems[19] proves that consistency as we have defined it is attainable only when all relations (micro-, macro-, and aggregation relations) are *linear*.[20] The implications of this result are quite extraordinary given that we are discussing exact relations. For the sociologist one practical conclusion is that consistency is ruled out by the use of distributional measures as macrovariables. This is troublesome when homogeneity-heterogeneity is a relevant dimension at both microvariables and macrolevels.[21] This conclusion, of course, holds *a fortiori* for stochastic aggregation problems.

Yet special problems arise in the case for stochastic k-variable models even when all relations are linear. To appreciate one of the more serious and unusual aggregation bias problems, we must shift our attention to relations which are estimated from a time-series of observations, i.e., situations in which we have measures for all microunits on the variables of concern at several points in time.[22] The use of such time-series, so basic to economic analysis, is still relatively rare in sociology. There seems to be an increasing emphasis on undertaking such studies, however. Examples of such studies are the cohort studies of high school or college classes where all individuals in the study are followed up and remeasured at regular time intervals. More common perhaps are the "synthetic cohort" studies in which retrospective measures of previous states are employed in the time-series (cf. Blau and Duncan, 1967).

The discussion must now become relatively concrete. We follow Theil's (1954) formulation.[23] We are requiring that all relations be linear. Consider the following *micromodel*:

$$y_i(t) = \alpha_i + \sum_{k=1}^{K} \beta_{ki} x_{ki}(t) + u_i(t) \tag{11}$$

$$(i = 1, \ldots, \mathcal{N})$$

where each microunit is permitted to behave idiosyncratically with respect

19. Green (1964) presents a more precise statement along with necessary theorems and associated lemmas. In general, they involve a mathematical restatement (in terms of partial derivatives and differentials) of the consistency formulation presented above.

20. Nonlinear functions that are easily transformed into linear functions (e.g., logarithmic functions) present no particular difficulties, however.

21. Boudon (1964) develops the implications for disaggregation of formulations in which this dimension is introduced. He argues that nonlinear formulations are generally appropriate in attempts at disaggregating data which has been grouped on some areal proximity basis.

22. We are concerned with a cross-sectional model estimated at numerous points in time rather than with dynamic formulations in which time plays a central role.

23. Excellent summary statements of Theil's analysis prepared for economists are found in Allen (1956, chap. 20) and Fox (1968, chap. 14).

to changes in the k micro explanatory variables, the t in parentheses denotes the time period of observation and the disturbance is assumed to have zero mean. We will restrict our attention to the simplest case of aggregation in which all macrovariables are the sums of corresponding microvariables (the extension to arithmetic means and proportions is straightforward):

$$y(t) = \sum_{i=1}^{N} y_i(t)$$

$$x_1(t) = \sum_{i=1}^{N} x_{1i}(t) \tag{12}$$

$$\vdots$$

$$x_K(t) = \sum_{i=1}^{N} x_{Ki}(t).$$

We assume that a *macromodel* is defined analogously to (11):

$$y(t) = \alpha + \sum_{k=1}^{K} \beta_k x_k(t) + u(t). \tag{13}$$

The analytic problem arises when we use least squares to estimate the macromodel directly,[24] and compare the obtained coefficients with those obtained from estimating the micromodel. The notion of simple consistency would suggest that we would want the macrocoefficients to be simple sums of the corresponding microcoefficients. We can use the consistency formulation to see this. Consistency is achieved when the two methods of generating predicted macro dependent variable values discussed above are identical. We can express changes in the macromodel as follows:

$$\Delta y(t) = \alpha + \sum_{k=1}^{K} \beta_k \Delta x_k + u(t). \tag{14}$$

For each equation in the micromodel, change is defined as follows:

$$\Delta y_i(t) = \alpha_i + \sum_{k=1}^{K} \beta_{ki} \Delta x_{ki} + u_i(t). \tag{15}$$

Consistency requires that:

$$\Delta y(t) = \sum_{i=1}^{N} \Delta y_i(t) = \sum_{i=1}^{N} \alpha_i + \sum_{i=1}^{N} \sum_{k=1}^{K} \beta_{ki} \Delta x_{ki} + \sum_{i=1}^{N} u_i(t). \tag{16}$$

24. Here we see the necessity of time-series observations. Since by definition only a single macrovalue corresponds to the array of microvalues of each corresponding variable at each time period, there would be no variation in the macromodel in a single cross-section.

In other words, when the aggregates are simple sums, aggregation is consistent if and only if:

$$\alpha = \sum_{i=1}^{N} \alpha_i; \quad \beta_k = \sum_{i=1}^{N} \beta_{ki}; \quad u(t) = \sum_{i=1}^{N} u_i(t). \tag{17}$$

There is nothing obscure in these definitions of the macroparameters. This is simply what intuition would suggest would be the appropriate set of definitions. We can see that the substitution of the values defined in (17) into the original macromodel (11) will yield (16) as required.

Theil's analysis is intended to demonstrate that we are not usually so fortunate as to obtain the required macroparameters. To pursue this and the resulting contradiction between micromodels and macromodels we need to define a new set of functions. We define a set of *auxiliary regressions* that express each microvalue (of explanatory variables) as a linear function of the whole set of macro explanatory variables. More precisely, they are the least squares estimates of the "time paths" of changes in the microvariables as functions of the macrovariables:

$$x_{ki}(t) = A_{ki} + B_{ki,1} x_1(t) + \ldots + B_{ki,K} x_K(t) + V_{ki}(t), \tag{18}$$

where $V_{ki}(t)$ are residuals which have zero mean and are uncorrelated with the T values taken by the macro-variables $x_{k'}$ $(k' = 1, \ldots, K)$. We need not assign any substantive meaning to these auxiliary regressions since they are simply a formal device by which we demonstrate the existence of aggregation bias.

Theil's Theorem 1 demonstrates that the parameters of (11) the macro-model are determined as follows (when the aggregates are simple sums):

$$\alpha = \sum_{i=1}^{N} \alpha_i + \sum_{k=1}^{K} \sum_{i=1}^{N} A_{ki} \beta_{ki};$$

$$\beta_k = \sum_{k'=1}^{K} \sum_{i=1}^{N} B_{k'i,k} \, \beta_{k'i} (k = 1, \ldots, K) \tag{19}$$

$$u(t) = \sum_{i=1}^{N} u_i(t) + \sum_{i=1}^{N} \sum_{k=1}^{K} \beta_{ki} V_{ki}(t).$$

Thus the macroparameters have some rather unusual properties:

(i) The macro-intercept is the sum of the corresponding micro-intercepts plus a series of terms involving noncorresponding parameters;

(ii) The macro regression coefficients that can be rewritten

$$\frac{1}{N} \sum_{i=1}^{N} \beta_{ki} + \sum_{i=1}^{N} (B_{ki,k} - \frac{1}{N} \beta_{ki} + \sum_{i=1}^{N} \sum_{k' \neq k} B_{k'i,k} \beta_{ki})$$

are composed of the sum of the arithmetic mean of the corresponding micro-parameters, plus a weighted mean of the corresponding microparameters plus a sum of weighted arithmetic means of noncorresponding coefficients;

(iii) The macrodisturbance is also composed of a sum of the sum of corresponding disturbances plus a weighted sum of noncorresponding parameters.

It is the presence of the terms involving noncorresponding parameters (Allen calls these "cross-effects") that is disturbing. Theil labels all terms other than $\sum\limits_{i=1}^{N} \alpha_1$, $\dfrac{1}{N} \sum\limits_{i=1}^{N} \beta_{ki}$ (or $\bar\beta_{ki}$), and $\sum\limits_{i=1}^{N} u_i(t)$ as *aggregation bias terms*.

We can further examine these aggregation bias terms by employing the second half of Theil's Theorem 1, which states that the following restrictions on coefficients of the auxiliary regressions must hold:

$$\sum_{i=1}^{N} A_{ki} = \Sigma V_{ki}(t) = 0;\ \Sigma B_{k'i,k} = \begin{matrix}1 \text{ if } k'=k \\ 0 \text{ otherwise}\end{matrix} \tag{20}$$

We want this requirement to be met since we have defined $x_k = \Sigma_{i=1}^{N} x_{ki}$ and the summation of expression (18) will not give this result unless the restrictions are met. Using these restrictions we can rewrite the expressions of (19) so as to represent the aggregation bias terms as covariances between micropara-meters and auxiliary regression coefficients:[25]

$$\alpha = \sum_{i=1}^{N}\alpha_i + N\sum_{k=1}^{K} \text{cov } (A_{ki},\ \beta_{ki})$$

$$\beta_k = \bar\beta_{ki} + N\sum_{k'=1}^{K} \text{cov } (B_{k'i,k},\ \beta_{ki}) \tag{21}$$

$$u(t) = \sum_{i=1}^{N}u_i(t) + N \text{ cov} \sum_{k=1}^{K} (V_{ki}(t),\ \beta_{ki}).$$

Thus, we see that the three macroterms (the two coefficients plus the distur-bance) are equal to linear combinations of corresponding microterms apart from certain covariance corrections. *These covariance corrections represent the aggregation bias in the macromodel.* In other words, it is the presence of these covariance corrections that will give rise to inconsistencies or contradictions between micromodels and macromodels. The reader may convince himself of this by pursuing our usual two-procedure method of generating predicted values for the macro dependent variable employing the coefficient values presented above for the macroparameters.

There are a number of special cases in which such aggregation bias

25. I will not derive these results here as the intervening steps are fully spelled out by Theil (1954, pp. 15–17).

vanishes. I will mention only one.[26] If we can write the micromodel with constant coefficients, all aggregation bias will disappear, since the covariance of a constant with any random variable is by definition zero. In other words, if all microunits behave exactly alike with respect to the variables in the model over the time period defined by the observations, one need not concern himself with aggregation bias. Theil proposed that it is highly unlikely that this condition would be realized in economic studies in which consumers or households are microunits. Economists expect wealthy families to behave differently economically from poor families. Sociologists would expect the same result and would stipulate further that many distinctions, rural-urban, black-white, conservative-liberal, etc. would be likely to produce similar kinds of differences. Malinvaud (1966) suggests that if there is only one dimension (e.g., wealth) which is suspected to be responsible for large differences in microparameters, one should stratify his sample on this dimension and run separate analyses. Within each subsample we might then reasonably expect the microparameters to be nearly constant. Sociologists are used to addressing the same problem in a very different context. The problem of variable microparameters can be seen as a classical statistical interaction problem: Other variables are changing the nature of the relationship across subsamples.

It is interesting to note that sociologists concerned with disaggregation have arrived at the identical conclusion about the aggregation problem. Goodman (1959), for example, arrives at a formulation for the two-variable cases in which disaggregation is consistent if the grouping criterion does not interact with the relationship of interest. That is, if the microparameters are reasonably constant across ecological areas, then aggregation is consistent and Goodman's disaggregation strategy will give reasonably good estimates of the microvalues. Boudon (1964); however, has argued vigorously that it is highly unlikely that such interactions will be weak or missing in most interesting cases.

What about the case in which the microparameters vary? Is aggregation bias an inevitable complication? Theil argues that it is not and proposes a strategy of "perfect aggregation." He advocates a peculiar sort of *fixed-weight aggregation*, which produces constant microparameters. Consider the following weighted aggregates (in place of simple sums):

$$y'(t) = \sum_{i=1}^{N} s_i \, y_i(t), \tag{22}$$

$$x'_k(t) = \sum_{i=1}^{N} w_{ki} x_{ki}(t), \tag{23}$$

26. The other cases are those in which the microvariables are all exact functions of the macrovariables (i.e., the auxiliary regression is deterministic rather than stochastic) or when we have additional knowledge that allows us to posit that the covariances are zero for the time span of concern.

where s_i and w_{ki} are fixed-weights (constant across time periods). We can write the micromodel in the form:

$$s_i y_i(t) = s_i \alpha_i + \sum_{k=1}^{K} \frac{s_i \beta_{ki}}{w_{ki}} x_{ki}(t) + s_i u_i(t)$$

$$= \alpha'_i + \sum_{k=1}^{N} \beta'_{ki} [w_{ki} x_{ki}(t)] + u'_i(t), \tag{24}$$

and see that it is equivalent to our earlier unweighted formulation. To see how fixed-weight aggregation can produce constant coefficients in the micromodel, we set the weights s_i equal to unity and assign the following values to w_{ki}:

$$w_{ki} = \frac{\beta_{ki}}{c_{ki}} \text{ for all pairs } (k,i)$$

where the c's are arbitrary constants. In other words, we weight microvariables by the corresponding microcoefficients. In this case, (24) is reduced to:

$$y_i(t) = \alpha_i + \sum_{k=1}^{K} c_k [w_{ki} x_{ki}(t)] + u_i(t), \tag{25}$$

so that the microcoefficients β'_{ki} of (24) are all identically equal to c_k.

> This implies that if aggregation is performed such that all microvalues of $x_{ki}(t)$ are weighted proportionately to their microparameters β_{ki}, both the intercept α and the rates of change β_k of the macro equation depend on microparameters corresponding only (Theil, 1954, p. 18).

This strategy, while mathematically sound, presents some obvious difficulties from the theory tester's perspective. Lancaster (1966) has presented perhaps the most compelling criticism of this approach in commenting on the issues in the context of the Keynesian Savings Function:

> The definition of Y (the macro explanatory variable) is not a "natural" definition; it does not conform to any standard statistical series; it is a solution only to the problem in hand and has no special use for any other aggregate income problem; it depends on the exact distribution of income at each period; but it makes the micro- and macro-relationships always consistent (Lancaster, 1966, p. 18).

In other words, the macrocoefficients are dependent on the exact distributions of the microvariables in the population under study for the time period specified. For this reason, the macrocoefficients are sensitive to changes in the distributions of the microvariables across time periods. Similarly, this characteristic of "perfect aggregation" makes it extremely difficult, if not impossible, to compare macroresults obtained from different populations or in the same population at different time periods.

The theorist operates in terms of general and abstract relationships that are neither time nor place specific. Of course, all operationalizations are to some extent time and place specific. Yet, this strategy seems more time and population bound than most procedures. In any particular application, "perfect aggregation" is likely to seem highly *ad hoc* and to have little intuitive or substantive appeal. None of these criticisms apply, however, to pure prediction problems. They are specific to attempts at theory testing or construction.

In an extremely interesting analysis, Boot and deWit (1960) estimated the aggregation bias in the coefficients of an investment model. They found such bias to be relatively small. Fox (1968), perhaps on the basis of this paper, suggests that in most economic applications aggregation bias should not exceed 10 per cent of the parameter values.[27] This is an encouraging result, since it suggests that until we operate in terms of highly precise models, aggregation bias will represent only a minor inconvenience.

It is interesting to recast this argument in causal terms, following Blalock's example. Examination of (21) shows that the presence of aggregation bias in the macroparameter estimates depends on nonzero coefficients in the auxiliary regressions. More specifically, it depends on nonzero coefficients associated with *noncorresponding* macrovariables. To this point we have followed the example of the economists and have treated the auxiliary regressions as purely formal. But it appears that insight into the aggregation problem arising in time-series can be gained by intensive examination of these relations. The question is, under what conditions are we likely to find microvariables associated across time with noncorresponding macrovariables?

Theil suggests that this is likely to result from multicollinearity of the macrovariables. But, since the corresponding macrovariable is included in the auxiliary regression along with the noncorresponding macrovariables, multicollinearity should not produce strong "partial" relationships of the kind required here. Reference to a simple specific model is helpful here. We can revise the first model presented in Figure 27.1 to include an arrow connecting one of the microvariables (X_1) with a noncorresponding macrovariable (X'_2), as in Figure 27.8. The multicollinearity explanation suggests that there is no direct causal link between the two variables, but that it is spurious due to high collinearity of X'_1 and X'_2. I have already suggested that most of this effect would be "credited" to X'_1 in the auxiliary regression. Three possibilities remain: (1) X_1 is systematically producing changes in X'_2 across time; (2) X'_2 is systematically producing changes in X_1 across time; (3) there is some omitted variable jointly affecting X_1 and X'_2 across time (the relationship is spurious owing to the effects of some "lurking" variable).

27. Boot and deWit found positive aggregation bias terms. It is, of course, possible for the covariance terms to be negative so that aggregation bias would deflate the parameter estimates.

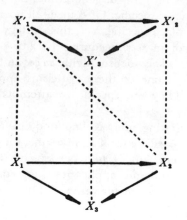

Figure 27.8.

Consider a model in which individual income and individual political radicalism are both included as explanatory variables. We might suspect that variations in individual radicalism will vary across time with variations in community (or national) income if there is enough variability in the latter during the time period of observation. Such a situation will give rise to aggregation bias if we estimate the analogous model across time with community radicalism and community income as explanatory variables. The third case listed above comes closest to the situation we have already analyzed. We see here a possibility of a temporal spuriousness at the macrolevel analogous to the areal spuriousness pointed out by Alker. In the model we have used, this spuriousness does not relate variables that are otherwise unrelated but simply inflates or deflates the microrelationship. The introduction of a time dimension raises the possibility of a kind of spuriousness that is not apparent when we restrict our attention to static models estimated at one point in time. The situation I am describing is pictured in Figure 27.9 for our three-variable model.

What of the other possibilities? It seems more plausible that a direct causal impact would flow from macrovariables to microvariables rather than *vice versa*, although there is no basis on which to rule out the possibility of direct impact of changes in microvalues on macrovalues (particularly given the simple definition of aggregate variables employed here).[28] Addressing this issue in any specific case demands the formulation of crosslevel theories. I

28. When such simple aggregates are used, some of the problems raised can be thought of as part-whole correlation problems. Recent discussions of this problem (Bartko and Pettigrew, 1968; Earle, 1969) do not seem to shed too much light on the problem that concerns us here.

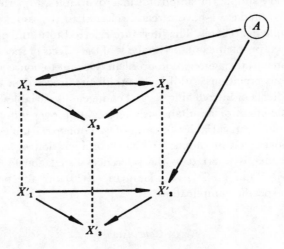

Figure 27.9.

would strongly endorse the statement made by Fox (1968, p. 496) relevant to aggregation problems in economics:

> If we are to avoid a naive empiricism in dealing with economic aggregates we must first do some rather careful bridge-building between the *micro-variables* and *micro-relationships* associated with individual consumers or firms and the *macro-variables* and *macrorelationships* associated with large aggregates of consumers or firms at a national or regional level.

Quite a few sociologists are willing to make strong arguments for the necessity of creating theories that include variables from different levels of social structure. There is no point in elaborating on this as the case is strongly made in many of the essays collected in the Doggan and Rokkan volume referred to previously. The analysis of some of the technical problems involved in changing units of analysis with empirical data (when the simplest of aggregates are used as macrovariables) brings us to the same conclusion. I would suggest that an examination of the work done to this point on the aggregation problem strongly suggests that progress in resolving the complex issues arising in attempts at changing levels of analysis is heavily dependent on theoretical advance in specifying crosslevel relationships.

5. Additional complications

I have indicated at numerous points that this analysis considers only the simplest cases of aggregation problems. In particular, we have limited our concerns to very simple (or simplistic) macrovariables, to perfectly specified recursive micromodels. I have already referred to the issues raised by the choice of simple aggregates. The literature referred to in the presentation of the aggregation problem contains analyses of the effects of specification error in aggregation and the aggregation problem relevant to nonrecursive systems of simultaneous equations. Additional problems discussed in this literature include the effects of introducing lagged endogenous variables in the micro-model and the effect of simultaneously aggregating over individuals (as we have done) and over variables (creating fewer macrovariables than micro-variables). Space considerations preclude consideration of such complications. The reader is referred to the references listed above. Theil (1954), Green (1964), Nataf (1968), and Hannan (1970) are the best sources of references on specific complications.

6. Conclusions

Two major conclusions emerge from this overview of aggregation problems. The first concerns the novelty of aggregation problems. We have pointed to specific statistical problems arising from the aggregation of functions or relationships. But the thrust of this presentation was to argue that the aggregation complications previously analyzed can be seen as special cases of more familiar causal modeling complications. The key insight is that when data-sets are aggregated nonrandomly (i.e., when the aggregation criterion is systematically related to one or more variables in the model), the relative variation in the variables tends to be affected. The most serious and also the most likely outcome of this process is the confounding of the variation of sets of variables. A special case of confounding effects is the production of spurious relationships at the aggregate level. Further, we noted that different but analogous mechanisms operate in cross-sectional and time-series analyses to produce similar effects. Unfortunately, many of these aggregation effects are only vaguely understood and considerable additional analytical and empirical analyses seem needed.

The second major conclusion is that the resolution of the kind of aggregation problems pointed to here seems to demand advances in cross-level theorizing. This conclusion emerges from the analysis of the aggregation bias mechanisms discussed above. The successful handling of any particular case of aggregation problems demands two things. First, one must specify the factors operating in the usually rather vague aggregation criterion (e.g., physical propinquity) to systematically affect variation in the variables of concern. Second, one must be able to specify the relationship of these factors to the variables in the model. Both tasks would seem to require theories that include in their scope both the microvariables being aggregated and the (presumably) macrolevel factors operating in the grouping or aggregation process. A theory seems required because of the extremely large number of possible factors that might be assumed to be operating in the type of grouping criteria usually encountered and the difficulties faced in attempting to specify the differential relationship of such factors to the variables in the model.

Finally, I would like to stress that this presentation of aggregation problems is in no way exhaustive. In economics, for example, aggregation problems have been raised and analyzed in a wide variety of theoretical models. There seems to have been a recent upsurge of renewed interest in aggregation problems in theoretical economics. Much of this recent work suggests interesting possibilities for the handling of the crosslevel theory problems just discussed.

References

ALKER, HAYWARD R., Jr. 1969. "A typology of ecological fallacies." In M. Doggan, and S. Rokkan (Eds.), *Quantitative Ecological Analysis in the Social Sciences*. Cambridge, Mass.: MIT Press.

ALLARDT, ERIK. 1969. "Aggregate analysis: the problem of its informative value." In M. Doggan, and S. Rokkan (Eds.), *Quantitative Ecological Analysis in the Social Sciences*. Cambridge, Mass.: MIT Press.

ALLEN, R. G. D. 1956. *Mathematical Economics*. London: Macmillan.

BARTKO, JOHN J., and PETTIGREW, KAREN D. 1968. "A note on the correlation of parts with wholes." *The American Statistician, 22* (October): 41.

BLALOCK, H. M., JR., 1964. *Causal Inferences in Non-Experimental Research*. Chapel Hill: University of North Carolina Press.

BOOT, J. C. G., and DEWIT, G. M. 1960. "Investment demand: an empirical contribution to aggregation problem." *International Economic Review, 1* (January): 3–30.

BOUDON, RAYMOND. 1963. "Propriétés individuelles et propriétés collectives: une probleme d'analyse ecologique." *Revue francaise de sociologie, 4* (July–September): 275–299.

CRAMER, J. S. 1964. "Efficient grouping: regression and correlation in Engel curve analysis." *Journal of the American Statistical Association, 59* (March): 233–250.

DOGGAN, MATTEI, and ROKKAN, STEIN (Eds.). 1969. *Quantitive Ecological Analysis in the Social Sciences*. Cambridge, Mass.: MIT Press.

DUNCAN, OTIS DUDLEY, and DAVIS, BEVERLY. 1953. "An alternative to ecological correlation." *American Sociological Review, 18* (December): 665–666.

DUNCAN, OTIS DUDLEY, CUZZORT, RAY P., and DUNCAN, BEVERLY. 1961. *Statistical Geography*. Glencoe, Ill.: The Free Press.

FOX, KARL. 1968. *Intermediate Economic Statistics*. New York: John Wiley.

GALTUNG, JOHAN. 1967. *Theory and Methods of Social Research*. New York: Columbia University Press.

GEHKLE, C., and BIEHEL, K. 1934. *Journal of the American Statistical Association Supplement, 29*: 169–170.

GOODMAN, LEO. 1953. "Ecological regression and the behavior of individuals." *American Sociological Review, 18* (December): 663–664.

GOODMAN, LEO. 1959. "Some alternatives to ecological correlation." *American Journal of Sociology*, 64 (May): 610–625.

GREEN, H. A. JOHN. 1964. *Aggregation in Economic Analysis*. Princeton, N.J.: Princeton University Press.

GRUNFELD, YEHUDA, and GRILICHES, ZVI. 1960. "Is aggregation necessarily bad?" *Review of Economics and Statistics*, 42 (February): 1–13.

HANNAN, MICHAEL T. 1970. *Problems of Aggregation and Disaggregation in Sociological Research*. Chapel Hill, N.C.: University of North Carolina, Institute for Research in Social Science.

KLEIN, LAWRENCE R. 1946. "Remarks on the theory of aggregation." *Econometrica*, 14 (October): 303–312.

———. 1953. *A Textbook of Econometrics*. Evanston, Ill.: Row, Peterson.

LANCASTER, KELVIN. 1966. "Economic aggregation and additivity." In Sherman Krupp (Ed.), *The Structure of Economic Science*. Englewood Cliffs, N.J.: Prentice Hall.

LAZARSFELD, PAUL, and MENZEL, HERBERT. 1965. "On the relations between individual and collective properties." In Amitai Etzioni (Ed.), *Complex Organizations*. New York: Holt, Rinehart and Winston.

LINZ, JUAN J. 1969. "Ecological analysis and survey research." In M. Doggan, and S. Rokkan (Eds.), *Quantitative Ecological Analysis in the Social Sciences*. Cambridge, Mass.: MIT Press.

MALINVAUD, E. 1966. *Statistical Methods of Econometrics*. Chicago: Rand McNally.

MAY, KENNETH O. 1946. "The aggregation problem for a one-industry model." *Econometrica*, 14 (October): 285–298.

NAROLL, RAOUL. 1968. "Some thoughts on comparative method in cultural anthropology." In H. M. Blalock, and Ann Blalock (Eds.), *Methodology in Social Research*. New York: McGraw-Hill.

NATAF, ANDRÉ. 1948. "Sur la possibilité de construction de certains macromodels." *Econometrica*, 16 (July): 232–244.

———. 1968. "Aggregation." In D. Sills (Ed.), *International Encyclopedia of the Social Sciences*. New York: Macmillan and the Free Press.

ROBINSON, WILLIAM S. 1950. "Ecological correlations and the behavior of individuals." *American Sociological Review*, 15 (June): 351–357.

SEARLE, S. R. 1969. "Correlation between means of parts and wholes." *The American Statistician*, 23 (April): 23–24.

THEIL, HENRI. 1954. *Linear Aggregation in Economic Relations*. Amsterdam: North Holland Publishing Company.

———. 1959. "The aggregation implications of identifiable structure macro-relations." *Econometrica*, 27 (January): 14–29.

THORNDIKE, EDWARD L. 1939. "On the fallacy of imputing the correlations found for groups to the individuals or smaller groups composing them." *American Journal of Psychology*, 52 (January): 122–124.

WAGNER, HELMUT R. 1964. "Displacement of scope: a problem of the relationship between small-scale and large-scale sociological theories." *American Journal of Sociology*, 69 (May): 517–584.

YULE, G. UDNY, and KENDALL, MAURICE G. 1950. *An Introduction to the Theory of Statistics*. London: Charles Griffin.

Index